M000096576

Table of Contents

Part Two: Advanced Drawing and Animation

Part Three: Adding Interactivity

Part Four: Delivering Your Animation to Its Audience

Part Five: Appendixes

The Missing Credits

About the Author

 Christopher Grover is a veteran of the San Francisco Bay Area advertising and design community, having worked for over 25 years in print, video, and electronic media. During that stint, he's had freelance articles published in a variety of magazines from *Fine Homebuilding* to *CD-ROM World*. Chris is owner of Bolinas Road Creative (*www.BolinasRoad.com*), an agency that helps small businesses promote their products and services. He's also the author of *Word 2007: The Missing Manual* and co-author of *Digital Photography: The Missing Manual*.

E.A. Vander Veer (previous editions) started out in the software trenches, lexing and yaccing and writing shell scripts with the best of them. She remained busy and happy for years writing C++ programs and wresting data from recalcitrant databases. After a stint as an Object Technology Evangelist (yes, that's an actual job title), she found a way to unite all of her passions: writing about cool computer stuff in prose any human being can understand. Books followed—over a dozen so far—including *Facebook: The Missing Manual*, *PowerPoint 2007: The Missing Manual*, *JavaScript for Dummies*, and *XML Blueprints*. She lives in Texas with her husband and daughter. Email: *emilyamoore@rgv.rr.com*.

About the Creative Team

Nan Barber (editor) is associate editor for the Missing Manual series. She lives in Massachusetts with her husband and G4 Macintosh. Email: *nanbarber@oreilly.com*.

Dawn Frausto (editor) is assistant editor for the Missing Manual series. When not working, she likes rock climbing, playing soccer, and causing trouble. Email: *dawn@oreilly.com*.

Nellie McKesson (production editor) lives in Jamaica Plain, Mass., where she makes t-shirts for her friends (*http://mattsaundersbynellie.etsy.com*) and plays music with her band Dr. & Mrs. Van Der Trampp (*myspace.com/drmrsvandertrampp*). Email: *nellie@oreilly.com*.

Dianne Russell (production manager) of Octal Publishing, Inc. When not frantically making book deadlines she enjoys gourmet cooking, jogging, taking care of 3 kids, 2 bunnies, 1 dog, 1 hampster, and a husband. Email: *dianne@octalpub.com*

Josh Buehler (technical reviewer) In 2001, Josh realized that his wife's homework was more fun that his was, so he signed up for the same Flash class she was taking. Since then, he has used Flash for everything from designing custom snowboards and displaying sheet music to sharing the Declaration of Independence. When not writing code, you can usually find him playing video games or talking like a pirate with his daughter Brooklynn. Josh is currently a Senior Flash Developer at RAIN. Web: *www.ghostRadio.net.*

Matthew Woodruff (technical reviewer) is a Web designer for O'Reilly Media and has enjoyed using Flash for the last six years. He has a degree in Interactive Media Design from the Art Institute of California–San Francisco. Email: *mattheww@oreilly.com.*

Alison O'Byrne (copy editor) has been a professional freelance editor for over six years. She lives with her family in Dublin, Ireland. Email: *alison@alhaus.com.* Web: *www.alhaus.com.*

Acknowledgements

It never ceases to amaze me how many talented pros it takes to turn some words on a page into a Missing Manual. A special thanks to Nan Barber, my editor, who has helped me through the process quite a few times now. (Where does she find the patience?) Many thanks to Josh Buhler and Matthew Woodruff, two great Flash and ActionScript experts, who checked and double-checked the technical details. Between my manuscript and all the new features in Flash CS4, they had their work cut out for them. My sincere appreciation to Alison O'Byrne and Lucie Haskins, who whipped through the copy editing and indexing in record time. Thanks to all the other Missing Manual folks who put in long weekends to get this book on the shelves. And, once again, thanks to Peter Meyers who gave me a crack at my first Missing Manual. Work really shouldn't be this much fun!

As always, thanks to my beautiful wife Joyce, my collaborator in that other project—life. And hugs for Mary and Amy who help me approach everything I do with fresh enthusiasm and a bundle of questions.

—*Chris Grover*

The Missing Manual Series

Missing Manuals are witty, superbly written guides to computer products that don't come with printed manuals (which is just about all of them). Each book features a handcrafted index; cross-references to specific pages (not just chapters); and RepKover, a detached-spine binding that lets the book lie perfectly flat without the assistance of weights or cinder blocks.

Recent and upcoming titles include:

Access 2007: The Missing Manual by Matthew MacDonald

AppleScript: The Missing Manual by Adam Goldstein

AppleWorks 6: The Missing Manual by Jim Elferdink and David Reynolds

CSS: The Missing Manual by David Sawyer McFarland

Creating a Web Site: The Missing Manual by Matthew MacDonald

David Pogue's Digital Photography: The Missing Manual by David Pogue

Dreamweaver 8: The Missing Manual by David Sawyer McFarland

Dreamweaver CS3: The Missing Manual by David Sawyer McFarland

Dreamweaver CS4: The Missing Manual by David Sawyer McFarland

eBay: The Missing Manual by Nancy Conner

Excel 2003: The Missing Manual by Matthew MacDonald

Excel 2007: The Missing Manual by Matthew MacDonald

Facebook: The Missing Manual by E.A. Vander Veer

FileMaker Pro 8: The Missing Manual by Geoff Coffey and Susan Prosser

FileMaker Pro 9: The Missing Manual by Geoff Coffey and Susan Prosser

Flash 8: The Missing Manual by E.A. Vander Veer

Flash CS3: The Missing Manual by E.A. Vander Veer and Chris Grover

FrontPage 2003: The Missing Manual by Jessica Mantaro

Google Apps: The Missing Manual by Nancy Conner

The Internet: The Missing Manual by David Pogue and J.D. Biersdorfer

iMovie 6 & iDVD: The Missing Manual by David Pogue

iMovie '08 & iDVD: The Missing Manual by David Pogue

iPhone: The Missing Manual by David Pogue

iPhoto '08: The Missing Manual by David Pogue

iPod: The Missing Manual, 6th Edition by J.D. Biersdorfer

JavaScript: The Missing Manual by David Sawyer McFarland

Mac OS X: The Missing Manual, Tiger Edition by David Pogue

Mac OS X: The Missing Manual, Leopard Edition by David Pogue

Microsoft Project 2007: The Missing Manual by Bonnie Biafore

Office 2004 for Macintosh: The Missing Manual by Mark H. Walker and Franklin Tessler

Office 2007: The Missing Manual by Chris Grover, Matthew MacDonald, and E.A. Vander Veer

Office 2008 for Macintosh: The Missing Manual by Jim Elferdink

PCs: The Missing Manual by Andy Rathbone

Photoshop Elements 7: The Missing Manual by Barbara Brundage

Photoshop Elements 6 for Mac: The Missing Manual by Barbara Brundage

PowerPoint 2007: The Missing Manual by E.A. Vander Veer

QuickBase: The Missing Manual by Nancy Conner

QuickBooks 2008: The Missing Manual by Bonnie Biafore

QuickBooks 2009: The Missing Manual by Bonnie Biafore

Quicken 2008: The Missing Manual by Bonnie Biafore

Quicken 2009: The Missing Manual by Bonnie Biafore

Switching to the Mac: The Missing Manual, Tiger Edition by David Pogue and Adam Goldstein

Switching to the Mac: The Missing Manual, Leopard Edition by David Pogue

Wikipedia: The Missing Manual by John Broughton

Windows XP Home Edition: The Missing Manual, 2nd Edition by David Pogue

Windows XP Pro: The Missing Manual, 2nd Edition by David Pogue, Craig Zacker, and Linda Zacker

Windows Vista: The Missing Manual by David Pogue

Windows Vista for Starters: The Missing Manual by David Pogue

Word 2007: The Missing Manual by Chris Grover

Your Brain: The Missing Manual by Matthew MacDonald

Introduction

Flash has been the gold standard in multimedia creation software for over 10 years. The program has come a long way since the mid-1990s, when professional animators—like those at Microsoft's MSN and Disney Online—used an early incarnation called FutureSplash. Over the years, Flash earned a following of programming geeks as an alternative to Java for creating vector-based Web graphics. In the 21st century, though, anyone with a desktop computer (or even a laptop) can be a Web animator. With Flash CS4's easy-to-use panels and toolbars, you can create sophisticated, interactive animations that run on the Web, standalone computers, handhelds, kiosks—virtually anywhere you find a screen (see Figure I-1).

Here are just some of the things you can create with Flash:

- **Drawings and animations.** Flash gives you the drawing tools to create original artwork and the animation tools to give it movement and life. Then you can edit your Flash document in another program, add it to a Web page, or burn it to a CD or DVD. Flash recognizes multimedia files created using other programs, so you can enrich your animations with image, sound, and video files you already have (or that you find on the Web).

- **Multimedia Web sites.** You can create original drawings and animations with Flash, add in voice-overs, background music, and video clips, and then publish it all to a Web page with the click of a button. Using Flash's built-in scripting language, ActionScript, you can add interactive features like hotspots and navigation bars. You can even position elements on the screen precisely and then change the layout at runtime. With Flash, even regular folks can create real-time video blogs and eye-grabbing splash pages. In fact, the most famous multimedia site of them all, YouTube, uses Flash to display videos.

Figure I-1:
The Yankee Candle Company's Web site is just one example of the movement, interactivity, and polish that Flash can add to a site. From the home page, clicking Custom Candle Favors → Custom Votives displays this Web-based Flash program.

• **Banner ads.** These blinking, flashing, animated strips of Madison Avenue marvelousness are easy to produce in Flash. Typically, banner ads consist of a skinny animation and a link to the sponsor site (see Figure I-2).

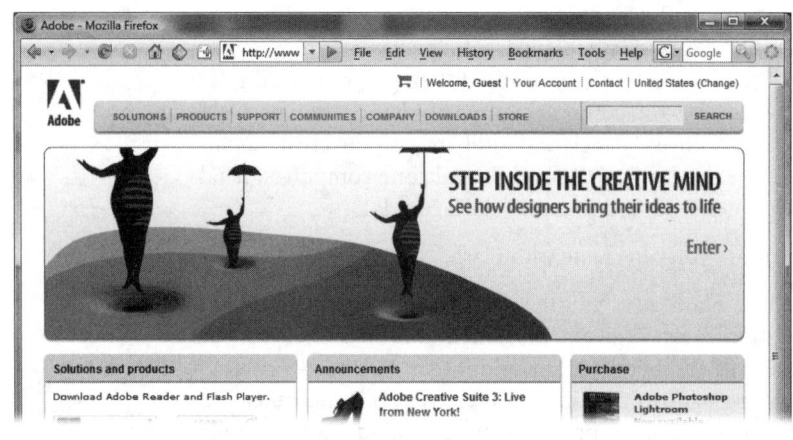

Figure I-2:
Over half of the banner ads you see on the Web were produced using Flash. The best ones combine creativity with action. Here, Magritte-like characters float up into the air, suspended from their umbrellas. Clicking the banner zips you to a different Web page, where you can place an order online.

• **Tutorials.** Web-based training courses, which often include a combination of text, drawings, animations, video clips, and voice-overs, are a natural fit for Flash. By hooking Flash up to a server on the back end, you can even present your audience with graded tests and up-to-the-minute product information.

You don't have to deliver your tutorials over the Web, though; you can publish them as standalone projector files (Chapter 19) and deliver them to your students via CDs or DVDs.

• **Full-length ads and product presentations.** Marketing types can use Flash to create slick, storyboarded, buy-our-stuff-now animations and program mock-ups.

- **Customer service kiosks.** Many of the kiosks you see in stores and building lobbies use Flash to help customers find what they need. For example, photo kiosks walk customers through the process of transferring images from their digital cameras and ordering their own prints; kiosks in banks let customers withdraw funds, check interest rates, and make deposits.

- **Television and film effects.** The Hollywood set has been known to use Flash to create spectacular visual effects for TV shows and even small feature films. But where the TV and film industry is seriously adopting Flash is on promotional Web sites, where they wed Flash graphics to scenes taken from their movies and shows to present powerful trailers, interactive tours of movie and show sets, and teasers. You can find hundreds of them on YouTube alone (Figure I-3).

- **Games and other programs.** With support for runtime scripting, back end data transfers, and interactive controls like buttons and text boxes, Flash has everything a programmer needs to create a cool-looking game (check out *www.addictinggames.com* for a few examples) or other *rich Internet applications* (Adobe's fancy term for "Web-based program").

Figure I-3:
YouTube has made great use of Flash's video abilities. You can check to see whether any site is using Flash behind the scenes. Just right-click (or ⌘-click) an image that you think might be Flash. If it says About Flash Player at the bottom of the pop-up menu, you guessed right.

Unfortunately, there's no such thing as a free lunch. If Flash is an incredibly powerful, useful program—and it is—it's also harder to use than a greased tightrope.

That's where this book comes in. You don't have to be a professional artist, animator, or software developer to create useful animations with Flash. All you need are this book and an idea of what you'd like to create. The examples, explanations, and step-by-step instructions in the next 19 chapters show you how to turn that idea into a working animation.

Flash CS4 Professional for Everyone

Previous versions of Flash came in two flavors: Professional and Standard. With Adobe Creative Suite 4, there's just one product: Flash CS4 Professional (Figure I-4). Flash Professional has everything for both professional developers and weekend Web mavens. Some of the pro-quality features include:

- **Additional graphic effects.** With Flash CS4 Professional, you get convenient extras like *filters* (predefined blurs, glows, and drop shadows), *blend modes* (transparency effects that make *compositing*, or combining images, easy), and *custom easing* (the ability to slow down or speed up animated tweens with the click of a button).

- **Support for mobile authoring.** Flash CS4 Professional comes with mobile templates (to help you size your animations for handhelds), an emulator (to let you see how your animations will appear on every handheld that Flash supports), and built-in publishing options.

- **Support for high-end video manipulation.** Flash CS4 Professional gives you extra tools, including the Flash Video Exporter (a QuickTime plug-in that lets you create Flash video files using any Apple QuickTime–compatible video authoring tool) and the Flash Video Encoder (a standalone program that lets you convert regular video files to Flash video files). Using Flash CS4 Professional, you can link to external video files and even layer video clips on top of each other to create sophisticated composite effects.

Figure I-4:
The Flash CS4 workspace looks familiar if you've used previous versions of Flash. Look closer and you'll notice Adobe has tweaked Flash to give it more of the look and feel of other Creative Suite programs. From the tool panels to the tabbed, docking palettes, this version bears resemblance to its Adobe cousins like Photoshop and Illustrator.

What's New in Flash CS4

When Adobe acquired Macromedia at the end of 2005, graphic artists and Web designers held their breath waiting to learn what this meant for Flash, as well as Dreamweaver (a favorite Web design tool). For the most part, there were sighs of relief when Adobe folded both beloved programs into its high-powered Creative Suite. The big change came with Flash CS3, which introduced a new workspace that was more consistent with other Adobe programs, including Photoshop. For example, without abandoning some of Flash's idiosyncratic drawing methods, CS3's pen tool took on Adobe Illustrator characteristics. CS3 was the first version of Flash to include ActionScript 3.0.

With Flash CS4, Adobe continues to update Flash at a rapid pace, adding powerful new features and improving the workspace, like making it easier to arrange and organize windows. If you've used other Adobe programs, you'll also welcome the consistency in drawing, text, and color-choosing tools. By the same token, if you're new to the Adobe family, the skills you learn in Flash will come in handy if you move on to Photoshop, Illustrator, Dreamweaver, Premiere, or After Effects.

Here's a short list of the new features in CS4:

- **Applying tweens directly to objects.** When you want something to change in your animation, you show Flash how it looks at the beginning and how it looks at the end. Flash creates all the in-between frames. The process is called *tweening*. Flash has always had tweens, but Flash CS4 introduces a new way of animating objects. Instead of applying tweens to keyframes, you apply tweens directly to the object you want to move. The new system for working with motion tweens is fast, easy to understand, and easy to use. Once you've crafted the perfect tween, it's easy to apply it to other objects.

- **New Motion Editor.** Adobe gives you more control than ever over your tweens. If you want to control every aspect of an object's motion, shape, color, and appearance as it changes over time, you'll love the motion editor that comes in CS4. It gives you the kind of power that video editors have enjoyed using Adobe After Effects.

- **Motion presets.** Flash comes with predesigned motion tweens that you can use in your animation. The presets that come in the box include actions like bounce, fly-in, fly-out, pulse, spiral, and wave. If that's not enough, you can save the tweens you create yourself and use them as presets.

- **Animating objects in 3D space.** Flash is dipping its graphic toe in 3D waters. You can animate movie clips in three dimensions, which is a great effect for text, still images, and other objects. To be sure, Flash isn't a full-blown 3D animation tool like 3DStudio, but it does let you do things that you've never done before.

- **IK Bones.** Flash's brand new *inverse kinematics* feature lets you link things together to create natural movements. The Bones tool and Binding tool will save you tons of time when you animate connected objects. (You may now start singing "The hip bone's connected to the thigh bone...") You can use the tools not only on bodies, legs, and feet, but also on machinery with moving parts like steam shovels, cranes, and desk lamps.

- **Designing Adobe AIR Projects.** Adobe AIR is a new Adobe technology for publishing programs for computer desktops and handheld devices like phones and palmtop computers. At the core of AIR are Flash Player and ActionScript 3.0. Using Flash, you can now design programs and animations for a wider audience.

- **Sound Samples Library.** Flash CS4 now includes dozens of sound samples that you can drop into your animations. Most of these are event sounds, like motors running, laughter, bells and the ever-popular gigantic explosion.

- **Adobe Media Encoder H.264 Support.** Flash CS4 shares the same media encoder with Adobe Premiere and After Effects. Translation: You can now create the same high quality video files you see in iTunes movies, AppleTV, and iPod video.

- **Workspace improvements.** Adobe continues to refine the Flash workspace. Flash CS4's Properties panel and Library are easier to use than ever, and more consistent with other Adobe products. Among dozens of other workspace improvements, the Properties panel is now displayed vertically, which is not only a better use of today's widescreen monitors, it makes it easier to group with other vertical panels. The Library panel has new search and sorting capabilities. Font selection is easier now that the font menus show previews of the typefaces.

Anatomy of an Animation

Animation is a complex subject, and Flash is a complex program. You'll have a much easier time plowing through the rest of the book if you start with a couple of basics under your belt: specifically, what an animation is and how you go about creating one in Flash. This section and the following one give you some background.

Animators used to develop animations in a frame-by-frame sequence, where every frame contained a different image. As the frames sped by on a projector, the hundreds (or hundreds of thousands) of static images created the illusion of moving characters.

Painstaking work? You bet. Before the age of computerized generation—which has really just come into its own in the last 20 years or so, with big names like Pixar—major animation houses employed whole armies of graphic artists, each charged with producing hundreds of drawings that represented a mere fraction of the finished work. What we chuckled at for a scant few minutes took weeks and dozens of tired, cramped hands to produce. One mistake, one spilled drop of coffee, and these patient-as-Job types would have to grab fresh paper and start all over again. When everything was done, the animation would have to be put together—much like one of those flip books where you flip pages real fast to see a story play out—while it was being filmed by special cameras.

Flash brings you the power of a design studio, expert tools, and the equivalent of a staff of highly trained detail people. You still have to come up with an idea for the animation, and you have to draw (or find and import) at least a couple of images. But beyond that, Flash can take over and generate most of the frames you need to flesh out your animation.

It's pretty incredible, when you think about it. A few hundred bucks and a few hours spent working with Flash, and you've got an animation that, just a few years ago, you'd have had to pay a swarm of professionals union scale to produce. Sweet!

UP TO SPEED

An Animation by Any Other Name

You may occasionally hear Flash animations referred to (by books, Web sites, and even Flash's own documentation) as *movies*. Perhaps that's technically accurate, but it sure can be confusing.

QuickTime .mov files are also called movies, and some people refer to video clips as movies; but to Flash, these are two very different animals. In addition, Flash lets you create and work with *movie clips*, which are something else entirely. And "movie," with its connotations of quietly sitting in a theater

balcony eating popcorn, doesn't convey one of the most important features Flash offers: interactivity.

Here's the most accurate way to describe what you create using Flash: a Web site or program with a really cool, animated interface. Unfortunately, that description's a bit long and unwieldy, so in this book, what you create using Flash is called an *animation*.

Flash in a Nutshell

Say you work for a company that does custom auto refinishing. First assignment: design an intro page for the company's new Web site. You have the following idea for an animation:

The first thing you want your audience to see is a beat-up jalopy limping along a city street toward the center of the screen, where it stops and morphs into a shiny, like-new car as your company's jingle plays in the background. A voice-over informs your audience that your company's been in business for 20 years and offers the best prices in town.

Across the top of the screen you'd like to display the company logo, as well as a navigation bar with buttons—labeled Location, Services, Prices, and Contact—that your audience can click to get more information about your company. But you also want each part of the car to be a clickable hotspot. That way, when someone clicks one of the car's tires, he's whisked off to a page describing your custom wheels and hubcaps; when he clicks the car's body, he sees prices for dent repair and repainting; and so on.

Here's how you might go about creating this animation in Flash:

- Using Flash's drawing tools, you draw the artwork for every *keyframe* of the animation: that is, every important image. For example, you'll need to create a keyframe showing the beat-up junker and a second keyframe showing the gleaming, expertly refurbished result. (Chapter 2 shows you how to draw artwork in Flash; Chapter 3 tells you everything you need to know about keyframes.)

- Within each keyframe, you might choose to separate your artwork into differ-ent *layers*. Like the see-through plastic cels that professional animators used in the old days, layers let you create images separately and then stack them on top of each other to make a single composite image. For example, you might choose to put the car on one layer, your company logo on a second layer, and your city-street background on a third layer. That way, you can edit and animate each layer independently, but when the animation plays, all three elements appear to be on one seamless layer. (Chapter 4 shows you how to work with layers.)

- Through a process called *tweening*, you tell Flash to fill in each and every frame in-*between* the keyframes to create the illusion of the junker turning slowly into a brand-new car. Flash carefully analyzes all the differences between the key-frames and does its best to build the interim frames, which you can then tweak or—if Flash gets it all wrong—redraw yourself. (Chapter 3 guides you through the tweening process.)

- As you go along, you might decide to save a few of the elements you create (for example, your company logo), so you can reuse them later. There's no sense in reinventing the wheel, and in addition to saving you time, reusing elements actually helps keep your animation files as small and efficient as possible. (See Chapter 6 for details on creating and managing reusable elements.)

- Add the background music and voice-over audio clips, which you've created in other programs (Chapter 10).

- Create the navigation bar buttons and hotspots that let your audience interact with your animation (Chapter 12).

- Test your animation (Chapter 18) and tweak it to perfection.

- Finally, when your animation is just the way you want it, you're ready to *publish* it. Without leaving the comfort of Flash, you can convert the editable .fla file you've been working with into a noneditable .swf file and either embed it into an HTML file or create a standalone *projector* file your audience can run without having to use a browser. Chapter 19 tells you everything you need to know about publishing.

The scenario described above is pretty simple, but it covers the basic steps you need to take when creating any Flash animation.

The Very Basics

You'll find very little jargon or nerd terminology in this book. You will, however, see a few terms and concepts that you'll encounter frequently in your computing life:

- **Clicking.** This book gives you several kinds of instructions that require you to use your computer's mouse or trackpad. To *click* means to point the arrow cursor at something on the screen and then—without moving the cursor at all—to press and release the clicker button on the mouse (or laptop trackpad). To *double-click*, of course, means to click twice in rapid succession, again without moving the cursor at all. To *drag* means to move the cursor while pressing the button continuously. To *right-click* or *right-drag*, do the same as above, but press the right mouse button.

    When you see an instruction like *Shift-click* or *Ctrl-click*, simply press the key as you click.

Note: Some Macintosh computers don't come with a right mouse button. With a one-button mouse, to do the same thing as a right-click or right-drag, press the Mac's Control key as you click or drag. (Or buy a two-button mouse.) See the next section for more Windows/Mac differences.

- **Keyboard shortcuts.** Every time you take your hand off the keyboard to move the mouse, you lose time and potentially disrupt your creative flow. That's why many experienced computer fans use keystroke combinations instead of menu commands wherever possible. Ctrl+B (⌘-B on the Mac), for example, is a keyboard shortcut for boldface type in Flash (and most other programs).

    When you see a shortcut like Ctrl+S (⌘-S on the Mac), which saves changes to the current document, it's telling you to hold down the Ctrl or ⌘ key, and, while it's down, type the letter S, and then release both keys.

- **Choice is good.** Flash frequently gives you several ways to trigger a particular command—a menu command, or by clicking a toolbar button, or by pressing a key combination, for example. Some people prefer the speed of keyboard shortcuts; others like the satisfaction of a visual command array available in menus or toolbars. This book lists several alternatives, but by no means are you expected to memorize all of them.

Macintosh and Windows

Flash CS4 works much the same way in its Mac and Windows incarnations except for a few interface differences. Naturally you may see slight variations in performance on different machines. This book's illustrations give Mac and Windows equal time, alternating by chapter, so you get to see how all of Flash's features look, no matter what kind of computer you're running.

There *is* one small difference between Mac and Windows software that you need to be aware of, and that's keystrokes. The Ctrl key in Windows is the equivalent of the Macintosh ⌘ key, and the key labeled Alt on a PC (and on non-U.S. Macs) is the equivalent of the Option key on American Mac keyboards.

Whenever this book refers to a key combination, therefore, you'll see the Windows keystroke listed first (with + symbols, as is customary in Windows documentation); the Macintosh keystroke follows in parentheses (with - symbols, in time-honored Mac tradition). In other words, you might read, "The keyboard shortcut for saving a file is Ctrl+S (⌘-S)." This book mentions any other significant differences between the Mac and Windows versions of Flash CS4 as they come up.

About This Book

Flash has gotten more powerful and more sophisticated over the years, but one thing hasn't changed: woefully poor documentation. If Flash were simple to use, the lack of documentation wouldn't be such a big deal. But Flash is a complex program—especially if you don't have a background in programming or multimedia authoring software. Basically, because Flash's documentation alternates between high-level market-speak and low-level computer engineering jargon, you're pretty much out of luck if you're a normal, intelligent person who just wants to use Flash to create a cool animated Web site, and then get on with your life.

Fortunately, there's an answer—and you're holding it in your hands.

This is the book that *should* have come in the Flash box: one that explains all the tools and shows you step-by-step not just how to create animations from scratch, but *why* you want to do each step—in English, not programmer-ese. You'll learn tips and shortcuts for making Flash easier to work with, as well as making your animations as audience-friendly as possible.

Flash CS4: The Missing Manual is designed for readers of every skill level *except* the super-advanced-programmer. If Flash is the first image-creation or animation program you've ever used, you'll be able to dive right in using the explanations and examples in this book. If you come from an animation or multimedia background, you'll find this book a useful reference for mapping how you created an element in your previous program, to how you do it in Flash. "Design Time" boxes explain the art of effective multimedia design (which is an art unto itself).

The ActionScript programming language is a broad, complex subject. This book isn't an exhaustive reference manual, but it gives you a great introduction to ActionScript programming providing working examples and clear explanations of ActioScript principles.

About the Outline

Flash CS4: The Missing Manual is divided into five parts, each containing several chapters:

- **Part One: Creating a Flash Animation** guides you through the creation of your very first Flash animation, from the first glimmer of an idea to drawing images, animating those images, and testing your work.

- **Part Two: Advanced Drawing and Animation** is the designer's feast. Here you'll see how to manipulate your drawings by rotating, skewing, stacking, and aligning them; how to add color, special effects, and multimedia files like audio and video clips; how to slash file size by turning bits and pieces of your drawings into special elements called *symbols*; and how to create composite drawings using layers. In this section, you'll learn about the Motion Editor. New to CS4, it gives you incredible control over motion tweens. There's a whole chapter that explains how to use the new inverse kinematics ("bones") feature (Chapter 8).

- **Part Three: Adding Interactivity** shows you how to add ActionScript 3.0 actions to your animations, creating on-the-fly special effects and giving your audience the power to control your animations. This section includes lots of examples and ActionScript code. You can copy and modify some of the practical examples for your own projects. You'll see how to loop frames and how to let your audience choose which section of an animation to play, and how to customize the prebuilt interactive components that come with Flash. You'll find specific chapters on using ActionScript with text and using ActionScript to draw.

- **Part Four: Delivering Your Animation to Its Audience** focuses on testing, debugging, and optimizing your animation. You'll also find out how to publish your animation so that your audience can see and enjoy it and how to export an editable version of your animation so that you can rework it using another graphics, video editing, or Web development program.

- **Part Five: Appendixes.** Appendix A, *Installation and Help*, explains how to install Flash and where to turn for help. Appendix B, *Flash CS4, Menu by Menu*, provides a menu-by-menu description of the commands you find in Flash CS4.

About → These → Arrows

Throughout this book, you'll find instructions like, "Open your Program Files → Adobe → Adobe Flash CS4 folder." That's Missing Manual shorthand for much longer sentences like "Double-click your Program Files folder to open it. Inside, you'll find a folder called Adobe; double-click to open it. Inside *that* folder is a folder called Adobe Flash CS4; open it, too." This arrow shorthand also simplifies the business of choosing menu commands, as you can see in Figure I-5.

Figure I-5:
When you see instructions like "Choose Text → Style → Italic," think, "Click to pull down the Text menu, and then move your mouse down to the Style command. When its submenu opens, choose the Italic option."

Unlike other programs you may have used, Flash makes extensive use of panels. The really complex panels are divided into subpanels, and this book uses the same arrow shorthand to navigate panels. So, for example, when working with a block of text, you may see an instruction like "Go to Properties → Paragraph → Format → Align Left." That means go to the Properties panel and find the Paragraph subpanel. In that subpanel, find the Format group of settings, and then click the Align Left button.

Flash Examples

As you read the book's chapters, you'll encounter a number of step-by-step tutorials. You can work through them using any Flash document of your own, or use the example files provided on this book's "Missing CD" page. You can download them using any Web browser at *http://missingmanuals.com/cds/*. You'll find raw materials (like graphics and half-completed animations) and, in some cases, completed animations with which to compare your work.

About MissingManuals.com

At *http://missingmanuals.com*, you'll find articles, tips, and updates to *Flash CS4: The Missing Manual*. In fact, we invite and encourage you to submit such corrections and updates yourself. In an effort to keep the book as up to date and accurate as possible, each time we print more copies of this book, we'll make any confirmed corrections you've suggested. We'll also note such changes on the Web site, so you can mark important corrections into your own copy of the book, if you like. (Go to *http://missingmanuals.com/feedback*, choose the book's name from the pop-up menu, and then click Go to see the changes.)

Also on our Feedback page, you can get expert answers to questions that come to you while reading this book, write a book review, and find groups for folks who share your interest in Flash.

While you're there, sign up for our free monthly email newsletter. Click the "Sign Up for Our Newsletter" link in the left-hand column. You'll find out what's happening in Missing Manual land, meet the authors and editors, see bonus video and book excerpts, and so on.

We'd love to hear your suggestions for new books in the Missing Manual line. There's a place for that on missingmanuals.com, too. And while you're online, you can also register this book at *www.oreilly.com* (you can jump directly to the registration page by going here: *http://tinyurl.com/yo82k3*). Registering means we can send you updates about this book, and you'll be eligible for special offers like discounts on future editions of *Flash CS4: The Missing Manual*.

Safari® Books Online

 When you see a Safari® Books Online icon on the cover of your favorite technology book, it means the book is available online through the O'Reilly Network Safari Bookshelf.

Safari offers a solution that's better than e-books. It's a virtual library that lets you search thousands of top tech books easily, cut and paste code samples, download chapters, and find quick answers when you need the most accurate, current information. Try it for free at *http://safari.oreilly.com*.

Part One: Creating a Flash Animation

1

Getting Around Flash

These days, computer programs strive to give you an intuitive work environment. A word processing document, for example, looks pretty much like a piece of paper and shows your words as you type them. Movie playing software has controls that look just like the ones on your home DVD player. Flash CS4 provides the powerful and flexible tools that you need to create interactive animations, which is a more complex affair than producing text or playing media. Problem is, if this is your first time in an animation program, it may not be immediately obvious what to *do* with all these tools.

When you start with a blank Flash document, you find yourself staring at a blank white square and a dizzying array of icons, most of which appear to do nothing when you click them (Figure 1-1). You'd pretty much have to be a Flash developer to figure out what to do next. In this chapter, you get acquainted with all the different parts of the Flash window: the stage and main work area, the main menu, the toolbars and panels, the timeline, and more. You'll also take Flash for a test drive and get some practice moving around the Flash screen. When you learn to create an animation of your own in Chapter 2 and Chapter 3, you'll feel right at home.

Tip: To get further acquainted with Flash, you can check out the built-in help text by selecting Help →
Flash Help. Once the help panel opens, click Workspace (on the left), and then "click Flash workflow and
workspace." You can read more about Flash's Help system in Appendix A.

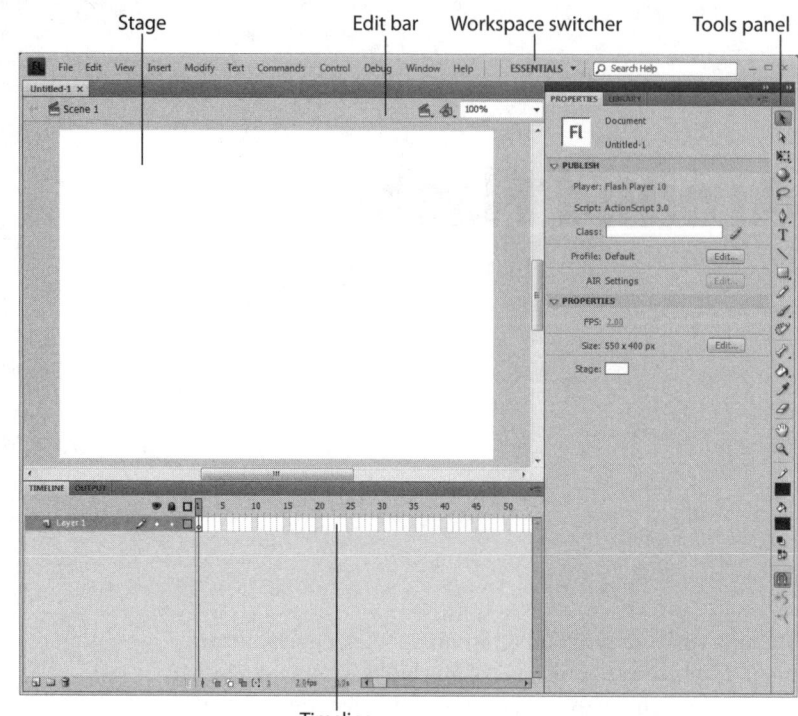

Stage   Edit bar   Workspace switcher   Tools panel

Figure 1-1:
The white rectangle in the middle of the main Flash window—the stage—is where you actually work on your animations. This entire window, together with the timeline, toolbars, and panels identified here, is called the Flash desktop, the Flash interface, or the Flash authoring environment.

Timeline

Starting Flash

Once you've installed Flash on your computer (page 662), you can launch it like any other program. Choose your method:

- **Double-click the program's icon.** You can find it on your hard drive in Program Files → Adobe → Flash CS4 (Windows) or Applications → Adobe Flash CS4 (Mac).

- **Click Start → All Programs → Adobe → Adobe Flash CS4 (Windows).** If you're running Mac, you can drag the Flash CS4 icon from the Adobe Flash CS4 folder to the Dock and from then on open it with a single click on the Dock icon.

Up pops the Flash welcome screen, as shown in Figure 1-2. When you open the program, you're most likely to start a new document or return to a work in progress. This screen puts all your options in one handy place.

Tip: If Flash seems to take forever to open—or if the Flash desktop ignores your mouse clicks or responds sluggishly—you may not have enough memory installed on your computer. See page 661 for more advice.

When you choose one of the options on the welcome screen, it disappears and your actual document takes its place. Here are your choices:

- **Open a Recent Item.** As you create new documents, Flash adds them to this list. Clicking one of the file names listed here tells Flash to open that file. Clicking the folder icon lets you browse your computer for (and then open) any other Flash files on your computer.

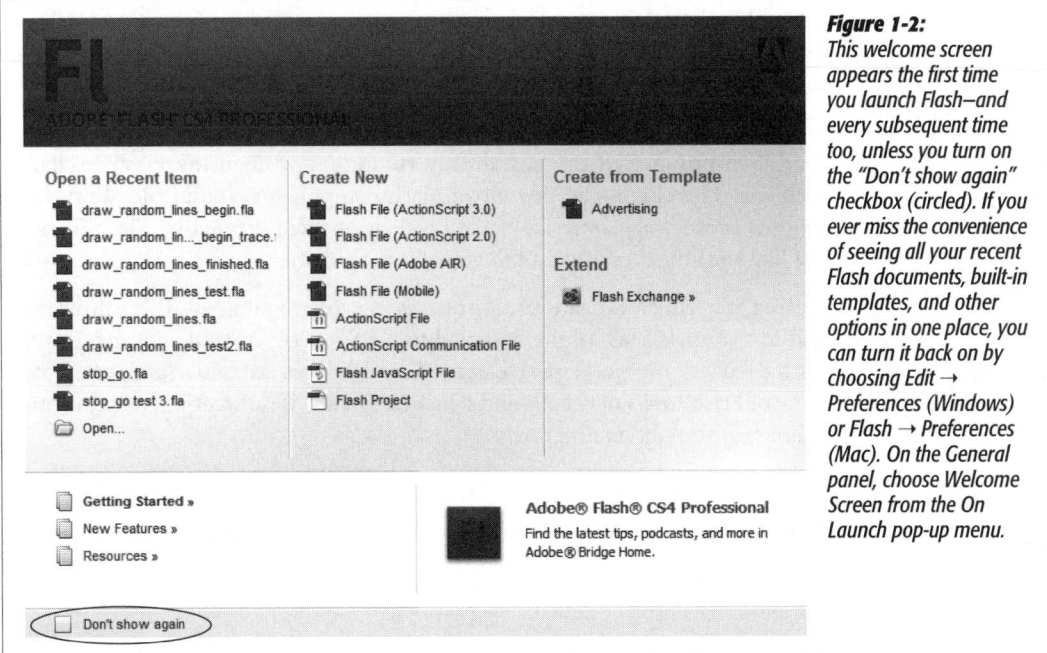

Figure 1-2:
This welcome screen appears the first time you launch Flash—and every subsequent time too, unless you turn on the "Don't show again" checkbox (circled). If you ever miss the convenience of seeing all your recent Flash documents, built-in templates, and other options in one place, you can turn it back on by choosing Edit → *Preferences (Windows) or Flash → Preferences (Mac). On the General panel, choose Welcome Screen from the On Launch pop-up menu.*

- **Create New.** Clicking one of the options listed here lets you create a brand-new Flash file. Most of the time, you'll want to create a *Flash File*, which is a plain garden-variety animation file. Flash gives you two choices: Flash File (Action-Script 3.0) and Flash File (ActionScript 2.0). This book focuses on Flash 3.0, so for the projects shown here, choose the first option: Flash File (ActionScript 3.0).

Tip: Old programming pros—you know who you are—may have reasons to prefer Flash File (ActionScript 2.0). For example, if you're continuing to work on a project originally created using ActionScript 2.0, or you're working with a team using ActionScript 2.0.

There are other options, too. You can use *Flash File (Adobe AIR)* and related developer tools to create programs that run in Web browsers called Rich Internet Applications. You can also create a *Flash File (mobile)*, a specialized animation for cellphones or other handheld devices; an *ActionScript file* (a file containing nothing but ActionScript, for use with a Flash animation); an *ActionScript Communication file* (a file that uses ActionScript to transfer data between an animation and a server); a Flash *JavaScript file* (used to create custom tools, panels, commands, and other features that extend Flash); and a *Flash project* (useful if you're planning a complex, multifile, multideveloper Flash production and need version control).

- **Create From Template.** Clicking one of the little icons under this option lets you create a Flash document using a predesigned form called a *template*. Using a template helps you create a Flash animation quicker because a developer somewhere has already done part of the work for you. You'll find out more about templates in Chapter 6.

- **Extend.** Clicking the Flash Exchange link under this option tells Flash to open your Web browser (if it's not already running) and load the Flash Exchange Web site. There, you can download Flash components, sound files, and other goodies (some free, some fee-based, and all of them created by Flash-ionados just like you) that you can add to your Flash animations.

- **Getting Started, New Features, Resources.** As you might guess, these three links lead to materials that Adobe designed to help you get up and running. Getting Started covers the very, very basics. New Features explains (and celebrates) some of Flash CS4's new bells and whistles. Finally, Resources introduces you to online help and discussion forums.

Note: Except for the Adobe Flash Exchange, which you find on the Help menu, all of the options on the welcome screen also appear on the File menu (shown in Figure 1-3), so you can start a new document at any time.

A Tour of the Flash Desktop

Even though it has more controls and gizmos than the cockpit of a jumbo-jet, don't let Flash's screen layout intimidate you. Each toolbar and panel plays a part in the life of an animation, and most are designed to give you, the animator, full and flexible control over your creation. Once you know why and how to use each type of control, all becomes clear. That's what this section does.

Menu Bar

Running across the top of the Flash desktop (or the very top of your screen, if you're on a Mac), is the menu bar. The commands on these menus list every way you can interact with your Flash file, from creating a new file—as shown on page 50— to editing it, saving it, and controlling how it appears on your screen.

Some of the menu names—File, Edit, View, Window, and Help—are familiar to anyone who's used a PC or Mac. Using these menu choices, you can perform basic tasks like opening, saving, and printing your Flash files; cutting and pasting sections of your drawing; viewing your drawing in different ways; choosing which toolbars to view; getting help; and more.

To view a menu, simply click the menu's title to open it, and then click a menu option. On a Mac, you can also drag down to the option you want. Let go of the mouse button to activate the option. Figure 1-3 shows you what the File menu looks like.

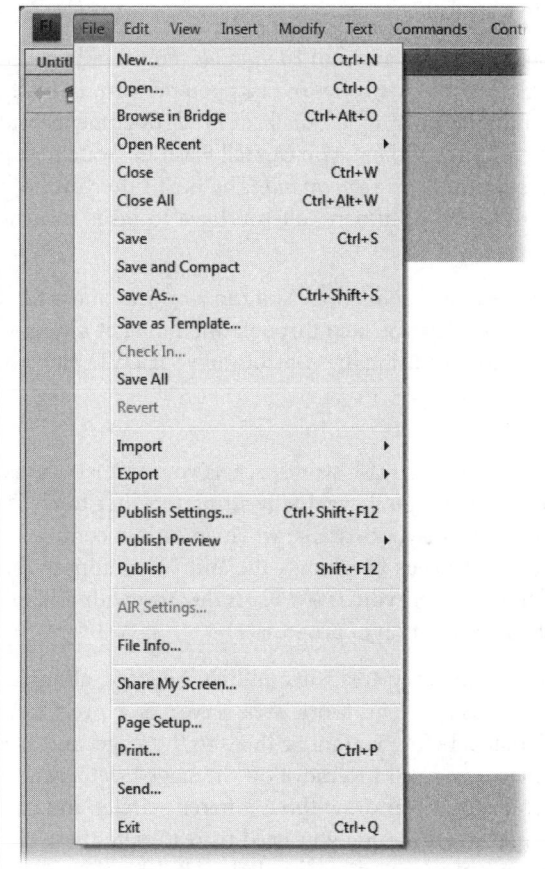

Figure 1-3:
Several of the options on each menu include keystroke shortcuts that let you perform an action without having to mouse all the way up to the menu and click it. For example, instead of selecting File → Save As, you can press Ctrl+Shift+S to tell Flash to save the file you have open. On the Mac, the keystroke is Shift-⌘-S.

Most of the time, you see the same menus at the top of the screen, but occasionally they change. For example, when you use the Debugger to troubleshoot Action-Script programs, Flash hides some of the menus not related to debugging. You'll learn all about these options in upcoming chapters. For example:

- **Insert.** The options you find in this menu let you create complex drawings and turn static drawings into Flash animations by adding *symbols* (reusable bits of drawings and animations, as you'll learn in Chapter 6); *layers* (virtual transparencies that let you manipulate the elements of a composite drawing separately, as shown in Chapter 3); and *frames* (virtual "flip pages" that, when displayed rapidly one after the other, turn a series of drawings into an animation, as discussed in Chapter 3); and so on.

• **Modify.** Selections here let you make changes to your work. For example, this is the menu you want when you want to rotate or *scale* (shrink or enlarge) a piece of your drawing.

• **Text.** The options in this menu let you work with the text you add to your drawings. Here, you can set standard text characteristics like font, alignment, and spacing; you can also run a spell check.

• **Commands.** Options here let you create and run *commands* (commonly called *macros* in other programs). Commands are series of tasks you perform in Flash. For example, if you know you'll be opening a bunch of Flash documents and making identical changes to each one of them, you can tell Flash to "watch" you make the changes once and save them as a *command*. The next time you need to make those changes to a different document, all you have to do is run the command.

• **Control.** This menu helps you test your animation. You can run your animation, rewind it, or even slow it down so that you step through one frame at a time—great for troubleshooting. It's a lot like using the controls on your DVD player.

The Stage

The *stage*, located at the dead center of your Flash workspace, is your virtual canvas. Here's where you draw the pictures that you'll eventually string together to create your animation. The stage is also your playback arena; when you run a completed animation—to test it out and see if it needs tweaking—the animation appears on the stage. At the beginning of this chapter, you saw a Flash desktop with a blank stage. Figure 1-4 shows one with an animation in progress.

Work area is the technical name for the gray area surrounding the stage, although many Flash-ionados call it the *backstage*. This work area serves as a prep zone where you can place graphic elements before you move them to the stage, and as a temporary holding pen for elements you want to move off the stage briefly as you reposition things. For example, let's say you draw three different circles and one box containing text on your stage. If you decide you need to rearrange these elements on the stage, you can temporarily drag one of the circles off the stage.

Note: The stage always starts out with a white background, which becomes the background color for your animation. Changing it to any color imaginable is easy, as you'll learn in the next chapter.

You'll almost always change the starting size and shape of the stage depending on where people will see your finished animation—in other words, your *target platform*. If your target platform is a Web-enabled cell phone, for example, you're going to want an itty-bitty stage. If, on the other hand, you're creating an animation you know people will be watching on a 50-inch computer monitor, you're going to want a giant stage. You'll get to try your hand at modifying the size of the stage in the Flash Test Drive later in this chapter.

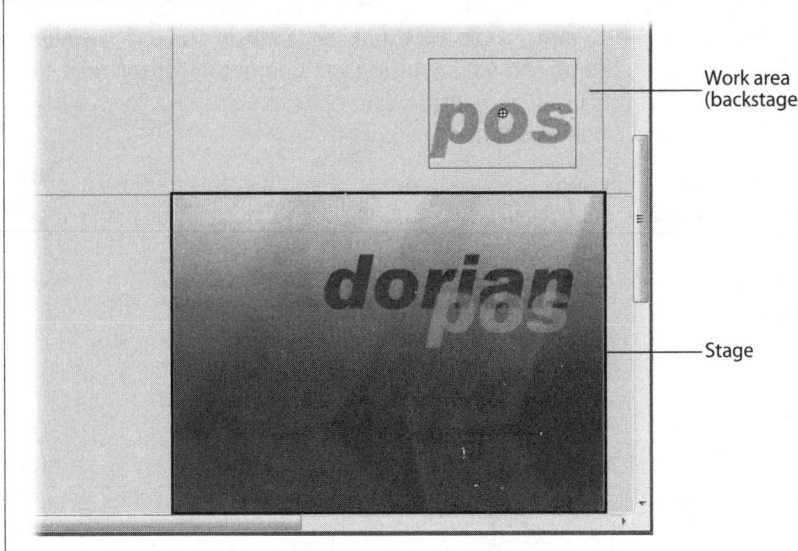

Figure 1-4:
The stage is where you draw the pictures that will eventually become your animation. The work area (gray) gives you a handy place to put graphic elements while you figure out how you want to arrange them on the stage. Here, a text box is being dragged from the work area back to center stage.

Work area (backstage)

Stage

Toolbars

Flash lets you put all the menu options you use most frequently at your fingertips by displaying *toolbars* and *panels* like those shown in Figure 1-1. Toolbars and panels are very similar: they're both movable windows that display Flash options. The difference is that toolbars are small and show only icons; panels are larger and show whole rafts of settings you can change. (You can learn all about panels in the next section.)

Toolbars pack some of the most commonly used options together in a nice compact space that you can position anywhere you like. (See the box on page 26 for tips on repositioning toolbars.) Displaying a toolbar means your options are right there in front of you, so you don't have to do a hunt-and-peck through the main menu every time you want to do something useful.

Tip: When you reposition a floating toolbar, Flash remembers where you put it. If, later on, you hide the toolbar—or exit Flash and run it again—your toolbars appear exactly as you left them. If this isn't what you want, you can wipe away all your changes and return to the way Flash originally displayed everything by choosing Window → Workspace → Default.

Flash has three toolbars, all of which you see in Figure 1-5:

- **Main (Windows only).** The Main toolbar lets you one-click basic operations, like opening an existing Flash file, creating a new file, and cutting and pasting sections of your drawing.

- **Controller.** If you've ever seen a video or sound recorder, you'll recognize the Stop, Rewind, and Play buttons on the Controller toolbar, which let you control how you want Flash to run your finished animation. (Not surprisingly, the Controller options appear *grayed out*—meaning you can't select them—if you haven't yet constructed an animation.)

- **Edit Bar.** Using the options here, you can set and adjust the timeline (page 38) as well as edit *scenes* (named groups of *frames*) and *symbols* (reusable drawings).

Note: The Edit Bar is a little different from the other toolbars in that it remains fixed to the stage. You can't reposition it.

Panels

A Flash *panel* is like a toolbar on steroids: bigger and loaded down with more options, but built for the same reason—to let you keep the stuff you work with the most visible, right there in front of you, where it's easy for you to find and use. Furthermore, unlike toolbars, panels have options you can't find on *any* menu.

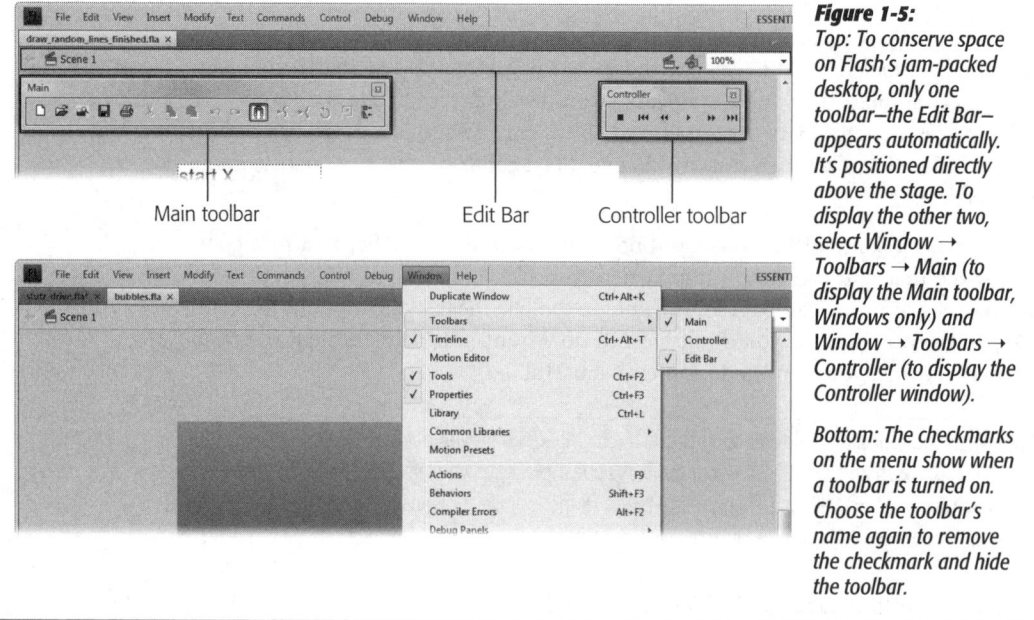

Main toolbar   Edit Bar   Controller toolbar

Figure 1-5:
Top: To conserve space on Flash's jam-packed desktop, only one toolbar—the Edit Bar—appears automatically. It's positioned directly above the stage. To display the other two, select Window → Toolbars → Main (to display the Main toolbar, Windows only) and Window → Toolbars → Controller (to display the Controller window).

Bottom: The checkmarks on the menu show when a toolbar is turned on. Choose the toolbar's name again to remove the checkmark and hide the toolbar.

Flash gives you a ton of panels, each of which appears initially in one of two flavors: *docked* or *floating*. Docked panels appear around the edge of the stage, like the Properties and Library panels shown in Figure 1-6.

You can have as few or as many panels showing at a time as you like docked or floating. The Window menu lists all of Flash's panels, and you show and hide them by selecting to turn their checkmarks on and off—exactly as with toolbars.

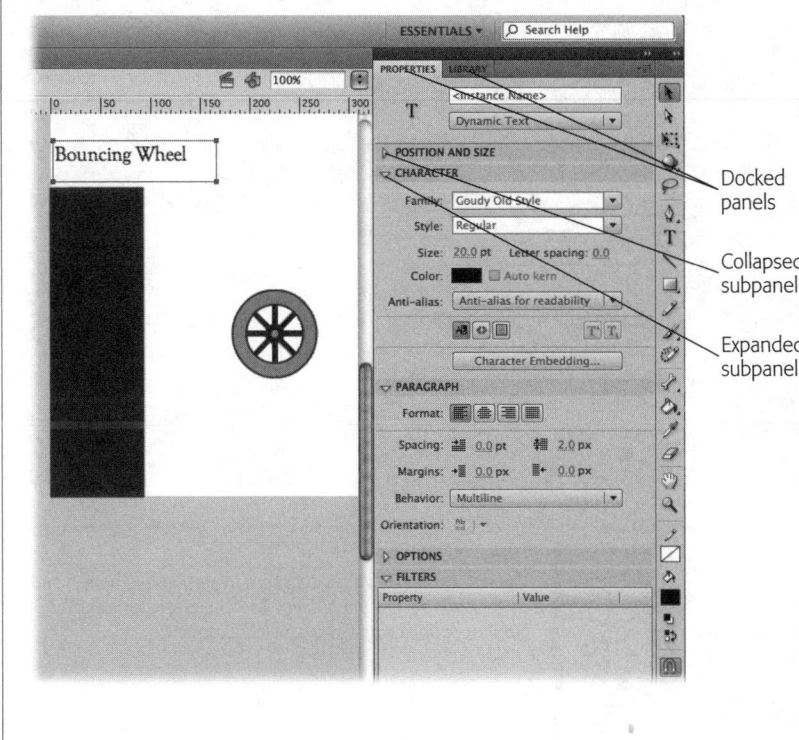

Docked panels

Collapsed subpanel

Expanded subpanel

Figure 1-6:
Panels like the ones shown here group useful options together, so you can find what you want quickly and easily. When there are lots of options and settings, panels are divided into subpanels. Click the triangular button to collapse or expand a subpanel. If all you see is a tab, the panel is collapsed and hiding its tools. To expand a collapsed panel and reveal its options, click the light gray bar near the tabs. To collapse a panel, another click will do the trick. Click the double arrows to shrink the panel down to icon size. To close a panel entirely, click the Options button and choose Close. To remove a floating panel, click the X button (not shown).

Besides keyboard shortcuts, there's only one way to display a panel—from the Window menu—but you have plenty of options for getting them out of your way. For example, you can click the X in the upper-right corner of a floating panel (Windows). On a Mac, click the red circular button in the upper-right corner.

For both docked and undocked panels, you can *collapse* (shrink) and expand them by clicking the dark bar at the top of the panel. Click the lower, lighter colored bar to shrink the panel down to icon size. There's also a collapse and expand button (two triangular arrows) in the upper-right corner, but it's usually easier just to click the bar—you don't have to be quite the mouse marksman. Another click, and you bring the panels back to their full glory. By dragging any edge of a panel—whether it's floating or docked—you can adjust its width.

Tip: To hide all the panels you've displayed in one fell swoop, select Window → Hide Panels or press the F4 key. Whoosh! The panels below the stage (or to the right of it) disappear, and you get to see a lot more of your workspace.

Docked vs. Floating Toolbars

A *docked* toolbar or panel appears attached to some part of the workspace window, while a *floating* toolbar or panel is one that you can reposition by dragging.

Whether you want to display toolbars and panels as docked or floating is a matter of personal choice. If you constantly need to click something on a toolbar—which means it needs to be in full view at all times—docked works best. But if you usually just need a toolbar or a panel for a brief time and want to be able to move it around on the screen (so it doesn't cover up something else you need to work with, for example), floating's the ticket.

To turn a docked toolbar into a floating toolbar:

1. **Click any blank spot on the panel's top bar and hold down the mouse button**. You may notice a

color change like the one shown in Figure 1-7, especially as you begin to move the panel. The actual visual effect is different on Mac and Windows computers, but the mechanics work the same.

2. **Drag the toolbar away from the edge of the workspace window and release the mouse button**. Flash displays the toolbar where you dropped it. You can reposition it anywhere you like simply by dragging it again.

To dock a floating toolbar, simply reverse the procedure: drag the floating toolbar to the edge of the workspace window and let go of the mouse button. You'll see a line or a shadow when the panel or toolbar is ready to dock. When you let go, Flash docks the toolbar automatically.

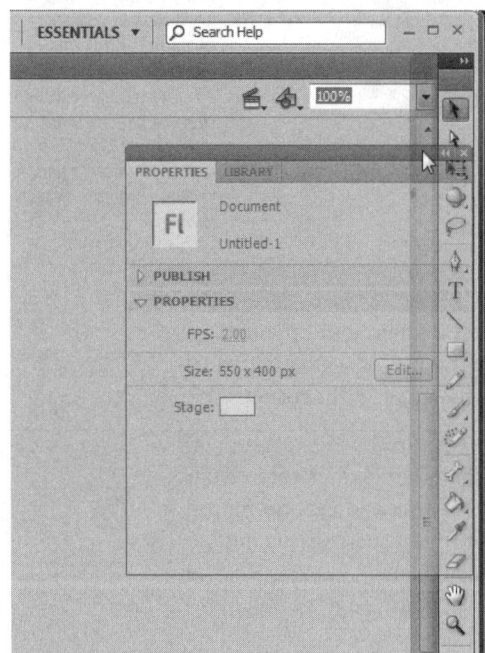

Figure 1-7:
You can customize your workspace by positioning panels and toolbars where you want them. To move a toolbar, click a blank spot and drag it to a new location.

Tip: In the upper-right corner of most panels is an Options menu button. When you click this button, a menu of options appears—different options for each panel. For example, the Color Swatch panel lets you add and delete color swatches. You'll find many indispensable tools and commands on the options menus, so it's worth checking them out. You'll learn about different options throughout this book.

Tools Panel

All animations start with a single drawing. And to draw something in Flash, you need drawing tools: pens, pencils, brushes, colors, erasers, and so on. The Tools panel, shown in Figure 1-8, is where you find Flash's drawing tools. Chapter 2 shows you how to use these tools to create a simple drawing; this section gives you a quick overview of the six different sections of the Tools panel, each of which focuses on a slightly different kind of drawing tool or optional feature.

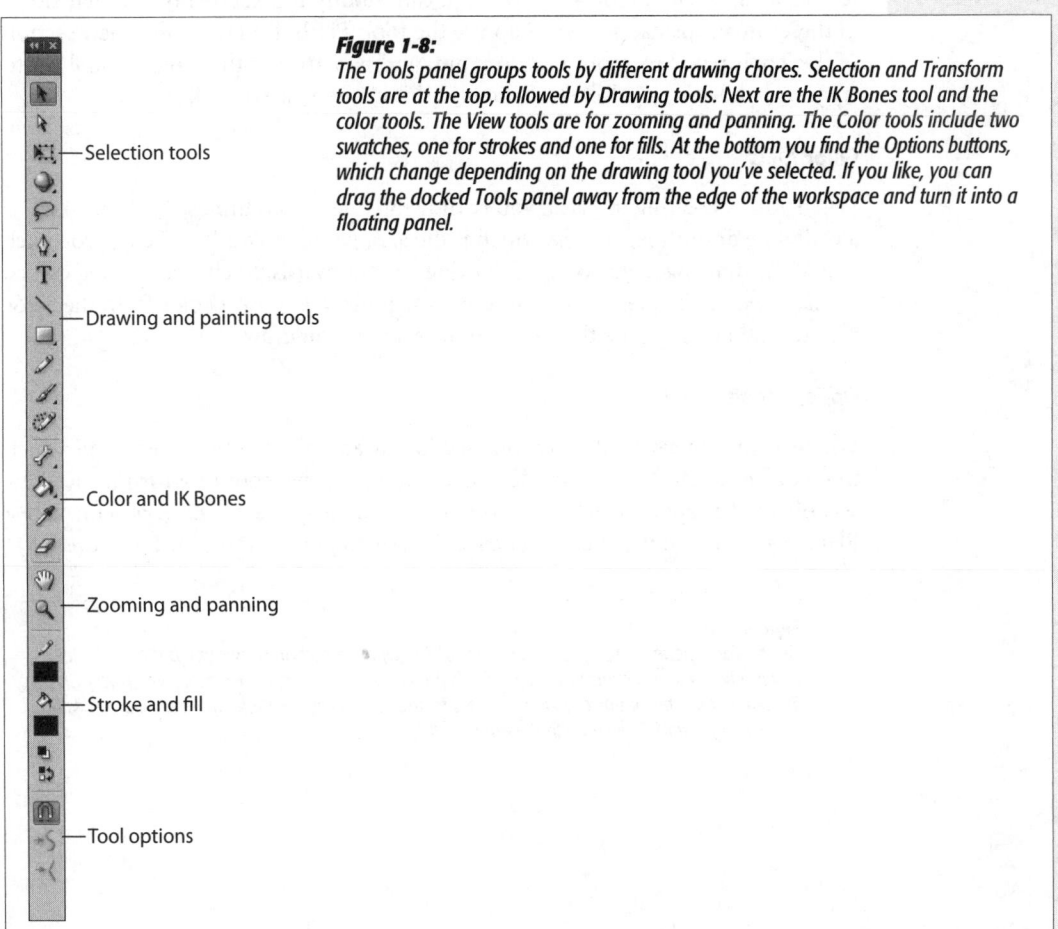

Figure 1-8:
The Tools panel groups tools by different drawing chores. Selection and Transform tools are at the top, followed by Drawing tools. Next are the IK Bones tool and the color tools. The View tools are for zooming and panning. The Color tools include two swatches, one for strokes and one for fills. At the bottom you find the Options buttons, which change depending on the drawing tool you've selected. If you like, you can drag the docked Tools panel away from the edge of the workspace and turn it into a floating panel.

Selection tools

Drawing and painting tools

Color and IK Bones

Zooming and panning

Stroke and fill

Tool options

Selection and Drawing tools

At the top of the Tools panel are the tools you need to create and modify a Flash drawing. For example, you might use the Pen tool to start a sketch, the Paint Bucket or Ink Bottle to apply color, and the Eraser to clean up mistakes.

Tip: If you forget which tool does what and can't tell by looking at the icon (and frankly, it's pretty tough to tell what a black or white arrow is supposed to do), move your mouse over the icon and hold it there (don't click). After a second or two, the name of the tool pops up onscreen.

View tools

At times, you'll find yourself drawing a picture so enormous you can't see it all on the stage at one time. Or perhaps you'll find yourself drawing something you want to take a super-close look at so that you can modify it pixel by pixel. When either of these situations happen, you can use the tools Flash displays in the View section of the Tools panel to zoom in, zoom out, and pan around the stage. (You'll get to try your hand at using these tools later in this chapter; see page 42.)

Color tools

When you're creating in Flash, you're drawing one of two things, a *stroke*, which is a plain line or outline, or a *fill*, which is the area within an outline. Before you click one of the drawing icons to begin drawing (or afterwards, to change existing colors, as discussed in Chapter 2) you can use these tools to choose a color from the color palette, and Flash applies that color to the stage as you draw.

Options tools

Which icons appear in the Options section at any given time depends on which tool you've selected. For example, when you select the Zoom tool from the View section of the Tools panel, the Options section displays an Enlarge icon and a Reduce icon that you can use to change the way the Zoom tool works (Figure 1-9).

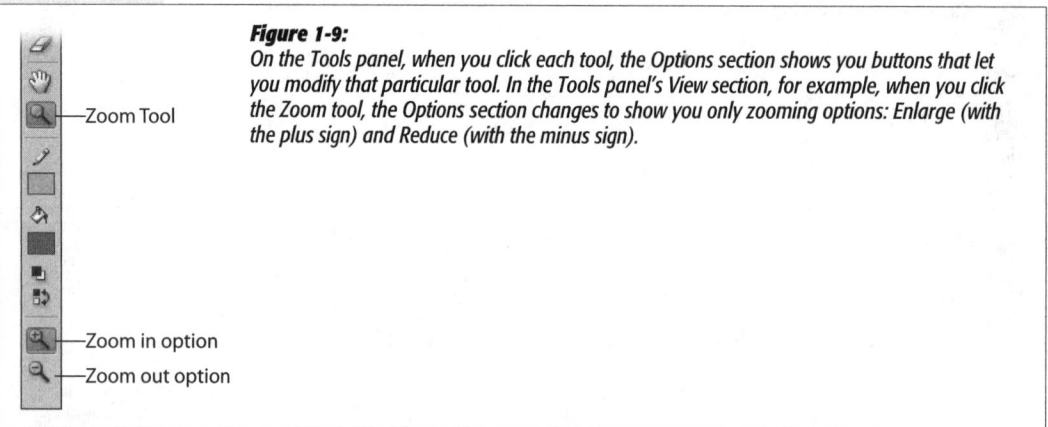

Figure 1-9:
On the Tools panel, when you click each tool, the Options section shows you buttons that let you modify that particular tool. In the Tools panel's View section, for example, when you click the Zoom tool, the Options section changes to show you only zooming options: Enlarge (with the plus sign) and Reduce (with the minus sign).

Zoom Tool

Zoom in option

Zoom out option

Accessibility Panel

Not everyone is blessed with perfect eyesight and hearing. To make sure vision- and hearing-impaired folks can enjoy the animations you create using Flash, you need to think about *accessibility*: the special techniques you can use to deliver your message via alternate means.

The Accessibility panel provides tools to help you create a design that provides at least some information to those whose vision or hearing is impaired. For example, using the Accessibility panel, you can give names and descriptions to certain sections of your drawings—descriptions that can be translated into speech by an assistive screen reader device, for example. Then, when a blind person surfing the Web loads your animation of a car crunching into a thick brick wall, the assistive reader can speak the words, "the car crashes into a brick wall."

Tip: Obviously, it's hard to translate any primarily visual medium like Flash into one that's spoken rather than seen. It's worth the effort it takes to try, though, because doing so gives impaired folks a chance to understand what you're trying to present. See the box on page 30 for more information.

To display the Accessibility panel, select Window → Other Panels → Accessibility (or press Shift+F11).

Actions Panel/ActionScript Debug Panels

ActionScript is a serious developer-level scripting language that lets you add inter- activity to your animations by tying a graphic element (say, a button) to a specific action (say, opening up a specific Web page). In fact, that's how ActionScript got its name: it lets you tie an *action* to an object or element you designate. You use the Actions panel to build the ActionScript code that turns regular animations into interactive animations like clickable splash pages, navigation bars, and type-in forms.

The Actions panel lets you mix and match snippets of ActionScript code to build what's called an ActionScript *script*, which you can then attach to one of the *frames* in your animation to make your animation "smart." After you create a script, the ActionScript debug panels let you troubleshoot any scripting code that's giving you trouble. You use different debug tools depending on the flavor of ActionScript used by your Flash file: ActionScript 2.0 or ActionScript 3.0. You'll learn how to write and debug ActionScripts of your own in Part 3.

Align Panel

Sometimes dragging stuff around the stage and eyeballing it works just fine; other times, you want to position your graphic elements with pinpoint precision. Using the Align panel, you can align graphic elements based on their edges (top, bottom, right, left) or by their centers. And you can base this alignment on the objects themselves (for example, you can line up the tops of all your objects) or on the stage (useful if you want to position, say, the bottoms of all your objects at the bottom of the stage, as shown in Figure 1-10). You can even distribute objects evenly with respect to each other.

To display the Align panel, select Window → Align or press Ctrl+K (Windows) or ⌘-K (Mac).

Tip: More help for aligning stuff on the stage comes from Flash's grids, guides, and rulers, which you'll learn about in Chapter 2 (page 77).

UP TO SPEED

Why Accessibility Matters

The term *accessibility* refers to how easy it is for folks with physical or developmental challenges (like low or no vision) to understand or interact with your animation.

As you can imagine, a Flash animation–which often includes audio in addition to video and still images–isn't going to be experienced the same way by someone who's blind or deaf as it is by someone who isn't impaired. But there is help. One of the features that conscientious Flash-ionados build into their animations is alternative information for those who can't see or hear. Often, sight and hearing-impaired folks use assistive devices to "report back" on what they otherwise can't access, so Flash animators build content into their animations that these assistive devices can access and translate.

Thanks to U.S. legislation referred to as *Section 508*, local, state, and federal Web sites absolutely have to be accessible and useable to the public. But if you're a private individual

planning to incorporate your animation into a Web site, you shouldn't ignore the issue of accessibility just because nobody's looking over your shoulder. If you ignore accessibility, you eliminate a whole audience who might otherwise benefit from your content.

For more information on accessibility, check out these Web sites:

- *www.adobe.com/accessibility/products/flash/*
- *www.DiveintoAccessibility.org*
- *www.Section508.gov*
- *www.paciellogroup.com*
- *www.WebAIM.org*
- *www.w3.org/wai*

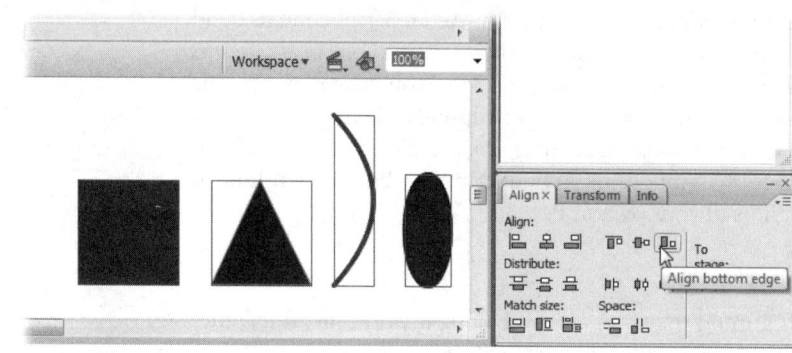

Figure 1-10:
The Align panel gives you the opportunity to align a single object (or whole groups of selected objects) along the left side of the stage, the right side, the top, the bottom, and more. Make sure you select the objects you want to align first, and then click the alignment icon from the Align panel.

Behaviors Panel

ActionScript 2.0 comes with several common, prescripted snippets of code called *behaviors* that you can add to your animations. You'll find a behavior for most of the really basic things you want to do with ActionScript, like triggering a sound file or jumping to a specific section of an animation.

All you have to do to use a behavior is display the Behaviors panel (Window → Behaviors) shown in Figure 1-11, and then click the Add Behavior icon to display a list of available behaviors. When you do, Flash pops up a helpful window (or two) to step you through the process of customizing the behavior.

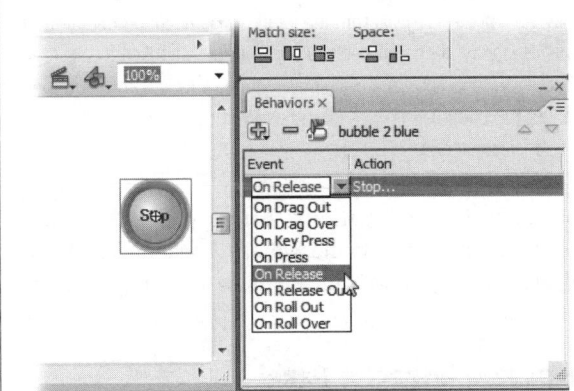

Figure 1-11:
The easiest way to add a behavior is to select a frame or object (like the Stop button shown here), and then select Window → Behaviors. In the Behaviors panel, click the big + button to add a behavior to the selected object. For example, this Stop button can stop a video from playing. Point to Embedded Video on the drop-down menu, and then choose Stop from the next menu. To finish up, choose the event that triggers the behavior, like "On Release" (in other words, the end of the mouse-click).

For example, if you want to trigger a sound file, you need to add the Play Sound behavior, tie it to an event—like a button clicking or a frame appearing—and then customize your newly added behavior by telling Flash which sound file you want it to play when the event happens.

Note: If you want to use behaviors, you have to start your Flash animation using the Flash File (ActionScript 2.0) option. The ActionScript examples in this book use ActionScript 3.0, and don't include Behaviors. For more details about using behaviors, see *Flash CS3: The Missing Manual*.

Color Panel/ Swatches Panel

A good painter can create custom colors by mixing and matching a bunch of other colors. In Flash, you can do that too, through the Color panel. And, if you like, you can save your custom color as a reusable color swatch in the Swatches panel. That way, when you get the urge to draw another puce-colored hedgehog, you'll be all set.

Note: Color in Flash is a huge topic. To explore it further (including how you can specify hue, saturation, and luminescence for a custom color) check out Chapter 5.

Common Libraries

The three Common Libraries panels—Buttons, Classes, and Sounds—display pre-built clips (in other words, self-contained, preconstructed Flash documents) that you can add to your animations simply by dragging them to the stage:

- **Buttons.** Here you'll find a wealth of cool-looking customizable push buttons, each as different from a dull gray HTML button as you can get.

- **Classes.** Useful only to heavy-duty ActionScript programmers, these compiled clips—DataBindingClasses, UtilsClasses, and WebServiceClasses—let you transfer information between your animation and server-side programs at runtime.

Note: To access the compiled classes that appear in the Common Libraries, you need to drag them from the Common Library to your document's Library; then you need to add specific ActionScript calls to your animation. Part 3 of this book introduces you to ActionScript and shows you how to add an action to your animation. You can find out more about the compiled classes Flash has by choosing Help → Flash Help and searching for the specific class you're interested in.

- **Sounds.** Need to add sounds to your animations? Before you grab a mic to record your own sound effects, check out the Sounds library. You'll find explosions, car sounds, phone sounds, sirens, male and female voices, laughing, coughing, and crying.

Components Panel/Component Inspector Panel

A Flash *component* is a reusable, self-contained, customizable, interactive graphic that you can add to your animation. Technically, you can create your own components using a combination of Flash and ActionScript. But right out of the box, the only components that appear on the Components panel are standard screen components (buttons, lists, text fields, and so on), animation controller components (MediaController, PlayButton, PauseButton, that kind of thing), and the handful of other assorted components that ship with Flash. To view and change a component's settings, all you have to do is click the component to select it, and then display the Component Inspector panel by selecting Window → Component Inspector or pressing Alt+F7 (Windows) or Option-F7 (Mac).

History Panel

Flash keeps track of every little thing you do to a file, starting with the time you created (or last time you opened) it: every shape you draw, every file you import, every color you change. This behind-the-scenes tracking—which you can view using the History panel shown in Figure 1-12—comes in handy when you want to revert to an earlier version of an animation. For example, you may want to go back to one in which the cartoon rabbits you drew actually look like rabbits instead of overfed mice. To display the History panel, click Window → Other Panels → History (or press Ctrl+F10).

Deciphering Components

Components aren't unique to Flash. Most programming languages provide a way to create components, which are nothing more than reusable hunks of code known in the trade as *black boxes*. What that means is that you don't have to know how the component code works behind the scenes in order to use it. All you have to do is put stuff in (change a couple of settings) and take stuff out (watch the component do its thing).

In days gone by, software pundits predicted that components would be the next big thing, since most people who sit down to work with Flash or similar programs tend to want to create the same kinds of things–menus, buttons, clickable images. Flash includes some very useful components, and you can find additional free and pay-to-play components on Adobe's Flash Exchange Web site (Help → Flash Exchange). For the complete rundown on components, see page 499.

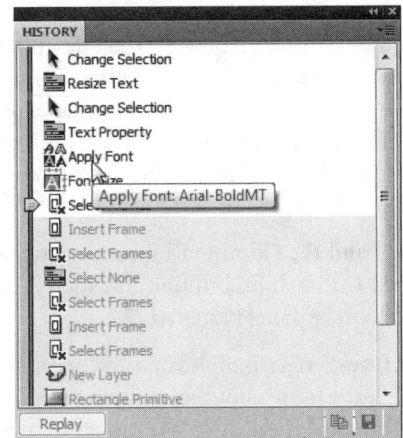

Figure 1-12:
When you move your mouse over one of the changes, Flash pops up a helpful detailed description of the change. To revert to an earlier version of your file, drag the slider until it's next to the last change you want to appear. To replay one or more changes, select the changes you want to replay, and then press Replay. If you do want to revert to an earlier version of your file, don't put it off: every time you close the file, Flash erases the file's history.

Tip: Unless you tell it otherwise, Flash keeps track of the last 100 changes you made to a document starting with the last time you opened it (or, if you've never saved the document, the last 100 changes since you created it). To increase this number, select Edit → Preferences. In the Preferences window that appears, select the General category. Then, in the Undo field, select Specify Document-level Undo, and then type in the number of levels (changes) you want Flash to track. You can specify any number you like from 2 to 300.

Info Panel

The more complicated your Flash creations become, the more likely it is that at some point you'll want to know specific details about the objects on your stage: details like the RGB values of one of the colors you used, the size of one of the objects in pixels, the XY coordinates of an object, and so on. This level of detail can be useful if you want to recreate a particular effect or if you want to rearrange objects on the stage down to the last little pixel.

To display the Info panel, first head to the stage, click an object to select it, and then choose Window → Info or press Ctrl+I (Windows) or ⌘-I (Mac). As shown in Figure 1-13, the Info panel displays information about the object you currently have selected.

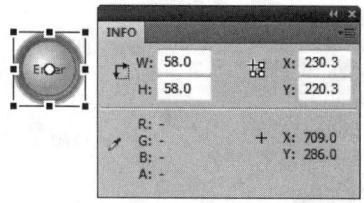

Figure 1-13:
Select an object on the stage, and the Info panel shows you the object's width, height, XY coordinates. Hold your cursor over an unselected object, and the color information appears (as RGB values and percentage of transparency). Move your mouse around the stage, and the bottom half of the Info panel shows you what color (and XY coordinates) your cursor is passing over.

Library Panel

The Library panel (Figure 1-14) is similar to the Common Libraries panel described on page 32: both display reusable components you can add to your Flash animations. The difference between the two is that while the Common Libraries panel displays components you can add to *any* Flash file, the Library panel displays objects you can add only to the file you currently have open. To show the Library panel, click Window → Library or press Ctrl+L (Windows) or ⌘-L (Mac).

Another difference between the Library panel and the Common Libraries panel is that the Library panel doesn't come preloaded with helpful buttons and such. You have to add your own reusable objects to the Library panel (Chapter 6).

Let's say, for example, that you create a picture-perfect bubble, or sun, or snowflake in one frame of your animation. (You'll learn more about frames on page 38.) Now, if you want that bubble, sun, or snowflake to appear in 15 additional frames, you *could* draw it again and again, but it really makes more sense to store a copy in the current project library and just drag it to where it's needed on those other 15 frames. This trick saves time and ensures consistency to boot.

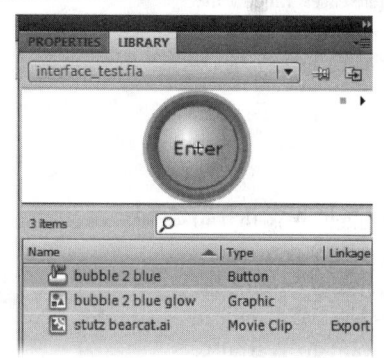

Figure 1-14:
Storing simple images as reusable symbols in the Library panel does more than just save you time: it saves you file size, too. (You'll learn a lot more about symbols and file size in Chapter 6.) Using the Library panel you see here, you can preview symbols, add them to the stage, and easily add symbols you created in one Flash document to another.

Movie Explorer Panel

After you finish creating a Flash animation (which you see how to do in Chapter 3), you can find and edit specific animation details quickly and easily by using the Movie Explorer panel, shown in Figure 1-15. To display the Movie Explorer panel, select Window → Movie Explorer (or press Alt+F3, or for the Mac, Option-F3).

If you're familiar with the Explorer tool in Windows, you may recognize the Movie Explorer panel. Much as the Windows Explorer shows you a collapsible outline of all the folders and files on your computer, the Movie Explorer panel shows you all the components of your animation, organized by scene: the video clips, sound files, text, images, and so on. (For more about scenes, check out the box on page 37.)

In addition to seeing an at-a-glance outline of your entire animation, you can use the Movie Explorer panel's Show icons to tell Flash which specific elements of your movie you want to view (just the buttons, say, or only the images, frames, and layers). Or you can use the Find box to view specific elements (for example, you can hunt for an ActionScript script named *openNewBrowserWindow*).

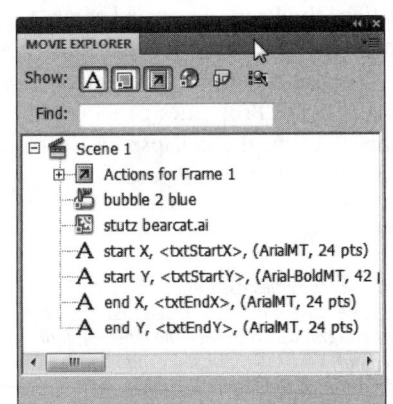

Figure 1-15:
The Movie Explorer panel lets you view the overall structure of your animation; it also gives you a way to find and edit specific elements quickly and easily. To find a specific element, use the Show icons or type the name of the element you're trying to find in the Find box. Right-clicking an element pops up a menu you can use to edit that element.

Output Panel

When Flash has something to tell you about your animation, it uses the Output panel. To view the Output panel, select Window → Output or press F2. For example, when you *export* your Flash animation (Chapter 19) or when you add buggy ActionScript code to your animation, Flash displays any problems it encounters in the Output panel and the Compiler Errors panel.

Tip: To tell Flash to include a file size report in the Output panel every time you publish your animation, select File → Publish Settings. Then, in the Publish Settings window that appears, click the Flash tab; finally, turn on the checkbox next to Generate Size Report. The next time you export your animation, Flash adds a file size report to the comments it displays in the Output panel. (You want to keep on top of file size if you plan to include your Flash animation in a Web page, because the larger the file size, the more likely folks will have problems viewing it over the Web.)

Properties Panel

In many ways, the Properties panel is command central as you work with your animation. It's Flash's most-used panel because it gathers all the pertinent details for the objects you work with and displays them in one place. It's not just an information provider; you use the Properties panel to change the settings and tweak the elements in your animation. When there's fine-tuning to be done, select an object and adjust the settings in the Properties panel. (You can learn more in the "Test Drive" section on page 40.)

The Properties panel usually appears when you open a new document. Initially, it shows information about your Flash document, like its dimensions and frame rate. Whenever you select an object in your animation, the Properties panel shows that object's details. For example, if you select a text field, the Properties panel lists the typeface, font size, and text color. You also see information on the paragraph settings, like the margins and line spacing. Because the Properties panel crams so many details into one place, you'll find yourself using the collapse and expand buttons to show and hide some of the information, as shown in Figure 1-16.

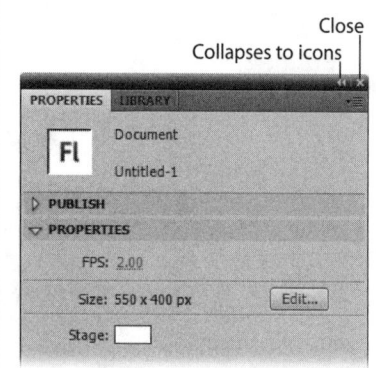

Close

Collapses to icons

Figure 1-16:
The Properties panel shows only those properties associated with the object you've selected on the stage. Here, because a text field is selected, the Properties panel gives you options you can use to change the typeface, font size, font color, and paragraph settings. Click the triangular expand and collapse buttons to show and hide details in the Properties panel.

Note: If you don't see the Properties panel, you can display it by selecting Window → Properties or by pressing Ctrl+F3 (⌘-F3 on a Mac).

Properties subpanels

On the Properties panel, you see different subpanels depending on the object you've selected, but, fortunately, the various panels and tools work consistently. For example, many objects have settings that determine their onscreen position and define their width and height dimensions. These common settings always appear at the top of the Properties panel and have the same tools for setting them. If you want to change colors or add special effects like filters or blends, you'll find the tools work the same way throughout Flash.

UP TO SPEED

Anatomy of a Scene

A *scene* is a collection of one or more frames tied to its very own timeline. Most of the time, you'll create animations consisting of just one scene; but if it makes sense to you organization-wise, you can choose to break your animation up into several scenes—for example, you might create an intro scene, a main scene, and a credits scene.

The benefit of breaking an animation up into a bunch of scenes is that it helps you reuse stuff. For example, say you use Flash to create 30-second Web advertisements for your company. If every single ad you create needs to contain

the same few seconds of animation at the beginning (a welcome message from your CEO) and the same few seconds at the end (a heartfelt "…and that's why you should buy from our company" appeal), it makes sense to designate these beginning and ending frames as separate, reusable scenes, perhaps naming them something descriptive like *Intro* and *Ending*. Then all you have to do to construct your next animation is create the meat of the new ad and sandwich it between the Intro and Ending scenes.

Scene Panel

You can create an animation in Flash that comprises just one scene, but you can choose to break your animations up into multiple scenes, too, if you like. (See the box above for the skinny on scenes and why you might want to organize your animation into multiple scenes.)

To add a scene to your animation (or to rename or delete an existing scene), use the Scene panel, which you display by choosing Window → Other Panels → Scene. Figure 1-17 shows you what the Scene panel looks like.

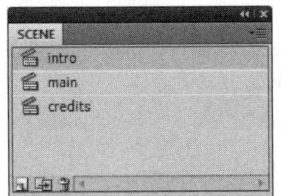

Figure 1-17:
Using the Scene panel, you can add a scene to your animation (either a duplicate of an existing scene, or a fresh, blank scene) or delete an existing scene. Just click the name of a scene, and then click Duplicate, Add, or Delete, respectively. To rename a scene, first double-click the name of the scene. Then, when you see an outline appear around the current name, click inside, and then type the new name.

Transform Panel

Transform is a fancy word meaning "to mess with." When you have an existing object that you want to mess with selected on your stage—to scale horizontally or vertically, rotate, compress, *distort* (pull out of shape like a wad of taffy), or *skew* (slant horizontally or vertically)—you want, in animation terms, to transform that object. You can learn how to do all these transformations in Chapter 5.

The Timeline

For a complex piece of software, Flash is based on a surprisingly simple principle—the old-fashioned slideshow. In case you're too young to remember, a slideshow consisted of a stack of slides loaded into a tray, a projector that displayed one slide at a time, and a human to run the show, determining the order in which the slides appeared and how long each stayed on screen. Well, a Flash animation is really nothing more than a souped-up slideshow. In Flash, the picture-containing slides are called *frames*, and instead of a person controlling the slide projector, you've got the *timeline*.

The timeline (see Figure 1-18) determines the order your frames appear in and how long each frame stays onstage. If you've decided to organize the images on your frames into separate *layers* (described in Chapter 4), the timeline is also where you specify how you want your layers stacked: which layer you want on top, which one beneath that, and so on.

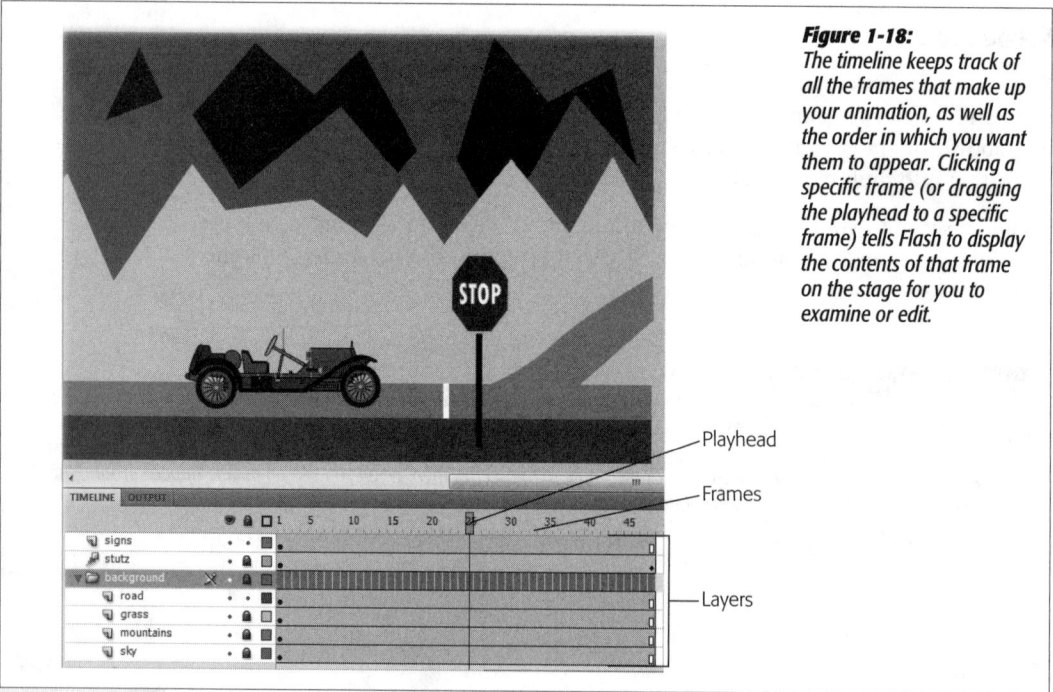

Figure 1-18:
The timeline keeps track of all the frames that make up your animation, as well as the order in which you want them to appear. Clicking a specific frame (or dragging the playhead to a specific frame) tells Flash to display the contents of that frame on the stage for you to examine or edit.

In addition to letting you put together a basic, plain-vanilla, frames-run-left-to-right, layers-run-bottom-to-top animation, the timeline also lets you create spiffy effects, like looping a section of your animation over and over again and creating tasteful fades.

Note: The first time you run Flash, the timeline appears automatically. But if you don't see it, you can display it by selecting Window → Timeline or pressing Ctrl+Alt+T (or for Mac, Option-⌘-T).

Using the Workspace Switcher

Tucked over on the right side of the menu bar is Flash's Workspace switcher. If you've read this chapter up to this point, you know just how many panels and windows and widgets and tools Flash has. Fortunately, Flash lets you customize the way the panels appear on your computer screen. After all, if you're a student doing a Flash project on a 13-inch laptop computer, your needs are different from those of a designer using two or more large monitors. So Flash lets you undock panels and move them around onscreen, or reduce them to show only icons. You can even set up one or more Flash environments for different projects. But doing all this customization can be a lot of work, so Flash gives you a tool to help you organize your tools—the Workspace Switcher.

The Workspace Switcher lets you save and reuse your favorite window and panel arrangements. You can adopt one of the predesigned workspaces (like the Essentials workspace used throughout this book) or you can create and save your own. Then, when you've completely discombobulated your workspace by undocking, closing and collapsing your favorite panels, you can return to the perfect workspace arrangement with one click, as shown in Figure 1-19.

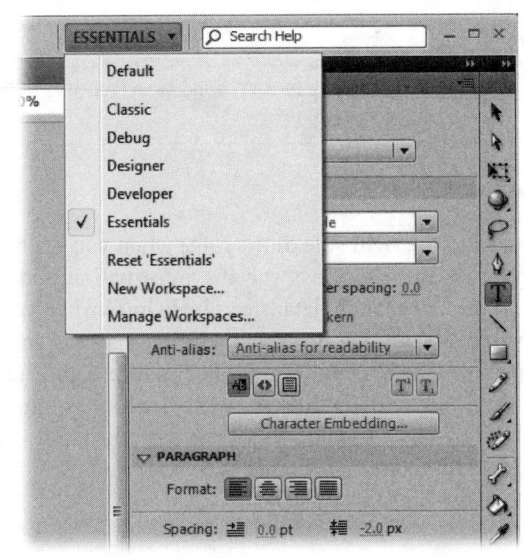

Figure 1-19:
The Workspace Switcher comes with several predesigned workspaces. Most of the exercise and pictures in this book are based on the Essentials workspace, which docks the Properties and Tools panels to the right of the stage.

In the rest of this chapter, you get to take Flash out for a test drive. You'll learn how to open, play, and save Flash animations; see the timeline in action; and try your hand at two of the program's most important panels—the Tools and Properties panels.

Note: This book doesn't cover the less-used Project, Screens, Strings, or Web Services panels.

The Flash CS4 Test Drive

For the tutorials in this section, you need a Flash animation to practice on. There's one ready and waiting for you on the "Missing CD" page at *http://missingmanuals.com/cds*.

Tip: Much of the time, you'll be working with files that already exist–either because you've created them yourself or because you want to incorporate them into Flash animation picture, sound, or movie files you've found on the Web. To avoid the agony of downloading a file and not being able to find it later, create a folder called, say, Downloads in the My Documents (Windows) or Home → Documents (Mac) folder and keep them there. You can even set your Web browser's Preferences to stash all downloads in that folder automatically.

Opening a Flash File

Download the file *rolling_ball.fla* and save it on your computer. Launch Flash, and then choose File → Open (the Welcome screen goes away automatically). When the Open dialog box appears, navigate to the file you just downloaded, and then click Open. Flash shows you the animation on the stage, surrounded by the usual timeline, toolbars, panels, and (at the bottom) the Properties panel. It should look like Figure 1-20. (To run the example animation, either press Enter or select Control → Play.)

Note: If you don't see the Properties panel, you can display it by selecting Window → Properties or by pressing Ctrl+F3 (⌘-F3).

Exploring the Properties Panel

The Properties panel appears docked to the right side of the stage when you open a new document. As shown in Figure 1-20, it displays specific information about whatever object you've selected on the stage. Such details can be helpful when you want to recreate an object precisely in another program, or incorporate your finished animation into a Web page you've already created. For example, the Size setting shows your animation's dimensions (550×200 pixels, say) which is information you need if you want to place your animation in a Web page by hand. (In Chapter 19, you'll learn how to tell Flash to create a simple Web page that includes your animation so you don't have to do this work by hand.)

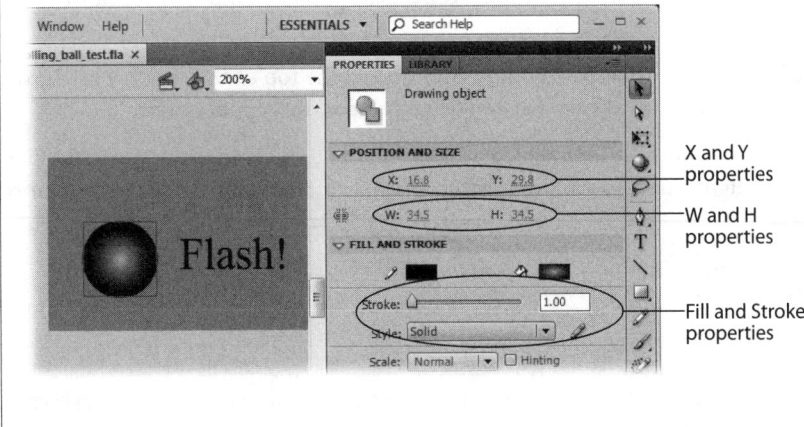

Figure 1-20:
Select an object on the stage, and the Properties panel automatically displays the properties (characteristics) of that object. You can change most of the properties in this panel; when you do, Flash redisplays the object on the stage to reflect your changes. Here, looking at the details for a drawing object, you can change the position (X and Y properties), dimensions (W and H properties) and the colors (Fill and Stroke properties).

To see how it works, click the ball in the *rolling _ball.fla* example animation. In the Properties panel, you'll see the following:

- **W.** The width of the ball is 34.5 px.

- **H.** The height of the ball is 34.5 px.

- **Stroke (pencil icon).** The stroke is black.

- **Fill (bucket icon).** The fill color is a blue to black gradient.

Note: If you don't see dimensions in the Properties panel, click the triangular expand button on the Properties subpanel.

By typing in new values or changing a setting, you can edit the selected object. To see the Properties panel in action, you'll use it to resize the stage itself, described next.

Resizing the Stage

In addition to just inspecting the properties of a selected object, you can also edit those properties using the Properties panel. In Flash, the size of your stage is the actual finished size of your animation, so setting its exact dimensions is one of the first things you do when you create an animation, as you'll see in the next chapter. But you can resize the stage at any time.

Here's how to change the size of your stage:

1. **Click the Selection tool, and then click on a blank area of the stage (to make sure nothing on the stage is selected).**

   Alternatively, you can click the Selection tool, and then chose Edit → Deselect All.

---

2. In the Properties panel, find the Properties subpanel, and then click the Edit button.

The Document Properties window appears. At the top of the window are boxes labeled Dimensions. That's where you're going to work your magic.

3. Click in the width box (which currently reads 800 px), and then type *720*. Click in the height box and change it from 600 px to 80 px. Click OK when you're done.

Flash accepts the new dimensions and resizes your stage, as shown in Figure 1-21.

Tip: If you resize the stage so big that you can't see the entire thing, check out the scrollbars Flash puts at the bottom and the right side of your work area. You can use them to scroll around and see everything.

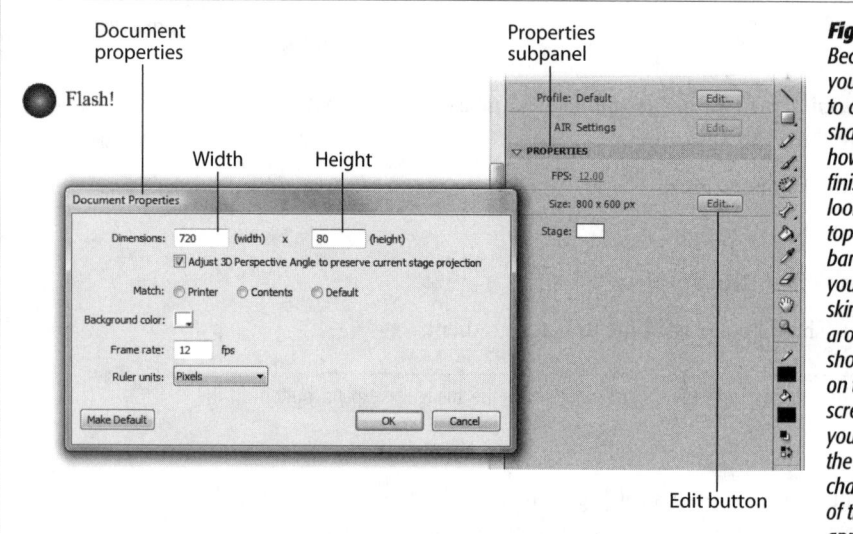

Figure 1-21:
Because the stage is your canvas, you'll want to change its size and shape depending on how you want your finished animation to look. For an across-the-top-of-a-Web-page banner ad, for example, you'll want a long, skinny stage–somewhere around 720 × 80 as shown here, depending on the size of your target screen. Any modification you make to the size of the stage immediately changes the dimensions of the stage itself as it appears in your workspace.

Zooming In and Out

Sometime in your Flash career, you'll draw a picture so enormous you can't see it all on the stage. The scroll bars let you move around a big stage, but they can't help you get a full overview. Next, you'll learn how to use the Zoom tools to pull back your view and see the entire animation at once. You can find these tools in the View section of the Tools panel. They let you zoom in, zoom out, and pan around the stage. You can even get in so close, you can modify your drawing pixel by pixel.

Here's how the Zoom tools work:

---

1. Click the Zoom tool (the little magnifying glass) in the View section of the Tools panel.

   The Tools panel usually sits at the right side of your screen (but you're free to move it, as described on page 23). As you can see in Figure 1-22, when you click the Zoom tool, the Options section at the bottom of the panel changes to show only zoom-related buttons.

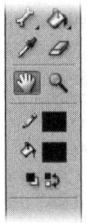 

Figure 1-22:
After you click the Zoom tool, each time you click your drawing, the stage (which contains your drawing) appears larger. If it gets so big that you can't see the whole thing, click the Hand tool; then click the stage again and drag to move the stage around (as shown here).

2. Move your cursor, which now looks like a magnifying glass with a plus sign on it, to the area on the stage that you want to zoom in on, and then click.

   Flash enlarges the stage and everything on it. The area where you clicked stays in full view.

3. Click the Hand tool.

   Your cursor turns into a little hand.

Tip: The quickest way to get to the hand cursor is to press the space bar. While you hold the space bar down, you can reposition the stage by dragging. When you let the space bar up, you're automatically returned to your previous tool.

---

4. Click anywhere on the stage, and then drag your cursor around.

   Flash moves the stage beneath your cursor so you can get a better look at whatever section of your bigger-than-life drawing you're most interested in.

Playing an Animation

Now that you've seen how to work on an animation while it's standing still, it's time for some action. After all, an animation by definition has to move. Using the Controller toolbar, which you display by choosing Window → Toolbars → Controller (see the box on page 45), you can play, pause, and rewind, much like a videotape or DVD. When you click Play on the Controller, your animation plays once through from beginning to end.

For finer control, you can use the timeline's playhead to click through your animation frame by frame, like the slideshows of yore. *Playhead* is nothing more than a fancy term for *currently selected frame.* Click a frame, and Flash displays the red playhead rectangle to show that you've successfully selected that frame (see Figure 1-23). If you select Control → Play to run your animation, your animation plays on the stage, beginning with the selected frame.

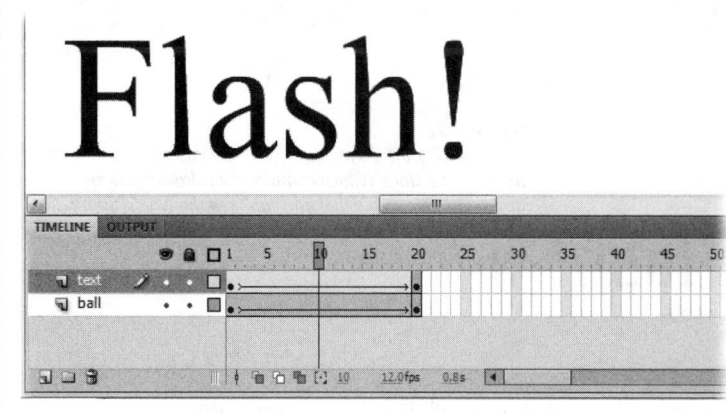

Figure 1-23:
You select a frame (specify a playhead position) the same way you select everything else in Flash: by clicking. In this example, the currently selected frame (playhead position) is the 10th frame. You can watch the playhead move from frame to frame by selecting Control → Play. Dragging the playhead back and forth (called scrubbing) is an even quicker way to test portions of your animation–and a fun way, too: dragging the playhead from right to left displays your frames in reverse order.

Saving a File

Saving your work frequently in Flash is a good idea. You might think you'll remember how to recreate a particularly great drawing or animated sequence if the unthinkable happens and your computer crashes, but why take the chance? You've got better things to do with your time.

The minute you finish a sizable chunk of work, save your Flash file by following these steps:

1. **Select File → Save As.**

   The Save As window appears (Figure 1-24). Choosing Save As (instead of Save) lets you create a new version of the file rather than overwriting the old one. Saving a new version of a file is always a good idea when you're experimenting, since some experiments invariably end up not working and you want to drop back to the previous working version of your file.

2. **Using the standard file and folder window, choose the folder where you want Flash to save your file.**

   PCs and Macs are slightly different, but Flash shows the standard file and folder window for each system. You can navigate to a new folder and save your Flash document there, or you can accept the folder Flash suggests, usually your Documents folder. You only have to choose a location once. After that, Flash will save your document in your chosen folder.

Controlling Playback with the Controller

If you've ever used DVD player or an iPod, the icons on the Controller toolbar (Window → Toolbars → Controller) look comfortingly familiar. Here's what each one does, from left to right as they appear onscreen:

Stop. Clicking this square icon stops playback.

Go to first frame. Clicking this icon rewinds your animation. That is, it moves the playhead back to Frame 1.

Step back one frame. Clicking this double-left-arrow icon moves the playhead back one frame. If the playhead is already at Frame 1, this button has no effect.

Play. Clicking this right-arrow runs your animation on the stage. Playback begins at the current position of the playhead. In other words, playback begins with the frame you selected in the timeline and runs either until the end of your animation or until you press the Stop button.

Step forward one frame. Clicking this double-right-arrow icon moves the playhead forward one frame (unless the playhead is already at the last frame).

Go to last frame. Clicking this icon fast-forwards your animation to the very end. That is, it sets the playhead to the last frame in your animation.

You can also access these six functions by choosing them from the Control menu in the menu bar.

Keep in mind that certain elements Flash shows you when you're testing on the stage—for example, *motion guide layers*, which you learn about in Chapter 3—don't appear in your finished animation. So while using the Controller panel is a great way to work the kinks out of your animation, it's no substitute for choosing Control → Test Movie, which exports (compiles) your Flash document and shows you *exactly* what your audience will see.

3. **In the File Name box, type a unique name for this file.**

A short, descriptive name that helps you easily identify the file later like *rolling_ball_changes*) is your best choice. Make sure you either include the standard Flash file extension (.fla) or don't type any extension at all, as shown in Figure 1-24.

4. **Click Save.**

Flash saves your file using the location and file name you specified.

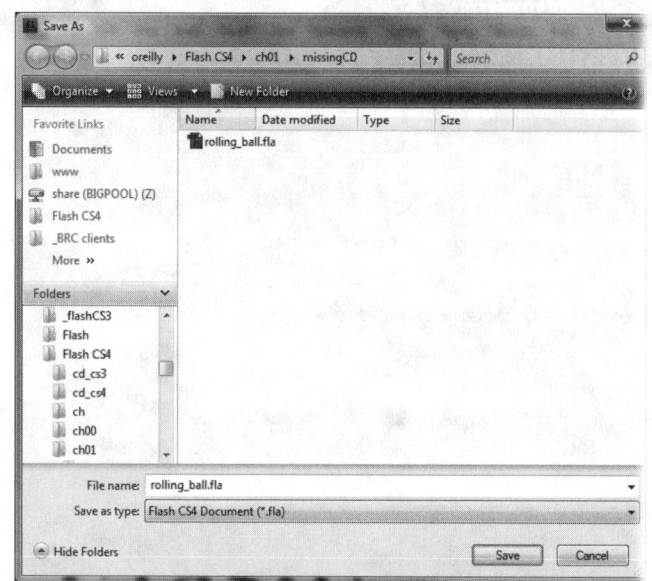

Figure 1-24:
You have only to specify a name and location for your file the first time you save it. After that, all you have to do to save your file (including any changes you've made since the last time you saved it) is select File → Save.

Flash File Extensions

Flash gives each different type of file its own extension to help it (and you) tell files apart. For example, when you save a Flash document, Flash automatically appends the .fla file extension. Here's a quick rundown of the file extensions Flash uses when you tell it to save or export a file:

- **Flash document files and Flash form application files (.fla)**. Flash form applications are HTML-like data entry forms you can create in Flash and hook up to a server on the back end to process the data that folks enter. This book doesn't cover Flash form applications.

- **ActionScript files (.as)**. ActionScript files let script jockeys write ActionScript code by hand and attach it to their Flash documents at runtime, rather than stepping their way through Flash's build-a-script interface to include their ActionScript code directly into their Flash documents. (This book doesn't cover Action-Script files, but you will learn how to write Flash scripts of your own in Part 3.)

- **ActionScript Communication files (.asc)**. Special ActionScript files that connect Flash animations to

database back ends. This book doesn't cover Action-Script Communication files.

- **Flash JavaScript files (.jsfl)**. JavaScript is a programming language built into Web browsers that Web designers use in conjunction with HTML to create interactive Web pages. Flash uses JavaScript a little differently. Programmers can automate Flash and use JavaScript to create custom tools. This book doesn't cover Flash JavaScript files.

- **Flash project files (.flp)**. If you need to create a large, complex Flash animation with a bunch of other people (for example, a corporate development team), you can use a Flash project file to keep track of all of the Flash documents, sound files, bitmaps, and other component files that make up that animation (including a copy of each version of the animation). This book doesn't cover Flash project files.

- **Flash runtime files (.swf, .exe, and .app)**. These published (compiled) files run in Flash Player (.swf), as an executable file that runs on Windows (.exe), and as an executable file that runs on a Mac (.app).

Creating Simple Drawings

The best way to get acquainted with Flash is just to dive in and create a simple animation. So this chapter starts with some tips for planning your work so you can get more done in less time (and be happier with the result). You'll see how to set up your Flash document and use the most popular Flash drawing tools—the Pen, the Pencil, the Shape tool, the Line tool, and the Brush—to draw a simple picture. Then you'll learn how to add color to your drawn shapes and move them around on the stage.

In the next chapter, you'll add a few more drawings and string them together to create a simple animation.

Planning Pays Off

Drawing a single picture is relatively easy. But creating an effective animation—one that gets your message across, entertains people, or persuades them to take an action—takes a bit more up-front work. And not just because you have to generate dozens or even hundreds of pictures: You also have to decide how to order them, how to make them flow together, when (or if) to add text and audio, and so on. In other words, you have to think like a movie director. With its myriad controls, windows, and panels, Flash gives you all the tools you need to create a complex, professional animation, but it can't do the thinking for you.

In this section, you'll see how the pros approach this crucial first step in the animation process: how to create a storyboard, come up with ideas, test your ideas, and benefit from others' successes.

Creating a Storyboard

Say you want to produce a short animation to promote your company's great new gourmet coffee called Lotta Caffeina. You decide your animation would be perfect as a banner ad. Now, maybe you're not exactly the best artist since Leonardo da Vinci, so you want to keep it simple. Still, you need to get your point across—BUY OUR COFFEE!

Before you even turn on your computer (much less fire up Flash), pull out a sketchpad and a pencil and think about what you want your animation to look like.

For your very first drawing, you might imagine a closeup of a silly-looking male face on a pillow, belonging to a guy obviously deep in slumber, eyes scrunched tight, mouth slack. Next to him is a basic bedside table, which is empty except for what appears to be a jangling alarm clock.

OK, now you've made a start. After you pat yourself on the back—and perhaps refuel your creativity with a grande-sized cup of your own product—you plan and execute the frame-by-frame action. You do this by whipping out six quick pencil-and-paper sketches. When you finish, your sketchpad may look something like this:

- The first sketch shows your initial idea—Mr. Comatose and his jangling alarm clock.

- Sketch #2 is identical to the first, except for the conversation balloon on the left side of the frame, where capped text indicates that someone is yelling to your unconscious hero (who remains dead to the world).

- In sketch #3, a disembodied hand appears at the left hand of the drawing, placing a cup bearing the Lotta Caffeina logo on the bedside table next to Mr. Comatose.

- Sketch #4 is almost identical to the second, except that the disembodied hand is gone now and Mr. Comatose's nose has come to attention as he gets a whiff of the potent brew.

- Sketch #5 shows a single eye open. Mr. Comatose's mouth has lost its slackness.

- The last sketch shows a closeup of the man sipping from the cup, his eyes wide and sparkling, a smile on his lips, while a "thought bubble" tells viewers, "Now, *that's* worth getting up for!"

In the animation world, your series of quick sketches is called a *storyboard*.

Figure 2-1 shows a basic storyboard.

Figure 2-1:
Spending time up-front sketching a storyboard lets you set up your basic idea from start to finish. Don't worry about how sophisticated (or unsophisticated) it looks; nobody but you will see this rough working model.

Five Questions for a Better Result

Creating your Flash animation will go more smoothly if you can answer these five basic questions before you even turn on your computer (much less start working in Flash):

- **What do you want to accomplish with this Flash creation?** Besides knowing whether you want your creation to be fun or serious, cutesy or slick, you should have a concrete, stated goal, like "show my company's new line of scooters" or "generate 1,000 hits per month for my personal Web page."

- **Who's your audience?** Different types of people require different approaches. For example, kids love all the snazzy effects you can throw at them; adults aren't nearly as impressed by animation for animation's sake. The more of a sense you have of the people most likely to view your Flash creation, the better you can try to target your message and visual effects specifically to them.

- **What third-party content (if any) do you want to include?** *Content* is the stuff that makes up your Flash animation: the images, text, video, and audio clips. Perhaps you want your animation to include only your own drawings, like the ones you'll learn how to create in this chapter. But if you want to add images or audio or video clips from another source, you need to figure out where you're going to get them and how to get permission to use them. (Virtually anything you didn't create—a music clip, for example, or a short scene from a TV show or movie—is protected by copyright. Someone somewhere owns it, so you need to track down that someone, ask permission, and—depending on the content— pay a fee to use it. Chapter 10 lists several royalty-free, dirt-cheap sources of third-party content.)

- **How many frames is it going to take to put your idea together, and how do you want them to be ordered?** For a simple banner ad, you're looking at anywhere from a handful of frames to around 50. A tutorial or product demonstration, on the other hand, can easily require 100, 200, or more frames. Whether you use storyboarding or just jot down a few notes to yourself, getting a feel for how many frames you'll need helps you estimate the time it's going to take to put your animation together.

Tip: Try to get your message across as succinctly as possible. Fewer frames (and, therefore, images) typically mean a smaller file size, which is important if you plan to put your Flash animation up on the Web. (Folks surfing with dial-up or on a cellphone often have trouble viewing large files.)

- **How will you distribute it?** In other words, what's your target platform? If you plan to put your animation up on a Web site, you need to keep file size to a minimum so people with slow connections can see it; if you plan to make it available to hearing-impaired folks, you need to include an alternative way to communicate the audio portion; if you're creating an animation you know will be played on a 100-inch monitor, you need to draw large, bold graphics. Your *target platform*—the computer and audience most likely to view your animation—always affects the way you develop your animation.

Preparing to Draw

Even if you're familiar with animation software (but especially if you aren't), you need to know a few quick things before you roll up your sleeves and dive into Flash—sort of like the quick where's-the-turn-signal once-over you do when you jump into a rental car for the first time.

In this section, you'll find out how to get around the stage and how to customize your Flash document's properties. You'll also learn a couple of basic Flash terms you need to understand before you use the drawing tools (which you'll see how to do on page 64).

But first you need to open a new Flash document page so you can follow along at home. To do so, launch Flash and, unless you've turned it off (page 19), the first thing you see is Flash's Welcome Screen. Under Create New, choose Flash File (ActionScript 3.0). If you've turned off the Welcome Screen, you can create a new file using the Flash main menu. Here's how:

1. **From the main menu, choose File → New.**

   The New Document window opens. If the window doesn't show the General tab as in Figure 2-2, click that tab to make it active.

2. **In the Type list, select the type of new file you want to create, and then click OK.**

   (If you're not sure what file type you want, choose Flash File (ActionScript 3.0); see page 19 for the reason why.) The New Document window disappears and Flash displays a brand-new blank document. You can tell it's a new document by the name Flash gives it: for example, *Untitled-1*.

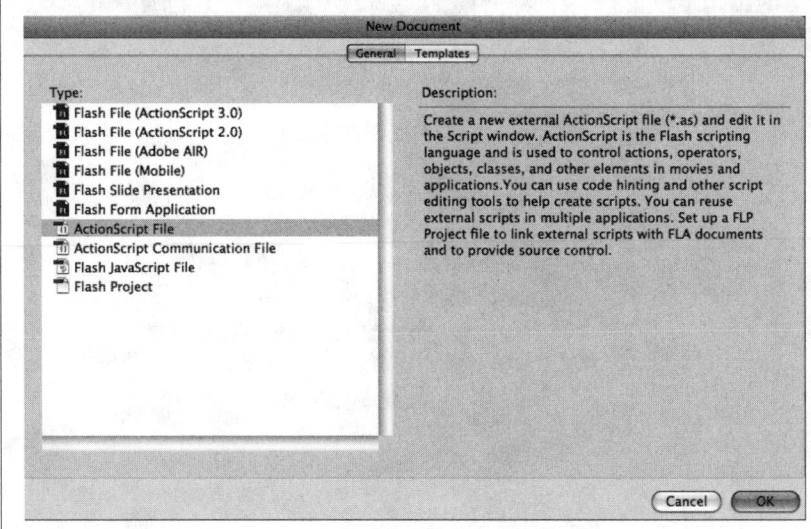

Figure 2-2:
In every case but one (Flash Project), selecting a document type and then clicking OK tells Flash to create a crisp, new document for you. (Flash projects are really nothing more than lists of other files with version control added so that multiple designers can work on the same Flash project without overwriting each others' changes.)

Both the Welcome Screen and the File → New menu show several types of Flash documents:

- Flash File (ActionScript 3.0) creates standard Flash animation documents with all the latest bells and whistles. Most of the examples in this book use this format.

- Flash File (ActionScript 2.0) is compatible with earlier versions of Flash that use the ActionScript 2.0 programming language and features.

- Flash File (Adobe Air) is a format for developers who create programs using Flash in combination with other Web page languages like HTML and JavaScript.

- Flash File (Mobile) is for creating programs for phones, and other handheld devices, a subject not covered in detail in this book.

Customizing Your Stage

The stage, as you may recall from Chapter 1, is your electronic canvas: it's where you draw your lines and shapes and add your text. Figure 1-1 shows what the stage looks like the first time you create a new document in Flash. There's certainly nothing wrong with it, but you may want to make yours larger (or smaller) or add helpful positioning guides, like rulers and gridlines. This section shows you how.

Change the size of the stage

The size of your stage is also the size of your finished animation. The standard 550 × 400 pixel Flash stage is a good compromise between large-enough-to-see-without-glasses and small-enough-not-to-hog-the-whole-screen. Flash automatically shows you this size stage because 550 × 400 is the minimum decent screen size for someone running a computer with a typical resolution of 800 × 600.

DESIGN TIME

Tips from the Trenches

Starting out on a learning curve as steep as Flash's can be daunting. Sometimes, it's helpful to hear what the pros think—to get advice from folks from who've been there, done that, and want you to know that you can, too.

Here are the top 10 recommendations from the experts:

1. **Analyze other people's animations**. As you begin to explore Flash content on other Web sites, think about it critically. Don't just focus on whether the result is dazzling or colorful, but also consider whether it's effective. What do you think it was designed to do? Get you to buy something? Get you interested in a product? Did it work? If not, why not? What detracts from the overall effect? Keep a notebook so you can apply what you learn to your own efforts.

2. **Don't sell yourself short**. Don't think you can't create great animations just because you're not a professional artist with a background in design. You'll find that Flash helps you through lots of tough spots (like correcting your shaky lines and generating frames out of whole cloth), and frankly, you're probably not shooting for a Picasso- or Tarantino-level result anyway. You get better at everything with practice; Flash is no exception.

3. **Always start with a storyboard**. Whenever you're working with anything but the simplest design (anything more than a couple of frames), create a storyboard (page 49). It can be as rough or as detailed as you want; some folks just jot notes to themselves. But do it you must. Every minute you spend planning will save you hours of hair-pulling later.

4. **Practice, practice, practice**. There are a lot of software programs out there that you can probably sit down and nail in 20 minutes flat. Flash isn't one of them. And while reading is a great way to begin learning Flash, no amount of book learning is going to substitute for rolling up your sleeves and actually producing an animation or two. (That's why this book includes hands-on examples for you to work through.)

5. **Join an online Flash community**. Real-time help from knowledgeable Flash-ionados is a beautiful thing. Use the online resources outlined in Appendix A Installation and Help to join a Flash community where you can ask questions, get help, and share ideas.

6. **Don't throw anything away**. You might be tempted to discard your mistakes. But if the "mistake" is interesting or useful, save it: you may be able to use it later for a different project. (While you're at it, write down a few quick notes about how you achieved the result so you can recreate it if you want to.)

7. **Spread yourself thin**. Many Flash pros like to have several different projects going at once, all of various types, so they can switch around when they get stuck on one. Keeping a lot of balls in the air can be an excellent way to help you think about things from different angles, which will help develop your skills.

8. **Always test your work in a live environment**. Don't rely on Flash's testing environment. If you're creating a Flash animation to display on a cellphone, test it on a cellphone before you go live. If you're targeting a Web site, upload your animation to a Web server and test it in a browser, or better yet, several different browsers, like Internet Explorer, Firefox, and Safari.

9. **Solicit (and incorporate) viewer feedback**. When you finish an animation, ask for feedback. Choose people you know will take the time to look at your work carefully and give you an honest evaluation.

10. **Never, ever sacrifice content for the sake of coolness**. The purpose of tools like Flash is to help you get your message across, not to see how many special effects you can cram into a 5-second spot. Pay more attention to whether you're creating an effective animation than whether you're adding enough colors, shapes, or audio clips.

But you may not want to keep that size. In some cases, you'll actually need the stage to hog the whole screen: for example, if you're designing an animation targeted for a very large size display monitor. If you're creating something for those itty-bitty mobile devices, you'll need to shrink the stage accordingly. In the case of the Lotta Caffeina banner ad, you want a wide, short stage (typically somewhere around 640×40).

The best way to ensure that your finished animation is the right size is to start with the right sized stage out of the gate. You set the size of the stage in the Document Properties dialog box (Figure 2-3), which you can open by using one of these methods:

- Right-click the stage. From the shortcut menu that appears, choose Document Properties.

- In Properties panel, find the Properties subpanel, where you'll see the Size properties displayed. To open the Document Properties, where you can make changes, click the Edit button (page 36).

- Choose Modify → Document.

Then, in the Document Properties window, type the new height and width in the Dimensions boxes. Figure 2-3 shows dimensions of 200×200 pixels, which is about the right size for a small pop-up ad. Click OK to close the window and return to the now-resized stage.

Tip: If you know you're going to be printing your work, you don't have to futz around with pixel dimensions; in the Document Properties box, you can just turn on the Match: Printer radio button, which automatically resizes your stage so that it prints out nicely on 8.5 × 11 paper.

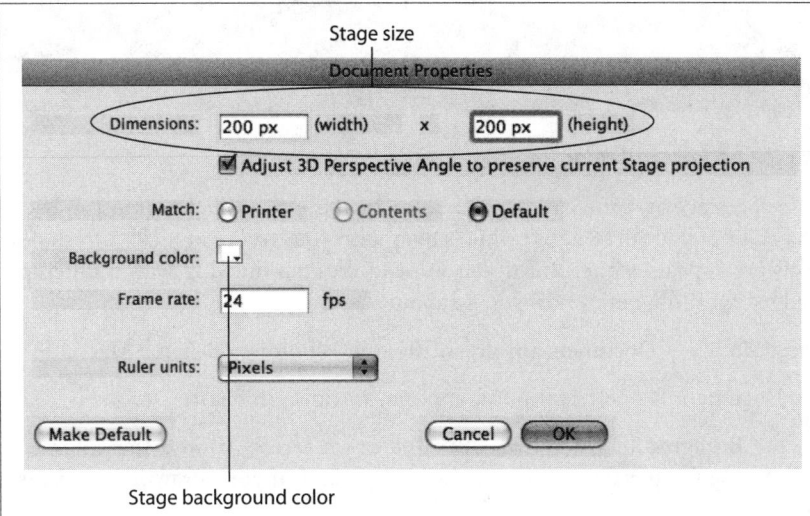

Stage size

Stage background color

Figure 2-3:
You use the Document Properties window to set the size and color of your stage (which will also be the size and background color of your finished animation). When you type the dimensions, you can type out the units of measurement (px, or even pixels, for example). But it's not necessary: The value in the Ruler units menu tells Flash which unit of measurement you're using.

Taking Advantage of Templates

How can some template designers I've never even met possibly know what kind of drawings I want to put in my animation, or how long I want my animation to be, or what kinds of sounds I want to add? They can't—so how on earth can Flash templates save me time?

The predesigned templates that come with Flash can save you time on the grunt work associated with several commonplace kinds of animations. For example, the Interactive Advertising Bureau (*www.iab.net*) recommends certain dimensions for certain types of Web ads, including pop-up windows and banner ads. When you open a template for a pop-up ad, for example, the stage is already preset to the dimensions for a standard sized pop-up in a standard sized browser window. You don't have to research the issue, and you don't have to customize the stage yourself.

Or say you want to create a slideshow in Flash, complete with buttons that let folks click forward and backward through your pictures. Putting an interactive animation like this together from scratch would require a fair bit of work, but if you use a slideshow template, all you have to do is add your images and captions. The template takes care of the rest.

On the downside, documentation for how each Flash template behaves and what you need to do to customize it is a bit skimpy. (When you select Help → Flash Help and, in the Help window that appears, search for *using templates*, you get some vague overall hints on what the templates to do and how to modify them, but no specific instructions.)

To see the templates Flash has, select File → New to display the New Document window, and then click the Templates tab. Here are the main categories:

- **Advertising**. Pop-up, skyscraper (skinny vertical), banner (skinny horizontal), and full-page ads.

- **BREW Handsets**. For Flash animations targeted for certain (Qualcomm) phones.

- **Consumer Devices**. For Flash animations targeted for certain media players and other portable electronics.

- **Global Handsets**. For Flash animations targeted for certain (Symbian) phones.

- **Japanese Handsets**. For Flash animations targeted for Japanese phones.

- **Photo Slideshows**. For Flash animations showing JPG images or other pictures overlaid with Forward and Back controls.

Setting the background color

Because the stage is your canvas, the color of the stage will become the background color of your drawing. If white's okay with you, you're in luck: A fresh new stage always appears white. But if you want to create a drawing with a different-colored background, here's how you go about it:

1. Select Modify → **Document (or press Ctrl+J in Windows; ⌘-J on a Mac).**

   The Document Properties window appears, as shown in Figure 2-4.

2. **On the Background color box, click the down-arrow, choose the color you want to use for the stage (and for the background of your drawing), and then click OK.**

   Flash turns the stage lime green (or whatever color you chose in step 2).

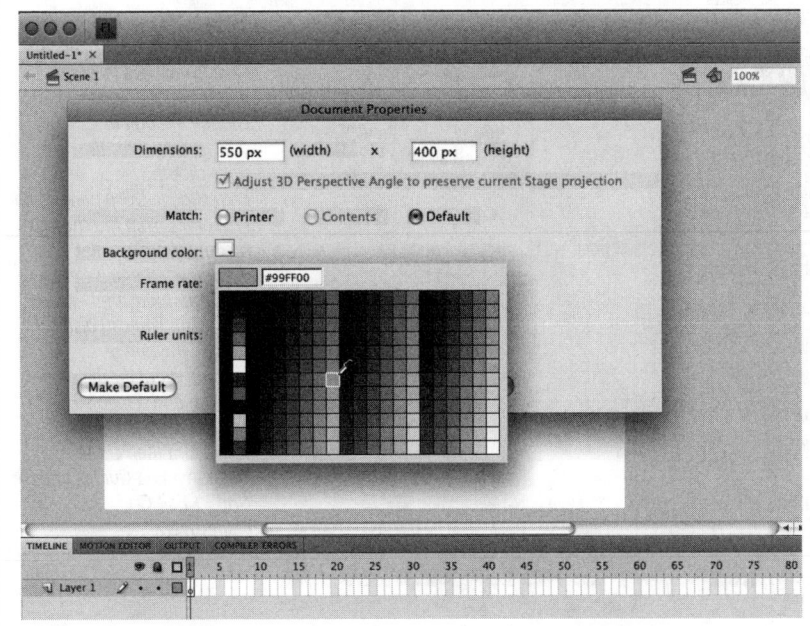

Figure 2-4:
Changing the color of the stage is an easy way to change the way your drawing looks. It can also make constructing your drawing easier. For example, if you're working with light-colored shapes, a nice dark background will help you see what you're doing better—even if you end up changing the stage back to a lighter color when your design is finished.

Tip: Because background color changes the way foreground objects appear, you might want to experiment with the color of the stage, beginning with one color and changing it as you add objects to the stage until you get the effect you want. (You can change the color of the stage at any time, even after you've completed your drawing.) When you're working on your animation, it may be easier to change the stage background color in the Properties panel. Select Properties → Properties → Stage, and then choose a color from the color picker.

Add helpful measurement guides

Even professional artists can't always draw a straight line or estimate three inches correctly. Fortunately, with Flash, they don't have to, and neither do you. Flash has several tools that help you spot precisely where your objects are on the stage and how much space they take up: rulers, a grid, and guides. You can see an example of these tools as they appear on the stage in Figure 2-5.

You can fine-tune your ruler, grid, and guides using the View menu or the shortcut menu that pops up when you right-click (or, on a Mac, Control-click) the stage. Here's what each tool does, and how to display each of them:

- **Rulers.** This tool displays a ruled edge along the left and top of the stage to help you determine the location and position of your objects. To turn on Rulers, right-click (Windows) or Control-click (Mac) the stage. Then, from the shortcut menu, choose Rulers.

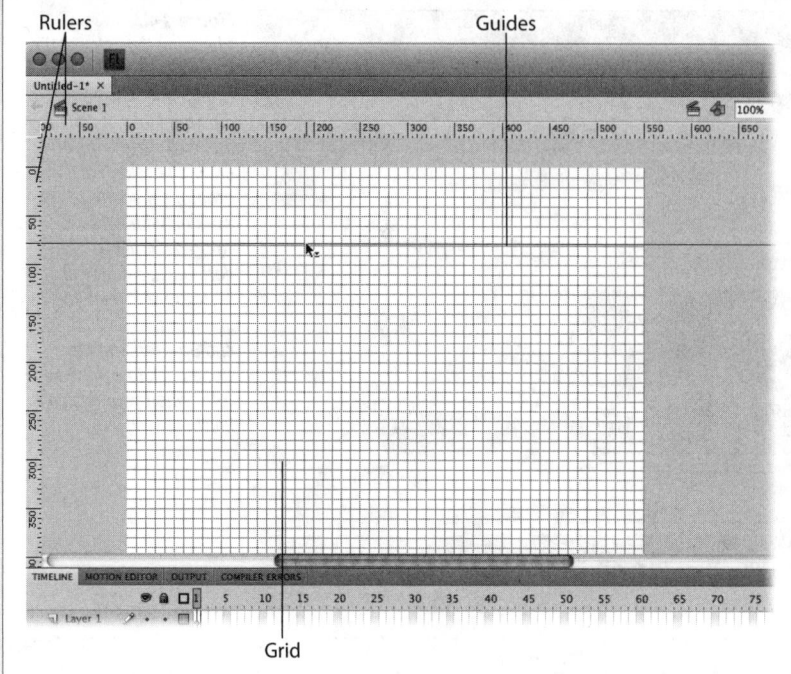

Rulers Guides

Figure 2-5:
Grids, guides, and rulers are Flash's answers to graph paper and a T-square. To change the unit of measurement for the ruler, right-click the stage, and then choose Document Properties from the shortcut menu. From the Ruler Units drop-down menu, select whatever measurement unit you want. You can also change the unit of measurement for the guides and the grid. To do so, right-click (Control-click) the stage, and then choose Guides → Edit Guides and Grid → Edit Grid, respectively.

Grid

- **Grid.** This tool divides the stage into evenly sized squares, which is great for helping you get the location of objects exact. To turn on the Grid, right-click (or Control-click) the stage. Then, from the shortcut menu choose Grid → Show Grid.

- **Guides.** If you want a tool that helps with straightedge alignment—like the grid—but you want more control over where the straight edges appear on the stage, you want guides. To add guides, you first have to turn on rulers (see above). Then, right-click (or Control-click) the stage and, from the shortcut menu, choose Guides → Show Guides. A checkmark appears next to Show Guides to indicate they're turned on, but you don't actually see any guide lines until you drag them onto the stage. You can drag as many guide lines as you want down from the top ruler or over from the left ruler. To add a guide, click a ruler (don't let go of the mouse) and drag your cursor to the stage. Release the button when you get to the spot where you want your guide to appear.

Tip: Grids and guides would be helpful enough if all they did was help you eyeball stuff, but Flash takes them one step further. If you turn on *snapping* and then drag, say, a circle around the stage, Flash helps you to align the circle precisely with either a grid or guide mark. When the circle is close to a grid or guide line, it snaps into position. To turn on snapping, simply right-click (Control-click) the stage, and then choose Snapping → Snap to Guides (or Snapping → Snap to Grid). For more on the joys of snapping, see page 197.

Choosing a Drawing Mode

Flash's selection tools, as you'll see in the next section, behave differently depending on which of Flash's two *drawing modes* you choose: the *merge* drawing mode (which was the only way you could draw before Flash 8) or the *object* drawing mode (which is more like the familiar drawing modes in Adobe Illustrator or Microsoft Word). The way you work with your drawings on the stage depends on the drawing mode you choose, so it pays to understand the differences between the two:

- **The merge drawing mode.** Flash assumes you want to use the merge drawing mode unless you tell it otherwise. In this mode, if you overlap one shape with another shape, Flash erases the overlapped portion of the first shape—a fact you discover only when you move the overlapping shape, as shown in Figure 2-6 (bottom).

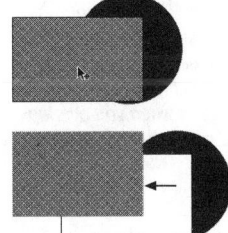

Figure 2-6:
Top: Say you're in merge mode and you drag a rectangle to overlap a circle, as shown here. Your only clue that you're in Flash's merge drawing mode is that the objects (or portions of objects) that you select appear to be covered by a dotted pattern.

Bottom: Drag the selected rectangle away, and you'll see that Flash has erased the overlapped portion of the circle. Notice that Flash repositioned the rectangle's fill, but left the outline in place. That's typical in merge drawing mode, where Flash treats shapes, not as complete objects, but as a collection of disparate elements.

- **The object drawing mode.** New since Flash 8, the object drawing mode tells Flash to think of shapes the way most humans naturally think of them: as individual, coherent objects. Overlapping shapes in object mode doesn't erase anything, and when you select a shape, you select the *entire* shape—not just the fill, or line, or portion of the shape you selected. Figure 2-7 shows you an example.

Note: You can mix and match modes in a single document. For example, you can use object drawing mode for some shapes and merge drawing mode for others. The drawing mode button on the Tools panel is a toggle, so the mode you choose remains in effect until you change it. Flash even remembers the setting from one document to another. So, if you decide to use only object drawing mode, you can set it once and forget it.

When to use merge drawing mode

As shown in Figure 2-6 (bottom), when you overlap objects in merge drawing mode, Flash erases the hidden portions of the objects underneath. You'll probably want to stay with the merge drawing mode if you fall into one of the following three categories:

- You're familiar (and comfortable) with an older version of Flash. (Merge was the *only* drawing mode before Flash 8.)

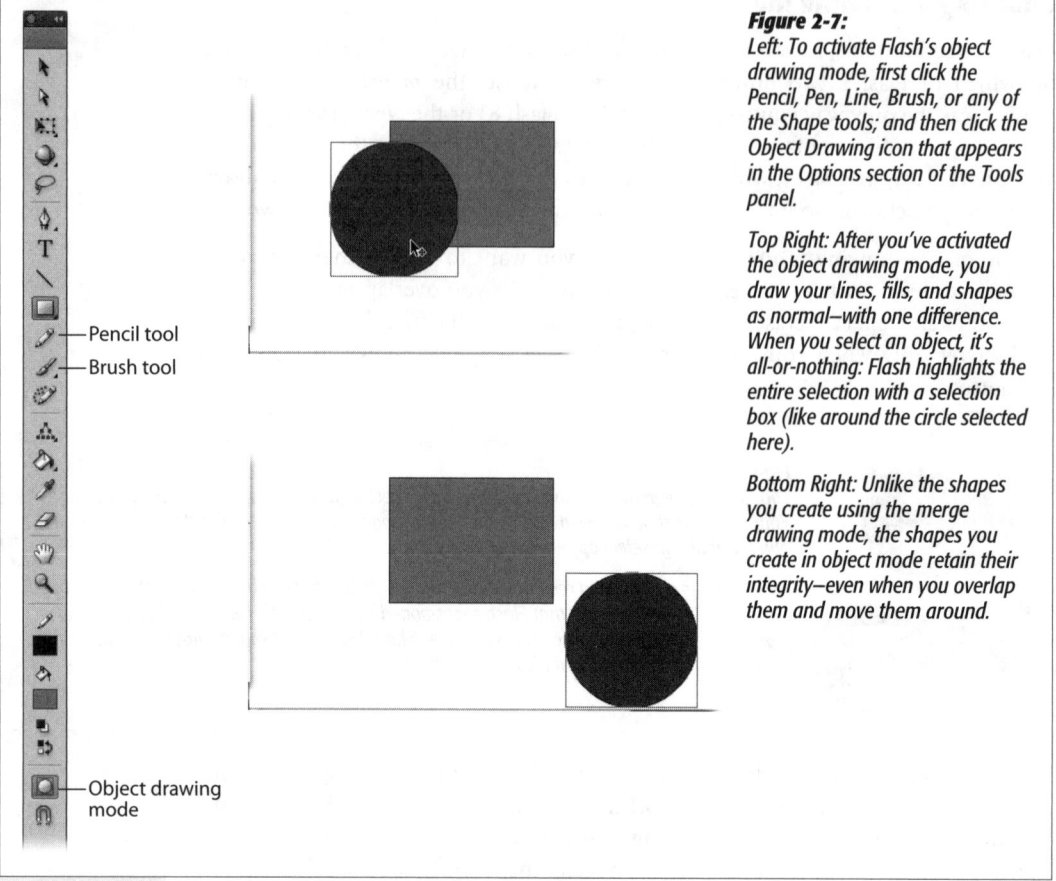

Pencil tool

Brush tool

Object drawing mode

Figure 2-7:

Left: To activate Flash's object drawing mode, first click the Pencil, Pen, Line, Brush, or any of the Shape tools; and then click the Object Drawing icon that appears in the Options section of the Tools panel.

Top Right: After you've activated the object drawing mode, you draw your lines, fills, and shapes as normal—with one difference. When you select an object, it's all-or-nothing: Flash highlights the entire selection with a selection box (like around the circle selected here).

Bottom Right: Unlike the shapes you create using the merge drawing mode, the shapes you create in object mode retain their integrity—even when you overlap them and move them around.

- You plan to create no more than one shape or object per layer anyway, so overlapping isn't an issue.

- You want to be able to select portions of objects, or create a deliberate "cutout" effect by overlapping objects and letting Flash do the cutting for you.

Out of the box, Flash assumes you want to work in merge drawing mode, so you don't have to do anything special to activate it the first time you use Flash. But if you (or someone you share your copy of Flash with) has activated object drawing mode (below), here's how to tell Flash to return to merge mode:

1. **Click to select one of the drawing tools (Line, Pencil, Pen, Brush, Oval, Rectangle, or Polygon).**

   In the Options section (bottom) of the Tools panel, Flash displays the Object Drawing icon (Figure 2-7, left). The icon (a circle in a square) appears pressed-down when it's selected.

2. **Click the Object Drawing icon to deselect it.**

   After you've deselected it, the Object Drawing button disappears, and it loses its outline and pressed-down look. You're then in merge drawing mode.

3. **Using the drawing tool you selected, draw an object on the stage.**

   Flash lets you work with your drawing (select it, overlap it, and so on) using merge drawing mode. Page 60 explains how the selection tools work in this mode.

Tip: If you've already created an object in object drawing mode, you can break it apart by selecting it, and then choosing Modify → Break Apart.

When to use object drawing mode

In early versions of Flash, you had to create your objects on separate layers if you wanted to overlap them with impunity. In Flash CS4, simply activate object drawing mode and bingo—Flash lets you stack and overlap your objects on a single layer as easily as a deck of playing cards. Choose object mode if you want to work with entire objects (as opposed to portions of them).

Here's how to activate object drawing mode:

1. **Click to select one of the drawing tools (Line, Pencil, Pen, Brush, Oval, Rectangle, or Polygon).**

   In the Options section (bottom) of the Tools panel, Flash displays the Object Drawing icon (Figure 2-7, left).

2. **Click the Object Drawing icon to select it.**

   The icon looks like an outlined, pushed-in button, meaning you're in object drawing mode.

3. **Using the drawing tool you selected, draw an object on the stage.**

   Flash lets you interact with your drawn item (select it, stack it, and so on) using object drawing mode. In the next section, you'll see how the selection tools work in this mode.

Tip: If you've already created an object in merge drawing mode, you can integrate it (in other words, tell Flash to treat it as a single, complete object just as though you'd created it in object drawing mode) by selecting the object, and then choosing Modify → Combine Objects → Union. If you want to go the other way, convert a drawing object (object mode) into a shape (merge mode), use Modify → Break Apart or Ctrl+B (⌘-B).

Flash's original drawing system, merge drawing mode, is unlike most other programs' drawing tools, while the object drawing mode will seem familiar if you're coming from other programs, like Adobe Illustrator. Even if this is your first adventure with a computer-based drawing program, you'll find the object drawing mode easier to learn and use. For that reason, the examples used in the rest of this book are based on the object drawing mode unless there's a note saying otherwise.

Note: This section gives you a quick introduction to Flash's selection tools. Page 60 shows you the finer points of selecting objects. Figure 2-8 shows some nifty tool keyboard shortcuts.

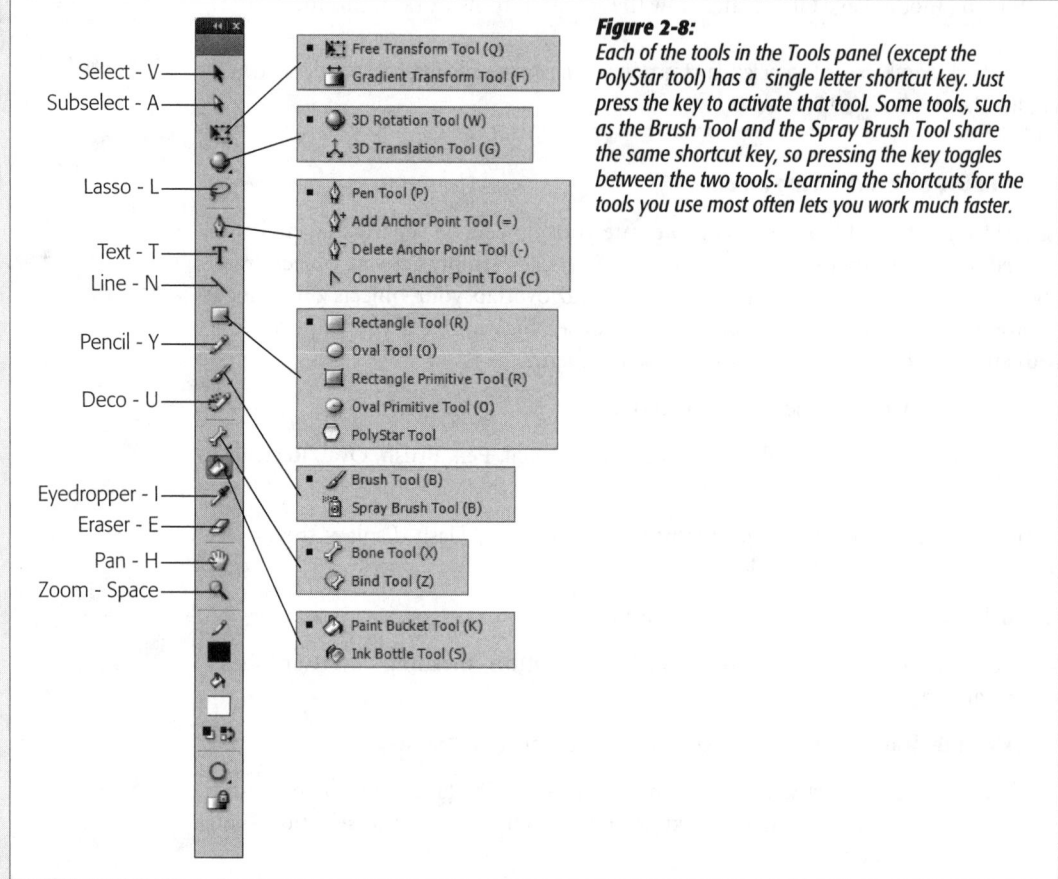

Figure 2-8:
Each of the tools in the Tools panel (except the PolyStar tool) has a single letter shortcut key. Just press the key to activate that tool. Some tools, such as the Brush Tool and the Spray Brush Tool share the same shortcut key, so pressing the key toggles between the two tools. Learning the shortcuts for the tools you use most often lets you work much faster.

Selecting Objects on the Stage

Once you draw a line or shape on your stage, you need to select it if you want to do anything else to it: for example, if you want to change its color, make it bigger, move it, or delete it.

As you can see in Figure 2-9, the Tools panel has three tools that let you select an object on the stage—Selection, Subselection, and Lasso. How these tools behave depends on whether you've created your drawings in merge or object drawing mode (see the previous section).

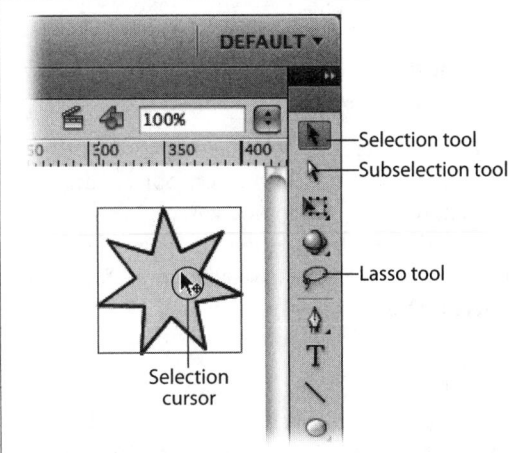

Figure 2-9:
Selecting an object on the stage to work with should be easy—and most of the time, it is; all you have to do is click the Selection tool (circled), and then either click your object or click near it and drag a selection box around it. But if your stage is crowded and you're trying to pick out just one little tiny angle of a line or portion of a drawing to manipulate, you'll need to use either the Subselection tool or the Lasso tool.

Selection tool

This tool lets you select entire shapes, strokes, and fills, as well as symbols and bitmaps. (If you've created objects in merge mode, the Selection tool also lets you select rectangular portions of those objects.) After you've made your selection, you can then work with it—move the object around the stage by dragging, for example.

- **Using the Selection tool in merge mode.** To select a rectangular portion of a shape you've drawn in merge mode, click near the shape and drag your cursor to create a selection box around just the portion you want to select. To select an entire shape, create a selection box around the whole shape, or double-click the shape.

  To select a symbol, a bitmap, or one element of a shape (just the fill portion of a rectangle, for example, or just the outline of a star) simply click the symbol, bitmap, or element. In merge mode, a single click on the stroke portion of a shape selects one line segment. Double-clicking selects the entire stroke. To show that an object is selected, Flash surrounds symbols and bitmaps with a rectangular outline; all other selections appear covered with a dotted white pattern.

- **Using the Selection tool in object mode.** To select an object created in object mode, click it. A rectangular outline appears around the selected object.

Subselection tool

The Subselection tool lets you reposition the individual points that make up your strokes and shape outlines.

- **Using the Subselection tool in merge mode.** To select a stroke or an outline created in merge mode, click the Subselection tool, and then click the line you want to move or change. Flash automatically redisplays that line as a bunch of individual points and lines. (Technically, these doohickeys are called *anchor* *points* and *segments*; see page 66 for more details.) As you move your cursor over the selection, Flash displays either a black (move) box or white (edit) box. Drag a black *move box* to move the entire stroke or outline; drag a white *edit box* to edit it (to change the individual points and segments).

- **Using the Subselection tool in object mode.** The Subselection tool works the same way on objects drawn in object mode as it does in on objects drawn in merge mode, except that on objects drawn in object mode you can also select an entire object by clicking the Subselection tool, and then clicking a fill. When you do, Flash displays a rectangle outline around the selected object, just as if you'd selected it using another selection tool.

Lasso tool

The Lasso tool is the one to use when you want to select a weirdly shaped portion of an object—say, you want to create a hand-shaped hotspot in the middle of a square bitmap—or when you need to select a weirdly shaped object that's super-close to another object.

- **Using the Lasso tool in merge mode.** To select a nonrectangular portion of an object drawn in merge mode, first click the Lasso tool; then click near (or on) the object and drag your cursor (as if you were drawing with a pencil) to create a nonrectangular shape.

- **Using the Lasso tool in object mode.** To select an entire object drawn in object mode, select the Lasso tool, click near the object, and then drag your cursor over the edge of the object. In object mode, dragging over a portion of the object selects the whole object.

Note: If you need to deselect an object after you've selected it (say, you changed your mind and don't want to change the object's color after all), you have three choices. You can press Esc; you can click somewhere else on the stage; or you can select Edit → Deselect All.

Special note to Photoshop fans: Ctrl+D (⌘-D on the Mac) works differently in Flash than it does in other Adobe programs. In Photoshop or Photoshop Elements Ctrl+D (⌘-D) is the keyboard shortcut that deselects an object. In Flash, the same keystroke creates a duplicate of the selected object.

Essential Drawing Terms

In Flash, a cigar isn't just a cigar. A circle isn't even just a circle. Every single shape you create using Flash's drawing and painting tools is composed of one of the following elements, as shown in Figure 2-10:

- **Strokes.** A *stroke* in Flash looks just like the stroke you make when you write your name on a piece of paper. It can either be a plain line or the outline of a shape. You draw strokes in Flash using the Pen, Pencil, and Line tools. When you use one of the Shape tools (for example, to create a square or polygon), Flash includes a stroke outline free of charge.

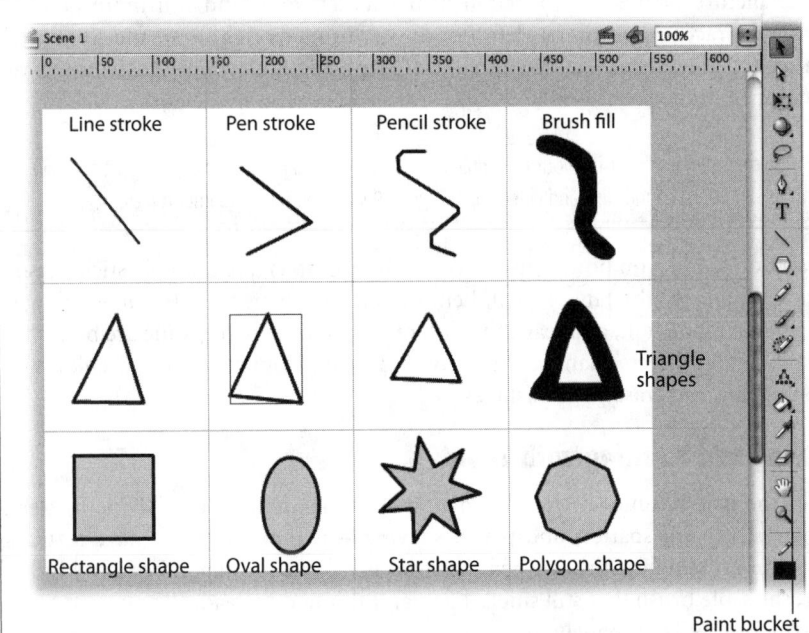

Figure 2-10:
Here you see the difference between strokes (lines and outlines) and fills. The strokes in this example appear black; the fills appear either light gray or white (Flash doesn't automatically add color to the fills you create by drawing outlines with the Line, Pencil, and Brush tool, so these fills stay the same color as the stage). You can change the color of any fill by clicking the Paint Bucket tool, and then clicking the fill you want to color.

Tip: You can quickly add a stroke to outline a shape that doesn't have a stroke. Choose the Ink Bottle tool, and then click the shape.

- **Fills.** Flash recognizes two different kinds of *fills*: the marks you make with the Brush tool, and the interior of a shape (in other words, everything inside the strokes that form the outline of a shape).

In a lot of cases, your shapes comprise both strokes and fills. You can create fill- and stroke-containing shapes in one fell swoop using Flash's shape tools—Oval, Rectangle, and PolyStar—or you can draw them by hand using the Pen, Pencil, and Line tools.

Why bother to learn the technical terms "stroke" and "fill" when all you want to do is draw a smiley face? For one very important reason: Flash treats strokes and fills differently. You use different tools to create them and different tools to modify them. If you don't know the difference between a stroke and a fill, you won't be able to do a whole lot with the drawing and painting tools described in this chapter.

Creating Original Artwork

Before you can create an animation, you have to have some drawings to animate. You start with one drawing and then create a bunch more (often by altering the first drawing slightly). For example, if you want to create an animation showing a raccoon marching in place, you need to draw a picture of a raccoon standing still;

another picture of the same raccoon lifting its left foot; and still more pictures showing the raccoon putting its left foot down, lifting its right foot, and so on. Put them all together using Flash's timeline (Chapter 3) and you've got yourself an animation.

Note: You're not limited to using your own drawings. Flash lets you *import*, or pull in, existing drawings and photos—and even sound clips and video clips. Page 319 shows you how to import files.

This section shows you how to use basic Flash tools to create a simple stick person drawing. You'll see the Line, Pencil, Pen, Brush, and shape tools (Oval, Rectangle, and PolyStar) in action, and learn the differences among them (some are better for creating certain effects than others). You'll also find out how to add color to a Flash drawing and erase your mistakes.

Drawing and Painting with Tools

One of the true beauties of creating digital artwork—besides not having to clean up a mess of paint spatters and pencil shavings—is that you don't have to track down your art supplies: the one pen that feels good in your hand, the right kind of paper, the sable brush that still smells like paint thinner. Instead, all you need to do is display Flash's Tools panel.

In this section, you'll see Flash's drawing and painting tools in action: the Line, Pen, Pencil, Brush, and shape tools. You'll also see the tools Flash provides (Lasso, Selection, and Subselection) that let you select drawings so you can modify them. And finally, you'll get a quickie introduction to color—specifically, how to change the colors of strokes and fills.

DESIGN TIME

To Thine Own Self Be True

When asked about her artistic process, a celebrated 20th century painter said that in order to create, she had to toss aside everything she knew about matching colors, standard techniques, and even the way she held her pencil and her paintbrush. As a right-handed person with a strongly analytical mind, she discovered her ability to create only after she started drawing with her *left* hand. She learned to ignore what everyone else told her about how she *should* be working.

There's a moral to this story: Just because one person finds the Pencil or Brush the easiest tool to use and sticks to it almost exclusively, that doesn't mean you should do the same. Experiment and find what works best for *you*!

To help get your juices flowing, the stick figure you see in this chapter shows several ways you can use Flash's painting and drawing tools. Each of these tools has its pros and cons, so try them all out for yourself. After all, the Flash police aren't going to arrest you if you sketch a beard and moustache on your stick figure using the Brush tool instead of the Pencil.

Line tool

You use the Line tool in Flash to draw nice, straight lines—perfect all by themselves or for creating fancy shapes like exploding suns and spiky fur.

Here's how to start drawing your stick figure using the Line tool:

1. **In the Tools panel, click the Line tool, as shown in Figure 2-11.**

   Flash highlights the Line tool in the Tools palette to let you know you've successfully selected it. When you move your cursor over the stage, you see it's turned into crosshairs.

2. **Click anywhere on the stage and drag to create a short horizontal line. To end your line, let go of the mouse.**

   Your line (technically called a *stroke*) appears on the stage.

3. **Click above the horizontal line and drag down to create a vertical line.**

   The result is a cross. Next, you'll add legs by drawing diagonal lines.

4. **Click the bottom of the vertical line and drag down and to the left; then click the bottom of the vertical line again and drag down and to the right.**

   Figure 2-11 shows the result. It doesn't look like much yet, but it's actually the basis for a stick figure you'll create as you experiment with Flash's drawing and painting tools in the following sections.

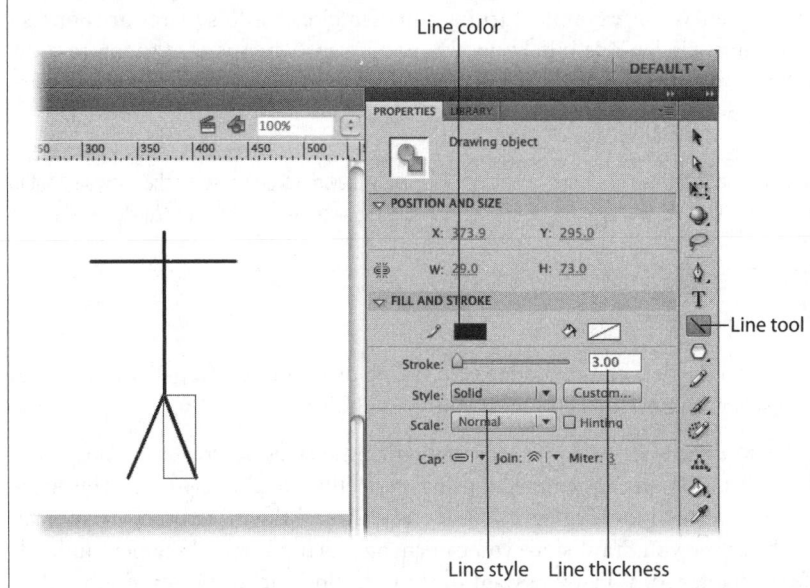

Line color

Line tool

Line style   Line thickness

Figure 2-11:
The Line tool is the easiest, quickest way to create straight lines in Flash (like the four straight lines you see here). If you'd like to customize the way your lines look, head to the Properties panel. There you find options that let you make the line thicker, change it to a different color–even turn it into a dashed or dotted line, instead of a plain solid line. (If you don't see the Properties panel, choose Window → Properties to display it.)

Pencil tool

The Pencil tool lets you draw freeform strokes on the stage, similar to the way you draw using a regular pencil on a regular sheet of paper. Unlike the Line tool, the Pencil tool doesn't make you stick to the straight and narrow, so it lends itself to curving lines and fine details, like hands and face. To use the Pencil tool:

1. **In the Tools panel, click the Pencil tool.**

   Flash outlines the Pencil tool to let you know you've successfully selected it, and Pencil-related options appear in the Options section at the bottom of the Tools panel. When you move your cursor over the stage, you see it's turned into a miniature pencil.

2. **In the Options section at the bottom of the Tools panel, click the down arrow.**

   A pop-up menu appears.

3. **In the pop-up menu, turn on the checkbox next to Smooth.**

   The *Smooth* option gently corrects any jiggles you make as you draw with the pencil—essential when you're trying to draw small lines, like this stick figure's face and hands.

4. **Click the stage and drag to draw a little face, hands, and feet similar to the ones in Figure 2-12.**

   While you're on the Options section, there are other ways you can modify how the Pencil tool works: The *Straighten* option emphasizes the corners you draw with the Pencil (for example, turning squarish circles into squares or roundish squares into circles—definitely *not* what you want when you're trying to draw the feet you see in Figure 2-12), and the *Ink* option leaves your Pencil strokes just as they are, jiggles and all.

Tip: You can also straighten or smooth a line you've already drawn. To do so, select the line you want to modify using the Lasso tool (page 62), then select Modify → Shape → Straighten or Modify → Shape → Smooth.

Pen tool

If you want to create a complex shape consisting of a lot of perfect arcs and a lot of perfectly straight lines, the Pen tool is your best choice.

To create straight lines with the Pen tool, click the stage to create *anchor points*, which Flash automatically connects using perfectly straight *segments*. The more times you click, the more segments Flash creates—and the more precisely you can modify the shape you draw, since you can change each point and segment individually (see Chapter 5). When you want to stop creating anchor points, double-click the mouse or press the Esc key.

If you drag the Pen tool (instead of just clicking), the Pen lets you create perfectly curved arcs.

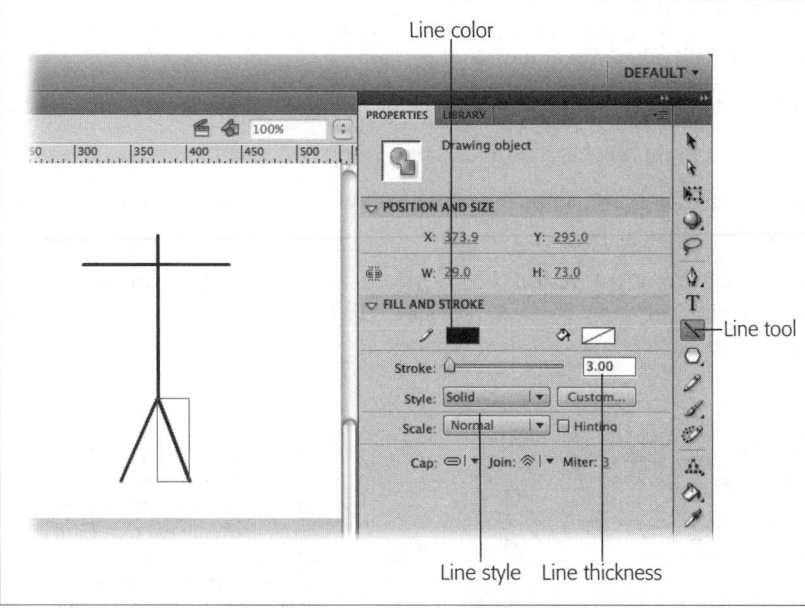

Line color

DEFAULT ▾

Line tool

Line style   Line thickness

Figure 2-12:
*Don't be surprised if your
results look a bit shakier
than you might expect. If
you've got an extra
hundred bucks lying
around, you can buy a
graphics tablet (see the
box below) to make
drawing in Flash a bit
easier, but most people
start out using a computer
mouse to draw—and it's a
lot harder to do than it
looks. Fortunately, Flash
has Pencil options you can
use to help you control
your drawing results.*

Mouse vs. Graphics Tablet

If you expect to do a lot of Flash work, do yourself a favor: ditch your mouse and get yourself a *graphics tablet* (sometimes referred to as a *digitizing tablet, graphics pad*, or *drawing tablet*). A graphics tablet is basically an electronic sketch board with a stylus that doubles as a pen, pencil, and brush. Today's graphics tablets connect through the Universal Serial Bus (USB) typically located at the front or back of your computer, so they're a snap to connect and remove.

With a graphics tablet, drawing and painting feels a whole lot more natural. Your results will look a lot better, too.

When you use a graphics tablet, Flash recognizes and records subtle changes, like when you change the pressure or slant of the stylus—something you don't get with a plain old mouse. (In fact, if you install your graphics tablet correctly, Flash displays extra icons on the Tools panel that relate only to graphics tablets.)

Expect to spend anywhere from $100 to $500 on a good graphics tablet.

Tip: Working with the Pen tool is a lot (a *whole* lot) less intuitive than working with the other Flash drawing tools. Because you can easily whip out a triangle with the Line tool or a perfect circle with the Oval tool, save the Pen tool for when you're trying to draw a more complex shape—like a baby grand piano—and need more control and precision than you can get free-handing it with the Pencil or Brush.

As you can see in the Tools panel in Figure 2-13, the Pen tool icon looks like the old-fashioned nib of a fountain pen.

To draw a straight line with the Pen tool:

1. **Select the Pen tool.**

   Your cursor changes into a miniature pen nib.

2. **Click the stage, move your cursor an inch or so to the right, and then click again.**

   Two anchor points appear, connected by a straight segment.

3. **Move the cursor again, stopping where you want to anchor the line, and then change direction again.**

   Figure 2-13 shows the results of several clicks. Flash keeps connecting each anchor point every time you click the stage. To break a line and start a new one, double-click where you want the first line to end.

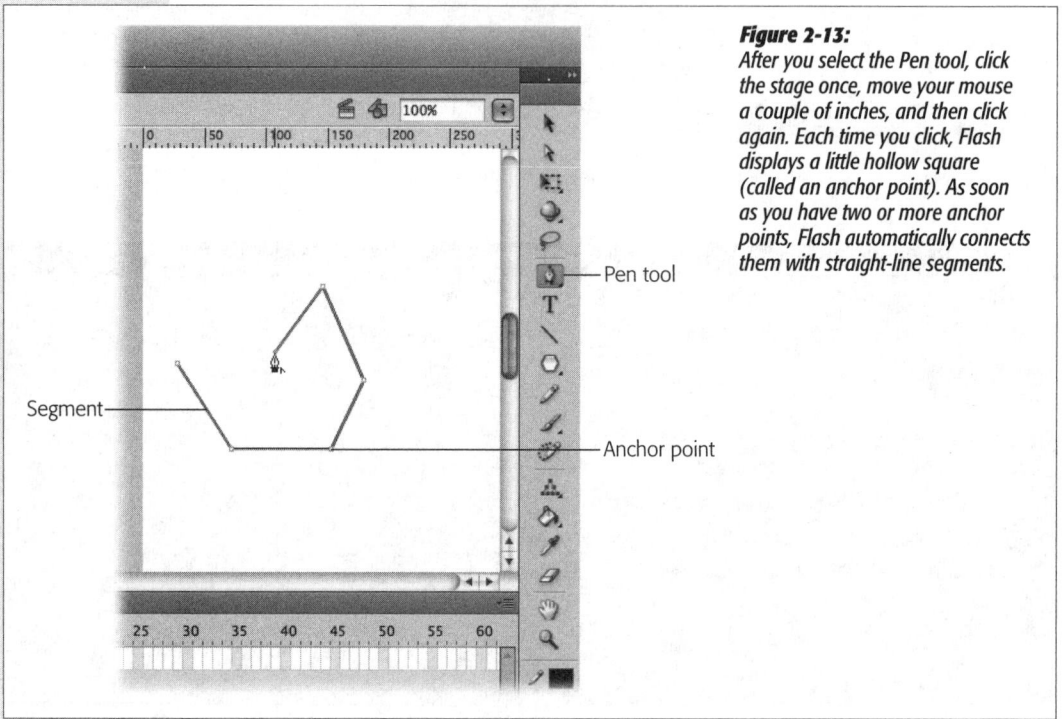

Segment

Pen tool

Anchor point

Figure 2-13:
After you select the Pen tool, click the stage once, move your mouse a couple of inches, and then click again. Each time you click, Flash displays a little hollow square (called an anchor point). As soon as you have two or more anchor points, Flash automatically connects them with straight-line segments.

To draw a curve with the Pen tool:

1. **Select the Pen tool.**

   Your cursor changes into a miniature pen nib.

2. **Click the stage once, and then move your cursor an inch or so to the right.**

   A single anchor point appears.

Note: Flash lets you change the way it displays anchor points as well as the way your cursor appears when you're using the Pen tool. You can even tell Flash to preview line segments for you, much as it previews curves. To change any of these preferences, select Edit → Preferences (Flash → Preferences for the Mac). Then, in the Preferences window, select the Drawing category. The Pen tool preferences appear at the top of the Preferences window.

3. **Click again; but this time, without letting go of the mouse button, drag the cursor around.**

   As you drag, the anchor point you create sprouts two control lines, and your cursor turns into an arrow. As you can see in Figure 2-14, something different is happening. Flash displays a preview curve and a control line that lets you adjust the angle of the curve. Drag the end of the control line, and the shape of the curve changes.

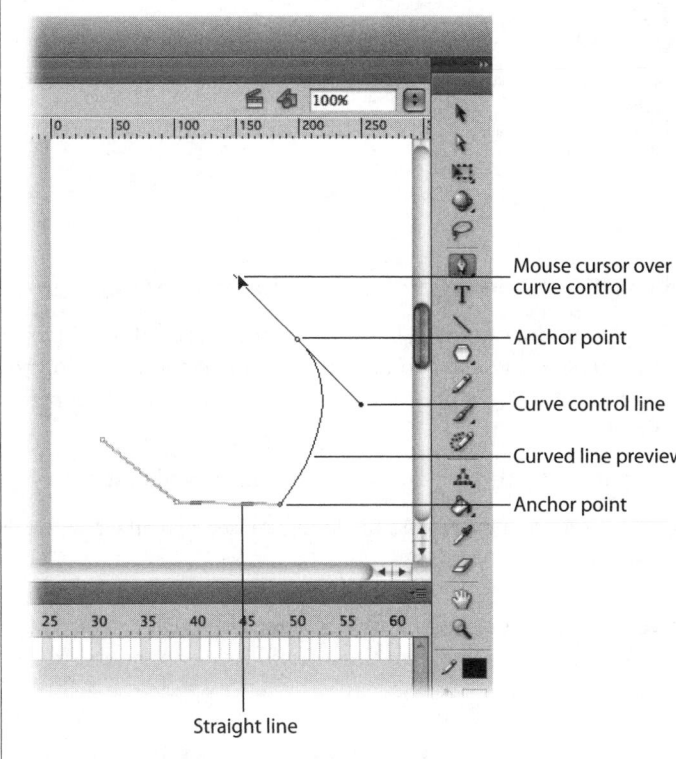

Mouse cursor over curve control

Anchor point

Curve control line

Curved line preview

Anchor point

Straight line

Figure 2-14:
To create a curve using the Pen, click the stage to begin the curve. Then move your cursor an inch or so, click again, and then drag. While you're dragging, Flash displays a temporary line with two small handles. These control lines don't show in your document; you use them to shape your curve. Drag the handles on the ends of the control lines. As you adjust the control lines, the curve changes shape.

4. **Release the mouse button.**

   When you let go of the mouse button, Flash draws the curve on the stage. The control lines disappear when you choose another tool. Using the pen tool, you can create both straight lines and curves as shown in Figure 2-15.

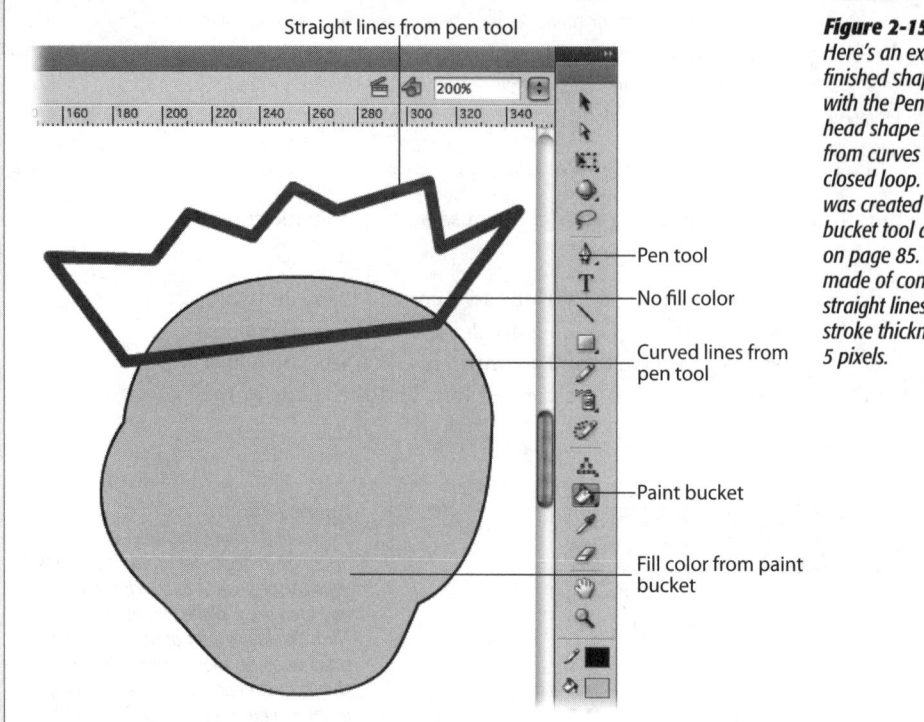

Straight lines from pen tool

Pen tool

No fill color

Curved lines from pen tool

Paint bucket

Fill color from paint bucket

Figure 2-15:
Here's an example of two finished shapes drawn with the Pen tool. The head shape is made from curves that create a closed loop. The fill color was created with the bucket tool as described on page 85. The hat is made of connected straight lines with the stroke thickness set to 5 pixels.

5. **Continue drawing connected lines by clicking other points on the stage.**

   Click, move, and click to draw straight lines. Click, move, and drag to create curves. Adjust the curves using the handles on the end of the curve control lines. If you've never used tools like these before, don't worry; you'll get better with a little practice.

6. **Create a closed loop shape by clicking the first point you created in step 2.**

   When the cursor is over a point that closes the loop, you see a small circle to the right of the Pen tool cursor.

Tip: If you want to adjust a curve after the fact, choose the Subselection tool, and then click an anchor point adjacent to the curve. The control lines appear, and you can change the shape of the curve by dragging the control points.

7. **Once you feel comfortable drawing straight lines and curved lines, use curves to create a cartoon head, similar to the one in Figure 2-15. Then use straight lines to make a hat for your creation.**

Drawing curves can be a bit tough until you get the hang of controlling the shape of the curves as you draw. One of the great things about the Pen tool is you can make adjustments after the fact. You can move anchor points by dragging the points. You can readjust curves by clicking an adjacent anchor point with the Subselection tool. The anchor point sprouts control lines, and you can adjust the curve by dragging the points on the end of the control lines. Once you get used to the Pen tool's drawing system, you'll find that you can draw very precise shapes. (Plus, all your practice with the Pen tool will pay off if you ever use Adobe Illustrator or similar programs that use the same drawing system, which is, by the way, called *Bezier curves*.)

Brush tool

You use the Brush tool to create freeform drawings, much like the Pencil tool described on page 66. The differences between the two are:

- **You can change the shape and size of the Brush tool**. You can choose a brush tip that's fat, skinny, round, rectangular, or even slanted. (You can't change either the size or the shape of the Pencil.)

- **You create fills using the Brush tool**. You create strokes using the Pencil. This distinction becomes important when it comes time to change the color of your drawings (see page 82).

Tip: The Brush tool really shows its stuff when you use it with a graphics tablet, as described in the box on page 67. That's because the brush tool makes great use of the tablet's ability to sense pressure. Press hard for thick bold lines. Lessen the pressure for thin delicate lines. With practice, you can create great calligraphic effects.

To use the Brush tool:

1. **On the Tools panel, click the Brush tool (the little paintbrush icon).**

   Flash displays your Brush options, including Brush size and shape, in the Options section of the Tools panel.

2. **From the Brush Size drop-down menu (Figure 2-16), select the third or fourth smallest brush size.**

   The larger brushes let you paint great sweeping strokes on the stage. But in this example, you'll be drawing hairs on your fellow's head, so a modest brush size is more appropriate. Your cursor changes to reflect your choice (you can see this change if you mouse over the stage).

Tip: Whenever you make a mistake, or simply want to wipe out the very last thing you did in Flash, select Edit → Undo.

---

3. **From the Brush Shape drop-down menu, choose the round brush shape.**

   Each brush shape gives you a dramatically different look. To draw hair, as in this example, you may choose round because it most closely approximates the results you get with a real brush. Once again, your cursor changes to reflect your choice.

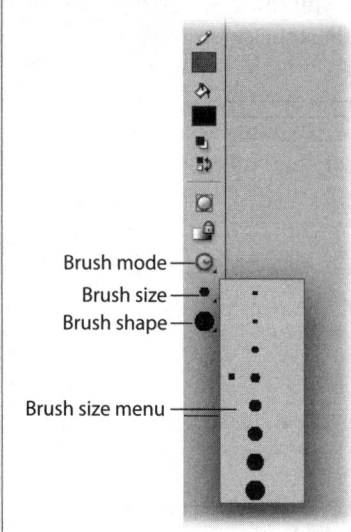

Figure 2-16:
The options for controlling the brush size, shape, and mode appear at the bottom of the Tools panel after you choose the Brush tool. To make a size adjustment, click the Brush Size button, and then select the size you want from the pop-up menu.

Brush mode

Brush size

Brush shape

Brush size menu

4. **Click the down arrow next to Brush Mode, and then, from the pop-up menu that appears, choose Paint Normal.**

   Brush modes change the way the Brush tool paints over or under strokes and fills already in your drawing. Figure 2-17 shows the different effects. Here you choose Paint Normal to draw hair that shows over the head shape and the hat. Later, you'll see how to tuck that hair under the hat.

   Here's a rundown of all the brush modes you can choose from:

   - **Paint Normal.** Flash uses this mode unless you tell it otherwise. If you brush over an existing object on the stage using Paint Normal, your brush stroke appears on top of the shape.

   - **Paint Fill.** If you brush over an existing object on the stage using Paint Fill, your brush stroke appears on top of the fill portion of the object, behind the stroke, and on the stage.

   - **Paint Behind.** If you brush over an existing object on the stage using Paint Behind, your brush stroke always appears behind the object.

   - **Paint Selection.** If you brush over an existing object on the stage using Paint Selection, your brush stroke only appears on the parts of the shape that are both fills and that you've previously selected.

   - **Paint Inside.** If you brush over an existing object on the stage using Paint Inside and begin *inside* the stroke outline, your brush stroke only appears inside the lines of an object (even if you color outside the lines). If you begin *outside* the lines, your brush stroke only appears outside (even if you try to color inside them).

5. **Click the stage just about where your stick person's hair should be and drag
   your mouse upward; release the mouse button when the hair is the length you
   want it.**

   Your paintbrush stroke appears on the stage.

6. **Repeat to create additional locks of hair.**

   You should see a result similar to the one shown in Figure 2-17.

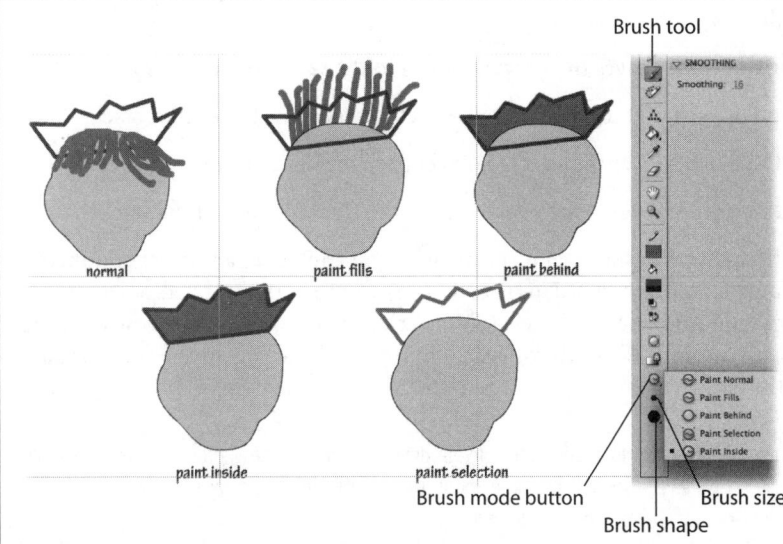

Brush tool

Figure 2-17:
*Here you get an idea of
how the different brush
modes work. The hair was
brushed into this picture
using the five different
brush modes.*

Brush mode button

Brush shape

Brush size

Arranging drawn objects forward and backward

When you draw in object mode, each part of your drawing (the head, the hat, the
hair) is an object, and you can place it in front of or behind the other objects.
Imagine that the head, hat, and hair are each cardboard cutouts that you're placing
on your desktop. You set them down so that the head is at the bottom, the hair
cutout covers the top of the head, and the hat covers part of the hair. Perfect! Flash
works the same way. When you draw objects, Flash places each new object in front
of the last. But what if you don't draw them in the proper order? Suppose, in the
cartoon face example, you drew the hair on top of the hat? Flash can help. Follow
these steps to move the hat to the front:

Note: If you don't have a drawing handy for this exercise, you can download *head_hat_hair.fla* from the
"Missing CD" page at *http://missingmanual.com/cds*.

---

1. **With the selection tool, click the hat's outline.**

   Before you can rearrange the stacking order, you need to select an object to move.

---

2. Go to Modify → Arrange → "Bring to Front" or press Shift+Ctrl+Up arrow (Windows) or Option-Shift-Up arrow (Mac) to move the hat to the front.

The hat moves in front of both the head shape and the hair as shown in Figure 2-18. You can still move the hat, hair, or head around the stage with the Selection tool. They stay in the same stacking order (head on bottom, hair in middle, hat on top) until you make another change using the Modify → Arrange commands.

There are four commands that help you arrange the stacking order of the objects you've drawn:

- **Bring to Front.** Moves the selected object to the very front of the stack.

- **Bring Forward.** Moves the selected object forward one level in the stack.

- **Send to Back.** Moves the selected object back one level in the stack.

- **Send Backward.** Moves the selected object to the very back of the stack.

As an alternative to using menu commands, you can select an object and then use Ctrl+Up or Ctrl+Down (⌘-Up or ⌘-Down) to move the selected object forward or backward. Add the Shift key (Shift+Ctrl+Up or Shift+Ctrl+Down for PCs; Shift-⌘-up or Shift-⌘-Down for Macs) to move all the way to the front or all the way to the back.

Note: There's another way to arrange parts of your drawing so that they're in front or behind each other. You can use Flash's layers. You'll learn more about layers in Chapter 4, but for the moment, and in this chapter, your works of art are all on a single layer.

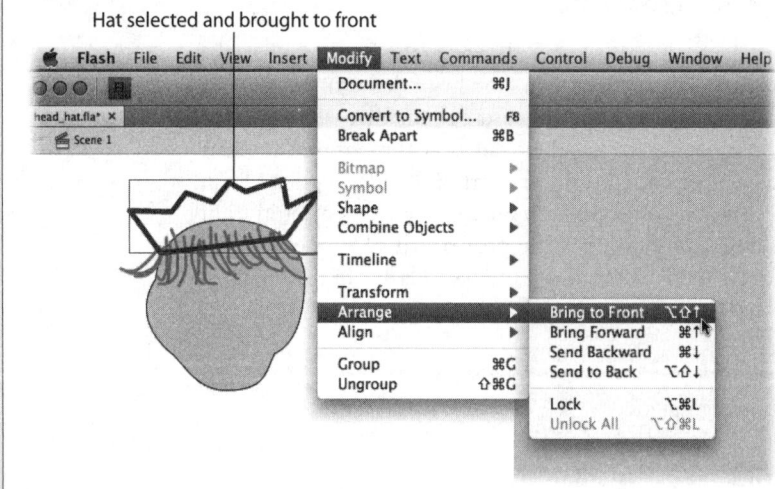

Hat selected and brought to front

Figure 2-18:
Use the Modify → Arrange commands to position parts of your drawing in front or behind other objects. Here the hat is brought to the front so that it partially covers the head and the hair.

Shape tools: Oval, Rectangle, and PolyStar

Flash gives you a quick way to create basic shapes: the Oval tool, which lets you draw everything from a narrow cigar shape to a perfect circle; the Rectangle tool, which lets you draw (you guessed it) rectangles, from long and skinny to perfectly square; and the PolyStar tool, which you can use to create multisided polygons (the standard five-sided polygon, angled correctly, creates a not-too-horrible side view of a house) and star shapes.

You can see the Oval, Rectangle, and PolyStar tools in Figure 2-19; Figure 2-20 shows you how to configure the PolyStar tool.

Note: You can always create a circle, a square, or a star using one of the other drawing tools, like the Pencil or the Line tool. But most people find the shape tools quicker and easier.

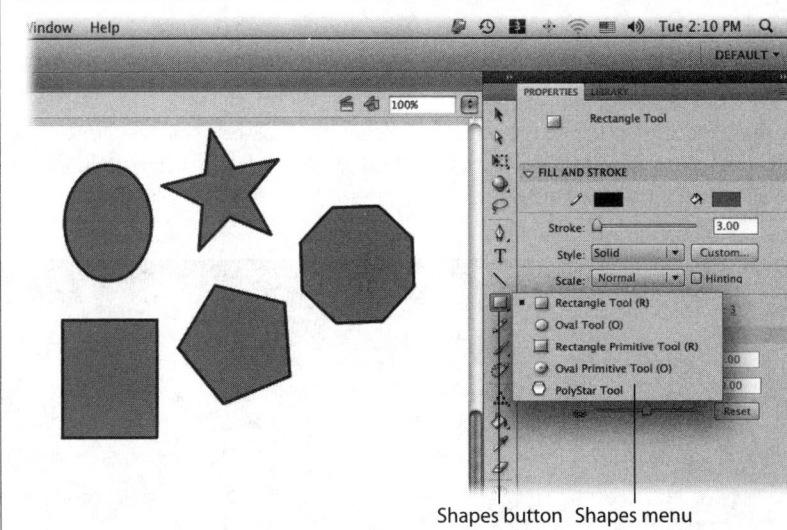

Figure 2-19:
The Oval, Rectangle, and PolyStar tools are all tucked under the same button on the Tools panel. The icon and related tooltip for the last-used shape appear on the button. The small triangle in the lower-right corner of the button is the clue that there are more options. To see the other shape options, click and hold down the button. A small menu appears showing all the options.

Shapes button   Shapes menu

To create a shape:

1. Click the shape tool you want (choose from Oval, Rectangle, or PolyStar, as shown in Figure 2-19).

   Your cursor changes into a cross.

2. Click the stage where you want to start your shape, and then drag your cursor to form the shape. When you're satisfied with the way your shape looks, release your mouse button.

   Flash displays your shape on the stage.

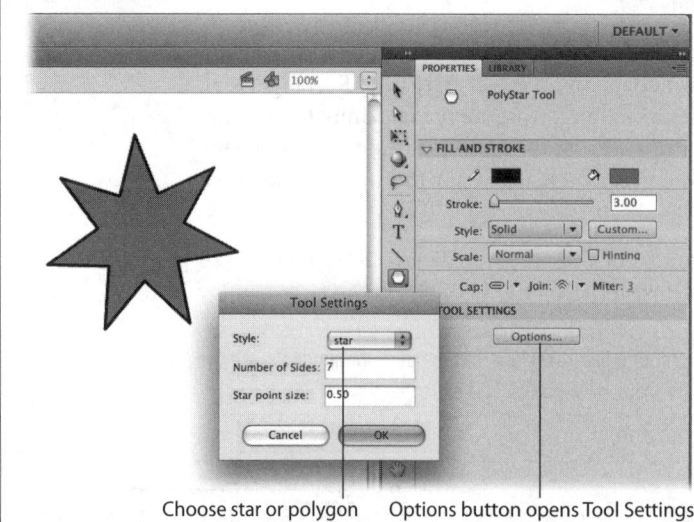

Figure 2-20:
One of the shape tools is called PolyStar because it creates, well, polygons and stars. After choosing PolyStar on the Tools panel, click the Options button in the Properties panel. Then, in the Tool Settings box, choose either polygon or star from the drop-down menu.

Choose star or polygon   Options button opens Tool Settings

Tip: To create a perfectly round circle or a perfectly square square, simply hold down the Shift key while you drag to create your shape. If you want to create beveled or rounded corners, before you release the mouse button, press the up or down arrow keys.

Rectangle and Oval Primitives

Flash has two special shapes: the rectangle and oval *primitives*. What makes these guys so primitive and where and how should you use them? When you draw a rectangle or an oval using the standard tools, Flash just considers them shapes. You see one as having corners and the other curves, but to Flash they're pretty much the same. When you draw them in merge mode, you can chop standard ovals and rectangles into little irregularly shaped pieces.

Primitives are different in that you can't erase part of a primitive or break it into parts. It's all or nothing. Primitives have some special features that you won't find in their counterparts. For example, using the Properties panel you can add rounded or beveled corners to your rectangle primitives. With the Oval primitive you can create pie slices by defining the arc angles.

And as with the shapes drawn in object mode, you can adjust the width and height of the objects by typing measurements in the Properties panel. Last but not least, when they're in the hands of an ActionScript programmer, these primitives can really jump through hoops.

Draw a rectangle, and then select it. Look in the Properties panel. If you drew it in object mode, the Properties panel lists it as a drawing object. Otherwise, it describes it as a Shape. Now draw a rectangle using the Rectangle Primitive tool. Sure enough, the Properties panel describes it as a Rectangle primitive.

Aligning Objects with the Align Tools

Sometimes dragging stuff around the stage and eyeballing the result works just fine. Other times, you want to position your graphic elements with pinpoint precision. Using the Align panel, you can align graphic elements based on their edges (top, bottom, right, left) or by their centers. And you can base this alignment on the objects themselves (for example, you can line up the tops of all your objects) or on the stage (useful if you want to position, say, several Freddy Flash heads precisely at the bottom of the stage, as shown in Figure 2-21). You can even distribute individual objects evenly with respect to each other.

To display the Align panel, select Window → Align or press Ctrl+K (Windows) or ⌘-K (Mac).

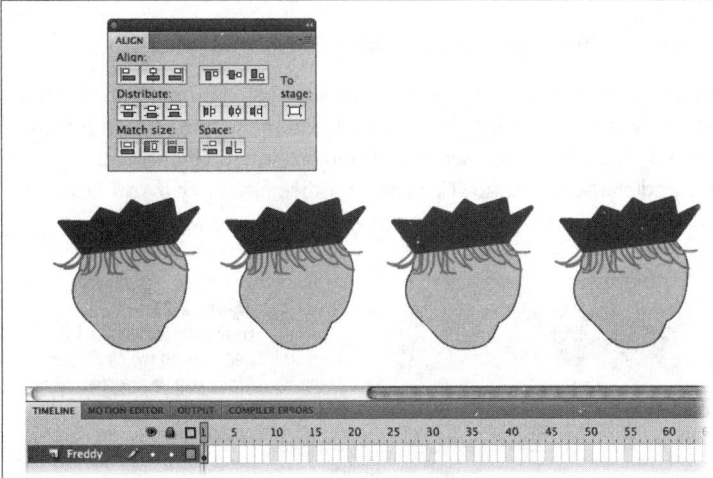

Figure 2-21:
The Align panel gives you the opportunity to align a single object (or whole groups of selected objects) along the left side, right side, top, or bottom of the stage, and more. First select Modify → Align → To Stage. Select the objects you want to align, and then click the alignment icon from the Align panel.

Erasing Mistakes with the Erase Tool

Only in the digital realm does an eraser work so effectively. Try erasing a goof on paper or canvas, and you not only have shredded eraser everywhere, you're also left with ghostly streaks of paint, lead, or charcoal.

No so in Flash. Using the Eraser tool (Figure 2-22), you can effectively wipe anything off the stage, from a little speck to your entire drawing.

Note: Using the Eraser tool is similar to selecting Edit → Undo, only in the sense that they both remove objects from your drawing. The difference: Edit → Undo tells Flash to work sequentially backward to undo your last actions or changes, last one first. The Erase tool, on the other hand, lets you wipe stuff off the stage regardless of the order in which you added it.

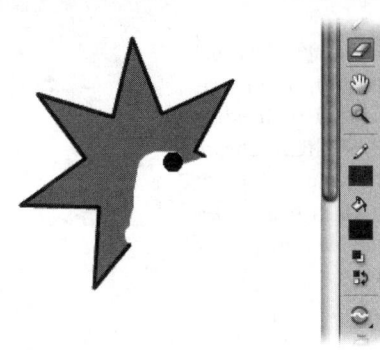

Figure 2-22:
Here the Eraser tool is rubbing out the PolyStar shape. Erasing in Flash isn't useful just for fixing mistakes; you can create cool effects (like patterns) by erasing, too. If you happen to start erasing the wrong thing, no problem; just click Edit → Undo Eraser.

To use the Erase tool:

1. **In the Tools section of the Tools panel, click the Eraser tool to select it.**

   Your cursor changes to the size and shape of eraser Flash assumes you want. To make your eraser larger or smaller, head to the Options section at the bottom of the Tools panel and, from the Eraser Shape pop-up menu (Figure 2-23), select the eraser size and shape you want. (You want a nice fat eraser if you have a lot to erase, or a skinny one if you're just touching up the edges of a drawing.)

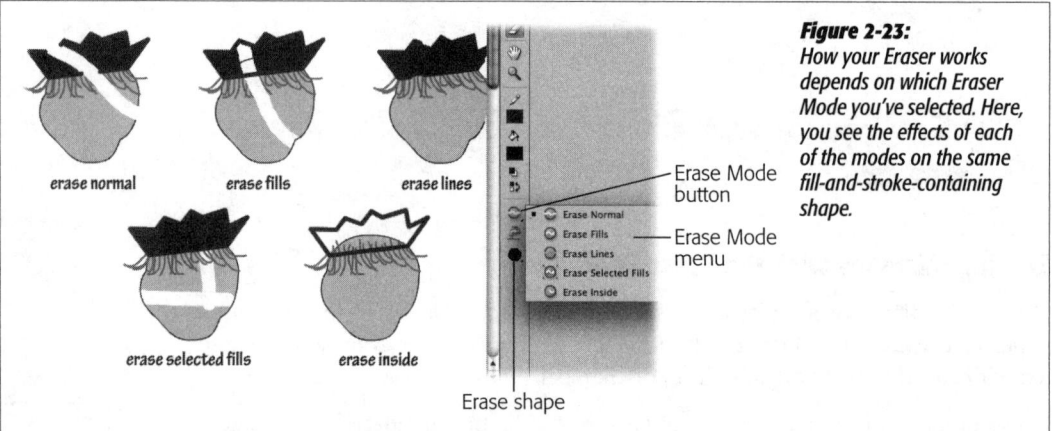

Figure 2-23:
How your Eraser works depends on which Eraser Mode you've selected. Here, you see the effects of each of the modes on the same fill-and-stroke-containing shape.

2. **On the stage, click where you want to begin erasing and drag your cursor back and forth.**

   Flash erases everything your cursor touches (or not, depending on the Eraser Mode you've chosen—see the following section for details).

Tip: To erase a line or a fill in one fell swoop, click the Faucet option, and then click the line or fill you want to erase. To erase everything on the stage and the Pasteboard (the area surrounding the stage) double-click the Eraser icon on the Tools panel.

Configuring the Eraser

Flash has a ton of Eraser modes you can use to control how the Eraser tool works (and what it erases). To see them, click the Eraser Mode button in the Options area (Figure 2-23), and then, from the pop-up menu that appears, select one of the following modes:

Note: The Eraser tool works only on editable objects. It doesn't work on grouped objects or symbols. To remove grouped objects and symbols, click them with the Select tool, and then press Delete.

- **Erase Normal.** Flash uses this mode unless you tell it otherwise. If you erase over an existing object on the stage using Erase Normal, Flash erases everything, fill and stroke included.

- **Erase Fill.** If you erase over an existing object on the stage using Erase Fill, only the fill portion of the object disappears.

- **Erase Lines.** If you erase over an existing object on the stage using Erase Lines, only the stroke portion of the object disappears.

- **Erase Selected Fills.** If you erase over an existing object on the stage using Erase Selected Fills, you erase only those parts of the object that are both fills and that you've previously selected (using one of the selection tools described on page 61).

Note: Oddly enough, if you configure your erase to Erase Selected Fills, and then rub your virtual eraser over *non*-selected fills, Flash pretends to erase them—until you let up on your mouse, when they pop right back onto the stage.

- **Erase Inside.** If you erase over an existing object on the stage using Erase Inside, Flash erases the inside (fill) of the object as long as you begin erasing inside the stroke outline; if you begin erasing outside the line, it only erases outside the line.

Cutting out an irregular shape from another object

You can cut an irregular shape out of the middle of an object using the Eraser tool. If you're going for precision, for example, you can use an eraser with a small head to outline the area that you're erasing, then use the Faucet tool to quickly erase the rest. For example, say you want to draw a donut. Here's how:

1. **Select the Oval tool on the Tools panel.**

   If you don't see the Oval tool, it's probably hiding under the Rectangle tool or the PolyStar tool. Notice the little triangle that indicates there are more options on the menu? Make sure you choose the Oval tool and not the Oval Primitive tool. The Oval Primitive tool has a dot in the center.

2. Drag out a decent sized oval on the stage.

You're drawing a donut, so there's no need to make a perfect circle, but do make it large enough so that you can cut out a donut hole.

3. On the Tools panel, click the Eraser tool.

When you move the cursor over the stage, you see that it's changed to a black dot. That's the eraser and the dot cursor shows how big the eraser head is.

4. In the Options section at the bottom of the Tools panel, choose a small eraser head.

At the bottom of the Tools panel is the drop-down menu that sets the size and shape of the eraser.

5. Using the Eraser, draw a circle within your oval to outline the donut hole.

As you drag, the fill color disappears, and you see the stage color beneath. (Make sure you complete the circle, or the Faucet will erase the entire fill color in your donut.)

6. On the Tools panel, click the Faucet, and then click the donut hole.

The donut hole disappears as the Faucet tool erases all the fill color from inside the cutout.

Copying and Pasting Drawn Objects

Copying graphic elements and pasting them—either into the same frame, into another frame, or even into another document—is much faster than drawing new objects from scratch. It's also the most familiar. If you've ever copied text in a word processing or spreadsheet document and pasted it somewhere else, you know the drill.

A simple copy-and-paste is the best way to go when you're experimenting: for example, when you want to see whether the blue-eyed wallaby you drew for one animation looks good in another. But if you're trying to keep your animation's finished file size as small as possible, or if you plan to include more than one copy of that wallaby, copying and pasting *isn't* the best way to go. Instead, you'll want to look into symbols (page 228).

To copy and paste an image:

1. On the stage, select the image you want to copy.

Page 61 gives you an overview of the selection tools. In Figure 2-24, Freddy Flash is selected.

2. **Choose Edit → Copy (or press Ctrl+C in Windows; ⌘-C on the Mac). Then select the keyframe into which you want to paste the image.**

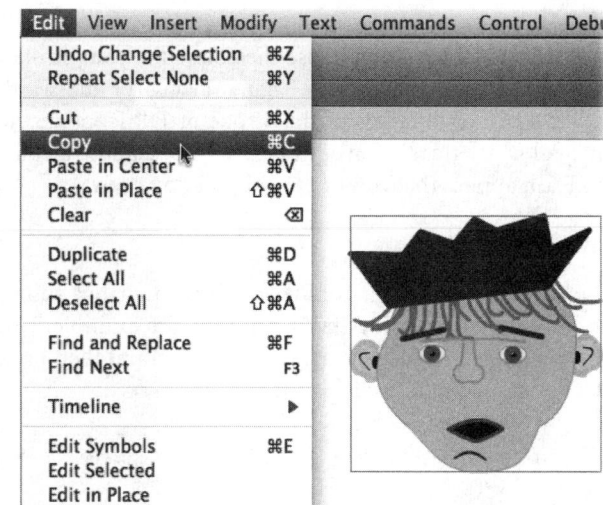

Figure 2-24:
Copying and pasting is the easiest way to try out a look. If you're copying a complex image, as shown here, you may want to group the selected image first by choosing Modify → Group. (There's much more detail on grouping objects on page 195.) For additional copies, simply choose Edit → Paste in Center or Edit → Paste in Place again.

You can paste the image in the keyframe you're in, or you can select another one. Flash doesn't restrict you to the document you currently have open; you can open another document to paste the image into.

3. **Choose one of the Paste commands. Your options include:**

   • **Edit → Paste in Center.** Tells Flash to paste the image in the center of the viewing area.

   • **Edit → Paste in Place.** Tells Flash to paste the image in the same spot it was on the original stage. (If you choose this option to paste an image to the same stage as the original, you'll need to drag the pasted copy off the original to see it.)

   • **Edit → Paste Special.** (Windows only.) Displays a Paste Special dialog box that lets you paste an image as a device-independent bitmap (an uneditable version of your image with a fixed background the size and shape of the selection box).

Flash pastes your image based on your selection, leaving your original copy intact.

Tip: If all you want to do is make a quick copy of an image on the same stage as the original, Flash gives you an easier way than copying and pasting. Select Edit → Duplicate (or press Ctrl+D in Windows; ⌘-D on the Mac). When you do, Flash pastes a copy of the image just a little below and to the right of your original image, ready for you to reposition as you see fit. For the fastest duplication method of all, with the Selection tool, just Alt-drag (Option-drag) the item you want to copy. The original stays put and you have a duplicate attached to your cursor. You can then drag the duplicate wherever you want on the stage.

Adding Color

The Colors section of the Tools panel lets you choose the colors for your strokes and fills. Before you click one of the drawing icons to begin drawing (or afterward, to change existing colors), you can click either of the Stroke or Fill icons in the Color Section to bring up a color palette, as shown in Figure 2-25. Choose a color from the color palette, and Flash applies that color to the objects you draw.

Changing the Color of a Stroke (Line)

One of the best things about drawing in Flash is how easy it is to change things around. If you draw a bright orange line using the Pencil tool, for example, you can change that line an instant later to spruce, chartreuse, or puce (and then back to orange again) with just a few simple mouse clicks.

Note: In Flash, all lines are made up of strokes. The Flash drawing tools that produce strokes include the Pencil, the Pen, the Line, and the shape tools (Oval, Rectangle, and PolyStar).

Flash gives you two different ways to change the color of a stroke: the Properties panel and the Ink Bottle tool.

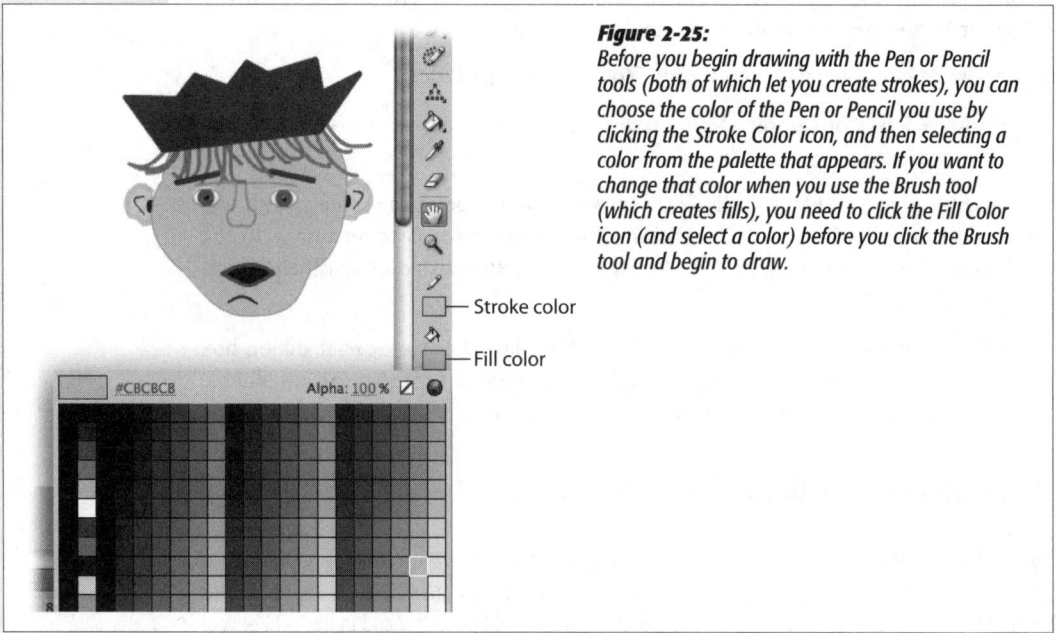

Figure 2-25:
Before you begin drawing with the Pen or Pencil tools (both of which let you create strokes), you can choose the color of the Pen or Pencil you use by clicking the Stroke Color icon, and then selecting a color from the palette that appears. If you want to change that color when you use the Brush tool (which creates fills), you need to click the Fill Color icon (and select a color) before you click the Brush tool and begin to draw.

Stroke color

Fill color

Coloring strokes with the Properties panel.

Changing the color of a stroke using the Properties panel is best for situations when you want to change the color of a single stroke or when you want to change more than just the color of a stroke (for example, you want to change stroke thickness or the color of the fill inside the stroke).

To change the color of a stroke using the Properties panel:

1. **On the stage, select the stroke you want to change.**

   A highlight appears around or on the selected stroke.

2. **If the Properties panel isn't open press Ctrl+F3 (⌘-F3).**

   The Properties panel shows settings related to the stroke as shown in Figure 2-26.

3. **In the Properties panel, click the Stroke Color icon.**

   A Color Picker appears.

4. **Click a new color for your selected stroke.**

   The Color Picker disappears, and Flash redisplays your stroke using the new color you chose.

Properties panel

Stroke selected   Stroke color picker

Figure 2-26:
Using the Properties panel is a quick and easy way to change the color of a single stroke. First, select the stroke you want to recolor; then, in the Properties panel that appears, click the Stroke Color icon. When you do, the Color Picker appears, complete with any custom color swatches you've added to it (if any). The instant you choose a color, the Color Picker disappears and the selected stroke changes to the new color. Here, the Fill Color icon has a slash through it, meaning that no fill color is currently selected.

Coloring strokes with the Ink Bottle tool

The Ink Bottle tool is great for situations when you want to apply the same color to a bunch of different strokes all in one fell swoop.

To change the color of a stroke (or several strokes) using the Ink Bottle tool:

1. **In the Tools panel, select the Stroke Color icon (Figure 2-27).**

   The Color Picker appears, and as you mouse over the different colors, you notice your cursor looks like a tiny eyedropper.

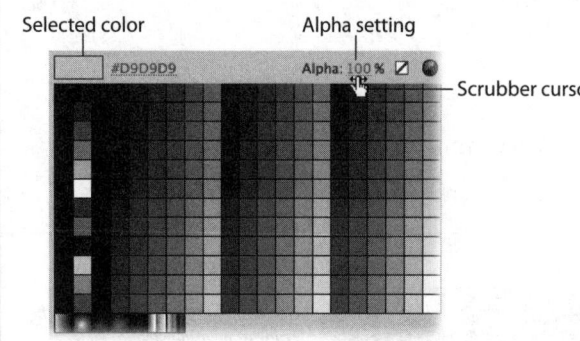

Selected color   Alpha setting

Scrubber cursor

Figure 2-27:
Clicking the Stroke Color icon displays the Color Picker. All Flash's color pickers work the same. Here, you can change not just the hue, but also the transparency of the color. To do so, click the number in the Alpha box and type in a new percentage or drag right or left to "scrub" in a new value. Numbers from 0%, (completely transparent) to 100% (completely opaque) are valid.

2. **Click a color to choose it.**

   The Color Picker disappears, and Flash redisplays the Stroke Color icon using the color you just selected.

3. **On the stage, select the stroke(s) you want to recolor.**

   Flash highlights the selected strokes.

4. **In the Tools panel, select the Ink Bottle tool.**

   The Ink Bottle and the Paint Bucket share the same Tools panel button. If the Ink Bottle isn't showing, click the Paint Bucket, hold the button down until you see the pop-up menu, as shown in Figure 2-28, and then select the Ink Bottle tool. Now, as you mouse over the stage, you notice your cursor looks like a little ink bottle.

5. **Click the selected strokes.**

   Flash recolors the selected strokes.

Tip: If all you want to do is change the color of one stroke, you don't need to select it first. Just click the Ink Bottle tool, and then click the stroke to recolor it.

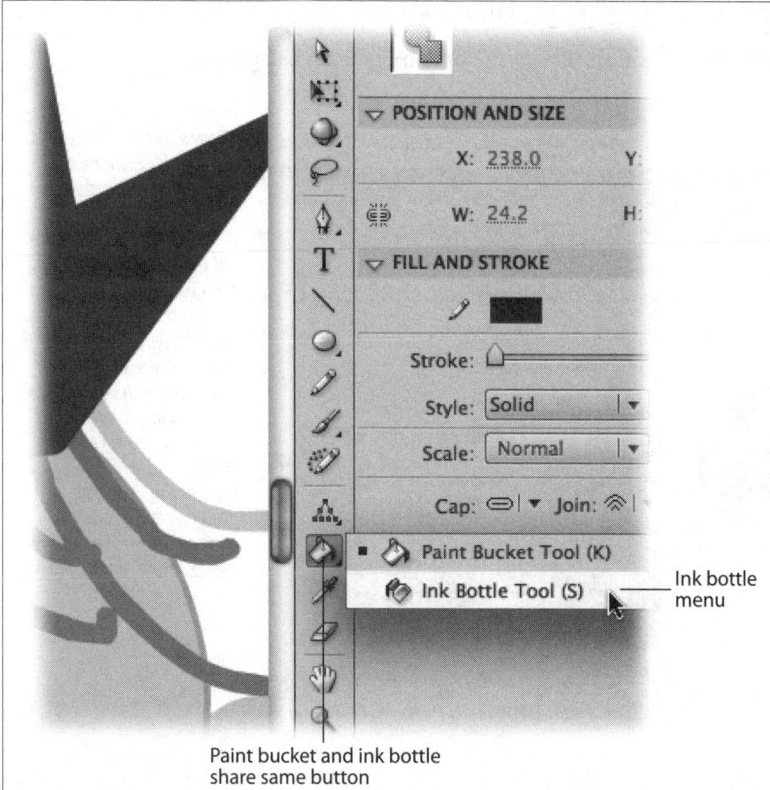

Figure 2-28:
After you select one or more strokes, click the Ink Bottle tool to change the color of all of the selected strokes. To change the color of strokes one by one, you don't need to select them first; simply click them with the Ink Bottle tool.

Ink bottle menu

Paint bucket and ink bottle share same button

Changing the Color of a Fill

If you change your mind about the color of any of the fills you add to the stage, no problem. Flash gives you two different ways to change the color of a fill: the Properties panel and the Paint Bucket tool.

Note: The Flash drawing tools that produce fills include the Brush tool and all of the shape tools (Oval, Oval Primitive, Rectangle, Rectangle Primitive, and PolyStar).

Coloring fills with the Properties panel

Using the Properties panel to change the color of a fill is great for situations when you want to change more than just fill color: for example, you want to change both fill color and the color of the stroke outline surrounding the fill.

To change the color of a fill using the Properties panel:

1. **On the stage, select the fill you want to change.**

   The selected fill is highlighted.

2. **If the Properties panel isn't open, go to Window → Properties to open it.**

The Properties panel similar to the one in Figure 2-29 appears.

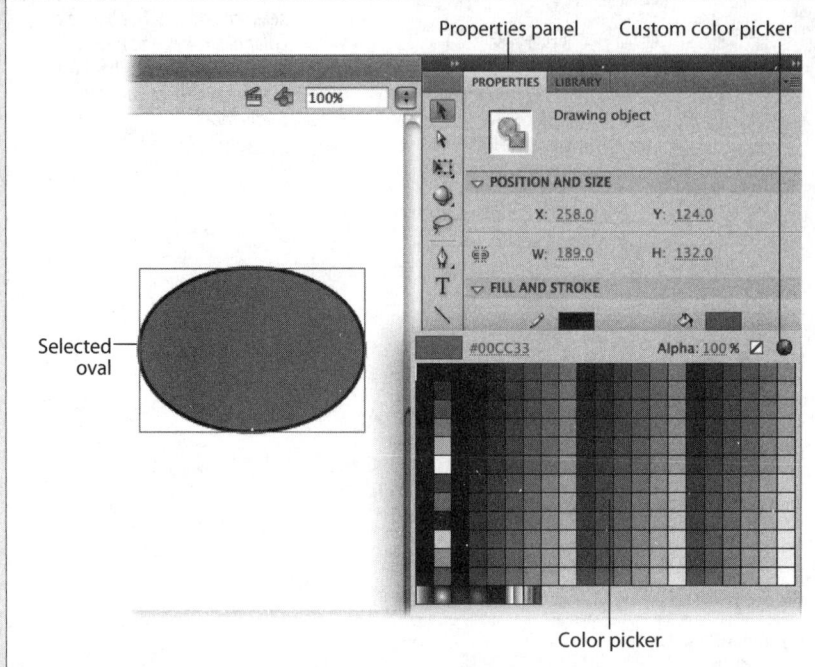

Properties panel   Custom color picker

Selected oval

Color picker

Figure 2-29:
Select a fill-containing shape (here, the inside of an oval). In the Properties panel, click the Fill Color icon to display the Color Picker, and then click to choose a new color for your fill. If you don't see the exact color you want, you can click the Custom Color icon to blend your own custom shade. And while you're here in the Properties panel, you can also change the stroke outline of the shape, if you like.

3. **In the Properties panel, click the Fill Color icon.**

The Color Picker appears.

4. **Click to choose a new color for your selected fill.**

As soon as you let go of your mouse, the Color Picker disappears, and Flash redisplays your fill using the color you chose.

Tip: To change the color of a bunch of fills quickly, select the fills you want to recolor first; then select the Fill Color icon and choose a new color. When you do, Flash automatically redisplays all your selected fills using your new color.

Coloring fills with the Paint Bucket tool

The Paint Bucket tool is great for situations where you want to apply the same color to one or more fills on the stage, either one fill at a time or all at once.

To change the color of a fill using the Paint Bucket tool:

1. **In the Tools panel, select the Fill Color icon (Figure 2-30).**

The Color Picker appears, and as you mouse over the different colors, you notice your cursor looks like a tiny eyedropper.

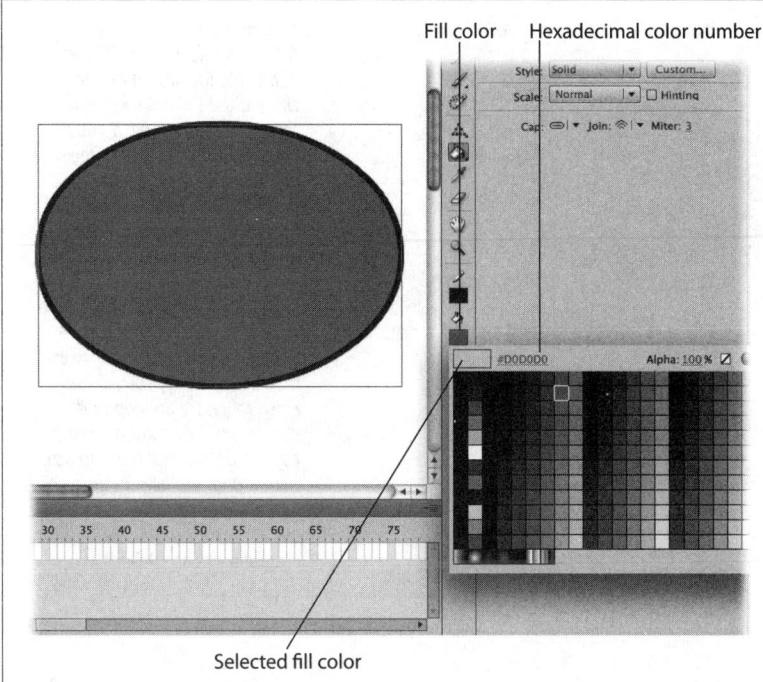

Fill color   Hexadecimal color number

Figure 2-30:
Click the Fill Color icon to choose a new color for your fills. As you move your cursor around the Color Picker, you notice the Preview Window displays the color your cursor happens to be over at any given time.

Selected fill color

2. **Click a color to choose it. (If you know the hexadecimal number of a specific color you want, you can type it into the field next to the selected color preview window.)**

   The Color Picker disappears, and Flash redisplays the Fill Color icon using the color you just selected.

3. **On the stage, click the fill(s) you want to recolor.**

   Flash recolors each fill you click, as shown in Figure 2-31.

Tip: If you don't have a completely closed outline around your fill, Flash might not let you apply a fill color. To tell Flash to ignore small gaps (or medium gaps, or even relatively large gaps) surrounding your fill: in the Options section of the Tools panel (Figure 2-31), click Gap Size. Then, from the pop-up menu that appears, turn on the checkbox next to Close Small Gaps, Close Medium Gaps, or Close Large Gaps. Then try to modify your fill again. (You may also want to consider closing the gap yourself using one of Flash's drawing tools.)

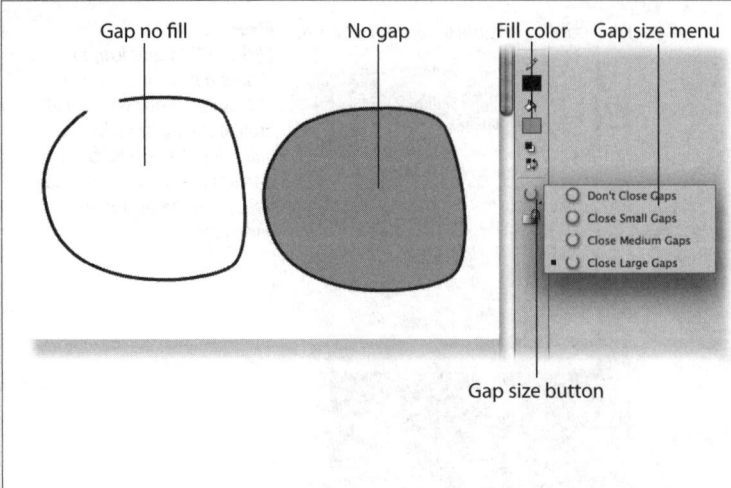

Gap no fill   No gap   Fill color   Gap size menu

Don't Close Gaps
Close Small Gaps
Close Medium Gaps
Close Large Gaps

Gap size button

Figure 2-31:
After you select a new fill color, apply it to the fills on the stage by clicking the Paint Bucket, and then clicking each fill. If you're adding a fill for the first time and you find that Flash doesn't add your fill color, make sure your fill is perfectly enclosed. If it isn't—if there's so much as a tiny gap in the outline surrounding your fill— Flash won't be able to tell where your fill stops and the stage begins, so your new color won't take. Fortunately, you can tell Flash to ignore the gap and change your fill color as best it can. To do so, click the Gap Size option and, on the pop-up menu that appears, turn on the checkbox next to Close Small (or Medium, or Large) Gaps.

Animating Your Drawings

Animation is what Flash is all about. Sure, Flash has tons of drawing and special-effect tools, but they are all a means to an end: a series of slightly different drawings that you can string together to create the illusion of movement.

In the old days, animators had to create each drawing, or *frame*, by hand—a daunting process when you consider that your average feature presentation clicks by at 24 frames per second. That's 1,440 drawings *per minute* of onscreen animation. Expensive? Hoo boy.

To keep those costs down, animation companies did what all self-respecting companies do: They figured out how to separate the highly skilled labor from the less-skilled labor. They figured out that there are key drawings (called *keyframes*) that show big changes in the finished animation, and a certain number of less-detailed, *in-between* drawings (regular frames) they could assign to lower-paid workers. For example, say you're a producer working on an animation showing a cartoon kangaroo jumping up into the air. If you get a skilled animator to draw the kangaroo-on-the-ground, kangaroo-midway, and kangaroo-at-the-top frames, you can hand these keyframes off to a low-paid tweener. All the tweener has to do is copy the keyframes, make a few adjustments, and bingo: You've got yourself a finished animation at a bargain-basement price.

Flash, like the animation studios of old, gives you the opportunity to use tweening to slash the time it takes to produce a finished animation. In this chapter, you'll see both approaches: frame-by-frame (still the best choice when you need to create highly complex, tightly controlled animations) and tweening (where Flash serves as your very own low-paid illustrator).

Frame-by-Frame Animation

An *animation* is nothing more than a series of framed images displayed one after the other to create the illusion of motion. When you create an animation by hand in Flash, you create each frame yourself—either by using Flash's drawing and painting tools (Chapter 2), or by importing images (Chapter 9) or movie clips that someone else has created.

The best way to gain an understanding of frames, keyframes, and Flash's animation tools is to start animating by hand, frame by frame. Most of the time, though, you'll use tweening (page 102) to save time and frustration. For more advice on when to use either technique, see the box on page 91.

Frames and Keyframes

Flash recognizes two different types of frames: *keyframes*, and plain old *frames*. Although in frame-by-frame animations most of the frames you create are keyframes, if you want to tell Flash to hold a particular image for effect, you need both types:

- **Keyframes** are the important frames—the frames you designate to hold distinct images.

- **Frames,** in a Flash animation, contain whatever image you associated with the last keyframe. Their purpose is to mark time. You use them to pace the action of your animation by telling Flash to skip a beat in the action here and there.

As you'll see in the following section, you add both keyframes and frames to an animation using the timeline.

Creating a Frame-by-Frame Animation

To build a frame-by-frame animation, you can use Flash's drawing tools to draw the content of each frame on the stage, or you can import (page 319) existing images created in another program. Either way, you have to place an image in each keyframe you create.

Here are the steps to creating a frame-by-frame animation:

1. **Open a blank Flash document.**

    As the timeline in Figure 3-1 shows, Flash starts you out in Layer 1, Frame 1. (If you don't see the timeline, select Window → Timeline.) Initially, a Flash document has only one frame, a keyframe at Layer 1, Frame 1.

Tip: You'll learn how to add more layers to your animation later in this chapter. When you've got more than one layer, you have to click a layer name in the timeline to select the layer you want to animate.

    The red rectangle over the Frame 1 is the *playhead*. It marks the current frame—the one that's displayed on the stage. When you begin a new document, you can't move the playhead until you add more frames, as described in step 3.

UP TO SPEED

To Tween or Not to Tween

The great thing about creating an animation frame by frame is that it gives you the most control over the finished product. If you're looking for a super-realistic effect, for example, you're probably not going to be satisfied with the frames Flash generates when you tell it to tween (page 319). Instead, you're going to want to lovingly handcraft every single frame, making slight adjustments to lots of different objects as you go.

Say, for instance, you're creating an animation showing an outdoor barbecue. Over the course of your animation, the sun's going to move across the sky, which is going to change the way your characters' shadows appear. Bugs are going to fly across the scene. When one character opens his mouth to speak, the other characters aren't going to remain static: Their hair's going to ripple in the breeze, they're going to start conversations of their own, they're going to drop pieces of steak (which the host's dog is going to come streaking over to and wolf down). You can't leave realistic, director-level details like this to Flash; you've got to create them yourself.

On the downside, animating by hand is understandably time-intensive. Even though many Web-based Flash animations run at a modest 12 *fps* (frames per second), that's a whole lot of frames. And compared to tweening, creating individual frames adds substantially to the file size of your movie—a big consideration if you intend to put your finished animation up on the Web. (Big files tend not to play so well over the Web, thanks to uncontrollable variables like Internet traffic and the connection speed of the folks viewing your animation. You can find tips for optimizing your finished animation's file size in Chapter 19.)

In other words, with frame-by-frame animation, you get more control—but it's going to cost you in time and hassle, and (potentially) it's going to make your finished animation harder for folks to view. The choice is yours.

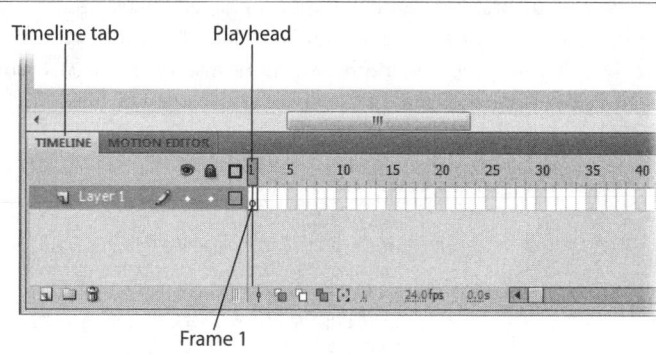

Timeline tab   Playhead

Frame 1

Figure 3-1:
When you create a new Flash document, as shown here, Flash automatically designates Frame 1 as a blank keyframe. You can tell that Frame 1 contains a blank keyframe by the little hollow circle Flash displays in Frame 1 (and by the fact that there's nothing on the stage).

2. **Using Flash's paint and drawing tools, draw an image on the stage.**

   Figure 3-2 shows an example drawing of a frog with a tempting fly overhead. As soon as you add a drawing or any visual content to a keyframe, the hollow circle fills in, becoming a solid circle.

Note: If you have an existing image stored on your computer, you can bring it onto the stage. Select File
→ Import → Import to Stage, and then, in the Import window that appears, type in (or browse to) the
name of the file you want to pull in. When you finish, click Open (Import on a Mac). (Chapter 9 covers
importing files in more detail.)

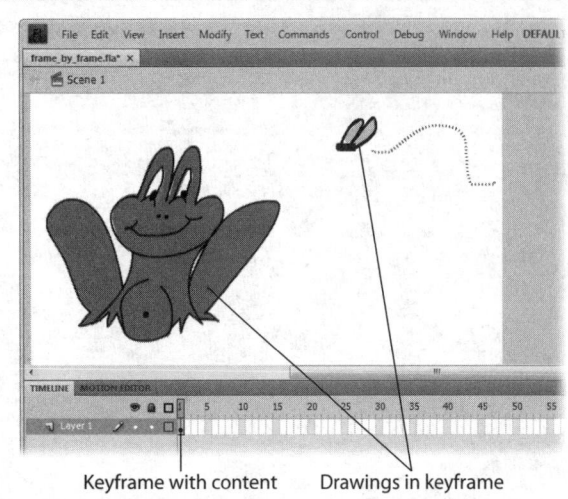

Figure 3-2:
*Flash associates the selected keyframe with all the
images you place on the stage—whether you draw
them directly on the stage using the drawing and
painting tools, drag them from the Library, or import
them from previously created files. Here, Flash
associates the frog-and-fly drawing with the
keyframe in Frame 1.*

Keyframe with content   Drawings in keyframe

3. **Click to select another frame further out in the timeline.**

   Which frame you select depends on how long you want Flash to display the
   content associated with your first keyframe. Since Flash usually plays at a rate of
   24 frames per second, selecting Frame 2 would tell Flash to display the two
   images so quickly that all you'd see is smooth, fast motion. For practice, so you
   can clearly see each frame of your work-in-progress, try Frame 20. Flash highlights the frame you select, as shown in Figure 3-3.

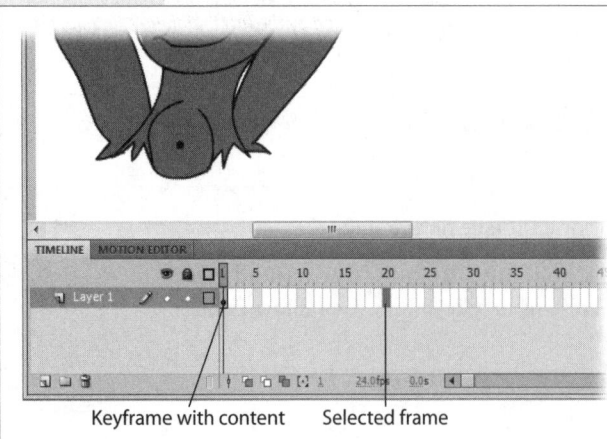

Figure 3-3:
*When you click a frame in the timeline, Flash
highlights it with a tiny blue rectangle, as shown
in Frame 20. The Properties panel starts out
blank since you haven't yet added a keyframe
(or a regular frame) at Frame 20.*

Keyframe with content   Selected frame

Note: Although Flash has a frame rate of 24 fps (frames per second) out of the box, you can change this setting. Learn how on page 475.

4. **Turn the selected frame into a keyframe by choosing Insert → Timeline → Blank Keyframe.**

Flash moves the playhead to the selected frame (Frame 20 in Figure 3-4), inserts a keyframe icon, and clears the stage. A quicker way to insert keyframes, or any type of frame, is to right-click the frame, and then choose from the shortcut menu.

Tip: Using three shortcut keys is the quickest way of all to work with frames. The F5 key inserts a frame. The F6 key creates a keyframe, including the content from the previous frame. The F7 key creates an empty keyframe.

Figure 3-4:
Here, the playhead is over the second keyframe, which tells Flash to place the content on the stage in the second keyframe (Frame 20). When it detects a new keyframe, Flash displays only the new content, so Frames 2–19 carry forward the content from Frame 1 (the first keyframe). You can verify this behavior by dragging the playhead (scrubbing) from Frame 20 back to Frame 1.

5. **Draw a second image on the stage.**

The second keyframe in Figure 3-4 shows the frog with a thought balloon instead of a fly. But if your two images are fairly similar, you can avoid having to completely redraw the image for your second keyframe, as you'll see in the next step.

6. **Click further out in the timeline (Frame 40, say), and choose Insert → Timeline → Keyframe.**

   Just as when you chose Insert → Timeline → Blank Keyframe, Flash still moves the playhead and inserts a keyframe icon; but instead of clearing the stage, Flash carries over the content from the previous keyframe, all ready for you to tweak and edit.

7. **Repeat the previous step to create as many keyframes as you want.**

   To get the hang of frame-by-frame animation, adding two or three keyframes is plenty. But when you're building an actual animation, you'll likely need to add dozens or even hundreds of keyframes (or even more, depending on the length and complexity you're shooting for).

Note: You can examine this sample animation to check your work. Simply download *frame_by_frame. fla* from the "Missing CD" page (*http://missingmanuals.com/cds*).

Making the Timeline Easier to Read

You can't create an animation—frame-by-frame or tweened—without the timeline. The timeline serves as a kind of indispensable thumbnail sketch of your animation, showing you at a glance which frames contain unique content (the keyframes) and which don't (the regular frames), how many layers your animation contains (page 154), which sections of your animation contain tweens (page 102), and so on.

Unfortunately, with its tiny little squares and cryptic symbols, the timeline can be pretty hard to read. And the more keyframes you add to your animation, the harder it is to remember which image you put in which keyframe.

You can always click a keyframe (or drag the playhead over a keyframe) to tell Flash to display the image associated with that keyframe on the stage—but there's an easier way.

You can tell Flash to expand the timeline and show miniature versions of each of your keyframes. In the timeline, click the Options menu in the upper-right corner, and then, from the shortcut menu that appears, turn on the checkbox next to Preview. Your timeline will look something like Figure 3-5.

Testing Your Frame-by-Frame Animation

You have two choices when it comes to testing your animation, and both of them are simple:

- **Control → Play.** The quickest and easiest approach is to test your animation inside the Flash development environment. Select Control → Play (or press Enter). When you do, Flash runs your animation right there on the stage. So, for example, if you create an animation containing just two keyframes (similar to the example on page 92), Flash displays the content for the first keyframe, followed by the content for the second keyframe.

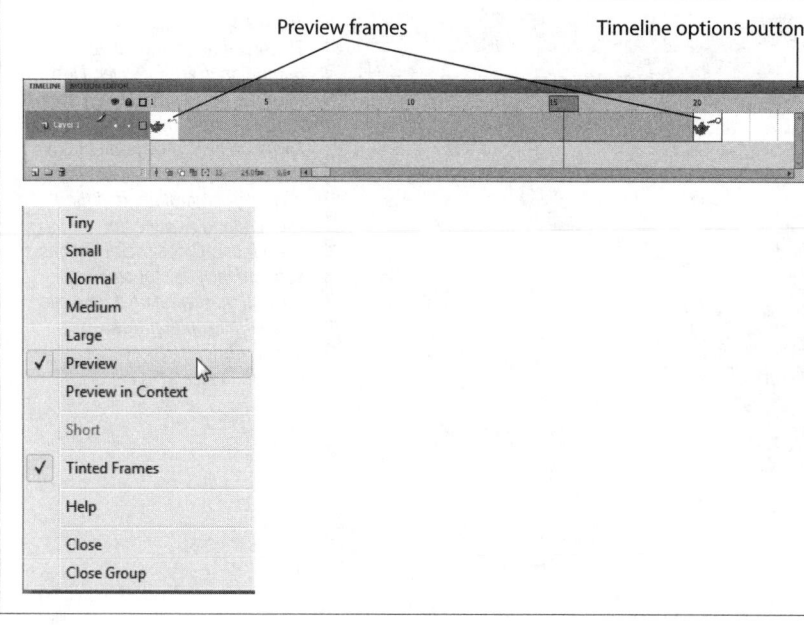

Preview frames · · · · Timeline options button

Figure 3-5:
*As shown at top, Flash
provides visual cues
about your keyframes
when you choose
Preview from the
timeline's Options menu.
The timeline options
(bottom) give you
several different ways to
adjust the view.*

Note: When you select Control → Play, Flash starts your animation beginning at whatever frame your playhead happens to be over—even if that's in the middle of your animation. To tell Flash to begin at the beginning, drag the playhead to Frame 1 before you select Control → Play.

- **Control → Test Movie.** Selecting Control → Test Movie *exports* your Flash document (compiles the .fla document into an executable .swf file) and automatically loads the .swf file into the built-in Flash Player. Figure 3-6 shows an example.

Testing your animation this way takes a bit longer, but it's more accurate: You're actually seeing what your audience will eventually see, from beginning to end. (In some cases—for example, if you've added a motion guide path as described on page 115 to your animation—selecting Control → Play shows a slightly different result than selecting Control → Test Movie does.)

Editing Your Frame-by-Frame Animation

It's rare that your first crack at any given animation will be your last. Typically, you'll start with a few keyframes, test the result, add a few frames, delete a few frames, and so on until you get precisely the look you're after.

This section shows you how to perform the basic frame-level edits you need to take your animation from rough sketch to finished production: inserting, copying, pasting, moving, and deleting frames.

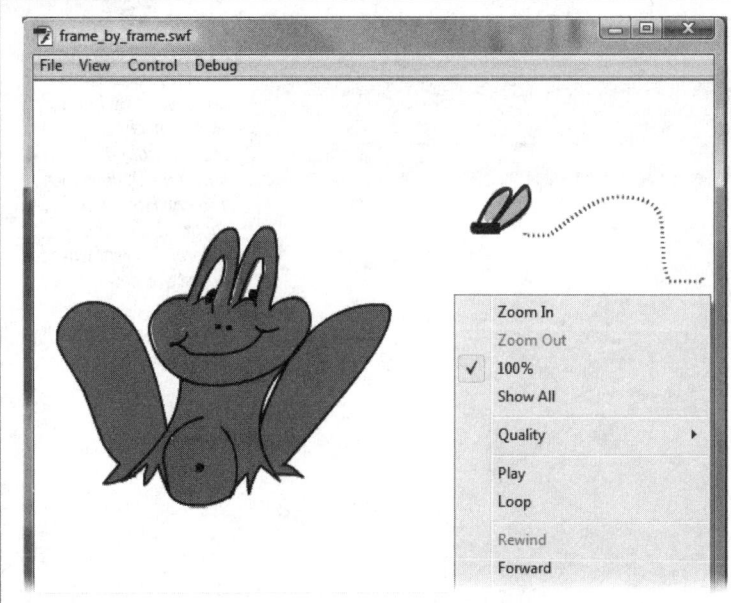

Figure 3-6:
The first time you run your animation in Flash Player, Flash assumes you want to run it over (and over, and over, and over). Fortunately, you can rid Flash of this annoying assumption. Right-click your animation, and then click Loop to remove the checkmark. Other useful options you find include stopping your animation, rewinding it, and even stepping through it frame by frame. Chapter 18 covers animation testing in depth.

Selecting frames and keyframes

Selecting a single frame or keyframe is as easy as zipping up to the timeline and clicking the frame (or keyframe) you want to select, as shown in Figure 3-7.

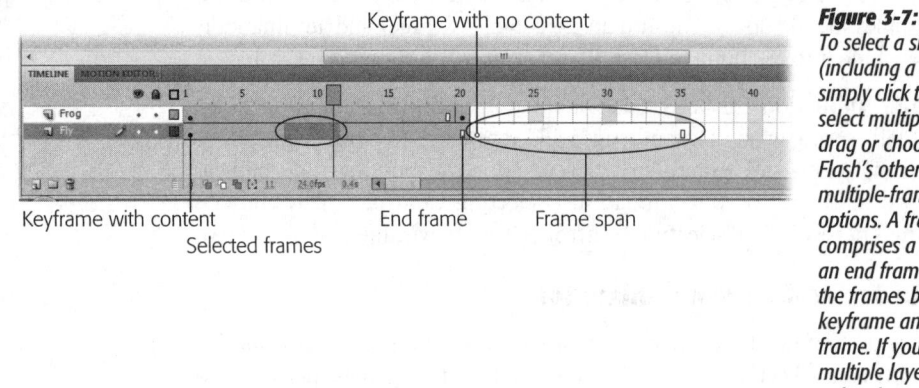

Figure 3-7:
To select a single frame (including a keyframe), simply click the frame. To select multiple frames, drag or choose one of Flash's other two multiple-frame-selection options. A frame span comprises a keyframe, an end frame, and all the frames between the keyframe and end frame. If you've added multiple layers to your animation, make sure you select frames from the correct layer.

But if you want to select multiple frames, Flash gives you four additional selection alternatives:

- **To select multiple contiguous frames.** Click the first frame you want to select, and then drag your mouse to the last frame you want to select. Alternatively, click the first frame you want to select, and then Shift-click the last frame you want to select.

Note: Dragging to select multiple frames can be highly annoying. Flash lets you move frames by selecting a series of frames, and then dragging it somewhere else on the timeline, so you may well end up moving frames when all you wanted to do was select them.

- **To select multiple noncontiguous frames.** Ctrl-click (on the Mac, ⌘-click) each frame you want to select.

Note: On the Mac, *Control*-clicking a frame brings up a context menu of timeline-related commands. To see this menu on a PC (or a Mac with a two-button mouse), right-click the frame.

- **To select an entire frame span.** Double-click any frame in the *frame span*. A frame span consists of all the frames between one keyframe (including that keyframe) and the next keyframe in the layer. So, for example, if you have a keyframe in Frame 15 and another keyframe in Frame 30, double-clicking *any* frame from Frame 15 through Frame 29 automatically selects *every* frame from Frame 15 through Frame 29.
- **To select all the frames on a layer.** Click the name of the layer. In the example in Figure 3-7, clicking "Fly" would automatically select all the frames in the Fly layer; clicking "Frog" would automatically select all the frames in the Frog layer.

No matter which alternative you use, Flash highlights the frames to let you know you've successfully selected them.

Inserting and deleting keyframes and frames

The smoothness of your finished animation depends on the number of keyframes and regular frames you've included. This section shows you how to add and delete both to an existing animation.

Inserting keyframes. Typically, you'll start with a handful of keyframes and need to insert additional keyframes to smooth out the animation and make it appear more realistic (less herky-jerky).

For example, say you're working on an animation showing a dog wagging its tail. You've got a keyframe showing the tail to the left of the dog; one showing the tail straight behind the dog; and a final keyframe showing the tail to the right of the dog. You test the animation and it looks okay, but a little primitive.

Inserting additional keyframes showing the dog's tail in additional positions (just a bit to the left of the dog's rump, a little bit further to the left, a little further, and *then* all the way to the left) will make the finished sequence look much more detailed and realistic.

Note: Technically speaking, you don't actually *insert* a keyframe in Flash; you turn a regular frame into a keyframe. But Flash-ionados speak of inserting keyframes, and so does the Flash documentation, so that's how this section presents it.

To insert a keyframe into an existing animation:

1. **In the timeline, select the regular frame you want to turn into a keyframe.**

   If you want to add a keyframe midway between Frame 1 and Frame 20 on Layer 1, for example, click in Layer 1 to select Frame 10, as shown in Figure 3-8.

   Flash moves the playhead to the frame you selected.

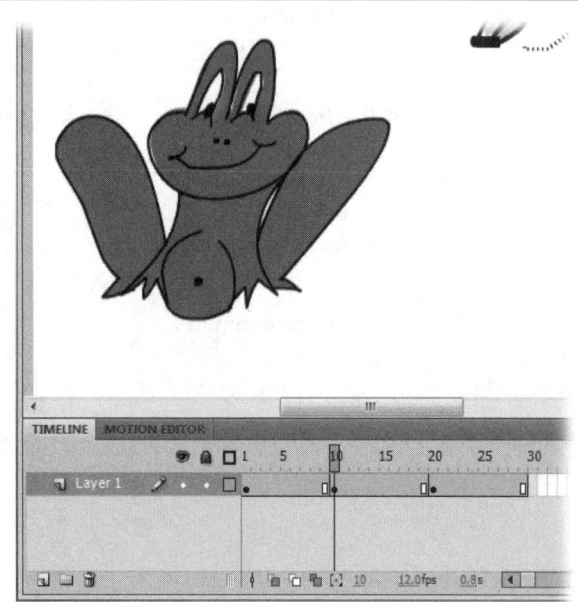

Figure 3-8:
Technically, you don't always add a keyframe in Flash (unless you're positioned over an existing keyframe or the very last frame in a layer). Instead, when you're positioned over a regular frame, you turn that regular frame into a keyframe. As you can see here, Flash displays its usual icons to show the results: The selected frame, Frame 10, is now a keyframe (you can tell by the solid black dot in the timeline), and Frame 9 is the end frame, or the last frame that'll display the contents of the previous keyframe, Frame 1 (you can tell by the hollow rectangle in Frame 9).

2. **Select Insert → Timeline → Keyframe (to tell Flash to carry over the content from the previous keyframe so that you can edit it) or Insert → Timeline → Blank Keyframe (to tell Flash to clear the stage).**

   On the stage, Flash either displays the image associated with the previous keyframe or, if you inserted a blank keyframe, displays nothing at all.

3. **Using the drawing and painting tools, add content for your new keyframe to the stage.**

   If you've already created drawings in another program, you can import them as described on page 319.

Inserting frames. Regular frames in Flash act as placeholders: They simply mark time while the contents of the previous keyframe display. So it stands to reason that you want to insert additional frames when you want to slow down the action a little. In fact, inserting frames is sort of like having a director yell, "Hold camera!" with the contents of the last keyframe remaining onscreen while the camera's holding.

To insert a frame into an existing animation:

1. **In the timeline, click to select the frame before which you want to add a frame. (Make sure the frame you select appears in the timeline after the keyframe you want to hold onscreen.)**

   Flash moves the playhead to the frame you selected.

2. **Select Insert → Timeline → Frame (or press F5).**

   Flash inserts a new frame *after* the frame you selected, bumping up the total number of frames in your animation by one.

Deleting keyframes. Technically speaking, a keyframe is just a regular frame to which you've added unique content. So to delete a keyframe, you first need to turn it back into a regular frame, and *then* delete it. If you try to delete a keyframe without converting it, Flash removes the next standard frame from the timeline, but the keyframe doesn't budge.

To clear a keyframe and turn it back into a regular frame (so you can delete it, as described next):

1. **On the timeline, click to select the keyframe you want to clear.**

   The playhead appears over the keyframe.

2. **Right-click the selected keyframe, and then, from the shortcut menu that appears, choose Clear Keyframe.**

   Flash removes keyframe status from the frame and whisks the associated image off the stage.

Tip: Because you can't tie a drawing to a regular frame, clearing a keyframe means *you lose anything you've drawn or imported to the stage for that keyframe*. To get the contents of the stage back—perhaps you'd like to save your drawing as a reusable symbol or save it off in its own separate file, as shown in Chapter 6, before you delete it from this frame—select Edit → Undo Clear Keyframe.

Deleting frames. Deleting frames—like inserting them—lets you control the pace of your animation. But instead of padding sections of your animation the way inserting frames does, deleting frames squeezes together the space between your keyframes to speed up sections of your animation. When you delete a frame, you're actually shortening your animation by the length of one frame.

For example, say you're working on the animation showing a frog catching a fly. You've created three keyframes: one showing the frog noticing the fly, one showing the frog actually catching the fly, and one showing the frog enjoying the fly. If you space out these three keyframes evenly (say, at Frame 1, Frame 15, and Frame 30), all three images spend the same amount of time onscreen. That's perfectly service-able—but you can create a much more realistic effect by shortening the number of frames between the second and third keyframes (in others words, by deleting a bunch of frames between Frame 15 and Frame 30 to speed up this portion of the animation).

To delete frames:

1. **In the timeline, select the frame (or frames) you want to delete.**

   Flash highlights the selected frame(s) and moves the playhead to the last selected frame.

2. **Select Edit → Timeline → Remove Frames.**

   Flash deletes the selected frames and shortens the timeline by the number of deleted frames.

Adding Layers to Your Animation

Imagine you're creating a complex animation in Flash. You want to show a couple of characters carrying on a conversation, a car speeding by in the background, and some clouds floating across the sky.

Theoretically, you could draw all of these elements together, in one *layer* (one set of frames). In the first frame, you could show the characters greeting each other, the car entering from stage left, and the first cloud drifting in from the right. In the second frame, the characters might begin speaking and waving their hands, the car might advance just a bit, more clouds might appear from the right, and so on.

Now imagine that your spec changes. It's not a car you need in the background, but a galloping dog. A relatively simple change, conceptually, but because you've drawn all the graphic elements on a single set of frames, you would now need to redraw *every single frame.* You'd need to slice away the car where it touches the other elements, and then draw in the dog. And because the dog needs to appear behind the two chatting characters, you can't even take advantage of Flash's motion tweening (which you can learn how to do on page 127), or even copying and pasting to speed up the animation process (page 80).

Fortunately, Flash gives you an alternative: *layers.* Layers in Flash are virtual clear plastic sheets that you stack on top of each other to create composite frames. So you can draw each element of your animation in a separate layer: the clouds, the car, the first character, and the second character. When you stack the layers together, your animation is complete.

Then, when you need to replace the car with a dog, all you need to do is delete the car layer and create a dog layer. You're working with a single object in your dog layer, so you can copy and paste, and even create motion and shape tweens, all without affecting any other part of your animation. And if you decide you want the dog to gallop in *front* of your characters instead of behind, you can make that change simply by restacking (reordering) your layers with the dog layer on top.

Creating Layers

When you create a new document, Flash starts you out with one layer, cleverly called Layer 1, in the Layers area of the timeline (Figure 3-9).

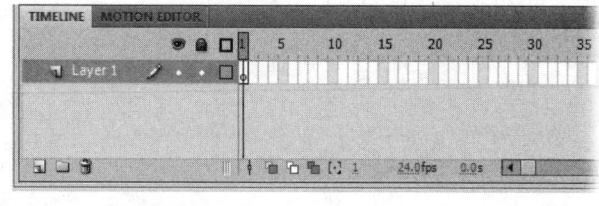

Figure 3-9:
A layer is nothing more than a set of frames, which is why Flash displays layer names to the left of the timeline (that way, you can easily spot which frames belong to which layer). When you create a new document in Flash, Flash names your first set of frames Layer 1. At some point, replace it with a more meaningful name that describes the content of the layer. (See the tip on page 116.)

To create an additional layer:

1. **In the timeline, click the name of the layer you want to add a layer above.**

   If you're starting out in a new Flash document, there's only one layer to select—Layer 1.

2. **Still in the timeline, right-click the layer name—in this example, Layer 1—and then, from the shortcut menu that appears, select Insert Layer.**

   Flash creates a new layer, named Layer 2, and places this new layer above the existing layer, as shown in Figure 3-10.

Note: Flash gives you two additional ways to create layers: by clicking the New Layer icon (Figure 3-10) and by selecting Insert → Timeline → Layer.

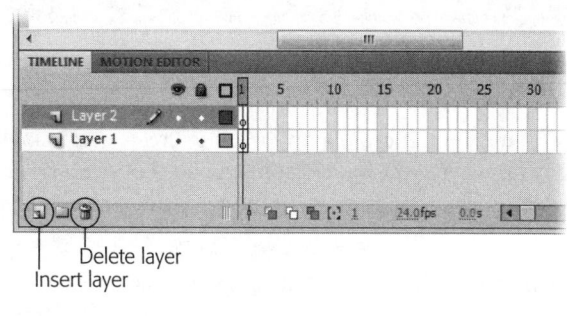

Delete layer
Insert layer

Figure 3-10:
To create a new layer, select an existing layer, and then click the New Layer icon. Flash immediately creates a new layer, names it (here, Layer 2), and places it above the selected layer. The fact that Flash places the new layer above (and not below) the existing layer is important because each layer's position determines how Flash displays your frames' contents. Change your layers' order by dragging them. If you can't see all the layers in the timeline, just click the bottom top edge of the timeline, and then drag to resize it.

Deleting layers

If you want to delete a layer, click to select the layer, and then click the trash can icon (Figure 3-10) in the lower-left corner of the timeline. Be careful though: when you delete a layer, you delete every frame in the layer and all the drawings, text, and other content in the frames.

Dividing Your Animation into Layers: The Common Sense Approach

When it comes to divvying your animation up into layers, there's no hard and fast rule. Some animators like to put every single element in its own separate layer; others take a more conservative approach. In general, the more layers you have, the more control you have over your animation, because you can change and position the content on each layer independently. You can use folders to group layers together. Just click the folder icon at the bottom of the timeline. To put a layer in the folder, just drag the layer onto the folder. (There's more on folders on page 162.)

On the downside, the more complex you make your timeline layers, the more time you spend organizing everything. Only you can decide what works best for your project. While this is one of those areas that's more art than science, here are a few questions to ask yourself when you're trying to decide whether (and how) to break up your animation into layers.

- **What's most likely to change?** If you know going into a Flash project that a particular design idea might change (for example, your team's still arguing over whether the ad you're developing should feature two people talking to each other or one person talking into a cellphone), by all means put those two people in their own layers so you can switch them out easily if you need to.

- **What moves independently of the objects nearest it?** Any moving object that you position on or near other objects needs to live in its own layer. Eyes and mouths are good examples; you want to be able to fine-tune eye and mouth movement to create different expressions on your characters without having to redraw the entire face every time. Same with characters' legs (you want to leave yourself the option of changing your characters' stroll to a sprint without having to redraw their bodies every time).

- **What do you want to tween?** You can't place more than one tween in a layer. (Well, technically, you can, but you don't want to: Flash generates unreliable results for multiple tweens in a single layer.) So if you know you want to create a specific motion tween—a star streaking across the sky, for example—place the tweened star in its own layer, whether or not it's positioned near any other objects in any other layers.

Animating Automatically (Tweening)

When you create a frame-by-frame animation, it's up to you to create every single keyframe and frame. And in cases where you want absolute control over every single image that appears in your finished animation, frame-by-frame animation is the way to go.

Often, however, you can get by with a little less control. If you want to create a scene of a ball rolling across a lawn, for example, you can create one keyframe showing a ball on the left side of the lawn, another keyframe showing the same ball on the right side of the same lawn, and tell Flash to create a *tween*, or all the keyframes in between. Bingo—scene done.

Tip: You can combine frame-by-frame animation with tweening. In fact, that's what a lot of professional animators do: Take care of the complex stuff themselves, and rely on Flash to fill in the spots that aren't as critical.

Tweening saves you more than just time and effort; when you go to publish your animation, it also saves you file size. That's because Flash doesn't save every single frame of a tweened animation the way it does with a frame-by-frame animation. Instead, for tweened animations, Flash saves only the keyframes you create, plus the information it needs to generate the tweened frames from your keyframes. And smaller file sizes are a good thing—especially if you're planning to put your finished animation up on a Web site. (You can find out more about file sizes, including tips for optimization, in Chapter 19.)

Choosing a Type of Tween

Flash gives you three choices for creating tweens: shape tween, classic tween, and the new Flash CS4 motion tween (see the box on page 104). Here's a guide to choosing the right type of tween for the job:

- **Shape tween.** Use a shape tween when you want to dramatically change an object's shape. For example, when you want to create a shape-morphing effect, like changing an acorn into a tree. (You can use a shape tween only when you're tweening an editable object.)

- **Classic tween.** This type of tween was called a motion tween in previous versions of Flash. Use it if you're working with a document created with an earlier version of Flash or if you prefer the old tween method for a particular job. In most cases, the new motion tween gives you greater control over how the tween looks and acts, as described in the box on page 104. Compared to the new motion tween, the classic tween is a simpler, no-nonsense way to make objects move on the stage, and it has a shorter learning curve. (You can use the classic tween on symbols and grouped objects.)

- **Motion tween.** Flash CS4's new motion tween is both more powerful and more complex than the classic version. Using its Motion Editor, you can move objects on the desktop and change their height, width, color, and transparency. You can create 3-D-style spinning effects. Motion tweening can handle most effects, but if you need to morph one shape into a completely different shape, use a shape tween instead. To use a motion tween, the object you're tweening has to be a symbol (page 228), or you have to convert it into one.

  Flash CS4's new motion tween has the steepest learning curve because you have to master the Motion Editor. But once you've put in the time, you'll find the effort was well worth it, since you can tween how your object looks as well as how it moves, and you'll probably end up using motion tween for most of your tweens.

If you're new to Flash in general and tweening in particular, for a thorough education, work your way through this entire section. You'll learn how to use all three types of tweens, plus all of Flash's tweening tools along the way, like shape hints, easing, and motion paths. If you're impatient, skip to the new motion tweening section on page 127.

If you've used Flash before, rest assured that shape tweening works just like it always has, and you can still create motion tweens the way you're used to—just use the Create Classic Tween command instead of Create Motion Tween. When you're ready to learn how to use the new Motion Editor for more powerful tweening, skip to page 134. There's even more detail on using the Motion Editor in Chapter 7 on advanced tweening.

Shape Tweening (Morphing)

Shape tweening—sometimes referred to as *morphing*—lets you create an effect that makes one object appear as though it's slowly turning into another object. All you have to do is draw the beginning object and the ending object, and Flash does all the rest.

For example, say you create a keyframe containing a yellow ball. Then, 24 frames along the timeline, you create another keyframe containing a green star. You apply a shape tween to the frame span, and Flash generates all the incremental frames necessary to show the ball slowly—frame by frame—transforming itself into a star when you run the animation.

Tip: Shape tweens work only on editable graphics. If you want to tween a symbol (page 228), you need to use a motion tween or a classic tween. If you want to tween a group of objects or a chunk of text, you need to ungroup the objects (page 169), break apart the text Modify → Break Apart, or use a motion tween.

Shape tweening lets you change more than just an object's shape over a series of frames. Using a shape tween, you can also change an object's size, color, transparency, position, scale, and rotation.

To create a shape tween:

1. **Select the frame where you want your tween to begin (for example, Frame 1).**

   Flash highlights the selected frame.

2. **If the selected frame isn't a keyframe (if you don't see a dot in the frame), turn it into a keyframe by selecting Insert → Timeline → Keyframe.**

   Flash displays a dot in the frame to let you know it's a keyframe.

3. **On the stage, draw the shape you want to begin your tween.**

   In Figure 3-11, the beginning shape's a ball—yellow circle with a black outline.

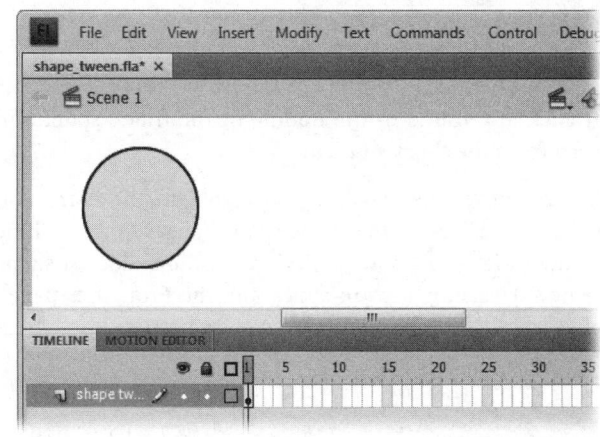

Figure 3-11:
You can use any or all of Flash's drawing and painting tools to create your first image. Just make sure you don't group objects (page 195) or convert your object into a symbol (page 228); shape tweening works only on ungrouped, editable objects in a single layer.

4. **Select the frame where you want your tween to end (for example, Frame 24).**

   Flash highlights the selected frame.

5. **Insert an ending point for your tween (and a clean, fresh stage on which to draw your ending shape) by selecting Insert → Timeline → Blank Keyframe.**

   The stage clears, the playhead moves to the selected frame, and Flash displays a hollow dot in the selected frame to let you know it's a keyframe.

Tip: As explained on page 97, you can carry over your beginning image from the first keyframe and make changes to it by choosing Insert → Timeline → Keyframe (instead of Insert → Timeline → Blank Keyframe).

6. **On the stage, use Flash's drawing and painting tools to draw the shape you want to end your tween.**

   Your ending shape can differ from your first shape in terms of position, color, transparency, rotation, skew, and size, so go wild. In Figure 3-12, the ending shape's a green, five-pointed star.

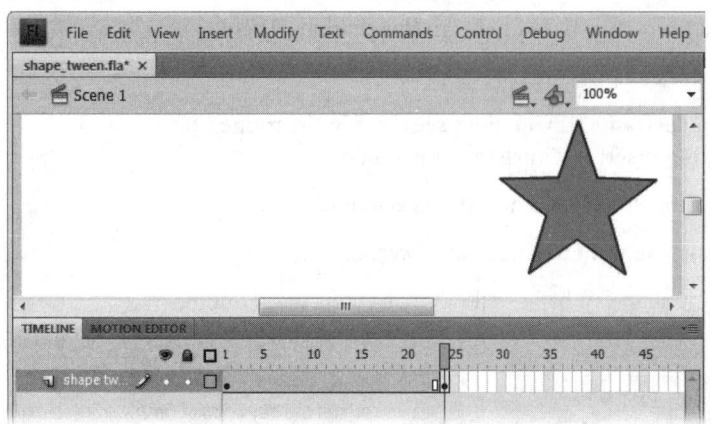

Figure 3-12:
Flash grays out all the frames in a frame span— in other words, all the frames beginning with one keyframe up to (but not including) the next keyframe—so you can spot them easily. As you can see here, each frame span ends with the end frame symbol, which looks like a hollow rectangle.

7. **On the timeline, right-click any frame in the middle of the frame span, and then choose Shape Tween from the shortcut menu.**

   When you right-click, Flash moves the playhead and highlights the frame you clicked. When you choose Shape Tween, the frame span changes to a nice lime color and inserts an arrow to let you know you've successfully added a shape tween (Figure 3-13). A new Tweening section appears in the Properties panel. (If the Properties panel isn't showing, choose Window → Properties.)

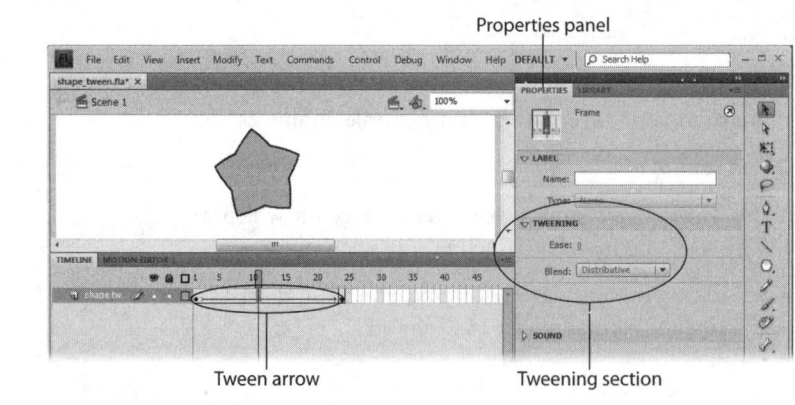

Properties panel

Figure 3-13:
As soon as you create a tween, Flash displays an arrow spanning the frames that make the tween. A new Tweening section appears in the Properties panel.

Tween arrow   Tweening section

Note: If you have Tinted Frames turned off, Flash doesn't change a color behind the tweened frames. To turn on Tinted Frames, click the Options menu (the tiny, striped icon on the far right of the timeline, just above the frame numbers, as shown in Figure 3-12); and then select the Tinted Frames option. A checkmark indicates the option is turned on.

8. **If you like, set the Ease and Blend shape tween options (Figure 3-14).**

- **Ease** tells Flash to speed up (or slow down) the tween. To change the Ease value, type a number or drag to change the number. If you want your tween to start out normally but speed up at the end, set the Ease value to a negative number. To tell Flash to start your tween normally but slow down at the end, use a positive number. (Zero means that when you play your animation, the tween appears to be the same speed throughout.)

- **Blend** tells Flash how picky you want it to be when it draws its in-between frames. If you want to preserve the hard angles of your original shape, click the Blend drop-down box, and then select Angular; if you want Flash to smooth out the hard edges so that the tween appears softer, select Distributive.

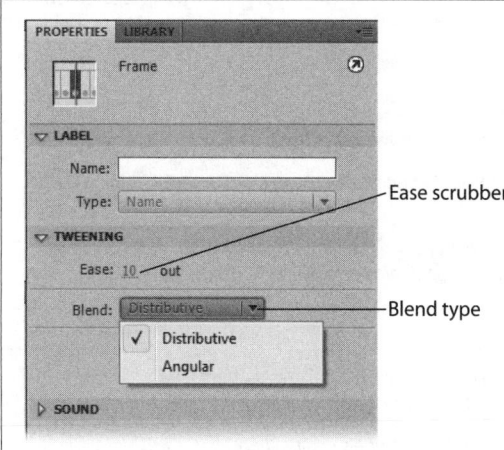

Figure 3-14:
Shape-related tweening options appear in the Properties panel: namely, Ease (to speed up or slow down your tween) and Blend (to tell Flash to preserve hard corners and angles from frame to frame or smooth them out). To preview the in-between frames Flash generated for you, just select any frame in the frame span.

9. **Test your shape by selecting Control → Play.**

Flash plays your shape tween on the stage (Figure 3-15).

Shape Hints

Flash does a bang-up job when it comes to tweening simple shapes: circles, squares, stars, rain drops. But the more complicated the images you want to tween, the harder Flash has to work to calculate how to generate the in-between images.

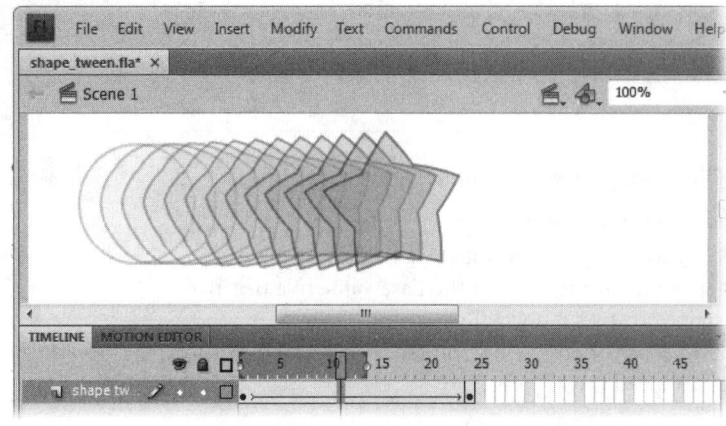

Figure 3-15:
When you run your animation, your beginning image appears to morph into your ending image, thanks to the in-between frames Flash generates when you create your shape tween. Because the pages of a book can't show motion, here onionskin outlines (page 145) represent the animated tween you'd see on the stage.

And if you think about it, that difficulty makes sense. Because complex beginning-and-ending images like a stylized acorn and tree (Figure 3-16 and Figure 3-17) contain a bunch of editable lines, shapes, and colors, Flash has to guess at which elements are most important and how you want the morph to progress from the first keyframe to the last.

Figure 3-16:
Left: The original acorn drawing: so far, so good.

Middle: Flash's first attempt at generating an in-between frame is a little scary.

Right: Clearly, the acorn is changing and growing, but that's about all you can say for this generated image.

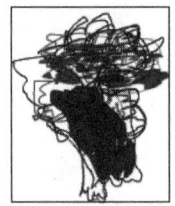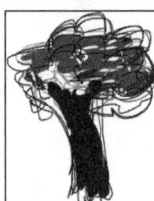

Figure 3-17:
Left: You can almost make out the outline of a tree now.

Middle: This one's getting there...

Right: And finally, at the end of the tween, Flash makes it to your original ending image.

Sometimes, Flash guesses correctly; other times, you need to give it a few hints. Adding *shape hints* to your tweens tells Flash how you want it to create each in-between frame, with the result that your finished tween appears more realistic—more how *you* want it to be.

In short, shape hints give you more (but not complete, by any means) control over the shape-tweened sections of your animation.

Note: Shape hints are especially valuable when you're working on an animation that moves at a relatively slow frame rate; in other words, in situations when each separate frame will be visible to your audience's naked eye.

To add shape hints to a shape tween:

1. **Select the first frame of your tween.**

   Flash highlights the selected frame.

2. **Choose Modify → Shape → Add Shape Hint (or press Ctrl+Shift+H [Windows] or Shift-⌘-H [Mac]).**

   Flash displays a hint (a red circle containing a letter from A–Z) in the center of your shape, as shown in Figure 3-18 (top).

Figure 3-18:

Top: When you add a shape hint, Flash places it at the center of your object. All you have to do is drag it to the edge of your object.

Bottom: The more shape hints you use (and the more accurately you place them around the edge of your object), the more closely Flash attempts to preserve your shape as it generates the tween frames. Make sure you place the hints in alphabetical order as you outline your shape. If you find after several tries that Flash doesn't seem to be taking your hints, your shapes might be too complex or too dissimilar to tween effectively. In that case, you'll want to create additional keyframes or even consider replacing your tween with a frame-by-frame animation.

---

3. **Drag the hint to the edge of your shape.**

   Figure 3-18 (bottom) shows the result of dragging several hints to the edge of your shape.

4. **Repeat as many times as necessary, placing hints around the outline of the object in alphabetical order.**

   The bigger or more oddly-shaped your object, the more hints you'll need. Placing a hint at each peak and valley of your object tells Flash to preserve the shape of your beginning object as much as possible as it morphs toward the shape of your ending object.

5. **Go to the last frame of the shape tween and adjust the shape hints to match the final shape.**

   When the animation runs, Flash uses the hints in both the beginning and ending keyframe to control the shape of the morphing object.

6. **Test your animation by clicking Control → Play.**

   The tweened frames of your animation conform, more or less, to the hints you provided. Figure 3-19 and Figure 3-20 show you an example.

  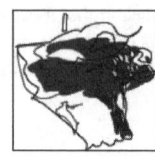

Figure 3-19:

Left: The original acorn is the same here as it was in Figure 3-16.

Middle: Compare this attempt at generating a first in-between frame to the one in It's not exactly a prize pig, but it's better.

Right: Already, you can see the form of the tree taking shape.

Figure 3-20:

Left: Here, the already-pretty-well-shaped tree looks as though it's about to burst out of the acorn outline.

Middle: Compared to tweening without shape hints (see Figure 3-17), this tween appears much smoother; you don't see the Flash-generated squiggly lines that you see in Figure 3-19, and break the grafs.

Right: The final frame of any tween appears the same, whether or not you use shape hints.

Using Multiple Layers for Shape Tweens

It's easier for Flash to morph two simple shapes than one complex shape. So, if shape hints don't help Flash solve shape tween confusion, try tweening parts of your drawing separately. For example, put the cap of an acorn on a layer by itself and put the bottom shell in a separate layer. Then you can shape tween the cap into the leaves of the tree, and shape tween the shell into the trunk of the tree, with results as shown in Figure 3-21.

Figure 3-21:
If you add a shape tween to a layer with more than one object, the results usually aren't pretty. It's best to place objects on separate layers. Here the cap of the acorn tweens into the leaves and the shell tweens into the trunk and branches. Using tweens on multiple layers, gives you more control over your animation.

Note: You can find the finished Flash document with the acorn tweening into a mighty oak at *http:// missingmanual.com/cds*. The file is named *shape_acorn.fla*.

Classic Tweening

Classic tweening is similar to shape tweening: To create both types of tweens, all you need to do is create a beginning image and an ending image, and then tell Flash to generate all the "in-between" frames to create an animated sequence. And you can create a lot of the same effects using both types of tweens: You can create a series of frames that, when run, show an object changing size, position, rotation, and skew.

Note: As explained in the box on page 104, what's called a classic tween used to be called motion tween in the Flash before CS4. The new motion tween (page 127) is easy-to-use and puts a lot of tweening power in your hands. Classic tween is provided primarily for compatibility with older Flash documents.

But beyond that, there are two important differences between shape tweening and classic tweening:

- **Tweenable objects.** While shape tweening works only on editable objects, classic tweening works only on noneditable objects: symbols, grouped objects (page 195), and text. And classic tweening, unlike shape tweening, limits you to one object per layer. (The single object can be a grouped object or a symbol containing multiple shapes; it just has to be a single object as far as Flash is concerned.)

- **Nonlinear paths.** With classic tweening and motion tweening (page 127), you can create a series of frames that show an object moving across the stage in a nonlinear fashion: for example, swooping, diving, arcing, rotating, or pulsing. You can't do that with shape tweening.

To create a classic tween:

1. **Select the frame and layer where you want your tween to begin (for example, Frame 1 in Layer 1).**

   Flash highlights the selected frame.

Note: If you try and apply a classic tween to a layer with more than one object, Flash groups the objects before it applies the tween. This may not be the effect you wanted. If you want multiple items to tween independently, put each item in its own layer.

---

2. **On the stage, draw the shape (or create the text) you want to begin your tween.**

   In Figure 3-22, the beginning shape is a fly on the right side of the stage.

3. **Convert the drawing to a noneditable form by selecting all the elements of your drawing, and then choosing either Modify → Group (to flatten all the elements into a single group) or Modify → "Convert to Symbol" (to convert the editable drawing into a reusable symbol).**

Tip: For a quick refresher on symbols, see "Symbols and Instances" on page 228. For the full story, see Chapter 6.

   Flash displays a box around the entire drawing to show that it's now a single, noneditable entity (Figure 3-22).

4. **If the selected frame isn't a keyframe (if you don't see a dot in the frame), turn it into a keyframe by selecting Insert → Timeline → Keyframe.**

   Flash displays a dot in the frame to let you know it's a keyframe.

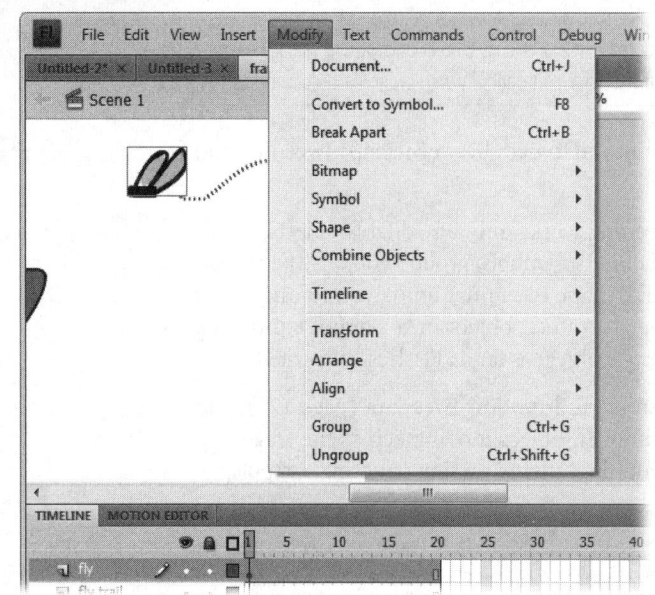

Figure 3-22:
If you apply a classic tween to an editable object, Flash groups the all the parts before creating the tween. This might seem capricious, but it's actually practical. If you drew a complex object consisting of seven different shapes and didn't flatten it into a symbol or a group, Flash wouldn't know which shape to move where.

5. **Select the frame where you want your tween to end (for example, Frame 10).**

   Flash highlights the selected frame.

6. **Insert an ending point for your tween by selecting Insert → Timeline → Keyframe.**

   The playhead moves to the selected frame, and Flash displays a solid dot in the selected frame to let you know it's now a keyframe, as shown in Figure 3-23.

Figure 3-23:
Here, you see a symbol being dragged from the right side of the stage to the left side. Moving a symbol is the quickest way to create a classic tween, but it's certainly not the only way. Using the Properties, Color Mixer, and Transform panels, you can create a tween that morphs an object's color, transparency, rotation, scale, and skew.

7. **On the stage, drag the object to somewhere else on the screen.**

   You can create a classic tween most easily by carrying over your beginning image from the first keyframe and moving it, but you can also create something much more sophisticated. To change the size, rotation, or position of your ending object, you can use the Properties and Transform panels.

8. **Right-click any frame in the frame span, and then choose Create Classic Tween from the shortcut menu.**

Flash highlights the selected frame. The frame shortcut menu (sometimes called a context menu) shows nearly two-dozen frame-related commands, as shown in Figure 3-24. The tweening options are at the top. You can also create a tween by selecting a frame, and then choosing Insert → Classic Tween.

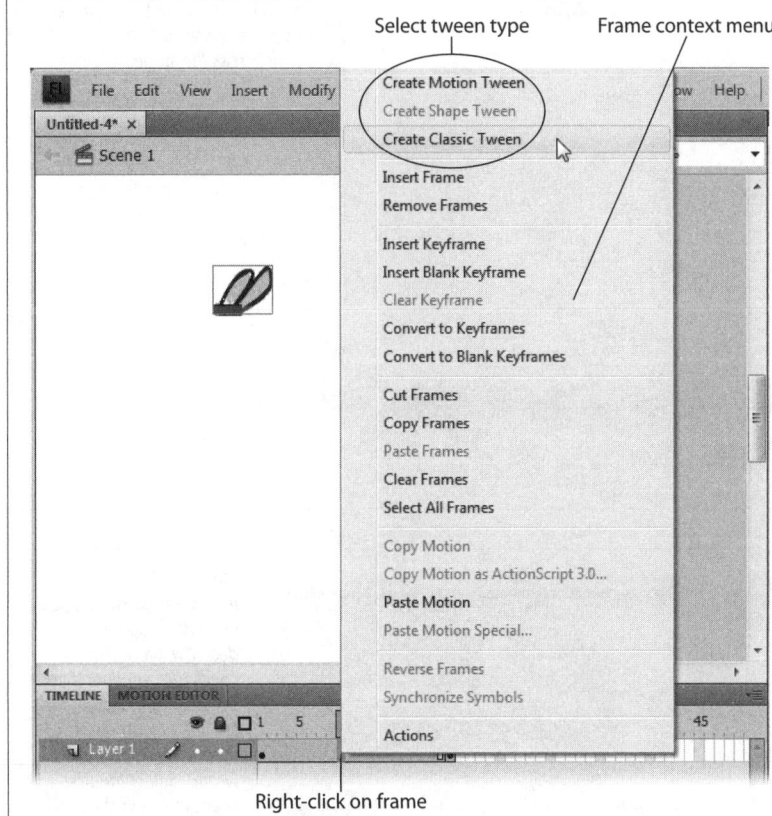

Figure 3-24:
Right-click the timeline to see related commands including the one used to Create a Classic Tween. All the tween commands appear at the top of the context menu.

Flash tints the background of the frame span and inserts an arrow (Figure 3-25) to let you know you've successfully added your classic tween. And in the Properties panel, motion-related tween options appear: Scale, Ease (Edit), Rotate, Orient to path, Sync, and Snap.

Tip: If you see a dashed line in the frame span (instead of an arrow), that's Flash telling you that your classic tween is broken, as shown in Figure 3-26. Check to make sure you're tweening noneditable objects (symbols, grouped objects, or text blocks) and that you've created both a beginning and an ending keyframe for your tween.

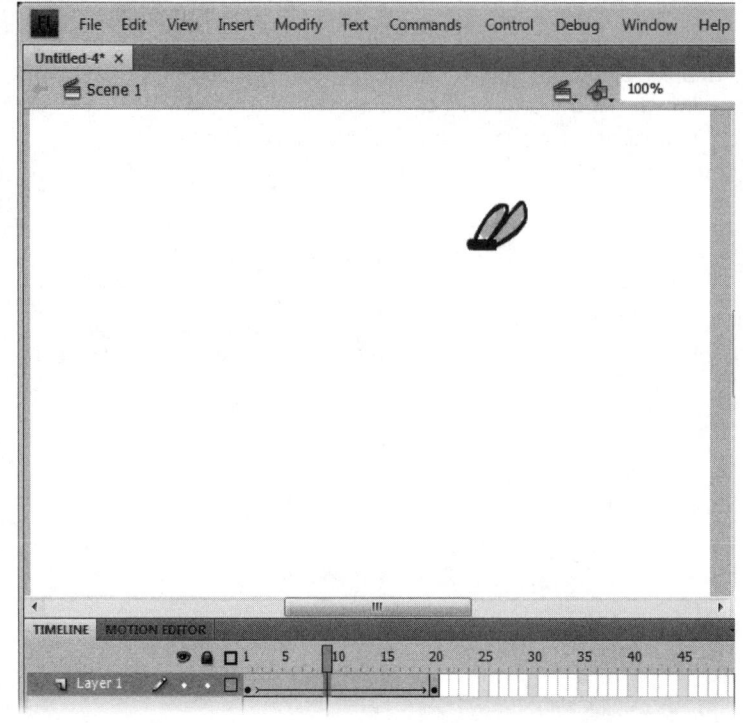

Figure 3-25:
Flash adds a classic tween automatically (the instant you select Create Classic Tween from the shortcut menu), so depending on the frame you selected, the content on the stage might change. For example, here, Frame 9 is selected, so the contents of Frame 9 appear—a tweened image of the fly part way across the stage.

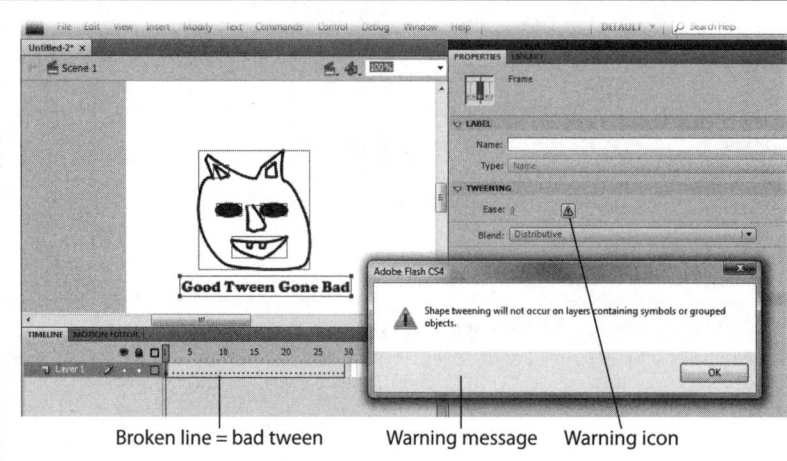

Broken line = bad tween   Warning message   Warning icon

Figure 3-26:
If a tween goes bad, you need to do some detective work. First check the timeline. If you see dashes in the tweened frame, that means something's wrong. Select the first keyframe, and then check to see if you have a yellow warning icon in the Properties panel. Click the warning icon to display a mildly helpful message.

9. **If you like, set the Ease option.**

Ease tells Flash to speed up (or slow down) the tween. To change the Ease value, type a number or drag to change the number. Zero means that when you play your animation, the tween appears to be the same speed throughout. If you want your tween to start out normally but speed up at the end, set the Ease value to a negative number. To tell Flash to start your tween normally but slow down at the end, use a positive number.

You can even create a custom speed that varies throughout the tween. (Perhaps you're tweening a scene of a mouse running past a gauntlet of cats, and want your mouse to speed up every time it passes a cat and slow down in-between.) To do so, click Edit easing (pencil icon). Then, in the Custom Ease In/Ease Out window that appears, drag the diagonal tween line to specify the relative speed for each frame of your frame span. When you finish, click OK.

Tip: The other classic tween–related options are useful only in the context of specific motion-related effects. Use Rotate to control the direction and number of times a tweened object spins. "Orient to path" and Snap are described beginning on page 118. The Sync option synchronizes the animation of graphic symbol instances by changing the number of frames in the symbol. The Scale checkbox allows (or prevents) changes to the H and W properties. For more finely-tuned motion effects, use the new motion tween (page 17) rather than the classic tween.

---

10. **Test your classic tween by selecting Control → Play.**

   Flash plays your classic tween on the stage.

Motion guide layers (moving along a nonstraight path)

The previous section showed you how to create a straight-line classic tween, where an object appears to move from one point on the stage to another. This section takes classic tweening a little further by explaining how you can use a motion guide layer to create a nonlinear classic tween.

Note: In Flash, there are more layers than just the generic ones you learned to create earlier in this chapter. There are also *guide layers* to help you position objects precisely on the stage (page 199), *mask layers* to hide and display specific portions of your images (page 118) for a peek-a-boo effect, and *classic motion guide layers* to create a nonlinear classic tween (these are the layers you get acquainted with in this section).

Using a motion guide layer to create a nonlinear classic tween is surprisingly easy. All you have to do is create a regular straight-line classic tween, as described on page 110. Then, you create a special type of layer called a *motion guide layer*. In the motion guide layer, you draw the path you want your object to follow. You can draw a twisty line, a curve, or whatever you like. Then you drag your objects to the beginning and the end of the path, respectively. The step-by-step example below takes you through the simple process.

You don't see the actual path when you run your animation; you see it only when you're editing your animation and testing it. You can think of a path as a kind of guideline that "shows" your objects how to move along a classic tween.

Note: You can find the finished Flash document with the frog fly and classic tween along a guide path at *http://missingmanual.com/cds*. The file is named *classic_tween_guide.fla*.

To create a tween along a nonlinear path using a motion guide layer:

1. **Create a basic, straight-line classic tween.**

   The steps for creating one begin on page 110.

2. **In the timeline, select the keyframe that begins your tween.**

   Flash highlights the selected keyframe as well as the name of the layer you're working in (the *active* layer). In Figure 3-27, the active layer is "frog".

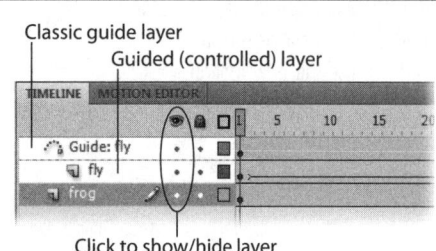

Classic guide layer
Guided (controlled) layer
Click to show/hide layer

Figure 3-27:
When you create a motion guide layer, Flash places it directly above the active layer—and indents the active layer—to give you a visual reminder that the motion guide layer controls the active layer. As you see in the steps on these pages, the path you draw on your motion guide layer determines how the objects on your active layer behave during a classic tween.

Tip: You can rename a layer from Flash's unimaginative Layer 1, Layer 2, and Layer 3 to something more meaningful, like Fly, Frog, or Fly Motion. (Doing so will help you remember what each layer contains—especially useful if you create animations with multiple layers.) To rename a layer: In the timeline, double-click the name of the layer you want to rename. In the editable name field that appears, type a new name, and then press Enter.

3. **Right-click the name of the layer you want to control, and then choose Add Classic Motion Guide from the shortcut menu.**

   The layer you right-click is indented, and a new guide layer appears above it. The name of the guide layer includes the name of the layer it controls. For example, if the layer being guided is called "fly," the guide layer is named "Guide: fly" as shown in Figure 3-27.

4. **With the motion guide layer still selected, draw a path (the line you want your classic tween to follow) on the stage.**

   The Pencil is an easy tool to use for this task—especially with the Smooth option turned on, as described on page 66. But you can use any of Flash's drawing tools to draw your path. Figure 3-28 shows you an example.

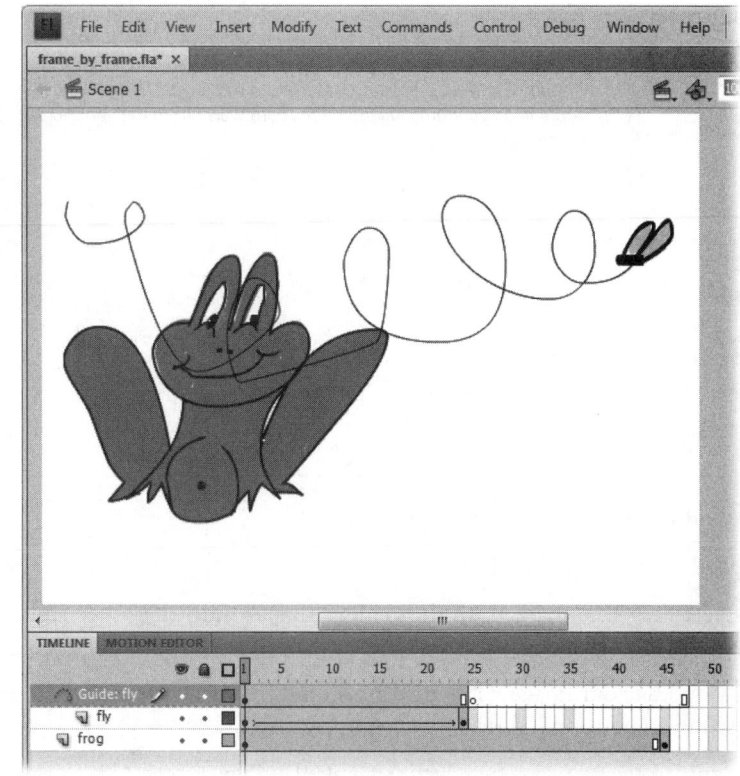

Figure 3-28:
*You can use any drawing
or painting tool you like to
create your path. If the path you
create is a closed shape (like a
circle) Flash will decide which
direction the tween should go.*

Tip: Some folks find it hard to concentrate on drawing a path with objects in the way. To temporarily hide the objects on the stage: On the timeline next to your *non*–motion guide layer, click the dot below the Show/Hide All Layers icon (the icon that looks like an eye, as shown in Figure 3-27). After you finish drawing your path, click the Show/Hide All Layers icon again to redisplay the objects on the stage.

---

5. **In the non–motion guide layer, click to select the beginning keyframe for your animation.**

   Flash highlights the selected keyframe.

6. **Click the center of your image to select it, and then drag the image until the center "snaps" onto one end of your path.**

   Flash displays a little circle in the center of your image to help you center the image directly onto your path, as shown in Figure 3-29.

   Your image doesn't have to be at the very *end* of the path, but it *does* have to be exactly *on* the path. Flash helps you find the sweet spot if you turn on Snap to Objects (View → Snapping → Snap to Objects). Doing so tells Flash to widen the center circle and to jump to the path, when you move your image near the path. After you sense the snapping motion, release the mouse button.

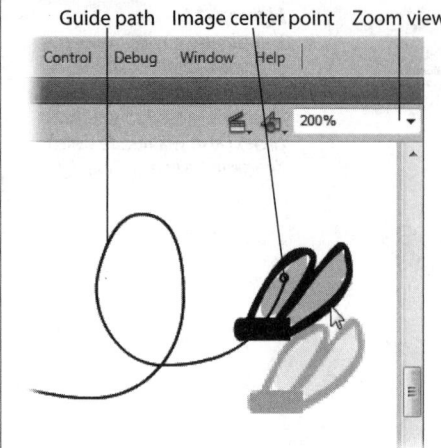

Guide path   Image center point   Zoom view

Figure 3-29:
If your eyesight's less than stellar, you might have a hard time positioning your image right on top of the path. But you have to position it correctly, or your classic tween won't work. It may help to zoom in on your drawing using the Zoom View box in the upper-right corner.

7. **Select the ending keyframe for your animation.**

   Flash highlights the selected keyframe.

8. **On the stage, drag the image until the center "snaps" onto the other end of your path.**

   Again, as you drag your image, Flash displays a little circle in the center of your image to help you position it directly onto your path.

9. **Test your guided classic tween by selecting Control → Play.**

   Flash plays your classic tween on the stage, moving your object along the path you defined in step 4. Figure 3-30 shows you an example.

Orient to path

If you've created a nonlinear path using a motion guide layer (page 115), you may have noticed that the object stays right-side up as it moves along the path—even if the path's a loop-de-loop, like the one in the fly example. That effect might be what you want. If it isn't, and you want your object to turn to face the path as it moves along, you can do so easily by turning on the "Orient to path" checkbox in the classic tween section of the Properties panel (Figure 3-31).

Spotlight Effect Using Mask Layers

Imagine placing a sheet of red construction paper containing a cutout of a star over a piece of green construction paper. The result you see, when you look at the two sheets stacked on top of each other, is a green star on a red background. That's the concept behind *mask layers*, a special type of layer that lets you create shaped "portholes" through which an underlying (*masked*) layer appears.

Figure 3-30:
Here you see the effect of a motion guide layer: The fly buzzes along according to a nonlinear, loopy path—much more realistic and interesting than a straight shot from right to left. But notice that the fly always faces straight ahead, even when it's upside down. If this isn't the effect you want in your classic tweens, check out the "Orient to path" section on page 118.

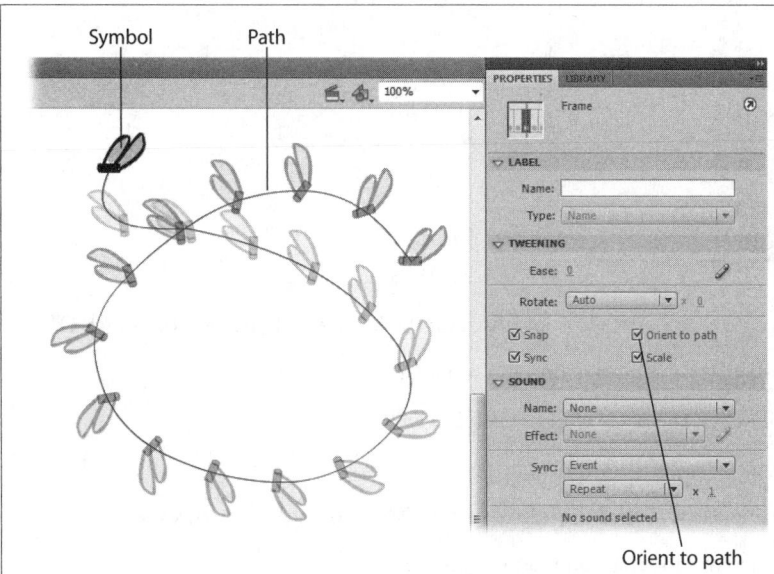

Figure 3-31:
Turning on "Orient to path" in the Properties panel (click any frame in your classic motion tween layer to view Frame properties in the Properties panel) tells Flash to turn the object as it moves along the path. Here, onion skinning (page 145) is turned on to show the fly's position in different frames.

At a masquerade ball, masks hide the important stuff—your face. It's a little different in Flash and other graphic arts endeavors. Masks hide part of a picture in order to reveal the important stuff—the subject. You use masks to direct the eye of your audience. And when you apply a classic tween to the porthole, you can create an effect that looks like a spotlight playing over an image—mighty cool, indeed.

Here's how you go about it:

1. **Open the file *mask_begin.fla*.**

   You can download this file, a working example of the file (*mask_finished.fla*), and all the other examples shown in this chapter from the "Missing CD" page at *http:// missingmanuals.com/cds*.

2. **Click Layer 1 to select it.**

   In the example file for this section (*mask_begin.fla*), Layer 1 contains a bitmap image.

3. **Click the Insert Layer button. (The Insert Layer button is on the bar below the layer names and looks like a folded-over page.)**

   Flash creates a new layer named Layer 2 and places it above Layer 1.

4. **Double-click the layer icon next to Layer 2.**

   The Layer Properties window appears (Figure 3-32).

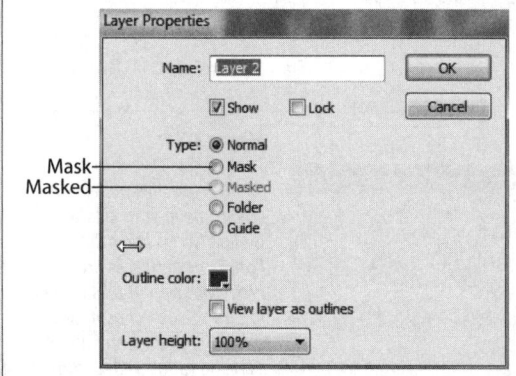

Figure 3-32:
Use the Layer Properties window to change the layer from one type to another. In this example, you create a Mask layer and a Masked Layer.

5. **In the Layer Properties window, turn on the Mask checkbox, and then click OK.**

   Flash displays the mask icon next to Layer 2.

6. **Double-click the layer icon next to Layer 1.**

   The Layer Properties window appears again.

7. **This time, turn on the checkbox next to Masked, and then click OK.**

   Flash displays the masked icon next to Layer 1.

Tip: Flash gives you a bunch of ways to create masks and masked layers (by right-clicking an existing layer, and then choosing Mask or Masked, for example), but one thing doesn't change: Masked layers have to appear directly below mask layers in the Layers window for the effect to work. If you create a mask layer and a masked layer in the wrong order, just drag the mask layer above the masked layer, and you're all set.

8. **Click to select the first frame in Layer 2 (the mask layer). On the stage, click the Oval tool, and then draw a circle in the upper-right corner of the stage (Figure 3-33).**

   The oval can be any color you choose, since it won't appear in the finished effect; instead, it'll act as a see-through portal.

Mask shape

Figure 3-33:
The shape you use as a portal has to be either a fill (like the circle shown here) or a symbol. Because the Brush tool creates fills, you can use the Brush to draw a freehand portal. (Strokes on the mask layer have no effect.)

CHAPTER 3: ANIMATING YOUR DRAWINGS

9. In Layer 2, click Frame 20, and then select Insert → Timeline → Keyframe.

Flash inserts a keyframe in Frame 20. On the stage, the bitmap image disappears so that all you see is the circle you drew in step 8.

10. Click the Select tool, and then drag the circle to the lower-right corner of the stage (Figure 3-34).

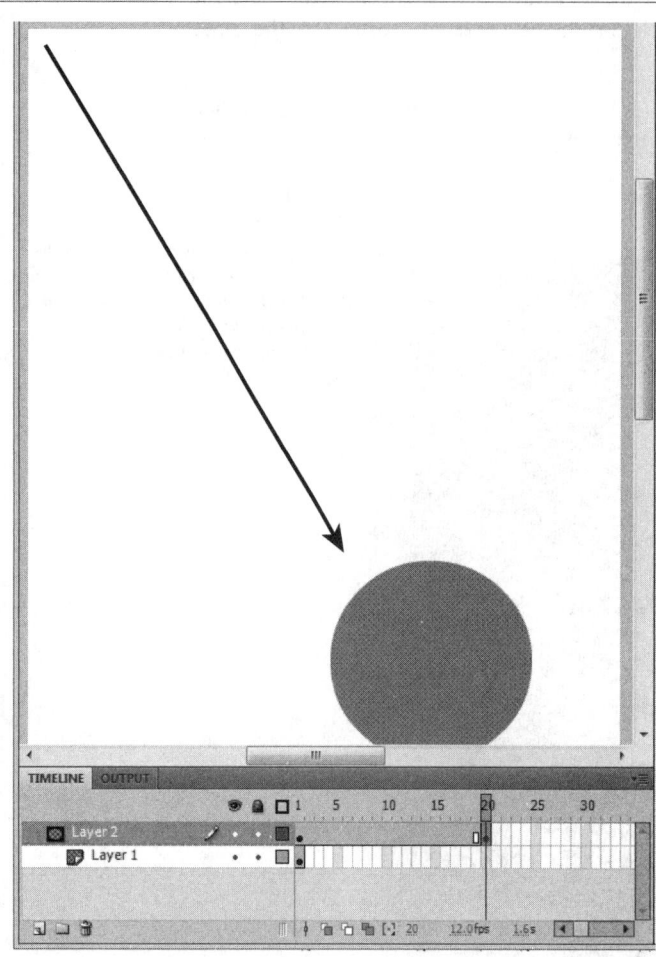

Figure 3-34:
In this example, you're creating a simple tween in Layer 2, so that the portal moves across the bitmap image showing only a circle's worth of image at any one time (a spotlight effect). But you can create static portals (masks), too. The simplest is a circle or a square, but nice thick letters also make a compelling effect.

11. In Layer 2, click Frame 2.

The circle jumps back into the upper-left corner of the stage, and the Properties panel appears.

12. Select Insert → Shape Tween.

Flash displays an arrow in Layer 2, from Frame 2 through Frame 19, showing you it's created a successful shape tween.

13. In Layer 1, click Frame 20, and then select Insert → Timeline → Keyframe.

Flash inserts a keyframe. On the stage, the bitmapped image appears behind the circle (Figure 3-35).

Figure 3-35:
At Frame 20 (notice the position of the playhead), the bitmapped image appears on stage along with the circle. At this point, testing the animation by choosing Control → Test Movie shows you the mask effect. But to see the mask effect on the stage, in edit mode, you need to lock both the mask and masked layers.

14. Click the lock icon you see above the layers once to lock both Layer 1 and Layer 2.

Flash shows you the mask effect on the stage (Figure 3-36).

15. Run the animation by choosing Control → Test Movie.

In the test window, you see the circle move in a diagonal line, revealing the bitmap beneath just as though you were looking through a tube sweeping diagonally across the image.

Adding a Motion Path to a Mask

In the previous section, you saw an example of an animated mask that moves in a straight line across the image on the masked layer. Wouldn't it be great if you could add a motion path to the mask to make the spotlight dip and weave and wiggle its way around the image?

Well, you *can*—but not in the usual way.

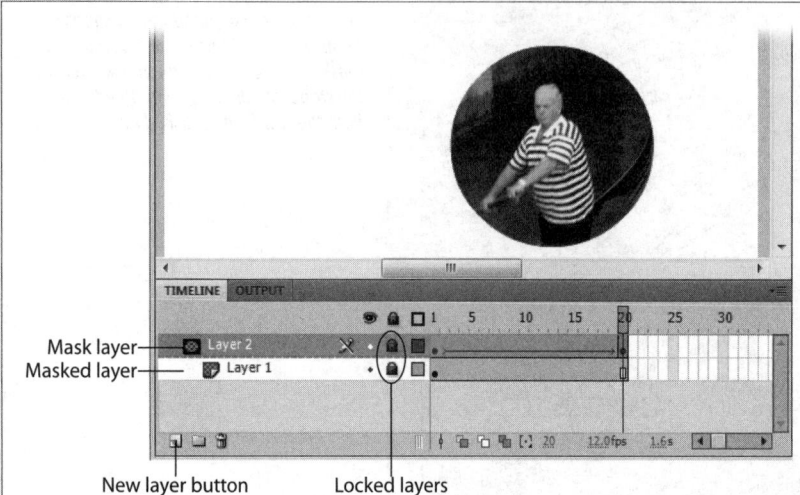

Mask layer
Masked layer

New layer button   Locked layers

Figure 3-36:
Here you see the effect at Frame 20: a circle's worth of bitmap, just like that cutout star showing the green construction paper underneath. You can test the effect quickly on the stage by dragging the playhead backward, from Frame 20 to Frame 1.

Flash doesn't let you apply a motion guide layer (page 115) to a mask layer. (Selecting a mask layer and clicking the Add Motion Guide icon has no effect, and right-clicking a layer, and then trying to choose Add Motion Guide from the shortcut menu doesn't work, either: The Add Motion Guide option appears grayed out.) But you *can* add a motion path to a mask indirectly, by using an animated movie clip symbol as the mask shape. It's a simple matter of creating the mask shape, and then converting it to a movie clip symbol before applying your motion tween. (You can learn a lot more detail about movie clip symbols on page 228.)

Note: You can find a copy of the example shown in this section, at the "Missing CD" page (*http://missingmanuals.com/cds*). Look for *mask_guide_begin.fla* (ready for you to begin the exercise) and *mask_guide_finished.fla* (a completed, working example).

Here's how to animate a mask layer, step by step:

1. **Open the file spotlight_begin.fla. Click the first frame of a new document, and then add the image or drawing you want in the masked layer (Layer 1).**

   As you can see in Figure 3-37, the background image for this example file is a Venice scene.

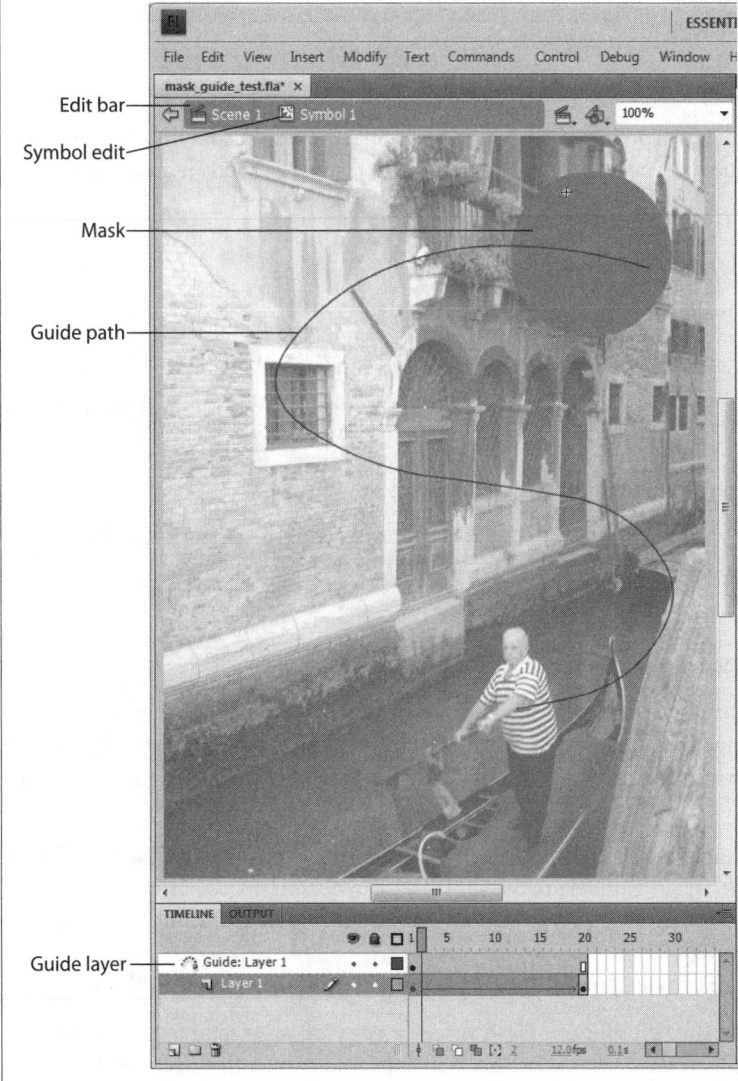

Figure 3-37:
Here's a motion path superimposed on the Venice scene (the masked layer). When you finish the steps in this example, the mask (the circle) will "shine a spotlight" on the gondolier after following the curved motion path.

Edit bar

Symbol edit

Mask

Guide path

Guide layer

2. **Choose Insert → Timeline → Layer.**

   Flash creates a new layer named Layer 2 and places it just above Layer 1.

3. **Double-click the layer icon next to Layer 2.**

   The Layer Properties window appears.

4. **In the Layer Properties window, turn on the checkbox next to Mask, and then click OK.**

   Flash displays the mask icon next to Layer 2.

5. Double-click the layer icon next to Layer 1.

   Once again, the Layer Properties window appears.

6. **This time, turn on the checkboxes next to Masked and Lock, and then click OK.**

   Flash displays the masked icon next to Layer 1; there's also a little padlock that lets you know Layer 1 can't be edited (you don't want to modify it inadvertently).

7. **Click the first keyframe in Layer 2.**

   Flash highlights the selected keyframe.

8. **Use the Oval tool to draw a circle on the stage.**

   So far, these are the same steps you take to create a straight-line motion tween.

9. **Select the entire circle (including its outline if it has one), and then choose Modify → Convert to Symbol.**

   The Convert to Symbol dialog box appears.

10. **In the Convert to Symbol dialog box, choose Movie Clip from the drop-down menu, and then click OK.**

    The dialog box disappears.

11. **On the stage, double-click the circle symbol.**

    Flash pops you into symbol editing mode: The content you placed in the masked layer appears grayed out, the name of your symbol appears in the Edit bar, and you see a fresh, clean timeline (the symbol's timeline) containing just one layer.

12. **On the stage, select the entire circle again (including its outline), and then choose Modify → Convert to Symbol.**

    The Convert to Symbol dialog box appears.

13. **Leaving the Movie Clip option selected in the drop-down menu, click OK.**

    The dialog box disappears. Flash places a copy of this second symbol into the Library. On the stage, a selection box appears around the circle and a center point appears at the center's circle.

14. **Click Frame 20, and then select Insert → Timeline → Keyframe.**

    Flash inserts a keyframe into Frame 20.

15. **Right-click Layer 1, and then choose Add Classic Motion Guide from the shortcut menu.**

    Flash creates a guide layer and places it directly above Layer 1.

16. **In Guide: Layer 1, click Frame 1 (the first keyframe). Then use the Pencil tool to draw a line (a motion path) on the stage.**

The motion path you draw can be curved, circular, jagged—anything you like. Figure 3-37 shows an example.

Tip: If you'd like a nice smooth path and the pencil line is a little rough, double-click to select the entire line, and then, at the bottom of the Tools panel, click the Smooth button once or twice.

---

17. **In Layer 1, click Frame 1. Using the Selection tool, drag the circle until its center snaps to the first end of the motion path. Click Frame 20, and then drag the circle until its center snaps to the second end of the motion path.**

    You've just created the beginning and end points for the spotlight animation. Now you can tween it, as described next.

18. **In Layer 1, right-click Frame 2, and then choose Create Classic Tween from the shortcut menu.**

    Flash saves the movie clip symbol and brings you back to your main timeline.

19. **In the Edit Bar above the stage, click Scene 1.**

    Flash closes the Symbol Edit window and shows you the main timeline again, with a single frame.

20. **Lock Layer 2, and then test your animation using Ctrl+Enter (⌘-Return on a Mac).**

    Locking Layer 2 masks the image in the layer except for the circle. When you test the animation, the circle moves around the image, like a spotlight. The motion repeats itself, as the movie clip symbol with the mask loops through its separate timeline.

The movie clip symbol takes up just one frame (Frame 1) of the mask layer, which is Layer 2. You know it's a symbol because you see both the cross and circle that are the symbol's registration point and transformation point, respectively; you know it's in the first frame because when you click the first frame of Layer 2, Flash displays a selection box around the symbol, as shown in Figure 3-38.

Motion Tweening

If you're a tween fan, you're going to love all the new motion tween features introduced in Flash CS4. One of the biggest changes from the classic tween is the ability to make size, rotation, and color changes in *any* frame throughout the tween. The tools you use to make changes in your tween are much more precise and have more features than the old tools.

Note: If you're learning Flash tweening for the first time, the new motion tween is a great place to start. It's easy to use and very logical. If you're a tween veteran from previous versions of Flash, consider this your re-education camp. The old motion tween is now called classic tween (page 110). The new, improved motion tween uses different tools and techniques, but you'll love the results.

Figure 3-38:
When you've finished adding the movie clip symbol to the mask layer, this is what you see: the selected symbol on top of the Layer 1 background. (You know it's the mask layer—Layer 2—that contains the selected symbol because you can see that Layer 2 is highlighted.)

The next few examples show how to make a billboard sign, convert the sign to a symbol, and then use motion tweening to animate its position, size, color, and rotation. There are a few motion tween rules you need to keep in mind:

- **Motion tweens work on a single object.** If you need to animate more than one object, put your objects on separate layers, and then apply motion tweens to each.

- **Motion tweens use symbols as the target object.** If you combine several objects into one symbol, that's considered a single object as far as motion tween is concerned.

- **Motion tweens use *property keyframes* to change the target object's properties over the course of the tween.** Don't confuse property keyframes with plain old keyframes—they're different beasts. Property keyframes are used only in motion tweens, and, as the name implies, they mark the points where the properties (position, size, color) of an object change.

Note: you can find the finished Flash document with the motion tween at *http://missingmanual.com/cds*. The file is named *motion_tween_finished.fla*.

The following example shows how to create a billboard sign using rectangle primitive and text tools. Then you use the Properties panel to change the appearance of the two parts that make the sign. The final step is to combine and convert the rectangle and text into a single Movie Clip symbol.

1. **From the Tools palette, choose the Rectangle Primitive tool, and then draw a rectangle.**

    If the Tools palette isn't showing, choose Window → Tools.

2. **Use the Properties panel (Figure 3-39) to fine-tune the appearance of the rectangle with the following settings:**

    • Under Position and Size: Click the numbers next to W (width) and type *300*. Click the H (height) and type *150*.

    • Under Fill and Stroke: Change the stroke to a dark brown and the fill to a pale yellow. Type *8* in the Stroke text box to change the thickness of the stroke.

    • Under Rectangle Options: Type *36* into a rounded-corner box. (If all the corners are going to be the same, you only need to enter a value in the upper-left corner.)

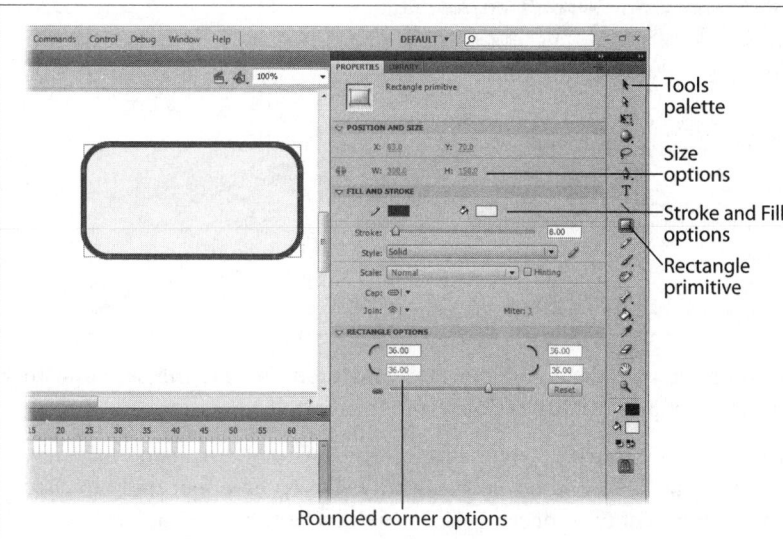

Tools palette

Size options

Stroke and Fill options

Rectangle primitive

Rounded corner options

Figure 3-39:
After you create your rectangle, you can adjust its size, color, and all other aspects of appearance using the controls in the Properties panel. Just select your rectangle and tweak away.

Tip: When you see blue numbers with tiny dots, that means you can change the value by scrubbing (clicking the number and dragging your mouse left or right). Most number values in the Properties panel are scrubbable. If your mouse has a wheel, you can move the cursor over the number, and then spin the mouse wheel.

3. Type a message for your sign, like *Stutz Bearcats*, and then use the Properties panel to fine-tune its appearance so it looks good on your sign. For example:

  • Press Enter to put one word on each line.

  • Under Character: Choose a bold typeface, like Cooper Black, as shown in Figure 3-40.

  • Adjust the Size to fit on the signboard. Cooper Black set to 55 points works for this example.

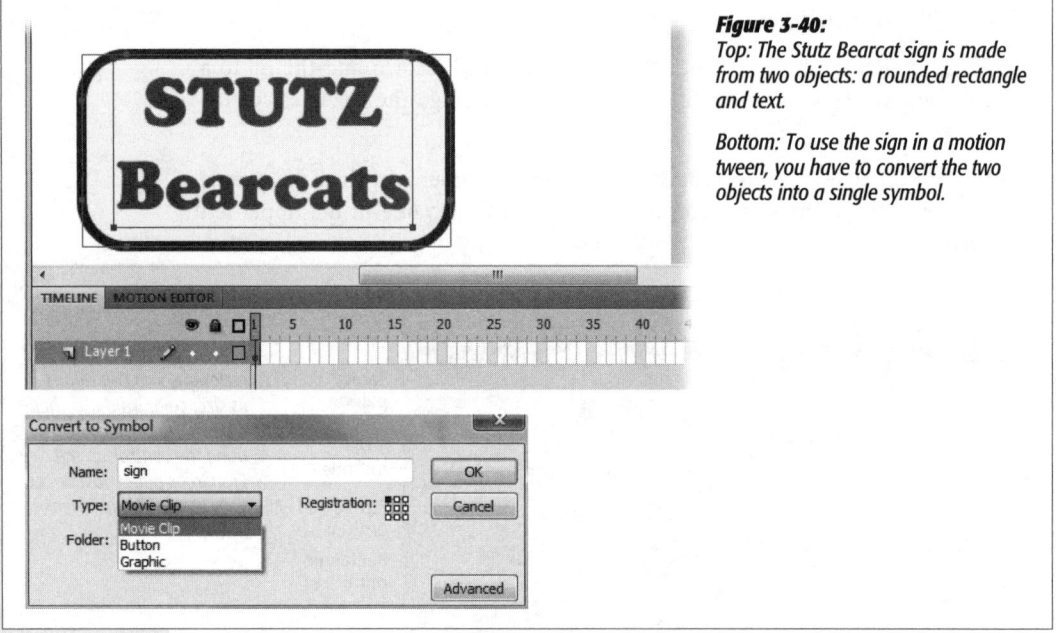

Figure 3-40:
Top: The Stutz Bearcat sign is made from two objects: a rounded rectangle and text.

Bottom: To use the sign in a motion tween, you have to convert the two objects into a single symbol.

4. Select both the rectangle and the text, and then convert the selection to a Movie Clip symbol (Modify → Convert to Symbol).

A dialog box opens where you can give your symbol and name like *sign* as shown in Figure 3-40. A drop-down menu gives you an opportunity to choose from three different types of symbols: MovieClip, Button, or Graphic.

Creating a Motion Tween Path

Now that you've got a fancy billboard sign to animate, it's time to put some motion in the motion tween. In the following steps, you'll start with the sign in the upper-left corner, and then make it drop to the bottom of the stage and take a couple of bounces along the bottom as it moves to the right. After that, it will ricochet off the right wall and end up in the middle of the screen. Sound complicated? Not so with Flash. Creating a motion tween is simply a matter of deciding where you want to place the sign at different points of the timeline. Here are the steps:

1. **Drag the sign to the upper-left corner of the stage.**

   You don't have to be precise about the placement. Wherever you drag it becomes the starting position for the sign in the first frame of the tween.

2. **Click Frame 60, and then hit F5 to insert a frame.**

   Flash adds 59 frames to the timeline, creating a timeline that's 60 frames long. The first frame in the timeline is a keyframe holding your sign.

3. **Right-click one of the frames in the middle of the timeline, and then choose Create Motion Tween from the shortcut menu.**

   The frames in the timeline layer turn blue to indicate a motion tween.

4. **Drag the playhead to the 10th frame, and then drag the sign to the bottom of the stage.**

   As you drag the sign, a line with little round points appears marking the motion across the sage. Each of the small points indicates the sign's position at a particular frame. So, the third dot represents the third frame on the timeline.

   A small diamond marks the point in the timeline where you changed the position of the sign. This point is called a property keyframe.

Note: The property keyframe is a new concept in Flash CS4. While it's similar to a keyframe, it's important to understand the differences. In keyframes, you can add and remove drawings from the stage. In property keyframes, you can only change the properties of the target object. You can't add new elements to the stage.

---

5. **Drag the playhead to the 20th frame, and then drag the sign up above the midpoint of the stage, as shown in Figure 3-41.**

   A new line appears on the stage following the motion of the sign, and a new property keyframe appears in the timeline at Frame 20.

6. **Drag the playhead to the 30th frame, and then drag the sign back down to the bottom of the stage.**

   This frame marks the second time the sign bounces on the bottom of the stage. You can even position it so the bottom of the sign is below the bottom of the stage to indicate a deeper bounce!

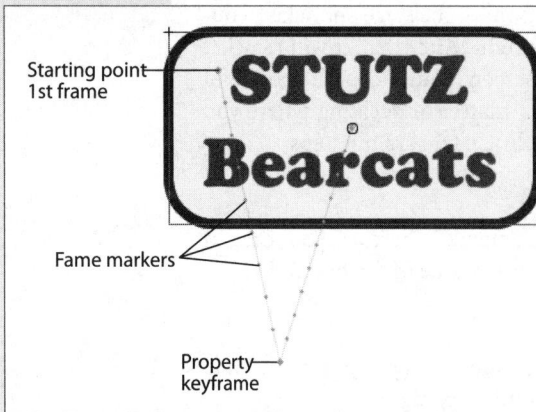

Starting point
1st frame

Fame markers

Property
keyframe

Figure 3-41:
The motion path shows the position of the animated object over time. The small diamonds mark frames. The larger dots mark the property keyframes.

7. **Drag the playhead to the 40th frame, and then drag the sign to the middle of the right edge of the stage.**

   Now you're bouncing off the walls, but then you knew it would come to this, didn't you?

8. **Drag the playhead to the 50th frame, and then drag the sign to the center of the stage.**

   Center stage makes for a good dramatic stopping point.

9. **Test your animation to check out the motion by pressing Enter to run it within Flash or Ctrl+Enter (⌘-Return) to test the movie in Flash Player.**

   Your sign should follow the path from the upper-left corner down to the bottom of the stage for a couple of bounces, ricochet once off the right wall, and then come to a stop in the center.

Scaling an Object with a Motion Tween

Part of the power of the new motion tween method is that you can change almost any type of property anywhere along the timeline. This gives you much more control than was possible with the classic tween where Flash made most of the decisions between two standard keyframes. This section shows how change the W (width) and H (height) properties and following sections explain how to change the transparency and how to rotate an object, all in the same tween.

Motion alone is fine and dandy, but there have to be some ways to make this animation a little more exciting. For example, it would be more dramatic if the sign starts out small and then grows throughout the tween. Here's a quick and easy way to make that happen:

1. **Drag the playhead back to the first frame.**

   As you scrub (drag) the playhead, the sign moves along the motion path.

2. Select the sign, and then, in the Properties panel under Position and Size, change the sign's dimensions to 100 × 50 pixels, as shown in Figure 3-42.

If you click the "link" symbol next to W (width) and H (height), the width to height proportions remain linked. Otherwise, you can change the width and the height independently.

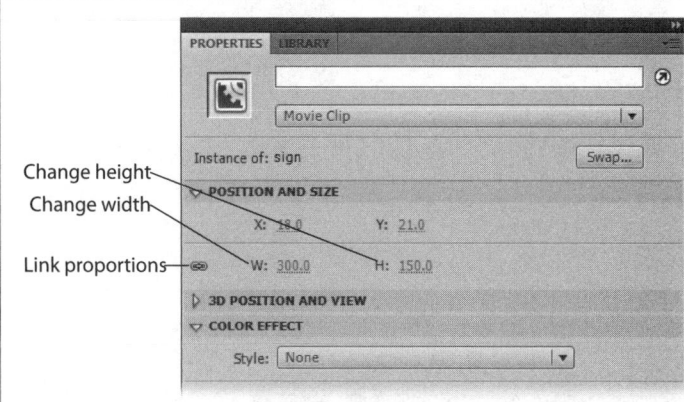

Change height
Change width

Link proportions

Figure 3-42:
Change the size of your symbol in the Properties panel to change the size throughout the timeline. To scale your symbol at a certain point in the tween, use the Scale tool on the Tools palette.

3. Drag the playhead to the last frame (Frame 60).

As you drag, the smaller sign makes the journey along the motion path.

4. Click the Scale tool in the Tools palette, and then scale the Sign so that it nearly fills the stage.

Shift-click one of the corners to keep the sign proportions as you scale it. You can use the Scale tool to change both the size and the rotation of an object. If you need a refresher on using the Scale tool, see page 182.

5. Scrub the playhead to see the scaling effect.

The sign starts off at Frame 1 and gradually grows to its monstrous size at the end of the animation.

6. Use the Select arrow from the Tool palette to bend curves into the motion path.

The cursor shows a small curve icon when it's close to the path, indicating that you can drag to shape the curve. You can edit the motion path by moving and bending the path as shown in Figure 3-43. When you hold the Select cursor over the path, a small curve appears next to the arrow. As you change the path, the number of frames between property keyframes may change. If you're unhappy with a path edit, just press Ctrl+Z (or ⌘-Z on a Mac) to undo the change.

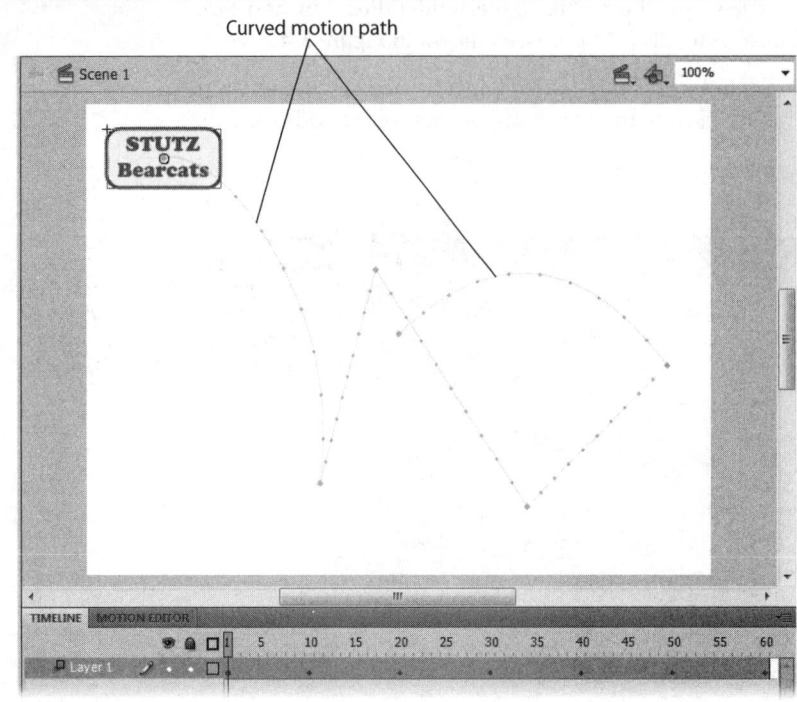

Curved motion path

Figure 3-43:
*Your motion tweens
don't have to be made
up of straight lines. Use
the Select arrow to add
curves to the motion
paths.*

7. **Test your animation either within Flash (Enter) or in the Flash Player (Ctrl-Enter).**

   The sign follows the curves you created in the motion path. The sign starts off small and grows throughout the animation until Frame 50, where it nearly fills the screen. For the last 10 frames, the sign stays the same size, because there were no further changes in its scale.

Property keyframes are markers in the timeline where a property value changes. If there's a difference in a value between two property keyframes, Flash tweens (creates in-between frames) to accommodate the change. That's what happened between Frame 1, where the sign dimensions were 100×50 pixels, and Frame 50, where the sign nearly fills the screen. There were no further size changes, so the sign's dimensions don't change for the last 10 frames of the animation.

Changing Transparency with the Motion Editor

You can create another dramatic effect for your sign by adjusting the transparency, or as the techies like to say, the *alpha channel*. Typically, computer video has RGB channels for red, green, and blue. To store information about the opacity and transparency of an image, programmers needed another channel, and they dubbed it the alpha channel because they needed another letter and why not start at the beginning of the alphabet?

Making your sign semi-transparent at the beginning, and then fully opaque at the end, increases the illusion that the sign is coming towards the audience. You can easily adjust transparency during a tween in Flash CS4's new Motion Editor window. Chapter 7 in its entirety is devoted to the intricacies of the Motion Editor, but the next two sections will give you a working introduction. You'll get a feeling for the way you set values for different motion tween properties:

1. **Drag the playhead to Frame 1, and then click the layer to make sure that the motion tween is selected.**

   Your sign is back to its starting position on the motion path. When you select the motion tween, the words Motion Tween appear at the top of the Properties panel.

2. **Click the Motion Editor tab next to the Timeline tab.**

   If you don't see the Motion Editor tab, choose Window → Motion Editor to make it visible, as shown in Figure 3-44.

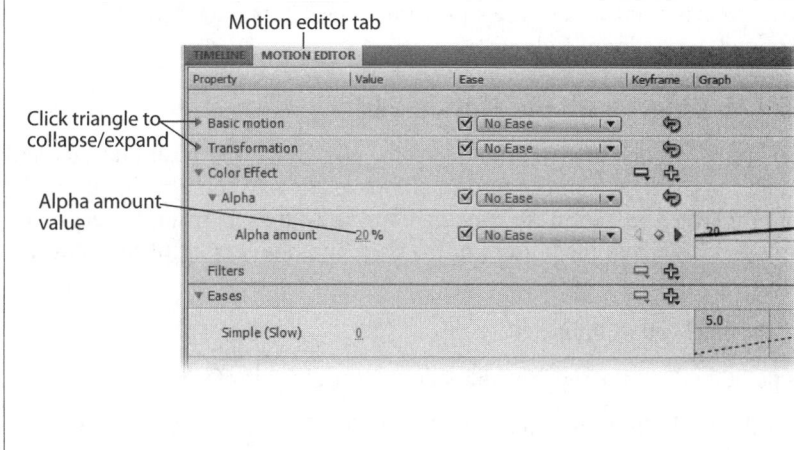

Figure 3-44:
The Motion Editor is command central for tweaking every little detail in your motion tween. It's made up of panels that give you access to properties, effects, and filters. Click the triangles to expand and collapse the different panels. Click the + and – buttons to add and remove effects and filters. The properties that use numeric values work just like the ones in the Properties panel: either click and type a number or use your mouse to scrub in a value.

3. **In the Motion Editor window, find the Color Effect section, and then click the + sign to add an Alpha color effect to the tween.**

   If some of the panels are expanded, you may not see the Color Effect panel right away. Either close the open panels by clicking their flippy triangles, or use the scroll bar to find the Color Effect panel. When you click the + button, a shortcut menu gives you four color related choices: Alpha, Brightness, Tint, and Advanced Color. After you choose Alpha, a new subpanel opens showing an Alpha amount as a percentage.

4. **Next to "Alpha amount", change the value to 20 percent.**

   You can click the number, and then type *20,* or you can scrub the value until 20 appears in the box. Notice how the graph to the right changes as you change the value. More on that in Chapter 7.

5. **Click the Timeline tab, and then drag the playhead to the last frame.**

   By moving the playhead to a new location, you can enter a different Alpha value to create the tween.

6. **Click the Motion Editor tab, and then change the Alpha amount to 100 percent.**

   Setting the Alpha amount to 100 percent makes the sign symbol completely opaque.

7. **Test your animation in Flash or using the Flash Player.**

   At this point, the animation looks pretty much the same whether you run it inside of Flash (Enter) or you compile the animation and test it in the Flash Player (Ctrl+Enter). Position, size, and alpha properties are all visible inside of Flash, but that's not always the case with some filters, components, timeline effects, and ActionScript code.

Rotating an Object with the Motion Editor

The previous examples used motion tweening to change the position, size, and transparency of the sign. This last tutorial shows you how to spin the sign using the rotation property. You can make your sign appear to tumble from its height and spin while it skips across the bottom of the stage and bounces off of the right side of the stage.

1. **Drag the playhead to Frame 40.**

   This point is where the sign hits the wall on the right side of the stage.

2. **Go to the Basic Motion section of the Motion Editor, and then change the Rotation Z value to 1800.**

   The Rotation Z value (Figure 3-45) rotates an object around its center point. The value refers to the degrees of a circle, so 360 is one complete rotation. A value around 1800 gives your sign a good spin in a clockwise direction.

3. **Drag the playhead to Frame 50, and then change the Rotation Z value to –360.**

   A negative value rotates an object in a counter-clockwise direction, so this value creates the effect of the sign hitting the wall and taking on a counterspin.

4. **Test your animation.**

   At this point your sign moves, grows, changes from semi-transparent to opaque, and spins around in different directions. If you want to explore, go ahead and continue to experiment with some of the other properties in the Motion Editor.

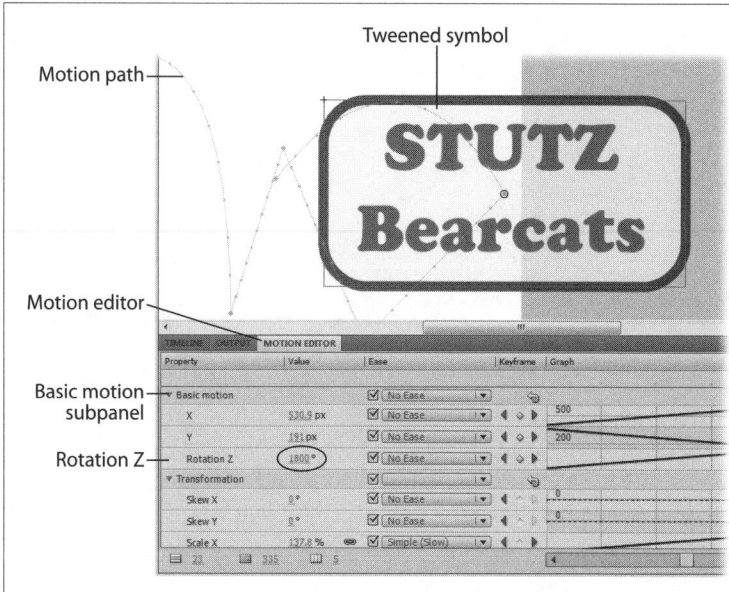

Motion path

Tweened symbol

Motion editor

Basic motion subpanel

Rotation Z

Figure 3-45:
The Motion Editor is made up of numerous subpanels. Each subpanel gives you access to tweenable properties. Here the Rotation Z property is set to 1800. You can click and type in a value or drag to "scrub in" a value.

Depending on your computer power and personal taste, you may find that the sign spins a bit too fast as it bounces around. There are a couple of ways to change the spin speed. First of all, you can change the number of rotations by using smaller numbers in the Rotation Z value. Or, you can increase the length of time it takes your tween to run by adding frames to the timeline. The easiest way to do that is to click the edge of the last frame in the tween, and then drag it to the right. Flash inserts frames as you drag and keeps the changes (property keyframes) proportionally spaced.

You can insert more frames into the tween at any point along the timeline. Or you can change the number of spins, by using lower numbers in the Rotations Z value.

Note: This section gives you an introduction to the motion tween and Motion Editor. For a more complete rundown on using the Motion Editor to modify your tween, see Chapter 7.

Part Two:
Advanced Drawing and Animation

2

Organizing Frames and Layers

Part 1 of this book gets you started launching Flash, creating your own drawings, and transforming them into moving animations. Most animation work, though, takes place after you've got all the frames and layers in place. Like a film director slaving away in the cutting room, as an animator you spend most of your time testing, editing, and retesting your movie.

This chapter is your crash course in Flash animation editing. Here you'll learn how to reorganize your animation horizontally (over time) by cutting, pasting, and rearranging frames in the timeline. You'll also see how to reorganize your animation vertically by shuffling and restacking the layers you've added to it.

Working with Frames

When you create an animation, you build it from frames and keyframes. Editing your document is a simple matter of moving, cutting, and pasting those frames until they look good and work well. You can perform these operations on individual frames or on multiple frames by combining them into groups, as you'll see at the end of this section.

Copying and Pasting Frames

Copy and paste are the world's favorite computer commands with good reason. These functions let you create a piece of work once (a word, line, shape, drawing, or what have you) and then quickly recreate it to build something even more complex with a minimum of effort. Well, Flash lets you cut, copy, and paste not just the content of your frames but your frames themselves, from one part of your timeline to another.

Copying and pasting frames is a great way to cut down on your development time. Here's how it works. Say you have a series of frames showing a weasel unwrapping a stick of chewing gum. It's a gag scene, one you want to repeat throughout your animation for comic effect. Instead of having to insert all the keyframes and regular frames every time you want to slip in the weasel gag, all you need to do is copy the weasel frames once, and then paste them onto your timeline wherever you want them to go.

Furthermore, copying and pasting isn't just useful for those times when you want a carbon copy of a scene. If you want to change something in each pasted scene—the brand of chewing gum the weasel's unwrapping, for example—you can do that, too, after you've pasted the frames.

Copying and pasting frames works almost exactly like copying and pasting words or drawn objects—with a few twists. Here are some points to keep in mind:

- As usual, you have to select what you're going to copy before you set off the command. You select frames in the timeline (see page 96 for a refresher).

- If the frames you're selecting span more than one layer, make sure you select all the layers for each frame, as shown in Figure 4-1.

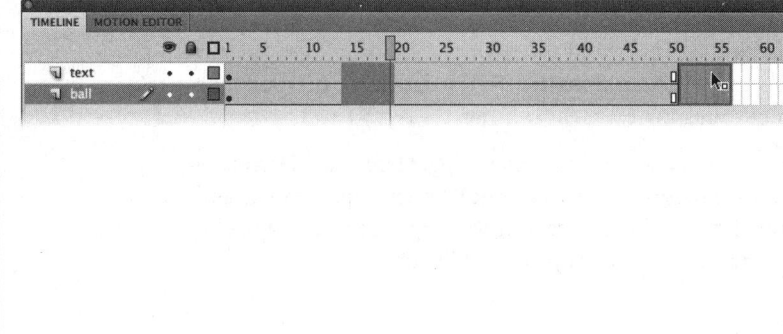

Figure 4-1:
To select multiple frames, click the first frame of the series you want to select, and then Shift-click the last frame. Flash automatically selects all the frames in between. To copy and paste frames in the same document, press the Alt key (Windows) or the Option key (Mac) while you drag a copy of the selected frames to a new spot.

- Copying and pasting tweened frames varies depending on the type of tween: motion, shape, or classic. While tweened frames are displayed as separate, distinct images, they're not. As you learned in Chapter 3, only keyframes contain distinct images. If you want to copy and paste an entire Shape or Classic tween, you have to select the beginning and end keyframes. The newer Motion tween is much easier-going when it comes to copying and pasting frames. You can select any frames from the middle of a Motion tween and paste them (as a tween) into another layer.

- Flash doesn't limit you to pasting within the same document. After you copy, you can open any other Flash animation and paste the frames right in.

Note: Although Cut, Copy, and Paste usually travel as a threesome, in Flash things work a little differently. The Cut Frames command on the Edit → Timeline submenu doesn't actually cut *frames*; instead, it cuts the *contents* of the selected frame. To get rid of the frame itself, you need to use Edit → Timeline → Remove Frames, as described in the box on page 145.

The process of copying and pasting frames follows the same basic steps every time:

1. **In the timeline, select the frames you want to copy.**

   You probably want to make sure that the set of frames you choose begins with a keyframe, as described in the third bullet point above. Either way, Flash highlights the selected frames and moves the playhead to the last selected frame.

2. **Choose Edit → Timeline → Copy Frames (or press Ctrl+Alt+C on Windows; Option-⌘-C on the Mac). Select the keyframe where you want to begin pasting the copied frames.**

   In other words, select the frame after which you want to add the copied frames. You can paste copied frames into the document you currently have open or into another document (select File → Open to open another Flash document). If the frames you copied have multiple layers, make sure the keyframe you select contains the same number of multiple layers.

3. **Select Edit → Timeline → Paste Frames.**

   Flash pastes the copied frames, replacing the currently selected keyframe with the first copied frame. If you pasted frames into the middle of a timeline, Flash repositions your existing frames *after* the last pasted frame.

Moving Frames (Keyframes)

The timeline is serial: When you run your animation, Flash displays the content in Frame 1, followed by the content in Frame 2, followed by the content in Frame 3, and so on. If you change your mind about the order in which you want frames to appear, all you need to do is move them.

Simple in theory—but moving frames in Flash isn't quite as cut and dried as you might think. As you may recall, if you've had a chance to read through Chapter 3, only keyframes can contain actual images; regular frames contain either tweened or "held over" copies of the images placed in the previous keyframe. So whether you move a frame or a keyframe, you end up with a keyframe. Here's how it works:

- **Moving a keyframe.** When you move a keyframe, what Flash actually moves is the keyframe's content and keyframe designation; Flash leaves behind a regular frame in the original keyframe's place. (And that regular frame may or may not be empty, depending on whether or not a keyframe precedes it on the timeline.)

- **Moving a regular frame.** Flash moves the regular frame, but turns the moved frame into a keyframe. (If you move a series of regular frames, Flash turns just the first moved frame into a keyframe.)

Tip: There's another way to change the order in which Flash plays frames: by creating an ActionScript action, as described in Chapter 11. Creating an action lets you tell Flash how to play your frames: backwards, for example, or by rerunning the first 10 frames three times and then moving on. You want to use ActionScript (as opposed to moving frames) when you want to give your audience the choice of viewing your animation in different ways.

To move frames, you simply select and then drag them. The process is the same whether you're moving frames, keyframes, or both, and all the usual rules of frame selection described earlier in this chapter still apply.

Here are the steps in detail:

1. **In the timeline, select the frame(s) you want to move.**

   Flash highlights the selected frame (or frames) and moves the playhead to the last selected frame.

2. **Drag the selected frame(s) to the frame after which you want to place the selected frames.**

   As you drag the selected frames, Flash highlights the frames you're moving to help you position them (Figure 4-2).

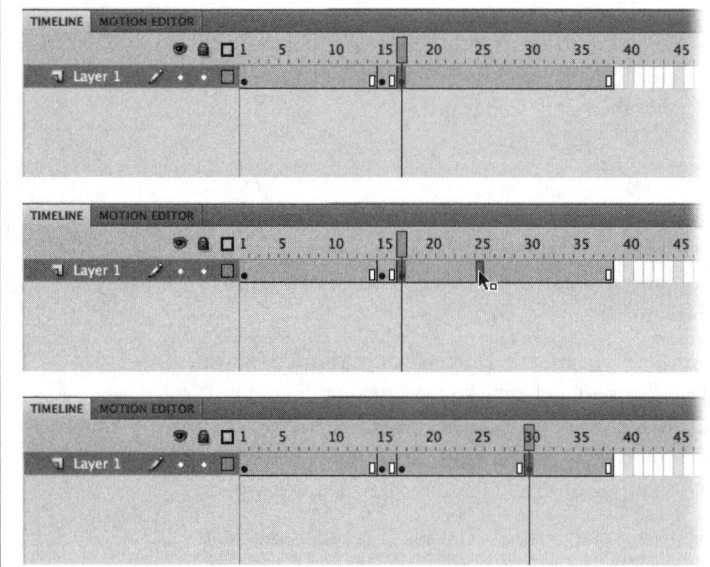

Figure 4-2:
Top: Click to select the frame you want to move, and then let go of your mouse. Then, drag to move the frame.

Middle: As you make the move, Flash displays a highlighted frame, or group of frames if you selected more than one.

Bottom: Here, you can tell the frame moved to frame 30 because the keyframe and end frame indicators have disappeared from their original locations (Frames 16 and 17) and reappeared in their new locations (Frames 29 and 30).

Tip: To select multiple frames, drag in the timeline. You have to release the mouse button to complete the selection. Then, you can drag the selected frames to move the whole bunch of highlighted frames to a new location. If dragging your frames isn't working, you can always copy and paste the frames you want to move (page 141). Then use Edit → Timeline → Remove Frames to delete them from their original location (see the box on page 145).

Flash clears the selected frames from their original position, and then inserts them in their new location.

Remove vs. Cut vs. Clear

Flash has several commands you can use to get rid of your frames (and the content associated with those frames): remove, cut, and clear. When you're new to Flash, it may not be immediately clear which command does what.

Here's what these commands do to selected frames:

- **Edit → Timeline → Remove Frames**. Removing a frame deletes that frame or group of frames from the timeline, as if you'd reached into the timeline and yanked them out. When a keyframe is involved, the result is a little different. If you attempt to remove a keyframe followed by a regular frame, Flash deletes the frame immediately to the *right* of the keyframe instead (go figure). To be safe, if you want to remove a keyframe—in other words, if you want to delete a keyframe from the timeline—you first want to clear the keyframe (strip the frame of its keyframe status); then you can remove the frame itself.

- **Edit → Timeline → Cut Frames**. Cutting a frame deletes the content on the stage associated with that frame (in other words, turns the frame into a blank keyframe). If the immediately succeeding frame is a regular frame, Flash turns that succeeding frame into a keyframe. Flash stores the contents of the cut frames on the Clipboard, so that you can restore them by choosing Edit → Timeline → Paste Frames.

- **Edit → Timeline → Clear Frames**. Clearing frames is identical to cutting them, with one difference: Flash doesn't store the contents of the cleared frames (so you can't restore them).

Editing Multiple Frames

Imagine you've just completed a 250-frame animation showing a character in a red t-shirt demonstrating your company's latest product, an electronic egg slicer. Suddenly, your boss comes in and declares that red's out. (Red is the color your competitor is using for *their* egg slicer launch.) You have, your boss declares, until the end of the day to change all 250 frames.

Now, if you had to change all 250 frames one at a time, you'd never be able to meet your deadline; and even if you did, you'd probably make a few mistakes along the way, like accidentally repositioning the t-shirt in a couple of frames or missing a few frames altogether. But it's precisely this kind of en masse editing job that Flash's multiple frame editing capability was designed to handle.

Using a technique called *onion skinning*, you can see the contents of several frames at once. There are three different modes for onion-skinning: Onion Skin, Onion Skin Outlines, and Edit Multiple Frames. Each is helpful for a different type of task. You use the buttons at the bottom of the timeline to choose an onion skin mode, as shown in Figure 4-3; use the *onion markers* in the timeline to choose which frames are displayed.

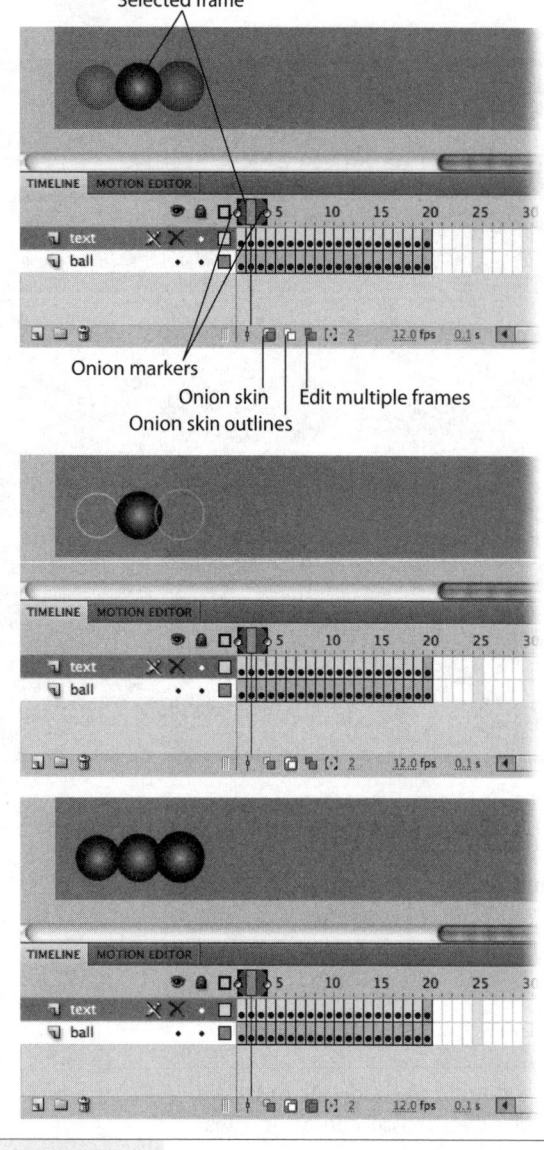

Selected frame

Onion markers

Onion skin | Edit multiple frames

Onion skin outlines

Figure 4-3:

Top: Click the Onion Skin button, and the image for selected frame appears bold. The images on the adjacent frames appear faded out.

Middle: Click Onion Skin Outlines, and images on the non-selected frames appear as outlines.

Bottom: Click the Edit Multiple Frames button, and all the images within the onion markers appear 100% opaque.

The Edit Multiple Frames mode makes it easy to deal with that red t-shirt issue, because you can quickly identify (and change) the frames containing red t-shirts. Onion skinning is also useful for those times when you want to hand-draw an "in-between" frame because you can see both the preceding and succeeding frames on the stage at the same time.

Note: Technically speaking, when you edit multiple frames in Flash, you're actually editing multiple *key-frames*. Keyframes are the only frames that contain unique, editable art. (Regular frames just "hold over" the contents of the previous keyframe, and Flash stores tweened frames not as editable images, but a bunch of calculations.)

To edit multiple frames using onion skinning:

1. **In the timeline, click the Edit Multiple Frames icon.**

   Flash displays multiple frames on the stage and adds onion markers to the frame display (bottom Figure 4-3). These beginning and ending onion markers tell Flash which frames you want it to display on the stage.

2. **Click the Modify Onion Markers icon.**

   Flash displays a pop-up menu.

3. **From the pop-up menu, select Onion All (Figure 4-4).**

   Flash displays onion markers from the beginning of your timeline's frame span to the end, and shows the contents of each of your frames on the stage. (If you don't want to edit all the frames in your animation, you can drag the onion markers independently to surround whatever subset of your frame span you want.)

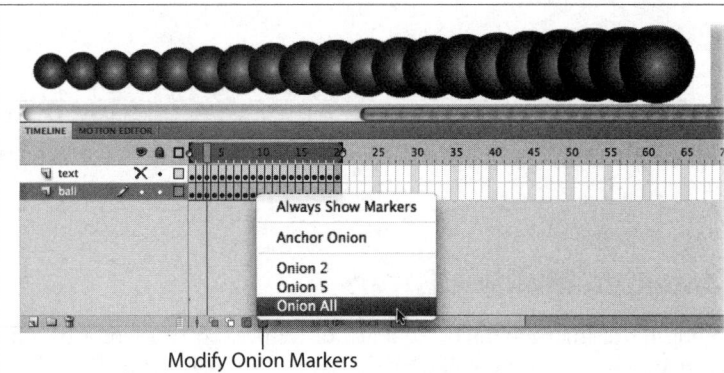

Figure 4-4:
Here you see the result of selecting Onion All. The onion markers surround the entire frame span (Frame 1 through Frame 20) and all 20 images appear on the same stage, ready for you to edit en masse.

Modify Onion Markers

4. **Edit the frames.**

   Because you can see all the content on a single stage, you can make your edits more easily than having to hunt and peck individually through every frame in your animation. In Figure 4-5, four frames are selected with the onion markers. The contents are first re-colored and then moved in one fell swoop. When the move is complete, your stage looks like Figure 4-6.

5. **Click Edit Multiple Frames again.**

   Flash returns to regular one-frame-at-a-time editing mode and displays only the contents of the current frame on the stage.

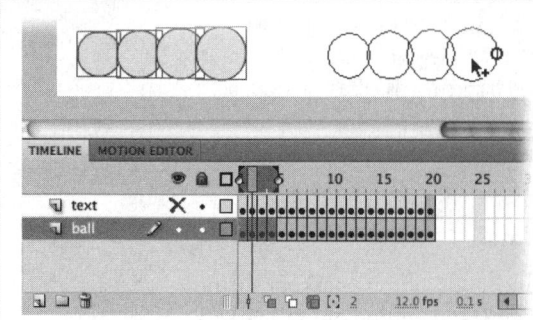

Figure 4-5:
You can work with multiple images just as easily as single images. For example, you can select several (or all of them) and apply whatever edits you like—moving them, coloring them, reshaping them, and so on.

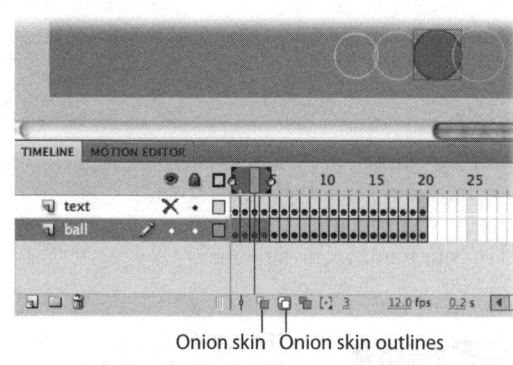

Figure 4-6:
With onion skinning turned on, you can see multiple frames, but you can edit only the content of the selected frame. Use the Edit Multiple Frames mode when you want to see and edit several frames at once.

Onion skin   Onion skin outlines

Note: You can't edit multiple frames on a locked layer (page 160). In fact, when you click Edit Multiple Frames on a locked layer, Flash doesn't even show you the content of the frames in the locked layer (not even in onion skin form).

Adding Content to Multiple Layers

A layer is nothing more than a named sequence of frames. So you won't be surprised to learn that, after you create a couple of layers as described in Chapter 3, you need to fill up each layer's frames with content. This section shows you how.

When you're working with a single layer, adding content to frames is easy because you don't have to worry about which layer you're working with: You simply click a keyframe and use Flash's drawing and painting tools to create an image on the stage.

But when you're working with multiple layers—for example, when you're creating a composite drawing by adding a background layer, a foreground layer, and a separate layer for your sound clips—you may find adding content a bit trickier because you have to be aware of the layer to which you're adding your content. Fortunately, as you see in the steps below, the timeline's Show/Hide icon helps you keep track of which content you've placed on which layers.

Here's how to add content to multiple layers:

1. **Open the file *multiple_layers_begin.fla*.**

   You can find this file (and all the other example files for this book) on the "Missing CD" page at *http://missingmanuals.com/cds*.

2. **Click the first keyframe in Layer 1.**

   Flash highlights the selected frame, as well as the layer name. You also see a little pencil icon that lets you know this frame is now ready for editing.

3. **Use Flash's drawing and painting tools to draw a fence on the stage.**

   Your fence doesn't have to be fancy; a quick "wooden" fence, like the one in Figure 4-7, is fine.

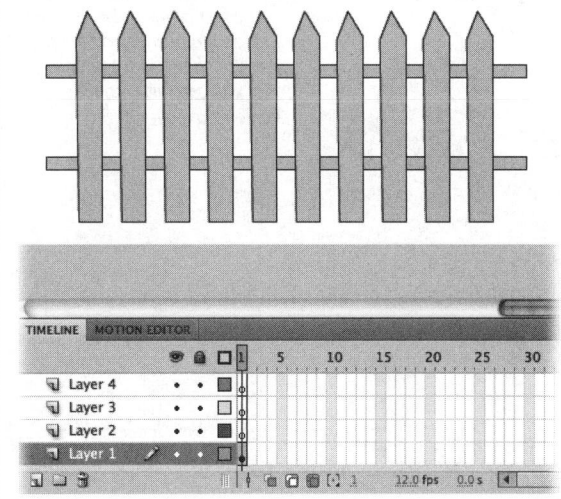

Figure 4-7:
You can tell at a glance which layer is active (editable) by the pencil icon next to the layer's name. Here, Layer 1 is active.

4. **Hide Layer 1 by clicking the Show/Hide button next to Layer 1.**

   The content on the stage temporarily disappears. Flash replaces the Show/Hide icon with an X and draws a slash through the pencil icon next to Layer 1 to let you know this layer is no longer editable.

Note: Technically, you don't *have* to hide the contents of one layer while you're working with another; in fact, in some cases, you *want* to see the contents of both layers on the stage at the same time (page 153). But for this example, hiding is the best way to go.

---

5. **Click the first keyframe in Layer 2.**

   Flash highlights the selected frame, as well as the layer name (Layer 2). Now the pencil icon is next to Layer 2.

6. Use Flash's drawing and painting tools to draw a few flowers on the stage.

Your workspace should now look like the one in Figure 4-8.

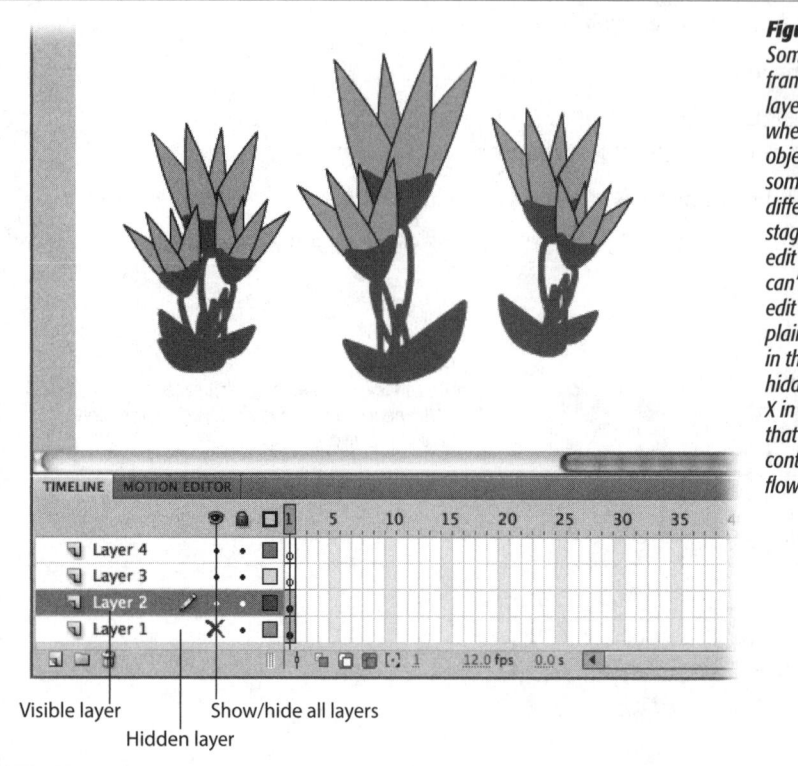

Figure 4-8:
Sometimes you want to see the frame contents of two or more layers at the same time, like when you're trying to line up objects in multiple layers. But sometimes seeing all those different objects on the same stage—some of which you can edit and some of which you can't, since Flash only lets you edit one layer at a time—is just plain confusing. Here, the fence in the first frame of Layer 1 is hidden (you can tell by the big X in the Show/ Hide column) so that you can focus on the contents of Layer 2 (the flowers).

Visible layer
Hidden layer
Show/hide all layers

7. Hide Layer 2 by clicking the Show/Hide icon next to Layer 2.

The content on the stage temporarily disappears. Flash replaces the Show/Hide icon with an X and draws a slash through the pencil icon next to Layer 2 to let you know that this layer is no longer editable.

8. Repeat steps 4–6 for Layers 3 and 4, adding some gray clouds to Layer 3 (Figure 4-9) and some flying birds to Layer 4 (Figure 4-10).

9. To see the content for all four layers, click to remove the Show/Hide X icon next to Layer 3, Layer 2, and Layer 1, as shown in Figure 4-11.

Flash displays the content for all four layers on the same stage.

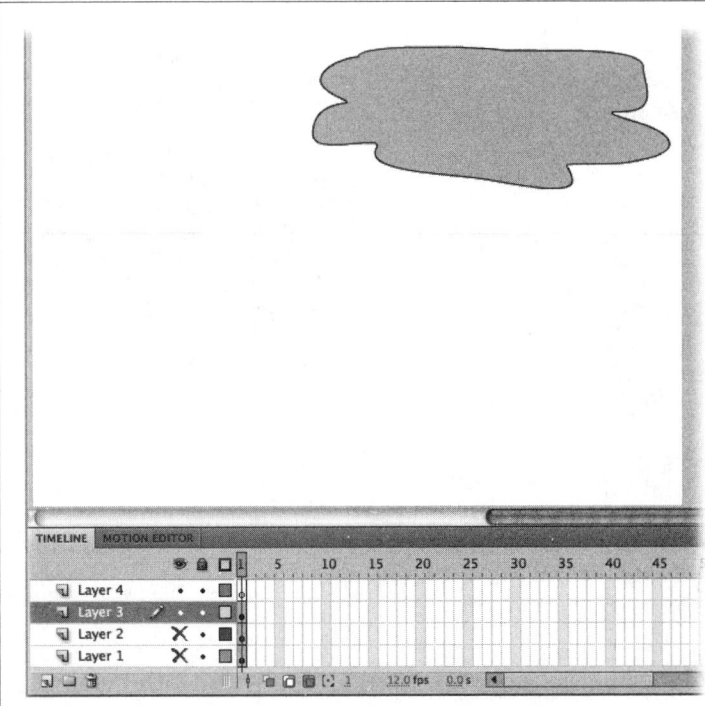

Figure 4-9:
Creating separate layers for different graphic elements gives you more control over how each element appears in your finished animation.

Figure 4-10:
In this example, the images are static, but you can place everything from motion and shape tweens to movie clips, backgrounds, actions, and sounds on their own layers. Hiding layers affects only what you see on the stage; when you select Control → Test Movie to test your animation, Flash displays all layers, whether or not you've checked them as Hidden.

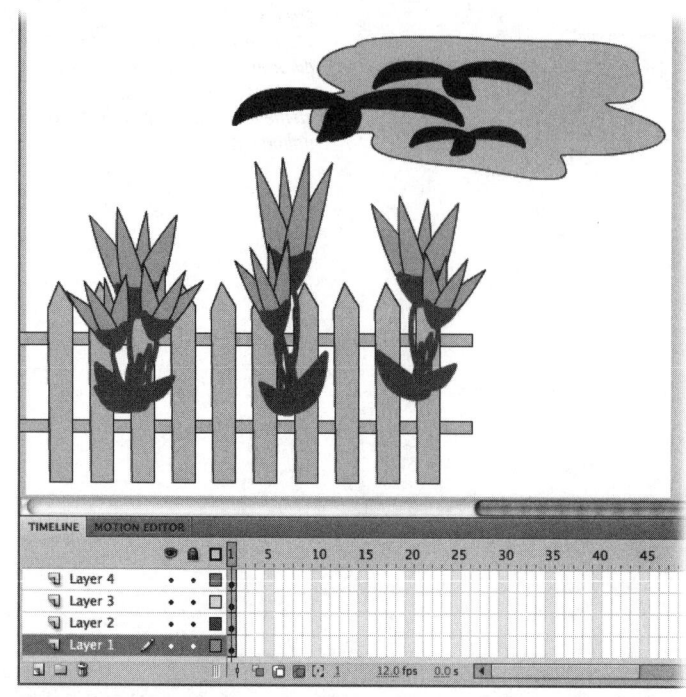

Figure 4-11:
Here's what the composite drawing for Frame 1 looks like: the fence, the flowers, the cloud, and the birds, all together on one stage. Notice the display order: The flowers (Layer 2) appear in front of the fence (Layer 1), and the birds (Layer 4) in front of the cloud (Layer 3). Flash automatically displays the layer at the bottom of the list first (Layer 1), followed by the next layer up (Layer 2), followed by the next layer (Layer 3), and so on. But you can change this stacking order, as you see on page 158.

GEM IN THE ROUGH

Editing Multiple Frames with Find and Replace

Another way to edit the content of multiple frames is to use Flash's Find and Replace function. Similar to the find and replace you've undoubtedly used in word processing programs, this function lets you search every frame of your animation for a specific bit of text (or even a certain color or bitmap file) and either replace the occurrences yourself, or tell Flash to replace them for you using the text (or color or bitmap file) you tell it to use.

To use this function, select Edit → Find and Replace. Then, in the Find and Replace window that appears, head to the For drop-down menu and select the item you want to find. Your choices include Text, Font, Color, Symbol, Sound, Video, and Bitmap.

To change the occurrences yourself, click Find Next or Find All (and then make your changes on the stage). To tell Flash to change the occurrences, add a Replace With option (for example, the color or text you want to insert), and then click Replace or Replace All.

Viewing Layers

This section shows you how to use Flash's layer tools (including locking/unlocking and hiding/showing) to keep from going crazy when you're editing content in multiple layers (Figure 4-12). (Two layers aren't so bad, but if you need to add 6, 8, 10, or even more layers, you'll find it's pretty easy to lose track of which layer you're working in.) Then, in the following section, you see how to edit the content in your layers.

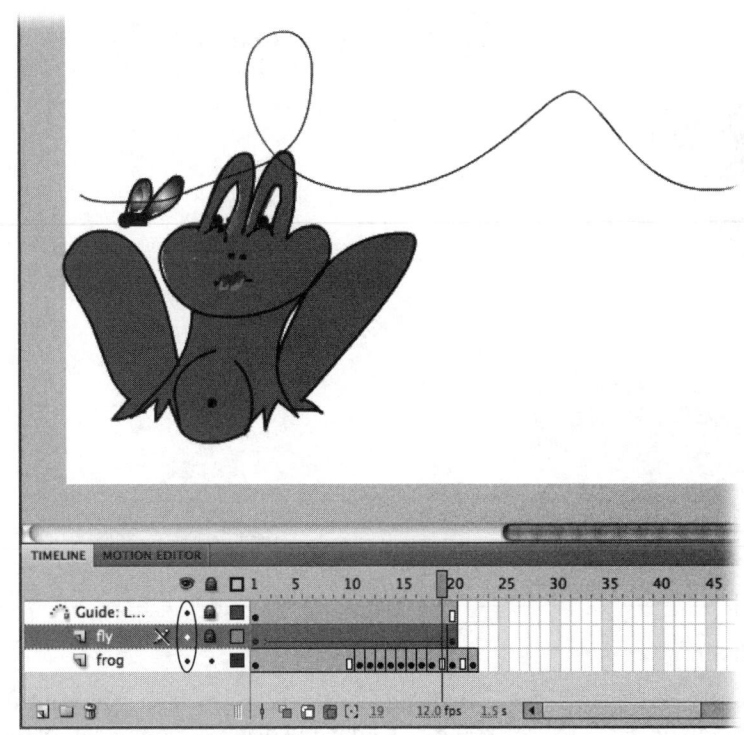

Figure 4-12:
This animation contains three layers: one containing a motion tween of a buzzing fly; one containing the path the fly takes as it buzzes around the frog's head; and one containing the highly interested frog. In some situations, showing all layers is fine, but here it's confusing to see all those images on the stage at the same time.

Showing and Hiding Layers

Whether or not you want Flash to show the contents of your layered frames on the stage depends on the situation. Typically, when you're creating the content for a new layer, you want to hide all the other layers so that you can focus on what you're drawing without any distractions. But after you've created a bunch of layers, you're probably going to want to see them all at once so that you have an idea of what your finished animation looks like and make adjustments as necessary.

Flash shows all layers until you tell it otherwise.

***

Tip: You can tell Flash to show (or hide) *all* your layers by clicking the Show/Hide All Layers icon you see in Figure 4-8. Click the icon again to turn off showing (or hiding).

***

To hide a layer

In the timeline, click the dot (the Show/Hide icon) next to the layer you want to hide. When you do, Flash redisplays the dot as an X, and temporarily hides the contents of the layer (Figure 4-13).

***

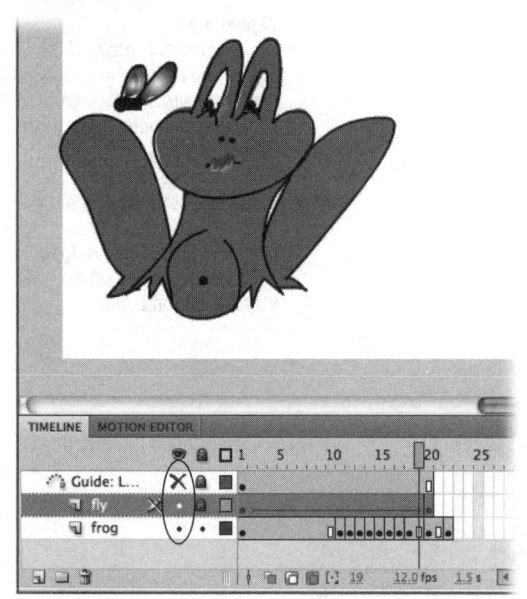

Figure 4-13:
Hiding the motion guide layer lets you focus on the two main elements of this animation: the frog and the fly.

To show a layer

In the timeline, click the X (the Show/Hide icon) next to the layer you want to show. When you do, Flash redisplays the X as a dot and displays the contents of the layer on the stage.

To hide (or show) all layers except the one you're currently editing

In the timeline, Alt-click (Windows) or Option-click (Mac) the Show/Hide icon next to the layer you're editing. Flash immediately hides (or shows) all the layers, except the one you're editing.

GEM IN THE ROUGH

Distribute to Layers

If you have a bunch of graphic elements on one layer that you want to put on separate layers (because, for example, you want to be able to tween them all), you can save time by telling Flash to do the work for you. First, select the objects you want to put on different layers and then select Modify → Timeline → Distribute to Layers.

Unfortunately, like any automatic process, this approach may not create the precise results you want. Flash can't possibly know that you want both an eye and an eyebrow to go on

the same layer, for example. And this trick *doesn't* break apart bitmaps, symbols, or grouped objects.

If you want to distribute the elements of a bitmap or symbol to individual frames, you first need to break up that bitmap, symbol, or grouped object by selecting it, and then choosing Modify → Break Apart or Modify → Ungroup, respectively.

Tip: If you try to edit a hidden layer by drawing on the stage, Flash displays a warning dialog box that gives you the opportunity to show (and then edit) the layer. Not so if you try to drag a symbol onto the stage–Flash just refuses to let you drop the symbol on the stage. Oddly enough, however, Flash *does* let you add a keyframe to a locked layer.

Working with Layers

The more layers you have, the more important it is to keep them organized. In this section, you see how to give your layers meaningful names, so that you can remember which images, sounds, or actions you placed in which layers. You also learn how to order your layer so that your composite images appear just the way you want them, and to copy and paste your layers (to cut down on the work you have to do to create similar layered effects).

UP TO SPEED

Why Layer?

In addition to making it much, much easier for you to change your animations, working with layers gives you the following benefits:

- **You can create multi-tweened animations**. Flash lets you create only one tween (Chapter 3) per layer. So if you want to show two baseballs bonking a parked car–one ball sailing in from the right, and one from the left–you need to either draw the entire animated sequence for each ball by hand, or use two separate layers, each containing one tween.

- **You can create more realistic effects**. Since you can shuffle layers, putting some layers behind others and even adjusting the transparency of some layers, you can add depth and perspective to your drawings. And because you can distribute your drawings to layers at whatever level of detail you want, you can create separate layers that give you independent control over, say, your characters' facial expressions and arm and leg movements.

- **You can split up the work**. TV and movie animators use layers (technically, they use transparent sheets of plastic called *cels*, but it's the same concept) to divvy up their workload, and so can you. While you're crafting the dog layer, one of your teammates can be working on the cloud layer, and another two can be working on the two character layers. When you're all finished, all you need to do is copy everyone's layers, and then paste them into a single timeline. Bingo–instant animation.

- **You can organize your animations**. As you begin to create more sophisticated animations, which may include not just images and animated effects, but symbols (Chapter 6), sounds (Chapter 10), and actions (Chapter 11), you quickly realize you need to organize your work. Layers help you get organized. If you get into the habit of putting all your animation's actions into a single layer (called *actions*), all the sounds into a single layer (called *sounds* or *soundtrack*), all the text into a single layer (called *text*), and so on, you can quickly spot the element you're looking for when it comes time to edit your animation.

Renaming Layers

The names that Flash gives the layers you create—Layer 1, Layer 2, Layer 3, and so on—aren't particularly useful when you've created 20 layers and can't remember which layer contains the ocean background you spent 10 hours drawing. Get into the habit of renaming your layers as soon you create them, and you'll have an easier time locating the specific elements you need when you need them.

Layer Properties

Flash gives you two different ways to change the properties associated with your layers: for example, the name of your layer, whether you want to show the content of a layer on the stage or hide it, whether you want to lock a layer or leave it editable, and so on.

One way is clicking the show/hide button in the timeline. (That's the approach described in this chapter.) The other way is by using the Layer Properties dialog box shown in Figure 4-14.

To display the Layer Properties dialog box, click to select a layer, and then do one of the following:

- Double-click the layer icon you find just to the left of the layer name. Right-click the layer name, and then choose Properties from the shortcut menu that appears.

- Select Modify → Timeline → Layer Properties.

The Layer Properties dialog box lets you change any or all of the following layer properties in one fell swoop:

- **Name**. Type a name in this text box to change the name of your layer.

- **Show**. Turn on this checkbox to show the contents of this layer on the stage; turn it off to hide the contents of this layer.

- **Lock**. Turn on this checkbox to prevent yourself (or anyone else) from editing any of the content in this layer; turn it off to make the layer editable once again.

- **Type**. Click to choose one of the following layer types:

  - **Normal**. The type of layer described in this chapter.
  - **Guide**. A special type of layer that you use to position objects on a guided layer, and which doesn't appear in the finished animation (page 199).
  - **Guided**. A regular layer that appears below a guide layer (page 114).
  - **Mask**. A type of layer you use to carve out "portholes" through which the content on an underlying masked layer appears (page 118).
  - **Masked**. A regular layer that appears below a mask layer (page 124).
  - **Folder**. Not a layer at all, but a container you can drag layers into to help you organize your animation (page 162).

- **Outline color**. Click to choose the color you want Flash to use when you turn on the checkbox next to "View layer as outlines."

- **View layer as outlines**. Turning on this checkbox tells Flash to display the content for this layer on the stage, but to display it as outlines (instead of the way it actually looks, when you run the animation). Find out more on page 162.

- **Layer height**. Click the arrow next to this drop-down list to choose a display height for your layer in the timeline: 100% (normal), 200% (twice as big), or 300% (three times as big). You may find this option useful for visually setting off one of your layers, making it easier to spot quickly.

After you make your changes, click OK to tell Flash to apply your changes to the layer.

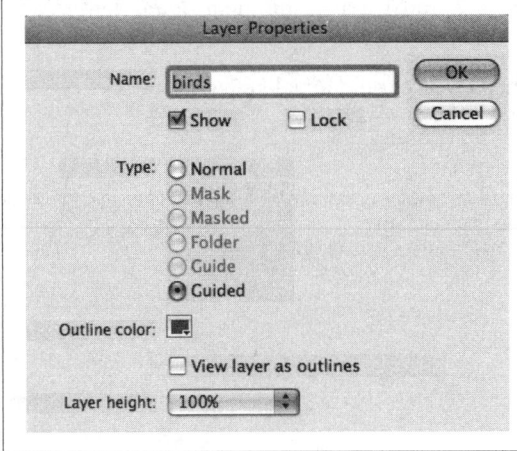

Figure 4-14:
When you open the Layer Properties box you've got all the layer settings in one place. You can change the layer name, show, hide, or lock your layer, and much more.

This section builds on the example you created earlier in this chapter. If you haven't had a chance to work through that section, you can download *flowers.fla* from this book's "Missing CD" page (*http://missingmanuals.com/cds*) and use it instead.

To rename a layer:

1. **Open the file *flowers.fla*.**

   If you created your own Flash document when you worked through "Adding Content to Multiple Layers" (page 148), you can use that document instead.

2. **Double-click the name Layer 4.**

   Flash redisplays the layer name in an editable text box (Figure 4-15). On the stage, you see the content for this layer (the birds) selected.

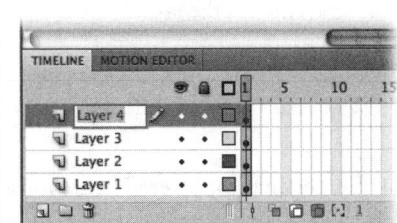

Figure 4-15:
If you can't remember what a particular layer contains, check the stage: When you double-click a layer name to rename it, Flash automatically highlights the content associated with that layer.

Note: Instead of double-clicking the layer name, you can use the Layer Properties dialog box to rename your layer. Check out the box on page 156 for details.

3. **Click inside the text box, type *birds*, and then click anywhere else in the workspace.**

   Flash displays the new name for your layer.

4. Repeat steps 1 and 2 for Layers 3, 2, and 1, renaming them *cloud*, *flowers*, and *fence*, respectively.

When you're done, your renamed layers should look like Figure 4-16.

Figure 4-16:
The Layers area of the timeline isn't particularly big, so it's best to keep your layer names short and sweet. If you need more room, just drag the bar that separates the names from the frames.

Copy and Paste a Layer

Earlier in this chapter, you saw how to copy and paste individual series of frames. But Flash also lets you copy and paste entire layers—useful when you want to create a backup layer for safekeeping, or when you want to create a duplicate layer you'll later change slightly from the original.

For example, if you want your animation to show an actor being pelted with tomatoes from different angles, you can create a layer that shows a tomato coming in from stage right—perhaps using a motion or shape tween (Chapter 3). Then you can copy that layer, paste it back into the Layers window, rename it, and tweak it so that the tomato comes from stage left. Maximum effect for minimum effort: That's what copying and pasting gives you.

To copy and paste a layer:

1. **In the Layers window, click the name of the layer you want to select.**

   Flash highlights the layer name, as well as all the frames in the layer.

2. **Select Edit → Timeline → Copy Frames.**

   If you don't have a layer waiting to accept the copied frames, create a new layer now before going on to the next step.

3. **In the Layers window, select the name of the destination layer. Then choose Edit → Timeline → Paste Frames.**

   Flash pastes the copied frames onto the new layer, beginning with the first frame. It also pastes the name of the copied layer onto the new layer.

Reordering (Moving) Layers

Flash always draws layers from the bottom up. For example, it displays the contents of the bottom layer first; then, on top of the bottom layer, it displays the contents of the next layer up; then, on top of both of those layers, it displays the contents of the third layer up; and so on. Figure 4-17 shows you an example.

Figure 4-17:
Flash treats layers the same way you treat a stack of transparencies: The image on the bottom gets covered by the image above it, which gets covered by the image above it, and so on. Stacking isn't an issue if none of your images overlap. But when they do, you need to decide which layers you want in front and which behind.

Because Flash always displays layers from the bottom up, if you want to reorder your layers, you need to reorder their position in the layers list. Doing so is simple: All you have to do is click the name of a layer to select it and then—without letting up on your mouse—drag the layer to reposition it. Figure 4-18 shows you an example.

Delete a Layer

Flash gives you three different ways to delete a layer:

- In the timeline, right-click (on the Mac, Control-click) the layer you want to delete, and then, from the shortcut menu that appears, choose Delete Layer.

- Drag the layer you want to delete to the Trash can (see Figure 4-19).

- Click the layer you want to delete to select it (or Shift-click to select several layers), and then click the Trash can.

Whichever method you choose, Flash immediately deletes the layer or layers (including all the frames associated with that layer or layers) from the Layers window.

Tip: If you delete the wrong layer by mistake, choose Edit → Undo Delete Layer.

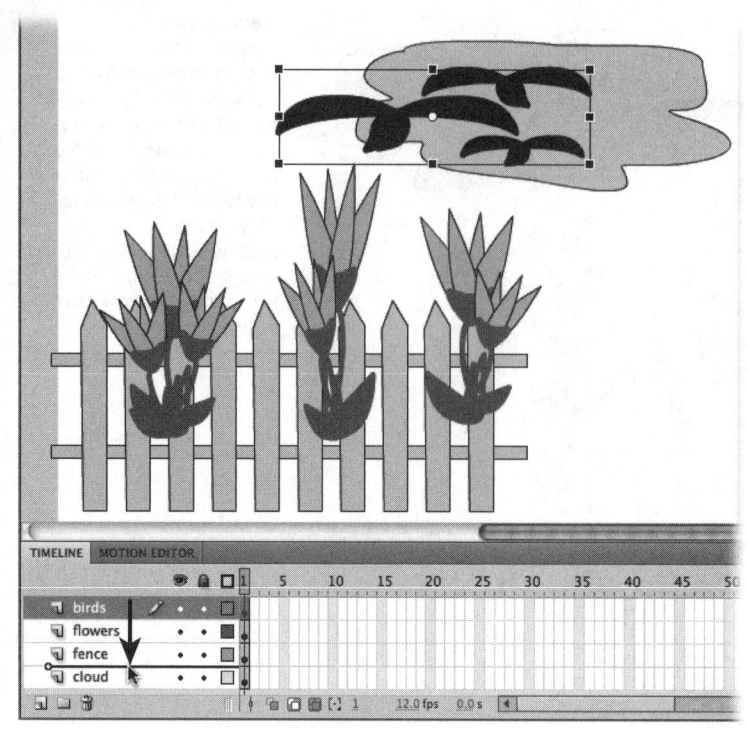

Figure 4-18:
Moving a layer is easy: Just click to select a layer, and then drag it to reposition it (and change the order in which Flash displays the content of your frames). Here, the cloud layer has been moved to the bottom of the list, so it now appears behind the other images. The birds layer is in the process of being moved; you can tell by the thick gray line you see beneath the cursor.

Figure 4-19:
The quickest way to dispose of a layer is to select it, and then click the Trash can. All Flash animations have at least one layer, so you can't delete the last layer. If you try, Flash doesn't display any error—it just quietly ignores you.

Locking and Unlocking Layers

Working with layers can be confusing, especially at first. So Flash lets you lock individual layers as a kind of safeguard, to keep yourself from accidentally changing content you didn't mean to change:

- **To lock a layer,** click the Unlocked icon (the dot in Figure 4-20) next to the layer you want to lock. When you do, Flash turns the dot into a little padlock icon and deselects any objects that you'd selected on the stage in that layer. If you locked the active layer, Flash draws a slash through the pencil icon next to the layer's name as a visual reminder that you can't edit it.

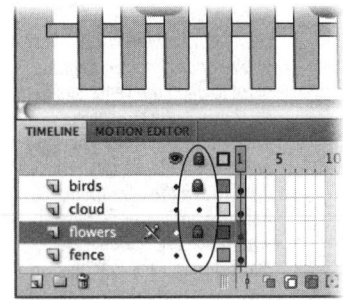

Figure 4-20:
Here, the cloud and fence layers are unlocked, and the birds layer (and the selected flowers layer) are locked. Some people get into the habit of locking all the layers they're not currently editing. That way, they can't possibly add a shape or a tween to the wrong layer.

- **To unlock a layer,** click the Locked icon (the padlock in Figure 4-20) next to the layer you want to unlock. Instantly, the padlock turns into a dot, Flash reselects your objects, and you can edit them once again on the stage.

- **To lock (or unlock) all of your layers all at once,** click the Lock/Unlock All Layers icon. Click the icon again to return to unlocked (or locked) layers. Ctrl-click (⌘-click) on any show/hide button also locks or unlocks all layers.

- **To lock (or unlock) all layers except the one you're currently editing,** Alt-click (Windows) or Option-click (Mac) the unlocked icon next to the layer you're editing.

___

Note: If you try to edit a locked layer, Flash displays a warning dialog box that gives you the opportunity to unlock (and then edit) the layer.

___

Organizing Layers

Flash gives you a couple of options that help you organize your layers both in your finished animation and in Flash. The *outline view* helps you tweak the way the content of your layers appears in your finished animation. You use the outline view to help position the objects on one layer with respect to the objects on all the other layers. *Layer folders* help you organize your layers in the timeline so that you can find and work with them more easily.

Outline View

To help you fit your layers together just the way you want them, Flash lets you display the contents of your layers in outline form. Instead of seeing solid pictures on the stage, you see wireframe images, as in Figure 4-21. Looking at your layer content in outline form is useful in a variety of situations: for example, when you want to align the content of one layer with respect to the content of another.

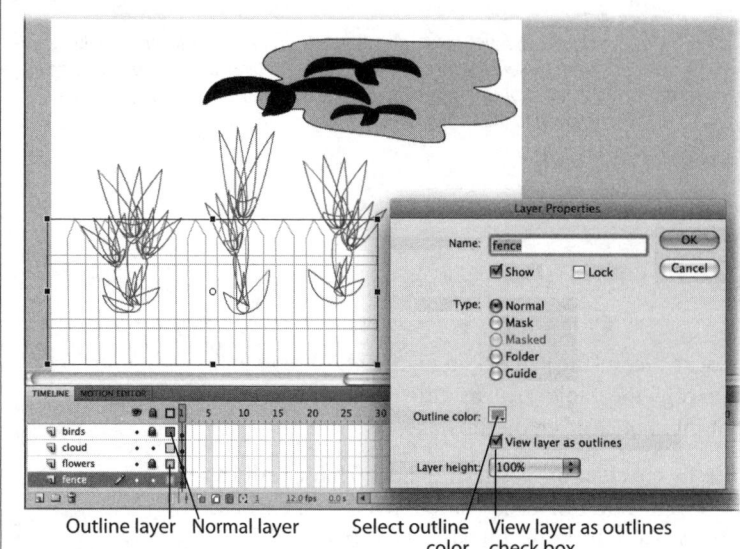

Figure 4-21:
Depending on the visual effect you're going for, you might want to align the centers of your flowers with the crosspieces of your fence. But when you look at the content normally, it's hard to see the alignment, because both your flowers and your fence are opaque. Here, Flash displays the flowers and fence layers in outline form so that you can concentrate on shape and placement without being distracted by extraneous details.

Outline layer   Normal layer   Select outline   View layer as outlines
color   check box

Tip: To display the content of *all* your layers as outlines, click the Show All Layers As Outlines icon. (Clicking it again redisplays your layers normally.) Or, to outline the contents of every layer *except* the one you're working on, Alt-click (Windows) or Option-click (Mac) the outline icon for that layer.

- **To show layer content in outline form,** in the Layers window, click the Non-Outline icon (the filled square in Figure 4-21) displayed next to the layer. When you do, Flash changes the filled square to a hollow square (the Outline icon) and displays your layer content in outline form on the stage.

- **To return your layer to normal,** click the Outline icon (the hollow square) next to the layer.

Tip: You can change the color that Flash uses to sketch your outlined content. For example, you can change the color from light to dark so that you can more easily see the outline against a light background or so that there's more contrast between two overlapping outlines. To change the outline color for a layer, first select the layer, and then select Modify → Timeline → Layer Properties. From the Layer Properties dialog box (Figure 4-21) that appears, click the Outline Color swatch, and then select a color from the Color Picker that appears.

Organizing Your Layers with Layer Folders

When your animation has only a handful of layers, organization isn't such a big deal. But if you find yourself creating 10, 20, or even more layers, you'll want to use layer folders to keep your layers tidy (and yourself from going nuts).

A *layer folder* is simply a folder you can add to the Layers window. Layer folders aren't associated with frames; you can't place images directly into them. (If you try, you see the error message shown in Figure 4-22.)

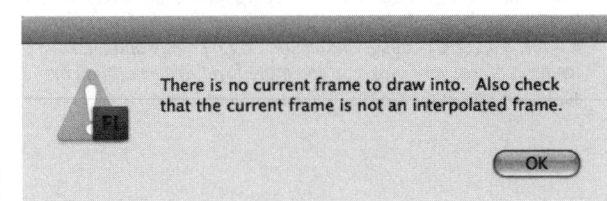

Figure 4-22:
If you try to draw on the stage when you've selected a folder instead of a layer, Flash lets you know in no uncertain terms. (An interpolated frame is a tweened frame; as you learn in Chapter 3, you can't place images in a tweened frame, either.)

There is no current frame to draw into. Also check that the current frame is not an interpolated frame.

OK

Instead, layer folders act as containers to organize your layers. For example, you might want to put all the layers pertaining to a certain drawing (like a logo or character) into a single layer folder, and name the folder *logo* or *Ralph*. That way, you don't have to scroll through a bunch of layers to find the one image you're looking for.

Note: As you might expect, showing, hiding, locking, unlocking, and outlining a layer folder affects every layer inside that folder.

Creating layer folders

When you start working with layer folders, you may want to drag to increase the size of the timeline so that you can see all your layers. If so, proceed as follows:

1. **Click the name of a layer to select it.**

   It doesn't much matter which layer you select since you'll be moving layers as well as the layer folder.

2. **Click the Insert Layer Folder icon. (If you prefer, you can choose Insert → Timeline → Layer Folder or right-click the layer, and then, from the shortcut menu that appears, choose Insert Folder.)**

   Flash creates a new layer folder named Folder 1 and places it above the layer you selected (Figure 4-23).

3. **Drag layers onto the layer folder.**

   If the folder is already expanded, you see the layers appear beneath. If the folder is closed, click the triangle button to view the layers inside.

Tip: You can place layer folders inside other layer folders, but don't go wild; the point is to organize your layers so that you can find them easily, not to see how few folders you can display in the Layers window.

Figure 4-23:
Newly created layer folders appear expanded, like Folder 1 here (note the down arrow). Clicking the down arrow collapses the folder and changes the down arrow to a right arrow. When you drag layers into an open folder (or expand a collapsed folder), the layers appear beneath the folder. You rename a layer folder the same way you rename a layer: by double-clicking the existing name and then typing in one of your own. You can move layer folders around the same way you move layers around, too: by dragging.

Deleting a layer folder

To delete a layer folder, *and all the layers and folders inside*, right-click the layer folder, and then, from the shortcut menu that appears, select Delete Folder. Flash pops up a warning message informing you that you're about to delete not just the folder, but also everything in it. If that's what you want, click Yes; otherwise, click No.

Advanced Drawing and Coloring

Chapter 2 showed you how to create a simple drawing using Flash's drawing and painting tools. But in real life—whether you're pounding out Flash animations for your boss or for your own personal Web site—you're rarely going to be satisfied with a simple drawing. For each keyframe of your animation, you're going to want to start with a basic sketch and then play with it, changing its color, moving a line here and there, adding a graphic element or two, and repositioning it until it looks exactly the way you want it to look.

This chapter shows you how to take a drawing from simple to spectacular. Here, you get acquainted with Flash's *selection* tools—the tools you use to tell Flash which specific part of a drawing you want to change. Then you apply Flash's editing tools from basic (copying, pasting, and moving) to advanced (scaling, rotating, stacking, grouping, and more).

You can also do more with color in Flash drawings than you saw in Chapter 2. After a quick background in color theory, this chapter covers applying color effects like brightness and transparency, and even creating your own custom colors.

Selecting Graphic Elements

With few exceptions, before you can modify an object on the stage, you first have to *select* the object. It's the same in a word processor, where you have to highlight a word with your cursor before you can edit or delete it. Since Flash deals with more complex objects than words, it gives you a variety of selection tools for different purposes. The Tools panel (Figure 5-1) has three different selection tools. Each is good for selecting different types of objects.

Selection

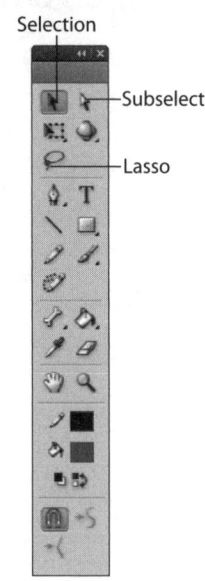

—Subselection

—Lasso

Figure 5-1:
Flash gives you three different ways to select the strokes, fills, bitmaps, symbols, and other graphic elements that make up your images: Selection, Subselection, and Lasso. As you see in the following sections, each has its advantages and drawbacks.

There are a couple of exceptions to this rule: specifically, modifying fill color using the Paint Bucket tool (page 86) and reshaping lines and curves using the Selection tool (next page). But in general, you need to select stuff in Flash before you can work with it.

Tip: To select everything on the stage, choose Edit → Select All or use the shortcut key Ctrl+A (⌘-A).

- **Selection.** The black arrow selects entire strokes, fills, shapes, and objects (like bitmaps and symbols), as well as individual portions of those strokes, fills, shapes, and objects.

- **Subselection.** The white arrow lets you select the individual points that make up lines and curves.

- **Lasso.** This tool, which looks like a miniature lasso, is great for selecting groups of objects, oddly shaped objects, or portions of objects. When objects are close together on the stage, you can use the lasso to carefully select around them.

The following sections describe each of these tools in detail.

Note: The selection tools behave differently depending on whether you've drawn your objects on the stage using object drawing mode or chosen to stick with merge drawing mode (which Flash assumes you want until you tell it differently). This chapter shows the selection tools in object drawing mode (page 57 explains the differences between the two modes).

The Selection Tool

The aptly named Selection tool is the workhorse of Flash's selection tools; with it, you can select individual graphic elements like strokes, fills, shapes, symbols, text blocks, and grouped objects. You can also use the Selection tool to select a portion of any object, as shown in Figure 5-2, or to move or reshape an object (a process sometimes referred to as *transforming* an object).

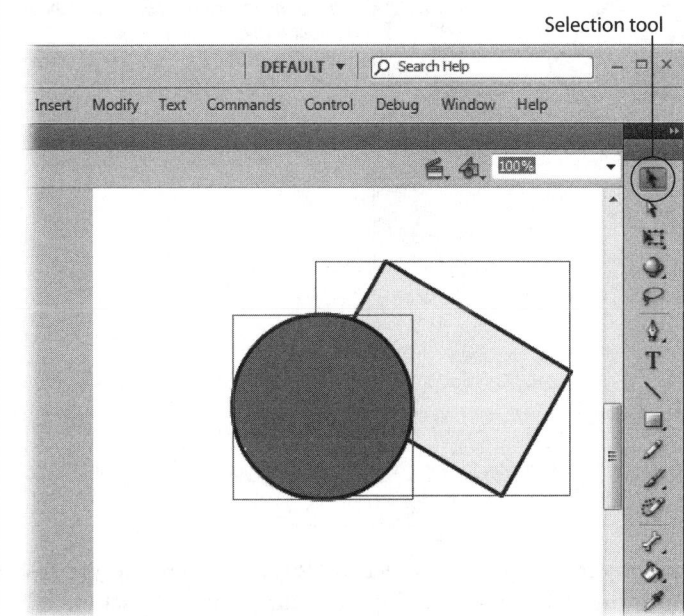

Selection tool

Figure 5-2:
Using the Selection tool is the easiest way to select just about any object, whether it's a shape, a stroke, a bitmap, a fill, or a text block. To use the Selection tool: In the Tools panel, click the tool; then, on the stage, click the object you want to select. To select groups of objects, you have a choice: You can either Shift-click each object, or click outside the group, and then drag until Flash displays a selection box around your group.

Selecting a graphic element

The most common thing you're going to want to do with the Selection tool is select an entire graphic element—a circle, a line, a block of text, a bitmap, a hand-drawn kangaroo—so that you can apply color to it, copy it, skew it, or make some other modification to it.

Note: To deselect a selected object (regardless of which tool you used to select it), simply click any blank spot on the stage.

To select an entire graphic element (or groups of elements) using the Selection tool:

1. **In the Tools panel, click the Selection tool.**

   Flash highlights the Selection tool, and Selection-specific options appear in the Options section at the bottom of the Tools panel (Figure 5-3). On the PC (not Mac), Flash displays a tiny gray selection box.

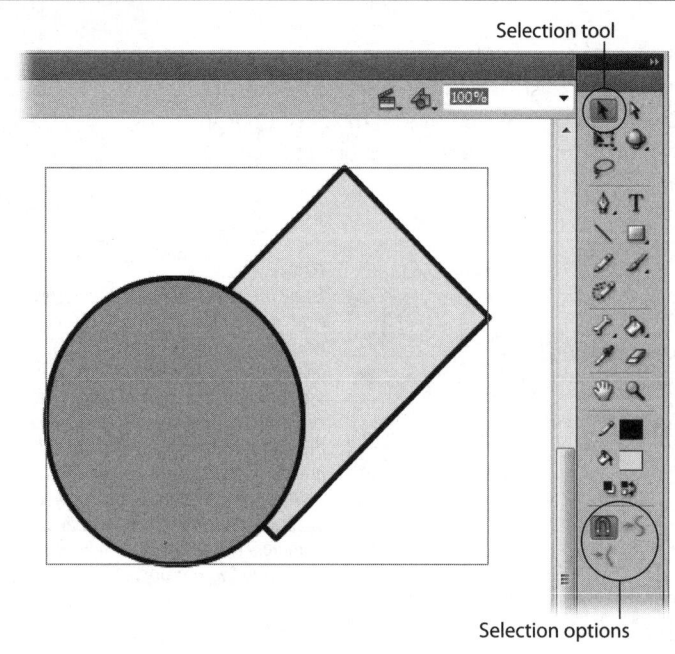

Selection tool

Selection options

Figure 5-3:
Flash displays a selection box around grouped objects (like the circle and rectangle shown here), symbols, and text blocks to let you know you've successfully selected them. When you're using the selection tool, you see special options at the bottom of the Tools panel. For example, the magnet button toggles the "Snap to Objects" option described on page 197.

Note: You use the "Snap to Objects" option to help you align an object you've selected using the Selection tool. You'll find out more about this option on page 197.

2. **Either click the object you want to select, or (best for lines and groups of objects) click near the object, and then drag your cursor until the selection box surrounds the object.**

Tip: You can also select groups of objects with the Selection tool when you Shift-click each object you want to select.

Flash highlights the selected object either by displaying a selection box around the object as shown on the left in Figure 5-4 or covering the selected area with the selection pattern on the right. Either way, the Properties panel changes to reflect the object you've selected.

Note: When you select a straight line or a rectangular object, you may find it tough to see the selection box because Flash draws it so closely around the line that it almost looks like part of the line itself.

With the object selected, you can make any modifications you want to the object using the main menu options, Flash's color or transform tools (page 208 and page 181), or any of the panels, like the Properties panel.

Note: If you use the Selection tool to select an ungrouped line or shape, Flash displays the Straighten and Smooth options (check out the Options section of the Tools panel). These options let you tweak your lines and shapes—useful if you've got a shape almost the way you want it, but not quite (and you don't want to have to start over and redraw the whole thing). To incrementally straighten a curved line, with the line selected, click the Straighten option. To incrementally turn a series of straight-line angles into a curve, with the line selected, click the Smooth option.

Selecting part of a graphic element

Sometimes you want to carve a chunk off an object to work with it separately: to apply a gradient effect, to cut it out of your image entirely, or whatever strikes your fancy. Using the Selection tool, you can drag a rectangle anywhere over an object to tell Flash to select just that portion of the object, but first you need to learn a couple of tricks.

When you draw shapes using object mode (described on page 57) Flash automatically groups the shape. One click on the oval or rectangle you just drew selects the entire object, both the fill and the stroke. To select specific parts of a shape, you need to ungroup it first. Select the shape, and then choose Modify → Ungroup. Flash gives you visual clues so you can tell a grouped shape from an ungrouped shape as shown in Figure 5-4. Once ungrouped, shapes behave differently when you use the Selection tool. Specifically, clicking an ungrouped shape once selects only the fill. A double-click selects both the fill and the stroke.

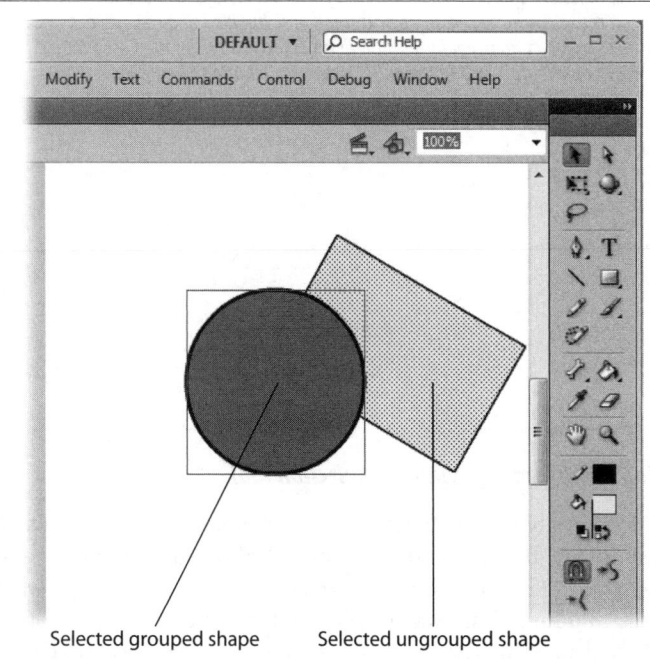

Figure 5-4:
Grouped shapes and ungrouped shapes behave differently when it comes to selection tools. They even look different when you select them. The circle here is a selected grouped shape; it shows a marquee. The rectangle is a selected ungrouped shape; it shows a highlight pattern on the selected portions.

Selected grouped shape   Selected ungrouped shape

Note: If you want to select a freeform portion of an object—for example, you've drawn a jungle scene and you want to cut the shape of a baboon's head out of it—you need the Lasso tool (page 174). The Selection tool lets you select only a rectangular shape.

To select just a portion of an ungrouped graphic element using the Selection tool:

1. **In the Tools panel, click the Selection tool.**

   Flash highlights the Selection tool.

2. **Click near the object, and then drag your cursor until the selection box surrounds just the portion of the ungrouped object you want to select (Figure 5-5).**

   When you let go of the mouse, Flash highlights the selected portion of the object as in Figure 5-5, right.

Note: Flash doesn't let you select a portion of a grouped object, a bitmap, or an object created using object drawing mode. To select a portion of a grouped object (or a single object created in object drawing mode), you need to ungroup it first (Modify → Ungroup). To select a portion of a bitmap, you need to break it apart first (Modify → Break Apart). To learn how to draw an object using merge drawing mode, check out "When to use object drawing mode" on page 59.

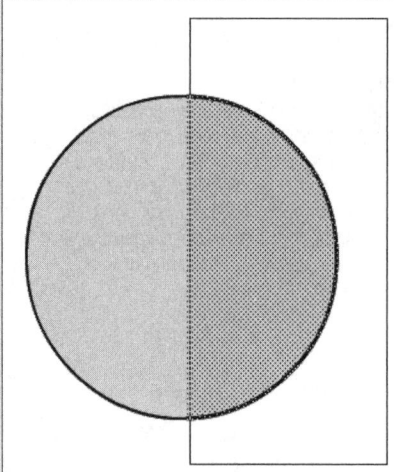

Figure 5-5:
The Selection tool lets you select using only a rectangular selection box. You can make it a large rectangle or a small one, but it's still a rectangle. If you need to select an irregular portion of an object, you need the Lasso tool. If Flash insists on selecting the entire shape (or bitmap) when all you want to do is select a piece of it, ungroup the shape (or break apart the bitmap).

Moving and reshaping (transforming) with the Selection tool

The Selection tool does double-duty: It lets you select objects and portions of objects, as described in the preceding section, but it also lets you move and reshape, or *transform,* them. This double-duty is great—as long as you know what to expect. (Many's the budding Flash-ionado who's sat down to select part of an image and been totally dismayed when the object suddenly, inexplicably, developed a barnacle-like bulge.)

Note: Whether or not Flash treats your shape as a single cohesive entity (for example, an outlined circle) or a combination of independent elements (the circle's outline plus the circle's fill) depends on whether you drew that shape in object or merge drawing mode. Grouped and ungrouped shapes also behave differently, as explained in the note on the previous page.

Here's how it works. If you click the Selection tool, and then position your cursor directly over an unselected fill or stroke, Flash displays, next to your cursor, one of three icons: a hooked cross, a curve, or an angle.

- **Moving (hooked cross).** The hooked cross (Figure 5-6) tells you that you can click to move the object directly beneath your cursor. Double-click if you want to select both the fill and stroke before you move the object.

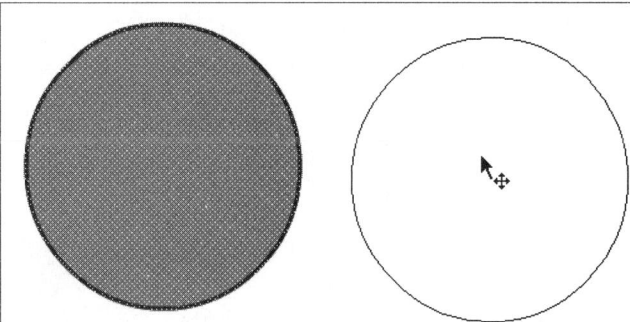

Figure 5-6:
The hooked cross shown here tells you that if you drag this fill, you can move it across the stage. Release the mouse when the object is where you want it.

- **Reshaping (curve).** When you see the curve icon shown in Figure 5-7, dragging reshapes the line beneath your cursor (in other words, it lets you add or modify a curve).

- **Reshaping (angle).** Dragging the angle icon (Figure 5-8) lets you reshape one of the corners of your object.

Tip: To add an angle rather than a curve, when you see the curve icon, press Alt (Windows) or Option (Mac) before dragging.

The Subselection Tool

When you want to modify the individual points and segments that make up your shapes, use the Subselection tool.

As shown in Figure 5-9, the Subselection tool (the white arrow) lets you redisplay shapes as a series of points and segments. You can drag any point to modify it (as well as the attached segments) or drag the tangent handle (temporary slope guide) for a curve to adjust the curve. You can also move a shape—both its outline strokes and inside fill—using the Subselection tool.

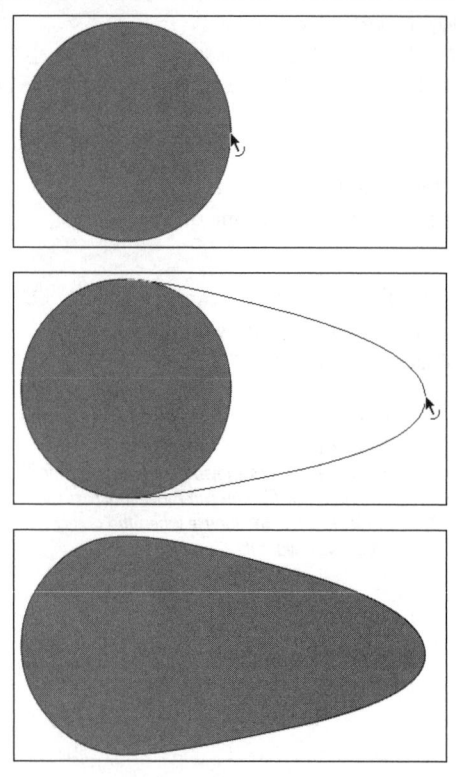

Figure 5-7:
When you see the curve icon (top), you can drag to pull the line in any direction you like (middle). Releasing the mouse finishes the modification (bottom).

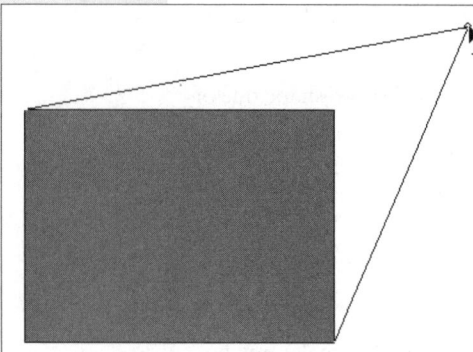

Figure 5-8:
When you mouse over an object's corner and see the angle icon shown here, dragging lets you pull the corner in any direction to reshape it. Releasing the mouse finishes the modification. Here, the upper-right corner of a rectangle is being reshaped.

To use the Subselection tool to move an object:

1. **In the Tools panel, click the Subselection tool (Figure 5-9).**

   Flash highlights the Subselection tool.

2. **Click the object you want to work with (or click near the object, and then drag your cursor until the selection box surrounds the object).**

   Flash redisplays the object as a series of segments and selectable points.

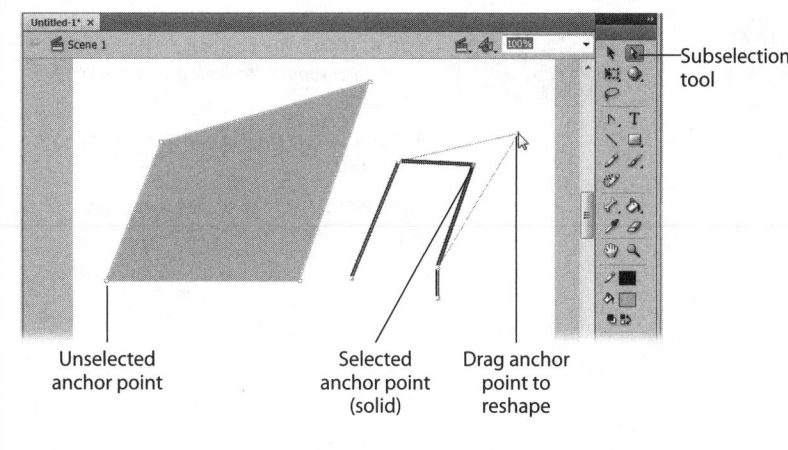

Subselection tool

Unselected anchor point

Selected anchor point (solid)

Drag anchor point to reshape

Figure 5-9:
If you click the Subselection tool, and then click an object you've created using any drawing tool (Pen, Pencil, Brush, Line, or Shape), Flash redisplays the line as a series of segments and points. Click any segment (the cursor displays a tiny black square as you mouse over a segment), and Flash lets you move the entire object. Click a point (a hollow square) instead, and Flash lets you change the object's shape.

3. **Mouse over any of the segments in the object.**

   Flash displays a black square.

4. **Drag to move the object. When you're satisfied, let go of the mouse.**

   Flash displays your moved object.

To use the Subselection tool to modify a point (and, by association, the segments attached to that point):

1. **In the Tools panel, click the Subselection tool.**

   Flash highlights the Subselection tool.

2. **Click the object you want to work with (or click near the object, and then drag your cursor until the selection box surrounds the object).**

   Flash redisplays the object as a series of segments and selectable points.

3. **Mouse over the point you want to modify.**

   Flash displays a hollow square.

4. **Click once, and then drag the point to reshape your object. When you're satisfied, let go of the mouse.**

   Flash displays your modified object. You can see an example in Figure 5-10.

Tip: If the point defines a curve (in other words, if you see a hollow square at the end of a curved line), clicking the point tells Flash to display a temporary slope guide, or *tangent handle*. You can click either end of the tangent handle, and then drag to adjust the curve. To convert a point to a curve, press Alt (Option) as you drag.

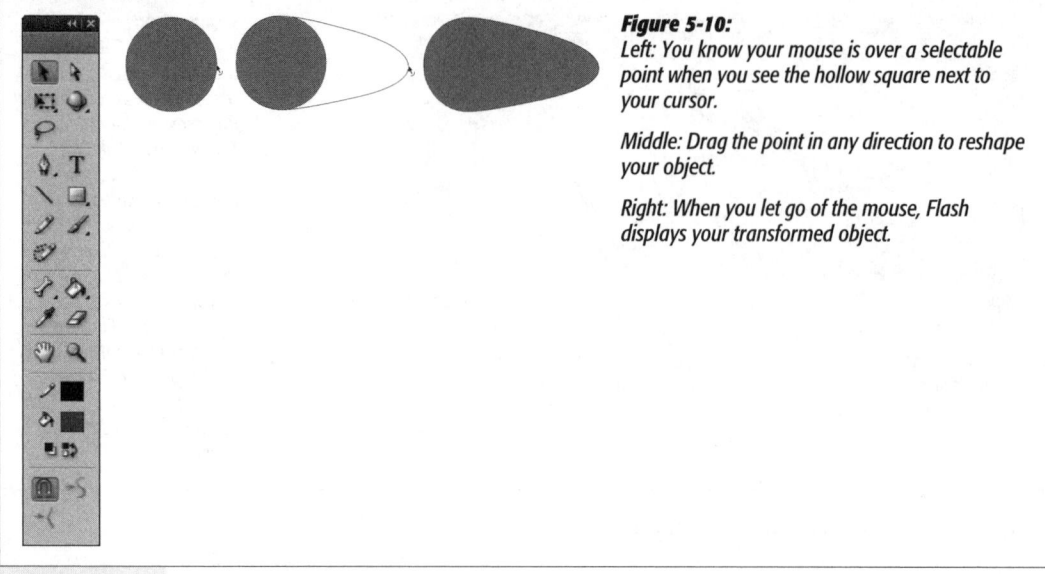

Figure 5-10:
Left: You know your mouse is over a selectable point when you see the hollow square next to your cursor.

Middle: Drag the point in any direction to reshape your object.

Right: When you let go of the mouse, Flash displays your transformed object.

The Lasso Tool

Say you want to select just part of an object to work with: to cut, recolor, and so on. The Selection tool (page 167) works just fine if your objects are nicely spread out on the stage with lots of room around each one. But if your stage is jam-packed with images, you can't select the image you want with the Selection tool without inadvertently selecting parts of images you *don't* want. Figure 5-11 shows an example.

You can use the Lasso tool to select nonrectangular portions of objects both by drawing freehand and by pointing and clicking.

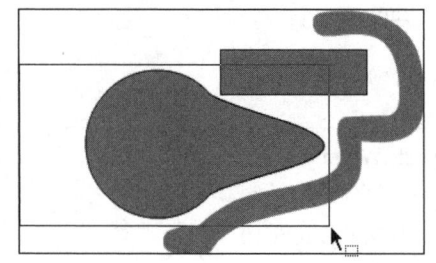 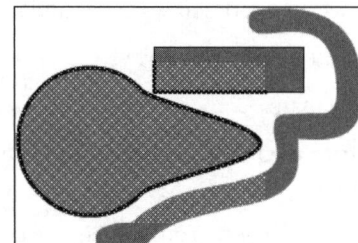

Figure 5-11:
Selecting an object that "overhangs" other objects on the stage (left) doesn't work with the Selection tool, which only gives you a one-size-fits-all selection rectangle. If you try it, you end up selecting portions of other, nearby objects. Use the Lasso tool (right) for pinpoint control over objects and the portions of objects you select.

Tip: The Lasso tool only lets you select portions of objects if those objects are either ungrouped lines or fills or broken-apart bitmaps. You create ungrouped shapes by using merge drawing mode, but you can also ungroup them after the fact by choosing Modify → Ungroup. To break apart a bitmap, select it, and then choose Modify → Break Apart.

Freehand selecting with the Lasso

Depending on how steady your hands are, drawing a freehand lasso around an object (or around the portion of an object you want to select) is the quickest way to select what you want. Straight out of the box, this is how the Lasso works.

To use the Lasso tool to select objects (and portions of objects) freehand:

1. **In the Tools panel, click the Lasso tool (Figure 5-12, left).**

   Flash highlights the Lasso tool; and in the Options section of the Tools panel, the Lasso-related options appear.

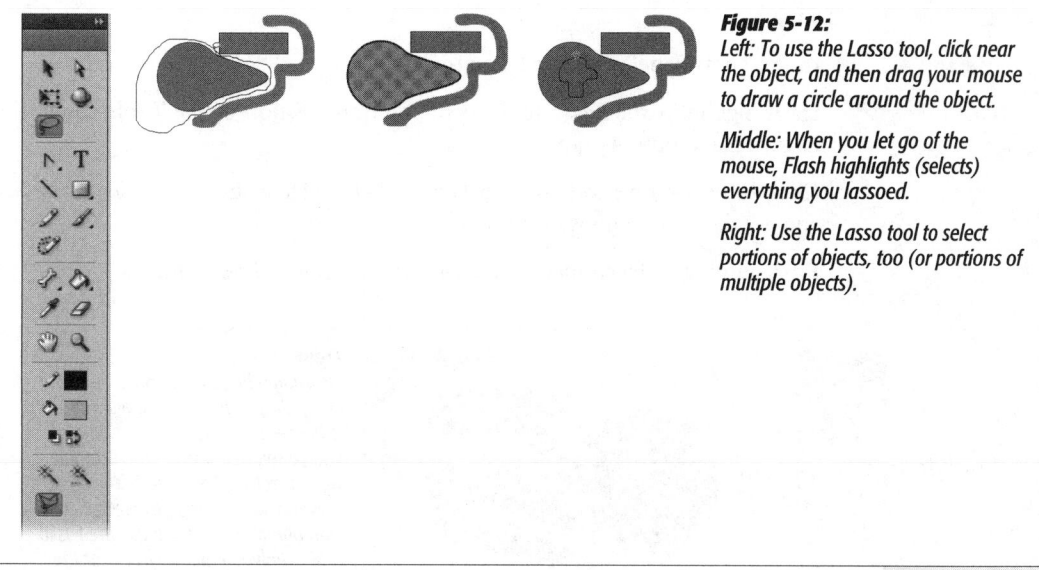

Figure 5-12:
Left: To use the Lasso tool, click near the object, and then drag your mouse to draw a circle around the object.

Middle: When you let go of the mouse, Flash highlights (selects) everything you lassoed.

Right: Use the Lasso tool to select portions of objects, too (or portions of multiple objects).

2. **Click near the object you want to select, and then drag your mouse to encircle the object.**

   Figure 5-12 (right) shows you an example.

3. **When you've completely encircled your object, let go of the mouse.**

   Flash selects everything inside the loop you drew with the Lasso tool.

Tip: You can have a tricky time describing a precise loop using the Lasso, especially if you're using a mouse instead of a graphics tablet. Fortunately, Flash has got your back; if you don't completely close the loop, Flash closes it for you, using a straight line. If this action isn't what you want, just select Edit → Undo Lasso, and then start over. If you're still having trouble, try using the Zoom tool to enlarge the stage or try the Lasso's Polygon mode, described in the following section.

Pointing and clicking with the Lasso

At times, you may find you need to select an object that's *really* close to another object on the stage. Or you may find you need to select a very precise portion of an object, like a perfect triangle.

In these cases, freehand just doesn't cut it; one slip, and you have to start over. You're better off taking advantage of the Lasso tool's Polygon Mode, which lets you click to surround an area. (Flash takes care of filling in the straight lines between your clicks so you don't have to.)

To use the Lasso tool to select objects (and portions of objects) by pointing and clicking:

1. **In the Tools panel, click the Lasso tool.**

   Flash highlights the Lasso tool. In the Options section of the Tools panel, the Lasso-related options appear.

2. **Click the Polygon Mode option (Figure 5-13). Then, using a series of clicks, enclose the object you want to select.**

   Flash automatically connects your clicks with straight-line segments.

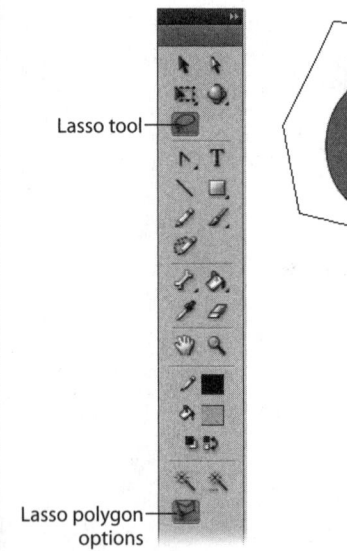

Lasso tool

Lasso polygon options

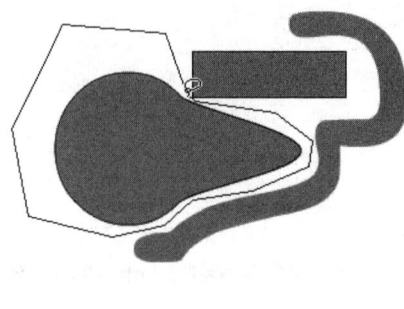

Figure 5-13:
Drawing a lasso freehand around the curvy shape on the left side of the stage is harder than it looks: one slip, and you've selected part of the rectangle right next to it. Fortunately, the Lasso's Polygon Mode combines precise control with automatic help. To use the Lasso tool in Polygon mode, click near the object you want to select, and then click again (and again and again) around the area you want. As you click, Flash connects your clicks for you, letting you create an enclosing shape quickly and easily.

3. When you've completely enclosed your object, let go of the mouse.

Flash selects everything inside the loop you drew with the Lasso tool.

Tip: You may find the Lasso—especially in Polygon Mode—doesn't want to quit when you do. In other words, when you go to use the main menu or a panel or another drawing tool, you find you can't because Flash keeps insisting you need to draw another lasso. Normally, to deactivate a tool, all you have to do is click the Selection tool in the Tools panel. If this doesn't work, try right-clicking an empty spot on the stage before you click the Selection tool.

Selecting ranges of color in bitmaps with the Magic Wand

Flash treats *bitmaps*—the GIF, JPEG, and other image files that you can pull into a Flash document, described in Chapter 9—differently from the way it treats the images you create using its drawing tools. And if you take a look at Figure 5-14, you see why.

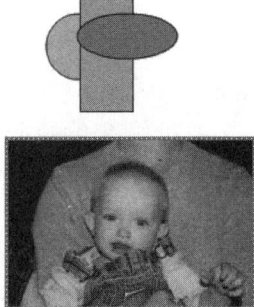

Figure 5-14:
Top: The drawing is clearly composed of three shapes, each of which you can click to select separately.

Bottom: The bitmap image is much more complex, with no easily identifiable shape outlines. When you click to select the image on the bottom, Flash highlights the entire rectangular image; it makes no distinction between the colors and shapes inside.

While you can't manipulate bitmaps in Flash anywhere near as easily or as completely as you can manipulate the shapes and lines you draw directly onto the stage, Flash does have a special tool specifically for selecting ranges of colors in bitmaps: the Magic Wand. After you select color ranges, you can then recolor them or cut them out of the bitmap completely.

To select color ranges in a bitmap using the Magic Wand:

1. On the stage, select the bitmap with which you want to work.

Flash displays a light-colored border around the selected bitmap.

2. Choose Modify → Break Apart.

Flash redisplays the bitmap as a selected fill.

3. From the Tools panel, select the Lasso. Then, in the Options section of the Tools panel, click the Magic Wand (Figure 5-15, top).

As you mouse over the bitmap, your cursor turns into a tiny magic wand.

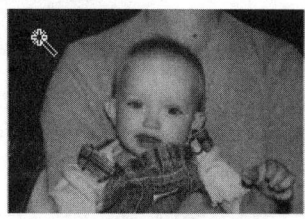

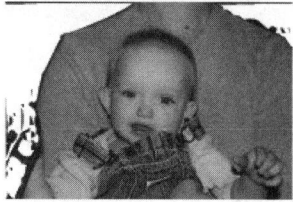

Figure 5-15:
Top: The first time you click the Magic Wand, Flash notes the color you choose.

Bottom: The second (and subsequent) times you click the Magic Wand, Flash selects the bits of color nearby that match your first selection. Selecting colored areas of bitmaps with the Magic Wand can be slow going. Don't expect the precision you enjoy when you're working with primitive shapes, like squares and circles. Still, depending on the effect you're after, the Magic Wand can be useful. Here, most of the background was selected with the Magic Wand tool and primed for repainting.

4. **Click the bitmap to select a color range.**

   Flash highlights bits of selected color.

5. **Click the bitmap again (click a similarly colored area).**

   Flash highlights the bits of color that match your selection.

You can modify the highlighted bits of fill color as you go (cut them, recolor them using the Eyedropper tool described on page 222, and so on), or continue to click the bitmap as you did in step 4 to add to the selection.

In Figure 5-15 (bottom), the designer first selected, and then cut (Edit → Cut) the pixels to make the selected areas easier to see.

Manipulating Graphic Elements

Flash gives you a gazillion tools to modify the drawings that make up your animations. You can stack, rearrange and reposition each individual graphic element, transform (shrink and squish) them, move them, apply color effects, and more until you're completely satisfied with the way they look. It's a cliché, but it's true: When it comes to drawing in Flash, you're pretty much limited only by your imagination.

This section acquaints you with the most powerful tools Flash has for modifying the lines, shapes, bitmaps, symbols, and other graphic elements you add to your drawings.

Modifying Object Properties

Flash's Properties panel is a beautiful thing. Select any element on the stage, and the Properties panel responds by displaying all the characteristics, or *properties*, that you can change about that element.

In Figure 5-16, for example, you see several graphic elements on the stage: a painted fill, a bitmap of a frog, a line of text, and a star. When you select the star, the Properties panel shows all the properties associated with the star: the color, width, and type of outline, the fill color, and so on. When you select the text, the Properties panel changes to reflect only text properties.

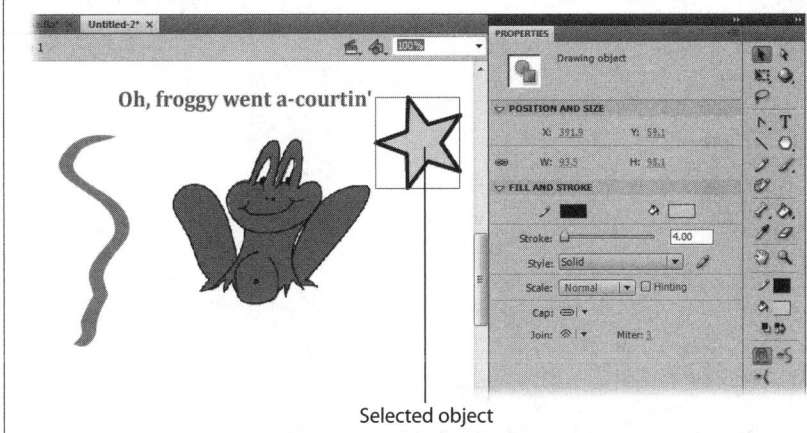

Figure 5-16:
Selecting an object tells Flash to display that object's properties right there in the Properties panel. Here, the star shape is selected, so the properties all relate to this particular star. As long as the property isn't grayed out, you can change it in the Properties panel.

Selected object

Note: If you don't see the Properties panel, choose Window → Properties, and then, in the pop-up menu that appears, turn on the checkbox next to Properties. If you still don't see it, check to see whether you've expanded your stage and pushed it out of the way or collapsed the Properties panel.

You can change any of the object properties you see in the Properties panel. For example, in the Properties panel on the left side of Figure 5-16, you can change the color, width, or style of the star's outline color. (You can change all these properties by using Flash's selection and drawing tools, too, of course, but using the Properties panel is a lot quicker for most changes.)

Moving, Cutting, Pasting, and Copying

After you have an object on the stage, you can move it around, cut it (delete it), paste it somewhere else, or make copies of it.

Tip: All the things you can do to an object—cutting, pasting, copying, and moving—you can also do to a *piece* of an object. Instead of selecting the entire object, just select whatever portion of the object you want to work with, and then go from there.

Moving

To move an object, simply select it (page 167), and then drag it around the stage. Figure 5-17 shows an example of using the Selection tool to select a group of objects, and then move them together.

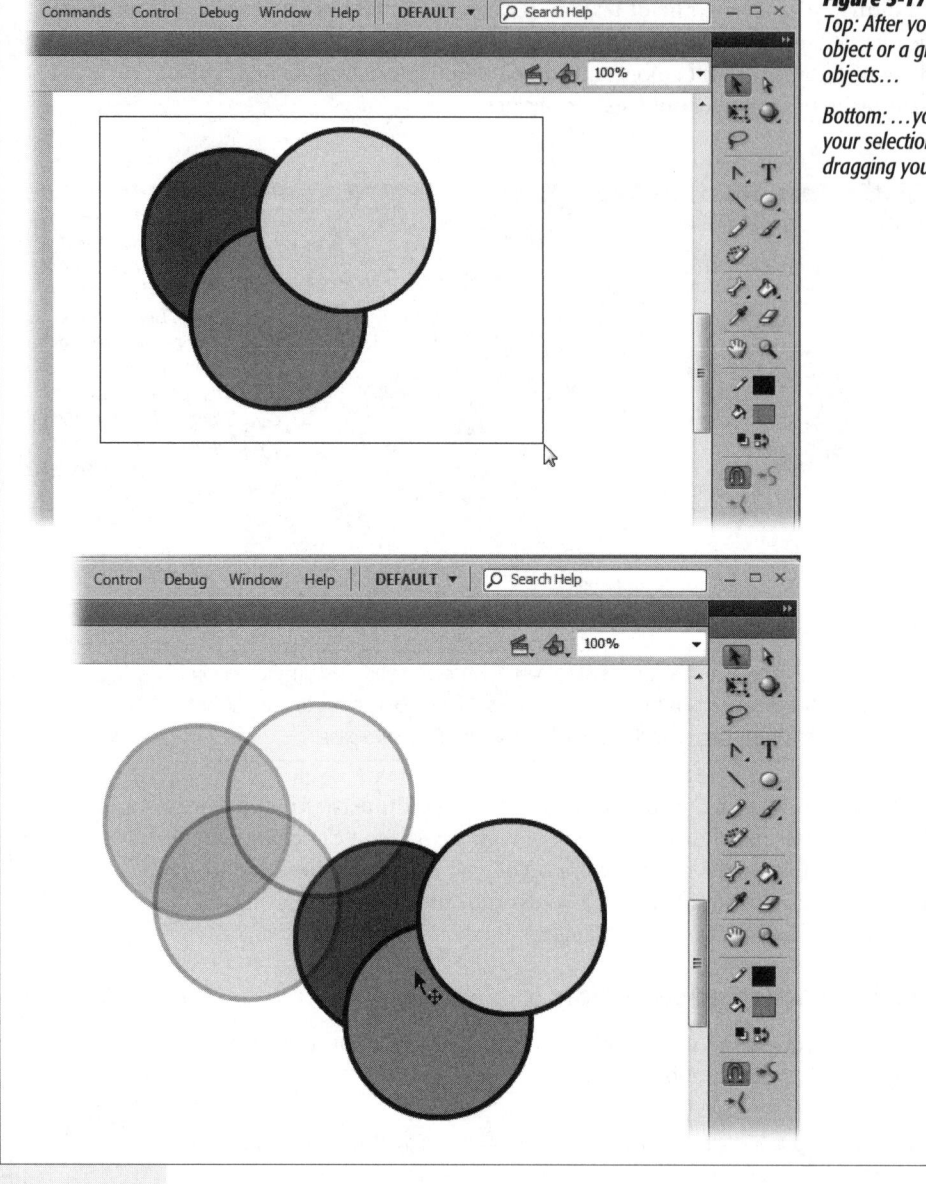

Figure 5-17:
Top: After you select an object or a group of objects…

Bottom: …you can move your selection simply by dragging your cursor.

Cutting

To cut an object, select the object (page 167), and then choose Edit → Cut. Flash deletes the object from the stage and turns on the Paste functions.

Note: Choosing Edit → Clear deletes the selected object, too, but doesn't turn on the Paste functions. In other words, after you choose Edit → Clear, it's gone, baby, gone (unless you quickly choose Edit → Undo Delete).

Copying

To copy an object, select the object (page 167), and then choose Edit → Copy. Flash leaves the object on the stage and turns on the Paste functions (see the next section).

Tip: You can perform a quick copy-and-paste operation by selecting an object, and then choosing Edit → Duplicate. Flash displays a movable copy of the selected object just above the selected object. For even faster duplication, press Alt (Option) as you drag the object.

Pasting

To paste an object that you've either cut or copied, choose one of the following:

- **Edit → Paste in Center.** Tells Flash to paste the cut (or copied) object smack in the middle of the stage's visible area, on top of any other image that happens to be there.

- **Edit → Paste in Place.** Tells Flash to replace the cut object, or to put the copied object square on top of the original. This command is especially useful when you want to move an object from one frame to another and place it in exactly the same position in the new frame.

Transforming Objects (Scaling, Rotating, Skewing, Distorting)

In the graphics world, *transforming* an object doesn't just mean changing the object; transforming means applying very specific shape and size changes to the object. These changes—called *transforms*—include:

- **Scaling.** Among graphic designers, scaling means resizing. You can scale (shrink or enlarge) a selected shape based on its width, height, or both.

- **Rotating.** You can rotate (turn) an object as far as you want, in any direction.

- **Skewing.** A limited kind of distortion, skewing means slanting an object either horizontally or vertically.

- **Distorting and Enveloping.** You distort an object by pulling it out of shape: in other words, by repositioning one or more of the object's angles. The Envelope transform is similar, but it doesn't preserve the lines of the shape the way distortion does; instead, it lets you pull any angle, line, or curve out of shape to create fantastic effects.

- **Flipping.** Flipping an object creates a mirror image of the object. Flash has commands for flipping both horizontally and vertically.

You have three choices when it comes to applying a transform to a selected object (or group of objects):

- You can click the Free Transform tool (Figure 5-18), choose the appropriate option from the Options section of the Tools panel, and then, on the stage, drag your selection to apply the transform. This approach is described in the following sections.

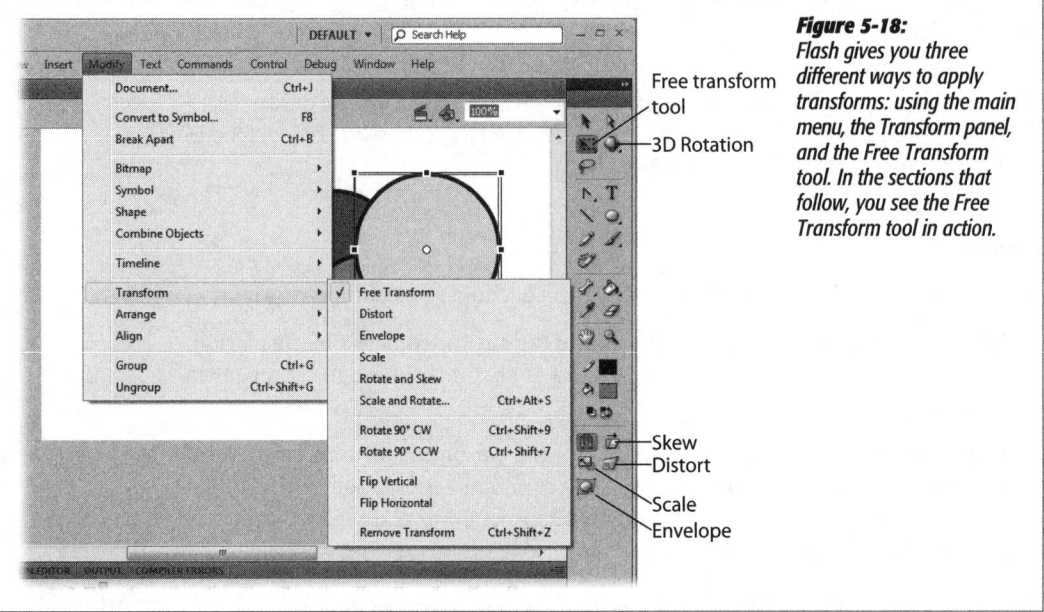

Figure 5-18:
Flash gives you three different ways to apply transforms: using the main menu, the Transform panel, and the Free Transform tool. In the sections that follow, you see the Free Transform tool in action.

- You can type information (for example, the number of degrees you want to rotate an object) directly into the Transform panel.

- You can choose Modify → Transform, and then, from the pop-up menu that appears, turn on the checkbox next to the transform you want to apply.

Scaling objects

To resize a drawn object, first select the object on the stage, and then proceed as follows:

1. **Select the Free Transform tool's Scale option.**

   Black squares appear at the corners and sides of your selection.

2. **Position your cursor over one of the black squares.**

   Your cursor turns into the double-headed *scale arrow* (Figure 5-19, top).

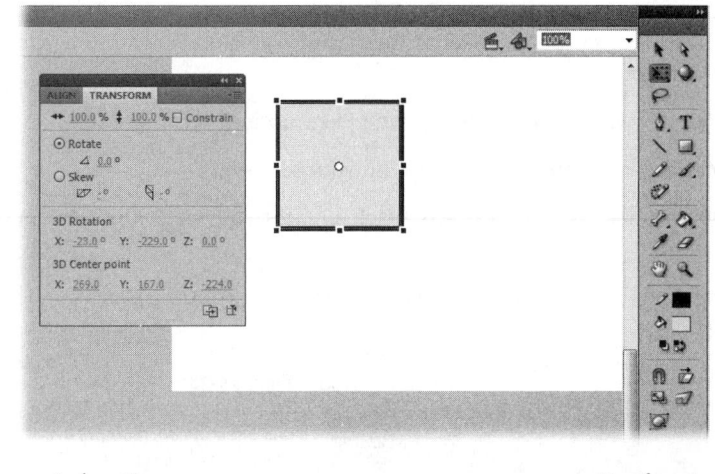

Figure 5-19:
Top: Mousing over any of the black squares on the sides and at the corners of your object displays a scale arrow. By dragging a square, you can scale an object vertically, horizontally, or both. Notice that before the scaling begins, the Transform panel displays the original width/height dimensions as 100% and 100%.

Bottom: Flash automatically plugs the new dimensions into the Transform panel on the bottom. Instead of dragging the object to scale it, you can also type or scrub the scale dimensions into the Transform panel yourself.

Scale settings   Transform tool

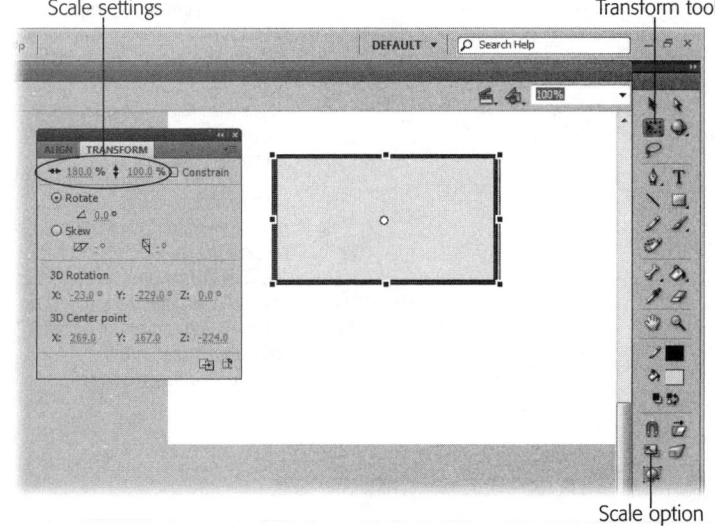

Scale option

3. **Drag to scale the selection.**

   As you drag outward, the selection gets larger; as you drag inward, the selection gets smaller. You can see an example of a scaled object at the bottom of Figure 5-19.

Tip: You can use modifier keys to constrain objects as you scale them. For example, press Shift to lock the proportions or press Alt (Option) to scale an object around its transformation point (indicated by a circle).

Rotating objects

To rotate a drawn object around its axis, first select the object on the stage, and then proceed as follows:

1. **Select the Free Transform tool's Rotate and Skew option.**

   Flash displays a black bounding box around your selection.

2. **Position your cursor over one of the black squares you see at the corners of your selection.**

   Your cursor turns into a circular *rotation arrow* (Figure 5-20, top).

Rotate settings   Transform tool

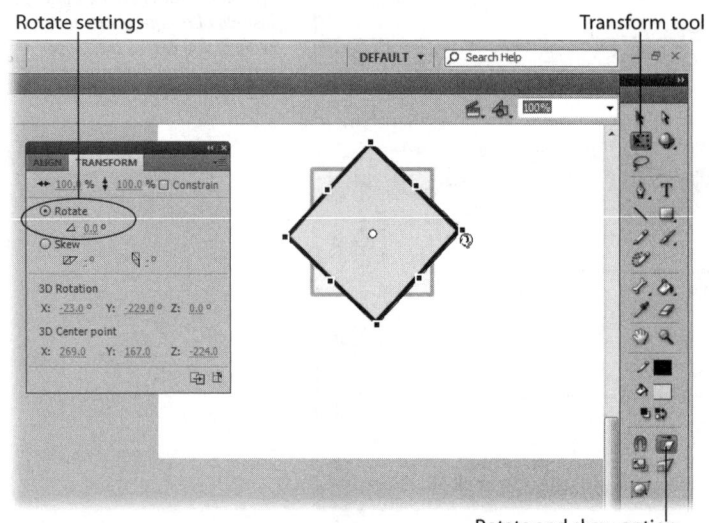

Rotate and skew option

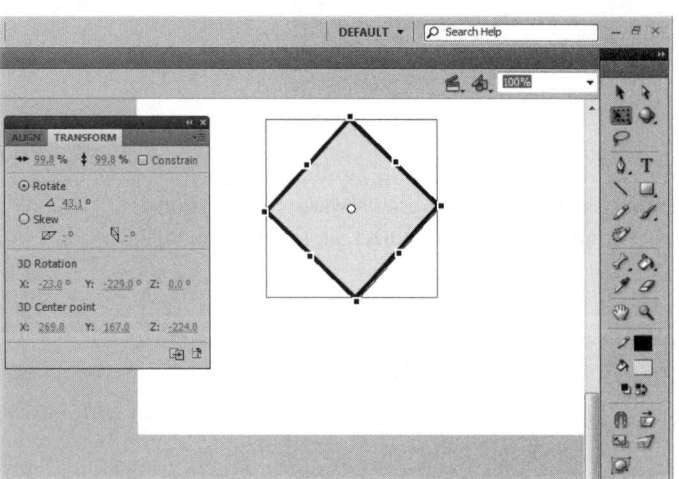

Figure 5-20:
Top: After you select the Rotate and Skew option, mousing over any of the black squares at the corners of your object displays a rotation arrow. Notice that before the rotation begins, the Transform panel displays the original rotation degrees as 0.0%. Drag to rotate the object on its center axis (its transformation point).

Bottom: After you let go of your mouse, Flash automatically records the rotation degrees into the Transform panel on the right. Instead of dragging the object to rotate it, you can also type the rotation degrees into the Transform panel yourself.

3. **Drag to rotate the selection.**

If you drag your cursor to the right, the entire selection rotates right; if you drag your cursor to the left, the selection rotates to the left. There's a rotated object in Figure 5-20 (bottom). Shift-drag to make an object rotate 90 degrees at a time. Alt-drag (Option-drag) to make your selection rotate around the anchor point on the opposite side from the cursor.

Tip: You can flip your objects, too by using Modify → Transform → Flip Vertical and Modify → Transform → Flip Horizontal. The effects are a little different from rotating, as explained in Figure 5-21.

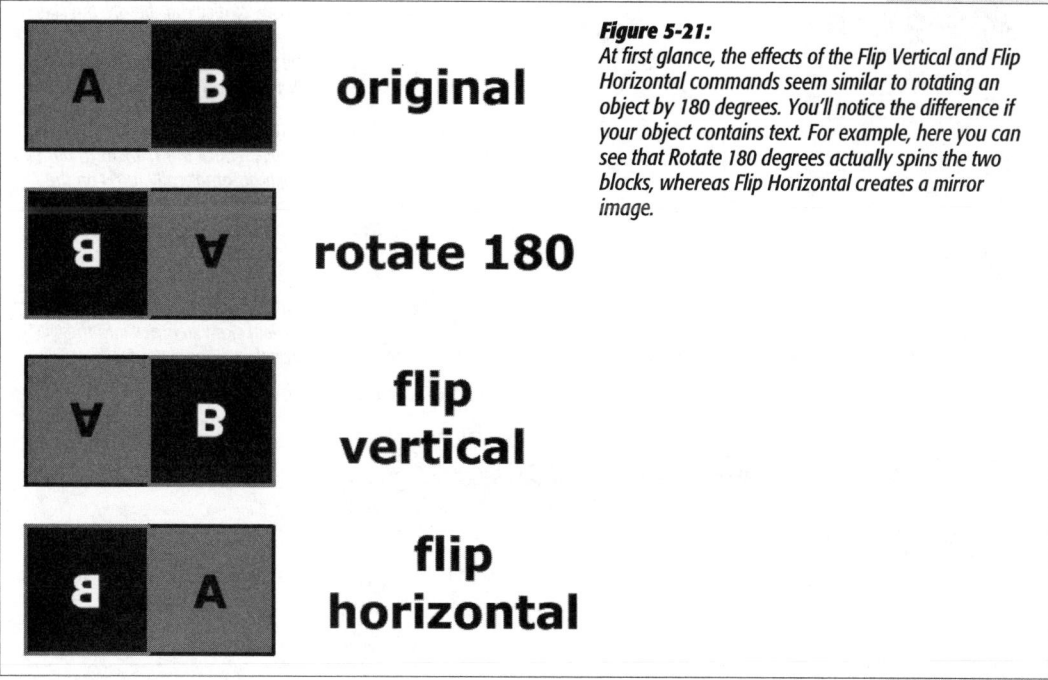

Figure 5-21:
At first glance, the effects of the Flip Vertical and Flip Horizontal commands seem similar to rotating an object by 180 degrees. You'll notice the difference if your object contains text. For example, here you can see that Rotate 180 degrees actually spins the two blocks, whereas Flip Horizontal creates a mirror image.

Skewing objects

To give your drawing a slanted shape, first select the object on the stage, and then proceed as follows:

1. **Select the Free Transform tool's Rotate and Skew option.**

Flash displays a black bounding box around your selection.

2. **Position your cursor over one of the black squares at the sides of your selection.**

Your cursor turns into a *skew arrow* (Figure 5-22, top).

---

3. **Drag to skew the selection.**

Dragging slants the selection along one of its axes (the one marked by the skew arrow you clicked) in the direction you're dragging. Figure 5-22 (bottom) shows a skewed object. Alt-drag (Option-drag) to make the selected object skew around the transformation point.

Skew settings   Transform tool

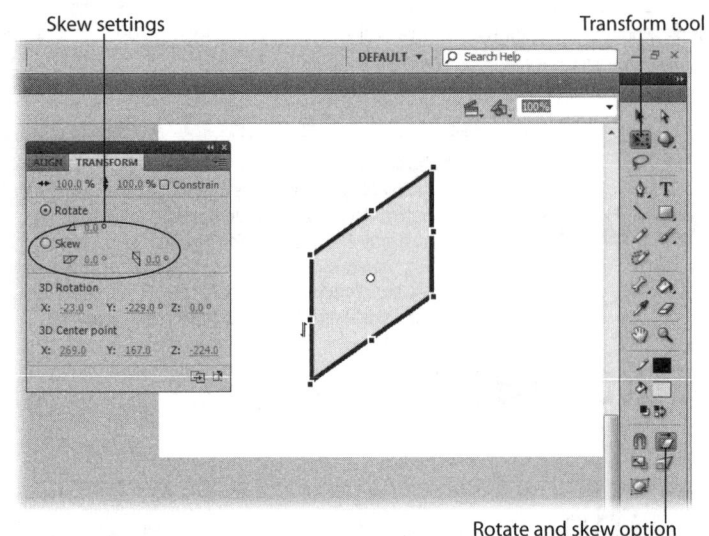

Rotate and skew option

Figure 5-22:
Top: After you select the Rotate and Skew option, mousing over any of the black squares at the sides of your object displays a skew arrow. Notice that before the skew begins, the Transform panel shows the Skew radio button turned off. Drag to skew the object.

Bottom: After you let go of your mouse, check the Transform panel: Flash automatically turns on the Skew button and logs the horizontal and vertical skew degrees. Instead of dragging the object to skew it, you can also turn on the Skew button and type the horizontal and vertical skew degrees into the Transform panel yourself.

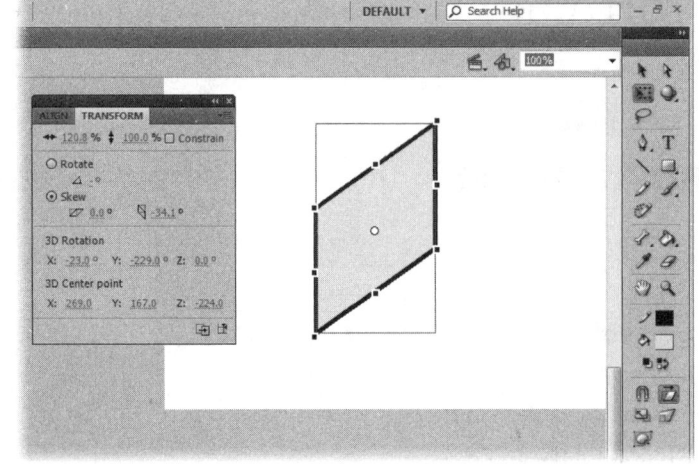

Distorting objects

For more freedom than simple skewing, you can distort your drawn objects in any way or direction:

1. **First, select the object you want to distort, and then select the Free Transform tool's Distort option (Figure 5-18).**

   Flash displays black squares around the sides and corners of your selection.

2. **Position your cursor over one of the black squares.**

   Your cursor turns into a tail-less *distortion arrow* (Figure 5-23, top).

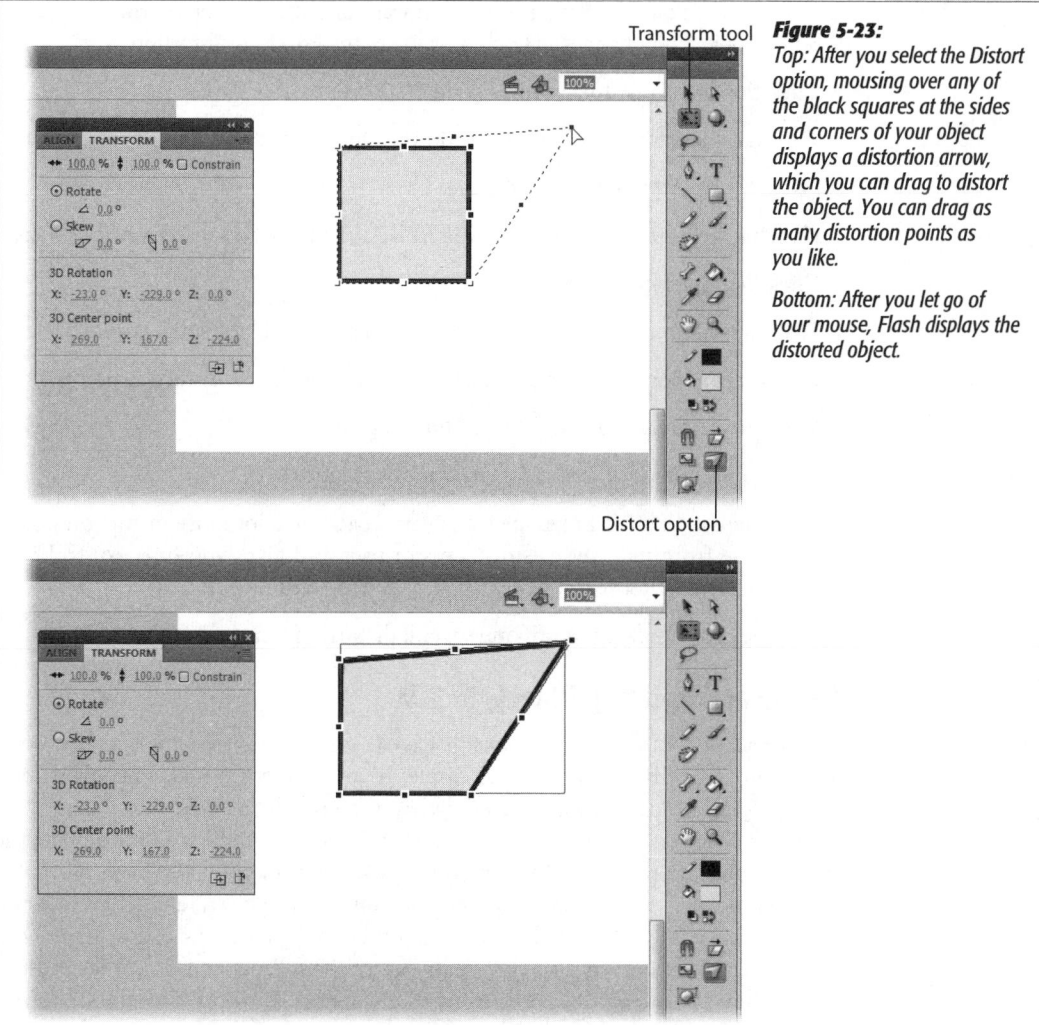

Transform tool

Distort option

Figure 5-23:
Top: After you select the Distort option, mousing over any of the black squares at the sides and corners of your object displays a distortion arrow, which you can drag to distort the object. You can drag as many distortion points as you like.

Bottom: After you let go of your mouse, Flash displays the distorted object.

3. **Drag to distort the selection.**

As you drag outward, the shape bulges outward; drag inward, and the shape dents inward. Figure 5-23 (bottom) shows a distorted object.

Tip: Shift-dragging a corner point lets you *taper* a shape; that is, move that corner and the adjoining corner apart from each other an equal distance.

Applying an Envelope transform

As discussed on page 181, an Envelope transform is the most radical distortion. It gives you more distortion points than the regular Distort option, and also gives you finer control over the points by letting you drag inward or outward to create rounded bulges or dents (not just pointy ones). Here's how to use the Envelope distortion.

1. **Click the Free Transform tool.**

The Free Transform options appear in the Options section of the Tools panel.

2. **Select the object you want to distort.**

Flash highlights the selected object with a black bounding box and tiny black squares.

3. **Click the Envelope option.**

The selected object appears surrounded by a series of black squares and circles.

4. **Position your cursor over one of the black squares or circles (distortion points).**

Your cursor turns into a tail-less *distortion arrow.*

5. **Drag to pull the selection into a new shape (Figure 5-24).**

You'll notice that the Envelope transform gives you a lot more distortion points to choose from than the Distort transform; it also gives you finer control over the points you choose to distort (by dragging inward or outward).

You can see the results of modifying several distortion points in Figure 5-24.

Moving and Rotating Objects in 3-D

Until Flash CS4 came along, it wasn't easy to make an object look as if it were moving in three dimensions. For example, if you wanted to make an image look like as if it were moving away from the viewer, about all you could do was move it slightly on the stage and make it smaller. There was no real science to the effect; the best you could do was eyeball it. Creating a 3-D rotation effect was even more difficult. But no more. Flash CS4 has tools that automatically create exactly these two effects. Next to the select tools, there's another tool that looks like a globe with some circles drawn around it, shown in Figure 5-25. Press and hold that button, and you find the two tools that turn the stage into a 3-D world. The globe lets you rotate an object three-dimensionally, while the tool with three arrows lets you move an object around in 3-D space.

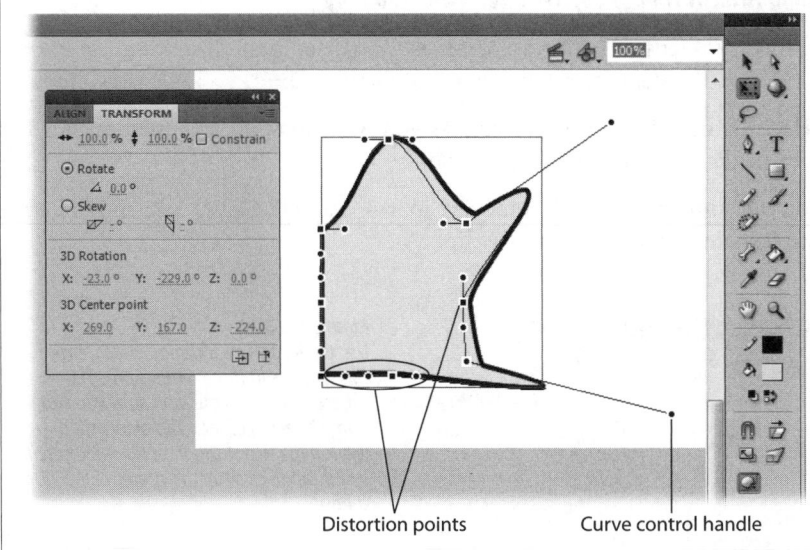

Figure 5-24:
This shape began life as a square. The top and left side were transformed using the Envelope option. Mousing over any of the black squares or circles at the sides and corners of your object displays a distortion arrow. Drag to reshape your object. The squares remain attached to the outline as you drag. The circles are curve control handles.

Distortion points   Curve control handle

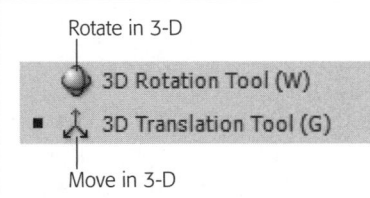

Rotate in 3-D

Move in 3-D

Figure 5-25:
Flash has two tools that let you move movie clip symbols in three dimensions. The tool that looks like a globe rotates movie clips. The tool with the three arrows lets you move movie clips in three dimensions.

One catch is that the object has to be a movie clip. This isn't too much of a catch, because you can put any object inside of a movie clip—like your logo or some text—and then make it fly and spin in 3-D. The other catch is a bit more limiting, since Flash's drawing tools only create two-dimensional images. For example, you can create squares but not cubes, and circles but not spheres. The text tool only creates two-dimensional type, not 3-D letters. But once these objects are placed inside of movie clips, you can move those movie clips around in three dimensions. It's sort of like moving a photo of a car around in 3-D space as opposed to moving a model car around the same space. But even with those limitations, you can create some pretty snazzy effects.

Note: Because the 3-D tools are new to Flash CS4, they only work when you start your document using the ActionScript 3.0 option (see page 19). You also need to publish your document for Flash Player 10.

Rotating (transforming) objects three-dimensionally

The 3-D pros refer to rotating an object as *transforming* an object or a *transformation*. Here are the steps for rotating a movie clip in 3-D:

1. **Select the object or group of objects you want to spin, and then press F8 to convert them into a movie clip symbol.**

   You can combine objects in a movie clip. For example, Figure 5-26 shows a circle and text combined in one movie clip.

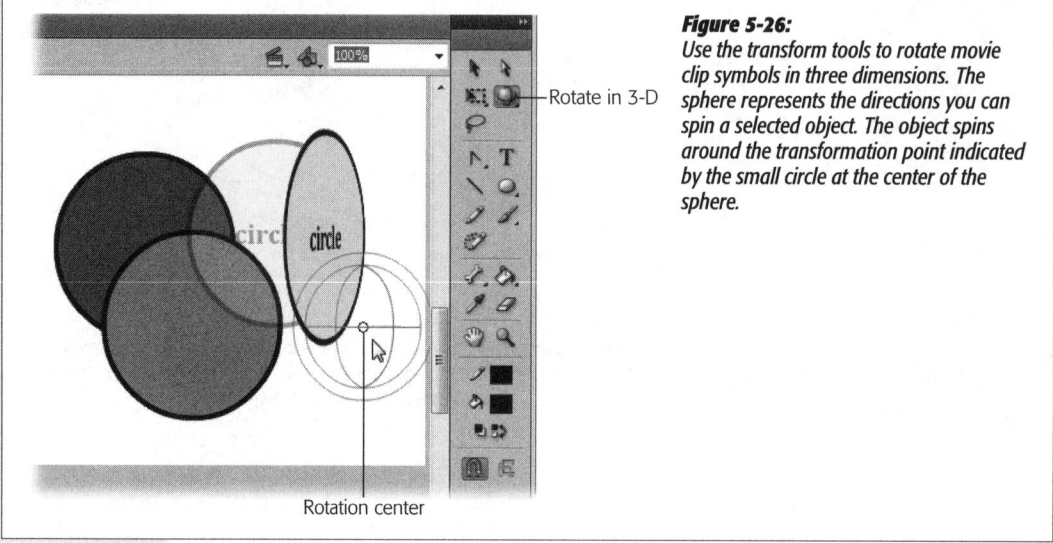

Rotate in 3-D

Rotation center

Figure 5-26:
Use the transform tools to rotate movie clip symbols in three dimensions. The sphere represents the directions you can spin a selected object. The object spins around the transformation point indicated by the small circle at the center of the sphere.

2. **On the stage, select the movie clip, and then click the 3-D Rotation tool in the Tools palette.**

   A globe-like image appears near the movie clip, made up of colored circles. Each color represents a 3-D axis. The small circle in the center marks the point around which the rotation happens.

3. **Drag the center point to change the point around which the rotation takes place.**

   You can drag the center point to any location on the stage.

4. **Click one of the colored lines in the 3-D rotation tool to rotate the movie clip along that axis.**

   As you hold the cursor over one of the colored axes, a tool tip appears indicating the direction of the axis. Green does top-to-bottom or bottom-to-top rotation (the Y axis). Red does horizontal rotation (the X axis). And blue rotates the object front-to-back or back-to-front (the Z axis). Drag a colored circle to spin the movie clip around that axis. If you don't want to be limited to spinning along a single axis, drag the orange ring around the outside of the other circles. That way, the object is free to follow your mouse movement in any direction.

Moving (translating) objects in three dimensions

The 3-D pros refer to moving an object in three dimensions as *translating* an object or a *translation*. Here are the steps for moving a movie clip in 3-D.

1. **On the stage, select the movie clip you want to move in 3-D.**

   Make sure the object you want to move is a movie clip symbol. If not, press F8 to make it into one.

2. **In the Tools palette, click and hold the button for 3-D rotation tools, and then choose 3-D Translation tool from the menu.**

   After you click the button, a 3-D translation symbol appears over the selected movie clip on the stage. The 3-D Translation tool and the translation symbol on the stage look like three arrows pointing in different directions. As shown in Figure 5-27, each arrow is a different color to represent an axis along which the movie clip can be moved. Green moves the object vertically (the Y axis). Red moves it horizontally (the X axis). And blue moves it towards or away from you (the Z axis).

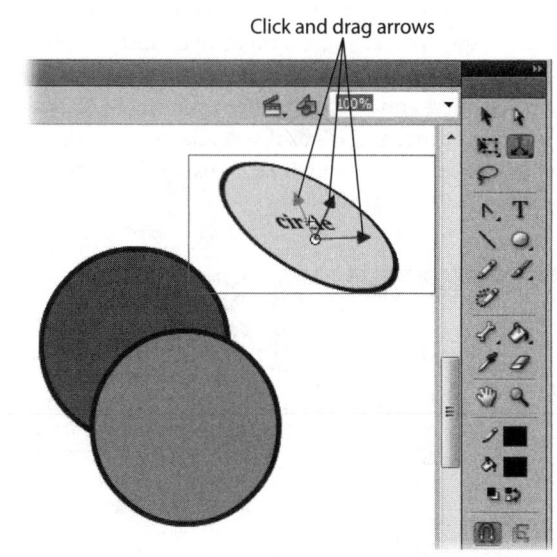

Click and drag arrows

Figure 5-27:
The 3-D Translate tool lets you move movie clips along the X, Y, or Z axis on the stage. Drag along one of the colored arrows representing each of the axes.

3. **Drag one of the colored arrows to move the movie clip along that axis.**

   When you hold the cursor over one of the arrows, a tooltip appears indicating the direction of the axis: X, Y, or Z.

In addition to using the 3-D Translate tool, you can also use the Properties panel to move objects along the three axes (Figure 5-28). Select the movie clip you want to position, and then use the 3-D Position and View X, Y, and Z settings to move it around the stage. Click a setting and type a number, or drag to scrub in a number.

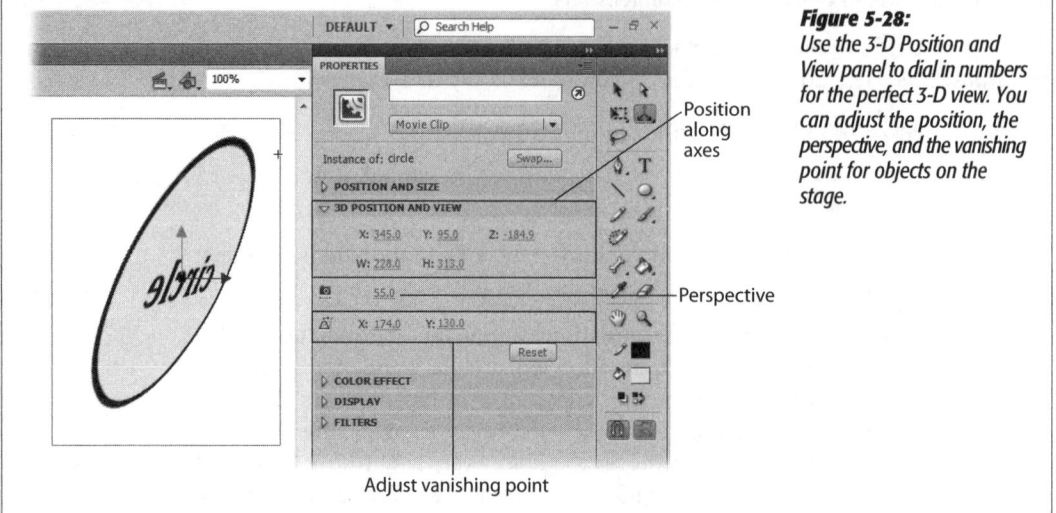

Figure 5-28:
Use the 3-D Position and View panel to dial in numbers for the perfect 3-D view. You can adjust the position, the perspective, and the vanishing point for objects on the stage.

Position along axes

Perspective

Adjust vanishing point

Adjusting the perspective and vanishing point in 3-D

You can set two 3-D properties in the Properties panel: Perspective and Vanishing Point (Figure 5-29). Choosing a perspective setting is similar to choosing a lens for your camera. Flash starts you off at 55, a "normal" point of view similar to a 55mm lens on a camera. Set the number higher, and it's like you're zooming in or attaching a telephoto lens. Choose a lower setting, and it's as if you attached a wide-angle lens. You can add some creative distortion to your images using the Perspective setting along with some of the other 3-D tools.

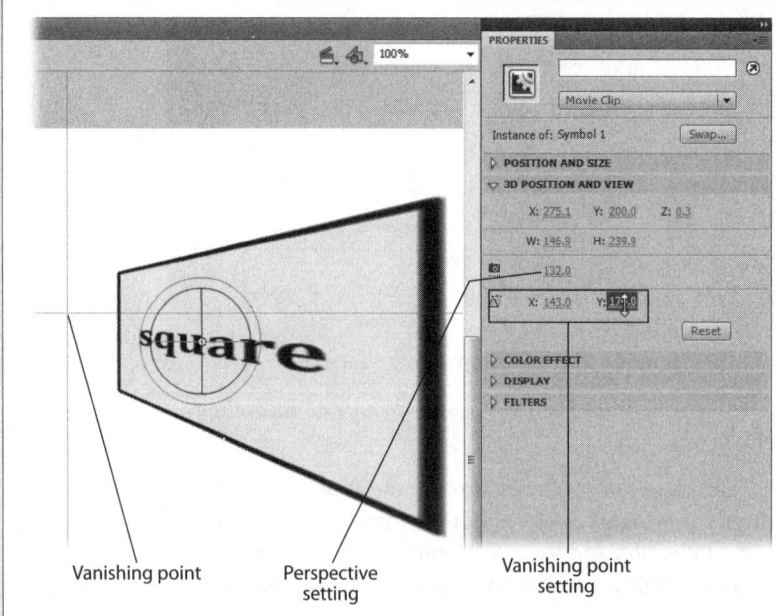

Figure 5-29:
The icon for setting the perspective looks like a camera because it's similar to changing camera lenses between normal, telephoto and wide angle. Use the X/Y Vanishing Point settings to position the vanishing point in your animation.

Vanishing point   Perspective setting   Vanishing point setting

Think back to your art class days when you learned how to add a vanishing point to your drawings to help you draw in perspective. The vanishing point is that place way off in the distance where all parallel lines seem to converge. In Flash, you can move the vanishing point around in your animation using the X/Y settings in the Properties panel (Figure 5-29).

Note: You can add these same 3-D effects to your motion tweens when you use the Motion Editor. For the details, see page 288.

Stacking Objects

In Chapter 4, you learned how to stack objects to create composite drawings using *layers*. But you don't need layers to place one item on top of another. You can overlap two or more objects on the same layer—as long as you don't need to tween them separately. The instant you create two or more overlapping shapes on the stage, though, you need to think about *stacking*, or arranging, those shapes. Stacking tells Flash which shape you want to appear in front of the other.

Note: You can't stack ungrouped objects, which includes any lines and fills you've created in merge drawing mode. See the box on page 193 for details.

In Figure 5-31, for example, you see three shapes: a rectangle, a circle, and a star. The shapes were created in that order, so Flash stacks them one on top of the other with the rectangle first, then the circle on top of the rectangle, and the star at the top of the stack. Flash keeps track of the stacking order even if the shapes aren't overlapping each other. So, when you drag the rectangle and drop it on top of the star, Flash displays the rectangle *behind* the star. Then, when you drag the circle and drop it on top of both the rectangle and the star, Flash displays the circle *behind* the star, but in front of the rectangle, as shown in Figure 5-30. If that's the effect you want, great; if not, you can change the stacking order of all three shapes.

To stack objects on the stage:

1. **Select the object you want to rearrange (either to push behind or pull in front of another object).**

   In Figure 5-30, the circle's selected.

2. **Choose Modify → Arrange, and then, from the pop-up menu that appears, change the object's stacking order.**

   Here are your options:

   • **Bring to Front.** Pulls the selected object all the way forward until it's on top of all the other objects.

   • **Bring Forward.** Pulls the selected object forward one position, in front of just one other object.

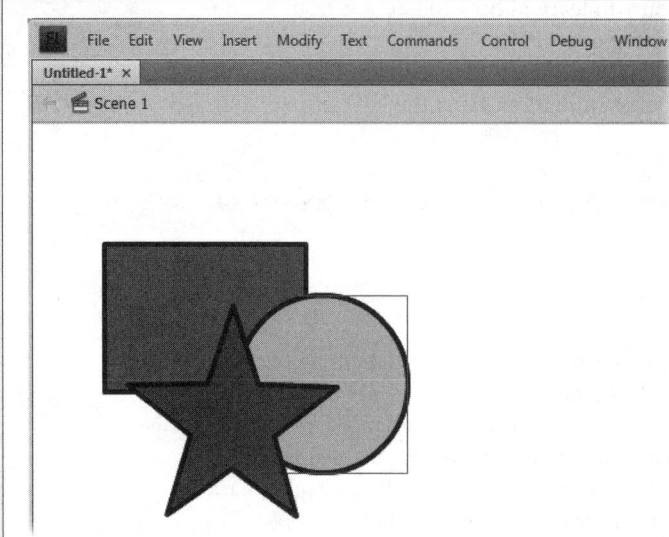

Figure 5-30:
When you create shapes in object mode, Flash puts the first shape on the bottom of the stack and each new shape is placed on top of the stack. Ungrouped objects are an exception to the rule. Ungrouped objects are always placed behind the other objects. See the box on page 193 for more details.

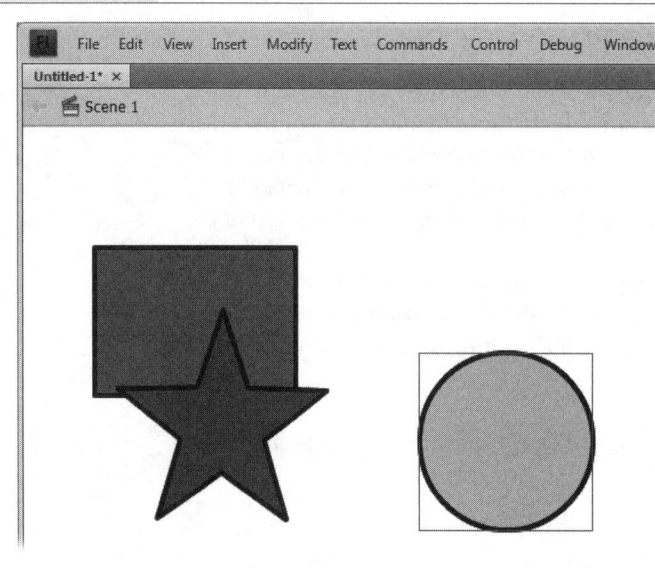

Figure 5-31:
Stacking isn't an issue when your objects don't touch each other. The instant you drag one object on top of another, though, you have to decide which object you want to appear on top, and which behind.

- **Send Backward.** Pushes the object back one position, behind just one other object.

- **Send to Back.** Pushes the selected object all the way back, until it's behind all the other stacked objects.

Tip: To quickly move a selected object forward and backward, use Ctrl+Up or Ctrl+Down (⌘-Up and ⌘-Down on a Mac). Shift+Ctrl+Up (Shift-Option-Up) brings the selected object all the way to the front and Shift+Ctrl+Down (Shift-Option-Down) sends it all the way to the back.

Figure 5-32 shows you an example of choosing Bring Forward with the circle selected.

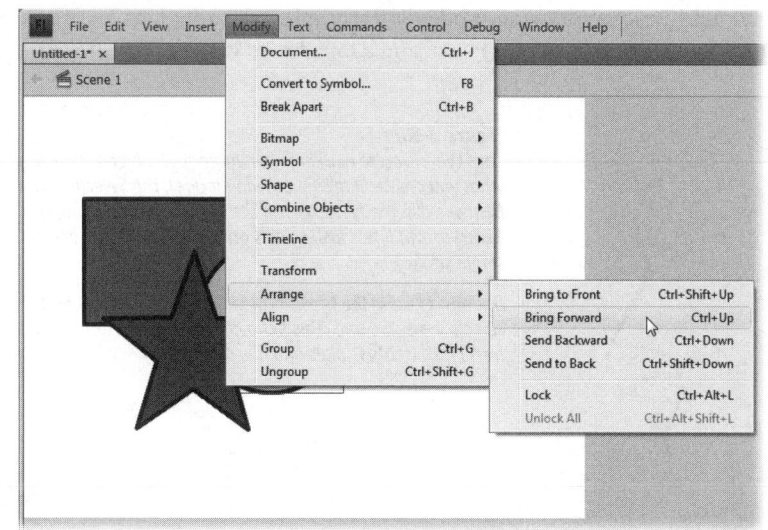

Figure 5-32:
To restack an object, you need to select it first. Here, you see the circle selected. Choosing Bring Forward will bring the circle forward one position, placing it on top of the star. The "Bring to Front" and "Send to Back" commands give you a quick way to move objects to the top or bottom of the stack.

WORKAROUND WORKSHOP

Safety in Groups

If you plan to move your graphic elements around a lot—stack them, unstack them, and reposition them on the stage—make sure you create them in object drawing mode (page 57), which tells Flash to group each object individually. If you want to stick with merge drawing mode (because it's the only way Flash let you draw pre-Version 8 and you're used to it, for example), draw your objects on a fresh, clean corner of the stage, and then group them individually yourself.

Here's why. Say you're working in merge drawing mode and you create a rectangle on the stage using Flash's Rectangle drawing tool. What you've really created are two separate animals: a rectangular fill, and a rectangular outline, or stroke. If you want to select the entire rectangle, outline and all, you need to drag the Selection tool to surround the entire rectangle—which is a problem if you didn't draw your rectangle on a fresh part of the stage and your rectangle happens to be sitting on top of another shape.

Selection is no problem, you say? Well, try dragging your selected (ungrouped) rectangle and dropping it onto another ungrouped shape, like a circle. When you go to move the circle, you see that it's no longer a circle at all: Flash has taken a pair of scissors to it.

Here's one last reason to group your objects before you begin rearranging or moving them: Flash uses a different automatic stacking order depending on the type of objects you drag on top of each other. Whichever way Flash stacks your objects, you can change the stacking order to suit yourself—with one exception. *Flash doesn't let you place an ungrouped object on top of a grouped object or a symbol—no way, no how.*

If you need to place an ungrouped object on top of a grouped object (or on top of a symbol), either group the ungrouped object, and then restack it (to group a selected object, choose Modify → Group), or move the ungrouped object to a separate layer (page 148).

Converting Strokes to Fills

As you saw in Chapter 2 (page 62), Flash treats lines and fills differently when you're working in merge drawing mode. For example, take a look at Figure 5-33, which shows a line drawn with the Pencil and a line drawn with the Brush.

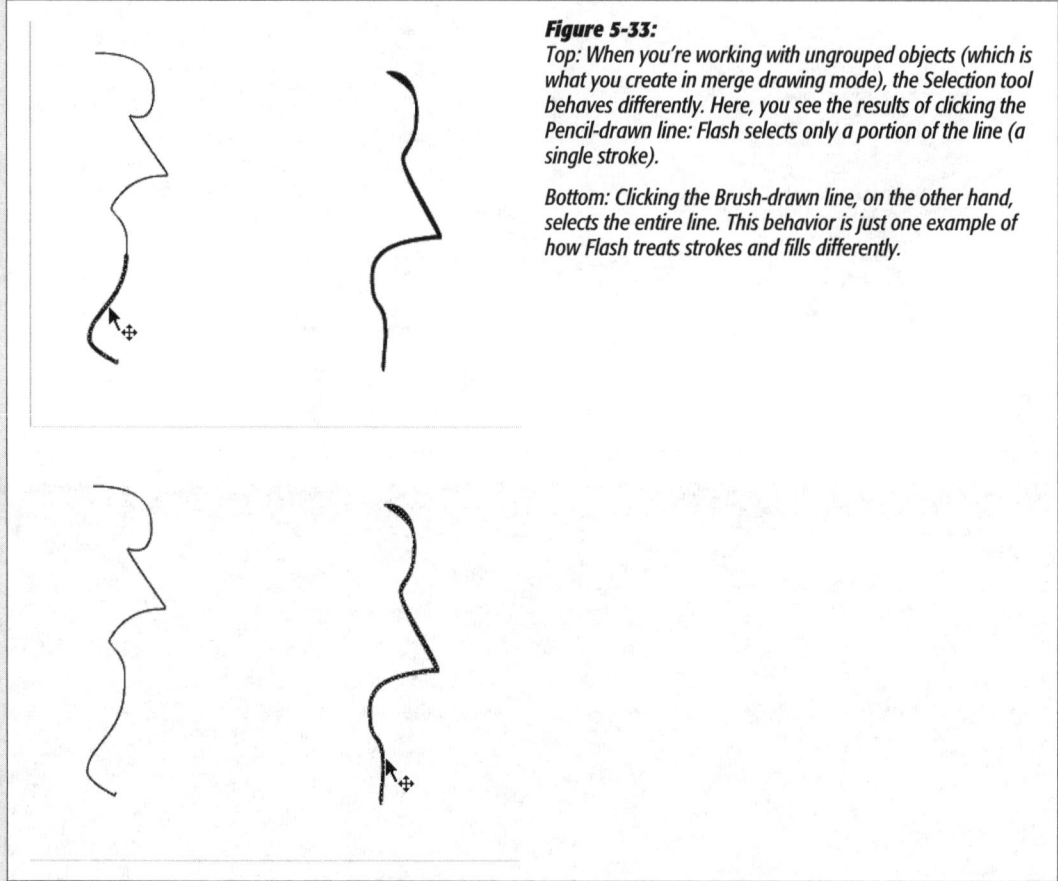

Figure 5-33:
Top: When you're working with ungrouped objects (which is what you create in merge drawing mode), the Selection tool behaves differently. Here, you see the results of clicking the Pencil-drawn line: Flash selects only a portion of the line (a single stroke).

Bottom: Clicking the Brush-drawn line, on the other hand, selects the entire line. This behavior is just one example of how Flash treats strokes and fills differently.

If you click the Selection tool, and then click to select the Pencil-drawn line, Flash highlights just one stroke of the line. But performing the very same operation on the similar-looking Brush-drawn line selects the *entire* Brush-drawn line.

When you convert a line into a fill, Flash lets you interact with the line just as you would with any other fill. This technique is especially useful when you're working with shapes, no matter which drawing mode you're using. That's because when you create a shape using one of Flash's shape tools—a star, say, or a circle—Flash actually creates two separate elements: the inside of the shape (a fill), and the outline of the shape (a stroke). If you want to change the color of the entire shape, you need to use two tools: the Paint Bucket tool (which lets you change the color of fills), and the Ink Bottle tool (which lets you change the color of strokes, or add a stroke to an existing fill). When you convert the outline to a fill, Flash lets you manipulate both the outside and the inside of the shape in the same way using the same tools. Converting also lets you create scalable shapes (images that shrink evenly) and nice straight corners (thick strokes appear rounded at the corners; thick fills shaped like lines don't).

To convert a line into a fill:

1. **Select the line (or outline) you want to convert into a fill.**

   Flash highlights the selected line.

2. **Choose Modify → Shape → Convert Lines to Fills.**

   Flash redisplays the line as a fill, and the Properties panel changes to display fill-related properties (as opposed to line-related properties).

Aligning Objects

In Chapter 2 (page 55), you saw how to use Flash's grid, guides, and rulers to help you eyeball the position of objects as you drag them around on the stage. You also see how to use the Alignment panel to line up objects with respect to each other or to one of the edges of the stage.

Both these approaches are useful—but Flash doesn't stop there. Snapping and guide layers give you even more control over where you place your objects with respect to each other on the stage.

Snapping

Snapping is one of those features you're going to either love or hate. When you turn snapping on, you tell Flash to help you out when you're moving an object around by giving you a visual cue when you start to get too close to (or actually touch) a gridline, a guideline, or another object.

For example, in Figure 5-34, you see a circle being dragged across the stage. Because Snap Align is turned on, Flash displays a faint dotted line (top) when the circle is dragged within range of the other object on the stage (in this case, a bitmap image). And because Snap to Objects is turned on, Flash displays a thick "O" at the very center of the object as it's dragged over the edge of the bitmap (Figure 5-34, bottom).

Tip: For snapping to work, you can't speed around the stage; if you do, you'll miss Flash's cues. Instead, drag your objects slowly.

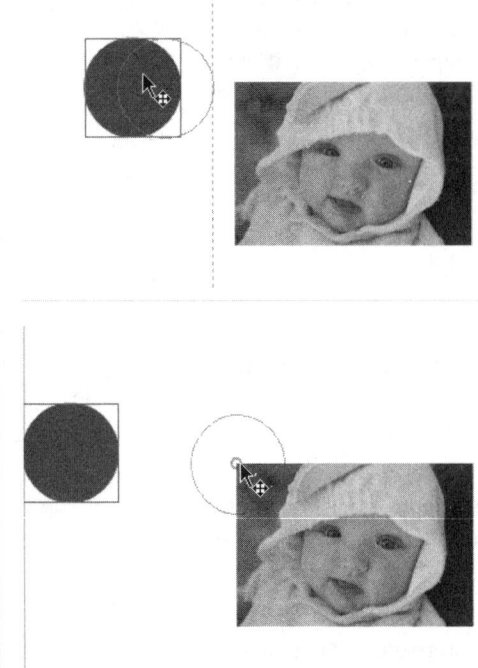

Figure 5-34:
Top: When you turn on snapping, Flash gives you a visual cue when you drag one object close to another object: a gridline or a guideline. Here, Snap Align is turned on, so Flash displays a dotted line when the circle is dragged near the bitmap. You tell Flash how close is close enough using the Horizontal and Vertical Object Spacing fields of the Edit Snapping window, which you display by choosing View → Snapping → Edit Snapping, and then, in the Edit Snapping window that appears, clicking Advanced.

Bottom: In this example, Snap to Objects is turned on too, so if you continue dragging past the dotted line, you see another helpful hint: Flash displays a circle when you center the circle directly over the bitmap's edge.

To turn on snapping, select View → Snapping, and then, from the shortcut menu that appears, choose one of the following:

- **Snap Align.** Displays a dotted line when you drag an object within a certain number of pixels (you see how to change this number in the box on the next page) of another object or of any edge of the stage.

- **Snap to Grid.** Displays a small, thick circle in the middle of your object when you drag that object close to a gridline (page 56).

- **Snap to Guides.** Displays a small, thick circle in the middle of your object when you drag that object close to a guideline (page 56).

- **Snap to Pixels.** Useful only if you want to work at the single-pixel level (your stage has to be magnified to at least 400% for this option to work), this option prevents you from moving an object in any increment less than a whole pixel. (To magnify your stage by 400%, select View → Magnification → 400%; when you do, a single-pixel grid appears.)

- **Snap to Objects.** Displays a small, thick circle in the middle of your object when you drag that object close to another object on the stage.

The next time you move an object on the stage, Flash displays the snapping behavior you chose.

Guide layers

If you've ever traced a drawing onto a piece of onionskin paper, you understand the usefulness of guide layers in Flash.

A *guide layer* is a special kind of layer that doesn't appear in your finished animation, but that you can hold beneath your stage while you're drawing to help you position objects on the stage. Say, for example, you want to align objects in a perfect circle, or on a perfect diagonal, or you want to arrange them so that they match a specific background (say, an ocean scene). You create a guide layer and, on it, draw your circle or diagonal or ocean scene. Then, when you create your "real" layer, your guide layer shows through so you can position your objects the way you want them. When you go to run your animation, though, you don't see your guide layer at all; it appears only when you're editing on the stage.

FREQUENTLY ASKED QUESTION

Object Snapping: How Close Is Too Close?

Everybody says Snap Align is so great, but I'm not sure why I'd use it or how close I should set the snapping range.

Whether or not you'll find Snap Align useful depends entirely on you (some folks prefer to freewheel it, while others appreciate hints and advice) and what you're trying to create on the stage. Snap Align is most useful in situations where you're trying to custom-position objects down to the pixel. For example, say you've drawn a row of different-sized flowers, and you're trying to position a row of bees, one bee at a time, exactly 25 pixels above the flowers. You can use the Align panel for a lot of basic alignment tasks, but this kind of custom alignment isn't one of them: Snap Align's your best option.

Initially, the Flash has all the Snap Align settings set to 0. To change either of these buffer zones:

1. Choose View → Snapping → Edit Snapping. The Edit Snapping window appears as shown in Figure 5-35.

2. In the Edit Snapping window, click Advanced to display expanded Edit Snapping options.

In the Object Spacing fields, type the buffer zone you want in pixels (you can specify both horizontal and vertical). For example, under Object Spacing, if you type *20 px* in the Horizontal and Vertical boxes, the edge of one object will snap to the edge of another when they're within 20 pixels of each other.

Note: Technically speaking, a guide layer is a motion guide layer (just without the motion). You learned more about motion guide layers in Chapter 3.

To create a guide layer:

1. **On the stage, draw your guide shapes, lines, or images.**

   In Figure 5-36 (top), the guide's a diagonal line.

2. **Position your cursor over the name of the layer you want to turn into a guide layer, and then right-click.**

   Flash displays a pop-up menu.

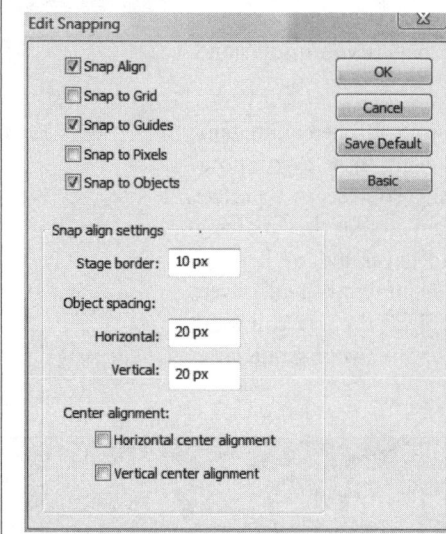

3. **From the pop-up menu, select Guide.**

   Flash displays a little T-square just before the layer name, as in Figure 5-36 (bottom).

4. **With the guide layer still selected, create a new, regular layer for your objects by choosing Insert → Timeline → Layer.**

   Flash creates a new layer and places it above the guide layer, as in Figure 5-36.

Tip: Working with layers—especially guide layers—can be confusing if you're not used to it (and, frankly, it can be confusing even if you *are* used to it, especially if you're working with a lot of layers). To make sure you don't inadvertently modify your guide layer, you can *lock* it (tell Flash not to let you edit it temporarily). To lock your guide layer, click to select it, and then turn on the checkbox beneath the Lock/Unlock icon. The dot changes to a padlock. Then, when you click to select your regular layer, you can align away without worrying about accidentally changing your (locked) guide layer.

---

5. **Select View → Snapping, and then, in the context menu that appears, turn on the checkbox next to "Snap to Objects". You've turned snapping on.**

   Turning snapping on helps you position your objects on your guide layer.

6. **With the regular layer selected, draw your objects.**

   You can then drag each object to your guideline (or guide object, or guide background), as shown in Figure 5-37.

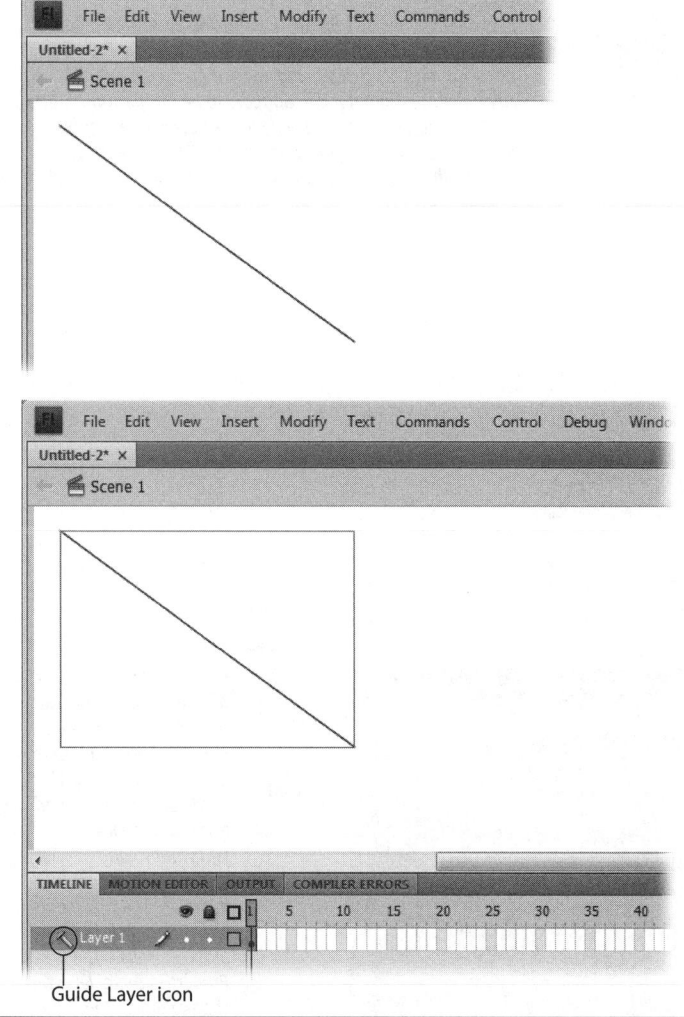

Figure 5-36:
Top: First, draw your guide. You can import a bitmap (useful if you want to display a background image as your guide) or use any of Flash's drawing tools. Here, the guide's a simple diagonal line.

Bottom: To tell Flash that this layer's going to be a special, only-see-it-while-you're-editing guide layer, right-click the layer name, and then, from the menu that appears, select Guide. After you do, Flash designates a guide layer by displaying the little T-square icon in front of the layer name (here, Layer 1).

Guide Layer icon

Adding Text to Your Drawing

Just as Flash has tools for adding shapes and lines to your drawings, it also has a tool specifically designed to let you add text to your drawings—the Text tool.

To use the Text tool:

1. **In the Tools panel, select the Text tool (Figure 5-38, top).**

    Flash highlights the Text tool; when you mouse over to the stage, your cursor changes to crosshairs accompanied by a miniature letter "T".

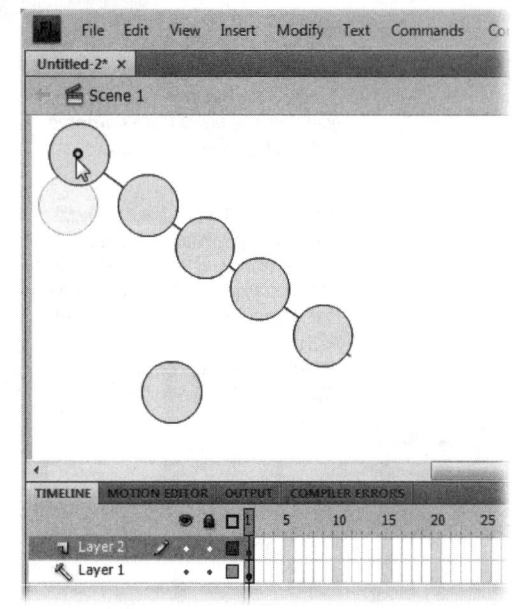

Figure 5-37:
Flash designates a "regular" layer using an icon of a little page turning. Guide layers have a T-square icon. Here you see a handful of circles being aligned on the diagonal. Although the diagonal line appears to be on the same stage as the circles, it's not; it's safely tucked away in the guide layer. When you run your animation, all you see are your objects; the guide layer doesn't appear at all in your finished animation.

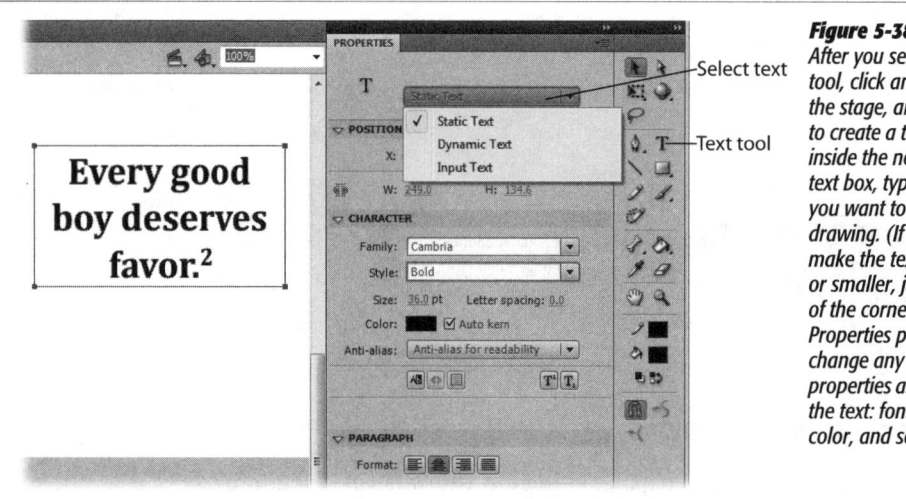

Figure 5-38:
After you select the Text tool, click anywhere on the stage, and then drag to create a text box. Then, inside the newly created text box, type the text you want to add to your drawing. (If you want to make the text box bigger or smaller, just drag one of the corners.) The Properties panel lets you change any of the properties associated with the text: font size, style, color, and so on.

2. **Click the stage where you want your text to begin.**

   Flash displays a squished-up empty text box, and the Properties panel displays text-related properties.

3. **Drag the box a few inches.**

   Flash widens the text box.

4. **If you like, in the Properties panel, change the font size, color, or any other font-related properties.**

Use one of the several subpanels like: Position and Size, Character, Paragraph, Options, and Filters (Figure 5-39) to fine-tune your text:

- **Text Type (Static, Dynamic, Input).** *Static text* is the text you add directly to your drawing, as shown in Figure 5-38; *dynamic text* is a placeholder for text that changes when your finished animation plays (for example, the current date or stock prices); *input* text is a text placeholder into which your audience can type text (and which you can then manipulate) when your finished animation runs. Find out more about input and dynamic text in Chapter 16.

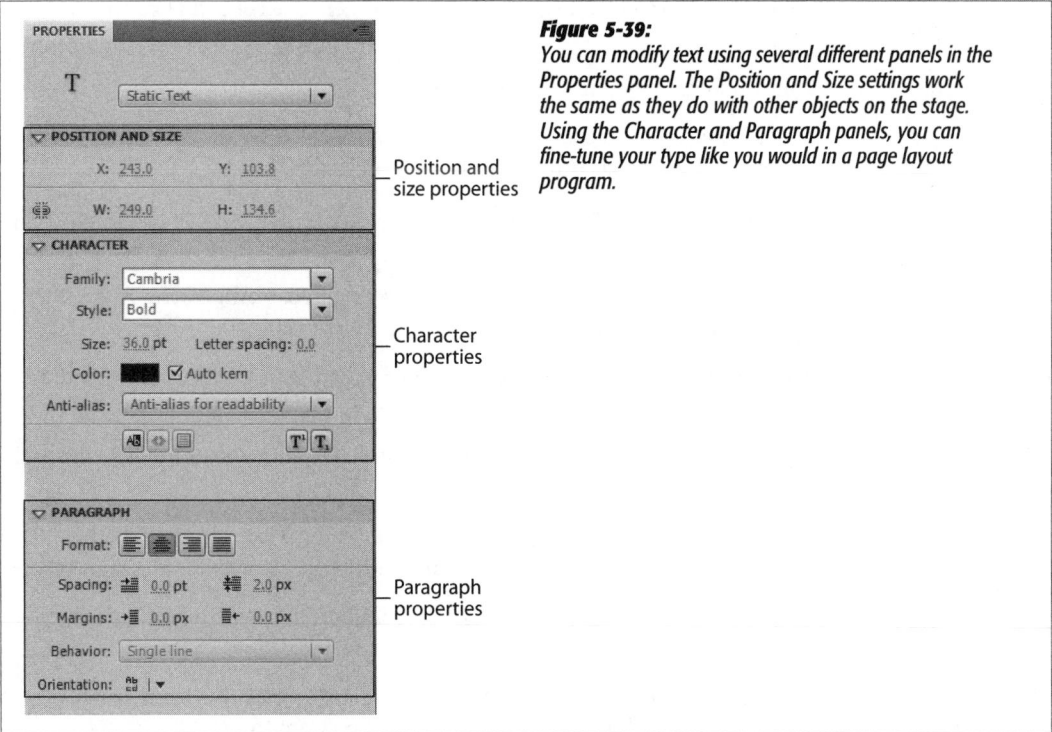

Figure 5-39:
You can modify text using several different panels in the Properties panel. The Position and Size settings work the same as they do with other objects on the stage. Using the Character and Paragraph panels, you can fine-tune your type like you would in a page layout program.

Position and size properties

Character properties

Paragraph properties

- **Position and Size: X and Y.** Type pixels to reposition the text box.

- **Position and Size: W and H.** Type pixels to change the size of the text box.

- **Character: Family.** Click to select from a long list of text fonts.

- **Character: Style:** Select styles like Bold and Italic.

- **Character: Size.** Type or scrub a font size from 8 (super-small) to 96 (gigantic).

- **Character: Letter Spacing.** Drag the slider to squish letters together (or pull them apart), a process called *manual kerning*.

- **Character: Color.** Click the color picker to choose a new color for the text.

- **Character: Auto kern.** Turn on this checkbox to make your font looks as natural as possible. (Turn it off if you prefer to kern manually; see the Letter Spacing option.)

- **Character Position.** Choose from Normal, Superscript (raised slightly), or Subscript (lowered slightly).

- **Character: Anti-alias.** Click to choose from Use Device Fonts, Bitmap Text (No Anti-Alias), Anti-Alias for Animation, Anti-Alias for Readability, and Custom Anti-Alias. Applying one of the first two options to fonts from 12 to 24 points can make the text appear a bit crisper.

- **Character: Selectable.** Click to let your audience select text at runtime.

- **Character: Render text as HTML.** Tells Flash to interpret any HTML code it encounters in dynamic text instead of just displaying it.

- **Character: Show Border Around Text.** Select to place border around dynamic or input text to set it off from other text.

- **Character: Superscript and Subscript.** Select to add superscript or subscript to your text, as in ™.

- **Paragraph: Format.** Click the buttons to choose Align left, Align center, Align right, or Justify.

- **Paragraph: Spacing.** Click and type or scrub in a number for indentation and line spacing.

- **Paragraph: Margins.** Click and type or scrub in a value for left and right margins.

- **Paragraph: Behavior.** For Dynamic and Input Text, choose whether Flash accepts multiple lines, wraps text, and hides text being entered as a password.

- **Edit Format Options.** Click to change indent, line spacing, and margins for your text.

- **Paragraph: Orientation.** Flash assumes Horizontal, but you can click to choose "Vertical, Left to Right" or "Vertical, Right to Left".

- **Options: Link.** Type a URL (like *http:// missingmanuals.com*) to display text in your finished animation as a clickable link.

- **Options: Target.** Used, as it is in HTML, to tell the browser how to open the linked Web page: *_self* (the standard option) opens the page in the current browser window; *_blank* opens the page in a new window; *_parent* opens the page in the parent of the current frame; and *_top* opens the page in the top-level frame of the current window.

5. **In the text box, type the text you want to add to your drawing.**

Flash displays your text based on the properties you set in the Properties panel.

Tip: To change the properties of individual letters, simply select the letters you want to work with, and then, in the Properties panel, make the changes you want. If you want to apply other, non–Properties panel effects to individual letters, though (for example, if you want to skew or flip certain letters and not others, or apply a *gradient*), you first need to break the text apart. To break text, select the text box, and then choose Modify → Break Apart *twice*. (Choosing Modify → Break Apart once breaks text into individual text boxes. Choosing the text a second time turns the text into a fill, in effect turning the text into shapes, so you can no longer edit it as text.)

6. **Click a blank part of the stage to exit text-editing mode.**

   Flash removes the bounding box, and the text properties disappear from the Properties panel. At this point you can move your text, resize it, and reshape it just as you can any other object. To change the text itself, though, you need to double-click the text box to get back into text-editing mode and redisplay the text properties.

Tip: You can apply *filters* (special effects) like Drop Shadow, Blur, and Glow to your text by using the Properties → Filters subpanel. Check out page 258 for details.

Spray Painting Symbols

Instead of simply spraying blobs of color, the Spray Brush tool can spray complex images, by using Symbols as its paint source. Symbols, as you see in Chapter 6, are graphic elements stored in the Library (Window → Library). When you know you're going to use a graphic, a movie clip or a button more than once, you save it as a symbol so you can reuse it to save time later.

The Spray Brush tool takes the concept of reusing a copy of something to an extreme. Suppose you want a sky filled with flashing yellow stars. You can load the Spray Brush tool with a movie clip blinking stars, and then spray them across the horizon. In the Tools panel, the Spray Brush tool is hidden underneath the Brush tool. (You can use the *B* shortcut key to toggle between these two tools.)

Note: For the following steps, you can download the file *spray_brush.fla* from the "Missing CD" page at *http://missingmanuals.com/cds*.

1. **Open the file *spray_brush.fla.***

   The background color of the stage is a nice midnight blue. There are two symbols in the Library: a Graphic called Star and a Movie Clip called BlinkingStar.

2. **In the Tools panel, select the Spray Brush tool, or press B until your cursor changes to the Spray Brush cursor as shown in Figure 5-40.**

   The Spray Brush tool looks like a spray paint can. When the Spray Brush tool is selected, the Properties panel (Window → Properties) shows related settings.

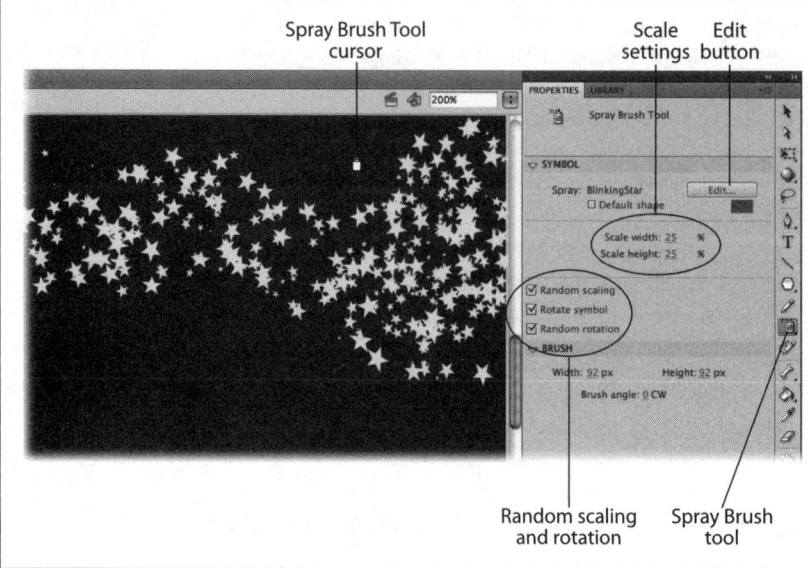

Spray Brush Tool cursor

Scale settings

Edit button

Figure 5-40:
Once the Spray Brush tool is selected the cursor (circled) changes into a spray paint can. Use Edit button in the Properties panel to load the Spray Brush tool with a symbol. Then, use the other property settings to adjust the size and randomize the spray.

Random scaling and rotation

Spray Brush tool

3. Under Properties → Symbol, click the Edit button, and then choose the BlinkingStar symbol.

The Swap Symbol dialog box opens displaying the symbols you can use with the Spray Brush tool.

4. **Select the BlinkingStar symbol, and then click OK.**

The BlinkingStar symbol is loaded in the Spray Brush tool and its name is displayed next to the "Spray:" label.

Tip: If you plan to spray the same symbol frequently, turn on the Default checkbox and it will load automatically when you choose the Spray Brush tool.

5. **In the same Symbol subpanel, set both the "Scale width" and the "Scale height" to 25%.**

Use the "Scale width" and "Scale height" to adjust the size of the symbol as it's sprayed. Often symbols are drawn at a size larger than needed for spraying.

6. **Turn on the checkboxes for "Random scaling," "Rotate symbol," and "Random rotation."**

Starry skies (and many other natural patterns) don't have standard sizes. Using random for these settings creates a much more natural effect for your starry sky.

7. **Click the sky, and then spray in some stars.**

Drag to spray stars across the sky. Hold the mouse button down for as long as you want to create new stars.

Drawing with the Deco Drawing Tool

The Deco Drawing tool lets you draw multiple, complex shapes easily. In that way, it's similar to the Spray Brush tool, described above (page 205). After you select the tool in the Tools panel, the Properties panel shows you the settings and options you use with the tool. Click the drop-down menu in the Drawing Effect subpanel (Figure 5-41), and you see that the Deco Drawing tool is actually three different tools: Vine Fill, Grid Fill, and Symmetry Brush.

- Use **Vine Fill** to create patterns on the stage or a selected symbol. Used on a background, the Vine Fill tool could create wallpaper for an interior scene. Used on a shape, Vine Fill could create the giftwrap for a present. Flash comes loaded with a leafy vine that you can use, as shown in Figure 5-41. Or you can provide your own symbols for the leaf and flower parts of the vine.

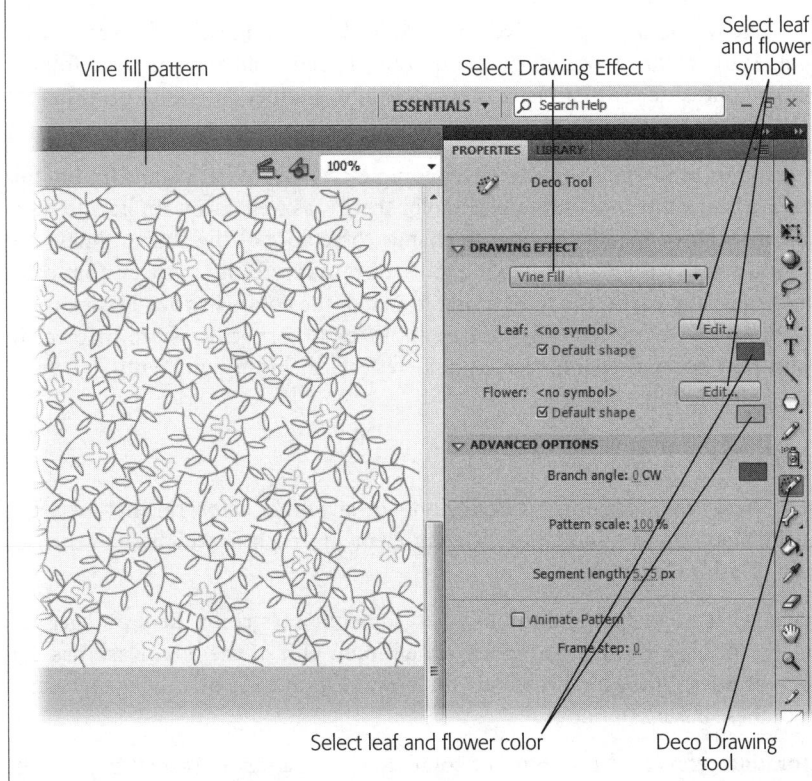

Vine fill pattern   Select Drawing Effect   Select leaf and flower symbol

Select leaf and flower color   Deco Drawing tool

Figure 5-41:
The Deco Drawing tool creates three different drawing effects chosen by the drop-down menu in the Properties panel. Here you see the Vine Fill effect and the options that let you select symbol patterns and colors to create interconnected vine patterns.

- Use the **Grid Fill** effect to create a repeating effect that's more uniform than the Vine Fill. For example, you could use your company logo as the symbol and apply the Grid Fill effect to a background layer in your animation. Then you can adjust the Alpha (transparency) to soften its appearance and make the logo fade into the background, giving text or images in other layers precedence.

- Use **Symmetry Brush** to arrange symbols symmetrically around a central point. If you've ever seen a Busby Berkeley movie with all those symmetrical dancers, you have an idea of the kaleidoscope effects you can create with symmetry. If you're not feeling quite so Hollywood, you can use the Symmetry Brush tool to create clocks, speedometers, or other circular gauges. As with the Vine Fill and Grid Fill tools, you can load the Symmetry Brush with any symbol. If you want to experiment and don't have a shape handy, use the preset rectangle to create patterns. When you drag on the stage, the Symmetry Brush creates multiple images using the loaded symbol. Use the drop-down menu in the Advanced subpanel to select a pattern. The options include: Rotate Around Point, Reflect Across Line, Reflect Around Point, and Grid Translation. Select the Test Collisions button to keep symbols from overlapping.

Advanced Color and Fills

Color is one of the most primitive and powerful communicative devices at your disposal. With color, a skillful animator can engender anxiety or peacefulness, hunger or confusion. She can jar, confuse, delight, soothe, entertain, or inform—all without saying a word.

Color theory is too large a topic to cover completely here. What you *do* find in this chapter is a quick introduction to basic color theory, as well as tips on how to work with color in Flash. You'll see how to change the colors of the shapes, lines, and images you create with Flash's drawing tools; how to create and reuse custom color palettes (especially useful if you're trying to match the colors in your Flash animation to those of a corporate logo, for example, or to a specific photo or piece of art); and how to apply sophisticated color effects including gradients, transparency, and bitmap fills.

Color Basics

The red you see in a nice, juicy watermelon—or any other color, for that matter—is actually made up of a bunch of different elements, each of which you can control using Flash's Color panel:

- **Hue** is what most people think of when someone says color. Red, orange, yellow, green, blue, indigo, and violet are all hues. Out of the box, Flash has 216 different hues. You can also blend your own custom hues by mixing any number of these basic 216 hues.

- **Saturation** refers to the amount of color (hue) you apply to something. A light wash of red, for example, looks pink; pile on more of the same color and you get a rich, vibrant red.

- **Brightness** determines how much of any given color you can actually see. A lot of light washes out a color; too little light, and the color begins to look muddy. At either end of the spectrum, you have pitch black (no light at all) and white (so much light that light is all you can see). In between these two extremes, adding light to a hue creates a tint. For example, if you add enough light to a rich strawberry-ice-cream pink, you get a delicate pastel pink.

- **Transparency** refers to how much background you can see through a color, from all of it (in which case the color is completely transparent, or invisible) to no background at all (in which case the color is opaque). In Flash, you set the transparency (technically, the opacity) for a color using the Alpha field.

RGB and HSB

Color doesn't exist in a vacuum. The colors you get when you mix pigments aren't the same as the colors you get when you mix different colored lights (which is how a computer monitor works). Artists working in oil paint or pastel use the red-yellow-blue color model, for example, and commercial printers use the cyan-magenta-yellow-black color model. In the world of computer graphics and animation, though, the color model you use is *red-green-blue*, or *RGB*.

This model means that you can tell Flash to display any color imaginable just by telling it precisely how much red, green, and blue to display. But if you don't happen to know how much red, green, and blue makes up, say, a certain shade of lilac, Flash gives you three more ways to specify a particular color:

- **HSB.** You can tell Flash the hue, saturation, and brightness you want it to display.

- **Hexadecimal.** You can type the hexadecimal number for the color you want Flash to display. Because hexadecimal notation is one of the ways you specify colors in HTML, you can use hexadecimal numbers to match a Web page color precisely to a color in Flash.

- **Selection.** In the Color panel, you can drag your cursor around on the Color Picker (Figure 5-34) until you find a color you like. This option's the easiest, of course, and the best part is, after you decide on a color, Flash tells you the color's RGB, HSB, and hexadecimal numbers (all of which come in handy if you want to recreate the color precisely, either in another Flash animation or in another graphics program altogether).

In the next section, you see how to specify a custom color using Flash's Color panel.

Creating Custom Colors

Out of the box, Flash has 216 Web-safe colors. But if you can't find the precise shade you want among those 216 colors, you're free to mix and match your own custom colors using Flash's Color panel.

Here's how:

1. **Select Window → Color.**

   The Color panel shown in Figure 5-42 appears with the Color tab selected.

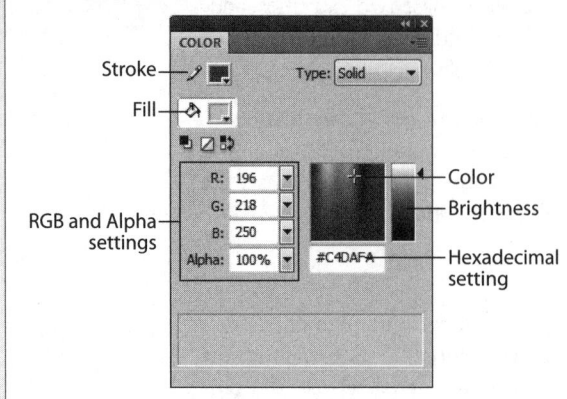

Stroke

Fill

RGB and Alpha
settings

Color

Brightness

Hexadecimal
setting

Figure 5-42:
Flash packs a lot of power into the tiny Color tab. But most of the time, you can safely ignore everything except the Stroke and Fill icons (one of which you need to choose before you begin working with the Color tab) and the Color and Brightness windows, which you use to select a custom color. Out of the box, Flash lets you specify red, green and blue values, as shown here; if you'd prefer instead to specify hue, saturation, and brightness, check out Figure 5-43.

2. **On the Color tab, click either the Fill icon or the Stroke icon, depending on whether you plan to apply your custom color to a fill or a stroke.**

   Page 62 gives you the lowdown on the difference between the two.

3. **Select a custom color. You can do this one of four ways:**

   • You can drag around on the Color Picker until you see a color you like in the Preview window (Figure 5-42).

   • If you know them, you can type values for the red, green, and blue color components of the color you want. (See the box on page 213.)

   • You can type a hexadecimal value in the Hexadecimal Color Designator box. (Hexadecimal, or base 16, values can only contain the following digits: 0-9 and A-F. Folks who spend a lot of time writing HTML code are usually comfortable with hex numbers; if you're not one of them, you can safely skip this option.)

   • You can type values for hue, saturation, and brightness. Click the Options menu, and then, from the pop-up menu that appears, turn on the checkbox next to HSB. The Color tab changes to displays fields for Hue, Saturation, and Brightness, as shown in Figure 5-43.

4. **To customize your color even further, you can also specify one of the following:**

   • **Color type.** Choose from Solid (what you want most of the time), Linear (a type of gradient effect described on page 216), Radial (another type of gradient also described on page 216), and Bitmap (lets you color an object using an image rather than a hue, as on page 215).

   • **Transparency (opacity).** You can tell Flash to make your color more or less transparent, so that the images and backgrounds you put behind the color show through (Figure 5-44). Click the arrow next to Alpha, and then drag the slider that appears. Zero percent tells Flash to make your color completely transparent (see-through); 100% tells Flash to make your color completely opaque.

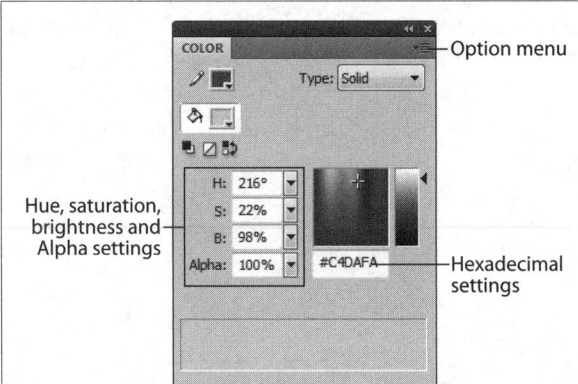

Figure 5-43:
Clicking the Options menu, and then turning on the checkbox next to HSB results in this version of the Color tab, which lets you specify a color by typing in values for hue (in degrees), saturation (as a percentage), and brightness (also as a percentage).

Option menu

Hue, saturation, brightness and Alpha settings

Hexadecimal settings

Tip: Invisible color sounds like an oxymoron, but zero percent opacity actually has a place in your bag of Flash tricks. As you'll see on page 294, you can create a nifty appearing/disappearing effect using see-through color and a shape tween by changing Alpha settings.

- **Brightness.** To tint a color (in other words, to add light, or brightness), click the Brightness window (Figure 5-44), and then drag until you see the exact shade you want in the Preview window.

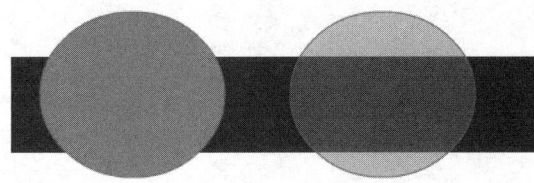

Figure 5-44:
When you use a transparent color, background objects and the stage itself show through, giving the appearance of a different color altogether. Here, the two ovals are actually the same color, but they don't look like it: The selected oval on the right is 50% opaque, while the oval on the left is 100% opaque.

5. **In the Tools panel, select a drawing tool, and then begin drawing on the stage.**

Your strokes (or fills, depending on which icon you selected in step 1) appear in your brand-new custom color.

Tip: You don't have to create a custom color before you draw an object. You can draw an object first, select it, and then create a custom color. When you create a color, Flash automatically changes the object's color to your new custom color.

The Six Commandments of Color

Whether you're using Flash to create an interactive tutorial, an animated art short, a slick advertisement, or something else entirely, you need to be aware of color and how it supports (or detracts from) the message you're trying to get across. Color is at least as important as any other design element, from the fonts and shapes you choose to the placement of those shapes and the frame-by-frame timing of your finished animation.

Although the psychology of color is still in its relative infancy, a few color rules have stood the test of time. Break them at your own risk.

1. **Black text on a white background is popular for a reason**. Any other color combination produces eyestrain after as little as one sentence.

2. **Color is relative**. The human eye perceives color in context, so the same shade of pink looks completely different when you place it next to, say, olive green than it does when you place it next to red, white, or purple.

3. **For most animations, there's no such thing as a Web-safe color**. Web-safe colors—the handful of colors that supposedly appear the same on virtually all computers, whether they're Mac or Windows, laptop or desktop, ancient or new—were an issue in the old days. If you chose a non-Web-safe color palette, your audiences might have seen something different from what you intended (or might have seen nothing at all, depending on how their hardware and software were configured). But time marches on, and any computer newer than a few years old can display the entire range of colors that Flash lets you create. Of course, if you know for a fact that your target audience is running 15-year-old computers (as a lot of folks in other countries and in schools are), or if you suspect they might have configured their monitor settings

to display only a handful of colors (it happens), you should probably play it safe and stick to the Web-safe colors that Flash already has. (To display Web-safe colors, choose Window, and then, in the pop-up menu that appears, turn on the checkbox next to Swatches. In the Swatches panel, click the Options menu, and then, from the pop-up menu that appears, select Web 216. The Swatches tab displays 216 Web-safe colors.)

4. **Contrast is at least as important as color**. Contrast—how different or similar two colors look next to each other—affects not just how your audiences see your animation, but whether or not they can see it at all. Putting two similar colors back-to-back (putting a blue circle on a green flag, for instance, or red text on an orange background) is unbearably hard on your audience's eyes.

5. **Color means different things in different cultures**. In Western cultures, black is the color of mourning; in Eastern cultures, the color associated with death and mourning is white. In some areas of the world, purple signifies royalty; in others, a particular political party; in still others, a specific football team. In color, as in all things Flash, knowing your audience helps you create and deliver an effective message.

6. **You can never completely control the color your audience sees**. Hardware and software calibration, glare from office lighting, the amount of dust on someone's monitor—a lot of factors affect the colors your audience sees. So unless you're creating a Flash animation for a very specific audience and you know precisely what equipment and lighting they'll be using to watch your masterpiece, don't waste a lot of time trying to tune your colors to the nth degree.

Specifying Common RGB Colors

RGB is a funky system based not on the way humans think, but on the way computers think. So the numbers you type in the Color Mixer to describe the red, green, and blue components of a color need aren't in percentages, as you might expect, but instead need to range from 0 (no color at all) to 255 (pure color).

Here are a handful of common colors expressed in RGB terms:

Red	Green	Blue	Result
49800	0	0	Black
503255255	255	255	White
508255255	0	0	Red
51300	255	0	Green
51800	0	255	Blue
523255255	255	0	Yellow
52800	255	255	Cyan
533255255	0	255	Magenta

Specifying Colors for ActionScript

ActionScript is Flash's programming language. As you'll learn in later chapters, you can use ActionScript to automatically perform the same tasks that you do by hand—including specify colors. Suppose you're animation is selling cars. Using ActionScript, you can let your audience change a car's color with the click of a button. ActionScript uses the RGB color system described in the previous section, but identifies individual colors using hexadecimal numbers. *Hexadecimal* numbers are base 16 instead of the base 10 numbers people use. (How's that for a flashback to math class?) The hexadecimal number system uses 16 symbols to represent numbers instead of the usual 0-9. When the common numeric symbols run out, hexadecimal uses letters. So, the complete set of number values looks like this: 0, 1, 2, 3, 4, 5, 6, 7, 8, 9, A, B, C, D, E, F.

Hexadecimal RGB numbers use six places to describe each color. The first two numbers represent shades of the color red, the second two numbers represent shades of the color green and the final two numbers represent shades of the color blue. So a color specification might look this: 0152A0. Or this: 33CCFF. At first, it seems odd to see the letters in numbers, but after a while you get the hang of it. So, the hexadecimal number FF0000 is a bright, pure red, while 0000FF is a bright blue. When you choose a color from a color picker, or Flash's Color panel (Window → Color) as shown in Figure 5-45, you're actually choosing an RGB color, whether you know it or not. Select a color, and then find the hexadecimal number in the box in the lower-right corner.

But you do need to use the hexadecimal notation when you choose colors in ActionScript. You have to write the RGB number into your ActionScript code. Notice that the hexadecimal number in the color picker box is preceded by a pound sign (#), which is one common way to indicate that this is a hexadecimal number. (Not all hexadecimal numbers include letters, so this notation prevents hexadecimal numbers from being confused with regular numbers.) ActionScript code uses another method to indicate that a number is a hexadecimal number. In ActionScript, you precede all color codes with two characters *0x*. So, if you want to use the color red shown in Figure 5-45 in your ActionScript code, you'd specify the color as *0xFF0000*. You'll see plenty of other examples of specifying colors in ActionScript, starting with Chapter 11.

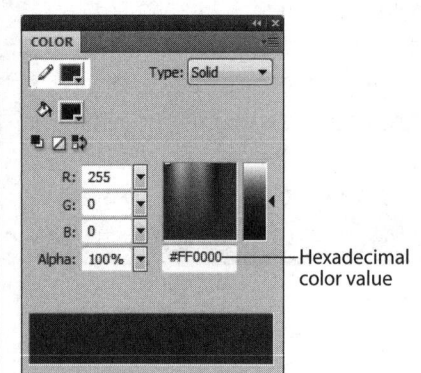

Figure 5-45:
Flash's color pickers display the hexadecimal color value in the box in the lower-right corner. You can use any color picker to look up the hexadecimal value for use in your ActionScript code.

Hexadecimal color value

Saving Color Swatches

After you go to all the hard work of creating a custom color as described in the preceding section, you're probably going to want to save that color as a virtual *swatch* so that you can reuse it again without having to try to remember how you mixed it.

To save a custom color swatch, first create a custom color as described in the preceding section. Then follow these steps:

1. **In the Color panel, select the Swatches tab.**

   (If you don't see the Swatches panel, choose Window, and then, from the drop-down menu that appears, turn on the checkbox next to Swatches.)

   Flash displays the Swatches panel in Figure 5-46.

2. **Move your cursor over the bottom half of the panel, anywhere below the color chart.**

   Your cursor turns into a miniature paint bucket.

3. **Click anywhere below the color chart.**

   Flash adds your new custom swatch to the bottom of the color chart on the left.

After you've saved a custom swatch, you can use it to change the color of a stroke or a fill, as you see in Figure 5-47.

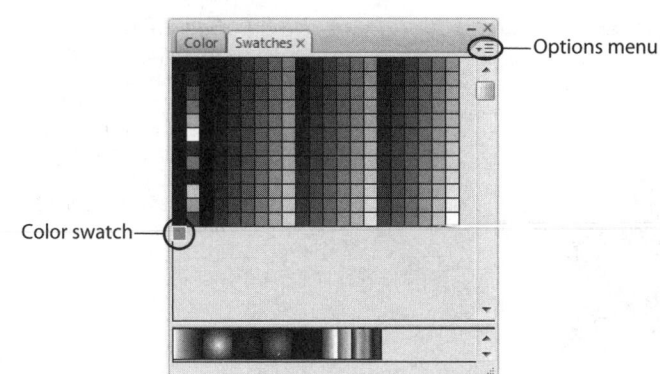

Options menu

Color swatch

Figure 5-46:
*Saving a specific color as a color swatch—
whether it's one you custom-mixed or a
standard color you found on the palette
and liked—is kind of like saving the empty
paint can after you paint your kitchen. The
next time you want to use that particular
color, all you have to do is grab the swatch
(instead of relying on your memory or
spending hours trying to recreate the exact
shade). If you work with color a lot, swatches
can make your life a whole lot easier.*

Tip: If you want to simplify your Swatches panel and remove colors that you don't need, Ctrl-click (⌘-click) any color that you want to remove. Later, if you want to return to the original colors, click the Options menu in the Swatches panel, and then choose Load Default Colors.

Using an Image as a Fill "Color"

Instead of choosing or blending a custom color, you can select an image to use as a fill "color" as shown in Figure 5-47. You can select any image in Flash's Library panel (page 34), or from anywhere on your computer, and apply that image to any size or shape of fill to create some pretty interesting effects.

As you can see in the following pages, the result depends on both the size and shape of the fill and the image you choose.

To use an image as a fill color:

1. **Select all the fills you want to "color."**

    Figure 5-48 shows an example of two fills: a star, and a freeform fill created using the Brush.

2. **In the Color panel, click the arrow next to Type, and then, from the drop-down list that appears, choose Bitmap (Figure 5-48).**

    Flash displays the Import to Library window (Figure 5-49).

Tip: To import additional image files to use as fills: in the Color panel, click the button marked Import. Then, with the fill on the stage selected, click the image you want to use.

3. **In the Import to Library window, select the image file you want, and then click Open.**

    Flash displays the image in the bottom of the Color panel, as well as next to the Fill icon, and "paints" your image with the bitmap. You can apply the bitmap to both fills and strokes as shown in Figure 5-50. If your fill's larger than your image, Flash tiles the image.

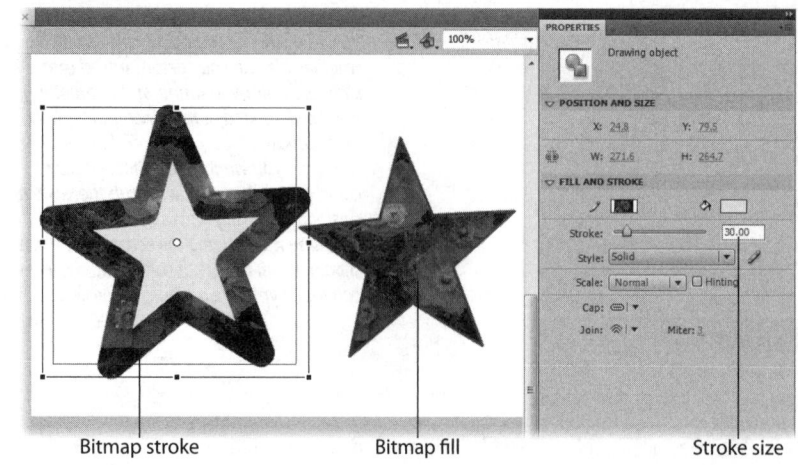

Figure 5-47:
You can apply your bitmap swatch to any shape or object that accepts a fill or stroke. If you're using a bitmap on a stroke, you'll want to set the stroke size to 30 or more.

Bitmap stroke   Bitmap fill   Stroke size

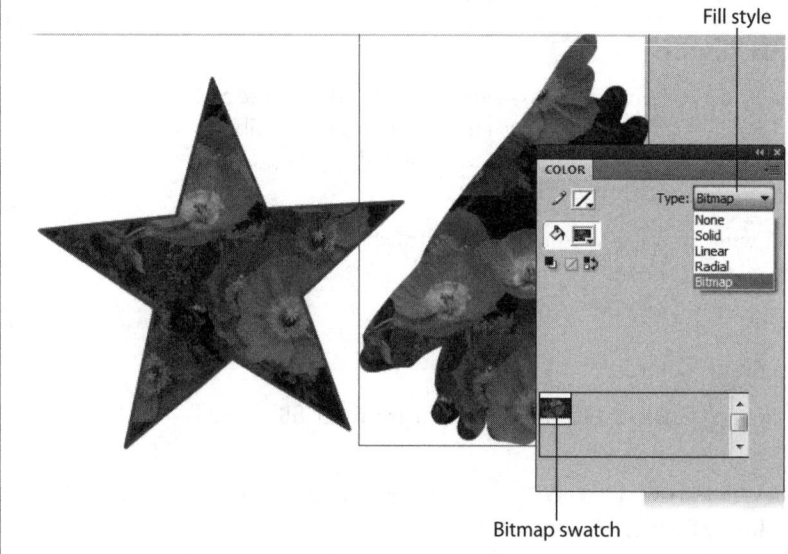

Fill style

Figure 5-48:
Click the Type drop-down menu in the Color panel, and then choose Bitmap to see your bitmap swatches. After you've added a bitmap, it appears as a swatch in your Color panel.

Bitmap swatch

Tip: If you apply the new fill "color" to an image by clicking the Paint Bucket icon, and then clicking the fill, Flash tiles super-tiny versions of the image inside the fill to create a textured pattern effect.

Applying a Gradient

A *gradient* is a fill coloring effect that blends bands of color into each other. Flash has *linear gradients* (straight up-and-down, left-to-right bands of color) and *radial gradients* (bands of color that begin in the center of a circle and radiate outward).

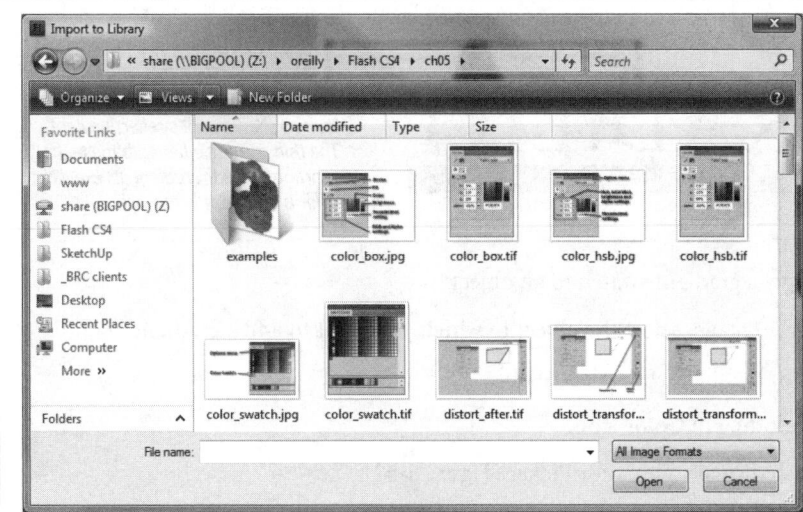

Figure 5-49:
The first time you head to the Color panel and set the Type menu to Bitmap, Flash pops open this Import to Library window. Despite the name (Bitmap), Flash lets you import JPEG and other types of image files; you're not limited to .bmp files. Browse your computer for the image file you want, and then click Open.

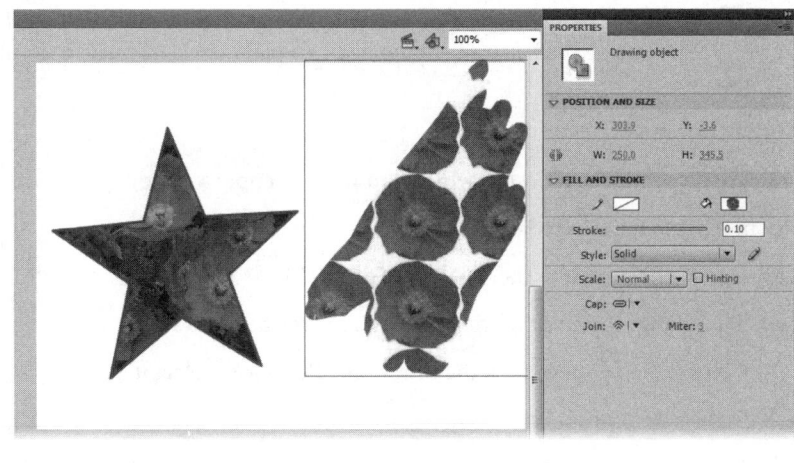

Figure 5-50:
How Flash applies your image to your fill depends on the size of your fill and the size of your image (and whether you select the fill, and then change the Style Type to Bitmap, or vice versa). Here, the star is smaller than the image imported into Flash, so Flash shows a single image framed by the star's outline. Because the freeform fill is larger than the image, Flash tiles the image inside the freeform fill. Note, too, that Flash sticks the image you imported into the Library panel.

By applying a gradient to your fills, you can create the illusion of depth and perspective. For example, you can make a circle look like a sphere, a line that looks like it's fading, and text that looks like it's reflecting light (Figure 5-51).

You can apply a gradient swatch to your fills, or you can create your own custom gradients in Flash, much the same way you create your own custom colors (page 209).

Figure 5-51:
Applying one of the preset radial gradients that Flash provides turns this circle into a ball, and makes this text look so shiny that it's reflecting light. The thin rectangle beneath the text is sporting a linear gradient; its bands of color blend from left to right.

To apply a gradient swatch to an object:

1. **On the stage, select the object to which you want to add a gradient.**

   Flash highlights the selected object.

2. **Click the Fill Color icon.**

   Flash displays the Color Picker (Figure 5-52).

3. **From the Color Picker, choose one of the seven gradient swatches that come with Flash.**

   Flash automatically redisplays your object using the gradient swatch you chose. Figure 5-52 shows a red radial gradient applied to a plain circle to create a simple 3-D effect.

To create a custom gradient:

1. **On the stage, select the object to which you want to apply a custom gradient.**

   Flash highlights the selected object.

2. **Apply a gradient swatch to the object (see page 214).**

   If you like, change the color of the gradient, as described next.

3. **In the Color panel, double-click the first Color Pointer to select it.**

   Flash displays a Color Picker.

4. **In the Color Picker, click to select a color.**

   In your selected object, Flash turns the color at the center (for a radial gradient) or at the very left (for a linear gradient) to the color you chose. Repeat these two steps for each Color Pointer to change the color of each band of color in your gradient.

   If you like, change the thickness and definition of your gradient's color bands, as described next.

5. **In the Color panel, drag the first Color Pointer to the right.**

   The farther to the right you drag it, the more of that color appears in your custom gradient. The farther to the left you drag it, the less of that color appears in your custom gradient. Repeat this step for each band of color in your gradient.

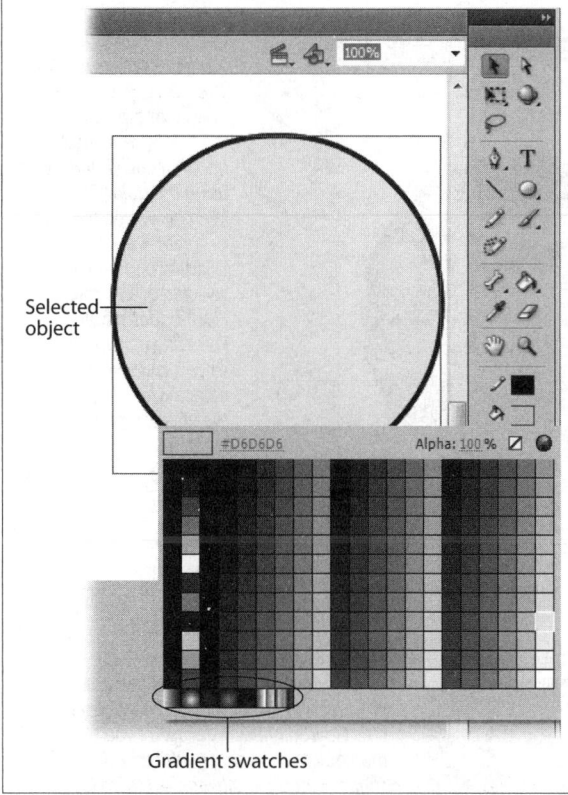

Selected object

#D6D6D6   Alpha: 100 %

Gradient swatches

Figure 5-52:
Applying a gradient swatch is just as easy as applying a color. Flash comes with four radial gradient swatches (white, red, green, and blue) and three linear gradient swatches (white/ black, blue/orange, and rainbow). If one of these creates the effect you want, great. If not, you can change any of them to create your own custom gradient effects, as you see on page 218.

Next, if you like, you can add a new band of color to your custom gradient.

6. **In the Color panel, click anywhere on the Gradient Edit Bar.**

   Flash creates a new Color Pointer (see Figure 5-53), which you can edit as described in step 3. You can add as many Color Pointers (new bands of color) to your gradient as you like.

   For even more excitement, apply one or more *gradient transforms* to your object, as described next.

7. **In the Tools panel, hidden under the Free Transform tool, click the Gradient Transform tool.**

   Flash displays a rotation arrow, a stretch arrow, and a reposition point.

   You can drag the *rotation arrow* to rotate the gradient; drag the *stretch arrow* to stretch the bands of color in your gradient, as shown in Figure 5-54; or drag the *reposition point* to reposition the center of the gradient, also shown in Figure 5-54.

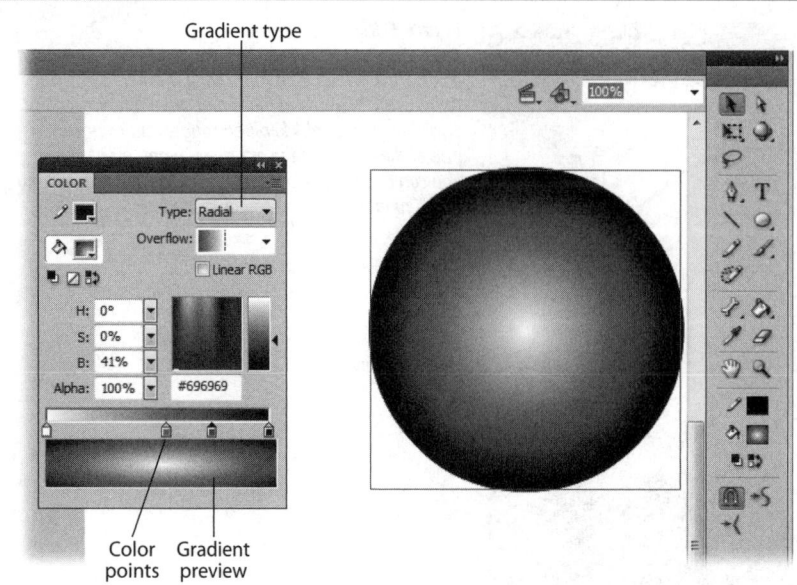

Gradient type

Color points   Gradient preview

Figure 5-53:
Creating a custom gradient is more art than science. As you create new color bands, adjust the colors, and widen and thin each band using the Color Points, keep an eye on the Gradient Preview Window and on your selected object, too; Flash updates both as you edit your gradient, so you can see at a glance whether you like the effects you're creating.

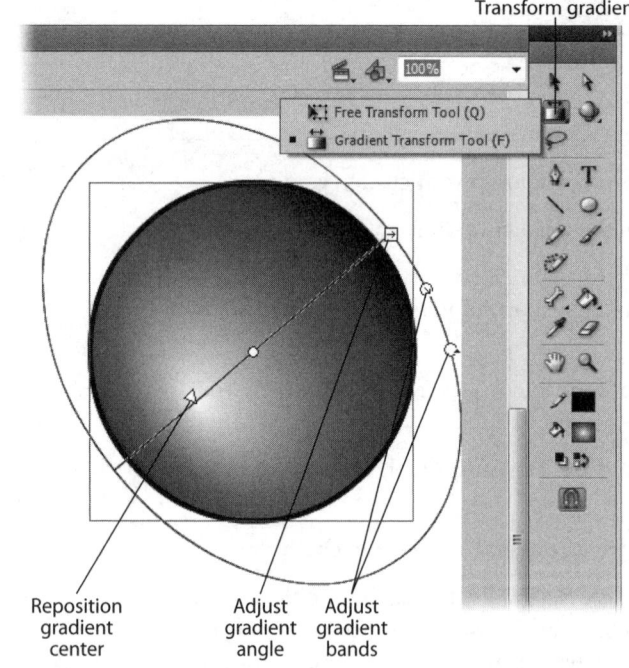

Transform gradient

Reposition gradient center   Adjust gradient angle   Adjust gradient bands

Figure 5-54:
Just as regular transforms let you poke and prod regular images to create interesting effects, gradient transforms let you manipulate gradients (with respect to the shapes you originally applied them to) to create interesting effects. Here, dragging the stretch arrow pulls the bands of color, widening the bands at the center and discarding the bands at the edges. Use the circular rotate control to adjust the gradient angle. Drag the reposition point to move the center of the gradient away from the center of the object. This effect is especially useful for creating the illusion that the object is reflecting light streaming in from a different angle.

Importing a Custom Color Palette

Depending on the type of animation you're creating in Flash, you might find it easier to import a custom color palette than to try to recreate each color you need.

For example, say you're working on a promotional piece for your company, and you want the colors you use in each and every frame of your animation to match the colors your company uses in all its other marketing materials (its brochures, ads, and so on). Rather than eyeball all the other materials or spend time contacting printers and graphics teams to try and track down the RGB values for each color, all you need to do is import a GIF file into Flash that contains all the colors you need: a GIF file showing your company's logo, for example, or some other image containing the colors you need to match.

To import a custom color palette:

1. **In the Swatches panel (Window → Swatches), click the Options menu.**

    A pop-up menu appears.

2. **From the pop-up menu, select Clear Colors.**

    Flash clears out the entire color palette on the Color Swatches tab, leaving just two swatches: black and white (Figure 5-55, right).

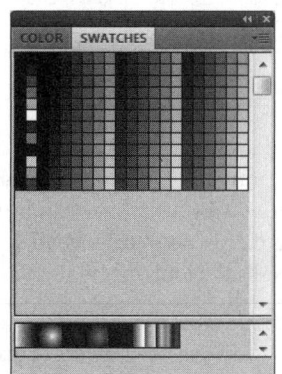 

Figure 5-55:
Left: Here's what the typical Swatches tab looks like before you clear it (by clicking the Options menu, and then selecting Clear Colors). Think twice before you clear the palette: You can get back Flash's basic color palette, but you lose any custom color swatches you've saved in this document.

Right: After you clear the color palette, you're left with just two swatches: black and white.

3. Once again, click the Options menu.

    The pop-up menu reappears.

4. **From the pop-up menu, select Add Colors.**

    Flash displays the Import Color Swatch window.

5. **In the Import Color Swatch window (Figure 5-56), click to choose a GIF file, and then click Open.**

    Flash imports the custom color palette, placing each separate color in its own swatch in the Swatches panel (Figure 5-55, left).

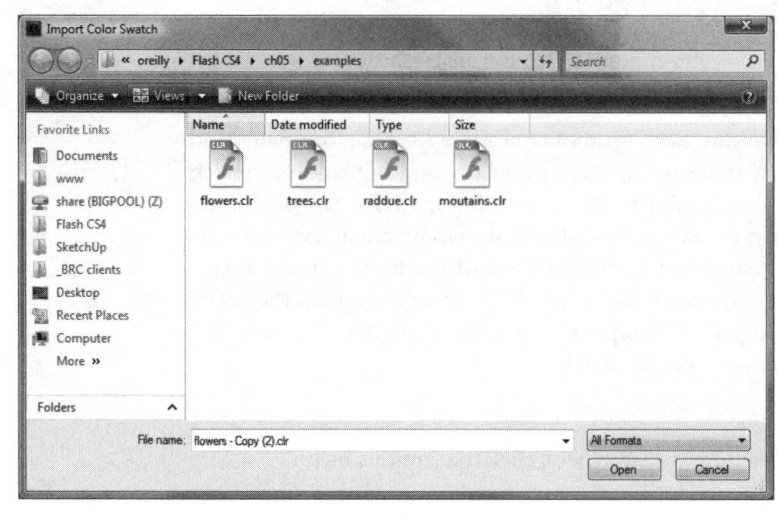

Figure 5-56:
*When you head to the
Swatches panel, click the
Options menu, and then
choose Add Colors to
import a custom color
palette, Flash displays an
Import Color Swatch
window that should look
pretty familiar if you've
ever had occasion to open
a file on a computer. Here,
you click to browse the files
on your computer. When
you find the GIF file
containing your custom
color palette, click Open.
Flash brings you back to
your Color Mixer panel,
where you'll see that Flash
has pulled in each separate
color in your GIF file as a
separate swatch, ready for
you to use.*

Note: To restore the standard Flash color palette: From the Swatches panel, click the Options menu, and then, from the pop-up menu that appears, select Load Default Colors.

Copying Color with the Eyedropper

Tying color elements together is a subtle—but important—element of good design. It's the same principle as accessorizing: Say you buy a white shirt with purple pinstripes. Add a pink tie, and you're a candidate for the Worst Dressed list. But a purple tie that matches the pinstripes somehow pulls the look together.

In Flash, you may find you've created a sketch and colored it just the right shade of green, and you want to use that color in another part of the same drawing. Sure, you could slog through the Color panel, write down the hexadecimal notation for the color and then recreate the color. Or, if you know you're going to be working a lot with that particular color, you could create a custom color swatch (page 214). But if you want to experiment with placing bits of the color here and there on the fly, the Eyedropper tool's the way to go. The Eyedropper tool lets you click the color on one image, and apply it instantly to another color on another image.

Note: The Eyedropper tool lets you transfer color only from a bitmap or a fill to a fill, and from a stroke to another stroke. If you want to transfer color *to* a bitmap, you need the Magic Wand (Lasso).

To copy color from one object to another:

1. **Select Edit → Deselect All.**

   Alternatively, you can press Ctrl+Shift+A (Windows) or Shift-⌘-A (Mac) to deselect everything on the stage.

2. **From the Tools panel, click to select the Eyedropper tool.**

   As you mouse over the stage, your cursor appears as an eyedropper while it's over a blank part of the stage; an eyedropper and a brush when it's over a fill (as shown in Figure 5-57, top); and an eyedropper and a pencil when it's over a stroke.

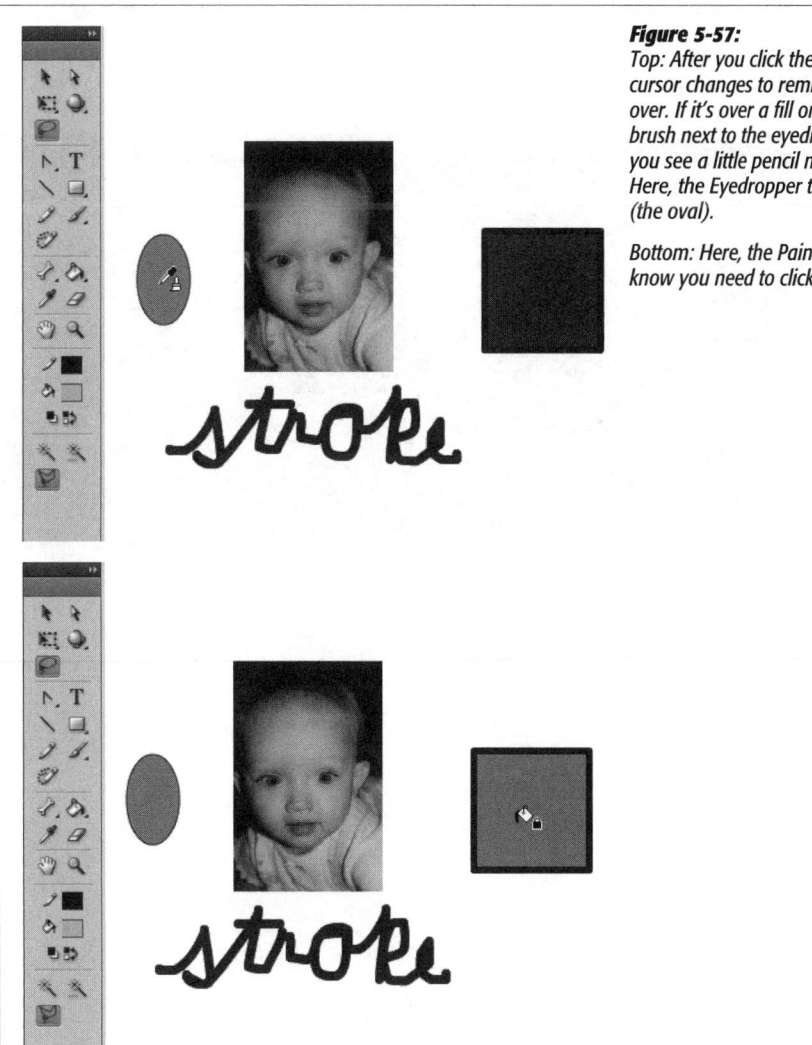

Figure 5-57:
Top: After you click the Eyedropper tool, your cursor changes to remind you what it's passing over. If it's over a fill or a bitmap, you see a little brush next to the eyedropper; it it's over a stroke, you see a little pencil next to the eyedropper. Here, the Eyedropper tool is selecting a fill (the oval).

Bottom: Here, the Paint Bucket icon lets you know you need to click a fill.

3. **Click the bitmap, fill, or stroke color you want to copy from (imagine sucking the color up into your eyedropper).**

   If you click to copy from a fill or a bitmap, your cursor turns immediately into a paint bucket; if you click to copy from a stroke, the cursor turns into an ink bottle.

Note: You can copy from a stroke, a fill, or a bitmap using the Eyedropper tool; you *can't* copy from a symbol or a grouped object.

---

4. **Click the bitmap, fill, or stroke you want to copy to (imagine squeezing the color out of your eyedropper). If you copied color from a bitmap or a fill, you need to click a fill; if you copied color from a stroke, you need to click a stroke.**

   Flash recolors the stroke, fill, or bitmap you click, applying the *from* color to the *to* color as shown in Figure 5-57, bottom.

UP TO SPEED

Kuler: Color Help from the Community

In an office full of designers, water cooler discussion often revolves around color palettes. What color combinations best represent autumn, or the Rocky Mountains, or surfing in Hawaii. Kuler is Adobe's way of providing that kind of designer know-how to everyone (Figure 5-58). Simply put, Kuler is a panel that shows named color combinations with five colors to a palette. Anyone can provide a color palette, even you. All these color combinations are stored online, so when you use Kuler, your computer connects to the Web.

Using the buttons and menus on the Kuler panel you can browse through all the color combinations provided by the Kuler community. You can choose a palette, edit the colors, and then save it under a different name. You can create your own color palettes, and then upload them for others to review and use. If you see the perfect color combination for your project, you can add the palette to your Swatches panel by clicking Add to Swatches.

Create theme

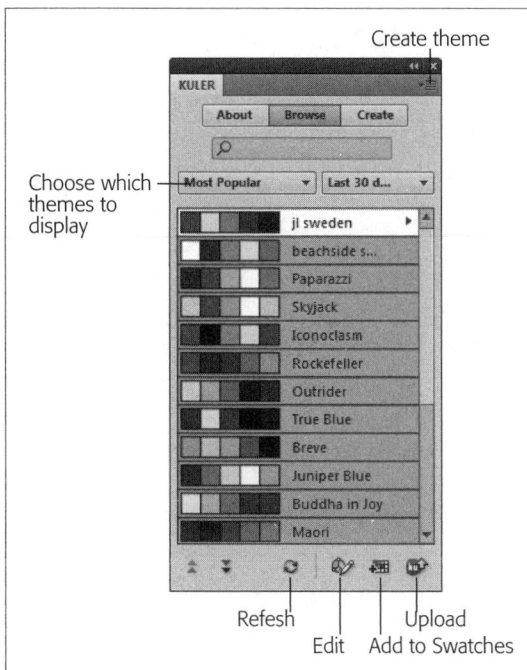

Choose which
themes to
display

Refresh

Edit   Add to Swatches

Upload

Figure 5-58:
When you find a palette that you want to use in your Flash project, click the Add to Swatches button and those colors appear in your Swatches panel. If you want to create your own theme for the Kuler community, click the button in the upper-right corner.

Reusable Flash: Symbols and Templates

The secret to productivity is to work smarter, not harder. And the secret to smart work is to avoid doing the same thing more than once. Flash understands. The program gives you ways to reuse bits and pieces of your animations—everything from simple shapes to complex drawings, multiframe sequences, and even entire animations. Create something once; reuse it as many times as you like.

Reusing animation elements can save you more than just time and effort—Flash lets you store pieces of animation as reusable master copies that can actually whittle the size of your finished animation file. That's great news if you plan to put your animation up on a Web site or shoot it out to handhelds. The smaller your file size, the faster it downloads, which makes *you* less likely to lose your audience to impatience.

Finally, if your work requires you to create animations that are so many variations on a theme, you can save documents as templates. Flash has templates representing many common document sizes like banner ads and cellphone screens so that you don't have to start from scratch. You can also save templates containing the pictures, logos, and other elements that appear in just about all your documents.

Note: Flash gives you two additional reuse options that are useful only in certain situations, and so are covered elsewhere in this book. You can export and import images (and animated clips) that you've created in either Flash or some other program (Chapter 10), and you can use layers to reuse chunks of composite drawings (Chapter 4).

Symbols and Instances

Copying and pasting is the most obvious way to reuse something you've created, but while that time-honored technique saves *time*, it doesn't save *space*. Say, for example, you need to show a swarm of cockroaches in the Flash advertisement you're creating for New and Improved Roach-B-Gone. You draw a single cockroach, then copy and paste it a hundred times. Congratulations: You've got yourself a hundred cockroaches…and one massive Flash document.

Instead, you should take that first cockroach and save it in Flash as a *symbol*. Symbols help keep your animation's finished file size down to a bare minimum. When you create a symbol, Flash stores the information for the symbol, or master copy, in your document as usual. But every time you create a copy (an *instance*) of that symbol, all Flash adds to your file is the little bit of information it needs to keep track of where you positioned that particular instance.

Then, to create the illusion of a swarm, you drag a hundred instances of the symbol onto the stage (and a hundred more for each frame of the animated sequence showing the swarm). Instead of swelling your document with all the kilobytes it would take to draw thousands of individual roaches in your running animation, all Flash has to do is increase your file size by the kilobytes it takes to draw *one* roach (plus a little extra, for the thousands of instances pointing to the one "real" roach). You can even vary the roach instances a little for variety and realism (so important in a pesticide ad) by changing their color, position, size, and even their skew.

If symbols offered only file optimization, they'd be well worth using. But symbols give you two additional benefits:

- **Consistency.** By definition, all the instances of a symbol look pretty much the same. You can change certain instance characteristics—color and position on the stage, for example—but you can't redraw them; Flash simply won't let you. (You can't turn a roach into a ladybug, for example.) For situations where you really need basic consistency among objects, symbols help save you from yourself.

- **Instantaneous update.** You can change an instance without affecting any other instances or the symbol itself. (You can turn one roach light brown, for example, without affecting any of the dark brown roaches.) But when you edit the symbol, Flash automatically updates all the instances of that symbol.

So, for example, say you create a symbol showing the packaging for Roach-B-Gone. You use dozens and dozens of instances of the symbol throughout your animation, and *then* your boss tells you the marketing team has redesigned the packaging. If you'd used copy-and-paste to create all those boxes of Roach-B-Gone, you'd have to find and change each one manually. But with symbols, all you need to do is change the symbol. Flash automatically takes care of updating all the symbol's instances for you.

- **Nesting.** Symbols can contain other symbols. Sticking symbols inside other symbols is called *nesting* symbols, and it's a great way to create unique, complex-looking images for a fraction of the file size you'd need to create them individually. Suppose you've drawn the perfect bug eye. You can turn it into a symbol and place it inside of your symbols for roaches, ladybugs, and any other insect you want.

- Flash lets you create three different types of symbols: graphic symbols, movie clip symbols, and button symbols. As you see in Figure 6-1, Flash stores all three types of symbols in the Library.

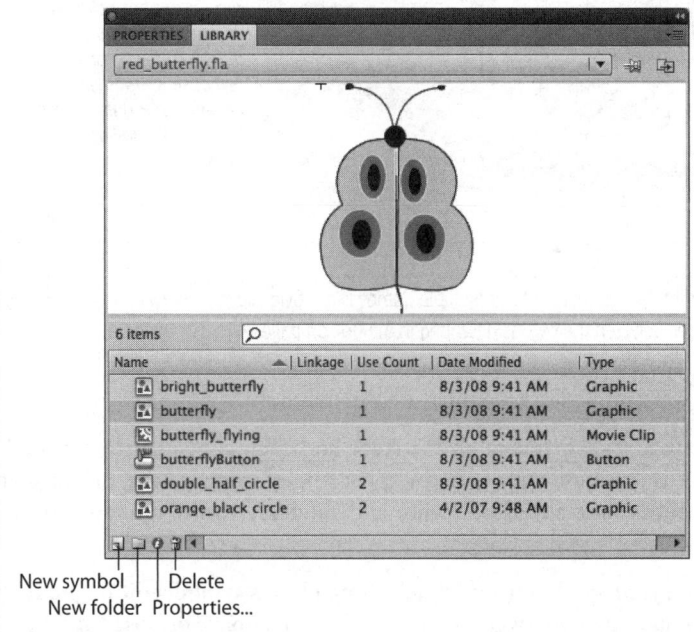

New symbol
New folder Properties...
Delete

Figure 6-1:
The Library is your one-stop shop for symbols. From this panel, you can create symbols, edit them, and drag instances of them onto the stage. Note the icons and descriptions that tell you each symbol's type—graphic, button, or movie clip. If you don't see the Library panel, select Window, and then turn on the checkbox next to Library. To display all the information in the Library panel, move your cursor over the bottom-right corner of the panel until your cursor turns into a diagonal two-headed arrow, and then drag to resize the panel.

Note: The button symbol is nothing more than a specialized form of the movie clip symbol. For example, you can add an instance of a movie clip symbol to a single frame in a button symbol to create a button that plays an animation when you mouse over it. You'll learn how to add this kind of interactivity to your animations in Part 3.

Graphic Symbols

You can tell Flash to turn everything from a simple shape (like a circle or a line) to a complex drawing (like a butterfly) into a symbol. You can also nest graphic symbols. For example, you can combine circle and line symbols to create a nested butterfly symbol (Figure 6-2).

A graphic symbol isn't even limited to a static drawing. You can save a series of frames as a *multiframe* graphic symbol that you can add to other animations.

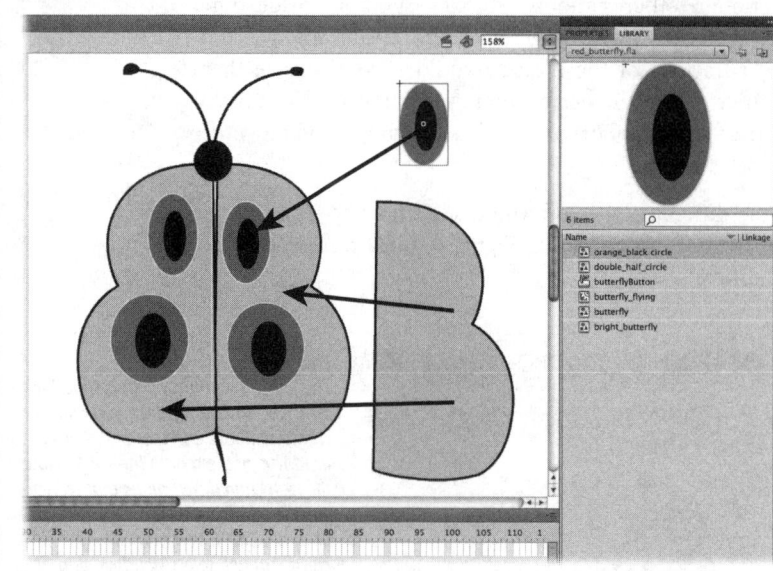

Figure 6-2:
If you're really serious about paring down the size of your animation file, consider nesting your symbols. Here, a couple of basic graphic symbols (double_ half_ circle and orange_ black_circle) combine to form a more complex graphic symbol (bright_ butterfly). Flash lets you flip, resize, and recolor symbol instances, so you can create surprisingly different effects using just a few basic shapes—all while keeping your animation's file size as small as possible.

Note: Another kind of symbol that contains multiple frames is a movie clip symbol (page 247). But there are two big differences between the two, as described in the box on page 231.

Flash gives you two options for creating a graphic symbol:

- **You can create a regular image on the stage and then convert it to a graphic symbol.** This is the best approach for those times when you're drawing an image (or a multiframe animated scene) and suddenly realize it's so good that you want to reuse it.

- **You can create your symbol from scratch using Flash's symbol editing mode.** If you know going in that you want to create a reusable image or series of frames, it's just as easy to create it in symbol editing mode as it is to create it on your main animation's stage and timeline—and you get to save the conversion step.

The following sections show you both approaches.

Converting an existing image to a graphic symbol

If you've already got an image on the stage that you'd like to turn into a symbol, you're in luck: The process is quick and painless.

To convert an existing image on the stage to a graphic symbol:

1. **On the stage, select the image (or images) you want to convert.**

   Flash's selection tools are described on page 60. Converting a grouped or editable image into a graphic symbol is quick and easy. Figure 6-3 shows three separate images selected that, all together, form a star.

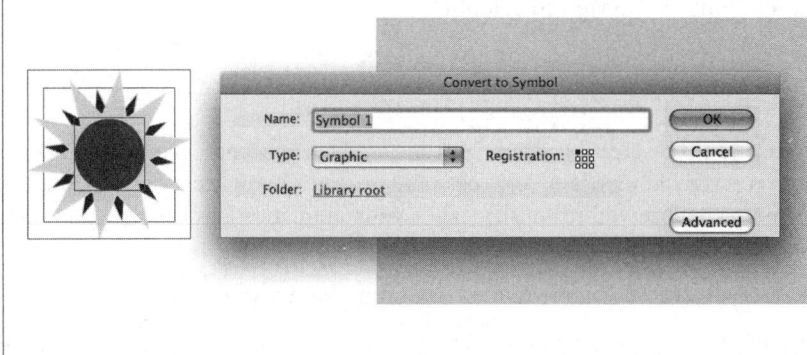

Figure 6-3:
You use the little grid labeled Registration to position the registration point of your symbol. Most of the time, it's fine to leave the registration point in the upper-left corner; see the box on page 234 for the full story. If necessary, you can reposition it later by editing your symbol (page 238).

FREQUENTLY ASKED QUESTION

Multiframe Graphic Symbol vs. Movie Clip

A movie clip symbol is a series of frames, but a graphic symbol can have multiple frames, too. So what's the difference between the two?

Leave it to the Flash development team (the people who let you add motion to a shape tween and manipulate shapes with a motion tween) to refer to a multiframe animation clip as a *graphic* symbol (instead of a movie clip symbol). The truth is, there are some big differences between a multiframe graphic symbol and a movie clip.

- **A multiframe graphic symbol has to match the animation to which you add it, frame for frame.** For example, suppose your main timeline has 20 frames and you add a 15-frame graphic symbol to Frame 1. Frame 1 in the main timeline shows Frame 1 of your graphic symbol. Frame 2 in the main timeline shows Frame 2 of the graphic symbol, and so on. If your main timeline only has five frames, you'd only see five frames of the graphic symbol. A movie clip symbol, on the other hand, *doesn't* have to match the animation you add it to frame by frame because

movie clips have their own timelines. So if you add a 15-frame movie clip symbol to a main timeline with only a single frame, you'll still see all 15 frames of the movie clip symbol. It'll loop until it encounters either a keyframe or an ActionScript statement telling it to stop playing.

- **A multiframe graphic symbol can't include sound or interactivity; a movie clip symbol can.** Movie clip symbols take up just one frame in the main timeline, so you can drop instances of them into button symbols and other movie clip symbols to create interactive nested symbols. Because they're not tied frame-for-frame to the animation you drop them into, they're able to hang fire while your animation plays and spring into action only when an audience member clicks them.

Chapter 10 and Chapter 11 show you how to add sounds and ActionScript actions to your symbols, respectively.

2. **Select Modify → "Convert to Symbol".**

The "Convert to Symbol" dialog box appears.

3. **In the Name text box, type a name for your symbol.**

Because you'll be creating a bunch of instances of this copy over the course of the next several hours, days, or weeks (and because you may end up with dozens of symbols before you're finished with your animation), you want a unique, short, descriptive name.

4. **Set the Type drop-down menu next to Graphic, and then click OK.**

Flash creates the new graphic symbol, places it into the Library, and automatically replaces the selected image on the stage with a selected instance of the symbol (Figure 6-4). Notice the instance's single bounding box (the original three images in this example had three).

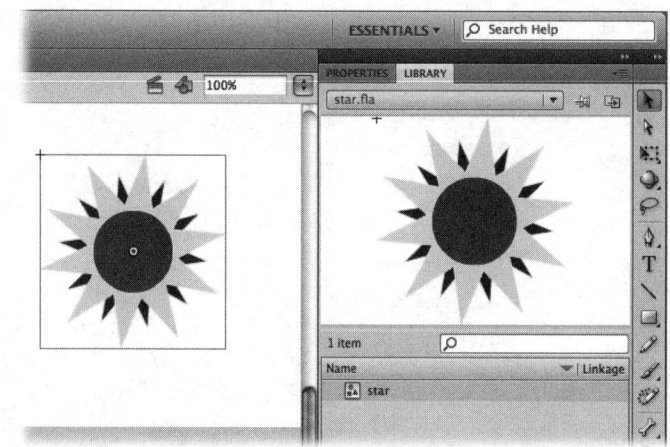

Figure 6-4:
You can tell that Flash has converted your image on the stage to an instance of the newly created symbol in two ways: the cross in the upper-left corner of the instance (the instance's registration point) and the little round circle (the instance's transformation point). Flash uses the transformation point if you decide to transform the instance, as described in Chapter 5. You'll learn more about these points in the box on page 234.

Tip: If you're already poking around the Library panel, you can create a new graphic symbol quickly by clicking the Library panel's New Symbol button (Figure 6-1) or by clicking the Library panel's Options menu, and then, from the pop-up menu that appears, selecting New Symbol. Either way tells Flash to display the Create New Symbol dialog box.

Creating a graphic symbol in symbol editing mode

If you want to create a symbol from scratch without going through the conversion step described above you can use Flash's symbol editor—the same symbol editor you use to edit, or modify, your symbols.

To create a graphic symbol in symbol editing mode:

1. **Select Insert → New Symbol.**

The Create New Symbol dialog box shown in Figure 6-5 (top) appears.

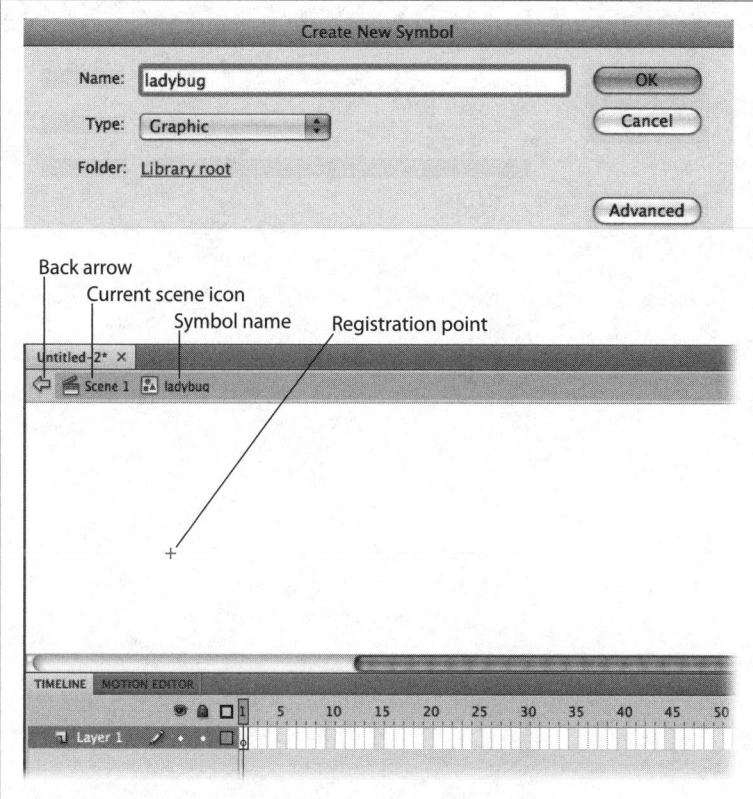

Figure 6-5:
*Top: You use the same Create
New Symbol dialog box to
create a symbol from scratch as
you do to convert an existing
image to a symbol.*

*Bottom: Here, you see the
symbol editing workspace, which
looks deceptively similar to the
regular animation workspace.
The only way you know you're
in symbol editing mode is the
graphic icon and symbol name
(ladybug) in the Edit bar and the
registration point (cross) in the
middle of the symbol editing
stage.*

2. **In the Name text box, type a name for your symbol.**

   Shoot for unique, short, and descriptive.

3. **From the drop-down menu choose Graphic, and then click OK.**

   Flash displays the symbol editing workspace shown in Figure 6-5 (bottom). The
   symbol editing workspace looks very much like an animation workspace, even
   down to the background color. The key differences to look for that tell you
   you're in symbol editing mode:

   • The name of the symbol you're currently editing appears in the Edit bar. To
     see the Edit bar, select Window → Toolbars, and then turn on the checkbox
     next to Edit Bar. There's no "stage" when you're editing symbols, so you
     won't see any backstage work area either.

   • The Back arrow and Current Scene icons in the Edit bar appear clickable, or
     active.

Registration Point vs. Transformation Point

Flash associates two different points with each symbol you create: a transformation point and a registration point. Both reference a specific point in the symbol, but you use them in very different ways. Here's the scoop:

- The symbol's *transformation point* is the little circle Flash displays in every symbol and graphic element. Flash uses the symbol's transformation point when you transform a symbol—for example, when you rotate a symbol, it spins around the transformation point. You can move the transformation point to any spot in or even outside of your symbol. The center of your symbol is a good starting spot for the transformation point, until you have a reason to place it elsewhere. If you want to reposition the transformation point, select a symbol or graphic element, and then click the Free Transform tool. The transformation point appears as a circle, usually on or near the symbol. Reposition the point by dragging it to a new location.

- The symbol's *registration point* appears as a little cross on the symbol. The registration point is the set of coordinates Flash uses to position an instance of a symbol on the stage. Often called X/Y coordinates, X equals the distance from the left side of the stage and Y is the distance from the top. You can place a symbol precisely on the stage by typing in the position coordinates in the Properties panel, as shown in Figure 6-6. You also use the position coordinates when

you position and move objects on the stage with ActionScript programming, as explained in Chapter 11. When you create new visual elements, like shapes and text, Flash automatically places the registration point in the upper-left corner. That's a good place to have the registration points for the symbols you create, unless you have a particular need to place it elsewhere. For example, if want to align several symbols on their center point, your may prefer to have the registration point in the center. To reposition the registration point for a symbol, double-click the symbol to edit it. The image opens in symbol edit mode as described on page 238, and the registration point appears as shown on the bottom of Figure 6-5. If you want the registration point centered, move your graphic element over the registration point, so it's centered. If you want the registration point in the lower-right corner, position your graphic above and to the left of the registration point.

In most cases, you don't have to think twice about the registration point. Let Flash put it in the upper-left corner and leave it there. If you're planning to manipulate the symbol in ActionScript, be aware that you can reposition the registration point if that upper-left corner doesn't work for your project, as described on page 238.

- A cross (the registration point for the symbol you're about to create) appears in the middle of the symbol editing workspace. The registration point is the reference point Flash uses to position your symbol on the stage, as explained in the box above. Technically, you can position your symbol anywhere you like with respect to the registration point; but out of the box, Flash puts the registration point for most graphics in the upper-left corner. For consistency's sake, you may want to do the same when you create symbols. Just create your artwork below and to the right of the registration point.

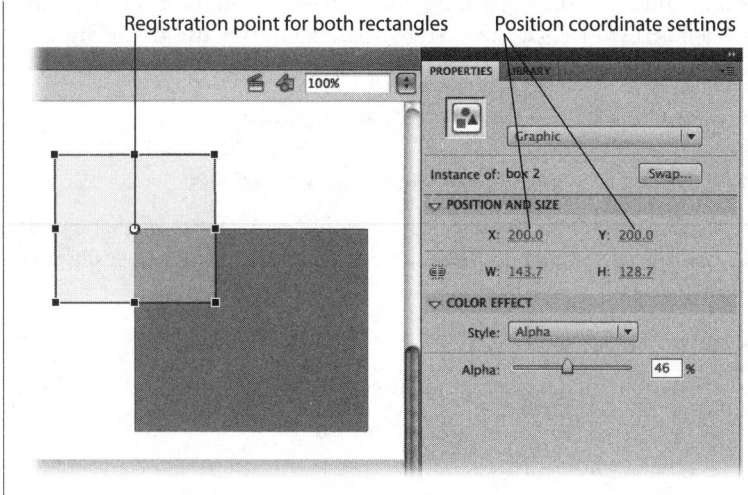

Registration point for both rectangles   Position coordinate settings

Figure 6-6:
Using the X, Y settings in the Properties panel, both of these rectangles are positioned at 200, 200. The difference? The small rectangle (selected) has a centered registration point, while the larger rectangle has its registration point in the upper-left corner.

4. **On the symbol editing workspace, create a graphic symbol.**

You can use Flash's drawing tools, instances of other symbols, or even an imported image (Chapter 9), just as you can on the main stage. As you draw, Flash displays a thumbnail version of your symbol in the Library preview window as shown in Figure 6-7. Note that the use count is zero, until you drag an instance of the symbol onto the stage. The *use count* is the number of instances of this particular symbol that have been dragged onto the main animation stage.

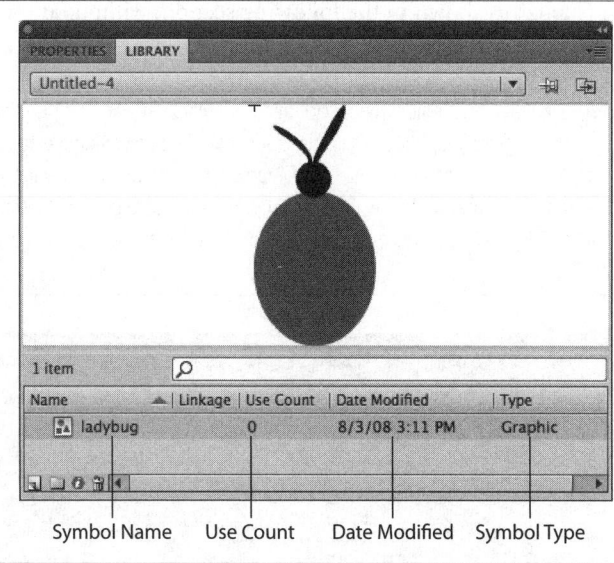

Symbol Name   Use Count   Date Modified   Symbol Type

Figure 6-7:
The ladybug symbol here was just created and, so the Library's showing a use count of 0. The registration point appears in the upper-left corner. The Library panel provides other details including when the symbol was last changed and how it's linked to other Flash and ActionScript documents.

5. When you're finished creating your symbol, head to the Edit bar, and then click the Back arrow or click the current scene icon. (Or use the menu command Edit → Edit Document.)

Flash brings you back to your main animation workspace.

Using a graphic symbol (creating an instance of a graphic symbol)

After you've created a symbol, you use it by creating an instance of that symbol, and then placing the instance somewhere in your animation. You can easily create a symbol, as the following steps show:

To create an instance of a graphic symbol:

1. **Make sure the Library panel containing the graphic symbol you want is visible. If it isn't, select Window, and then turn on the checkbox next to Library.**

Flash displays the Library panel.

2. **On the timeline, click to select the keyframe and layer where you want to put the instance.**

Flash highlights the selected keyframe.

3. **In the Library panel, click the name of the symbol you want to use.**

A thumbnail version of the symbol appears in the Library's preview window.

4. **Drag the thumbnail onto the stage (Figure 6-8).**

Flash creates an instance of the symbol and places it on the stage. You can transform or recolor this instance, as shown in the following section, without affecting any other instances or the symbol itself.

Tip: You can always convert an instance of a graphic symbol back into an editable image. You lose the file optimization benefits that an instance gives you, but on the other hand, you get to rework the graphic using Flash's drawing and painting tools. To convert an instance of a graphic symbol back into an editable image, first select the instance, and then choose Modify → Break Apart. If your instance contains nested instances, you need to choose Modify → Break Apart once for each level of nested instance to convert the entire symbol into editable pixels.

In the Mode

It's astonishingly easy to get confused about where you are when you're working in symbol editing mode. If you think you're in your main animation when you're actually in symbol mode, for example, you get frustratingly unexpected results when you try to test your animation by selecting Control → Play or Control → Test Movie.

You can most easily tell where you are when you make sure the Edit bar's visible (select Window → Toolbars, and then turn on the checkbox next to Edit Bar). If your symbol's name appears in the Edit bar, you're in symbol editing mode; if it doesn't, you're not.

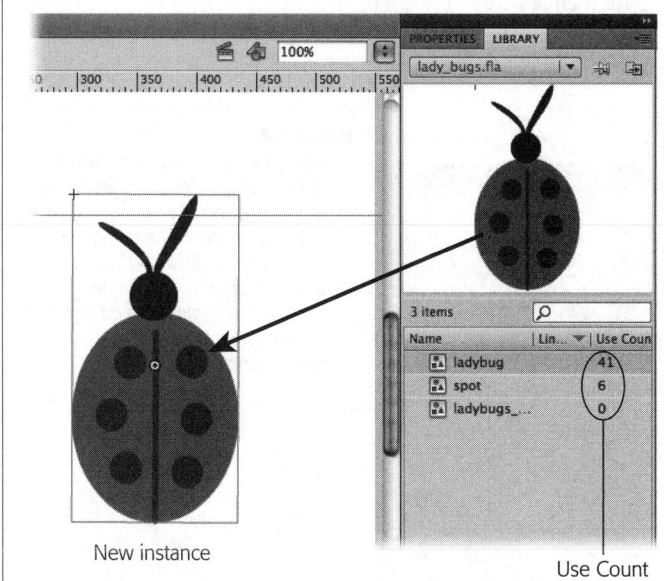

Figure 6-8:
Creating an instance of a symbol is as easy as dragging the symbol from the Library and dropping it onto the stage. Flash has bumped up the use count for the ladybug symbol to 1. Because the ladybug uses spot symbols, the count for spot has bumped up to 6.

New instance

Use Count

Editing an instance of a graphic symbol

The whole point of graphic symbols is to help you reuse images (and to help Flash keep down file size while you're doing it). So it should come as no surprise that you can't completely rework the instances you create. You can't, for example, create an instance of a ladybug, erase it, draw a toad in its place, and expect Flash to consider that toad an instance of the ladybug symbol.

But while you can't use Flash's drawing and painting tools to change your instance, you *can* change certain characteristics of an instance, including color, transparency, tint, and brightness using the Properties panel; and scale, rotation, and skew using the Transform panel.

Note: When you transform or recolor an instance, only that instance changes; the other instances you've added to your animation aren't affected, and neither is the symbol itself. If you want to change multiple instances en masse, you need to edit the symbol itself (page 238).

You can also edit an instance by swapping one instance of a graphic symbol for another. Say, for example, that you've created a nature backdrop using multiple instances of three symbols: a tree, a bush, and a flower. If you decide you'd rather replace a few trees with bushes, Flash gives you a quick and easy way to do that, as shown in the following steps:

1. **On the stage, select the instance you want to replace.**

   Flash redisplays the Properties panel to show instance-related properties. (If you don't see the Properties panel, choose Window → Properties to display it.)

2. **In the Properties panel, click Swap (Figure 6-9).**

The Swap Symbol dialog box appears.

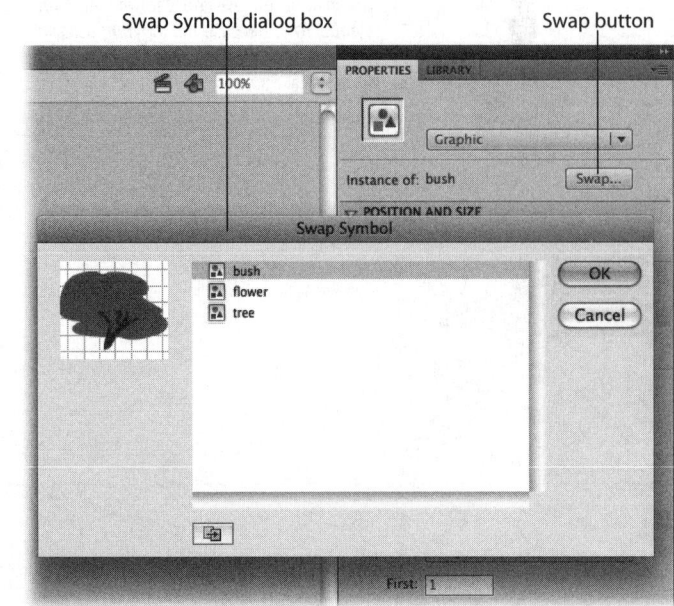

Swap Symbol dialog box

Swap button

Figure 6-9:
The Swap button is active only when you have a single instance selected on the stage. The Swap Symbol dialog box is misnamed; it should be called the Swap Instance dialog box. That's because you use it to replace an instance of one symbol with an instance of another symbol; the symbols themselves don't change.

3. **In the Swap Symbol dialog box, click to select the symbol with which you'd like to replace the original. When you finish, click OK.**

On the stage, Flash replaces the selected instance with an instance of the symbol you chose in the Swap Symbol dialog box.

Editing a graphic symbol

Recoloring or transforming an instance changes only that instance, but editing a symbol changes *every single instance* of that symbol, immediately, wherever you've placed them in your animation.

The good news about editing symbols, of course, is that it can save you a boatload of time. Say you've added hundreds of instances of your company's logo to your animation and the brass decides to redo the logo. Instead of the mind-numbing chore of slogging through your animation finding and changing each instance by hand, all you have to do is edit one little image—your logo symbol. The minute you do, Flash automatically ripples your changes out to each and every instance of that symbol.

The bad news, of course, is that you might edit a symbol by mistake, thinking you're editing an instance instead (page 237). Editing a symbol is for keeps. You can select Edit → Undo if you realize your mistake in time, but once you close your Flash document and Flash erases your Undo history, it's all over but the crying: You're stuck with your edited symbol, for better or for worse.

Tip: If the thought of editing a symbol makes you leery–say you've got 500 instances of your symbol scattered around your animation and you don't want to have to redraw it if you goof up the edit job–play it safe and make a duplicate of the symbol before you edit it. In the Library panel, click the Options menu. Then, from the pop-up menu that appears, select Duplicate. When you do, Flash displays the Duplicate Symbol window, which lets you give your backup copy a unique, descriptive name (like logo_backup).

UP TO SPEED

Exchanging Symbols Between Documents

Flash puts all the symbols you create in a Flash document–as well as all the bitmaps, sound files, and other goodies you import into that document–into the Library panel, which you display by choosing Window → Library.

Technically speaking, the stuff you put in the Library is good only for that Flash document or project (unlike the Common Libraries, which you access by choosing Window → Common Libraries, and which always list the same preinstalled files, no matter which document you have open).

But you can pull a symbol from one document's library and put it into another by copying and pasting. To do so:

1. Open the two documents between which you want to exchange symbols (File → Open).

2. Open the Library panel from which you want to copy a symbol (Window → Library), and then choose the document from the drop-down list in the Library panel.

3. In the Library panel, right-click the name of the symbol you want to copy, and then, from the pop-up menu that appears, choose Copy.

4. Above the timeline, click the tab displaying the name of the other document.

5. In the new document, click to select the keyframe where you want to paste the symbol.

6. Choose Edit → Paste in Center. Flash pastes a copy of the other document's symbol on the stage.

To open a document's library without having to open the document itself: Select File → Import → Open External Library, choose the document whose symbols you want to copy, and then click Open. When you do, Flash opens the document's Library (but not the document). With two libraries open, you can drag symbols directly from one library to another.

Flash gives you three ways to edit symbols: Edit, Edit in Place, and Edit in New Window.

- **Edit** is the most common way to edit symbols, and it's the method Flash uses when you right-click a symbol name in the Library, and then choose Edit. You can also use the menu command Edit → Edit Symbols or keyboard shortcut Ctrl+E (⌘-E for Macs). The stage temporarily disappears, to be replaced by a window showing only the contents of the symbol. If you have the Edit toolbar showing (Windows → Toolbars → Edit Bar), you see the symbol's name, as shown in Figure 6-10. After you finish your edits, click the Scene name or the Back button to return to the stage.

- **Editing in place** lets you edit a symbol right there on the stage, surrounded by any other objects you may have on the stage. (Flash grays out the other objects; they're just for reference. The only thing you can edit in this mode is the symbol.)

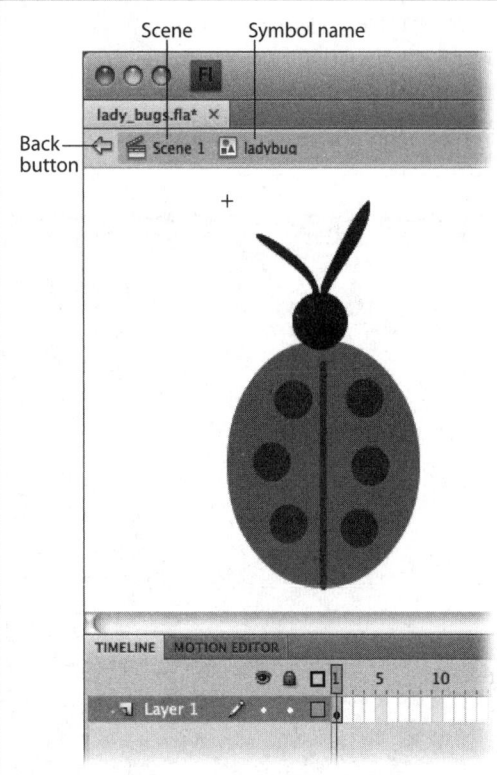

Scene   Symbol name

Back
button

Figure 6-10:
When you edit your symbol in its very own window, there's no ambiguity: You know you're editing a symbol (and not merely an instance). You edit a symbol using the same tools and panels you use to edit any other image. As you make your changes, Flash automatically updates the symbol in the Library, as well as all the instances of that symbol, wherever they may be in your Flash document.

If you're not ready for it, this option is right up there with the more confusing features the Flash design team has ever come up with. As you can see in Figure 6-11, mixing the symbol editing mode with the appearance of the main stage makes it incredibly easy to assume you're changing an *instance* of a symbol (instead of the symbol itself) with frustrating results. Double-clicking a symbol on the stage or selecting Edit → Edit in Place from the main menu or from the pop-up menu that appears when you right-click an instance on the stage all tell Flash that you want to edit in place.

Note: One man's meat is another man's poison. If you absolutely have to see your symbol in context (surrounded by all the other stuff on the stage) to be able to edit it properly, editing in place is just what you want.

- **Edit in New Window** creates a new window tab where you edit your symbol, as shown in Figure 6-12. Right-click (or Control-click) a symbol on the stage, and then choose "Edit in New Window" from the pop-up menu. Flash opens the symbol under a new tab and your work area looks similar to the basic Edit mode. As you make changes, Flash updates all existing instances to match the newly edited symbol. This makes it easy to jump back and forth between symbol editing workspace and the stage, so you can see how the edited symbol looks in context. When you're finished making changes, just click the Close button.

Symbol name

Figure 6-11:
It's hard to tell that the large ladybug (the one that's not grayed out) is a symbol and not just an instance of a symbol. (Your one clue: the symbol name "ladybug" that Flash displays above the stage.) Editing a symbol when you mean to edit an instance can have pretty serious consequences, so if you find yourself second-guessing, stick to editing in a new window, as described in Figure 6-10.

In a nutshell, to tell Flash you want to edit a symbol, do any of the following:

In the Library panel:

- Double-click the symbol, either in the list or in the preview window. The symbol opens in Edit in Place mode.

- Select a symbol from the list, and then click the Options menu. From the pop-up menu that appears, choose Edit. The symbol opens in Edit mode, where you see the symbol by itself.

- Right-click a symbol in the list. From the pop-up menu that appears, choose Edit, Edit in Place, or Edit in New Window. The pop-up menu lets you select exactly how you'd like view the symbol while editing.

On the stage:

- Select Edit → Edit Symbols.

- Select an instance of the symbol, and then choose Edit → Edit Selected.

- Right-click an instance of the symbol, and then, from the pop-up menu that appears, choose Edit, Edit in Place, or Edit in New Window.

New window tab   Close window button

Figure 6-12:
*"Edit in New Window" is one of three ways that Flash gives you
to edit a symbol. Both the Edit and "Edit in New Window"
options give you a nice, uncluttered view of your symbol.*

• In the Edit Bar (Window → Toolbars → Edit Bar), click Edit Symbols (the icon
on the right that looks like a jumble of shapes).

No matter which method you choose—editing, editing in place, or editing in a new
window—you get out of symbol editing mode and return to the main stage the same
way: by selecting Edit → Edit Document (Ctrl+E on a PC or ⌘-E on a Mac).

Deleting a graphic symbol

You can delete the graphic symbols you create. Just remember that when you do,
Flash automatically deletes all the instances of that symbol, wherever you've placed
them in that document.

To delete a graphic symbol:

1. **In the Library panel, click to select the graphic symbol you want to delete.**

   Flash highlights the selected symbol's name and type.

2. **Right-click the graphic symbol icon, and then, from the pop-up menu that
   appears, choose Delete.**

   Flash removes the graphic symbol from the Library panel. It also removes all
   the instances of that symbol from your animation. Another option is to click the
   trash can icon at the bottom of the Library panel.

Multiframe Graphic Symbols

Multiframe graphic symbols are a kind of hybrid symbol halfway between single-frame graphic symbols and movie clip symbols. Multiframe graphic symbols can't contain sounds or actions the way movie clip symbols can, but they *can* contain multiple frames, which regular single-frame graphic symbols can't. As explained in the box on page 231, multiframe graphic symbols synchronize frame-for-frame to the animation in which you place them.

Tip: For many common Flash chores, it makes sense to use movie clips instead of multiframe graphics. As a designer, you have more control over movie clips, and you don't have to worry about the synchronization issues that come with multiframe graphics. However, one advantage multiframe graphic symbols have over movie clips is that they take up less space in the SWF file when you publish your animation.

Creating a multiframe graphic symbol

Flash gives you the same two options for creating multiframe graphics symbols as it does for single-frame graphic symbols: You can create a series of frames as usual and then convert it into a reusable symbol, or you can use Flash's editing mode to create a multiframe graphic symbol from scratch and save yourself the conversion step. This section shows both approaches.

To convert a series of frames to a multiframe graphic symbol:

1. **On the timeline, select the frames you want to convert.**

   You can easily select a series when you click at one end of the series, and then Shift-click at the other end. Flash automatically selects all the frames in between.

2. **Choose Edit → Timeline → Copy Frames (or press Ctrl+Alt+C in Windows; Option-⌘-C on the Mac). Then choose Insert → New Symbol.**

   The Create New Symbol dialog box appears.

3. **In the Create New Symbol dialog box, turn on the Graphic radio button. Type a short, descriptive name for your symbol, and then click OK.**

   The name of your symbol appears in the Library panel and in the Edit bar above your stage to let you know you're in symbol editing mode. In addition, Flash replaces your animation stage with the symbol editing stage. You can recognize the symbol editing stage by the cross (your symbol's registration point) that appears in the middle of the symbol editing stage.

4. **In the symbol timeline, click to select the first keyframe (Frame 1).**

   Flash highlights the selected keyframe.

5. **Select Edit → Timeline → Paste Frames.**

   Flash pastes the copied frames in the symbol's timeline. The Library panel's preview window shows you the contents of your new symbol's first keyframe (along with a mini-controller, as shown in Figure 6-13).

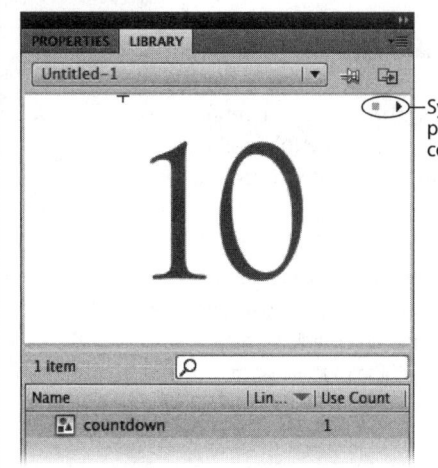

Symbol
preview
controls

Figure 6-13:
Get into the habit of previewing your multiframe graphic symbols in the Library before you add instances of each symbol to your animation. If you do, you'll save yourself the hassle that can result from incorporating instances of a symbol that doesn't run properly. To preview your symbol, click the Play button as shown. Flash displays the contents of each frame of your symbol, one after the other, in the Preview window.

6. **Preview your symbol by clicking the mini-controller's Play button.**

Flash runs a thumbnail version of the symbol in the preview window.

7. **Get out of symbol editing mode by choosing Edit → Edit Document.**

Flash hides the symbol editing stage and brings you back to your main animation's stage and timeline.

To create a multiframe graphic symbol from scratch in symbol editing mode, follow the steps you see on page 232, adding the content for as many frames as you need in step 5.

Creating an instance of a multiframe graphic symbol

Creating an instance of a multiframe graphic symbol is like creating an instance of a movie clip symbol, but it's not identical. When you insert a multiframe graphic symbol into a timeline, the graphic synchronizes frame-for-frame with that timeline. If the timeline doesn't have enough frames, Flash lops off any frames of the graphic that don't fit. If the timeline has more frames than the graphic, Flash loops the graphic frames unless you provide other instructions in the Properties panel. If it's important that every frame of the graphic plays, make sure the timeline has enough frames. The following steps show you how.

To create an instance of a multiframe graphic symbol:

1. **In your main animation, click to select the keyframe where you want to place an instance of a multiframe graphic symbol.**

Only keyframes can contain new content (see page 90 for the skinny on keyframes). So if you try to place a symbol in a regular frame, Flash "backs up" and places your symbol in the keyframe immediately preceding the selected frame anyway.

2. **Make sure you have exactly as many frames after the selected keyframe as you
   need for this instance.**

   If you're creating an instance of a symbol that contains 10 frames, make sure 10
   frames exist including the selected keyframe. If the symbol contains 20 frames,
   make sure 20 frames exist. To add frames after your selected keyframe, choose
   Insert → Timeline → Frame (or press F5) once for each frame you want to add.

   Warning: If you forget this step and add a multiframe graphic symbol to a timeline that *doesn't* contain
   exactly as many frames as the symbol, Flash doesn't issue any warnings. Instead, it matches as many of
   the instance frames to your timeline frames as it can. If you don't have enough room on your timeline,
   Flash quietly snips off the instance frames that don't fit. If you have too *much* room, Flash repeats the
   instance frames until all your main animation's frames are filled.

   ---

3. **In the Library, click to select the multiframe graphic symbol of which you want
   to create an instance.**

   You can either click the symbol's icon from the list or click the symbol's thumbnail in the preview window. The Library lists the type of both single and multiframe graphics the same—Graphic—but you can always tell a multiframe
   graphic by the mini-controller that appears along with the symbol's content in
   the Library's preview window as shown in Figure 6-13.

4. **Drag the symbol to the stage.**

   Flash creates an instance of the symbol and places it in the keyframe you
   selected in step 1. As you see in Figure 6-14, Flash colors your frames a nice
   solid gray to let you know they now contain content. But Flash *doesn't* display
   the individual keyframes of your instance in your main timeline. (By the same
   token, if your symbol contains multiple layers, you don't see those on your
   main timeline, either. This visual simplification is one of the benefits of using
   symbols, as opposed to just copying and pasting frames.) To preview your
   instance, select Control → Test Movie.

   Note: You can also test an instance of a multiframe graphic symbol by choosing Control → Play, or by
   dragging the playhead on the main timeline.

Editing an instance of a multiframe graphic symbol

If you need the flexibility to individually change each keyframe of a multiframe
graphic instance, you're out of luck, but you can use the Transform tool and the
Properties panel to make tweaks that affect every frame of your multiframe graphics. Use the Properties panel to change the size, position, and color of your graphic,
as shown in Figure 6-15. Changes you make here affect every frame in the multiframe graphic.

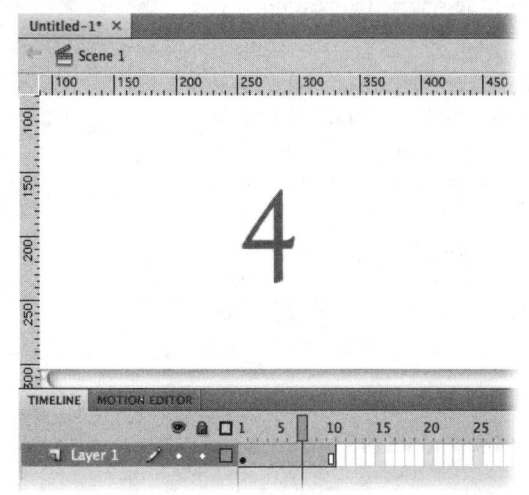

Figure 6-14:
The solid gray bar you see beginning with the keyframe (Frame 1) lets you know that Frames 1–10 now contain content: in this case, an instance of a multiframe graphic symbol. If testing your animation yields an unexpected result, check to make sure that the frame span to which you've added the symbol matches your symbol frame for frame.

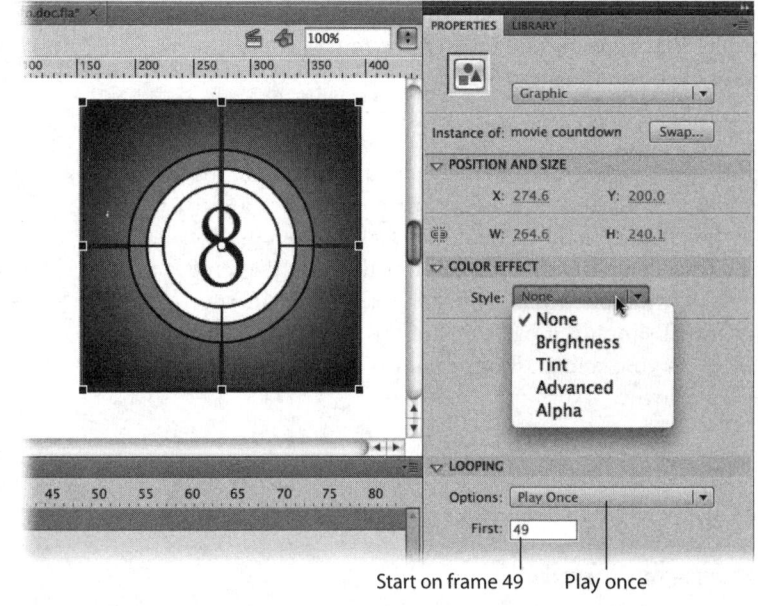

Figure 6-15:
This multiframe graphic shows a countdown similar to the ones that appear before old movies. In the Properties panel, the Looping → First option is set to Frame 49, so that the countdown begins with the number 8.

Flash lets you change the contents of the first keyframe of your instance, just the way you can an instance of a single-frame graphic (page 238). But Flash automatically applies those changes to the contents of *every* keyframe in your instance. Skew the frog in your first keyframe and turn it blue, for example, and every image in every frame of your instance appears skewed and blue.

Using the Properties panel, you can tweak the playback settings for a multiframe graphic. Under Looping → Options you can choose between Loop, Play Once, and

Single Frame. In the First box, you can choose the first frame that Flash displays. For example, suppose you have a nifty countdown multiframe graphic like the ones at the beginning of old newsreels. Your graphic counts down from 10, but for this project you'd like to start it at 8 like in the movies. Simply adjust the starting frame, so that it begins when the 8 is showing, as shown in Figure 6-15.

Note: The file *multiframe_countdown.fla*, shown in Figure 6-15, is available at *http://missingmanuals.com/cds*. It shows how multiframe graphic symbols can be made up of several different graphic elements, layers, and symbols.

Editing a multiframe graphic symbol

You edit a multiframe graphic symbol the same way you edit a single-frame graphic symbol: by switching to symbol editing mode (page 238). In both cases, Flash immediately applies the changes you make to the symbol to all the instances of that symbol.

Deleting a multiframe graphic symbol

You delete a multiframe graphic symbol the same way you delete any other symbol in Flash: through the Library panel. Just remember that when you delete a symbol, *Flash automatically deletes all the instances of that symbol*, wherever you've placed them.

To delete a graphic symbol:

1. **In the Library panel, click to select the graphic symbol you want to delete.**

   Flash highlights the selected symbol's name and type.

2. **Right-click the graphic symbol icon, and then, from the pop-up menu that appears, choose Delete.**

   Flash removes the graphic symbol from the Library panel. It also removes all the instances of that symbol from your animation.

Movie Clip Symbols

A *movie clip* symbol (Figure 6-16) is a reusable, self-contained chunk of animation, which you can drop into a single frame in another animation.

Unlike multiframe graphic symbols, you can add sounds (Chapter 10) and actions (Chapter 11) to movie clip symbols. Also unlike multiframe graphic symbols, movie clip symbols run independently from the animations to which you add them.

So movie clips give you the opportunity to create nonsequential effects like repeating, or *looping*, scenes, as well as interactive graphics—for example, buttons, checkboxes, and clickable images that tell Flash to display something different, depending on what your audience clicks.

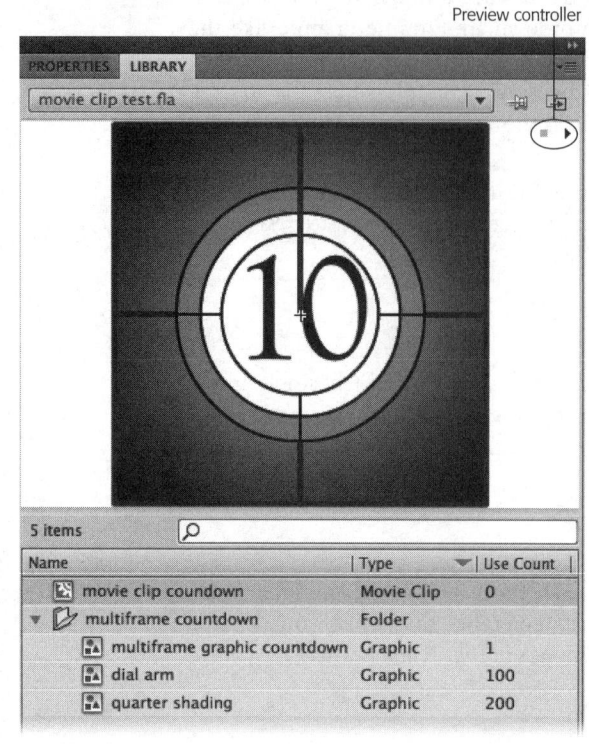

Preview controller

Figure 6-16:
When you select a movie clip symbol in the Library, the Library panel's preview window shows you the first frame of the symbol, as well as a mini-controller you can use to play (and stop) the movie clip right there in the Library before you go to all the trouble of dragging an instance of the movie clip to the stage. (You see this same mini-controller when you select a multiframe graphic in the Library.)

As you'll see in the following section, movie clip symbols have their very own timelines, so an instance of a movie clip symbol always takes up just one frame in the animation to which you add it, no matter how many frames the movie clip symbol actually contains.

Creating a movie clip symbol

Creating a movie clip symbol in Flash is similar to creating a multiframe graphic symbol (page 243). You can either create a series of frames (including sounds and actions, if you like) and convert it into a movie clip symbol, or you can use Flash's editing mode to create a movie clip symbol from scratch and save yourself the conversion step.

In fact, as the following steps show, only one minor but important difference exists between creating a multiframe graphic symbol and creating a movie clip symbol, and that's selecting the correct drop-down menu option in step 4.

Warning: Modify → "Convert to Symbol" works only when you're converting an image to a single-frame graphic symbol; it *doesn't* let you convert a series of frames into a movie clip symbol. But if you try it, Flash won't give you an error. Instead, it'll chug along happily, pretending it's creating a movie clip symbol. But in reality, the symbol you create this way contains just one frame.

To convert a series of existing frames to a movie clip symbol:

1. **On the timeline, select the frames you want to convert.**

   It's easy to select a series of frames. Click at one end of the series, and then Shift-click at the other end of the series. Flash automatically selects all the frames in between. If your frames contain layers, make sure you select all the layers in each frame.

2. **Choose Edit → Timeline → Copy Frames (or press Ctrl+Alt+C on Windows, or Option-⌘-C on Mac).**

   Flash copies the frames.

3. **Choose Insert → New Symbol.**

   The Create New Symbol dialog box appears.

4. **In the Create New Symbol dialog box, make sure to choose Movie Clip from the drop-down menu.**

   If it's not, click to select it.

5. **Type a name for your movie clip symbol, and then click OK.**

   The name of your movie clip symbol appears in the Library panel, and in the Edit bar above your stage, to let you know you're in symbol editing mode. Another tip-off that you're in symbol editing mode is the cross, or registration point, that appears in the middle of the symbol editing stage.

6. **In the symbol timeline, click to select the first keyframe (Frame 1).**

   Flash highlights the selected keyframe.

7. **Select Edit → Timeline → Paste Frames.**

   Flash pastes the copied frames onto the symbol's timeline and displays the first keyframe of the new symbol (along with a mini-controller) in the Library panel's preview window.

8. **In the Library panel, preview your symbol by clicking the mini-controller's Play button.**

   Flash runs a thumbnail version of the movie clip symbol in the preview window.

9. **Get out of symbol editing mode by choosing Edit → Edit Document.**

   Flash brings you back to the workspace and your main animation.

To create a movie clip symbol from scratch in symbol editing mode, follow the steps on page 232, adding the content for as many frames as you need.

Creating an instance of a movie clip symbol

Because movie clip symbols have their own timelines, they're completely self-contained. You don't have to worry about matching your movie clip symbol to your main animation's timeline the way you do with a multiframe graphic symbol (page 243); movie clip instances live on a single frame in your main animation, no matter how many frames the instances themselves contain. As a matter of fact, as you'll see next, creating an instance of a movie clip symbol is as easy as dragging and dropping.

To create an instance of a movie clip symbol:

1. **In your main animation, click to select the keyframe where you want to place an instance of a movie clip symbol.**

   Only keyframes can contain new content. So if you try to place a symbol in a regular frame, Flash "backs up" and places your symbol in the keyframe immediately preceding the selected frame anyway.

2. **In the Library, click to select the movie clip symbol of which you want to create an instance.**

   You can either click the symbol's icon from the list or click the symbol's thumbnail in the preview window.

3. **Drag the symbol to the stage.**

   Flash creates an instance of the symbol and places it in the keyframe you selected in step 1, as shown in Figure 6-17.

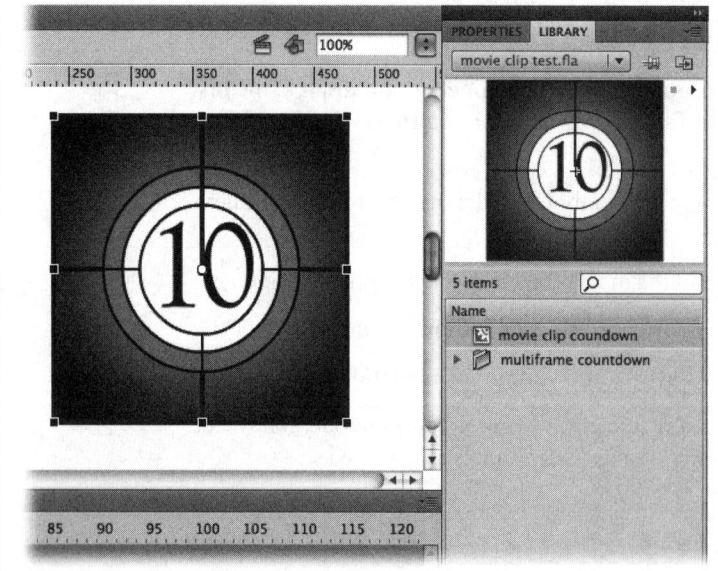

Figure 6-17:
Dragging a movie clip symbol from the Library to the stage tells Flash to create an instance of the symbol. No matter how many frames (or layers) your movie clip instance contains, it takes up only one frame on your animation (circled), which makes movie clips perfect for creating animated buttons.

4. **To preview your instance, select Control → Test Movie.**

You'll notice that even if you turn looping off in the Control panel (which you do by selecting Control, and then, from the pop-up menu that appears, turning off the checkbox next to Loop) your movie clip instance continues to loop. The movie clip behaves this way because it's running on its own timeline (not the timeline Flash associates with your main animation). One way to tell Flash to stop looping your movie clip instance is to add a keyframe (blank or otherwise) to your timeline *after* the keyframe that contains your movie clip instance.

Note: Flash automatically *loops* the movie clip instance (plays it over and over again) until it encounters the next keyframe on the timeline, or until it encounters an ActionScript statement that tells it to stop (like *stop( )* or *goToAndStop( )*). You can see an example of controlling playback with ActionScript in Chapter 11.

Editing a movie clip symbol

You edit a movie clip symbol the same way you edit a single-frame graphic symbol: by switching to symbol editing mode (page 238). In both cases, Flash immediately applies your changes to all the instances of that symbol.

Editing an instance of a movie clip symbol

Similar to multiframe graphic symbols, Flash lets you change the contents of the first keyframe of your movie clip instance, just the way you can an instance of a single-frame graphic (page 238). But Flash automatically applies those changes to the contents of *every* frame in your instance. So, for example, if you apply a sepia tint to the first keyframe, your entire movie clip instance looks old-timey.

You can also apply filters (page 258) and blending effects to movie clip instances, including buttons. (Button symbols, as discussed below, are nothing more than specialized movie clip symbols.)

Reuse Deluxe: Repurposing Symbols

When you think about it, it's the simple, classic shapes you use most often in drawing.

Sure, it's great to have a sun, flower, or cockroach symbol hanging around in the Library, but it's the ovals, wedges, and sweeps that you find yourself coming back to again and again. And because Flash lets you resize, reposition, and recolor each instance, you can create radically different drawings using the same handful of simply shaped graphic symbols. You optimize the size of your finished animation,

and, as a bonus, you get to focus on design at the graphic element level. (Even accomplished animators can find fresh ideas by limiting themselves to a handful of shapes.)

Expand and flip a raindrop symbol, and then add a tail, for example, and you've got yourself a whale as shown in Figure 6-18.

Figure 6-18:
*You'll find that simple
shapes are the easiest
to reuse because they're
the most adaptable. In
this image a raindrop is
resized and rotated to
become the body of
a whale. Creative
repurposing saves time
and reduces the size of
your Flash files.*

Button Symbols

The easiest way to make your animation interactive is to add a button someone
can click at runtime to perform a task, like replaying your entire animation, choosing which of several scenes to play, loading a Web page, and so on.

To make creating a button easy, Flash has button symbols (Figure 6-19). A *button
symbol* is a specialized form of movie clip symbol that contains four frames:

• **Up.** In this frame, you draw the button as you want it to appear *before* your
audience mouses over it.

• **Over.** In this frame, you draw the button as you want it to appear *after* your
audience mouses over it.

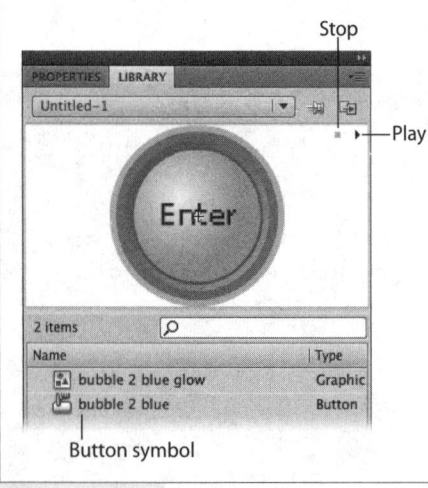

Figure 6-19:
*Because button symbols are nothing more than specialized movie clip
symbols, you see the same mini-controller in the Library's preview
window when you click a button symbol as you see when you select a
movie clip or multiframe graphic symbol. Clicking Play cycles through
the button symbol's four frames, so you get to see 1) how the button
looks before the cursor mouses over it, 2) how it looks after the cursor
mouses over it, 3) how it looks when clicked, and 4) the button's
clickable area. When you create a button symbol, Flash spots you the
four frames; all you have to do is customize them, as shown in the
following sections.*

- **Down.** In this frame, you draw the button as you want it to appear when your audience clicks it.

- **Hit.** In this frame, you draw the active, or "clickable," area of your button. In most cases, you want the active area to be identical to the button itself. But in other cases—for example, if you want to create a bullseye-shaped button that responds only when your audience clicks the tiny red dot in the center—you draw that center dot here, in the fourth frame (the Hit frame). You can also use this frame to create invisible buttons as explained on page 257, or buttons that are the shape of an image in your animation, like a car.

Of course, you can always create your own interactive button from scratch and save it as a movie clip symbol (page 247). But the better way to go is to create a button symbol. When you do, Flash automatically gives you the four Up, Over, Down, and Hit frames—all you have to do is plug in your drawings and go. As you see in the following section, Flash also gives you a handful of built-in graphic effects, called *filters*, which you can apply to your buttons to get professional-looking results.

Note: To get your button to actually *do* something when someone clicks it—to display a different section of the timeline, for example, or some dynamic text—you need to tie a snippet of ActionScript code to your button. Chapter 11 shows you how.

Creating a button symbol

When you create a button symbol, you start out basically as if you're creating any graphic symbol from scratch (page 232), but since button symbols have those four possible states, you can create up to four different graphics. When you choose Button in the New Symbol dialog box, Flash gives you a separate frame to hold each drawing so that you won't get confused.

In this example, you'll create a round, red button that turns yellow when your audience mouses over it and green when your audience clicks it.

1. Click Insert → New Symbol.

   The Create New Symbol dialog box appears.

2. In the Name text box, type bullseye. Make sure the drop-down menu is set to Button, and then click OK.

   When you create a new button symbol, Flash gives you four named frames (Figure 6-20). It's up to you which frames you want to modify, but at the very least, you need to add a drawing to the Up frame, to show the button before it's clicked. For a more sophisticated button, you'll also add a drawing to the Over frame (as shown below) to let someone know when his mouse is over the button.

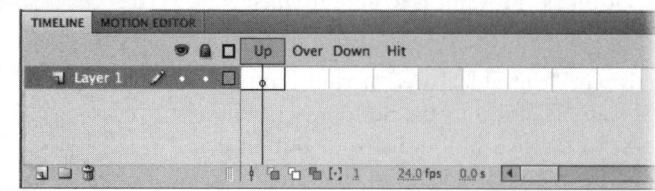

Figure 6-20:
Flash pops you into symbol editing mode. In the symbol's timeline, you see four named frames: Up, Over, Down, and Hit.

Tip: Flash comes with a blue million button symbols already spiffed up and ready for you to drop into your animations. So before you get too carried away drawing your own button, choose Window → Common Libraries → Buttons to see if Flash already has a button symbol that fits your bill. (You still have to add ActionScript code to the prebuilt button symbol to tell Flash what you want it to do when your audience clicks your button, of course; Flash isn't a mind reader. Find out how in Chapter 12.)

3. **Draw your button as you want it to appear initially by using the Oval tool to add a red circle to the first keyframe (the Up frame).**

   Keep the registration point (the cross) in the upper left corner of your button image as you draw. When you finish, your workspace should look similar to the one in Figure 6-21.

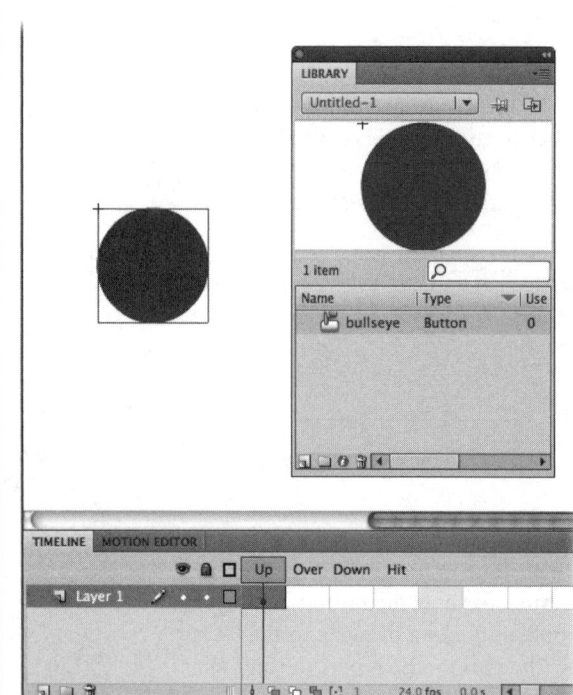

Figure 6-21:
Your button doesn't have to look like a button; it can be an image, a shape, a line–anything you like. But most people are used to circular buttons, so a circle's a good place to start. Notice that as you create your image, Flash automatically updates the Library's preview window.

4. **Right-click Frame 2 (the Over frame), and then, from the pop-up menu that appears, select Insert Keyframe.**

   Flash displays a circle in Frame 2 to let you know you've successfully added a keyframe. On the stage, you see a copy of the button you drew in Frame 1.

5. **Here's how you make the button change when a cursor passes over it: On the stage, select the circle. In the Properties panel, click the Fill Color icon, and then, from the color picker that appears, choose a yellow swatch.**

   Flash recolors the circle yellow. If you don't see the Properties Panel, select Window → Properties. If you still don't see it, make sure you've selected the circle on the stage.

6. **Right-click Frame 3 (the Down frame), and then, from the pop-up menu that appears, select Insert Keyframe.**

   Flash displays a circle in Frame 3 to let you know you've successfully added a keyframe (and, therefore, can change the content of the frame).

7. **Here's how you draw the button as you want it to appear when a cursor clicks it: Select the button. In the Properties panel, click the Fill Color icon once again, and then, from the color picker that appears, choose a green swatch.**

   Flash recolors the circle green.

8. **Right-click Frame 4 (the Hit frame), and then, from the pop-up menu that appears, select Insert Keyframe.**

   Flash displays a circle in Frame 4 to let you know you've successfully added another keyframe. As you can see on the stage, Flash assumes you want the entire button to respond to a mouse click—and in a lot of cases, that's exactly what you do want. But you can make the clickable portion of your button smaller or larger. To do so:

9. **On the stage, click the circle to select it. Then choose Window → Transform to display the Transform panel.**

   In the Transform panel, type *50* into the Width and Height boxes, and then press Return.

   Figure 6-22 shows you a scaled-down circle that should look similar to the one you see on your workspace.

10. **Return to your animation by choosing Edit → Edit Document.**

    Flash hides your symbol editing workspace and displays your animation workspace.

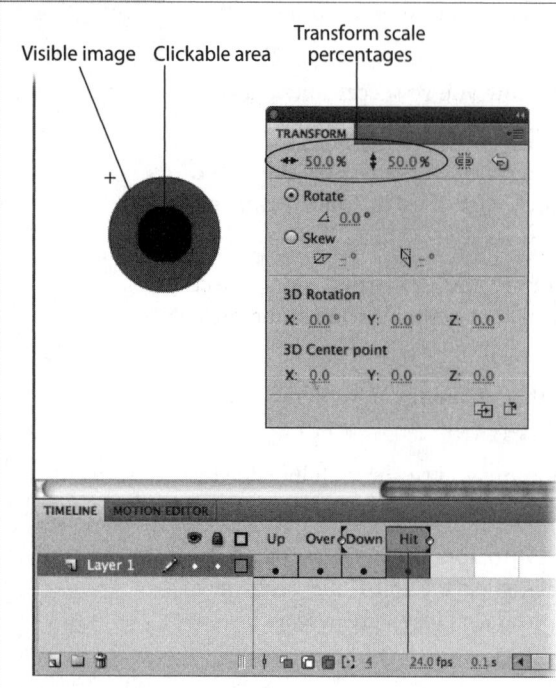

Visible image   Clickable area   Transform scale percentages

Figure 6-22:
Normally, you want to draw the same size shape in the Hit frame as you do in the other frames so that the entire button responds to mouse clicks. Drawing a smaller (or even different-shaped) image for the Hit frame lets you create more sophisticated buttons: clickable images, for example, or invisible buttons that let the content of your frame itself appear to respond to mouse clicks (see the box on page 257). Here, the clickable portion of the button is exactly half the size of the visible portion.

Using a button symbol (creating an instance of a button symbol)

You can find the work file *button_car.fla* at *http://missingmanuals.com/cds*.

To create an instance of a button symbol:

1. **Click to select the first keyframe (Frame 1) in your animation.**

   Flash highlights the selected frame.

2. **In the Library panel's preview window, drag your button symbol's thumbnail onto the stage.**

   On the stage, Flash creates an instance of the button symbol and surrounds it with a selection box.

3. **Test your button instance. To do so, choose Control → Test Movie.**

   A red circle appears in the middle of the test window (Figure 6-23).

Tip: To test your button instance on the stage, select Control → Enable Simple Buttons. When you do, your button responds to mouse movement and clicking right there on the stage.

---

4. **In the test window, drag your mouse over the red circle.**

   When your mouse nears the center of the red circle, your arrow cursor turns into a pointing finger, and the red circle turns yellow.

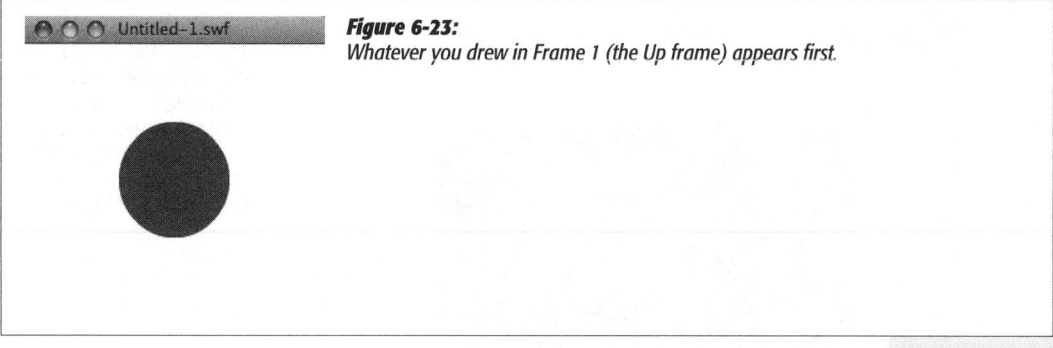

Figure 6-23:
Whatever you drew in Frame 1 (the Up frame) appears first.

5. **With your pointing-finger cursor, click the yellow circle.**

The yellow circle turns green.

Note: Chapter 11 shows you how to add an action to your button so that clicking it does something useful.

FREQUENTLY ASKED QUESTION

Oddly Shaped (and Invisible) Buttons

Why would I want to make my Hit frame smaller than the button itself? Won't that just make it harder for people to click?

One popular situation when you might want to make the Hit frame *smaller* than the button itself is when you're creating a hotspot. For example, say you're creating an interactive Web-based game for kids. On the stage, you've drawn several different animals: a pig, a duck, and a lamb. The audio file you've attached to your animation tells the player which specific part of each animal to click: the duck's bill, for instance, or the pig's tail. In this case, you want to limit the clickable portion of the image to the bill (or tail).

A situation when you might consider making the Hit frame *larger* than the button is when you want to give your audience a larger target. Instead of making someone center her cursor precisely over a teeny-tiny button, for example, you can let her click as soon as her cursor comes anywhere close to the button. This option is great for text-only buttons, too.

Otherwise, only the actual letters are clickable. (Obviously, this strategy works best when you have only a few buttons on the stage and they're not near each other.)

Finally, you can create *invisible* buttons by drawing a shape in the Hit frame and leaving the rest of the button frames empty. Suppose you have a picture and you want to make a car inside that picture a clickable button, as shown in Figure 6-24. Bring the entire picture into your button symbol. In the Hit frame, trace and fill the portion you want to be clickable, say, the car. Then delete the original picture, leaving only the filled shape. Exit symbol editing mode, and then drag your invisible button over the picture in the main timeline. To help you out in placing an invisible button on the stage, Flash provides a transparent blue hotspot shape. You can see this shape when you're working in Flash, but it doesn't appear in your published animation.

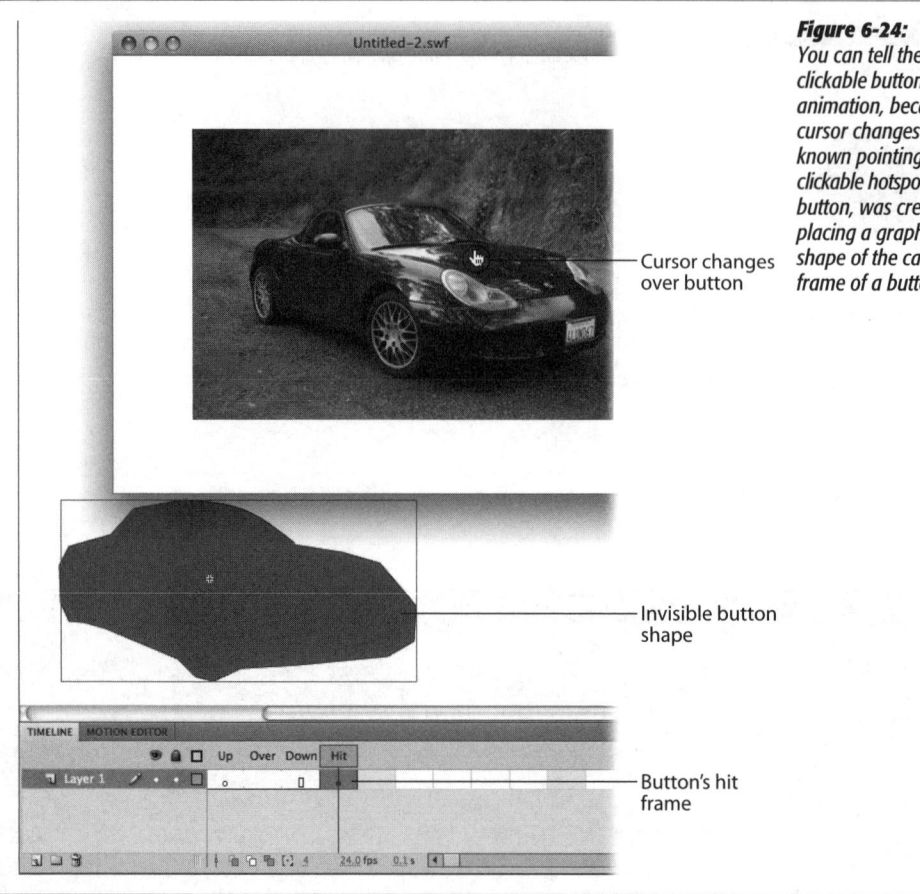

Figure 6-24:
You can tell the car is a clickable button in this Flash animation, because the cursor changes to the well-known pointing finger. This clickable hotspot, or invisible button, was created by placing a graphic, the shape of the car in the Hit frame of a button symbol.

Cursor changes over button

Invisible button shape

Button's hit frame

Editing an instance of a button symbol

You can't change the individual frames of your button instance individually. But Flash *does* let you apply the same changes to *all* the frames of your button instance.

Page 253 shows you the steps you can take to apply color, transparency, and transforms to your button instances. (The steps are identical to those you take to edit a single-frame graphic instance.) But you can also apply *filters*, or visual effects, to your buttons. Filters can turn even a plain oval button into something that looks like you spent hours tweaking it.

Note: Filters aren't just for buttons. You can also apply filters to text blocks (Chapter 16) and movie clip instances.

To apply a filter to a button instance:

1. **On the stage, select the button instance.**

   Flash draws a blue selection box around the instance.

---

2. **In the Properties panel, click the Filters subpanel.**

   If the Filters subpanel is closed, click the triangular button to expand it.

3. **Click the Add Filter button (lower left corner).**

   A pop-up menu appears (Figure 6-25) listing the following filter options.

   - **Drop Shadow.** Displays a shadow on the right and bottom edges of the button.

   - **Blur.** Redraws the surface of the button so that it appears soft and blurred.

   - **Glow.** Similar to a drop shadow, creates a fuzzy aura in the color of your choosing.

   - **Bevel.** Applies brightness and shadow on opposite sides of the button to create a 3-D effect.

   - **Gradient Glow.** Similar to Glow (above), but lets you specify bands of different colors (instead of just one color).

   - **Gradient Bevel.** Similar to Bevel (above), but lets you choose bands of different colors for the brightness and shadow.

   - **Adjust Color.** Lets you individually adjust the brightness, contrast, saturation, and hue of your button.

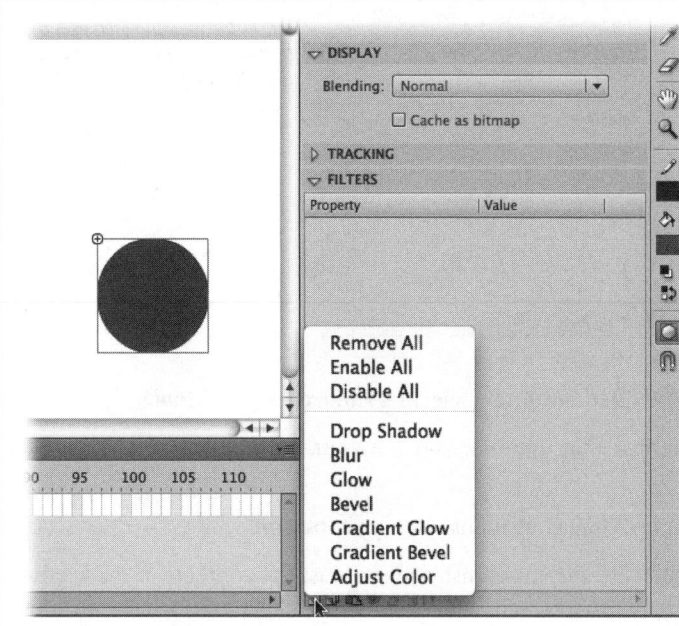

Figure 6-25:
When you click the Add Filter icon in the Filters panel, this pop-up menu appears, showing you all the effects you can add to your button instance.

4. **From the menu, select Glow.**

   A red glowing effect appears around your button, and the Filter panel displays the Glow properties.

5. **Click the down arrow next to Blur X, and then drag the slider to 40.**

   On the stage, the glow diffuses.

6. **Click the Shadow Color icon, and then, from the color picker that appears, click the black swatch.**

   On the stage, the glow turns from red to black, yielding a subtle 3-D effect (Figure 6-26).

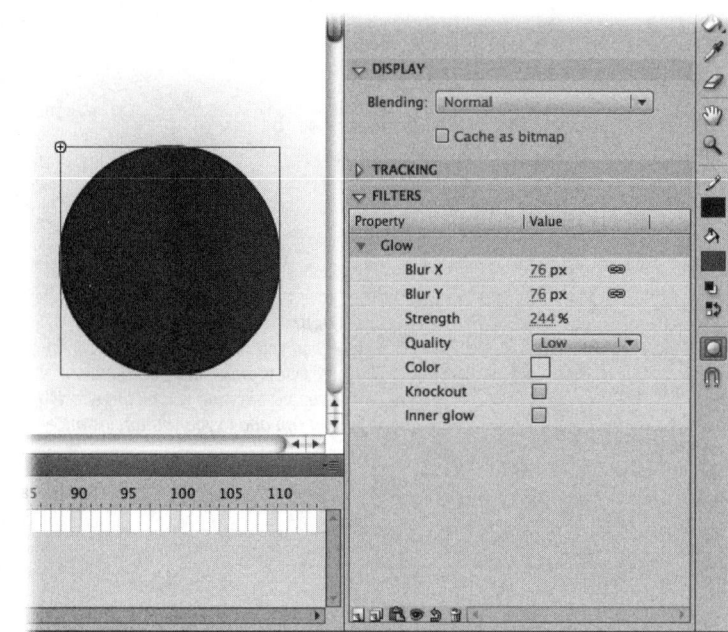

Figure 6-26:
When you apply a Glow filter to a button, you can change the horizontal and vertical width of the glow (Blur X and Blur Y), the density of the blur (Strength), and how far out the blur extends (Quality). You can also choose a different color for your blur or apply a Knockout effect (which leaves the blur but erases the button) or Inner Glow (which erases the blur and then uses the blur color to repaint the surface of the button).

7. **Test your newly edited button by selecting Control → Test Movie.**

   In the test window that appears, you see your button with the Glow effect applied.

8. **In the test window, drag your mouse over your button.**

   Flash applies filters to the entire instance (not just the contents of the keyframe to which you apply them), so the Glow effect remains even when you mouse over the button.

Tip: With filters, you can quickly make a button instance look both unique and spiffy. Flash lets you change the properties of your filters—for example, you can change the size of a blur or the color of a drop shadow—so the drop shadow you apply to one instance doesn't have to look the same as the drop shadow you apply to another instance of the same symbol.

To remove a filter you've applied: In the Filter panel, select the filter you want to remove, and then click the Delete Filter button (trash can).

Tip: Applying a filter isn't an either/or proposition. You can add multiple filters to the same instance to create different effects: For example, you can add both a Glow and a Drop Shadow as shown in Figure 6-27.

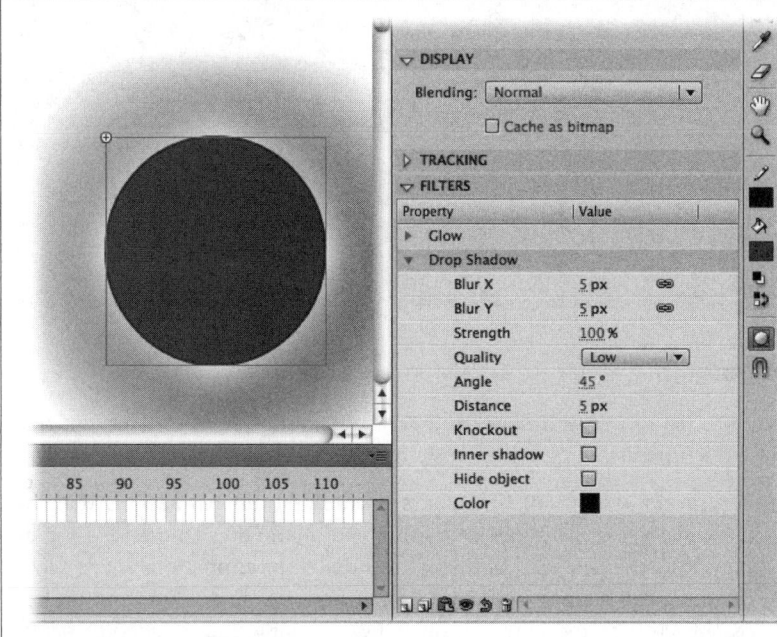

Figure 6-27:
Flash applies filters in top-down order, so adding a Glow and a Drop Shadow yields a different result than adding a Drop Shadow and then a Glow. You can even add the same filter more than once to compound the effect. To change the order of your filters, simply drag them to reposition them in the Filter panel.

Editing a button symbol

You edit a multiframe graphic symbol, like a button, the same way you edit a single-frame graphic symbol: by switching to symbol editing mode (page 238). In both cases, Flash immediately applies the changes you make to the button symbol itself, as well as all the instances of that button symbol.

Organizing Your Symbols

If you do a lot of work in Flash, chances are you're going to create a lot of symbols. But in Flash as in life, if you can't see what you've already got, you're apt to recreate it, or else go without—both of which lose you the benefits of reuse that you're using symbols for in the first place.

The answer? Organize your symbols into folders.

Flash lets you create folders inside the Library. You can use these folders to organize your symbols. For example, you might want to keep all your movie clip symbols in one folder, all your graphic symbols in another, and so on. Or you might want to keep all the symbols related to a composite drawing (like a cartoon character or a corporate logo) in a separate folder. Use whatever organization makes sense to you; you can always reorganize your files and folders later.

To create a folder in the Library:

1. In the Library, click the Options menu. From the pop-up menu that appears, choose New Folder.

2. A folder named *untitled folder 1* appears in the Library beneath your symbols.

3. Replace the folder name by typing in a new, more meaningful name, like *logo, spaceman*, or *intro_scene*. Flash selects the folder name automatically when it creates a new folder, but if you need to change the name after the fact, double-click it.

4. Drag all the logo-related symbols into the *logo* folder, all the spaceman-related symbols into the *spaceman* folder, and so on.

If you need more levels of organization, you can place folders inside folders.

Templates

While symbols let you reuse images and series of frames, *templates* let you reuse entire Flash documents.

Templates are useful when you find yourself cranking out animations that look and behave similarly. For example, say you create marketing animations for display on your corporate Web site. You may find that your animations share a lot of the same elements: your company's logo somewhere on the background, a copyright notice, the same sound clips of your CEO speaking, the same color palette, the same size stage, and the same intro and credit scenes.

Using a template, you can create all these basic elements just once. Then, the next time you're tapped to do a marketing spot, you can load the template and just add the new content you need. You've not only saved yourself a lot of time, but you've also ensured consistency among your animations (highly important in certain corporate circles).

In this section, you see how to create and use your own templates. You also see how to take advantage of Flash's prebuilt templates.

Using a Prebuilt Template

Flash comes with a bunch of templates all ready for you to customize. While they're obviously not specific to your particular company or project, they *can* save you time on a lot of basic animations, including banner ads, slideshows, and presentations. Here's a quick rundown of the templates you find in Flash:

- **Advertising.** Pop-up, skyscraper (skinny vertical), banner (skinny horizontal), and full-page ads.

- **BREW Handsets.** For Flash animations targeted for certain (Qualcomm) phones.

- **Consumer devices.** For Flash animations targeted for certain media players and other portable electronics.

- **Global handsets.** Stages targeted for certain (Symbian) phones.

- **Japanese handsets.** Stages targeted for Japanese phones.

- **Photo Slideshows.** For Flash animations showing drawings or bitmaps overlaid with Forward and Back controls.

- **Quiz.** Simplified data input forms that let your audience page through multiple screens and answer yes/no questions.

> **Note:** Flash's templates are useful—*if* you can figure out what they're supposed to do and how to customize them. To see what few hints the Help system offers, select Help → Flash Help, in the window that appears, type *using templates,* and then click Search. A better option: Check out one of the Flash developer support sites listed in Appendix A.

To use one of the prebuilt templates that comes with Flash:

1. **Select File → New.**

   The New Document window appears.

2. **In the New Document window, click the Templates tab.**

   The "New from Template" window in Figure 6-28 appears.

3. **In the Category box, click to select Photo Slideshows.**

   Modern Photo Slideshow appears selected in the Templates box. You see a thumbnail of the first keyframe in the preview window and, below the preview window, a short description of this template.

4. **Click OK.**

   Flash opens the Modern Photo Slideshow. You may need to adjust the timeline so you can see all the layers in the template, as shown in Figure 6-29.

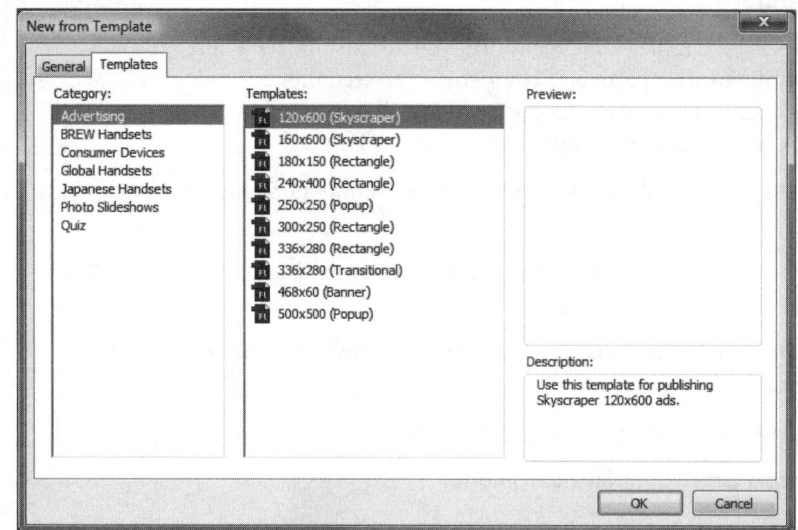

Figure 6-28:
Flash offers a ton of templates you can use to jump-start the animation process. They don't come with descriptions or instructions, but hints are included in each template file itself. In this section, you see how to customize the Photo Slideshow template to create a spiffy slideshow in just a couple of minutes.

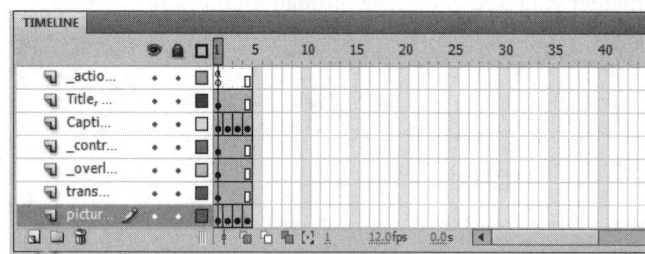

Figure 6-29:
Clicking the bottom of the timeline and dragging downward expands the timeline so you can see all the layers. Other than a few vague hints in the Flash Help, these layer names are your only clues for understanding what you need to do to customize this template.

5. **Select Control → Test Movie to preview the template.** It's always a good idea to preview a template before you begin to customize it.

   A test window similar to the one in Figure 6-30 appears.

6. **In the test window, select File → Close.**

   The test file closes, and Flash brings you back to the template workspace.

   Next, change the title of the slideshow.

7. **In the timeline, click to select the first keyframe in the Title, Date layer.**

   On the stage, you see a selection box around the text "My Photo Album" (Figure 6-31).

8. **Click the text box, and then replace "My Photo Album" by typing Custom Slideshow.**

   Next, replace the photos that appear in the slideshow.

Figure 6-30:
Notice the title (My Photo Album), the screen number (1 of 4), the photo itself (an ocean cliff), and the caption ("The elegant seashore"). You can customize all these items while keeping the nifty controller that lets you scroll forward and back through the photos.

Figure 6-31:
This template was set up to make customization easy: Its creators placed every element you can edit—from the slideshow title to the caption for each picture—on its own separate, appropriately named layer.

9. **Click the first keyframe in the layer named "picture layer". On the stage, click the photo to select it, and then choose Edit → Cut.**

   The photo disappears.

10. **Click the Oval tool, click the stage, and then drag your cursor to create a red circle.**

    This example shows a circle for simplicity's sake in demonstrating the Modern Photo Slideshow template, but after reading Chapter 9 you may prefer to add a scanned-in photo of your own to the stage (page 327).

11. **Repeat the previous step for the second and third keyframes of the picture layer.**

    Insert a square and a star, respectively. There's one more keyframe, which you're going to remove.

12. **Click the fourth keyframe of the picture layer. On the stage, right-click the photo, and then, from the pop-up menu that appears, select Cut.**

    Flash removes the solid black dot that indicates a filled keyframe and replaces it with a hollow dot that indicates an empty keyframe.

    Next, change the captions for your three new images.

13. **Click the first keyframe in the layer named Captions.**

    On the stage, a selection box appears around the text "The elegant seashore". (You may need to scroll down the stage to see the text.)

14. **Click the text box, and then replace "The elegant seashore" by typing** *Circle.*

    Repeat Steps 10 and 11 for the second and third keyframes of the Captions layer, replacing the existing captions with *Square* and *Star*, respectively.

15. **On the timeline, click to select the fourth frame in the "_actions" layer. Then Shift-click the fourth frame of the "picture" layer.**

    Flash highlights the fourth frame of all seven layers, as shown in Figure 6-32.

16. **Right-click the selected frames, and then, from the pop-up menu that appears, select Remove Frames.**

    Flash deletes the fourth frame of every layer.

17. **Test your customized template by selecting Control → Test Movie.**

    You should see something similar to Figure 6-33.

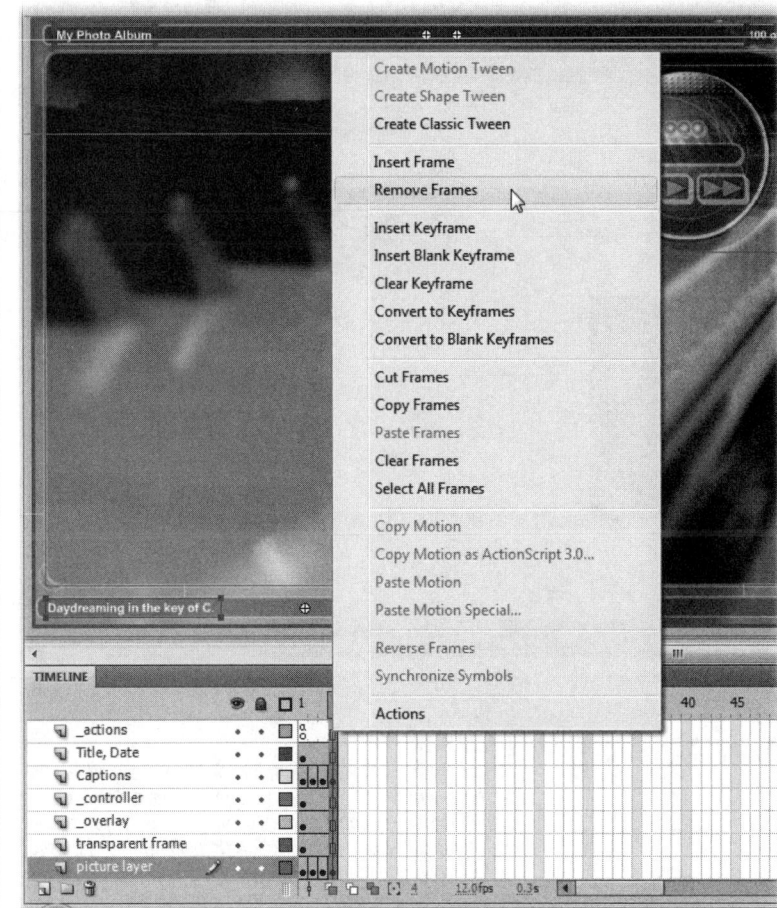

Figure 6-32:
This template displays the slide number (1 of 4, 2 of 4, 3 of 4, and so on) based on how many frames the timeline contains. So because in this example you're only replacing content for three of the frames, you want to remove the fourth frame of each layer so that the template (technically, the template's ActionScript code) can calculate and display the correct number of frames.

Creating and Using Your Own Custom Template

You create a custom template the same way you create a regular Flash document—with one exception, as you see in the steps below.

To create a custom template:

1. **Create a new Flash document. Add to it the images, frames, and layers you want your template to have.**

   Because you know you (or your colleagues) will be reusing this template, you need to think about reuse as you're deciding which graphic elements and effects to add. The box on page 270 gives you some ideas.

2. **Save your template. To do so, choose File → Save As Template.**

   The Save As Template window in Figure 6-34 appears, complete with a thumbnail preview of the first keyframe of your template.

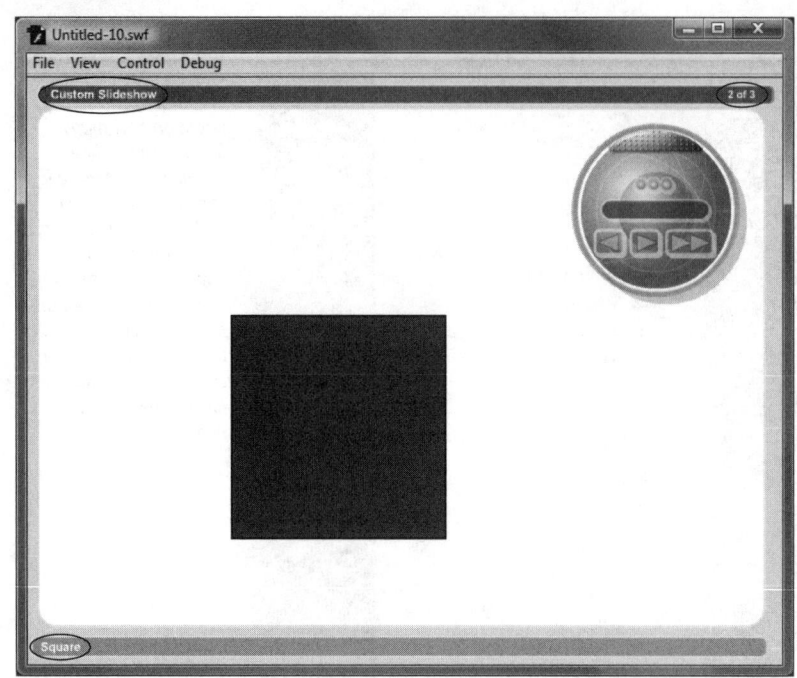

Figure 6-33:
Note the changes you made: the title (now Custom Slideshow), the number of pages (now 1 of 3), the content of the frame itself (a basic square), and the caption (Square). When you click the Next button, you step through your remaining frames containing the square and the star. You've got a professional-looking, fully functional, completely customized slideshow—all for just a few minutes' effort. Behold the power of templates.

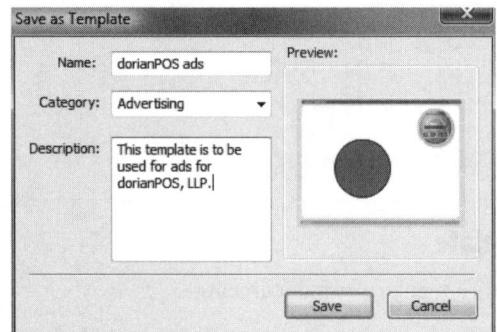

Figure 6-34:
Choosing File → Save As Template displays the window you see here, which lets you type a name (not a file name, but an actual human-readable name), a category (to let you group your templates), and a description (to help remind you which features you added to this template and which situations it's most appropriate for). Be sure to add as complete a description as you can in the 255 characters Flash gives you. The few minutes you spend now will pay off in the future, when you don't have to keep opening the template over and over again just to remind yourself what it does.

3. In the Name field, type a short, descriptive name for your template. Then, from the Category pop-up menu, choose a category.

The categories listed are the same categories you see when you use one of Flash's built-in templates: Advertising, Form Applications, Global Phones, Japanese Phones, PDAs, Photo Slideshows, Presentations, Quiz, and Slide Presentations. If none of these categories seems appropriate for your template, you can type your own category into the Category box.

4. In the Description box, type a complete, concise description of your template, and then click Save.

Flash saves your document as a template.

You use a custom template the same way you use one of Flash's prebuilt templates. To use (open) a custom template:

1. Select File → New.

The New Document window appears.

2. In the New Document window, click the Templates tab.

Your custom template appears in the "New from Template" window listed in the category you selected for it in step 3 above. Figure 6-35 shows you an example.

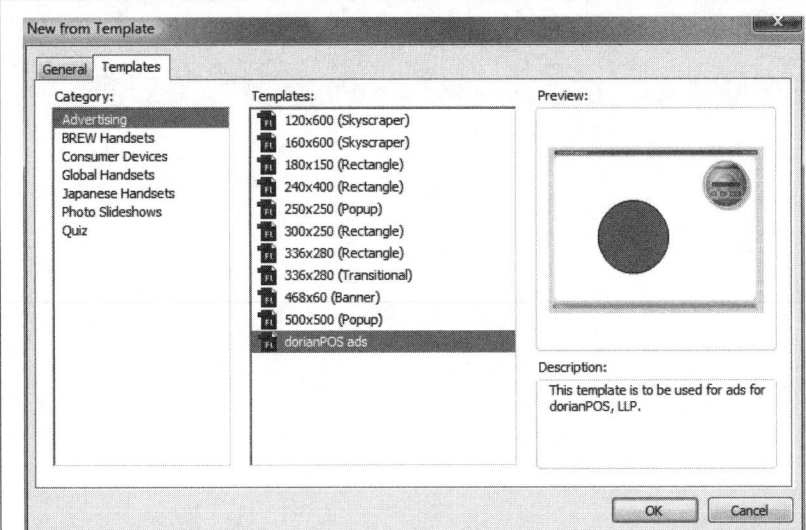

Figure 6-35:
The next time you go to open a template, you see your template listed in the category you selected for it, complete with a preview and the description you typed in when you saved it. Click OK to create a document from this template just as though it were one of Flash's prebuilt templates.

DESIGN TIME

Building a Better Template

Sometimes, you'll find yourself creating a template almost by accident. For example, imagine that you're hard at work on one animation when your boss comes in, peeks over your shoulder, and tells you to create another one "just like that one" for another client. Choose File → Save As Template, continue with the instructions you find on page 44, and you're on your way.

But if you know *beforehand* that you're creating a template, you can plan for reuse. And planning always results in a more useful template. Here are a few planning tips for creating a template you'll use over and over again:

- **Include only reusable stuff**. If you save a working animation as a template (complete with company-specific elements), you'll need to delete any unusable elements each time you reuse the template. Consider up front which elements apply across the board, and include only those in your template.

- **Name your layers**. Giving your layers meaningful names that describe what each layer contains (like actions, sounds, background, buttons, and so on) is always

a good idea. But it's even more important when you're creating a template, because it gives you (or your colleague, or whoever's reusing the template two weeks from now) an easy way to find and change the elements that need to be changed.

- **Document, document, document**. Have pity on the person who tries to reuse your template a month from now, and tell him up front what the template's for (a product demonstration combined with an order form, for example) and what needs to be changed (the company logo, demo movie clip, and three form fields). The quickie description you type when you create your template (below) is rarely enough. Instead, attach a script to the first frame and use ActionScript comments to document the template. Or—better yet—add documentation text to the first frame, where the person reusing your template can't miss it (but can easily delete it before putting the template into action).

Advanced Tweens with the Motion Editor

Tweens have always been a big tool in Flash's animation toolbox, and, as explained in Chapter 3, in Flash CS4 they can do more than ever. Flash's new motion tween (page 127) can do more than just show a car moving down a street—it can make the car stretch out and turn blazing red when it's going really fast and scrunch up when it stops. It can even make the car's shadow change position as the car and sun move across the screen.

You accomplish these sophisticated tweens by making multiple property changes at multiple points in time with the help of Flash CS4's shiny new Motion Editor. This chapter shows you in detail how to apply and fine-tune your motion tweens, focusing in particular on Motion Editor control. You'll start by learning how to use motion presets, which are simply predesigned tweens that you can apply to objects with a couple of mouse clicks. Then, you'll learn some of the different ways you can edit your tweens on the stage, in the timeline, and using the Motion Editor. Along the way, you'll learn how to apply filters for special effects and how to create more realistic motion (easing).

Note: If you need a primer on motion tween basics, or tweens in general, head back to page 127.

Applying Motion Presets

Designing a perfect tween can be a lot of work. It's not so much that it's difficult, but creating a complex motion tween where several properties change at different points in time can be time-consuming. Fortunately, right out of the box, Flash gives you a head start. Open the Motion Presets panel (Window → Motion Presets), and you see a handful of predesigned tweens, as shown in Figure 7-1. Initially, the motion preset panel comes with two folders: Default Presets, where the Adobe-designed presets live and Custom Presets, where you can store tweens you've perfected as motion presets, see page 274. Just click a motion preset to see a mini-preview at the top of the panel.

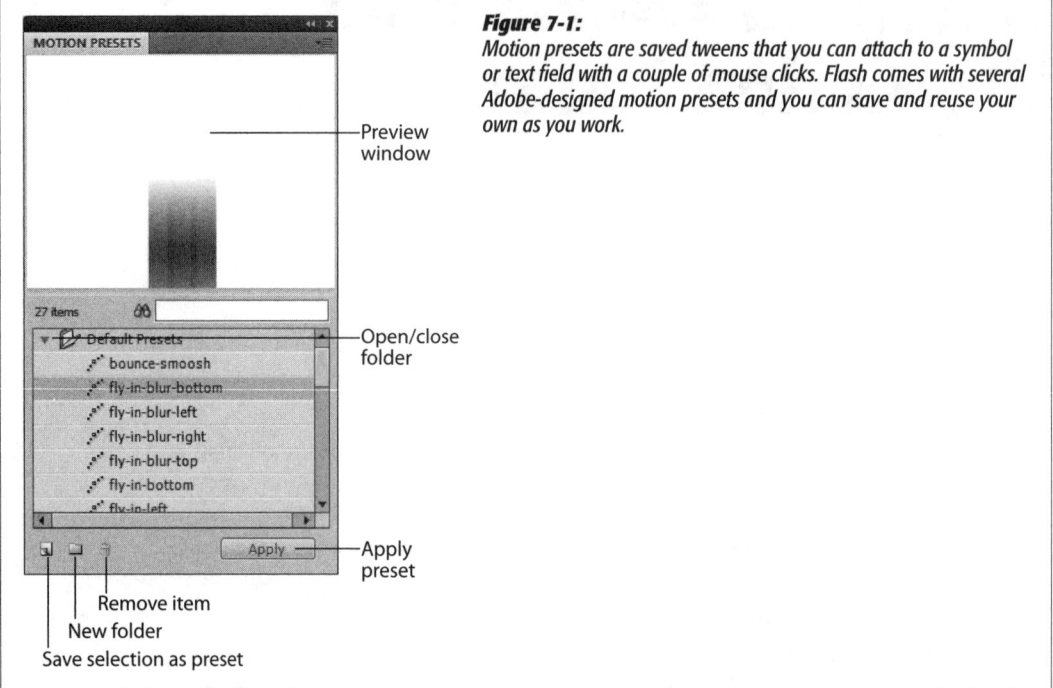

Figure 7-1:
Motion presets are saved tweens that you can attach to a symbol or text field with a couple of mouse clicks. Flash comes with several Adobe-designed motion presets and you can save and reuse your own as you work.

Not only are motion presets useful design tools, they're great learning tools. By dissecting some of the professionally designed presets that come with Flash, you can see how certain effects are created. After you've applied presets in your project, you can modify them, examine them, and steal some of their ideas for your own tweens. To get started, the following steps show how to apply and modify a motion preset called *bounce-smoosh*, which does exactly what the name suggests.

First, the easiest part: applying a motion preset. Like any motion tween, a preset can only be applied to a symbol or a text field. For this exercise, you can draw your own simple circle, or you can use the animated wheel in the file: *bouncing_wheel_begin. fla*, which you'll find on the "Missing CD" page at *http://missingmanuals.com/cds*.

1. **Open the Motion Presets panel by choosing Window → Motion Presets.**

   The Motion Presets panel is small, so you can easily let it float over your work area while you're making a selection, and then close it after you've applied a preset. You won't need it again until you need another preset.

2. Select the symbol you want to tween; in this case, your circle or the wheel from the example file.

The symbol or text field you tween has to be by itself in a layer in the timeline. If the layer holds more than one object, Flash creates a new layer for the object before it applies the tween. If the object can't be tweened (perhaps it's not a symbol), you see a warning like Figure 7-2.

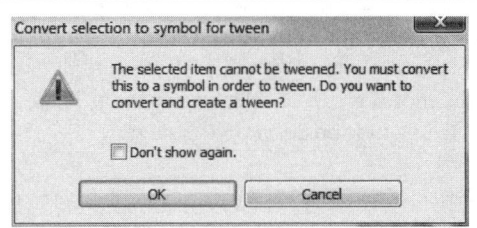

Figure 7-2:
If you try to apply a motion tween to an object other than a symbol or a text field, you'll see this warning.

3. In the presets panel, click the bounce-smoosh tween, and then click Apply.

A motion path appears attached to the object on the stage, and a blue tween appears in the main timeline, as shown in Figure 7-3.

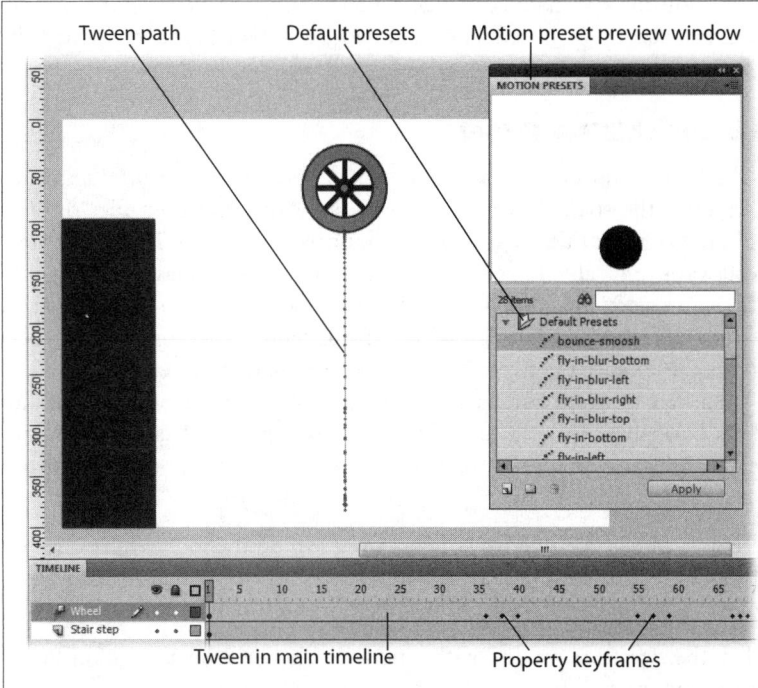

Tween path · Default presets · Motion preset preview window
Tween in main timeline · Property keyframes

Figure 7-3:
After you apply a tween to a movie clip or text field, you see a motion path attached to the tweened object. A blue tween appears in your animation's timeline complete with preset property keyframes.

4. **Press Enter to preview your tween in Flash.**

More often then not, you'll make changes to a preset motion after you apply it. Start by taking a look at how the motion preset behaves. In a bounce-smoosh, the wheel or circle drops straight down from a height, hits the ground and flattens a bit on impact with a cartoonish flair. It bounces a couple of times before coming to rest and regaining its circularity.

5. **Modify the tween just as you would any tween you created from scratch.**

For example, often the tween is working right, but you need to fine-tune the position of both the object and the motion path. With the Selection tool, drag a box around both the object and the motion path to select everything. Then you can drag the whole kit and kaboodle to a new position on the stage.

Note: In different places, this book explains how to make changes to the tween using the motion path (page 130), the timeline (page 282), the Motion Editor (page 286) and the Properties panel (page 127).

Once you've applied a tween using a motion preset, it's no different from a tween that you create from scratch. Also, there's no connection between the tween and the presets panel. If you make changes to the tween in your animation, it has no effect on the one stored in the Motion Presets panel. Vice versa is true, too. Unlike with symbols in the library, making changes to or deleting the tween in the Motion Presets panel has absolutely no effect on animations to which you've applied the preset.

Saving a Custom Motion Preset

Setting up the perfect motion tween can take time. Perhaps you've got a text banner that flies onto the stage, hovers for a readable while, and then flies out. Or maybe you spent time getting a basketball to bounce just right. With all that time invested, you want to be able to reuse that work, and as usual, Flash helps you do just that. You can save your carefully crafted tween as a motion preset, and then, in the future, apply it to new symbols and text fields with a click or two. Furthermore, because you modify the tweens created by presets, they're very versatile and adaptable to different uses. For example, a badminton shuttlecock might not bounce like a basketball, but it's probably faster to apply the basketball-bounce preset to the shuttlecock, and then tweak it a bit than creating a new motion tween from scratch.

Saving a preset is easy and you have couple of ways to do the job. Which one you use may depend on your own preferences or where your mouse happens to hover at the moment. You can choose one of these methods to save a motion preset:

- Right-click the tween or motion path, and then choose Save as Motion Preset from the pop-up menu.

- Select the tween or motion path, and then click the "Save selection as preset" button on the Motion Presets panel (Figure 7-1).

In either case, a dialog box opens where you name the preset, and then click OK. Once that's done, your newly named preset appears in the Custom Presets folder in the Motion Presets panel. (Your custom preset won't have an animated preview like the ones that come with Flash, but you can create one as instructed in the box below.)

DIY Preview

Can I create a preview for my custom motion preset?

If you've gone to the work of creating a custom motion preset, you may want it to have its own nifty preview animation just like the presets Adobe designed. As it turns out, you can do that easily. First, publish your preset to create a SWF file that shows the animation. (The details for publishing SWF files are on page 631.) Then place the SWF file in the folder that holds your motion presets.

That last bit is the tricky part. The motion presets storage location is different for different computers, as shown in the following examples. (The words in brackets, like <hard disk> and <your name>, represent the disk drives and user names on your computer, <locale> represents the locale or language for the computer, for example "en" is used for English.)

- **Mac OS X:** <hard disk>/Users/<your name>/Library/ Application Support/Adobe/Flash CS4/Configuration/ <locale>/Motion Presets/

- **Windows Vista:** <hard disk>/Users\<your name>\AppData\Local\Adobe\Flash   CS4\<locale>\ Configuration\Motion Presets

- **Windows XP:** <hard disk>\Documents and Settings\ <your name>\Local Settings\Application Data\Adobe\ Flash CS4\<locale>\Configuration\Motion Presets\

Deleting motion presets

If you decide that a particular motion preset isn't worthy, you can delete it from the Motion Presets panel. In the Motion Presets panel, click to select the offending preset, and then click the trash can icon at the bottom of the panel. The stored preset disappears from the panel, but it has no effect on any tweens that were created using the preset.

Modifying a Motion Preset

As discussed earlier in this chapter, Adobe gives you a bunch of snazzy motion tweens with Flash. But one designer's perfect tween is another designer's, well…nearly perfect tween. Fortunately, you can customize presets after you apply them. In fact, tweaking a motion preset is great learning ground for designing and perfecting your own tweens. Editing a motion preset is no different from editing a tween you created yourself, so the following sections on "Changing the Motion Path" (page 276) and "Editing a Tween Span" (page 282) apply to both motion presets and the tweens that you create from scratch.

Changing the Motion Path

Whether you used a motion preset or created your own tween, chances are you'll want to tweak the motion path. Perhaps the ball doesn't bounce in just the right places, or that car looks like it's driving off the road. The motion path looks like a line trailing off from the tweened object. As you drag the playhead in the timeline, you'll notice that the tweened object follows the motion path. You can change this path on the stage using the same Selection tool that you use to modify any line:

- **Move the entire motion path.** With the Selection tool, drag a box around the tweened object and any part of the path. Then drag everything to a new spot.

- **Move the starting point for the motion path.** With the Selection tool, drag the square selection point at the beginning of the motion path to a new location. The end of the path remains anchored where it was, while the motion path stretches or shrinks to accommodate the move.

- **Move the ending point of the motion path.** Select the square end point of the path and drag it to a new location. The starting point of the tween remains anchored in place, and the motion path adjusts to the move.

- **Create a curve in the motion path.** With the Selection tool, point to the path; when you see a curve appear next to the cursor arrow, drag to create a curved path (Figure 7-4). You can reshape the path by dragging different points along the path.

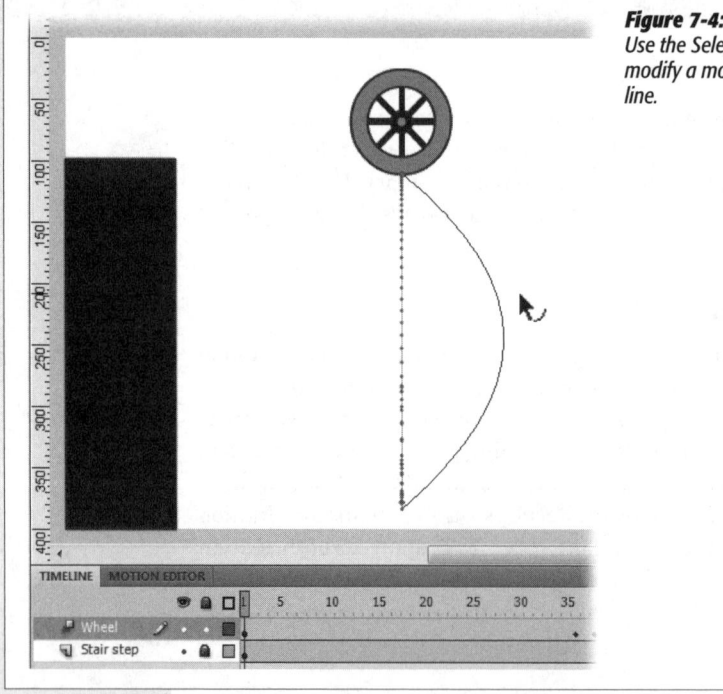

Figure 7-4:
Use the Selection and Subselection tools to modify a motion path just as you would any other line.

• **Change the tweened object's position at any point of the motion path.** In the main timeline, move the playhead to the frame where you want to reposition the tweened object, and then drag the object to a new position. Flash creates a new property keyframe in the timeline and adjusts the motion path to the new position. To use this method to move the start or end point, make sure that the playhead is on the first or last frame of the tween.

In the previous example, the animation would be much more interesting if the wheel rolled along the high step, dropped to the ground, and then bounced in a forward motion. Here's how to change the path for that effect:

1. **Move the playhead to Frame 1 and make sure that nothing is selected. Then drag the wheel so it sits on the step as shown in Figure 7-5.**

    If the entire path moves with the wheel, you've selected both the path and the object. To deselect everything, click an empty spot or press Shift+Ctrl+A (Shift-⌘-A).

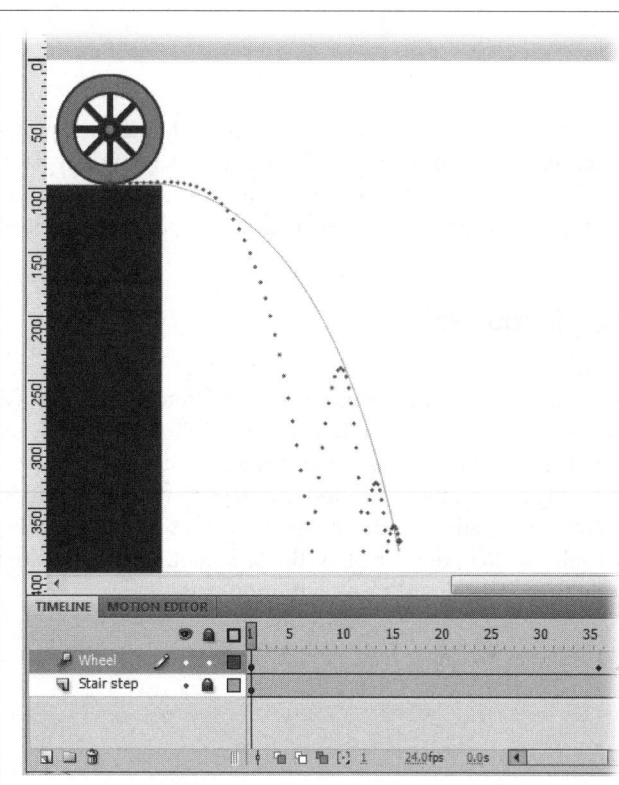

Figure 7-5:
To move the starting point of a motion path you can drag the square end point to a new position.

2. **With the Selection tool, adjust the curve so that the wheel appears to roll along the top of stair step.**

When you move the cursor close to the path, it changes to show a curved line next to the arrow. Drag to adjust the curve in the motion path. The solid line shows the general arc of the motion, while the small dots show the actual position of the tweened object at different points in time.

3. **Adjust the end of the motion path so the wheel moves to the right as it bounces.**

You can stretch the path to the right side of the stage, giving the wheel a feeling of increased forward motion as it bounces.

4. **Preview the animation and fine-tune it as necessary.**

If you got it perfect the first time, great! If not, try zooming in a little and fine-tuning the motion path as described in step 2. If you'd like to see an example, you can find *bouncing_wheel_finished.fla* on the "Missing CD" page at *http://missingmanuals.com/cds*.

Deleting a motion path

You can delete a motion path from a tween by simply selecting it, and then pressing Delete. The consequence, of course, is that your tween isn't going anyplace. The tweened object remains stranded at its starting point until you provide further instructions. For example, you can copy and paste in a new path, as described next.

Copying and Pasting a Motion Path

Flash gives you tools to create perfect shapes like circles, rectangles, polygons, and stars, not to mention the precise control that comes with the Pen tool. You can use any of these drawing tools to create a motion path. If you need a path that matches a perfect shape or is extremely complex, it's faster and easier to use Flash's drawing tools, rather than dragging tween objects around the stage to modify a motion path. First you need to create the path with one of the tools that creates a stroke; that is, any of the shape tools, the Pen, the Pencil, or the Line tool. Then, you paste that stroke into an existing tween that doesn't have a motion path.

Note: A file with a completed version of this project, *orient_to_path_finished.fla*, is available at *http://missingmanuals.com/cds*.

Here are the steps:

1. **In a new Flash document, create two layers, each with 48 frames.**

After you create the second layer, Shift-click to select the 48th frame in both layers, and then press F5 to add new frames on both layers.

2. Create a text field with the words *not oriented,* and then rename the layer *not oriented.*

    Make the text nice and bold and about 32 points in size. Double-click the layer name so you can edit it.

3. Right-click a frame in the timeline of the "not oriented" layer, and then choose Create Motion Tween from the pop-up menu.

    You now have a motion tween with no motion and no tween, because you haven't yet made any changes to the tweened-object's properties.

4. In the other layer, use the Oval tool to draw a circle, and then rename that layer *circle.*

    Set the oval fill color to "none" by clicking the swatch with the Paint Bucket, and then, in the upper right corner of the panel with color swatches, click the square with a stroke through it. Make the circle about 200 pixels in diameter. If necessary, you can set the size in the Properties panel.

5. Use the Eraser tool, with a small eraser size, to erase a little bit of the circle.

    You can't use a closed shape as a motion path, so you need to break the path at some point. When you're done erasing, your stage should look something like Figure 7-6.

6. Using the Selection tool, drag a box around the circle to select the entire circle. Copy it (Ctrl+C or Control-C), click the "not oriented" tween layer, and then paste it (Ctrl+V or Control-V) into the tween.

    As soon as you paste the circle into the tween layer, the text field attaches itself to the path. At this point, it's easier to examine your tween if you hide the original circle by clicking the show/hide button in the "circle" layer (Figure 7-6).

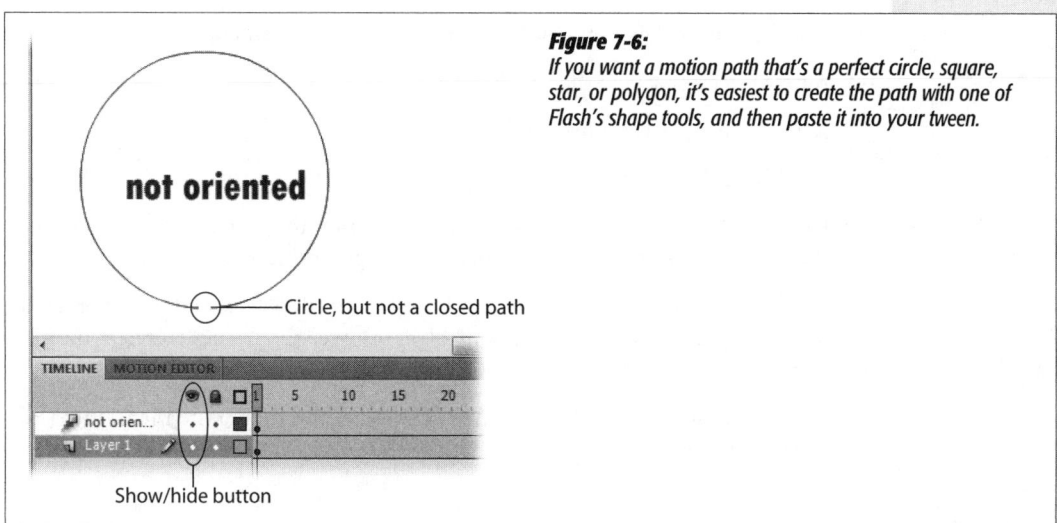

Figure 7-6:
If you want a motion path that's a perfect circle, square, star, or polygon, it's easiest to create the path with one of Flash's shape tools, and then paste it into your tween.

7. **Press Enter or Return to preview the animation.**

   Your "not-oriented" text field moves in a circular motion, but the text isn't oriented to the circle. It remains right-side up and oriented to the stage. That looks a little odd, but don't fret. You'll learn how to orient the text to the circle in the next section.

You can use any stroke as a motion path, even complex strokes created using the Pen tool with multiple complex Bezier curves. Just make sure you're not using a closed path. Even though the circle isn't a closed path, the motion of the text looks like it's making a complete circle. When the movie clip loops, no one in your audience will ever know there's a break in the circle.

Orienting Tweened Objects to a Motion Path

Orienting text fields and symbols to a motion path is as simple as clicking a checkbox. In this section, you'll learn how to do that as well as another handy technique—copying and pasting a motion from one layer to another in the same animation. When you're done, you'll have one Flash file with two examples of circular motion. In one, the text field is oriented to the circle; in the other, it's not (Figure 7-7).

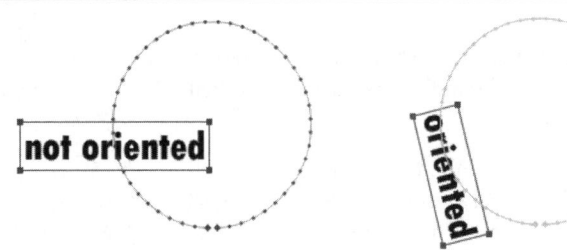

Figure 7-7:
The text field on the left follows the motion path in a circular motion. The text field on the right is oriented to the circular path, so the top of the text field always points to the middle of the circle.

1. **Click the Insert Layer button in the timeline's lower-left corner.**

   A new layer appears in the timeline.

2. **Rename the new layer** *oriented.*

   Double-click the layer, and then type the new name.

3. **Click the "not oriented" layer name to select all the frames in that layer, and then copy the frames (Edit → Timeline → Copy Frames).**

   When you click the layer name, Flash automatically selects all the frames in the layer. You can also Ctrl-drag (Control-drag) over the frames to select multiple frames.

4. **Click the first frame of the "oriented" timeline, and then paste the frames (Edit → Timeline → Paste Frames).**

When you paste frames into the timeline, Flash inserts the pasted frames, pushing any existing frames on down the timeline.

Note: You can also right-click the timeline to see a shortcut menu that has both the Copy Frames and Paste Frames commands.

5. **Shift-drag the end of the "oriented" timeline to the 48th frame so it matches the length of other layers.**

   At this point, your oriented timeline is almost identical to the not oriented layer.

6. **Edit the text field to read oriented.**

   With the Text tool still selected, you can resize the text field to fit the text by double-clicking the box in the text field's upper-right corner.

7. **Click the motion path, and then, in the Properties panel, turn on the "Orient to path" checkbox.**

   If the "Orient to path" checkbox isn't showing, click to open the Rotation panel in the Properties panel, as shown in Figure 7-8. Notice that in the timeline, Flash has added a property keyframe to every frame of the tween, since the rotation of the text field changes in every single frame.

8. **Preview your animation (Ctrl+Enter on a PC; ⌘-Return on a Mac).**

   Your animation has two text fields that follow a circular path. The text that says "oriented" is oriented toward the circle and rotates as it makes its rounds. The text that says "not-oriented" remains upright while it follows the motion path.

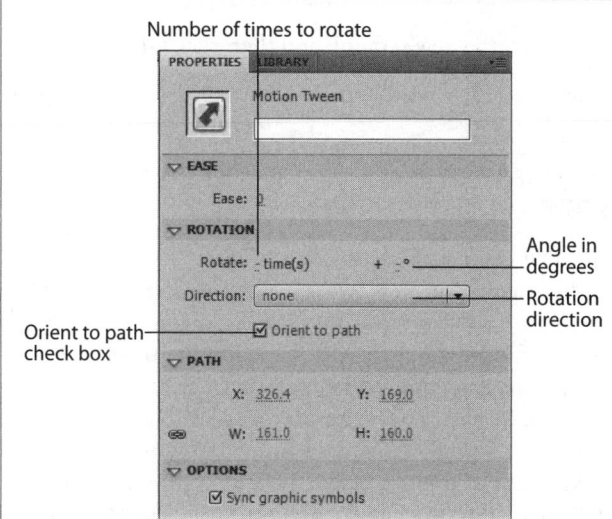

Number of times to rotate

Orient to path check box

Angle in degrees

Rotation direction

Figure 7-8:
Here the Rotation panel is set to align a symbol to the motion path. Other options (not set) control the direction, angle, and number of rotations.

Other things you can do in the Rotation panel

The Rotation panel in the Properties panel has a few other settings in addition to "Orient to path." You can use the Direction drop-down menu to choose clockwise (CW) or counter-clockwise (CCW) rotation for a tweened symbol or text field. This rotation refers to the tweened object rotating around its center point, not its path around the circular motion path; in other words, it makes a text field or symbol spin during the tween. Above the Direction drop-down menu, you can set the number of times the object spins and its angle at a particular point in time.

Note: If you turn on "Orient to path", these other settings become unavailable, as shown in Figure 7-8. Vice versa is true, too. Setting Direction to any setting other than "none" turns off the "Orient to path" option.

Swapping the Tweened Object

Suppose you create the perfect tween for logo or a text banner. It spins, it moves in 3-D, and even the transparency changes so it fades in and out at just the right moment. Then your client informs you of a big change—there's a new company logo or different text. Before you pull your hair out, read on to see how easy it is to swap the object of a motion tween. Remember, a motion tween is applied to a single object, so it's simply a matter of shifting all the property value changes over to a new movie clip or text field. To swap a symbol for a tweened object, follow these steps.

1. **In the original tween, select the symbol.**

   The tween's properties appear in the Properties panel.

2. **In the Properties panel, click the Swap button.**

   The Swap button appears beneath the symbol's name and type.

3. **In the Swap Symbol box, select the new symbol, and then click OK.**

   The new symbol replaces the old symbol and performs all the same property changes.

Editing a Tween Span

The tween span in the timeline deserves a closer look (Figure 7-9), since it gives you a good overview of what's going on in a tween. When you create a motion tween, Flash colors it blue to set it off from the other layers, so you can easily find your way around. Property keyframes are diamond shaped in the timeline to distinguish them from the circle-shaped standard keyframes. Clicking anywhere on the tween selects the entire tween and moves the playhead to that frame in the tween. What if you need to select a single frame in a tween? Suppose you want to copy and paste the tweened object at that particular position into another frame. In that case, Ctrl-click (⌘-click) the timeline to select a single frame, then use the Copy Frame (Ctrl+Alt+C or ⌘-Option-C) and Paste Frame (Ctrl+Alt+V or ⌘-Option-V) commands.

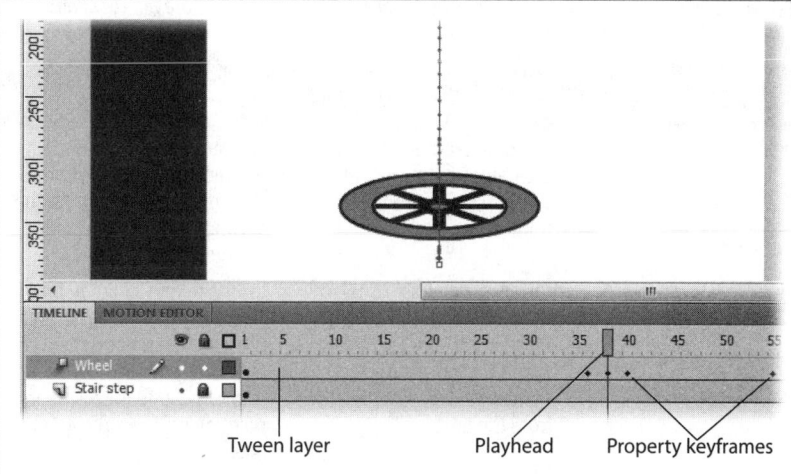

Tween layer　　　　Playhead　　Property keyframes

When you apply a motion tween to an object, Flash automatically sets aside a certain number of frames for the tween, marking them with the blue highlight. If there's only one keyframe on the layer, Flash uses all the layer's frames for the tween. Otherwise, if there are several keyframes on a layer, Flash uses all the frames between two keyframes. So, being the clever designer you are, you take this into account when you create your motion tweens; you lengthen or shorten the available space in the timeline to make your tweens just the right length. Still, there are times when you need to make a tween longer or shorter after the fact. The main thing to consider when you change the number of frames in your tween is the effect the change has on your carefully positioned property keyframes. For example, suppose you have the perfect tween for a basketball bouncing, but it seems to be running too slowly. You want to speed up the bouncing motion but keep the relative positions of the property keyframes the same. In that case, use the first option in Table 7-1—drag the end of the timeline. In another case, you may want to trim a few frames off the end of your time, making it shorter, but you don't want the property keyframes to change position at all. To do that, Shift-drag the end of the timeline.

Table 7-1. *Want to lengthen or shorten the timeline of your motion tween? Here are the commands and the way they affect the property keyframes.*

Action	How to do it...	Effect on property keyframes
Make a motion tween longer or shorter.	Drag the end of the timeline.	Property keyframes move proportionately, keeping their relative position along the tween.
Keep a tweened object on the stage after it's motion is complete.	Shift-drag the end of the timeline.	Has no effect on property keyframes.

Table 7-1. *Want to lengthen or shorten the timeline of your motion tween? Here are the commands and the way they affect the property keyframes. (continued)*

Action	How to do it...	Effect on property keyframes
Remove frames from a tween.	Ctrl-drag (⌘-drag) to select the frames to be deleted. Then press Shift-F5 to remove frames.	The number of frames between property keyframes stays the same, except for the segment where the frames are removed.
Insert frames into a tween.	Ctrl-drag (⌘-drag) to select the number of frames to insert in the timeline. Then right-click the selected frames. Choose Insert Frame from the time.	Inserts frames at the point of selection. Keyframes before the insertion point remain in the same position. Keyframes beyond the insertion point move down the timeline.
Move a tween span in the same layer.	Drag the tween span to a new point in the timeline.	The relationship of all the keyframes stays the same; however, the move erases the existing frames at the new location.
Change the breakline between two adjacent tween spans.	Drag the breakline to a new point.	Property keyframes move proportionately, keeping their relative position along the tween.
Delete a tween span.	Right-click the tween span, and then choose Remove Frames or Clear Frames to replace the selection with standard frames.	Deletes all the property keyframes.

Viewing and Editing Property Keyframes in the Timeline

Property keyframes appear in the tween span at the point when any property changes. Those properties can include:

- **Position** shown as X/Y coordinates in the Properties panel.

- **Scale** shown as H/W (height and width) coordinates.

- **Skew,** created with the Transform tool.

- **Rotation** around the transformation point.

- **Color** including Tint, Brightness, and Alpha (transparency)

- **Filters,** like Drop Shadow, Blur, and Glow.

Suppose you want to change the width of a symbol or text field in the middle of a motion tween. So, you drag the playhead to the point in the timeline where you want the change to happen. Then, with the tweened object selected, you make the width change using the W setting in the Properties panel. Flash automatically adds a diamond-shaped property keyframe to the tween span to mark the change. As seen on page 283, a single tween span can end up with bunches of property keyframes scattered all up and down the timeline. Single property keyframe markers can represent more than one type of tween, too; for example, you may have both a color change and a scale change in the same frame. Sometimes when you're working with your tween, you want to zero in on property keyframes for specific types of changes. Perhaps you want to double-check all the color property keyframes. In that case, right-click the timeline, and then choose View Keyframes from the shortcut menu, as shown in Figure 7-10. Toggle the different options until only the Color option is checked.

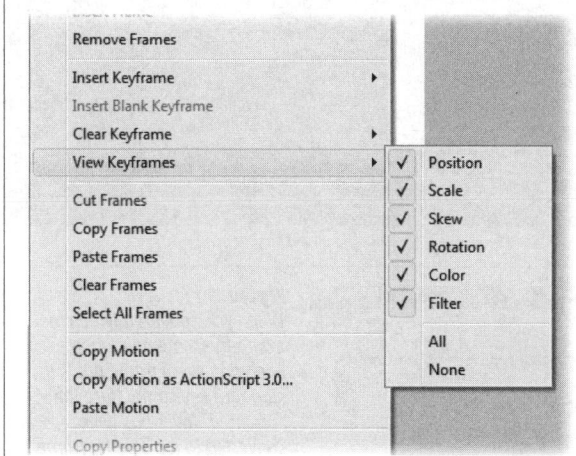

Figure 7-10:
You can select which property keyframes you want marked in the timeline. Right-click a tween span, and then choose View Keyframes to see this menu.

Tip: As you're trying out different effects with the Motion Editor, you may experiment your way from a good motion tween to a not so good motion tween. Don't forget about the History panel (Windows → Other Panels → History), where you can backtrack to a previous (and better) point in your work. Just drag the arrow handle on the left side of the panel back to where things looked good.

Copying Properties Between Property Keyframes

There may be times when you want to duplicate the properties in one property keyframe to another elsewhere in the tween span, or perhaps to an entirely different tween span. For example, it's a great way to freeze the action for a certain number of frames. Create two motion keyframes with identical properties. Insert frames inbetween the keyframes to lengthen the amount of time the action freezes. Or remove frames to make it shorter.

Start by Ctrl-clicking (⌘-clicking) the property keyframe you want to copy to select a single frame. Right-click that frame, and then choose Copy Properties from the shortcut menu. Head over to the destination frame where you want to paste the

properties and select that single frame using a Ctrl-click (⌘-click). Then, right-click
that selected frame; you can then choose Paste Properties to paste in all the properties, or Paste Properties Special, where you can specify which properties to paste.

FREQUENTLY ASKED QUESTION

No Longer a Tween

Can I change a tween to a frame-by-frame animation?

Yes. Sometimes you may want to work with the individual
frames inside of a tween. Perhaps you want to copy and use
them in another scene. Before you do that, you need to convert the tween to a frame-by-frame animation. What you're
basically doing is changing every frame in your tween to a
keyframe that contains a copy of the tweened object with all
the adjusted position, scale, rotation, and color properties.
Keep in mind, though, that doing so substantially increases
the size of your Flash animation.

Right-click the tween span you want to convert. Choose
"Convert to Frame by Frame Animation" from the shortcut
menu. The blue tween highlight disappears from the timeline and is replaced with keyframes lined up like dominoes,
as shown in Figure 7-11. These are standard keyframes,
mind you, not property keyframes.

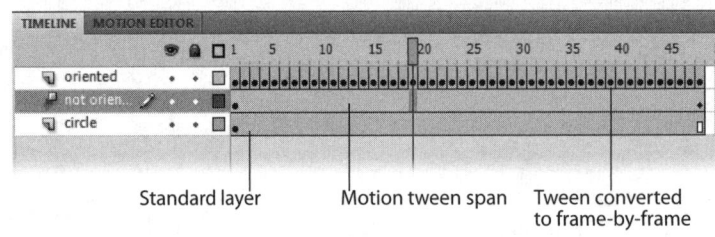

Standard layer   Motion tween span   Tween converted
to frame-by-frame

Figure 7-11:
*When you convert a tween to
frame-by-frame animation,
each and every frame holds a
standard keyframe. Here the
"oriented" layer has been
converted to a frame-by-frame
animation.*

A Tour of the Motion Editor

The Motion Editor, a new feature in Flash CS4, is like a powerful microscope that
lets you examine a motion tween's innards. Combining the features of the timeline and the Properties panel, the Motion Editor focuses on a single tween span,
showing you its workings at a seemingly molecular level. Not only that, the Motion
Editor gives you the power to make a change to any tweenable property at any
point in time. With all this firepower, you can create very complex tweens and
control them with better precision than ever before.

To open the Motion Editor, go to Window → Motion Editor. The Motion Editor
won't show its stuff unless you select either a tweened object on the stage or a
tween span in the timeline. (If you want to experiment with an existing tween, you
can download *bridge.fla* from the "Missing CD" page at *http://missingmanuals.com/
cds.*) At first glance, the Motion Editor may look a little intimidating, with lots of
properties, numbers, widgets and graph lines. Don't be put off—it's not tough to

master these elements and bend those motion tweens to your iron will. If you've used Flash's custom ease feature before (it's been around since Flash 8), you have a head start.

Tip: Using the Essentials workspace, which this book uses throughout, the Motion Editor appears as a tab below the stage, next to the timeline (Figure 7-12). If you have room, though, you may want to drag the tab to a new location—like a second monitor. Giving the Motion Editor more room makes your work easier and faster.

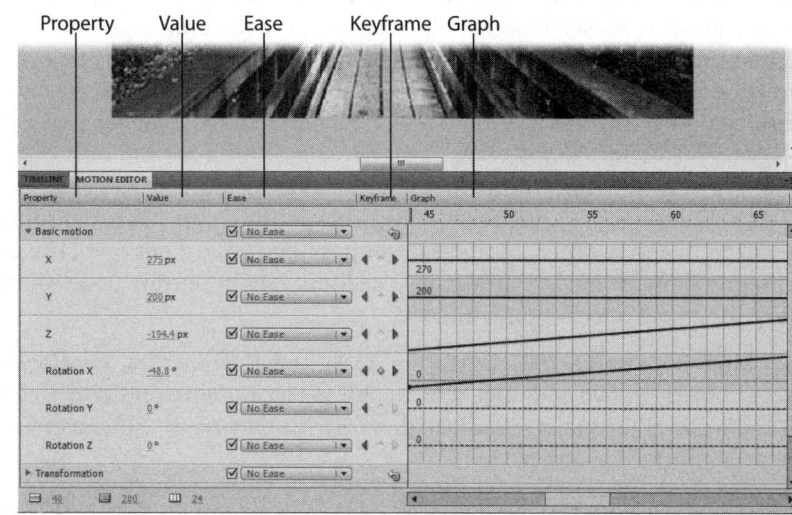

Figure 7-12:
Flash CS4 introduces a new way to create tweens and a shiny new tool to do the job: the Motion Editor. Now designers can control tweens with numeric precision and the help of graphic displays.

There's a lot going on with the Motion Editor, so it's best to introduce yourself a section at a time. At the very top, there are labels for each of its sections:

- Below the **Property** label, you see the same properties that you've used in the Properties panel, like the X/Y position coordinates, the W/H (width and height) properties, and so on.

- The **Value** settings should look familiar by now. For each property, you can click and type a new value, or you can drag to scrub in a value.

- The **Ease** tools (covered on page 293) let you speed up or slow down specific portions of your tweens. For example, you could make a moving car start off slowly, and then gain speed.

- The triangle buttons under **Keyframe** give you a way to jump forward and backward between the property keyframes. You use the diamond button to add and delete property keyframes.

• The **Graph** gives you a visual representation of the way properties change over time, showing the property values as they increase and decrease. The vertical axis displays property values, while the horizontal axis measures time—just the way things are in the main timeline. The squares on the graph represent property keyframes. The graph isn't just some way to show you the geeky innards of your tween, it's a design tool. You can drag the graph elements around to make changes in your animation. (More on that on page 290.)

Workflow for Common Tweens

You won't see anything at all in the Motion Editor unless you select a tween span in the timeline or a tweened object on the stage. Most of the time, you want to set up the basic framework of your tween in the main timeline before you work with the Motion Editor. That way, you can establish the timing for the major events in the tween, using some of the steps described in "Editing a Tween Span" on page 282. Using a famous cartoon example, you might have the roadrunner run off a cliff at Frame 6; then up to Frame 12 the roadrunner hangs in mid-air, feet churning; from Frame 12 to Frame 18, the roadrunner drops to the desert floor, and so on. After you have the basic timing for these major positions worked out, you can turn to the Motion Editor to perfect the details. The Motion Editor breaks down all the tweenable properties into five categories:

• **Basic Motion** is where you change the X, Y, and Z properties, positioning tweened objects in two and three dimensions. (You can move only movie clips and text fields in three dimensions, so those are the only types of objects where you can apply the Z property.)

• Under **Transformation** you tween properties like Scale X (width), Scale Y (height), Skew X, and Skew Y.

• **Color Effect** includes properties for Alpha, Brightness, Tint, and Advanced Color (a combination of color effects).

• Use the **Filters** panel to apply filters like Glow, Blur, and Drop Shadow.

• **Eases** give you the ability to speed up or slow down property changes at specific points in the timeline. The details are on page 293.

Within each of those categories you can:

• Add and remove property keyframes (page 289).

• Move property keyframes to change values and timing (page 290).

• Fine-tune and smooth property changes using Bezier curves (page 290).

• Add and remove color effects and filters (page 291).

• Apply easing to change the timing of property changes (page 293).

Tip: Keep in mind that a visual effect, like the aforementioned roadrunner, can be composed of several different tweened objects. The spinning legs can be a movie clip that stretches as gravity takes effect—the legs keep spinning but become elongated. Facial features like the beak and eyes can be separate tweened objects on different layers, giving you the opportunity to create lots of different facial expressions.

Adding and Removing Property Keyframes

In the Motion Editor, every property has its own graph line, as shown in Figure 7-13. Move from left to right along that graph line, and you're marking the passage of time. Like the main timeline, it's measured in frames. The vertical axis of the graph tracks changes in value for that particular property. The units used differ according to the property. For example, if it's the Y coordinate in the Basic Motion panel, the value relates to the vertical position of an object on the stage and it's measured in pixels. If it's the Alpha value in the Color Effect group, it's a percentage indicating the transparency (0%) or opacity (100%) of an object.

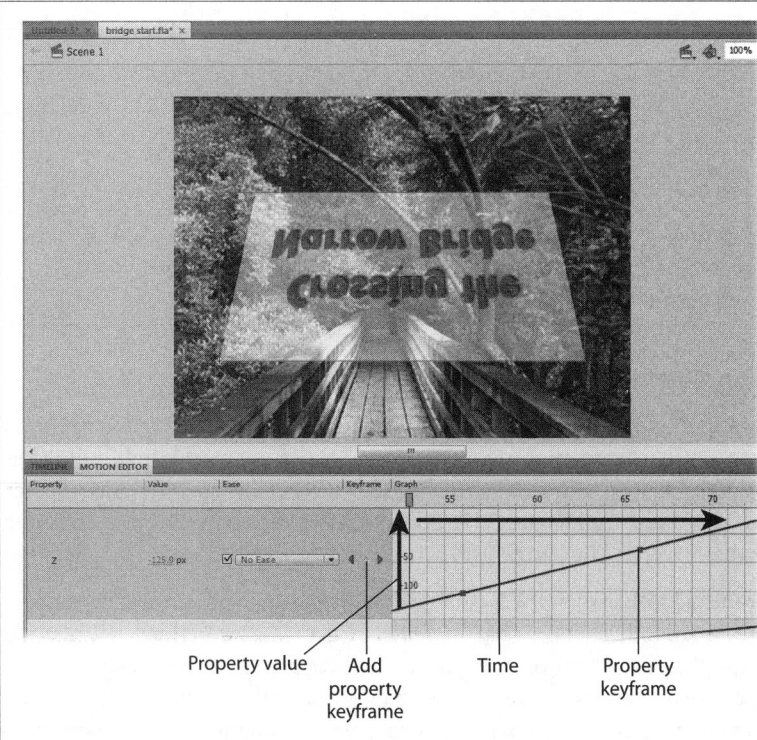

Figure 7-13:
Each property has a graph where the horizontal axis marks time in frames and the vertical axis shows the change in property values.

Property value · Add property keyframe · Time · Property keyframe

You apply tweens to values by placing property keyframes along the timeline; Flash calculates the changes for all the values between two property keyframes (Figure 7-13). To add a property keyframe, move the playhead to the frame where you want to record a change in value, and then click the diamond-shaped button under Keyframe. This button is a toggle: If there aren't any keyframes at that position, Flash creates one. If there's a keyframe at that position, Flash removes it.

There are other ways to add property keyframes to a graph line. One of the quickest is simply to right-click at a point in the graph line, and then choose Add Keyframe from the shortcut menu. Another way to add keyframes is to drag the playhead to a specific frame, and then make a change in a property's value. Flash automatically creates the property keyframe.

The Motion Editor uses a solid line in the graph to indicate values in-between keyframes—values that are changing. A dashed line indicates that the values of the property aren't changing—*static*, in Flash-speak.

Moving Property Keyframes

When you work with tweens, timing is everything. Whether you're controlling the movement of a jumping cheetah or a building changes color as it explodes, you control the timing by moving property keyframes up and down the timeline. You reposition property keyframes by dragging them with the Selection or Subselection tools. By moving the property keyframe up and down, you increase or decrease the value of that property. If you drag a property keyframe left or right along the timeline, you change the frame (time) at which the property change happens.

There's another way that you can move property keyframes up and down the timeline—with roving keyframes. Using this method, Flash keeps track of the relationship of keyframes even as you make changes to the timeline. See the box on page 297 for the details.

Tip: Sometimes when you move a property keyframe, the entire graph line moves. That's because you've somehow selected more than one property keyframe. To deselect all the property keyframes, just click an empty spot on the graph, and then try your move again.

Fine-tuning Property Changes

In the Motion Editor, the Basic Motion properties X, Y, and Z go everywhere hand-in-hand. Whenever you change one of the properties, the Motion Editor registers the values for the other two. It's Flash's way of keeping tweened objects pinned down in time and space. The Basic Motion properties are also the only properties that you can't fine-tune using Bezier line tools.

For any properties other than the Basic Motion properties, you can use Bezier controls to create smooth changes that increase or decrease over time. It's just like editing a line that you draw on the stage. The property keyframes can be either sharp-angled corner points where a value changes abruptly, or they can be gradual curves. Initially, property keyframes are corner points. Right-click a property keyframe to change a corner point to a curve, as shown in Figure 7-14. If there are property keyframes on both sides of the one you click, you can choose whether to add a single Bezier control handle ("Smooth left" or "Smooth right") or add two handles ("Smooth point"). If you right-click a property keyframe that's already a curve, you can turn it back into a corner point.

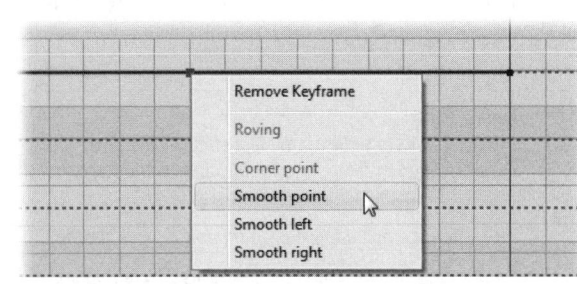

Figure 7-14:
Right-click a property keyframe to change a corner point to a curve. The menu shows different options depending on the position of the property keyframe.

Adding and Removing Color Effects

Your tween span has no Color Effects until you apply them (in the Properties panel or the Motion Editor). To add a color effect in the Motion Editor, position the playhead on the frame where you want to make a change, click the + button, and then choose the effect you want to add: Alpha, Brightness, Tint, or Advanced Color. Once you choose an effect, its subpanel appears under Color Effect. Click the Value setting to the right of the property name, and then type a new value.

Note: Alpha sets the transparency for an object. If you want to apply a combination of Alpha, Brightness, and Tint, use the Advanced Color option.

To remove a Color Effect, click the − button, and then choose the name of the effect from the pop-up menu. Flash removes the property changes from the tweened object and the effect's subpanel goes away.

Using Filters in Tweens

Flash includes a handful of standard filters that you apply to movie clips and text fields, and when you apply filters using the Motion Editor, you can change the values of these filters over time. Want a drop shadow to change its angle as the sun moves across your animation? You can do it with the Motion Editor (Figure 7-15).

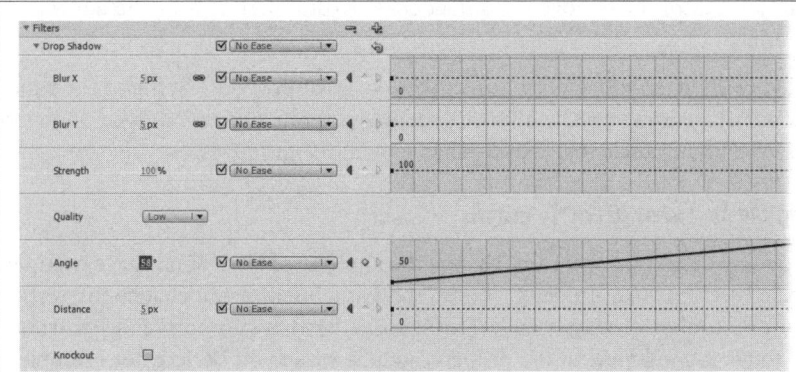

Figure 7-15:
Filters sometimes have multiple properties. The Drop Shadow filter shown here has properties for the shadow's blurriness, strength, quality, and angle. Not shown, there are even more properties for the color and type of shadow created.

Don't be afraid to experiment with the filter effects. A single filter can create dramatically different effects as shown in Figure 7-16.

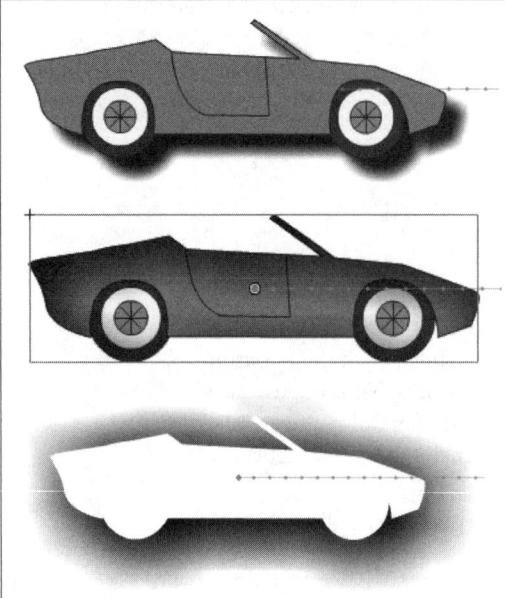

Figure 7-16:
You don't have to settle for the first effect a filter gives you. The Drop Shadow filter, for example, gives some remarkably different effects.

Top: When you first apply a drop shadow it looks like this.

Middle: Adjusting the Inner Shadow gives the car a more 3-D look.

Bottom: The Knockout property makes the car look like a paper cutout.

Customizing Your Motion Editor View

Working with Flash, you fight a constant battle to get a good view of the stage, the timeline, and all of the panels and windows. It's a balancing act where you're constantly expanding this and shrinking that. Adding the Motion Editor to the mix just makes the problem tougher. It's so packed with properties, graphs, and widgets that it requires tweaking to achieve a workspace that works for you. If you plan to do a lot of work in Flash and you don't have a two-monitor system, think seriously about upgrading to one. With two monitors, you can leave your Motion Editor open in one monitor and keep your stage and main timeline open on another. To move the Motion Editor, or remove it from a docked position, drag it by the tab with its name on it.

Initially, Flash gives you a fairly skimpy view of each property. Some of the panels are closed, depending on the kinds of changes in your tween. To open and close panels, click the triangle toggle buttons as shown in Figure 7-17.

Getting the best view property graphs

Unlike some windows, you can't change the amount of horizontal space occupied by labeled sections like Property, Value, and Ease, but you can change the vertical space in a number of ways. That vertical space is what's important when you're trying to get a good view of the property graphs while you perfect, for example, a custom ease (page 296). You can expand a single property graph by clicking anywhere in the panel to the left of the graph. That graph remains expanded until you click the panel again or click another property panel to expand a different graph. This feature means that only one graph can be expanded at a time. Two settings in the lower left corner of the Motion Editor control the height of graphs. A third setting controls the number of frames displayed in the Motion Editor timeline:

• **Graph Size** sets the height of all the graphs.

• **Expanded Graph Size** sets the height of the one expanded graph.

• **Viewable Frames** sets the number of frames showing in the graph timeline.

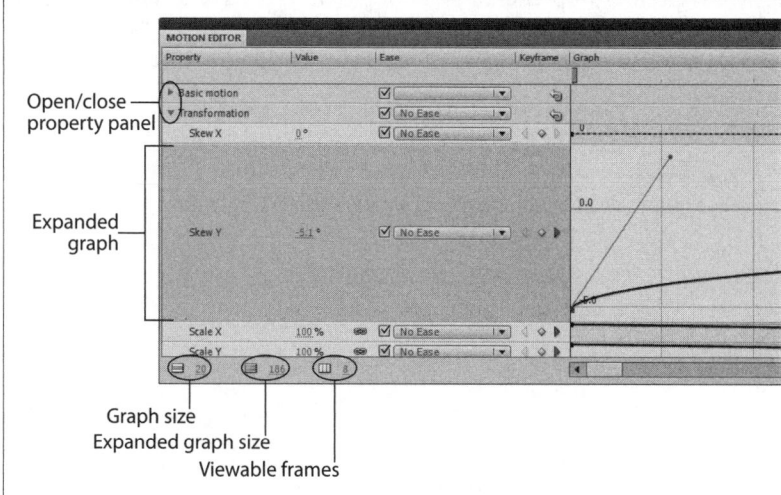

Figure 7-17:
Don't be afraid to make adjustments to the Motion Editor to improve your workspace. In the bottom-left corner are three settings that change the size of all the graphs, the expanded graph, and the number of frames shown in the timeline.

Easing Tweens

When Flash creates a tween, it doesn't use an artist's eye; it uses an accountant's calculator. If a cartoon roadrunner sprints across the desert, it moves exactly the same distance in each frame, even though we all know that cartoon roadrunners start slowly, build up speed, and then slow as they skid to a stop, usually with a little thwang motion at the end. It's up to you to add realistic (or, if you prefer, cartoonistic) motion to your animations and fortunately, the Ease tools are there to help. When you apply an *ease* to one of the properties in your tween span, Flash recalculates how much of a change takes place in each frame. Suppose you want an object, like a moving car, to roll gradually to a stop. You can apply an ease that makes the car move farther in the first few frames, and then shorter distances in the final frames until it stops, as shown in Figure 7-18.

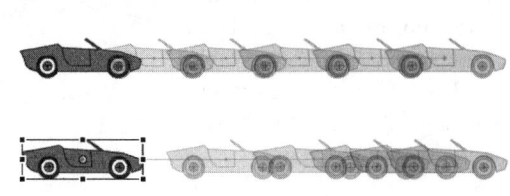

Figure 7-18:
These two tweens are onion-skinned to show the wheel in several different frames. The tween on the top has no ease. The Fast ease was applied to the tween on the bottom.

Applying an Ease Preset

Flash comes with several ease presets, as shown in the menu in Figure 7-19. Ease presets aren't limited to changing the position of an object; you can apply them individually to specific properties. For example, if you have a lamp shining a yellow light, you can make that light blink on and off by applying a "square wave" ease to the alpha value (transparency) of the light. (A square wave is binary, it's either on or off.)

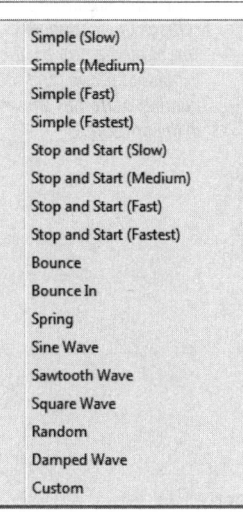

Figure 7-19:
Flash gives you ease presets that you apply in the Motion Editor's Eases panel.

There are a couple of steps for applying an *ease preset*. First, you need to add the ease preset to the Motion Editor's Eases panel. Then you apply the ease to one or more properties, using the drop-down menus that appear in the Ease section of each property. Here are the step-by-step details for adding the Square Wave ease to make a light blink. You can create your own lamp and light, or you can use the simple desk lamp provided in *lamp_begin.fla* found at *http://missingmanuals.com/cds*. In either case, make sure the light emanating from your lamp is a movie clip on its own layer, and give yourself about 48 frames for the tween span.

1. **With the light's tween selected, open the Motion Editor (Window → Motion Editor), as shown in Figure 7-20.**

   The Motion Editor panel opens, with the Eases panel at the bottom.

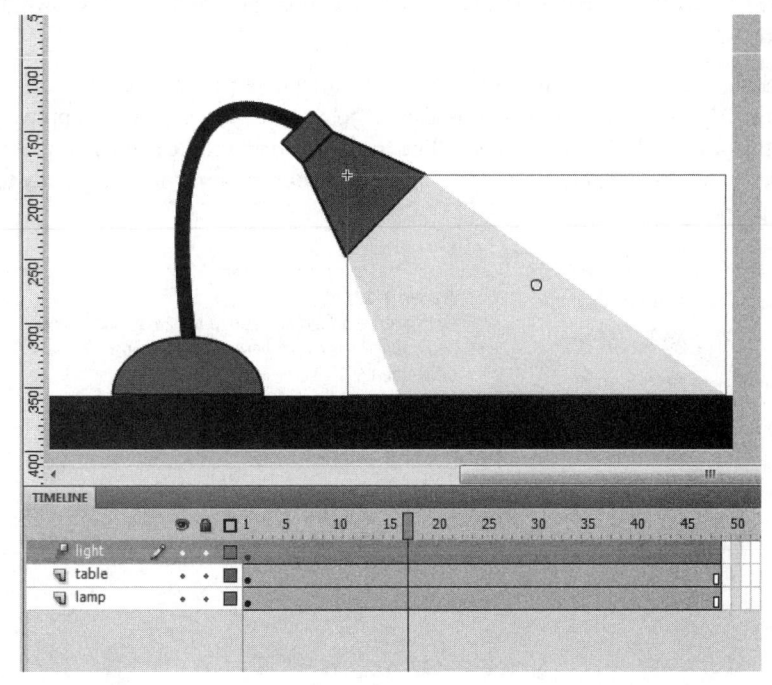

Figure 7-20:
Apply the Square Wave ease to the Alpha value (transparency) of an object and you can make it repeatedly disappear and reappear. The technique is used here to make this lamp blink.

2. **In the Eases panel, click the + button to add a new tween, and then choose Square Wave from the shortcut menu.**

    When you click the + button, you see the Eases menu (Figure 7-19). After you select the Square Wave ease, a subpanel for Square Wave appears under the Eases panel (with any other eases belonging to the tween span).

3. **In the Square Wave property subpanel, set the value to 6.**

    Eases have a related value, but the function of the value may be different depending on the ease. The Square Wave's value controls number of changes. In this case, it controls the number of times your lamp blinks on or off.

4. **In the Color Effect panel, click the + button, and then choose Alpha from the pop-up menu.**

    An Alpha subpanel appears under the Color Effect panel.

5. **In the Motion Editor's timeline, move the playhead to the last frame of the tween, and then set the Alpha value to 0.**

    Without any easing, this causes the light to gradually dim from 100% to 0%.

6. In the Color Effect panel, in the Ease section, choose Square Wave as shown in Figure 7-21.

The Square Wave ease is applied to all the Color Effect properties. You can see that the Alpha property subpanel is also set to Square Wave. You can apply an ease in some of the category panels, like the Transformation category, where it applies to all the properties in that category, or you can apply it individually to each property.

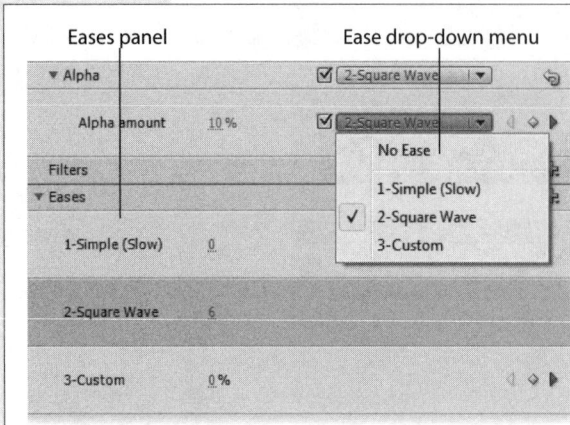

Eases panel   Ease drop-down menu

Figure 7-21:
Once you've added an ease to the Eases panel, you can apply it to any property, using the Ease drop-down menu.

7. Test your animation.

The light flashes from on to off and then back again. It changes six times, matching the Value in the Square Wave subpanel.

After you've applied an ease to a property, the graph shows two lines, as shown in Figure 7-22. The solid line shows any property changes that were originally in that tween span. The dotted line shows the property changes after you apply the tween.

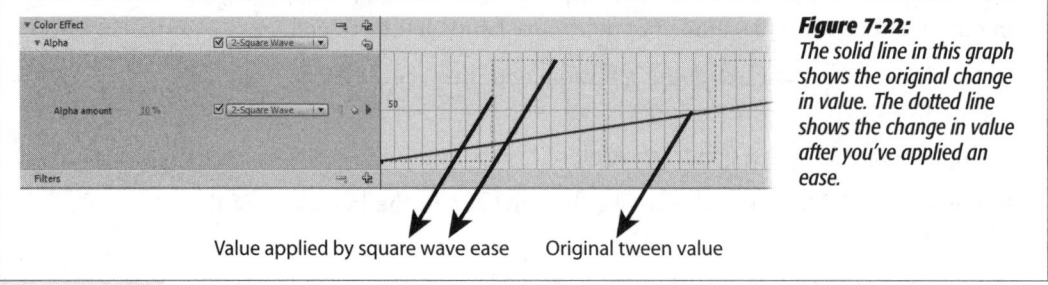

Value applied by square wave ease   Original tween value

Figure 7-22:
The solid line in this graph shows the original change in value. The dotted line shows the change in value after you've applied an ease.

Creating a Custom Ease Preset

You can create your own ease presets and store them in your Flash file. Once you've created a preset, you apply it just as you would any other ease preset. Flash names your preset for you, so you'll have to remember what your 3-Custom and 5-Custom ease presets do. Flash saves the presets in your Flash file, so you can use them with any property and they'll be there the next time you open the file. However, you can't use your custom ease in other Flash documents; they're only available in the document where you created them.

To create a custom ease, click the + button in the Eases panel, and instead of choosing one of Adobe's predesigned ease presets, choose Custom at the bottom of the menu. A custom preset appears in the panel with any other eases you may be using in your document. There's a line in the graph ready for you to edit (Figure 7-23). You use Flash's standard line and Bezier tools to change the shape of the line, and subsequently change the values of any property, once the ease is applied. Page 290 explains how to edit a graph line.

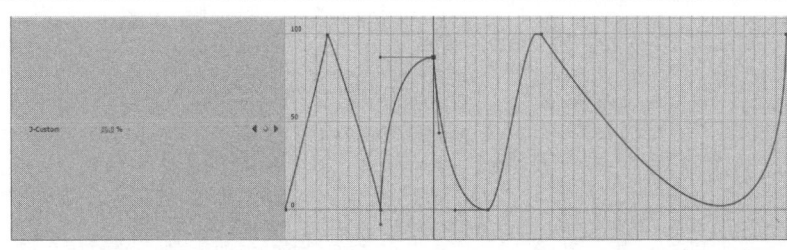

Figure 7-23:
Use Flash's Bezier tools to modify the graph line in a custom ease preset. It may take some trial and error to become proficient in designing custom ease presets.

FREQUENTLY ASKED QUESTION

The Keyframe Rovers

What's a roving keyframe…and why do I care?

Roving keyframes are a concept that migrated from Adobe's After Effects program to Flash CS4. Roving keyframes apply only to properties in the Basic Motion category (X, Y, and Z). You can think of a roving keyframe as a keyframe that's not tied down to a specific frame. You're letting Flash move that keyframe up and down the timeline so the speed of a motion remains consistent throughout the tween.

As for the second part of your question, roving keyframes are especially helpful if you've messed with the motion path on the stage by dragging the tweened object to different locations. Often, this type of editing changes the path segment in a way that affects its timing.

You can change an entire motion path to roving keyframes by right-clicking the motion path on the stage, or right-clicking the tween span in the timeline, and then choosing Motion Path → Switch keyframes to roving in the shortcut menu. Using the same technique, you can remove all the roving keyframes by choosing Motion Path → Switch keyframes to non-roving. If you want to convert a single keyframe, select the single frame in the timeline with a Ctrl-click (Control-click), right-click, and then choose the option from the Motion Path submenu.

Realistic Animation with IK Bones

Everywhere you look in the real world, you see things that are linked together: a dog and its tail, a ribbon and a bow, a train engine and its caboose. And then, of course, there's that song about the hipbone connected to the thighbone. In Flash, you've always been able to draw these objects, but not until CS4 could you link them together so they'd move in your animation as if they were actually connected. Now using the Bone tool, you can link objects, so when you move the hipbone, the thighbone automatically moves in a realistic manner. The animation tool you use is appropriately called a *bone*; specifically an *IK Bone*. IK stands for *inverse kinematics*, which is the type of animation algorithm at work here, but you don't have to remember that. You can just call them bones, and know that you're using the same technology that computer game developers use to make onscreen characters move realistically.

In this chapter, you'll learn about the two different ways you can use Flash's Bone tool—with symbols and with shapes. When you use bones with symbols, you link one symbol to another. For example, suppose you have a train in your animation. Each car is a separate, carefully drawn symbol. Using bones, you can link the engine to the coal car, the coal car to the boxcar, and so on, all the way down to the caboose. The other way you can use bones is with shapes. In the past, if you wanted to draw a snake, you'd have a hard time getting that snake to squirm and slither properly. You had to painstakingly reposition, distort, or even redraw several versions of the snake to make a good animation. Now you can draw a snake, place bones inside that single shape, and then bend that shape into realistic poses, which makes it easy to reposition or pose your snake for some realistic slithering and sliding.

Note: The IK Bones features discussed in this chapter work only with ActionScript 3.0 documents. When you want to use bones, make sure that you use the command File → New → Flash File (ActionScript 3.0) to create your new documents.

Linking Symbols with Bones

What better way to show how IK Bones link one symbol to another than with a chain made up of separate links? Just to show that all the linked symbols don't have to be identical, you can throw in a padlock at the end. If you want to get a feeling for the end result, open the file *chain_links_finished.fla*. If you're ready to start earning your bones, open the file *chain_links_begin.fla*. You'll find both files on the "Missing CD" page at *http://missingmanuals.com/cds*.

1. **Open the Flash document *chain_links_begin.fla*.**

   There are six hollow ellipses on the stage that look like the links in a chain. In the Library, there are two Movie Clip symbols: link and padlock. The links on the stage are different colors. Click a link to select it, and then in the Properties panel under Color Effect, you'll see that it's colored using the tint color effect.

2. **Drag the padlock symbol from the Library and position it on the stage so the lock's shackle overlaps the right-most link in the chain, as shown in Figure 8-1.**

   Before you start linking symbols together, you need to make sure you have every symbol on the stage. You can't add new symbols to the IK bones layer after you've created a bone with the Bone tool.

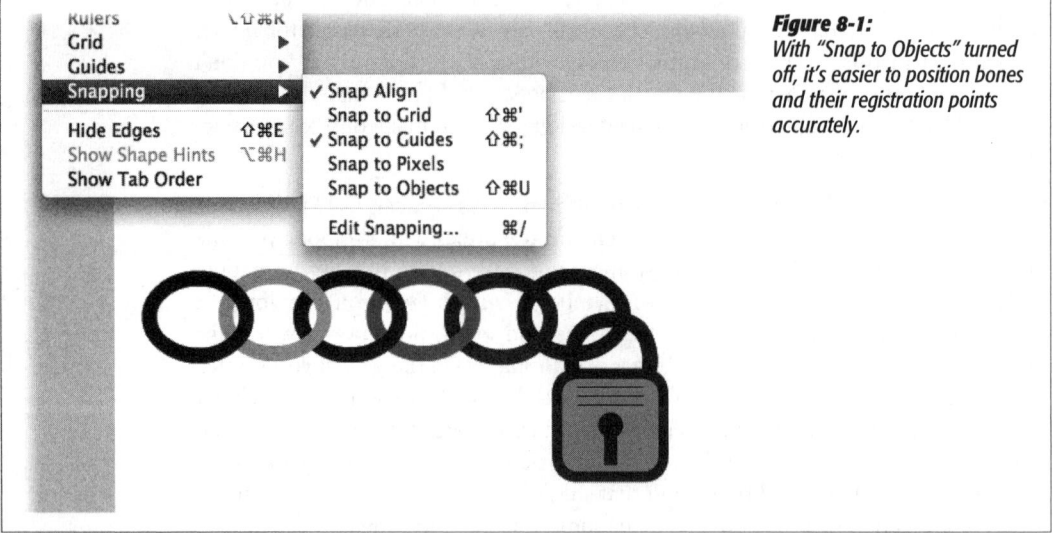

Figure 8-1:
With "Snap to Objects" turned off, it's easier to position bones and their registration points accurately.

3. Select View → Snapping → "Snap to Objects" to turn "Snap to Objects" off.

It's easier to position bones precisely in objects if you turn off the cursor's snapping action.

4. Click the Bone tool (or press *X*, the hot key for the Bone tool).

The Bone tool is in the middle of the Tools palette, and there are two tools under the Bone icon. The one on the top is Bone tool; the one on the bottom is the Bind tool. The cursor for the Bone tool is a bone and a + sign. When the Bone tool is over an object to which you can attach a bone, the solid black bone turns into a hollow bone.

5. Click the left side of the left-most link, and while holding the button down, drag to the right until you reach the left side of the next link, as shown in Figure 8-2.

You may want to zoom in, so that you can carefully place each bone. You drag to create a bone. The first place you click creates the head of the bone, when you release the mouse button, you create the tail of a bone. The head indicated by the large circle becomes the registration point for the bone, and the symbol to which it's attached. That means that the bone symbol pivots around the head of the bone. When you create a series of bones, known in Flash-speak as an *armature*, the first bone is known as the *root* bone. The head of the root bone takes on special importance, since it's the registration point for the entire armature or family of symbols.

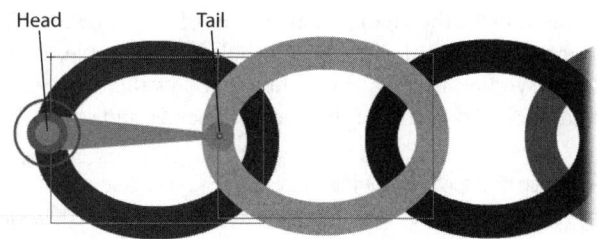

Head   Tail

Figure 8-2:
*Each bone has a head (your first click) and a tail
(when you release the mouse button).*

If you glance at the timeline, you notice that adding the first bone creates a new armature layer (also called *pose layer*) in the timeline (Figure 8-3). Similar to a motion tween layer, the pose layer has special properties.

6. From the tail of the first bone, drag to create another bone that connects to the next link in the chain.

You can attach bones to either the head or the tail of the first bone. In this case, you attach a second bone to the tail. As you drag, notice that the cursor shows a "no" symbol (circle with a line through it) when you're over the empty stage or some other object where it's not possible to link your bone. It turns back to a + when the cursor is over a suitable target.

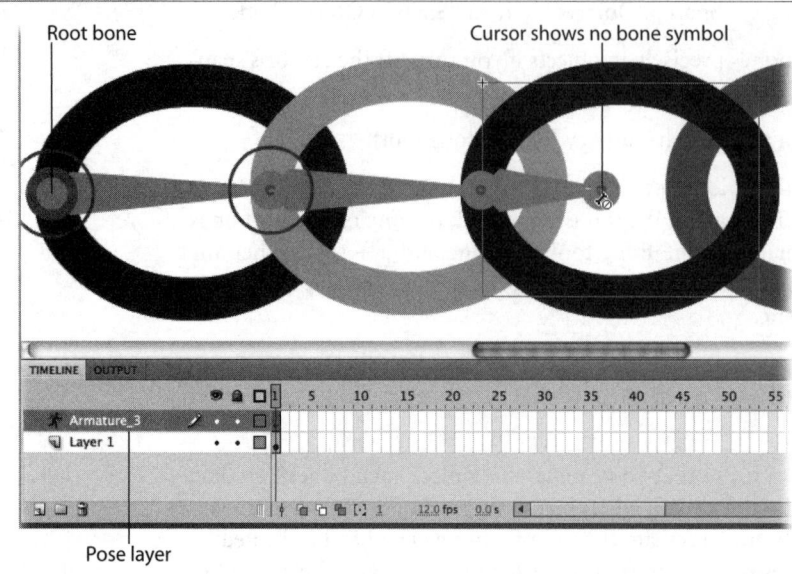

Root bone

Cursor shows no bone symbol

Figure 8-3:
When you create a bone, Flash automatically creates an "armature" or pose layer. The pose layer is similar to a motion tween layer but with a couple of twists to make it work with bones.

Pose layer

When you link to a new symbol, Flash automatically repositions the transformation point to the point where the bones connect. The transformation point is the point around which the symbol rotates.

7. **Repeat this process for the remainder of the chain links until you finally connect the last bone to the padlock's shackle.**

In this animation, all the links in the chain are instances of the same symbol, but often you'll use bones with lots of different symbols. For example, if you were applying bones to the symbols that make up a human body, there'd be separate symbols for the head, neck torso, parts of the arms and hands, and so on.

Tip: If necessary, you can switch to another tool, like the Hand tool, to get a better view of your work. You can then go back to the Bone tool and add more bones. The one thing you can't do is add new symbols or drawings to the pose layer.

8. **In the pose layer, click Frame 30, and then press F5 to create a frame.**

The pose layer extends to become 30 frames long. You can make the pose layer any length you wish, and you can add and remove frames from the pose layer as you would any other layer.

9. **With the Selection tool, click Frame 5, and then drag the padlock to a new position (Figure 8-4).**

The pose layer is similar to a motion tween layer (page 130). When you reposition the padlock in Frame 5, Flash creates a tween to animate the motion from Frame 1 to Frame 5. The frame where you create a new pose is marked with a small diamond, and it's called a pose frame.

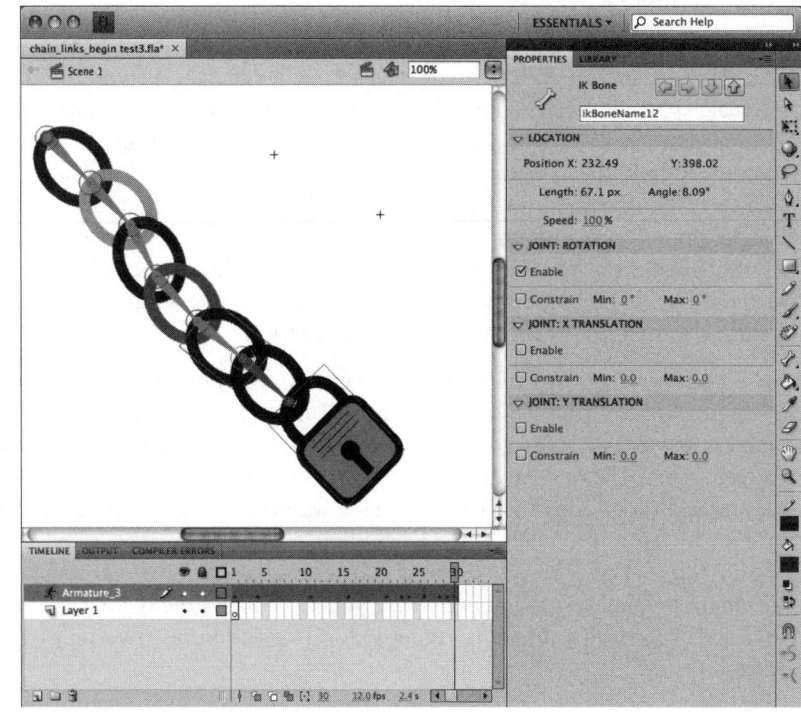

Figure 8-4:
Pose the chain by dragging the lock or by dragging individual links. When you drag a link, the links up to the top rotate around their transformation points; the links down to the lock don't rotate.

The bones connecting all the links in the chain and the padlock constrain the movement of each symbol, giving the entire family of symbols a realistic sense of motion. Not only that, it's easier for you, the artist, to position the symbols, because they really are connected to each other.

10. **Click Frame 10 and reposition one of the middle links in the chain.**

Bones have a parent-child relationship. When you move one of the middle links, the motion is different, in that the links on the tail end of the chain move as one group. With a little practice, you'll learn to use the parent-child relationship of the bones to quickly pose linked symbols.

11. **Every five frames or so, continue to pose the chain and padlock.**

Experiment to get a feeling for the motion. You can create a new pose by dragging either a bone or the symbol attached to the bone. You can use either the Selection tool or the Bone tool to create a pose. If you want a quick preview, press Enter to see the animation play. You can make it swing back and forth, like a chain attached to a wall or a door, or you can make it move like a snake charmer's cobra. Try some different techniques and positions.

12. **Press Ctrl+Enter (⌘-Return) to test the animation.**

The chain links and the padlock move. The head of the root bone acts as an anchor. The entire armature can pivot around the head, but it remains fixed at that point.

Changing the Pose Layer

Creating just the right motion is more art than science. Think about how many movement details there are in a running cheetah, or a swinging pendulum, or a slithering snake. Chances are you'll fiddle with the pose layer after you finish using the Bone tool. For example, you may want to slow down or speed up the action. You may want to hold the armature (that is, all the linked bones and their related symbols) in a certain position for a few beats, and then continue the motion. You may want to smooth the motion or make it more erratic. You can make those changes by changing the relationship of the pose frames in the pose layer. For example, adding or removing frames changes the timing of the animation. Copying and pasting frames can freeze the action for an interval.

For most actions, you need to select specific frames in the pose layer before you cut, copy, paste, and so on. In many respects, you manage the pose layer and its frames the same way you manage other layers. Its behavior is similar to that of motion tween layers. The pose layer is colored green so you can distinguish it from normal layers and tween layers, which are shaded with other colors. There's also a little figure of a person to the left of the layer name. Each frame with a small diamond is *pose frame*. These frames are similar to keyframes in a normal standard layer, they mark a point in the timeline where you've defined exactly how the animated object is positioned. Flash is responsible for positioning (tweening) the other frames.

FREQUENTLY ASKED QUESTION

Combining Bones and Tweening

How do I tween color, dimensions, and other properties when I use IK Bones?

There's one important difference between a pose layer and a motion tween layer: A pose layer only tweens the position of the symbols or shapes; you can't tween colors, dimensions or any of the other properties that you can change in a motion tween. If you want to change those properties too, the solution is to create your animation in the pose layer, and then wrap the entire animation in a movie clip or graphic symbol (Modify → "Convert to Symbol" or F8).

Once the bone's animation is contained in a symbol, you can add it to your main timeline as you would any symbol. Just drag it onto the stage. At that point, you apply a motion tween to the entire movie clip or graphic. This trick also lets you use filters or blends on the animation.

So, wrapping your pose layer in a movie clip or graphic symbol gives you the best of both worlds: IK bones' help in creating an animation and all the power of a motion tween to transform your animated object.

Here's the lowdown on some common operations you can perform in the pose layer.

- **Speed up or slow down animation.** Move the cursor to the end of the pose layer. When the cursor is over the right edge, the cursor changes to show arrowheads pointing left and right. Drag to extend or shorten the pose layer. Flash inserts or removes frames making the playing time longer or shorter. As much as possible, Flash keeps the pose frames in the same position relative to each other. Of course, if you really shrink the layer, all the pose frames get bunched together.

- **Select frames.** When you click the pose layer, you select the entire layer and it changes from green to blue. The playhead moves to the frame that you clicked, but a single click doesn't actually select the frame. To select a single frame Ctrl-click (⌘-click) a frame. When you select a single frame, it turns blue and the rest of the pose layer returns to its green color. To select a sequence of frames in the pose layer, Ctrl-drag (⌘-drag) over those frames. Once the frames are selected, you can copy, cut, or delete them.

- **Remove frames.** After you've selected the frames you want to remove, right-click (or Control-click) the selected frames. A shortcut menu appears, displaying options related to the pose layer, as shown in Figure 8-5. Click Remove Frames to remove all the selected frames. (This action removes the standard frames in the pose layer as well as pose frames.)

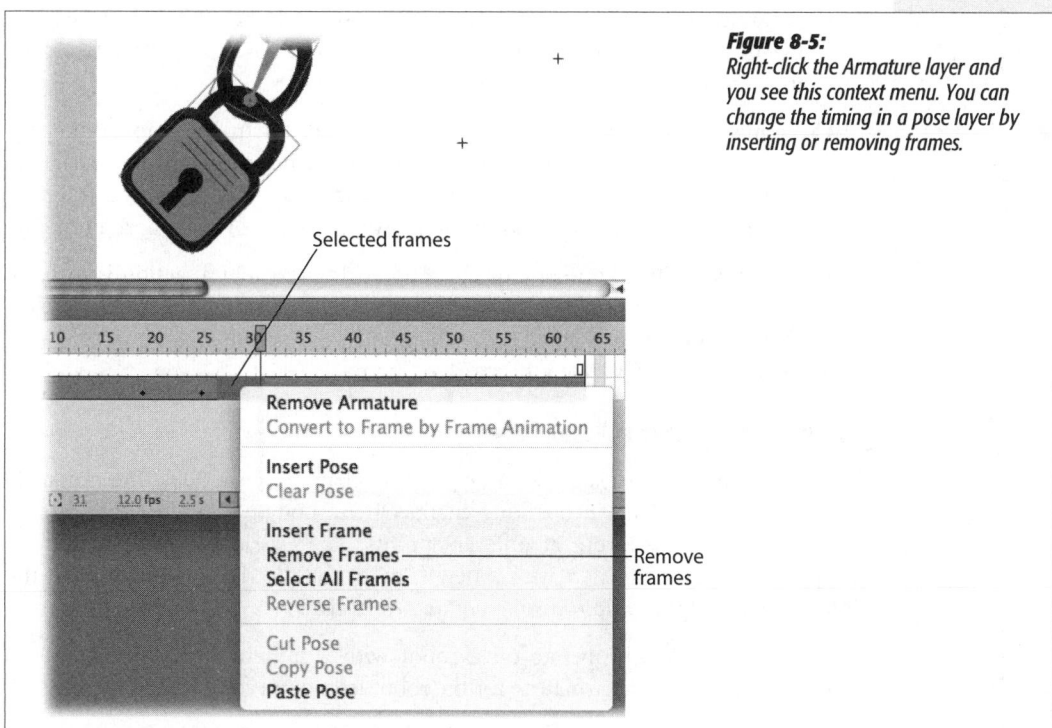

Figure 8-5:
Right-click the Armature layer and you see this context menu. You can change the timing in a pose layer by inserting or removing frames.

- **Insert a pose.** The pose layer has two types of frames. The pose frames, which display a small diamond, are like keyframes for the armature, where you position every part of the armature just the way you want. The other frames are tweened frames, where Flash determines the position of the armature. You can turn a tweened frame into a pose frame in a number of ways. First, move the playhead to the frame you want to change, and then press F6. Flash turns the frame into a pose frame. You can also right-click the frame in the pose layer, and then choose Insert Pose from the shortcut menu. Inserting a pose doesn't add any frames to the timeline; it simply converts the frame at the playhead to a pose.

- **Clear a pose.** If you want to clear a specific pose frame in your timeline, but leave the rest of it intact, click the frame you want to change. You don't need to Ctrl-click (or ⌘-click) in this case. The playhead moves to the clicked frame. Right-click (or Control-click), and then choose Clear Pose from the shortcut menu. This action removes the pose, but doesn't remove the frame. The position of the armature changes because it's now controlled by the closest pose frames before or after the displayed frame. If you want to clear several pose frames at once, you can Ctrl-drag (⌘-drag) to select several frames, right-click, and then choose Clear Pose to convert the pose frames to standard frames. Clearing a pose doesn't remove frames from the pose layer.

- **Copy a pose.** If you want your carefully positioned armature to remain in the same position for a few frames, one way to do that is to copy the desired pose, and then paste it back into the pose layer. The frames in between two identical pose frames will all be the same. To copy a pose, Ctrl-click (⌘-click) to select a frame in the pose layer, right-click it, and then choose Copy Pose from the shortcut menu.

- **Cut a pose.** Similar to copying a pose, except that it actually removes the pose from the frame at the playhead. You can then paste it somewhere else (earlier or later) in the pose layer. To cut a pose, Ctrl-click (⌘-click) to select a frame in the pose layer, right-click it, and then choose Cut Pose from the shortcut menu.

- **Paste a pose.** When you copy or cut a pose, the next logical action is to paste that pose into the pose layer on a different frame. Ctrl-click (⌘-click) to select the frame where you want to place the pose. Then, right-click (Control-click) and choose Paste Pose from the shortcut menu.

Creating Branching Armatures

In the lock and chain example earlier in this chapter (page 300), the armature linked symbols together in one long chain. Often, though, you want to create an armature that branches out at different points. The classic example is a human body. For this exercise, start with a new copy of the file *robot_begin.fla* from the "Missing CD" page at *http://missingmanuals.com/cds*.

In this example, you'll operate on a robot with a somewhat human shape. As shown in Figure 8-6, the armature for the robot isn't quite complete.

1. **Open the file *robot_begin.fla*. In the "right arm" layer, click the show/hide button (beneath the eye icon).**

   All the pieces for the right arm are in a separate layer from the pose layer and the armature. You can't draw directly in a pose layer with an existing armature, but you can add symbols from another layer to an existing armature.

2. **With the Bone tool, click the thick circle in the root bone, and then drag a new branching bone to the right shoulder, as shown in Figure 8-6.**

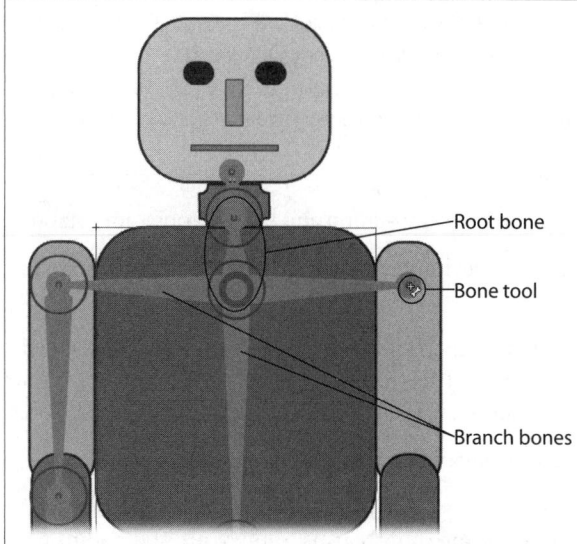

Figure 8-6:
The root bone (circled) goes from the upper torso to the neck. Branch bones are already created to the left arm and down to the hips. Here, a new branch is being created to the right shoulder.

—Root bone

—Bone tool

—Branch bones

When you connect from the root bone to the upper arm (technically called the *humerus*) the symbol is automatically moved from the "right arm" layer to the pose layer, and the bone is connected.

3. **Continue to create bones for the robot's right arm and hand.**

As each bone is added, the connected symbol is moved from the *right arm* layer into the pose layer.

You can add bones that branch from the head or tail of any bone, and, as you see in this example, you can create multiple branches from the same joint. So, if you want to create a spider, for example, you can create eight legs that all connect to the same joint.

Note: One thing you can't do is reconnect the tail of a bone to an existing bone. For example, you can't connect a bone from the hand to the hipbone.

Controlling the Degree of Rotation

Bodies, even robot bodies, have their limits. You don't want your robot flapping around like a rag doll. In terms of IK Bones, that means you don't want every bone in the robot armature to have full movement to rotate 360 degrees. Constraining rotation is one of the ways you can create realistic movement when you're using bones. Once you put constraints on rotation, it's easier for you to set up pose frames, too. Also, by turning off Joint: Rotation, you can prevent bones from pivoting around specific joints. If you want to provide a certain degree of motion around a point, you leave the Joint: Rotation turned on, but constrain the motion, by providing a minimum and maximum number of degrees for rotation.

Tip: When you work with more complex armatures with lots of branching bones, it's sometimes hard to control all the flopping parts. When you're just getting started it's helpful to save (File → Save As) multiple copies of your file with different names, like *robot_arms_down.fla* or *robot_running.fla*. Save a few versions where you're happy with the poses. Then if things get out of hand as you're working on your file, you have a saved file as a backup.

In the next few steps, you see how to prevent rotation and how to constrain rotation.

1. **In the *robot_begin.fla* from the previous section, click the bone you created in step 2 on page 306.**

   When you select the bone that connects the root bone to the top of the right arm, the Properties panel shows settings specific to that bone. There are four subpanels: Location, Joint: Rotation, Joint: X Translation, and Joint: Y Translation.

2. **In Properties → Joint: Rotation, click to turn off the Enable checkbox.**

   Once you turn off the Enable checkbox for Joint: Rotation, the armature won't pivot around that joint. You want the robot's arms to pivot around a joint near the shoulder, not in the center of the torso.

3. **With the bone still selected, click the Child button at the top of the Properties panel (shown in Figure 8-7), to select the bone that connects to the right forearm.**

   The humerus bone is selected, and the Properties panel shows the related settings.

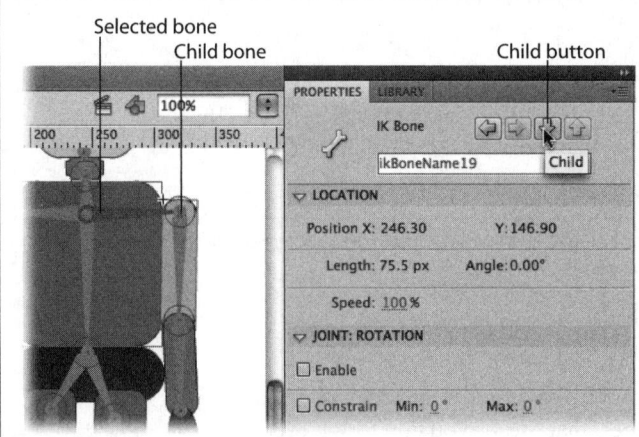

Figure 8-7:
You can use the four buttons at the top of the Properties panel to traverse the bones in an armature. From left to right the buttons are: Previous Sibling, Next Sibling, Child, and Parent.

4. **Drag the selected bone to examine its movement.**

   The horizontal bone from the torso to the top of the arm remains locked in place, in effect creating a shoulder. The humerus pivots around the joint at the top of the bone. It can pivot a full 360 degrees.

5. **Under Properties → Joint: Rotation, click the Constrain button.**

   With a check in the Constrain checkbox, the Min and Max settings come to life.

6. **Enter a value of *–132* in the Min box and a value of *45* in the Max box.**

Min and Max settings are displayed as degrees. You can click and type in a value or you can scrub in a value. Scrubbing is a good option, because Flash shows the joint's angle as you scrub, as shown in Figure 8-8. With the constraints, the robot arm has a more appropriate range of movement. (Well, appropriate for a robot, not what you'd want in a major league pitcher.)

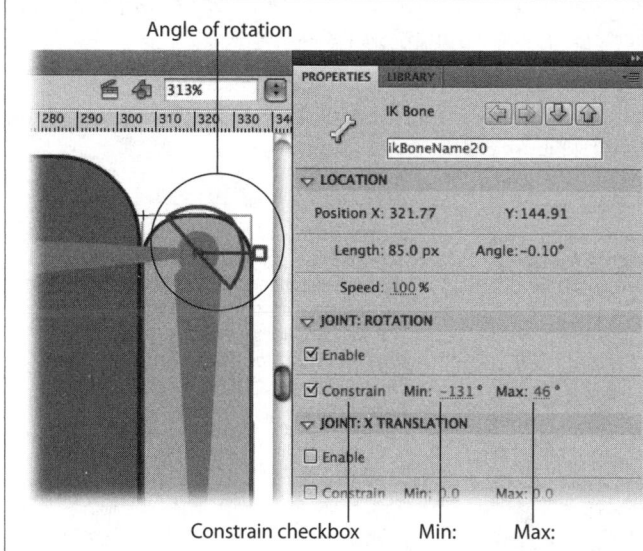

Angle of rotation

Constrain checkbox Min: Max:

Figure 8-8:
As you type or scrub in a Min and Max Joint: Rotation value, Flash shows you the angle of rotation superimposed over the joint.

If you want to create a well-behaved robot, you can repeat these steps to turn off or constrain the rotation in the other joints. Once you've done that, you can make your robot dance a jig by creating different poses in the pose layer.

Moving Bones

No matter how talented or lucky you are, it's unlikely you're going to get your IK Bones animations exactly right the first time you set them up. You can, and probably will, edit the pose layer (as shown on page 304), and edit the armature (as described in this section).

Here's a good example of a problem and solution continuing from the exercise begun on page 300. If you drag the padlock down as far as it can reach, it ends up beyond the bottom of the stage. The next few steps show how to move the entire chain and padlock up higher in the animation.

Here are the steps to move the entire armature to a new location:

1. **Open the Flash document *chain_links_begin.fla*.**

If you haven't done the steps on page 300, do so now. Then continue here with step 2.

2. **Click to select the first frame in the pose layer.**

The playhead moves to the first frame in the layer.

3. **Select the root bone.**

The root bone is the first bone that you created, and in this case, you need to actually select the bone; just selecting the symbol attached to the bone won't do the trick. A selected bone turns green; unselected bones are colored purple. When you move the root bone to a new location, the other bones (sometimes referred to as *children* or *child bones*) move with the root.

When you select any bone, the Properties panel displays settings related to the bone. The subpanels include: Location, Joint: Rotation, Joint: X Translation, and Joint: Y Translation (Figure 8-9).

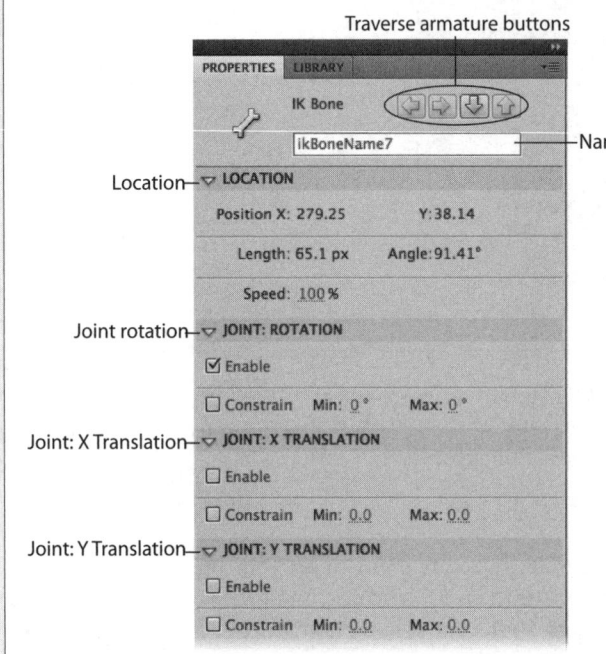

Figure 8-9:
Select a bone, and you see these settings in the Properties panel. Click the buttons at the top to change the selection to a different bone. Use the Joint: Rotation setting to let a bone pivot—or restrict the way a bone pivots. Turn on the Joint: Translation settings if you want to move a bone on the stage.

4. **In Properties → Joint: Rotation, click to turn off the Enable checkbox.**

When you first create a bone, Joint: Rotation is turned on and Joint: X Translation and Joint: Y Translation are turned off. These initial settings give you the kind of motion that you want most of the time.

Turning off Joint: Rotation on this bone prevents the entire armature from spinning around when all you want to do is move it.

5. In Properties → Joint: X Translation, turn on the Enable checkbox. Do the same in Properties → Joint: Y Translation.

   With Joint: X and Joint Y Translation turned on, you can move the root bone and the entire armature along the X and Y axes.

6. **Drag the root bone up to the top center of the stage.**

   The root bone and the armature move slowly as you drag them to a new location. There may be some rotation around the joints of some of the child bones as you move the armature. You can prevent this movement by turning off Joint: Rotation. Remove the check mark from Properties → Joint: Rotation → Enable.

7. **Turn Properties → Joint: Rotation back on. Turn both Properties → Joint: X Translation and Properties → Joint: Y Translation back off.**

   Now that you've moved the armature, you want to reset the properties of the root bone to their previous settings.

8. **Drag the padlock and some of the links on the chain.**

   Notice that the armature's movement and action hasn't changed; just the location.

In these steps, you changed the location of the chain in Frame 1. If you move the playhead along the timeline, you see that this move didn't change the chain's position in the other pose frames. This setup probably isn't what you want for this particular animation, but it shows a point. One way to create movement about the stage when you're working with an armature is to move the root bone between poses. Another way to animate movement is to wrap your armature inside of a movie clip or graphic symbol, and then use a motion tween to create movement around the stage.

Repositioning Symbol Instances

You don't always want your symbols to move in lockstep. There are times when you want some of the symbols to rotate on their own or even move away from the rest of the armature. For example, suppose you have a clown cartoon character who keeps losing his hat. The hat bounces around his head at different angles and perhaps it even flies off, only to snap back into place.

When you connect symbols to each other using bones, you can reposition the symbols independently using the usual transform tools. For example, you can "break" the chain in the previous example, as shown in Figure 8-10. Select the Transform tool, and then rotate one of the links in the middle of the chain. The link pivots around its transformation point. Using the Transform tool to rotate an instance of a symbol doesn't change the length of the bones in the armature.

Changing the Length of a Bone

If you want to move the symbol, including its transformation point, you have to change the length of the connected bones. That's also a job for the Transform tool. Select the Transform tool, and then move the cursor over the symbol you want to move. Drag the symbol to a new position. As an alternative, you can use the Selection tool to move a symbol; just press Alt (Option) as you drag.

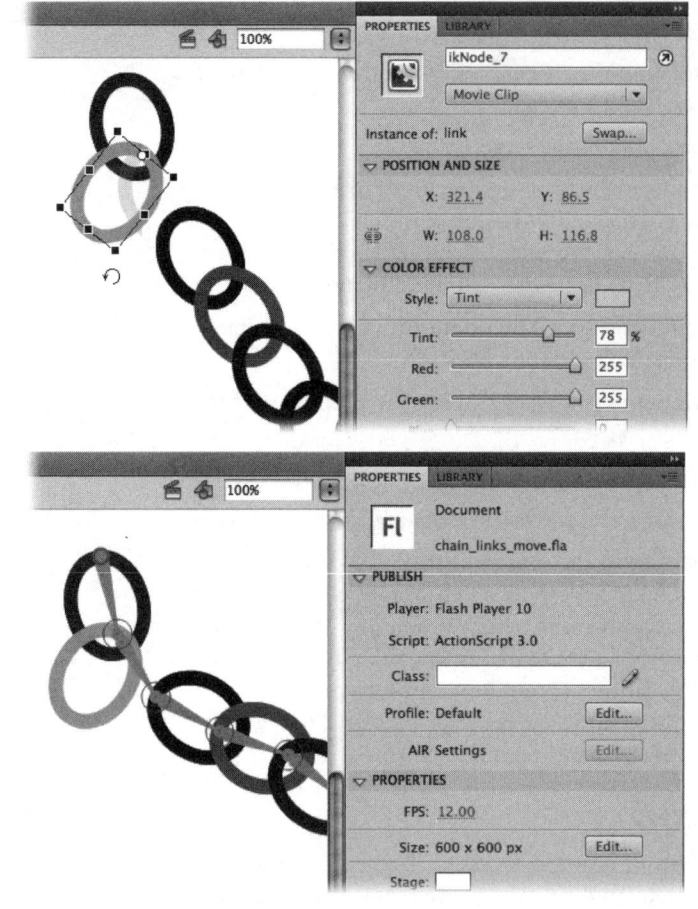

Figure 8-10:
Top: To reposition a symbol relative to the bone armature, use the Transform tool.

Bottom: The link has pivoted around its transformation point, but still moves with the rest of the armature.

Flash doesn't display the armature when you use the Transform tool. When you're done, select the symbol, and you'll see how the length of the bones have changed to accommodate the move, as shown in Figure 8-11.

Deleting Bones

Deleting bones from an armature is a pretty straightforward procedure. Just select the bone, and then press Delete. The bone disappears along with any child bones connected to it. The symbols that were connected by the bone remain in the pose layer, but they're no longer connected to the armature, so they aren't animated with the other symbols.

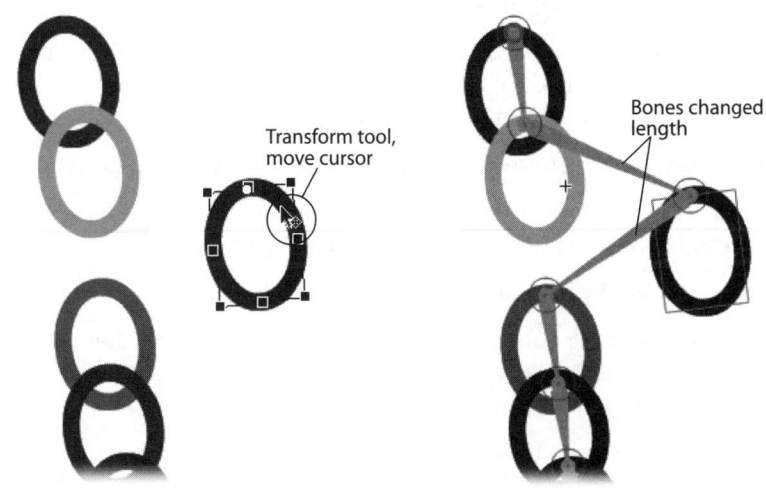

Figure 8-11:
Left: Use the Transform tool to move an instance of a symbol that's part of an armature. When the cursor changes to a cross with arrowheads, you can move the symbol.

Right: The bones linking the symbol change in length to accommodate the move.

Transform tool, move cursor

Bones changed length

Making Shapes Move with Bones

There are two different ways to use bones. You can use IK Bones to link symbols together, creating a chain of objects (as described on page 300) or you can add bones to the *inside* of a shape, making that shape bendable and flexible. It's kind of like dressing up a group of bones inside of a costume. Though both these methods rely on an armature made up of bones, the techniques you use to make them work are quite different.

You can add bones to a single shape or you can add bones to more than one shape. The word "group" isn't used here, since you can't combine the shapes using the Group commands. The way you add bones to more than one shape is to select all the shapes that you're going to include *before* you add the first bone. Flash then automatically places those selected shapes in the pose layer.

In this exercise, you'll animate a snake by placing several bones inside of it. Unlike a robot, snakes don't have limbs, but you can still give them plenty of different bones. Download *snake_begin.fla* from the "Missing CD" page at *http://missingmanuals.com/cds*.

1. **Open *snake_begin.fla*.**

   The lovely rattlesnake is made up of several shapes: a body, a tongue, and two eyes.

2. **Zoom in on the front section.**

   To place bones precisely inside of a shape, it helps to zoom in for a close view. Then, if you need to get a view of a different part of the shape, you can use the Hand tool to reposition the object on the stage.

3. **Select the tongue, the body, and the eyes.**

   You can add bones to more than one shape, but you can't group those shapes with the Modify → Group command when you add the bone. Instead, you have to select all the shapes you want to include in the IK shape object.

4. **With the Bone tool, drag to create a bone from the snake's head to the tongue.**

   When you create the first bone, Flash converts all the selected shapes and the bone into an IK shape object and places the object in a pose layer.

5. **Create a bone from the root bone down the body of the snake.**

   You can attach bones to both the head and tail of the root bone. You can also create branches in shapes. (Page 306 describes creating branching armatures when linking symbols.)

6. **Create several more bones inside the body of the snake down to the tail.**

   Use a total of about eight or nine bones for the snake's armature (Figure 8-12). If you use too many bones, it's more work for you when you try to pose the snake. Too few bones, and you won't be able to create the desired snaky slithering.

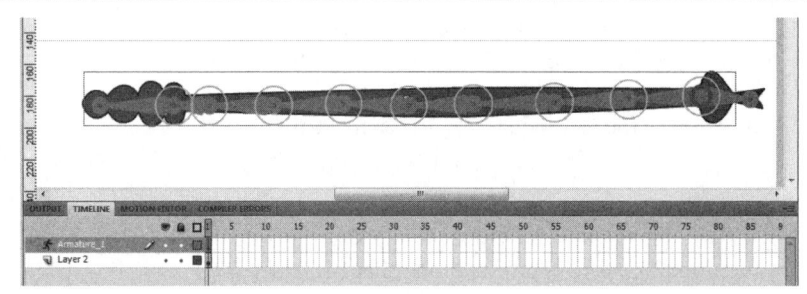

Figure 8-12:
The root bone in the snake starts at the head. One bone extends to the tongue. The rest of the bones extend down the body of the snake to the tail.

7. **In the pose layer, click Frame 50, and then press F5.**

   The green pose layer shows 50 frames for you to create some snaky movement.

8. **Create several poses to animate the snake so that it moves across the stage from left to right.**

   Here are some suggestions: In Frame 1, start with the snake offstage to the left. In Frame 5, pose the snake with just the head coming on to the stage. In Frames 10, 20, 30, and 40, pose the snake in different S-shaped curves to simulate snake propulsion across the stage. In Frame 45, show just the snake's rattle with the rest of the snake body already offstage. In Frame 50, move the snake entirely off stage to the right.

9. **Test the animation.**

   If you're not pleased with the movement at any stage, try to reposition the adjacent poses or create more intermediate poses.

You use the pose layer to animate the position and location of the armature. In many ways, the pose layer seems like a motion tween; however, you can't use the pose layer to tween properties like color, transparency, or dimensions. If you want to change these properties, you need to select the pose layer, and then wrap it in either a movie clip or a graphic symbol. There are more details in the box on page 304.

Working with Control Points

When you place bones inside of shapes, Flash automatically creates control points around the contour of the shape, as shown in Figure 8-13. The control points establish the perimeter of the shape as you create different poses. Some shapes, especially more complex and branched shapes, can get contorted in unexpected ways. You can solve the problem by repositioning the control points. With the Subselection tool, click the boundary of the shape. The control points and the edge of the shape appear highlighted. Then, just drag the control points to adjust the shape. Control points at a curve show Bezier-style curve control handles that you can use to modify the curve.

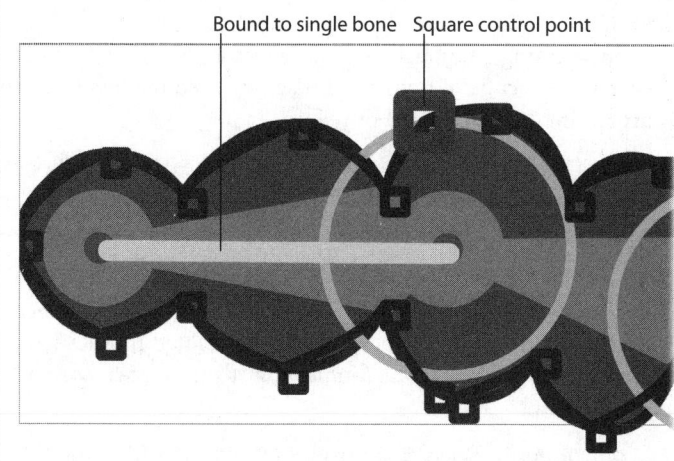

Bound to single bone   Square control point

Figure 8-13:
Flash automatically creates control points around the edge of shapes when you add bones. You can change the contour of a shape by dragging the control points.

When you add bones to a shape, Flash binds the control points on the perimeter of the shape to the nearest bone. In some cases, a control point may be bound to more than one bone as shown in Figure 8-14. If the control points aren't configured the way you'd like, you can edit them using the following techniques:

• **View control points bound to a bone.** Choose the Bind tool in the Tools panel, and then click a bone in the armature. The selected bone shows a red highlight. The control points bound the selected bone are highlighted in yellow. The other control points in the armature are colored blue.

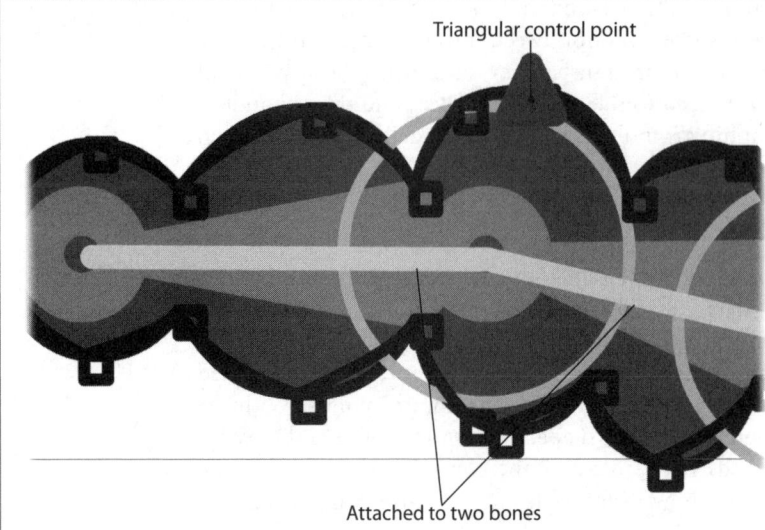

Triangular control point

Figure 8-14:
When a control point is a
triangle, that means it's
bound to more than one
bone.

Attached to two bones

- **View bones bound to a control point.** Choose the Bind tool in the Tools panel, and Flash displays the bones and control points in the armature. Square control points are bound to a single bone. Triangular control points are bound to more than one bone. Click a control point, and it shows a red highlight. Bones bound to the control point are highlighted in yellow.

- **Bind a control point to a bone.** Choose the Bind tool in the Tools panel, and then click a bone. The control points bound to the bone appear highlighted in yellow. With the Bind tool, Shift-click a control point that doesn't show a yellow highlight, and Flash binds it to the selected bone.

- **Remove (unbind) control points from a bone.** Use the Bind tool to select a bone. Ctrl-click (Option-click) a control point that's highlighted in yellow. The control point changes from yellow to blue, indicating it's no longer bound to the selected bone.

- **Bind a bone to a control point.** Select a control point with the Bind tool, and then drag to the bone you want to bind to. As an alternative, Ctrl-clicking (Option-clicking) acts as a toggle, binding and unbinding control points to adjacent bones.

- **Remove (unbind) a bone from a control point.** Select a control point with the Bind tool, and then drag away from the shape to unbind the control point. As an alternative, Ctrl-clicking (Option-clicking) acts as a toggle, binding and unbinding control points to adjacent bones.

Animating an Armature

Though it's not covered in this book, you can use ActionScript 3.0 to animate IK Bones armatures. The IK armature has to be connected to either shapes or movie clip symbols. You can't use ActionScript to animate graphic or button symbols. To prepare an armature for use with ActionScript, create a pose layer with only a single pose. If there's more than one pose in the layer, you can't use it with ActionScript.

1. **Select a frame in the pose layer.**

   The settings for the pose layer appear in the Properties panel (Figure 8-15).

2. **In Properties under Options → Type, choose Runtime from the drop-down menu.**

   When you first create an armature, Option → Type is set to Authortime, meaning you create the animation in the timeline as you design the animation. Once you change it to Runtime, you can use ActionScript code to control the movement of the armature and its elements.

3. **Change the instance name for the armature to** *amtrChain.*

   You can change the name of the armature to match your ActionScript naming conventions. Initially, Flash gives the armature instance the same name that's used to name the pose layer. You can change the name in either the layer in the timeline or in the Properties panel.

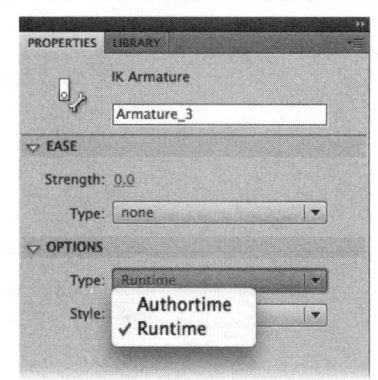

Figure 8-15:
Change the Properties → Options → Type to Runtime if you want to use ActionScript to control the movement of your IK Bones armature.

Incorporating Non-Flash Media Files

Flash gives you a ton of drawing and painting tools you can use to create original artwork, as you saw in Chapter 2 and Chapter 5. But if you've already got some cool logos or backgrounds that you created in another program (like Adobe Illustrator, Photoshop or the orphaned Macromedia FreeHand), you don't have to redraw them in Flash. All you have to do is pull them into Flash—*import* them. Once you do, you can work with them nearly as easily as you do the images you create directly on the stage. You can also add sound clips, video clips, and scanned-in photos to your animations.

This chapter introduces you to the different types of media files that Flash lets you work with. It also gives you tips for working with imported files: You'll see how to apply effects to bitmap graphics, edit video clips, and synchronize (match) sound clips to specific animated sequences.

Note: After you've incorporated non-Flash media into your animation, you can control that media using ActionScript. For more details, flip to Chapter 11.

Incorporating Graphics

Theoretically, you can cut or copy graphic elements from any other program you have open, paste them into Flash, and then tweak them. For example, say you've created a drawing in Microsoft Paint. In Microsoft Paint, you can choose Edit → Copy. Then, in Flash, you can choose Edit → Paste in Center to transfer the image from Microsoft Paint to your stage, and then edit it using Flash's drawing and painting tools. When you import or paste an image onto the stage, Flash stores a copy in your Library as shown in Figure 9-1.

Figure 9-1:
*After you import a bitmap, Flash throws
a backup copy of the image into the
Library as a convenience so you have
the option of dragging another copy
onto the stage without going through
all the trouble of importing the file
again. To see the properties of your
newly imported bitmap, click the
information icon.*

Properties button

Unfortunately, you can get hit-or-miss results by using the system clipboard in this way. Flash may decide to flatten (group) the drawing, limiting your ability to edit it. Flash may also decide to ignore certain effects (like transparency and gradients) so that the image you paste onto your stage doesn't quite match the image you cut or copied.

A much safer alternative: In your non-Flash program, save your graphic elements as separate files, and then import those files into Flash. Flash lets you import virtually all graphics file formats, including the popular .jpg, .gif, .png, .bmp, and .eps formats (see Table 9-1 for a complete list).

One of the major improvements in recent versions of Flash is the way that it imports Adobe Photoshop and Adobe Illustrator files. These programs use layers much like the layers in Flash, as explained on page 148. When you import Photoshop and Illustrator files in Flash, you can choose which layers you want to import, and the program converts them into Flash layers. Say you're creating a business presentation and you've got a Photoshop file of a map. The Photoshop PSD file has the map on one layer, city names on another layer, and stars on another layer to highlight where you've had increased sales. Flash imports the map, city names, and stars on separate layers, making it easy for you to show and hide these elements separately in your Flash animation. Also, if you need to make changes after you pull Photoshop or Illustrator files into Flash, you can edit the shapes and text within Flash.

Table 9-1. *Graphics file formats you can import into Flash*

File Type	Extension	Note
Adobe Illustrator	.eps, .ai, .pdf	Instead of automatically pulling these files in as flat, rasterized bitmaps, Flash lets you set import settings that help preserve the original images' layers and editable text.
AutoCAD DXF	.dxf	Flash imports 2-D DXF files, but not 3-D DXF. Font confusion can happen when Flash tries to match AutoCAD's non-standard font system. Flash only imports ASCII (text based) DXF files. Binary DXF files have to be converted to ASCII before they're imported to Flash.
Windows Bitmap	.bmp, .dib	If you're running a Mac, you need to have QuickTime 4 (or later) installed on your computer to import Windows bitmap files into Flash.
Enhanced Windows Metafile	.emf	Only works on Windows.
Macromedia FreeHand	.fh7, .fh8, .fh9, .fh10, and .fh11	Instead of automatically pulling these files in as flat, rasterized bitmaps, Flash lets you set import settings that help preserve the original images' layers and editable text.
Graphic Interchange Format (including animated GIF)	.gif	
Joint Photographic Experts Group	.jpg	
Portable Network Graphic	.png	Instead of automatically importing PNG files created in Fireworks as flat, raster-ized bitmaps, Flash lets you set import settings that help preserve the original images' layers, editable objects, and editable text.
Flash and FutureSplash (pre-Flash)	.swf, .spl	
MacPaint	.pntg	You have to have QuickTime 4 installed before you can import MacPaint files into Flash.
Portable Document Format (Adobe Acrobat)	.pdf	Instead of automatically pulling these files in as flat, rasterized bitmaps, Flash lets you set import settings that help pre-serve the original images' layers and editable text.
Photoshop	.psd	You have to have QuickTime 4 installed before you can import Photoshop files into Flash.

Table 9-1. *Graphics file formats you can import into Flash (continued)*

File Type	Extension	Note
PICT	.pct, .pict	You have to have QuickTime 4 installed before you can import PICT files into Flash.
QuickTime Image	.qtif	You have to have QuickTime 4 installed before you can import QuickTime Image files into Flash.
Silicon Graphics Image	.sgi	You have to have QuickTime 4 installed before you can import Silicon Graphics Image files into Flash.
Targa	.tga	You have to have QuickTime 4 installed before you can import Targa files into Flash.
Tagged Image File	.tif, .tiff	You have to have QuickTime 4 installed before you can import TIFF files into Flash.
Windows Metafile	.wmf	Only works on Windows.

Note: If you're looking for places to find third-party graphics files to import into Flash, check out the box on page 349.

Importing Illustrator Graphics Files

Flash lets you import graphics files that you've created with another image-editing program (like Adobe Illustrator or Photoshop) and then stored on your computer. After you import a graphics file, you can either edit the image it contains using Flash's tools and panels or just add it directly to your animation.

Note: Table 9-1 shows you a complete list of all the different graphics file formats you can import into Flash.

As you see in the steps below, after you've imported a graphics file, Flash stores a copy of the image in the Library panel (page 34) so you can add as many instances of the image to your animations as you like.

Of course, there's no such thing as a free lunch. Depending on the format of your graphics file (Table 9-1), Flash either pulls the image in as a collection of editable shapes and layers—which you can work with just as you work with any image in Flash—or as a flattened bitmap, which limits your editing choices a bit. (Page 333 gives you tips for working with flattened bitmaps.) Flash does its best to give you all the bells and whistles of the original file format. Flash really excels when you import a file from one of Adobe's Creative Suite programs, like Illustrator. As the example below shows, you get to choose the way Flash imports layers, shapes, and text. As a result, if you're importing Illustrator files, Flash lets you go ahead and modify the shapes (vector graphics) and edit the text after import.

Flash/QuickTime Cross-Pollination

Since the good old days of Flash 4, Flash has enjoyed a symbiotic relationship with Apple's QuickTime. Back then, you could import a QuickTime movie into Flash, and then add some Flash content (for example, buttons that Web surfers can press to start and stop the QuickTime movie). And you still can import QuickTime movies into Flash CS4 and link the two together, as you see on page 250.

But the relationship between Flash and QuickTime goes beyond video integration—it also affects your ability to import media files into Flash. If you have QuickTime installed on your computer, for example, Flash lets you import more types of graphic file formats than it does if you don't have QuickTime installed (see Table 9-1 for details).

The bottom line is, if you're working with others who use both Macs and PCs, it's well worth installing QuickTime. Fortunately, QuickTime's easy to install. It's free too. To download a copy, visit: *www.apple.com/quicktime/download*.

Tip: Adobe Illustrator files are frequently saved for printing on paper using a color space called CMYK (Cyan-Magenta-Yellow-Black). Before you import these files, use Illustrator to convert them to the RGB (Red-Green-Blue) color space used by Flash. To check and change the color space setting in Illustrator, choose File → Document Color Mode. Less frequently, you may find Adobe Photoshop files using the CMYK color space. In Photoshop, to check and change the color space, go to Image → Mode → RGB.

To import an Adobe Illustrator graphics file into Flash:

1. **Choose File → Import → Import to Stage.**

   Your standard file dialog box appears. If you're using a Mac, it looks like Figure 9-2, for example.

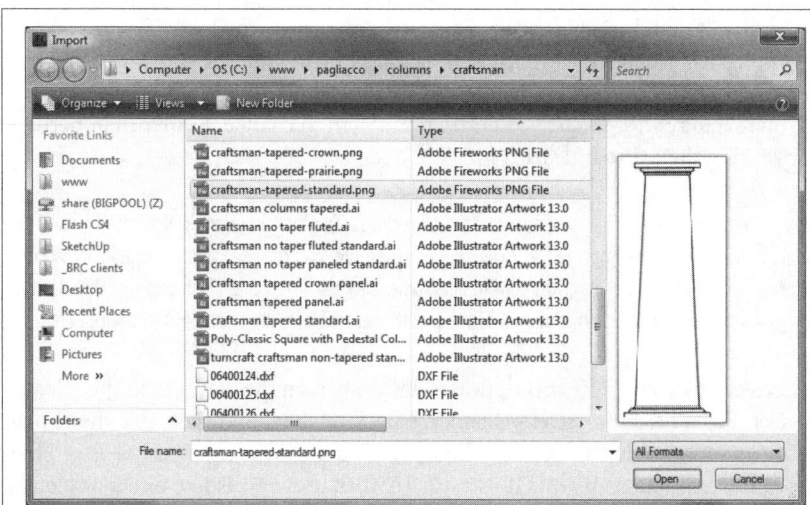

Figure 9-2:
You can import a graphic to the stage and the Library, as you see in the numbered steps, or just to the Library (by choosing File → Import → "Import to Library"). Either way, you first have to tell Flash, which file contains the graphic you want to import—and that's exactly what you do here, in the Import dialog box.

2. **In the "File name" field, type the name of the Adobe Illustrator (.ai) file you want to import (or, in the file window, click the file to have Flash fill in the name for you).**

Use the drop-down menu at the bottom to see all the different types of files you can import. Initially the drop-down menu is set to All Formats.

3. **Click Open (or Import on your Mac).**

The Import dialog box disappears, and then Flash displays an extra Import Settings window that lets you tell it how much editability you want to preserve: whether you want it to convert the original frames into Flash frames or Flash layers, pull in all the frames or just a few, include invisible layers or not, and so on. Figure 9-3 shows you the Import Settings windows you see when you import files created with Adobe Illustrator. You'll see limited but similar options when you import FreeHand files (.fh*), as explained in the box on page 326.

4. **When you see the Import to Stage dialog box (Figure 9-3), click to select one or more of the following options, and then click OK.**

   • **Check Illustrator layers to import.** Flash gives you a scrolling list of all the layers in the Illustrator file, with icons and labels describing the contents of the layers. Place checkmarks next to the layers you wish to import. To the right of the scrolling list, you see Layer Import Options that change depending on the content of the layer.

   • **Layer Import options for paths.** If the layer includes lines and shapes, you can choose to import the content as an *editable path*, meaning you can change it later within Flash. Or you can import it as a Bitmap, which gives you fewer editing options.

   • **Layer Import options for text.** You have three options for importing text. Choose "Editable text" if you wish to edit or rewrite the text. Choose "Vector outlines" if you want to change the shapes of letters in the same way that you change the shapes of polygons and circles within Flash. Choose Bitmap if you're happy with the text as is and don't plan to change it other than perhaps tweaking the color and size a bit.

Tip: If you see a yellow triangle with an exclamation point (!), Flash is warning you that one of the graphic elements may not be imported as expected. For example, you may see an incompatibility warning if you try to import text that has been rotated in Illustrator. Click the layer, and Flash explains that the best option is to import the text as vector outlines. Once you fix the problem, the warning sign disappears.

   • **Create movie clip.** Use this option to instantly turn the graphics in the selected layer into a Flash movie clip symbol. Check the box, and then give the clip an Instance name that's used for the copy of the movie clip symbol that Flash places on the stage. If your Illustrator artwork uses effects like filters or blends, choose the Create movie clip option. In Flash only movie clips can have filters and blends.

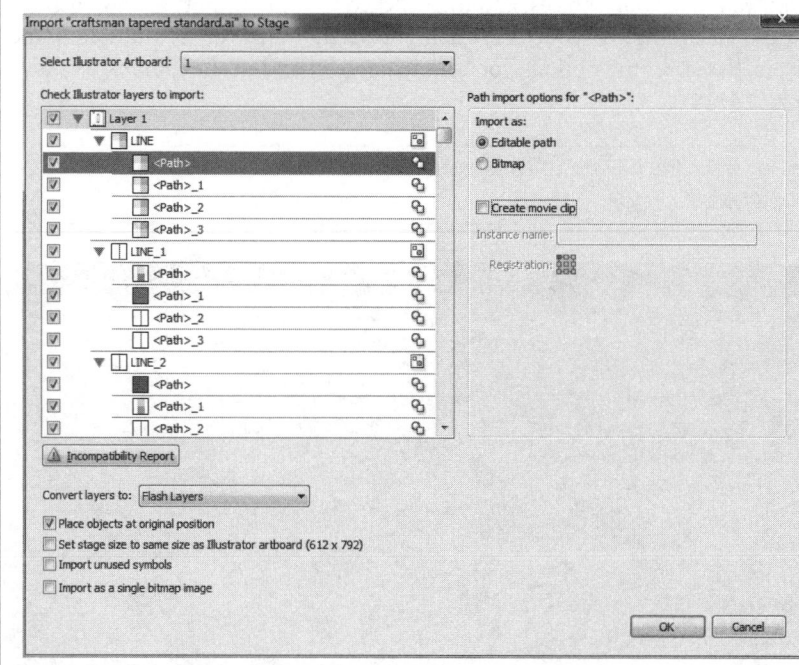

Figure 9-3:
*When you try to import
certain types of vector
files, Flash lets you
specify how much
editability you're willing
to sacrifice for good-
quality images. Here, you
see the dialog box Flash
displays when you try to
import an Adobe
Illustrator file.*

At the bottom of the Import to Stage dialog box, you see options that affect all the layers you're importing.

- **Convert layers to: Flash Layers/Keyframes/Single Flash Layer.** This option tells Flash to keep the layering structure of the original file intact, to place the content of each layer in a separate layer or keyframe. If you don't need to work with the image's layers separately, you can flatten the content of all layers onto a single Flash layer.

- **Place objects at original position.** This option keeps the different elements in a graphic positioned the same way they were in Illustrator.

- **Set stage to same size as Illustrator artboard/crop area.** Turning on this box automatically changes the Height and Width Document settings in Flash to match the page settings in the Illustrator file you're importing.

- **Import unused symbols.** Illustrator has a Symbols panel that's similar to Flash's Library. Turn on this option if you want to import all the symbols in the Illustrator panel, even if they don't appear in the document's page.

- **Import as a single bitmap image.** Sometimes you're not interested in multiple layers, editable shapes, and editable text. All you want is a single picture in your library that you don't want to change. Turn on this box to import the Illustrator file as a single, bitmap picture.

After you've made your choices, and then clicked OK, the Import settings window disappears. Flash imports your file, placing it on the stage (or in multiple frames and layers, based on the options you selected above) and in the Library, as shown in Figure 9-1.

Tip: You can import files into your Library without placing them on the stage. Just choose File → Import → "Import to Library".

Importing Other Vector Graphics Files

When you import Illustrator files, Flash gives you an amazing amount of control over the process. Not so with other programs, like the now orphaned program FreeHand (Figure 9-4). Specifically, when you import FreeHand files, the Import dialog box is divided into three sections:

Mapping. Here you choose how Flash imports FreeHand pages and FreeHand layers by mapping the import process. In other words, you show Flash where to put these items. You can turn FreeHand's pages into Flash Scenes (see Chapter 14) or Keyframes. In most cases, Keyframes are your best bet. You can turn FreeHand Layers into Flash Layers or Keyframes. You also have the option to flatten the layers into one single graphic element.

Pages. FreeHand files can include multiple pages, so when you import them you can choose to import all the pages, or you

can enter a starting page number in the From box and an ending page number in the To box.

Last but not least, in the **Options** section you have checkboxes where you can choose to:

- **Include Invisible Layer**. This option tells Flash to import all layers, including those marked as hidden in the original editing program.

- **Include Background Layers**. This tells Flash to import the layer that, in the original drawing program, is the equivalent of the stage.

- **Maintain Text Blocks**. This tells Flash to keep the text blocks it imports editable.

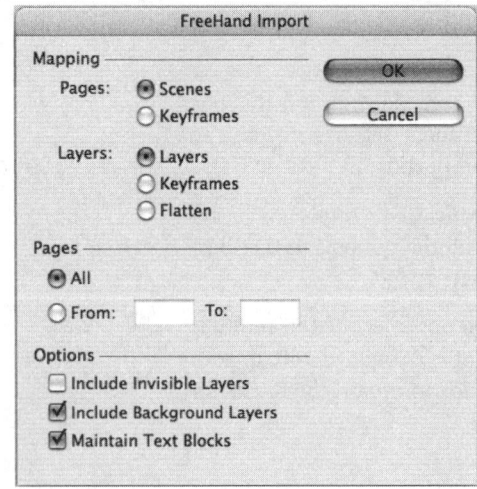

Figure 9-4:
You see this dialog box when you import graphics from Macromedia FreeHand files. You don't get to micromanage the import quite as much as you do with Adobe Illustrator files, but you can still choose to create save layers and pages as keyframes or Flash layers.

Graphic File Sizes: How Big Is Too Big?

To help you make important file size decisions, Flash gives you a Calculate Bitmap Size button in the Import to Stage dialog box. When you click this button, Flash reports the expected size of your graphic in computer speak kilobytes or (if you've got huge files) megabytes. For example, Flash may report that a file's compressed size is 39.9 kb. Files in the single- or double-digit kilobyte range will travel the Internet fairly quickly. Download times for files that are hundreds of kilobytes or (gasp!) megabytes may try your audience's patience as they download. You can keep tweaking the compression settings and clicking the Calculate Bitmap Size button until you find the right balance between file size and image quality.

Importing Photoshop Graphic Files

Now that Adobe has brought Flash into the Creative Suite fold, Photoshop files have a special relationship with Flash and the import process is very similar to importing Illustrator files, described on page 322. The Import dialog box (Figure 9-5) has the same look and layout, but when you look closely at the options, you see some differences. Not surprising, since Photoshop specializes in raster or bitmap images, while Illustrator focuses on vector graphics (sometimes called *drawings*).

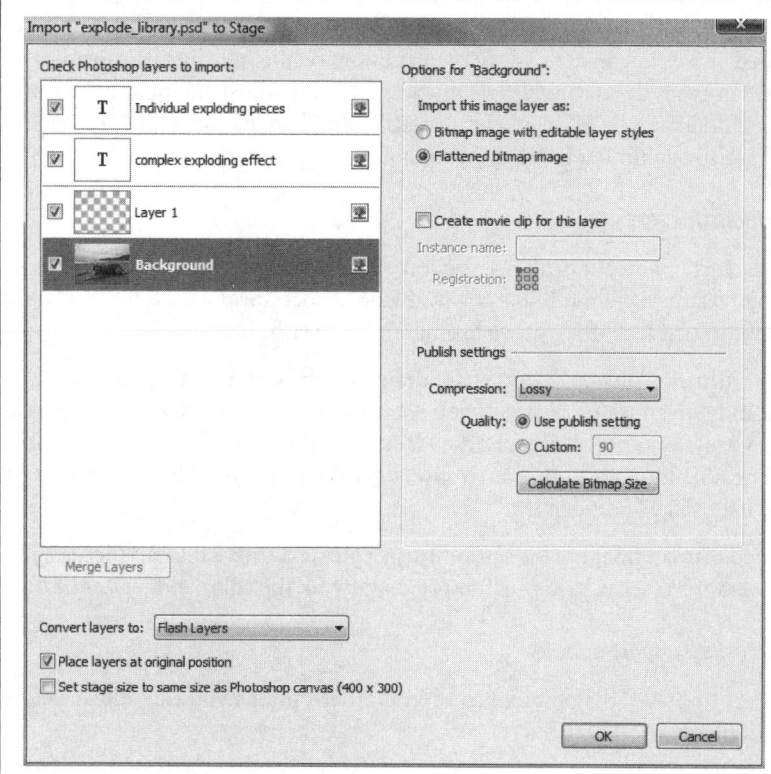

Figure 9-5:
When you import Photoshop graphics, Flash gives you a boatload of control over the process. Using the "Import to Stage" dialog box, you can tweak the settings on individual layers of the Photoshop file so you get exactly the tools you need for your animation.

The "Import to Stage" dialog box for Photoshop files shows you a scrolling list of Photoshop layers. Turn on the checkbox for each layer you want to include in the import process. Click the layer name to highlight the layer, and you see options listed on the right. The options differ depending on the content of the layer.

Here's the rundown on the import options you find in the Photoshop "Import to Stage" dialog box.

Import options for bitmaps

- **Import this layer as.** You have two choices for importing bitmap layers. Choose "Bitmap image with editable layer styles" if you want to tweak the layer settings in Flash. If all you need is a picture, choose "Flattened bitmap image."

- **Create movie clip for this layer.** Use this option to instantly turn the graphics in the selected layer into a Flash movie clip symbol. Turn on the box, and then give the clip an Instance name (which Flash uses for the copy of the movie clip symbol it places on the stage).

- **Publish settings.** You can adjust the quality of bitmaps as you import them into Flash. This option gives you control over the size of your Flash files, which is important when you're posting Flash movies on the Internet (better quality equals bigger files; see the box above). Using the Compression drop-down menu, you can choose between Lossy and Lossless. If you choose Lossy compression (similar to JPEG images), you'll get a compact file size at the risk of degraded image quality. Lossless compression retains all digital information, even when resized. As with JPEG images, you can adjust the quality of Lossy compression images by setting them to match your Flash publish settings (page 634) or by entering a number in the Custom box.

Import options for text

- **Editable text.** Photoshop places text on separate layers from photographs so that the text can be edited, like it's in a word processor. Choose this option if you want to edit text after you've brought it into Flash.

- **Vector outlines.** The letters in text are drawn on the screen in the same way that circles and polygons are drawn. If you want to be able to modify those letters as if they were any other shape, choose "Vector outlines" as your import option. You'll be able to distort your letters in all sorts of fun ways, but you won't be able to edit it like "Editable text".

- **Flattened bitmap image.** This option turns your text into a bitmap picture, like a photograph. You can't do much more than tweak the color and resize it a bit.

Other Photoshop import options

The "Import to Stage" dialog box has several other options you can adjust before you import files:

- **Create movie clip for this layer.** Select one or more layers, and you can turn them into a Flash movie clip symbol. As explained on page 228, movie clip symbols reduce file size and have special properties when it comes to animation.

- **Merge layers.** Below the scrolling list of layers is a Merge Layers button. Shift-click or Ctrl-click (Shift-click or ⌘-click on the Mac) to select multiple layers, and then click Merge Layers. Flash creates a new merged layer right in the scrolling list that you can import into your Flash document. (This process doesn't affect the original Photoshop file on your computer.)

- **Convert layers to: Flash layers/Keyframes.** This option tells Flash to keep the layering structure of the original file intact, to place the content of each layer in a separate layer or keyframe.

- **Place layers at original position.** This option keeps the different elements in a graphic positioned the same way they were in Photoshop.

- **Set stage to same size as Photoshop canvas.** Turn on this box to automatically change the Height and Width Document settings in Flash to match the page settings in the Photoshop file you're importing.

WORKAROUND WORKSHOP

Importing Unimportable Graphics

If you're not importing Adobe Illustrator, Photoshop, or Fireworks files, don't expect perfection when you're importing complex graphics. That's especially true if you're trying to preserve the ability to edit your graphics in Flash. Flash does the best it can, but there are an awful lot of variables involved, from the specific effects you applied to the graphics to the specific version of the program you used to create them.

If the graphics you import into Flash don't look or behave the way they do in the original program, try one or more of the following:

- **Ungroup the imported image.** You do this by selecting the image on the stage, and then choosing Modify → Ungroup.

- **Try using the Clipboard.** First, choose Edit → Preferences (Windows) or Flash → Preferences (Mac) to display the Preferences window. In the Category list, click

Clipboard. Then adjust the settings based on what you're trying to import. For example, if you're trying to import an image containing a gradient effect, click the Gradient Quality drop-down list, and then choose Best. If you're trying to import a FreeHand file, turn on the checkbox next to "Maintain as blocks." Then, in the original program, copy your image. Return to Flash, and then choose Edit → "Paste in Center".

- **Return to the original program and see if you can simplify the image.** Reduce the number of colors you're using, as well as the number of layers, and flatten (group) as much of the image as you can. Then try the import process again.

Importing Fireworks Graphics

Fireworks is another program that's part of Adobe's Creative Suite family. Fireworks' specialty is performing all sorts of graphics tricks for people who design Web sites. It has tools for creating buttons, rollover images, and other Web graphics. For example, Fireworks can take a photo and shrink it down to a very small file size, so it'll look fine on a Web site, but may not look so great in print. Fireworks creates most of its magic using the standard web language (HTML), and graphics files (JPG, GIF), with a little JavaScript for programming chores. Although Flash produces SWF files and uses ActionScript for programming, these two programs play well with each other, and you'll often find reasons for swapping files back and forth between them.

Note: Flash and Fireworks have a working relationship that precedes the Adobe era. Both were published by Macromedia until Adobe purchased the company.

Fireworks is a hybrid in that its working file format (PNG) holds both photographic images like Photoshop and vector drawings like Adobe Illustrator. Designers often create complex images in Fireworks that may include photographs, text, and shapes. They *save* their work in PNG files, but they *export* the files to smaller simpler formats to use on the Web. Flash can import almost any of the files that Fireworks saves or exports, but to get the most graphic goodness from Fireworks, it's best to save the file as PNG, and then import it into Flash. This section shows you how.

Tip: The PNG (Portable Networks Graphic) file format is a standard that was developed to replace GIF files on the Internet for both copyright and techie reasons. In Fireworks, you can save files as PNGs, or you can export files as PNGs. Exported files are very small and great for use on Web sites. However, if you want to use Fireworks' layers and other design goodies, use the Save or Save As command for files you want to import into Flash.

There are three ways to bring graphics from Fireworks into Flash. If you want to bring everything from all the layers in Fireworks into a Flash project, the best option is to import the entire PNG file. If you want specific graphic or type elements from a Fireworks file, you can drag and drop, or copy and paste as explained here:

- Use Flash's **File → Import** command to import a complete Fireworks PNG, including all its layers, both visible and hidden.

- **Drag images** from Fireworks to Flash as shown in Figure 9-6. Before you drag, select the graphics you want to copy. Make sure that any graphics you want to copy are visible and on unlocked layers.

- **Copy and paste** works, too, and sometimes it's easier than arranging your windows for a drag operation. The same rules apply, make sure that any graphics you want to copy are visible and on unlocked layers.

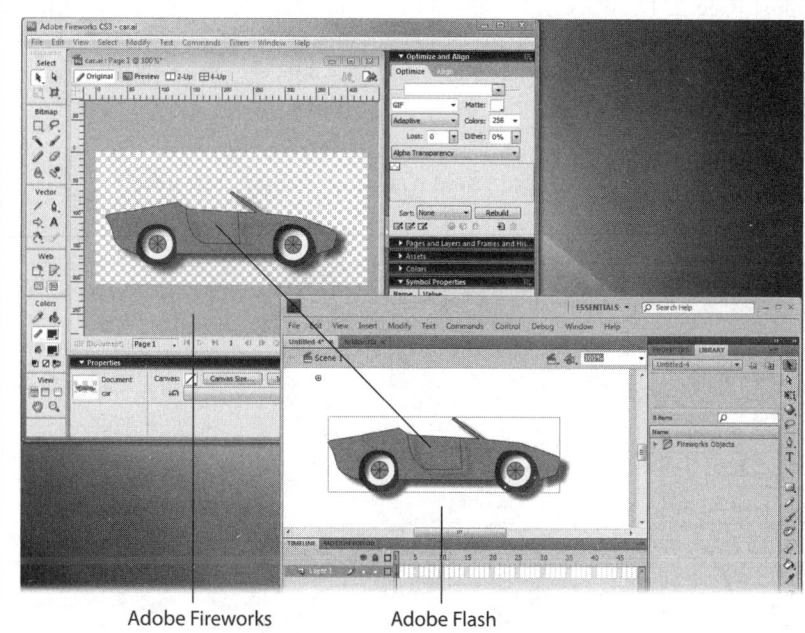

Figure 9-6:
*With Adobe Creative
Suite programs, like
Fireworks, you can drag
and drop graphics, from
one program to another.
An Import dialog box
opens, letting you choose
among the import
options.*

Adobe Fireworks   Adobe Flash

Whatever method you use to snag images from Fireworks, you see the Import Fireworks Document box as shown in Figure 9-7. You can also successfully import layers and drawing guides when you import files. Text and vector graphics (like those in Illustrator) can be preserved so that they're editable in Flash.

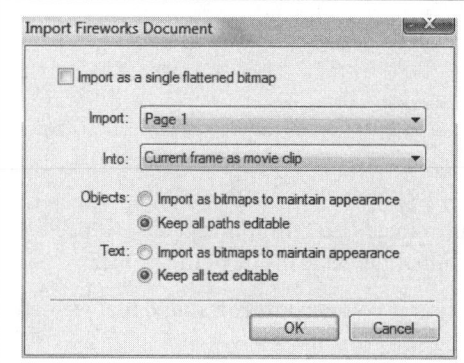

Figure 9-7:
*Fireworks import options are similar to those of Photoshop and
Illustrator. You can bring in editable objects or flattened images.*

Here's the rundown on the Fireworks import options:

- **Import as a single flattened bitmap.** Turn on this checkbox if all you need is a single image and you don't plan to make change the details within Flash. For example, you can scale the entire image, but you can't scale individual elements inside the image.

• **Import Page X.** Fireworks can store different images in different pages, similar to the way Flash keyframes can hold different images. When you import a multipage Fireworks file, you can choose to import a single page or all the pages, as shown in Figure 9-8.

• **(Import Page) Into.** When you import a multipage Fireworks file, you can choose to put the contents of different pages into frames or scenes.

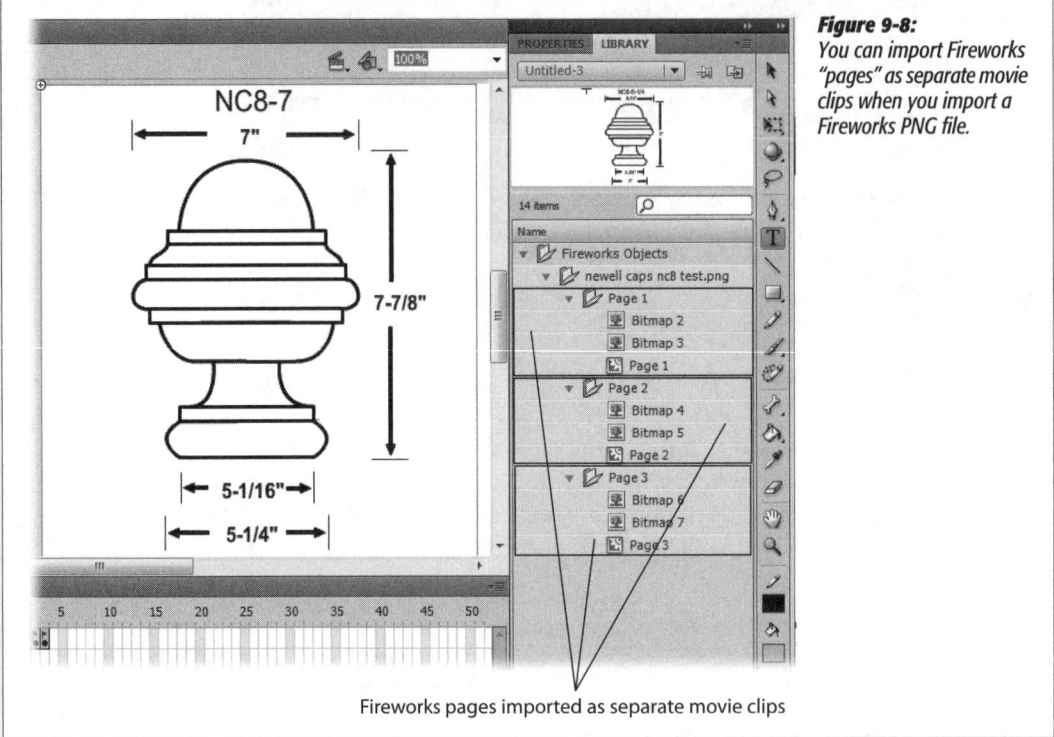

Figure 9-8:
You can import Fireworks "pages" as separate movie clips when you import a Fireworks PNG file.

Fireworks pages imported as separate movie clips

Import options for graphics

• **Import as bitmaps to maintain appearance.** Use this option if all you need is a single image. You can't change individual elements inside of the image.

• **Keep all paths editable.** Use this option if you need to edit individual elements within the Fireworks document.

Import options for text

• **Import as bitmaps to maintain appearance.** Lets you treat text as if it were a graphic image. You can't edit the text, but you can scale or skew the text's image.

• **Keep all paths editable.** Use this option if you need to go back and fix your spelling.

Copying Fireworks Effects and Blends

Like Flash, Fireworks has special effects called *filters* that you can apply to images. You can copy many of these effects from Fireworks to Flash, and they remain editable inside of Flash. If the filter isn't editable, Flash converts the image to a single image showing the effect as it appeared in Fireworks. Flash imports the following Fireworks effects as modifiable filters: Drop Shadow, Solid Shadow, Inner Shadow, Blur, Blur more, Gaussian blur, Adjust color brightness, and Adjust color contrast.

Blends are special effects created by overlapping images. Flash uses mathematical calculations to create different effects with descriptive names like: Darken, Lighten, Multiply, Difference, Add, Invert, Erase, and Alpha. Flash and Fireworks share many of the same blends. When imported into Flash, these blends remain editable. However, Flash doesn't use some of Fireworks' blends, so it simply ignores them when you import the file.

Editing Bitmaps

Depending on the graphic file format you import into Flash, you may be able to edit the edited image using Flash's tools, or you may not. If Flash recognizes the image as a *vector* image, with distinct strokes and fills, you're good to go. Just open the Tools panel, choose a selection, drawing, or painting tool, and then get to work.

But if the image comes through as a bitmap, you need to do a bit of finagling, because Flash treats bitmaps as big blobs of undifferentiated pixels. (See the box on page 336 for more details.)

With bitmaps, Flash's selection tools don't work as you might expect. Say, for instance, you import a scanned-in photo of the Seattle skyline. Flash treats the entire photo as a single entity. When you click the Space Needle, Flash selects the entire scanned-in image. When you try to use the Lasso tool to select the half of the image that contains Mount Rainier, Flash selects the entire image. When you try to repaint the sky a lighter shade of gray, Flash paints around or behind the imported bitmap, but not the sky.

Fortunately, Flash gives you a few options when it comes to working with bitmaps: You can break them apart, you can turn them into vector graphics, or you can turn them into symbols. The following sections describe each option.

Turning bitmaps into fills

Breaking apart a bitmap image transforms the image from a homogenous group of pixels into an editable fill. You still can't click the Space Needle and have Flash recognize it as a distinct shape (you can only do that with vector art), but you *can* use the Selection, Subselection, and Lasso tools to select the Space Needle, and then either cut it, copy it, move it, repaint it, or otherwise edit it separately from the rest of the scanned-in image.

To break apart a bitmap:

1. **On the stage, select the bitmap image you want to break apart.**

   Flash displays a selection box around the image.

2. **Choose Modify → Break Apart.**

   Flash covers the image with tiny white dots to let you know it's now a fill.

At this point, you can use the Selection, Subselection, and Lasso tools to select portions of the image (something you *couldn't* do before you broke the bitmap apart).

Turning bitmaps into vectors

Tracing a bitmap transforms a bitmap into a vector graphic. You can check out the box on page 336, for a rundown of the differences between the two; but basically, turning a bitmap into a vector gives you three benefits:

 • It produces a cool, stylized, watercolor effect.

 • It reduces the file size associated with the image (but only in cases where the image doesn't have a lot of different colors or gradients).

 • It turns a nonscalable image into a scalable image—one you can "zoom in" on without it turning all fuzzy on you.

Note: The fewer colors your bitmap has, the more faithful your bitmap-turned-vector is likely to be to the original. Tracing a bitmap of a hand-drawn sketch done in black charcoal, for example, is going to result in a vector graphic that resembles the original bitmap much more closely than a bitmap trace of a scanned-in photo. (Even photos that look to the naked eye as though they only have a handful of colors usually contain many, many more at the pixel level.)

To trace a bitmap, select the bitmap you want to turn into a vector graphic, and then select Modify → Bitmap → Trace Bitmap. Figure 9-9 shows you an example.

Turning bitmaps into symbols

Suppose you want to add an old-timey sepia color to a photo or you want your bitmap to gradually fade and then disappear. You can't change the color, brightness, or transparency (*alpha*) of an imported bitmap, but you *can* change them for a symbol. So if all you want to do is tint or fade a bitmap, you can use a quick and easy fix, and transform it into a symbol.

To turn a bitmap into a symbol:

1. **Select the bitmap, and then choose Modify → "Convert to Symbol".**

   The "Convert to Symbol" dialog box appears.

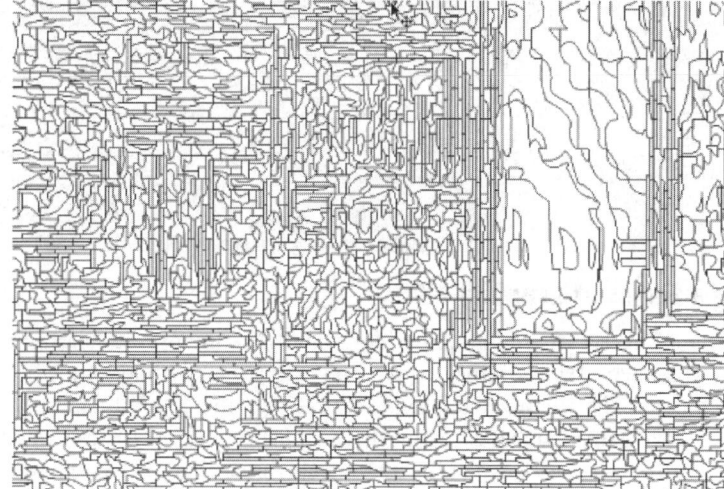

Figure 9-9:
Top: Here's the way a scanned-in image looks as a bitmap.

Bottom: Here's how it looks after Flash has traced it (turned it into vector art). With photos, the effect is more arty than realistic, which might be just what you're looking for. Even though the image is now a vector, you can't click to select individual objects—like the child or the open book—because Flash doesn't recognize meaningful shapes. Instead, it works off pockets of color saturation.

2. **In the "Convert to Symbol" dialog box, choose MovieClip from the drop-down menu, and then click OK.**

   In the Properties panel, click the drop-down list next to Color Effect to set the symbol's brightness, tint, and alpha (transparency) settings. If you convert bitmaps to MovieClip symbols you can apply filter effects in the Properties panel (page 36). If you don't intend to apply a filter and you want to create the smallest possible file size, choose Graphic from the drop-down menu.

   Note: For the skinny on symbols, check out Chapter 6; for more on color, brightness, and transparency, see Chapter 5.

Vector vs. Bitmap Images

Flash lets you import and work with two different types of graphics files: vector and bitmap. You can't tell by looking at the image—the difference is in the structure of the information that makes up the image. Here are the main points:

Computer programs, including Flash, store vector graphics (such as the original artwork you create on the stage) as a bunch of formulas. Vector graphics have the advantage of being pretty modest in size compared to bitmaps, and they're scalable. In other words, if you draw a tiny blackbird and then decide to scale it by 500 percent, your scaled drawing will still look like a nice, crisp blackbird, only bigger.

In contrast, computer programs store *bitmap*, or *raster*, graphics (such as a scanned-in photo) as a bunch of pixels. Bitmap graphics doesn't refer just to files with the Windows bitmap (.bmp) extension; it refers to all images stored in bitmap format, including gif, .jpg, and .png. (You can find a complete list of the file formats Flash lets you import on page 321.)

The good thing about bitmap graphics is that they let you create super-realistic detail, complete with complex colors, gradients and subtle shadings. On the downside, bitmaps typically take up a whopping amount of disk space, and they're *not* particularly scalable: If you scale a photo of a blackbird by 500 percent, it appears blurry because all Flash can do is enlarge each individual pixel: It doesn't have access to the formulas it would need to draw the additional pixels necessary to keep the detail crisp and sharp at five times the original drawing size.

Why do you care whether a graphics file is a vector or bitmap? Because you work with imported bitmap files differently in Flash than you do with imported or original vector files. As you see on page 333, you need to break bitmap images apart before you can crop them in Flash. You also need to optimize the bitmaps you import into Flash if you're planning to reduce the size of your finished animation. (Chapter 19 shows you how.)

Importing a Series of Graphics Files

At times, you may have a series of graphics files you want to import into Flash. Say, for example, you have a series of images you took with a digital camera showing a dog leaping through the air to catch a tennis ball. If you import all these images into Flash, one per frame, you've got yourself an animation. (How herky-jerky or smooth the animation appears depends on how many images you have; the more images, the smoother the animation.)

If you give your graphics files sequential names like *dog_01.gif*, *dog_02.gif*, *dog_03.gif*, and so on, Flash is smart enough to recognize what you're trying to do, and it imports the entire series in one fell swoop.

To import a series of graphics:

1. **Make sure the names of the files you want to import end with sequential numbers.**

   For example, *file1.bmp*, *file2.bmp*, and *file3.bmp*.

2. **Choose File → Import → Import to Stage.**

   The Import dialog box you see in Figure 9-10 (top) appears.

3. **In the Import dialog box, click to select the first file in the series, and then click Import.**

The confirmation dialog box you see in Figure 9-10 (bottom) appears.

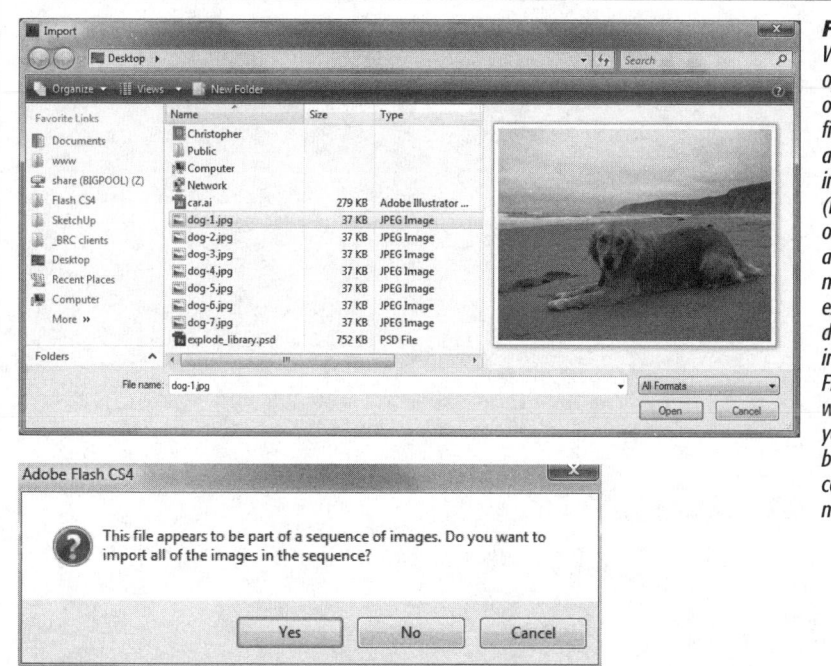

Figure 9-10:
When you tell Flash to open the first in a series of sequentially numbered files (top), the program asks if you'd like to import the entire series (bottom). This trick works only if the numbers appear at the end of the file name just before the extension and if you don't skip any numbers in the series. And since Flash begins importing with the numbered file you choose, it doesn't go back and pick up files containing lower numbers.

4. **Click Yes.**

The Confirmation dialog box disappears, and Flash imports the series of files. In the timeline you see one image (and one keyframe) per frame.

If you check the Library panel (Window → Library), you see that Flash has placed each of the image files in the Library.

Exporting Graphics from Flash

Sometimes you have artwork in Flash that you'd like to use in another program. Perhaps it's a single image that you want to place on a Web page, or maybe it's an entire animation that you want to save in a format other than Flash's SWF file. In either case, it's easy to save that artwork in a format that other programs can use. As you might expect, Flash plays especially well with other Adobe programs like Illustrator, Photoshop, and Fireworks.

DESIGN TIME

Using Bridge as a File Manager

A Flash chapter that discusses different graphic file formats isn't complete without a mention of Bridge, Adobe's program for managing media files of all types (Figure 9-11). If you got Flash as part of an Adobe Creative Suite collection, you probably have Bridge installed on your computer. If you think you're perfectly happy managing files with Mac's Finder or Windows Explorer, you don't know what you're missing. Bridge is much more powerful and customizable than either of those handy and necessary utility programs. Because Bridge is devoted to media files and because Adobe has the proprietary key to some of the most important file formats (Photoshop and Illustrator), Bridge is a more powerful graphics program than your typical OS utility.

Like Finder and Explorer, you can select a file from a thumbnail in Bridge, and then launch a program to open it. But Bridge is much more versatile and flexible when it comes to organizing media files and showing you the files you want at a given moment. Bridge tracks all sorts of information about the photos, graphics, videos, and sound files on your computer, and you get to decide exactly how those details are displayed. For example, if you manage a large collection of photographs, Bridge excels at managing photos descriptive *metadata*. (Cameras automatically store details about a photograph in the photo file. That includes details like the date a

picture was snapped, or edited, the exposure used, and the type of lens. As a photographer or photo archivist, you can also add other metadata tags to photos, to make them easier to find in searches.) Bridge gives you the tools to read the metadata in photos, and to find, sort and view photos based on those details.

There's not enough room here to fully describe Bridge, but here's a short list of some of the things it can do:

- Organize media assets including photos, graphics, video, and audio files.
- Show media files from different computer folders in a single catalog.
- Preview Flash SWF files, while using the file catalog.
- Compare and preview most media files.
- Show/hide/find files based on criteria that you provide.
- Automatically, import, name and store photos from digital cameras and card readers.
- Run automated tasks from programs like Photoshop.
- Manage the tags (metadata) embedded in photos and other graphic files.

To Export graphics from Flash, go to File → Export, and then choose either Export Image or Export Movie. Flash opens a box similar to Figure 9-12, where you can name your file and choose its format. After you click Save, Flash displays another box, where you can choose options specific to the movie or image file format you selected. The complete details for exporting single images and animations from Flash are covered in Chapter 19.

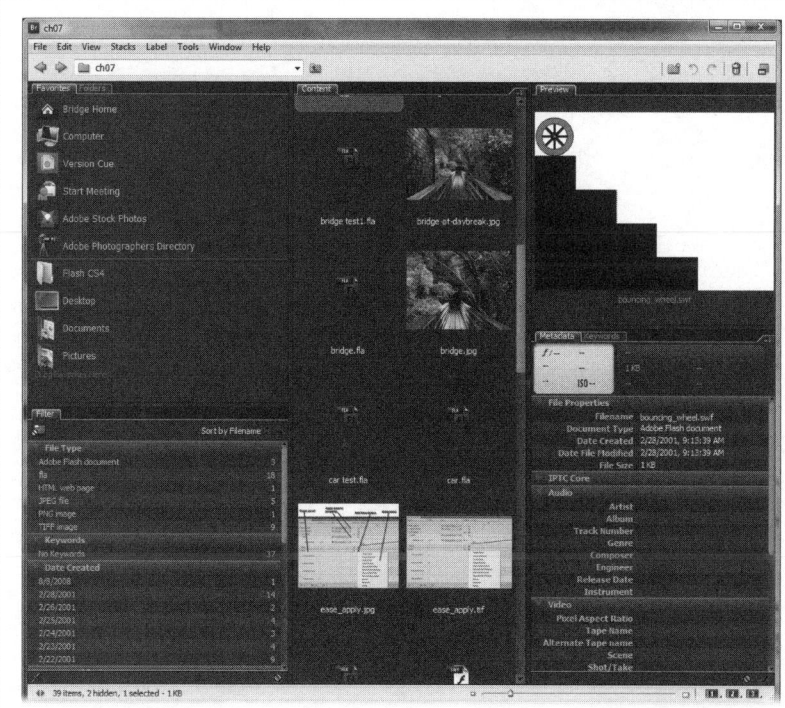

Figure 9-11:
Bridge is Adobe's program
for managing, organizing,
cataloging and previewing
media files of all flavors.
You can customize the
program to show the
details you need for your
media files.

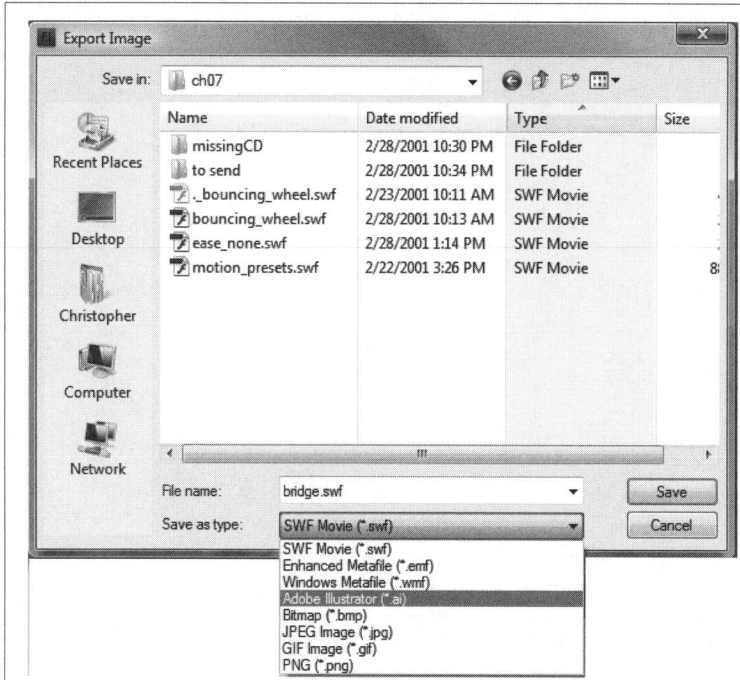

Figure 9-12:
You can export single images and
animated sequences from Flash
and save them in file formats
compatible with other programs.
For the complete details on
exporting, see page 654.

Incorporating Sound and Video

You can create almost any kind of picture or effect in Flash, but sometimes you already have the perfect piece of sound or video…and it's in another file. No problem: Flash lets you pull in all kinds of other media files—like songs in MP3 files or QuickTime videos. Whether you're showcasing your band's performances, creating an employee training Web site, or creating an online wedding album, Flash has all the multimedia tools for the job.

When Flash was born, it was a big deal to have moving pictures on the Internet. Most folks had pretty slow Internet connections, so it was kick to see pictures move, even if they were simple cartoonish images. The same was true of even the most basic sound effects. Today, we're used to full screen video delivered over the Net, and sounds have gone from beeps and bells to radio broadcasts, audio books, and entire albums of music. Things have changed, and Flash is at the center of the revolution.

One change, of course, is the number of people who use fast Internet connections. The other change came when Web developers began to use Flash video (FLV). Most of the Web browsers in the world have Flash capabilities—Adobe's estimates are way above 90%. For you, the good news is that when you wrap your audio and video offerings in Flash, you don't have to force your audience to download and install yet another plug-in. This chapter explains how to add sound to your animations and how to edit that sound for the best fit. You'll also learn how to present video in a predesigned component that gives the audience playback controls.

Incorporating Sound

Flash lets you score your animations much the same way a filmmaker scores a movie. You can add a soundtrack that begins when your animation begins and ends when it ends. Or you can tie different sound clips to different *scenes* (series of frames) of your animation. For example, say you're creating an instructional animation to demonstrate your company's egg slicer. You can play music during the opening seconds of your animation, switch to a voice-over to describe your product, and then end with realistic sounds of chopping, slicing, and boiling to match the visual of cooks using your product in a real-life setting.

You can also tie sounds to specific *events* in Flash. For example, say you want your instructional animation to contain a button someone can press to get ordering information. You can tie the sound of a button clicking to the Down state of your button, so when someone clicks your button, she actually *hears* a realistic clicking sound.

Note: Early on (that is, before version 8), Flash included a library of sound effects you could add to your animations. Now in Flash CS4, the Sounds Library is back, and crammed full of noises made by animals, machines, and nature. To add a library sound to your animation, choose Window → Common Libraries → Sounds, and drag a sound to the stage.

Importing Sound Files

Before you can work with sound in Flash, you need to import a sound file either to the stage, the Library, or both. Flash lets you import a variety of sound files, as you can see in Table 10-1.

Table 10-1. Audio file formats you can import into Flash

File Type	Extension	Note
MPEG-1 Audio Layer 3	.mp3	Works on both Mac and Windows.
Windows Wave	.wav	Works on Windows only, *unless* you have QuickTime 4 (or later) installed; then you can import .wav files into Flash on the Mac, too.
Audio Interchange File format	aiff, .aif	Works on Mac only, *unless* you have Quick-Time 4 (or later) installed; then you can import AIFF files into Flash running in Windows, too.
Sound Designer II	.sd2	Only works on Mac, and only if you have QuickTime 4 (or later) installed.
Sound-only QuickTime movies	.mov, .qtif	Works on both Windows and Mac, but only if you have QuickTime 4 (or later) installed.
Sun AU	.au	Works on both Windows and Mac, but only if you have QuickTime 4 (or later) installed.

To import a sound file:

1. **Select File → Import → "Import to Library".**

   The "Import to Library" dialog box appears.

2. **In the "File name" field, type the name of the sound file you want to import (or, in the file window, click the file to have Flash fill in the name for you).**

   To see the different types of sound files you can import, you can either click the drop-down menu at the bottom of the "Import to Library" dialog box, or check out Table 10-1.

3. **Click Open ("Import to Library" on a Mac).**

   The "Import to Library" dialog box disappears, and Flash places a copy of the imported sound file into the Library (Figure 10-1, top). When you click to select any of the frames in your timeline, the Sound subpanel appears in the Properties panel.

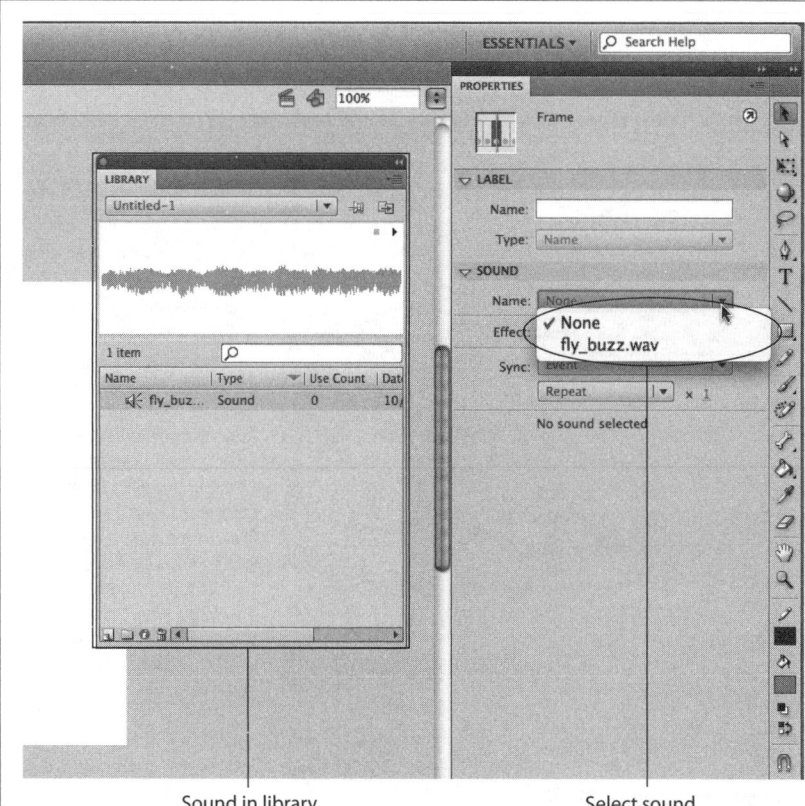

Sound in library   Select sound

Figure 10-1:
The visual representation Flash displays when you select an imported sound clip is called a waveform. *(As discussed on page 349, you use this waveform when you're editing a sound clip in Flash.) When you click the Play button that Flash displays along with the waveform, you can preview the sound. Flash puts a copy of your imported file in the Library and makes the imported file available in the Properties panel.*

Adding an Imported Sound to a Frame (or Series of Frames)

You can tell Flash to play an animated sound beginning with any frame of your animation. Depending on the settings you choose, Flash keeps playing the sound file either until it finishes (regardless of whether your animation is still playing or not) or until you tell it to stop.

The example below shows you how to use the *stream* option to synchronize a short sound clip of a fly buzzing with an animated sequence showing—what else?—a buzzing fly. Then you'll learn how to start and stop a second sound (the sound of the fly becoming a frog's lunch).

To add an imported sound to a series of frames:

1. **Open the file *happy_frog.fla*.**

   You can find this file on the "Missing CD" page at *http://missingmanuals.com/cds*. (To see a working version, check out *happy_frog_sound.fla*.)

2. **In the Layers window, click to select the topmost layer (Guide: Layer 1).**

   Flash highlights the layer name, as well as all the frames in that layer.

3. **Select Insert → Timeline → Layer.**

   Flash creates a new layer and places it above the selected layer.

   Double-click the new layer name, and then type in *soundtrack*, as shown in Figure 10-2.

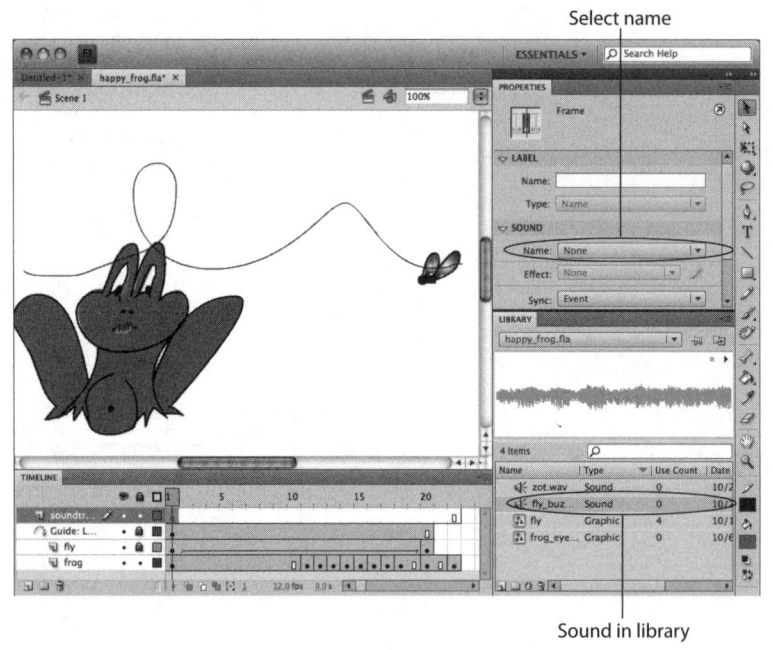

Select name

Sound in library

Figure 10-2:
Technically speaking, you can add a sound clip to any layer you like. But if you're smart, you create a separate layer for your sounds (some folks even create a separate layer for each sound). Creating separate layers helps keep your keyframes from becoming so cluttered that you can't see everything you've added to them. It also helps you find your sounds quickly in case you want to make a change down the road.

Tip: You add a sound to a button the same way you see shown here, but with two exceptions: You typically add a sound file for a button to the button's third, or Down, frame (so that the sound plays when your audience clicks *down* on the button) and you leave the synchronization option set to Event. To see an example, check out the file *button_sound.fla* on the "Missing CD" page.

DESIGN TIME

Using Sound Effectively

If you've ever watched a movie that had a breathtakingly beautiful (or laughably cheesy) musical score, you've experienced the power of sound firsthand. Effective sound can elevate a decent visual experience into the realm of art. Ineffective sound can turn that same visual experience into a nerve-shredding mess.

If you're thinking about adding sound to your animation, consider these points:

- **Why do you want to add sound?** If your answer is to add emotional punch; to cue your audience aurally to the interactive features you've added to your animation, like buttons that *click* or draggable objects that *whoosh*; or to deliver information you can't deliver any other way (like a voice-over explaining an animated sequence or realistic sounds to accompany the sequence); then by all means go for it. But if your answer is "Because I can," you need to rethink your decision. Sound—as much as any graphic element—needs to add to the overall message you're trying to deliver or it'll end up detracting from that message.

- **Are you sure your audience will be able to hear your sound?** Sound files are big. They take time to download. If you're planning to put your animation on a Web site, Flash gives you a couple of different options for managing download time—but keep in mind that not everyone in your audience may have a fast connection or the volume knob on her speaker turned up. (For that matter, some folks can't hear. Check out the box on page 30 for tips on providing hearing-impaired folks with an alternate way of getting your information.)

- **How important is it that your soundtrack matches your animation precisely?** Flash gives you options to help you synchronize your sound clips with your frames. But you can't match a 2-second sound clip to a 10-second animated sequence without either slowing down the sound or speeding up the animation. If you want to match a specific sound clip to a specific series of frames, you may need to edit one (or both) to get the balance right before you begin synchronizing them in Flash.

---

4. **Click the first keyframe in the soundtrack layer.**

   In the Properties panel, Flash activates the Frame properties. With a sound file in the Library, the Sound subpanel appears in the Properties panel.

5. **In the Sound subpanel, click the Name drop-down menu, and then choose the imported sound file *fly_buzz.wav*.**

   Alternatively, you can drag the sound file symbol from the Library to the stage. Either way, the sound properties for the file appear at the bottom of the Properties panel, and the waveform for the buzzing fly sound appears in the soundtrack layer (Figure 10-3).

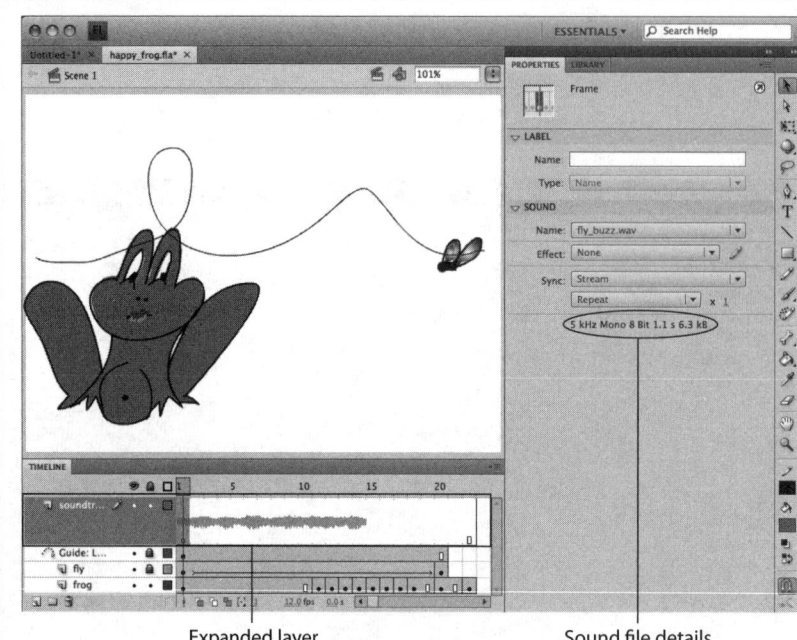

Figure 10-3:
It's rare that the length of a sound clip precisely matches the length of the animated clip to which you want to assign it. Here, the sound clip stretches only to Frame 14—but the layer showing the buzzing fly stretches all the way to Frame 20. You could cut and paste the sound to fill those last four frames so that the fly doesn't become uncharacteristically silent all of a sudden, but Flash gives you much easier ways to match a sound clip to a frame span: streaming, repeating, and looping.

Expanded layer   Sound file details

Note: If you don't see the waveform in the timeline after you've added it, click the first keyframe, and then Shift-click Frame 20 to select all of the frames, from 1 to 20. Finally, choose Insert → Timeline → Frame.

---

6. **In the Properties panel, click the Sync field, and then, from the first drop-down list that appears, choose Stream.**

   Your synchronization choices include:

   - **Event.** Tells Flash to give the sound its very own timeline. In other words, Flash keeps playing the sound until the sound finishes, regardless of whether or not the animation has ended. If you repeat (or loop) the animation in the Controller, Flash begins playing a new sound clip every time the animation begins again—with the result that, after a dozen or so loops, you hear a dozen flies buzzing! Flash assumes you want your sound to behave this way unless you tell it otherwise.

   - **Start.** Similar to Event, but tells Flash *not* to begin playing a new sound if the animation repeats.

   - **Stop.** Tells Flash to stop playing the sound.

   - **Stream.** Tells Flash to match the animation to the sound clip as best it can, either by speeding up or slowing down the frames-per-second that it plays the animation. This option is the one you want for *lip-synching*, when you're trying to match a voice-over to an animated sequence featuring a talking head. Because choosing this option also tells Flash to *stream* the sound file (play it before it's fully downloaded in those cases where you've put your animation on a Web site), someone with a slow connection can get a herky-jerky animation.

Tip: To preview your newly added sound on the stage, drag (*scrub*) the playhead along the timeline. You can scrub forward or backward. To hear just the sound in a specific frame, Shift-click the playhead over that frame. Flash keeps playing the sound until you let up on either the Shift key or the mouse.

---

7. **From the second drop-down menu next to the Sync field, choose Loop.**

   Loop tells Flash to repeat the sound clip until the animation ends. Repeat lets you tell Flash how many times you want it to play the sound clip (regardless of the length of the frame span).

8. **Test the soundtracked animation by choosing Control → Test Movie.**

   You hear a buzzing sound as the fly loops its way across the test movie.

9. **Add a second, short sound clip to your animation to make the scene more realistic. To do so:**

   In the soundtrack layer, click Frame 20.

   On the stage, you see the frog's tongue appear (Figure 10-4).

10. **Select Insert → Timeline → Blank Keyframe, or press F6.**

    Flash places a blank keyframe (a hollow circle) in Frame 20.

11. **In the Sound subpanel, click the arrow next to Name, and then, from the drop-down list that appears, choose *zot.wav*.**

    Flash places the waveform for the sound file into the timeline, beginning with Frame 20.

Tip: If you need a better view of the sound's waveform in your timeline, right-click the layer with the sound, and then choose Properties. The Properties panel opens. At the bottom set the layer height to either 200% or 300%, as shown in Figure 10-3.

---

12. **In the Properties panel, click the arrow next to Sync, and then, from the drop-down list that appears, choose Start. Then, in the soundtrack layer, click to select Frame 22.**

    On the stage, you see a very satisfied frog (Figure 10-5).

13. **Select Insert → Timeline → Blank Keyframe or press F6.**

    Flash places a blank keyframe (a hollow circle) in Frame 22.

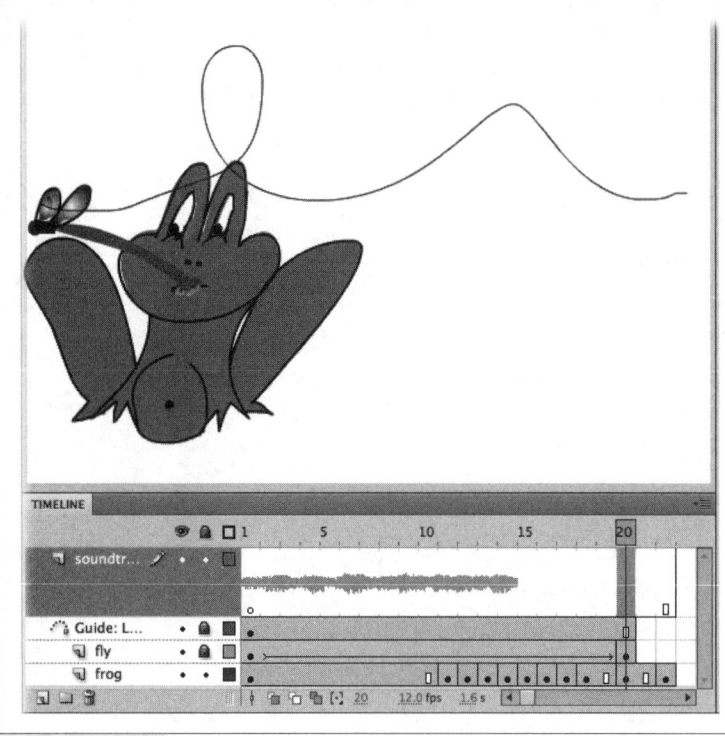

Figure 10-4:
Beginning sound clips in individual keyframes lets you change the soundtrack at the exact moment your visuals change. Here, you see the frog's tongue appear in Frame 20 of the frog layer, and it doesn't change until Frame 22 (which contains the final keyframe of the animation). So to match the "zot!" sound to the tongue action, you want to tell Flash to start playing the zot.wav file on Frame 20 and stop playing it on Frame 22.

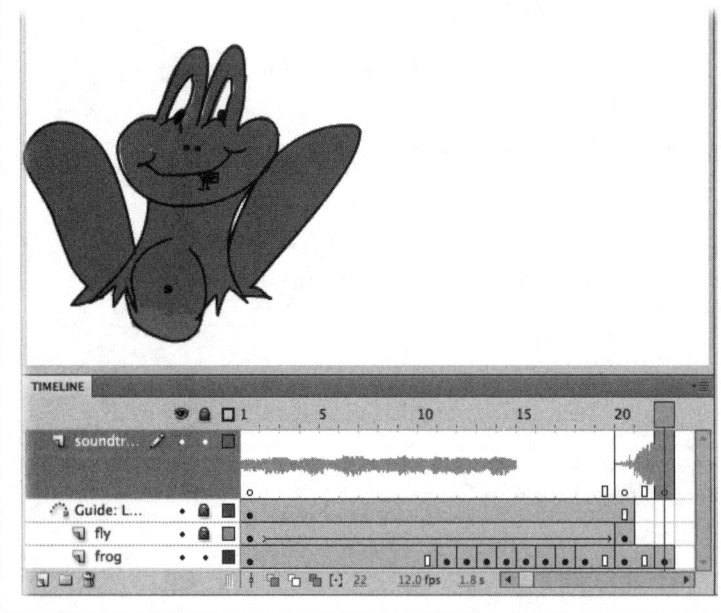

Figure 10-5:
Because the synchronization option for the "zot!" sound was set to start in Frame 20, Flash automatically stops playing the zot.wav sound file when the animation ends. Still, it's good practice to tell Flash specifically when you want it to stop playing a sound file. You'll be glad you did when you come back to the animation a week or two later because you won't have any cleanup to do before you add additional sounds to the timeline.

14. In the Sound subpanel, click the Name drop-down menu, and then choose zot.wav. Click the arrow next to Sync, and then, from the drop-down list that appears, choose Stop.

You're done!

15. Test the new sound by choosing Control → Test Movie.

You hear a buzzing sound as the fly loops its way across the test movie. But as the frog's tongue appears, the buzzing stops and you hear a satisfying "zot!"

Tip: If you don't hear any sounds, select Control and see whether the checkbox next to Mute Sounds is turned on. If it is, click it to turn it off.

Editing Sound Clips in Flash

You can change the way your imported sound clips play in Flash. You can't do anything super-fancy, like mix down multiple audio channels or add reverb—Flash isn't a sound-editing program, after all—but you *can* crop the clips, add simple fade-in/fade-out effects, and even choose which speaker (right or left) they play out of.

First, import the sound clip you want to edit, as described on page 342. To edit it, follow these steps:

1. **In the timeline, click any frame that contains a portion of the sound clip's waveform.**

   Flash activates the sound options you see in the Properties panel.

2. **In the Properties panel, click the drop-down box next to Effect, and then choose from the following menu options:**

   - **Left channel.** Tells Flash to play the sound through the left speaker.

   - **Right channel.** Tells Flash to play the sound through the right speaker.

   - **Fade left to right.** Tells Flash to begin playing the sound through the left speaker, and then switch midway through the clip to the right speaker.

   - **Fade right to left.** Tells Flash to begin playing the sound through the right speaker, and then switch midway through the clip to the left speaker.

   - **Fade in.** Tells Flash to start playing the sound softly, and then build to full volume.

   - **Fade out.** Tells Flash to start playing the sound at full volume, and then taper off toward the end.

   - **Custom.** Tells Flash to display the Edit Envelope window you see in Figure 10-6, which lets you choose the *in point* (the point where you want Flash to begin playing the sound) and the *out point* (where you want the sound clip to end). You can also choose a custom fading effect; for example, you can fade in, then out, then in again.

Note: Clicking the Property panel's Edit button displays the same Edit Envelope window you see when you choose the Custom option.

Incorporating Video

In the past few years, Flash has become the video champion of the Internet. You find Flash video on sites from YouTube to CNET. It wasn't long ago that a battle royale raged between Microsoft, Apple, and RealMedia for Web video bragging rights. Flash was seldom mentioned in the contest; after all, it was just for making little animations. But, like the Trojans with their famous horse, Flash Player managed to sneak onto about 90% of today's computers. And guess what? Flash does video, too. It's easy for you to add video to a Web page or any other project by adding it to a Flash animation. It's easy for your audience, too, since they don't have to download and install a special plug-in to watch your masterpiece. Flash is also fueling the recent surge in video blogging, or *vlogging*—adding video clips to plain-vanilla Web logs. You can find out more at sites like *www.vidblogs.com* and *www.wearethemedia.com*.

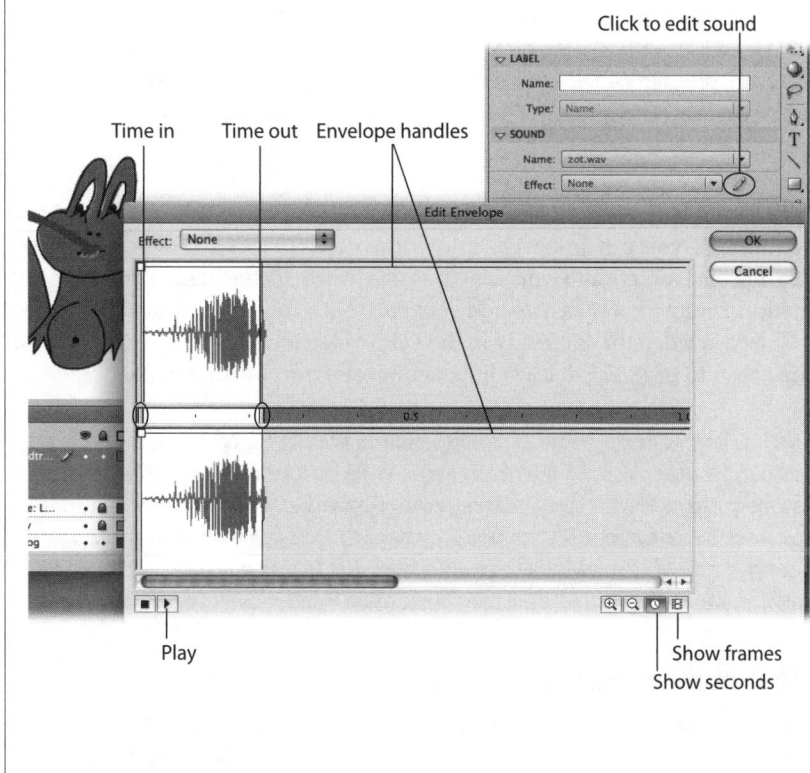

Click to edit sound

Time in   Time out   Envelope handles

Play

Show frames
Show seconds

Figure 10-6:
The sound file you see here is a two-channel (stereo) sound, so you see two separate waveforms, one per channel. To crop the sound clip, drag the Time In and Time Out control bars left and right. Flash ignores the gray area during playback and only plays the portion of the waveform that appears with a white background, so here Flash only plays the second half of the waveform. To create a custom fading effect, you can drag the envelope handles separately. These settings tell Flash to fade out on the left channel while simultaneously fading in on the right channel. To preview your custom effect, click the Play icon.

Tip: If you're watching a video on the Web and wondering whether the site uses Flash to publish it, right-click the video. If you see "About Flash Player…" in the shortcut menu, you know Flash is working behind the scenes.

May as well face it: sometimes video footage is more effective than even the most well-crafted animation. For example, video footage showing a live product demonstration, a kid blowing out the candles on his birthday cake, or an interview with a CEO can get the point across quicker than any other medium.

There are two basic steps to creating Flash video:

• **Convert your video to the Flash video file format: .flv or .f4v.** Before you can add video to your Flash animation, you have to convert it to a special file format. The process, which video techies call encoding, creates small files that can travel quickly over the Internet. Flash comes with the Adobe Media Encoder, which lets you convert most types of video into Flash video format. The next section describes the encoding process.

Note: Adobe is working hard to keep Flash at the forefront of the Internet video revolution. With version 9.0.124 of the Flash Player (codenamed Moviestar), Adobe added capabilities for HD (high definition) video and audio, similar to what you find in Blu-Ray DVDs. The amount of data needed for HD video would overwhelm most of today's Internet connections, but it's certainly an indication of what to expect in the future.

- **Import your video into a Flash animation.** Once your video clip is in Flash video format, you can import it into your project. Flash stores a copy of the video in the Library, and you can drag the video to the stage like any other graphic. It's remarkably easy to add video playback controls to your Flash video. If you have a video that's already in the Flash video format (.flv or .f4v), you can jump ahead to page 365 to learn how to import it into your Flash file.

Note: Neither Flash nor the Adobe Media Encoder let you do extensive editing. At best, they let you crop a segment out of a larger video clip. If you're interested in piecing together different video segments to create a movie or a scene, turn to a specialized video editing program like Adobe Premiere or Apple Final Cut Pro. If your needs are more modest, you can probably get by with Apple's iMovie or Microsoft's MovieMaker. Using those programs, you can either save clips as Flash video, or you can save clips in a different format (.mpg, .mov, or .avi), and then convert them using Adobe Media Encoder.

Encoding: Making Flash Video Files

Video files are notoriously huge, which means standard video files take a long time to travel the Internet. To solve this problem, Flash uses special video formats that shrink or compress video into smaller files. The quality might not be what you'd expect from your 50-inch plasma HDTV, but it's certainly acceptable for Web delivery. The process of converting a video from its original format to Flash video (.flv or .f4v) is called encoding. If you already have a file in the Flash video format or if someone else is responsible for this part of the job, you can jump ahead to "Importing Video Files" on page 365.

Using the Adobe Media Encoder, you can encode any of the common video files listed in Table 10-2. As explained in the box on page 356, it's best to start off with a high quality, uncompressed video. You can add prebuilt controls that let your audience control the playback and adjust the volume. You can even apply effects to a video clip in Flash: for example, skewing and tinting.

Table 10-2. video file formats you can convert to Flash Video with Adobe Media Encoder

File Type	Extension	Note
QuickTime movie	.mov	The audio/video format.
		Apple's video player uses. A free version of QuickTime player is available for both Macs and PCs.
Audio Video Interleaved	.avi	Microsoft audio/video format.

Table 10-2. *video file formats you can convert to Flash Video with Adobe Media Encoder (continued)*

File Type	Extension	Note
Motion Picture Experts Group	.mpg, .mpeg	MPEG-1 is an early standard for compressed audio and video media.
		MPEG-2 is what standard DVDs use.
		MPEG-4 Part 2 is used by the DivX and Xvid codecs.
		MPEG Part 10 is used by QuickTime 7 and the H.264 codec.
Digital video	.dv	Many camcorders use this digital video format.
Windows Media	.asf, .wmv	These Microsoft formats are for compressed audio/video files.
Flash video	.flv, .f4v	Flash's video format employs a "lossy" compression technique to produce very small files suitable for broadcast over the Internet.

The hardest part of encoding video files is the wait. It takes time to encode large video files, but it's getting better with today's faster computers. Flash CS4's installer automatically puts Adobe Media Encoder on your computer. Fire it up, and it looks like Figure 10-7. There are two basic things you need to do: locate the file you want to encode, and give Adobe Media Encoder instructions about how to process it. Here are the steps:

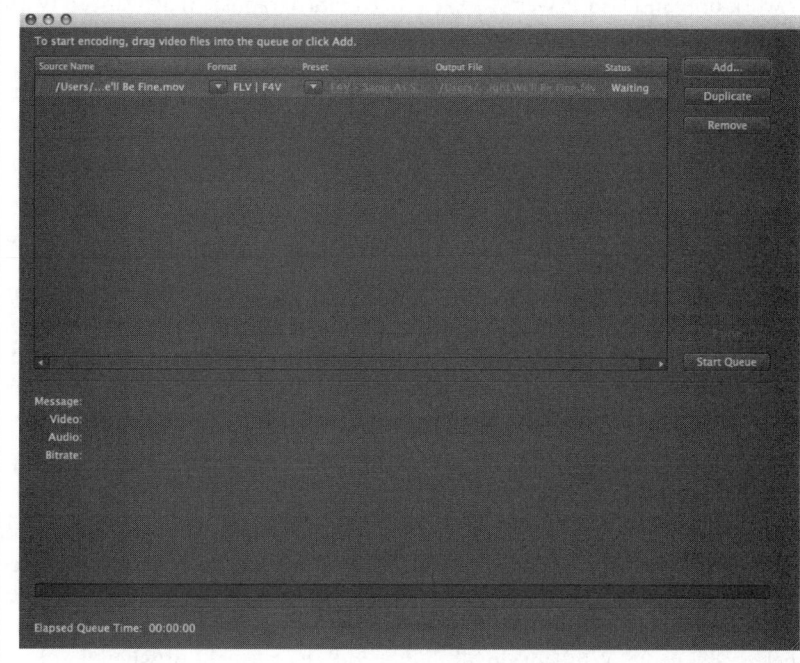

Figure 10-7:
Adobe Media Encoder is a multipurpose conversion tool that comes with several different Adobe products, including Flash. You add media files to the queue and tell Flash what type of file you want it to produce.

1. **In Adobe Media Encoder, click Add.**

   Flash displays a standard Open window similar to the one you use to open a Flash document.

2. **Navigate to the file on your computer that you want to encode, and then click Open.**

   The name of the video file appears under Source Name.

3. **Under Format, choose the Flash video format: FLV/F4V.**

   Flash video files automatically determine whether your fill is encoded in the FLV or the F4V format. That determination depends on the preset you choose in the next step. Flash gives you these presets (predetermined settings) because choosing all the settings to encode video can be ridiculously complicated. Even when you choose a file format like FLV or F4V, there are still dozens of settings you can choose based on how the video is distributed and viewed. Adobe helps you wade through the swamp of video settings by providing presets for common video needs.

4. **Under Preset, choose a preset format that matches your project.**

   Flash has what may seem like a bewildering number of presets as shown in Figure 10-8. The names are marginally descriptive. If your project is destined for a Web page, try FLV – Web Medium to start. The FLV format works with Flash Player 8 and 9. The F4V formats show better quality video in smaller files, but work only in Flash Player 9. Experienced videographers may want to tweak the encoding settings or trim the video clip before it's encoded.

5. **Under Output you can change the name or location of the file.**

   If you don't make any changes under Output, the encoded file appears in the same folder as the original video file. It has the same name, but will end with either .flv or .f4v.

6. **Click Start Queue.**

   Adobe Media Encoder starts to encode your file. A bar at the bottom of the window tracks the progress (Figure 10-9). If you have several files to encode, you add them all to the queue before you hit Start Queue. The encoder makes no changes to the original file. When the encoder is finished, a checkmark appears next to the file in the queue, and you have a new file with a *.flv* or *.f4v* extension.

Batch encoding to save time

No matter how you cut it, encoding video takes time and can slow down your computing workflow. If you have lots of video to encode, prepare several video clips for encoding using the steps described in this section. You can add several encoding jobs to the encoding queue, and then run them all at the same time when you click Start Queue. Why not do all that encoding overnight or when you head out to lunch?

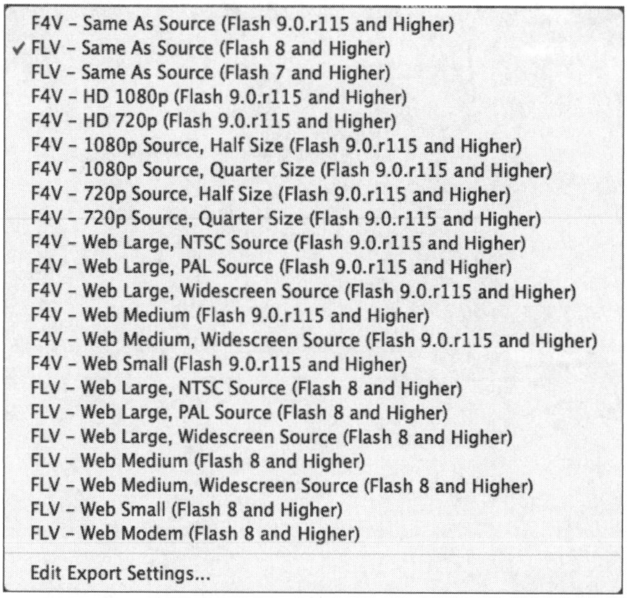

F4V - Same As Source (Flash 9.0.r115 and Higher)
✓ FLV - Same As Source (Flash 8 and Higher)
FLV - Same As Source (Flash 7 and Higher)
F4V - HD 1080p (Flash 9.0.r115 and Higher)
F4V - HD 720p (Flash 9.0.r115 and Higher)
F4V - 1080p Source, Half Size (Flash 9.0.r115 and Higher)
F4V - 1080p Source, Quarter Size (Flash 9.0.r115 and Higher)
F4V - 720p Source, Half Size (Flash 9.0.r115 and Higher)
F4V - 720p Source, Quarter Size (Flash 9.0.r115 and Higher)
F4V - Web Large, NTSC Source (Flash 9.0.r115 and Higher)
F4V - Web Large, PAL Source (Flash 9.0.r115 and Higher)
F4V - Web Large, Widescreen Source (Flash 9.0.r115 and Higher)
F4V - Web Medium (Flash 9.0.r115 and Higher)
F4V - Web Medium, Widescreen Source (Flash 9.0.r115 and Higher)
F4V - Web Small (Flash 9.0.r115 and Higher)
FLV - Web Large, NTSC Source (Flash 8 and Higher)
FLV - Web Large, PAL Source (Flash 8 and Higher)
FLV - Web Large, Widescreen Source (Flash 8 and Higher)
FLV - Web Medium (Flash 8 and Higher)
FLV - Web Medium, Widescreen Source (Flash 8 and Higher)
FLV - Web Small (Flash 8 and Higher)
FLV - Web Modem (Flash 8 and Higher)
Edit Export Settings...

Figure 10-8:
When you first use Adobe Media Encoder, it's best to use one of the presets that match your project. Later, you may want to create your own settings by clicking Edit Export Settings.

/Users/...e'll Be Fine.mov
FLV | F4V
Encoding
Duplicate
Pause
Stop Queue
Message: Encoding Item 1 of 1
Video: 640x480, Same as source [fps], Progressive
Audio: AAC, 128 [kbps], 44.1 kHz, Stereo
Bitrate: VBR, 1 Pass, Target 1.50 [Mbps], Max 2.00 [Mbps]
Encoding "Teddy Thompson - Tonight We'll Be F...
Elapsed Time: 00:00:16
Estimated Remaining: 00:08:37
Elapsed Queue Time: 00:00:18
Progress bar
Estimated remaining time

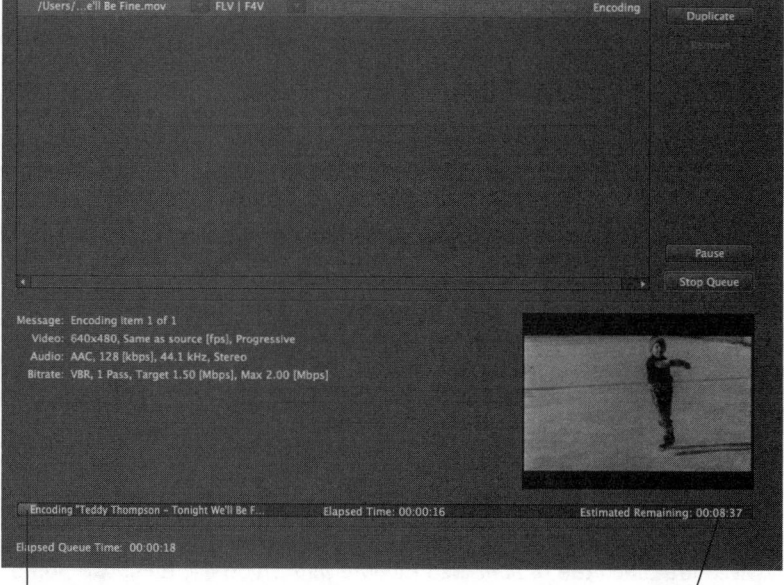

Figure 10-9:
While the Media Encoder processes your file, it keeps you updated with a progress bar and the Estimated Remaining time. The video also appears in a preview window.

Over-Compression: Too Much of a Good Thing

The final destination for many Flash projects is a Web site. One of Flash's great virtues is the ability to present animations, video, and sound over the Web without making the audience wait while humongous files travel the Internet. Flash makes big files small by compressing them. It uses different compression methods for images, sound files, and video files. Some types of compression actually degrade the image, sound, or video quality. It's a tradeoff, but it's the best way to create really small files that travel the Net fast. The idea is to keep as much information as is needed to maintain acceptable quality and throw out the extra bits. These types of compression schemes are called *lossy* formats because they lose data and as a result lose quality. Examples of lossy formats are: JPEG photo files, MP3 audio files, and FLV or F4V Flash video files. While compression is a good thing because it keeps the file size down and helps Web-based Flash animations load quickly, it's possible to over-compress a file. One way that happens is when you compress a file that's already been compressed.

If you repeatedly compress photos, sound files and video files you can end up with media mush. For example, take a JPEG and save it five times using 50% quality and you find that the last copy is much poorer in quality than the first. You can do the same thing to MP3 audio files and video files. Ideally, it's best to bring uncompressed files into Flash, and then let Flash do the compression once, when it publishes a SWF file. For audio files, that means it's best to use uncompressed AIFF files on a Mac or WAV files on a PC. For video files, use video that hasn't already been compressed. With video, the compression takes place when you use the Adobe Media Encoder to make .flv or .f4v files. So, if you just shot the video with your camcorder, feed the raw .dv file to Adobe Media encoder for the best results. If the file is coming from someone else, ask him to give you the best quality possible.

Encoding Part of a Video Clip

There are a few reasons why you might want to dig into Adobe Media Encoder's export settings before you encode a file. One of the most common scenarios is that you have a long video and you only need to bring a small part of it into your Flash project. To do so, follow the encoding steps that begin on page 354. When you reach step 4, instead of choosing one of Adobe's presets, click Edit Export Setting at the bottom of the list. The next thing you see looks like a video editing window, shown in Figure 10-10. You can't do extensive editing in this window like you can with Adobe Premiere or Apple's Final cut, but you can select a portion of a video clip to encode. Encoding is pretty slow business, and there's no reason to waste time converting video that you won't use.

In the upper-left corner of the Export Settings window is a small preview screen. Below the screen is a timeline with a playhead, similar to Flash's. Drag the playhead to see different frames in your video. The two markers in the timeline below the playhead are called the *In point* and the *Out point*. You use these two points to select a segment of the video. As you drag either point, the preview window shows the image (or video frame) for that point in time. A highlight appears on the selected segment of video.

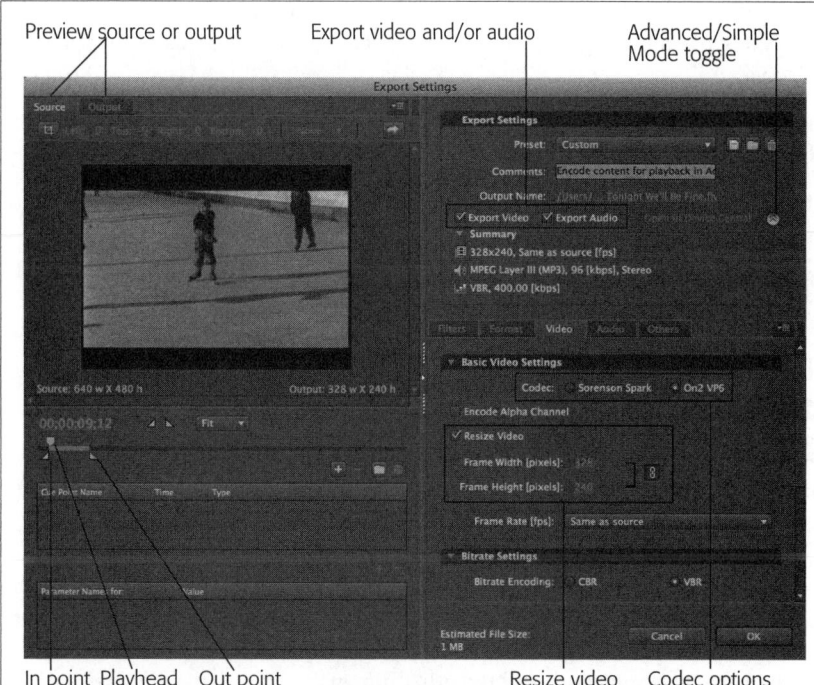

Preview source or output   Export video and/or audio   Advanced/Simple Mode toggle

In point   Playhead   Out point   Resize video   Codec options

Figure 10-10:
You can't do extensive editing in Adobe Media Encoder, but you can select the portion of a video file that you want encode. The program also provides tools to resize the entire video, select portions of the image, and fine-tune the video codec used to encode your Flash video file.

If you want to use one of Adobe's encoding presets, you can choose one in the upper-right corner of the Export Settings window. (If you'd rather tweak the export settings on your own, see page 359.) Click OK, and you're back at the Media Encoder, where you can change the name and location for your encoded file, as described in step 5 on page 354. Or, you can simply click the Start Queue button to encode the video segment you selected.

Resizing and Cropping a Video Clip

When you choose an encoding preset in Adobe Media Encoder, the preset determines the dimensions of the video image. For comparison, a wide-screen TVs might show a high-definition image that's 1920 pixels wide by 1080 pixels high. When you choose the FLV – Web Medium setting, the preset encodes an image that's 360 pixels wide by 264 pixels high. When you're in Export Settings, you can choose any size you want. Understandably, large dimensions, like those for that hi-def TV, mean much larger files. If your video is traveling the Internet, you can dramatically reduce the travel time by reducing the video dimensions. The 360×264 size of the FLV – Web Medium preset is a nice compact size for the Net. If you know everyone in your audience is going to have a fast cable or DSL connection, you can go ahead and bump the dimension up to 640×480, another fairly standard dimension for video.

After you've opened Adobe Media Encoder and added a video to the encoding queue, as described on page 354, follow these steps to choose a custom size for the encoded video:

1. **Instead of choosing one of Adobe's presets, click Edit Export Setting at the bottom of the list.**

   The Export Settings window appears, where you can fine-tune many aspects of the encoding process.

2. **On the left side of the Export Settings window, click the Video tab.**

   If you don't see tabs in the Export Settings window, click the Advanced/Simple Mode toggle button, as shown in Figure 10-10.

3. **Click the Resize Video checkbox.**

   Once you've checked the Resize Video box, the encoder uses the size dimensions entered in the next step.

4. **Change the height and width dimensions, as shown in Figure 10-11.**

   Most of the time, you want to maintain your video's proportions to keep the images from looking too tall or too fat. To constrain the proportion, make sure the Constrain width/height button is depressed. Then, you can enter either a width or height dimension, and the other dimension automatically sizes itself.

5. **Click OK.**

   The Export Settings window closes, and you see the Adobe Media Encoder queue.

Cropping a video while encoding

Cropping a video is just like cropping a photo. Instead of resizing the entire image, you select a portion of the image that you want to view. With moving pictures it's a little trickier, because the image is changing at multiple frames per second. The crop that looks great for the first 20 seconds of a clip might not look as good a minute later. Also keep in mind, when you crop a video, you're changing the dimensions and the quality of the image. When you crop into an image too far, you end up with a blurry picture.

To crop your video, follow the steps on page 358 to open the Export Settings window in Adobe Media Encoder. Above the preview window, click the Crop button. A frame appears around the video image with handles at the corner. Drag the handles to frame the portion of the picture you want to keep, as shown in Figure 10-12. If you need specific dimensions in pixels, you can click the Crop dimension numbers, and then type new values. Keep in mind, these numbers are showing the number of pixels being trimmed from the edges of the picture. To see the dimensions of the cropped image, point to one of the frame handles. A tooltip appears near the mouse cursor with the width/height dimensions in pixels.

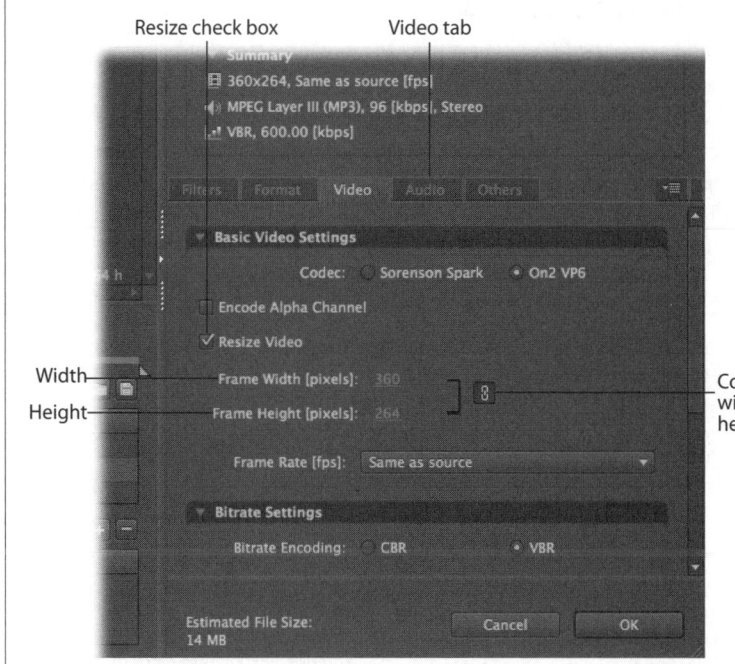

Resize check box   Video tab

Figure 10-11:
Open Adobe Media Encoder's Export Settings window to choose a custom size for your encoded videos. Click the Constrain width/height button to maintain the picture's original proportions.

Width

Height

Constrain width/height

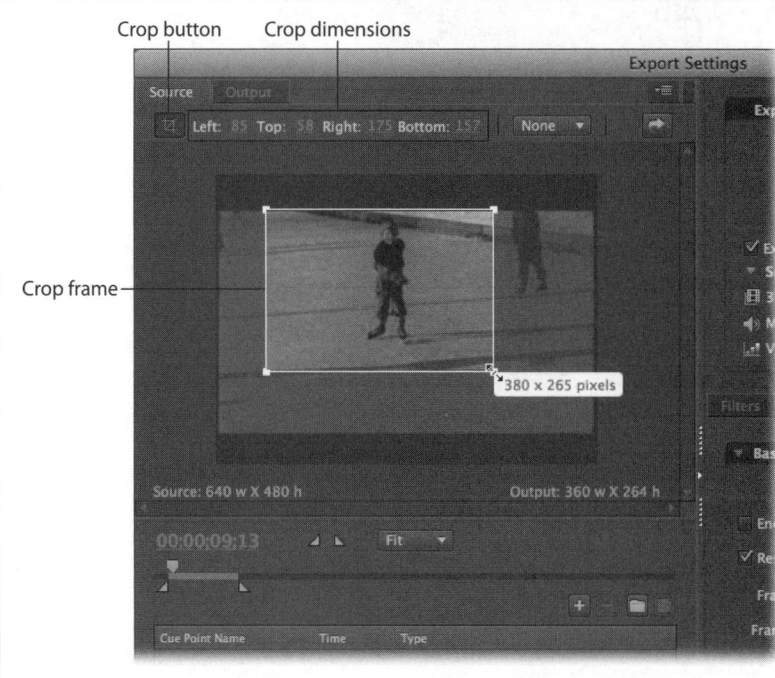

Crop button   Crop dimensions

Figure 10-12:
Drag the handles in the "crop frame" to select the portion of the video picture you want to keep in your encoded video.

Crop frame

Adding Cue Points to Your Video

Flash lets you place *cue points* (markers) in your movie clips, which you can then use to trigger other actions in your Flash animation. For example, perhaps you'd like to show text on the screen at a certain point in the video, or perhaps you'd like to trigger a certain sound or narration track. You give cue points names—like "narration"—as you create them. Then you use ActionScript code to identify the cue points and trigger the actions you want performed. (There's more on Action-Script starting in Chapter 11.)

You add cue points in Adobe Media Encoder, using the same Export Settings window that you use to resize or crop your video.

1. In Media Encoder select Edit → Export Settings to open the Export Settings window.

   You see a preview window showing your video, with a timeline underneath, as shown in Figure 10-13. Just as in Flash, the timeline has a playhead. Drag the playhead to a point in the timeline, and you see that frame in your video. Below the preview, there are two panels: one for cue points and one for parameters.

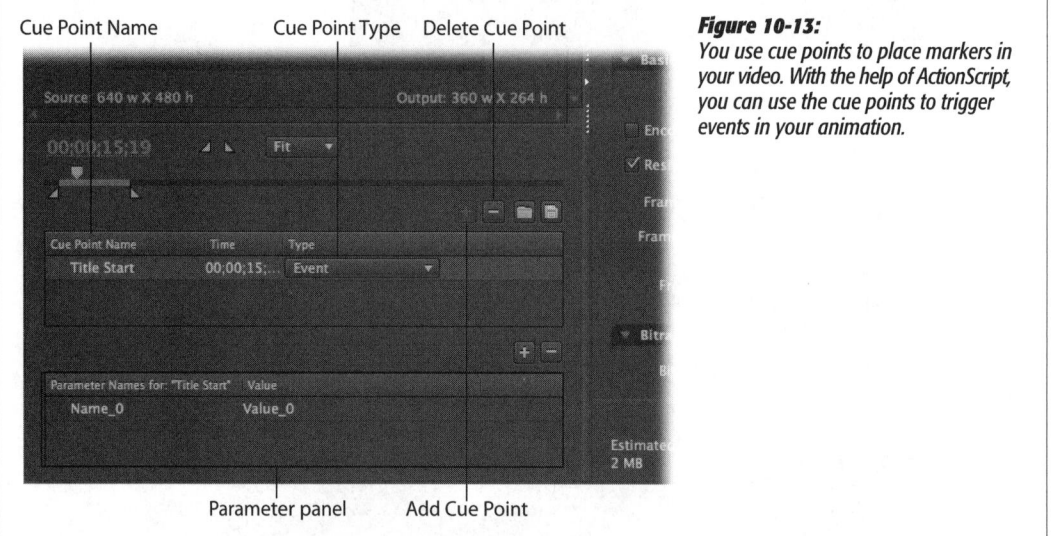

Cue Point Name   Cue Point Type   Delete Cue Point

Parameter panel   Add Cue Point

Figure 10-13:
You use cue points to place markers in your video. With the help of ActionScript, you can use the cue points to trigger events in your animation.

2. Drag the playback head to the point in your video you want to mark.

   The video image changes as you move the playback head.

3. Click the + button to add cue points; click the – button to remove them if you make a mistake.

   Flash creates a cue point in the list and gives it a name, a time setting, and a type. The time setting is determined by the playback head's position in the video clip. In the next steps, you'll change the name and type of cue point.

4. Click the name, and then type a descriptive name for your cue point.

Flash names all cue points "cue point" when it first creates them. It's up to you to type something more descriptive.

5. Choose the type of cue point you want to create—Event or Navigation. If you're an ActionScript hotshot, set parameters.

Event cue points trigger an action when the video reaches them. Navigation cue points let you locate and play certain portions of your video. Both Event and Navigation cue points require ActionScript to work their magic.

6. Click the + button to add parameters to your cue point; click the – button to remove them if you make a mistake.

Parameters are key-value pairs that programmers use to store and retrieve information. So the parameter values are available to ActionScript programs when the video reaches the cue point.

7. Repeat steps 2–6 to add more cue points, or click OK to go back to the encoder queue.

Choosing a Video Codec

Part of the encoding process is choosing the *codec* (*co*mpressor/*dec*ompressor...get it?) that shrinks your video as it converts it to the Flash video format. Over its short history, Flash video has used three different codecs. The makers of Flash have updated the Flash Player to use new codecs as they've become available. The new codecs provide new features and produce better quality video using smaller file sizes. As a Flash designer, you need to guess which version of the Flash Player your audience is likely to have when you choose the best codec for encoding.

Flash CS4 makes these decisions relatively easy for you. If you use one of the presets when you encode, all you need to do is choose the Flash player your audience will use, and then decide the relative size. For example, one of the choices is FLV – Web Medium (Flash 8 or higher). If you customize the Export Settings, you can choose the video codec that's used to shrink your video file to size. Here's a guide to the Flash Players that work with different codecs (the year the Flash Player was released is shown in parentheses):

• Sorenson Spark: Flash Player 6 (2002) and above. It's the safest choice; if your audience's Flash Player is video-capable, this codec will work.

• On2 VP6: Flash Player 8 (2005) and above. This choice is pretty safe, unless you're sure that your audience has older computers. One advantage of this codec is you can perform tricks like making part of the video image transparent, just like the news folks do when they put the weather guy in front of a map.

• F4V (H.264): Flash Player 9.2 (2008) and above. This choice produces the best quality video using smaller file sizes. If you choose the F4V Flash video format, it automatically uses the same H.264 codec that Apple uses for iTunes and Apple TV.

You can manually choose a codec from the Export Settings window of the Adobe Media Encoder. Here are the steps:

1. **In the Media Encoder, select Edit → Export Settings.**

   The Export Settings window opens, as shown in Figure 10-10.

2. **Click the Format tab, as shown in Figure 10-14.**

   If you don't see tabs in the Export Settings window, click the Advanced/Simple Mode toggle button, as shown in Figure 10-10.

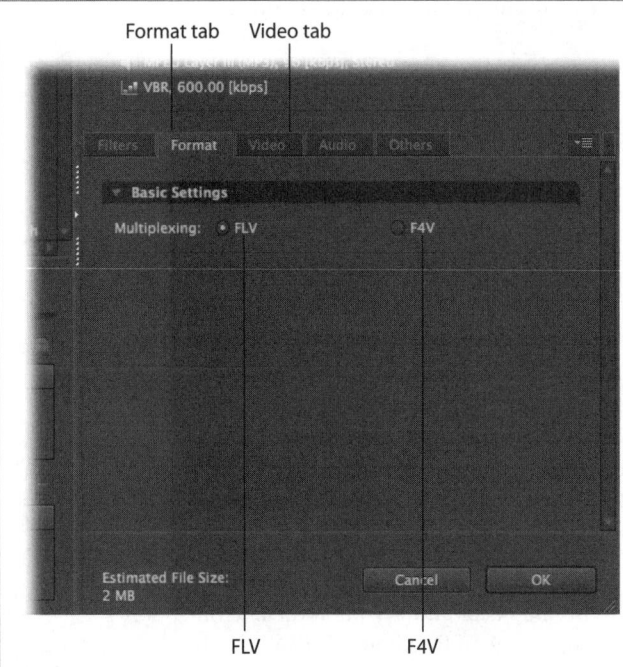

Figure 10-14:
Flash video uses two file formats. The FLV format works with more Flash Players, but the F4V format uses the latest, greatest technology to create good looking video in small file sizes.

3. **Choose either FLV or F4V format.**

   If you choose the F4V format to take advantage of its good looks and small file sizes, your job is done. The encoder uses the H.264 codec. If you choose the FLV file format so you have compatibility with the older Flash Players out there, then you need to go on to step 4 to specifically choose a codec.

4. **If you're using the FLV format, click the Video tab, and then select either Sorenson Spark or On2 VP6.**

   The bullet points before these steps explain the advantages between these two codecs. If you choose Sorenson Spark, you're done. If you choose On2 VP6, you can go on to the next step to choose whether or not to add an Alpha channel (transparency) to your video.

5. If you chose the On2 VP6 codec, you can click the Encode Alpha Channel checkbox.

   With an Alpha Channel encoded in your video, you have the ability to replace a specific color with transparency. Called *chroma-keying*, this technique is common in newscasts and feature films.

Other Techniques for Reducing Video File Sizes

No one likes to wait while a Web page loads. So when you're publishing video on the Web, life is a constant quest to shrink the size of your video files so they'll travel the Net faster. In addition to the encoding tricks already mentioned, here are some tips for shrinking those files while still providing a good video experience. Some of these techniques are related to creating the video, and others are related to Adobe Media Encoder and Export Settings.

Video techniques for reducing file sizes

- **Start out with good quality video.** When possible, use uncompressed video before you encode to Flash Video. If your video has blips and glitches (called noise by videographers) before you encode it, the video file ends up bigger.

- **Avoid fancy effects and transitions.** Special effects like fancy wipes or spiral transitions don't work as well in Flash video as a plain cut from one scene to the next. Even dissolves add to the size of your video file.

Encoding techniques for reducing file sizes

- **Reduce the dimensions of the video.** It's great to have a high-resolution video that looks beautiful when the audience clicks the full-screen button. But if it takes too long to download over the Internet, you won't *have* an audience. As described on page 357, you can change the dimensions of your video to reduce the file size.

- **Consider using a lower frame rate.** You can set the frame rate in the Video tab of the Export Settings window. The standard frame rate for American TV is 29.97 frames per second (don't ask about the decimal; it's a long story). The standard for film is 24 fps. Test your videos at 18, 15, or even 12 fps to see whether the quality/file size tradeoff is worth it.

- Use mono sound where possible. If your video is a musical performance, it may be important to have stereo sound, but otherwise you can save precious file space by clicking the Audio tab in the Export Settings window, and then choosing Mono.

- Use a lower bit rate for sounds that are mostly voices or don't require high-fidelity. Go to the Audio tab in Export Settings, and then use the drop-down menu to reduce the bit rate for sound. The encoder has bit rates from 16 to 256. A bit rate of 64 works for many Flash videos. You can go even lower if the sound track is primarily voice, with no music.

Preparing to Import Video Files

Before you can import a video clip into Flash, it's good to know up front how you expect to link the video file to your finished Flash animation file at runtime: by embedding the video file directly into your Flash timeline, or by linking to the video file at runtime, and so on.

This cart-before-the-horse consideration isn't quite as odd as it seems at first blush. Video files tend to be so huge you don't usually want to embed them directly into your Flash document the way you embed graphics and sound files (page 319 and page 342, respectively). The process of setting up your Flash animation and Flash video files for the public to view them is called *deploying*.

Note: Chapter 19 tells you all you need to know about publishing Flash files, including Flash files containing video clips.

Your deployment options include:

- **Progressive download from a Web server.** This option is one of the most popular because all you need to publish video on the Internet is a regular, garden-variety Web server. Your Flash animation files (.swf) and Flash video files (.flv or .f4v) are stored on the server. It's called progressive because the video starts playing for your visitors before the entire video file is downloaded. The downside to this option is the fact that the entire video is eventually stored on your visitor's computer, giving her the ability, if she's clever, to make a copy of your video. If you aren't comfortable with bootleg copies, then consider one of the next two options.

- **Stream from Flash Video Streaming Service.** This option is the most popular way to show videos without letting others copy them. Basically, you hire a company to stream your video from their computers to your Web site visitors. Your visitors never have a complete copy on their computers, making it more difficult for them to swipe it. You can find a long list of companies that provide this service on Adobe's Web site (*www.adobe.com/products/flashmediaserver/fvss/*). These companies have a program called Flash Media Server on their computers, which detects the speed of your Web visitor's Internet connection and sends the video at a speed it can handle. Your visitor gets a higher-quality video experience, and you get added security for copyrighted material. All you have to do is pay for the service.

- **Stream from Flash Media Server.** This option is similar to the second option above, except that you (or, more likely, your organization's IT department) buy the server hardware, install the server software, and maintain the resulting system. This option is best if you have deep pockets (Flash Media Server costs $4,500) and don't mind the hassle of maintaining a media server.

Note: If you have your own Web server and want to dip your toe in the Media Server water, you may want to investigate Red5, an open source (free) Flash Server (*http://osflash.org/red5*).

- **As mobile device video bundled in SWF.** Use this option in combination with Flash's templates for consumer devices and handsets to create animations for small handheld devices. This option is used to place video inside of SWF files used with phones and handsets.

- **Embed video in SWF and play in timeline.** This option represents the simplest way to embed video into your animation, but it only works for very short video clips (somewhere between 5 and 10 seconds or less). Any more than that, and the size of your animation file grows so large that you have trouble editing the file in Flash *and* your audience has trouble viewing it in their Flash Player.

Importing Video Files

Once you have access to a video in the Flash Video format (*.flv* or *.f4v*), you're ready to begin importing the video file into Flash. When you begin this process, your video can be on your computer or it can be on the Web, where it's served up by a Flash Media Server. In this section, you see step-by-step examples for both scenarios.

Importing a Flash Video File Stored on Your Computer

When you have a video on your computer in one of Flash's two video formats (.flv or .f4v), it's easy to import it into your Flash project. By making a couple of choices along the way, you can give your Flash audience standard controls to play and pause your video and adjust its sound. To work on the following exercise, you can download the video *building_implode.flv* from the "Missing CD" page at *http://missingmanuals.com/cds*.

Note: If you need to convert a video to one of the Flash video formats (.flv or .f4v), see page 352.

When you add video to your Flash project using this method, Flash creates a link between the Flash file and your project. Even after you publish a Flash .swf file for final distribution, the Flash file and your video file remain separate. If the project is for a Web site, you need to place both the Flash .swf file and the video file (.flv or .f4v) on the Web site, ideally in the same folder. To make things easy for yourself, it's best to put your Flash video in same folder where you save your Flash work file (.fla) and publish your Flash animation (.swf).

1. **Create a new Flash document, and then save it.**

   It's always good to name and save your Flash projects at the beginning. It's even more helpful when you work with external video files as you do in this project. A name like *building_bye_bye.fla* might be appropriate for this one.

2. Place the Flash video *building_implode.flv* in the same folder where you save your Flash file (.fla) and your published flash file (.swf).

This step makes it easier for Flash to create a link to the video file. After publishing the *.swf*, as long as both files are located in the same folder, the link between the two will continue to work.

3. In Flash, select File → Import → Import Video.

The Import Video dialog box appears, as shown in Figure 10-15, with several options you can choose using radio buttons. The question is: Where is your video file? Either it's on your computer, or it's stored on a Web server with Flash Media Server software.

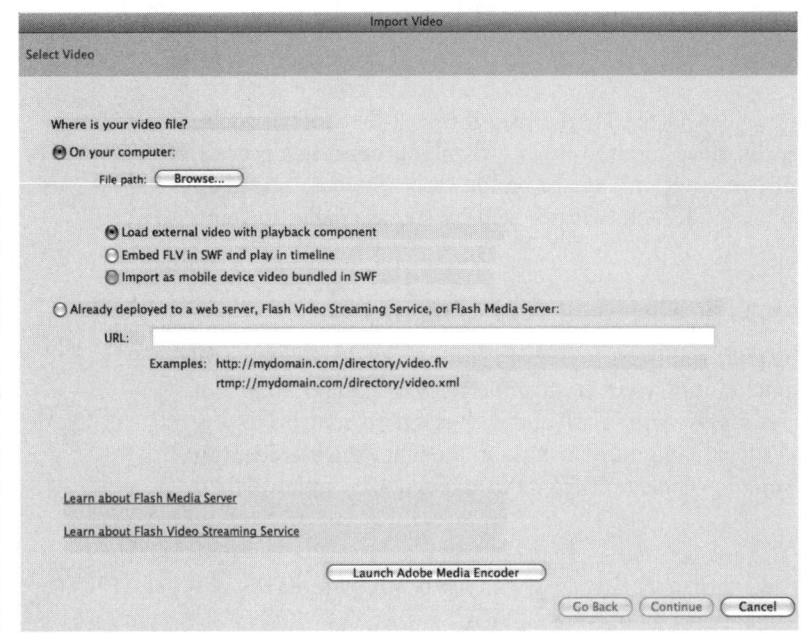

Figure 10-15:
The large Import Video dialog box walks you through adding video to your Flash project. In the first step, shown here, you answer questions about the location of the video file and how you want to use it in your project.

4. Click the radio button for "On your computer."

Flash wants to know where the file is right now, so it can load it into your project. At this step, don't jump ahead and start thinking about where the final project is going to be published.

5. Click the Browse button, and then locate your video file.

Flash displays a standard Open window similar to the one you use to open a Flash document. It should be easy to locate *building_implode.flv*, because it's in the same folder as your Flash file. After you select the file, its name and path show up under the Browse button. Now that Flash knows where the file is located, it can work with the video.

6. **Tell Flash how you want to work with the video by clicking the radio button labeled: "Load external video with playback component."**

   • **Load external video with playback component** creates a link between your Flash file and an external video file. When Flash gets a command to play the video, it finds and plays the external file.

   The other two options are used less frequently, but they're useful for special cases:

   • **Embed FLV in SWF and play in timeline.** This option embeds video into your animation. Each frame of video becomes a frame in the Flash timeline. The result is the Flash file gets huge very fast, and your audience will be frustrated trying to download and play the video. Don't try this option with clips any larger than 5 or 10 seconds.

   • **Import as mobile device video bundled in SWF.** Use this option in combination with Flash's templates for consumer devices and handsets to create animations for small handheld devices (a topic not covered in this book).

7. **Click Continue to move to the next Import Video step.**

   The Import Video box changes to show skinning options for your video. A *skin* is a sort of container that adds play/pause/stop type controls to your video, as shown in Figure 10-16.

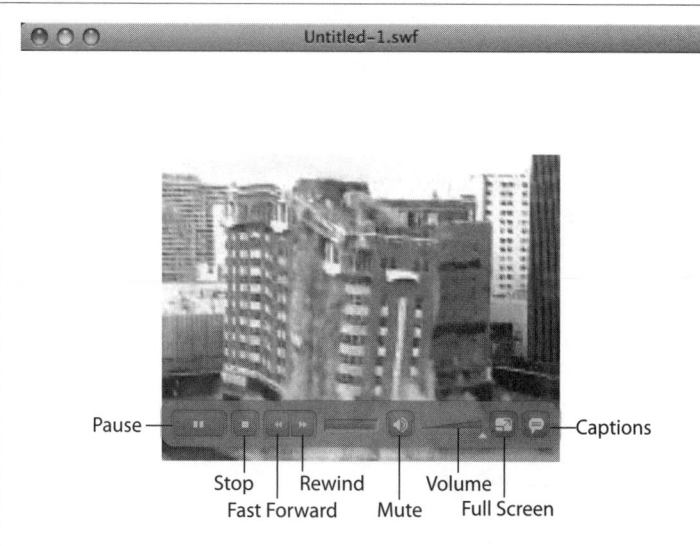

Figure 10-16:
There are two basic types of skins for Flash video. "Over" skins like the one shown here sit on top of the video image, hiding some parts of the picture. "Under" skins are completely outside of the image.

8. **From the Skin drop-down box, choose SkinOverAll.swf.**

Use the drop-down menu to choose an Adobe predesigned skin, as shown in Figure 10-17. Adobe supplies a whole slew of skins with different combinations of controls. SkinOverAll includes all of the controls, so this exercise shows you what's available. When you tackle a real-world project, you may find you don't need quite so many gadgets on your videos.

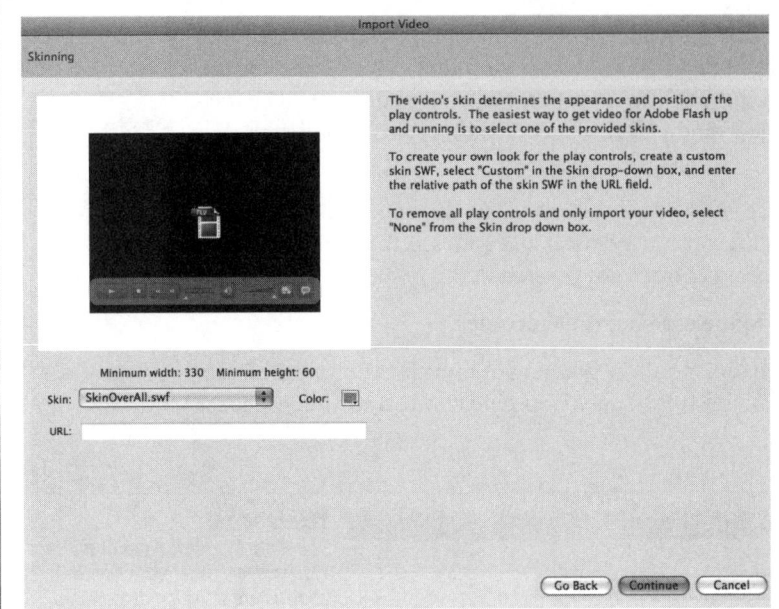

Figure 10-17:
Give your audience snazzy video controls by simply choosing from the Skin drop-down menu. Use the buttons in the lower-right corner of the Import Video dialog box to move forward (Continue) or backward (Go Back) in the Import Video process. Or you can give up entirely (Cancel).

There are also options to provide no controls at all (usually not the best option) or to use a custom-designed skin. For example, you might want to put your client's logo on the video skin as another way to establish their brand.

9. **Click Continue.**

Flash displays the Import Video: Finish Video Import dialog box you see in Figure 10-18. The details shown may not seem that important until it's time to publish your Flash project on a Web page. Here's a translation for each of the lines:

• **The video you are using is located at:** This line lists the folder where the video file lives. If your final project is going on a Web server, you have to give both *building_implode.flv* and *building_bye_bye.swf* to your Webmaster.

• **The video will be located at: (relative paths are relative to your .swf)** This line explains the relationship of your files when you publish your Flash animation. It shows you the path that has to exist between the .swf and your video file (*building_implode.flv*). In this case, there is no path (just a file name) because you're planning on keeping both the .swf and the .flv in the same folder, whether it's on your computer or a Web server.

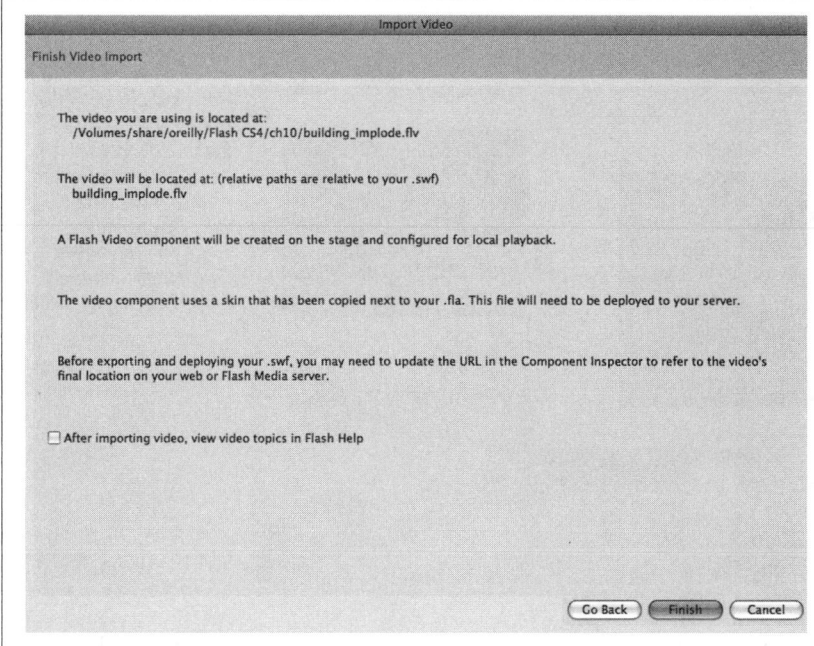

- **A Flash video component will be created on the stage and configured for local playback.** This line simply tells you that your video and whatever skin you selected will appear on the stage in your Flash document.

- **The video component uses a skin that has been copied next to your .fla. This file will need to be deployed to your server.** These sentences are a roundabout way of saying that the skin for your video is stored in a separate .swf file. Flash places it in the same folder on your computer with *building_bye_bye.fla*. This skin has a name similar to the name you choose in step 8. In this case, it's named *SkinOverAll.swf*, and it has to be in the same folder with *building_bye_bye.swf* and *building_implode.flv* when you publish your Flash animation.

- **Before exporting and deploying your .swf you may need to...** If *building_bye_bye.swf* and *building_implode.flv* aren't in the same folder when you put your animation on a Web server, you need to change the path in the video component. For more on video components, see the next section, page 371.

10. **Click Finish.**

The Import Video: Finish Video Import dialog box disappears. As promised, you see the video on your stage along with the skin (video controls). There's also copy of the video in the Library, as shown in Figure 10-19.

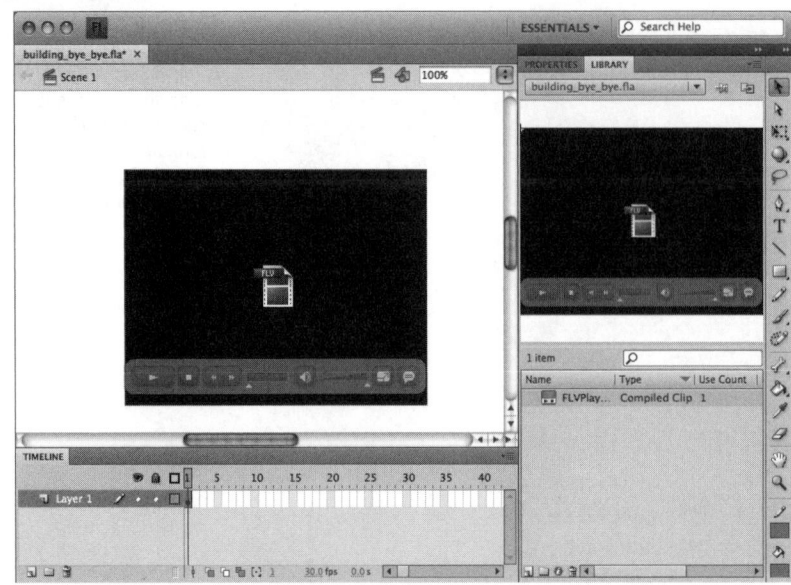

Figure 10-19:
When you finish importing your video to Flash, it shows up in the Library and there's an instance already placed on the stage. If you need another instance of the video, say in another scene, you can simply drag it from the Library to the stage in that scene.

11. **Press Ctrl+Enter (⌘-Return on a Mac) to test your Flash project and view the video.**

    In the Flash animation, you see your video running. Using the skin controls, you can start and stop the playback.

Deploying your flash video on the Web

Most of the time, Flash projects that incorporate videos end up on the Web. Whether you're uploading the video to a Web page or someone's doing it for you, make sure that three files make the journey: the Flash animation (.swf), the Flash video file (.flv or f4v), and the skin file (named something like *SkinOverAll.swf*).

Importing a Flash Video from the Web

Surprisingly, importing a video file that's stored on the Web isn't much different from importing one that's on your computer, as described on page 365. The Flash video file may be in a standard Web server or one that has Flash Media Server software. (Don't worry if you don't have a video file stored on a Web server; there's an example file you can practice with, as you'll see in the following steps.)

The only differences in the importing process happen at the very beginning.

1. **Select File → Import → Import Video.**

    The Import Video: Select window appears.

2. **Turn on the radio button next to "Already deployed to a web server, Flash Video Streaming Service, or Flash Media Server" (Figure 10-15). In the URL box, type the Web address where the file lives, and then click Continue.**

   The URL for the practice file is *http://examples.oreilly.com/flashcs4mm/building_ implode.flv*. When you click Continue, the Import Video: Skinning window you see in Figure 10-17 appears.

The rest of the steps are identical to those for importing a Flash video file on your own computer. You can pick up the process at step 8 on page 368.

Customizing the Video Playback Component

In Flash-speak, once your video is added to your Flash file, it's called the FLVPlayback component. Components are prebuilt widgets that you drop into your animations. Someone else went to all the trouble of building (and hopefully testing) the component. All you have to do is drop a component into your Flash project and let it do its stuff. Components save you design and programming time, so it's worthwhile to learn about them. There's a whole chapter on components (Chapter 15), but since you're already using one in this example, it's worth covering some of the specific ways you can customize the FLVPlayback component.

Most components provide a few options that let you customize them for your nefarious purposes. For example, in the case of the FLVPlayback component, you can change the playback behavior of the video and the appearance of the video controls. You can even change the video source file if you have a newly edited and improved video. You change the settings for a component by changing its parameters. Here's how to view and edit the FLVPlayback parameters:

1. **In Flash, click the FLVPlayback component on the stage.**

   You don't see many settings in the Properties panel for the FLVPlayback component. Instead, you use the Component Inspector to make most adjustments, as described in the next step.

2. **Select Window → Component Inspector.**

   The Component Inspector panel opens in Flash. The name of each parameter (setting) is listed on the left, and its value is shown on the right.

3. **Make changes to the FLVPlayback parameters.**

   You can change multiple parameters without closing the Component Inspector. For example, to change the appearance of the skin (video playback controls), click skinAutoHide, and then set the value to *true*. To change the color of the skin, click the skinBackgroundColor swatch, and then choose a new color from the Color Picker.

Here's a complete description of the parameters for the FLVPlayback component:

- **align.** Determines the alignment of the video image when the video scaleMode (below) isn't set to exactFit.

- **autoPlay.** If set to true, the video automatically plays when the Flash animation frame that holds it is loaded.

- **cuePoints.** You can add cue points to your video when it's encoded, as explained on page 360. Or you can add them using the FLVPlayback component. Click the magnifying glass to open a window where you can add manual cue points by typing in a name and a time.

- **islive.** Used with a Flash Media Server, this value is set to *true* when streaming a live performance.

- **preview.** Used for the live preview feature that helps you test the parameter settings. Click the magnifying glass to see your video with the current settings.

- **scaleMode.** This setting determines how the video image sizes itself after it's loaded. There are three options: *noScale*, where the video uses the size of the Flash video source file; *maintainAspectRatio*, where the video retains its proportions when enlarged or shrunk; and *exactFit*, which forces the video to fit the dimension of the component as shown in the Properties panel.

- **skin.** The name and path for the .swf file that adds playback controls to the video.

- **skinAutoHide.** If set to true, the playback controls disappear unless the mouse is hovering over the video image.

- **skinBackgroundAlpha.** Playback controls can be transparent. A value of 1.0 = opaque and 0 = invisible. So, a value of .8 provides an 80% opacity effect.

- **skinBackgroundColor.** Click the color swatch, and then choose a new color from the color picker.

- **source.** The name and path for the Flash video file.

- **volume.** Sets the audio volume for video playback. A value of 1.0 = full volume and 0 = no volume. So a value of .5 provides half the available volume for audio playback.

Part Three:
Adding Interactivity

3

Introduction to ActionScript 3

When your Flash document is on your computer, you're in control. You can make it do whatever you want, whenever you want. But eventually, your creation has to strike out on its own. You won't be there to tell your animation what to do when someone clicks a button or to remind it to turn off the sound after the first three times through. You need to provide instructions to make your animation perform automatically—that is, *automate* it.

To automate your animation or make it interactive, you use ActionScript—Flash's built-in programming language—to act on, or *script*, the different parts of your animation. For example, you can instruct your animation to load a Web page when someone clicks a button you've added, to start playing an audio clip at the beginning of a certain scene, to play your animation in reverse, to loop certain sections of your animation, and so on.

Flash calls the chunks of ActionScript code you attach to your animation *actions*, which is a great reminder that ActionScript exists to help your audience *interact* with your animation.

The first section part of this chapter explains how ActionScript has grown up from a simple macro language for animations into a full-blown programming language. After that, the chapter introduces you to some of ActionScript's basic concepts, with examples each step of the way. Follow the examples and try some experiments of your own. Go ahead, you won't break anything. You're on your way to a whole new level of Flash animation.

Getting to Know ActionScript 3

ActionScript is a serious programming language. As explained in the box below, folks in cubicles use ActionScript to develop major programs—like ticket purchasing and reservation systems. ActionScript incorporates geeky programming concepts like variables, functions, parameters, and so on. Delve deep and you find the scripting *object model* (the internal, Flash-designated names of all the parts of your animation). But none of that will stop you from using ActionScript for your own needs. In fact, Flash has some great tools to ease you into programming, like the Actions Panel introduced in this chapter. The visual nature of Flash gives you instant feedback, letting you know when your script works and when it doesn't. Combine those features, and you've got a great way to dip your toe in the programming waters. You can even apply the skills you gain with ActionScript to other programming languages, including that Web developer favorite, JavaScript.

The Flash/ActionScript Partnership

ActionScript is a great name for a programming language. All computer programs perform actions, but the cool thing about Flash and ActionScript is that those actions are so visible. You're not just "assigning a value to a variable," as you would in typical computer lingo, you're making the moon move across the sky, or playing a video clip, or turning up the volume of the music. ActionScript programming is satisfying because many of the actions it performs are so apparent.

IN THE NEWS

ActionScript Hits the Big Time

Now is an exciting time to learn ActionScript. Not only is ActionScript the programming language Flash uses to control animations, it also lets you create lots of other programs that run via the Internet or on your desktop just like word processors and spreadsheets. Adobe is taking advantage of the fact that nearly every computer on earth plays the SWF files that Flash creates. ActionScript programs can sit on a Web site and run in people's browsers. Adobe calls these programs *Rich Internet Applications* (RIAs), and they're at the front of the next big wave in computer software. Traditional (non-artist) programmers use Adobe's Flex Builder tool to create these RIAs.

It doesn't end with the Internet. Flash Player is the little unit that plays Flash movies on your computer desktop. The pocket protector set calls it a *runtime* program, since Flash Player provides all the support needed to run programs in a given computer operating system. There are Flash Players for Windows, Mac, and Linux computers, making it a virtually universal system. So if you create your program in Flash, it can run just about anywhere. Adobe is working to expand this universality into a new standard dubbed *Adobe Integrated Runtime* (AIR). AIR combines several standards to produce desktop programs: Flash, ActionScript, JavaScript, PDF (Adobe Acrobat), and HTML. You can build AIR programs using Flash, Dreamweaver, or Flex Builder. Depending on your program's version, it may require either an upgrade or an extension.

In the earliest versions, ActionScript was sort of tacked on to the Flash animation machine, the way macro programming was added to early word processors and spreadsheets. You used drop-down menus and dialog boxes to move parts of your drawing around the stage. You could start and stop animations on specific frames using familiar programming techniques like loops and conditionals (more on those later). In short, you could create some pretty snazzy visual effects.

At first, programming and animation seemed a curious match, since artists and programmers often seem to be such different people. But when you think about it, programming and drawing are both creative activities. Just like the artist, a programmer needs imagination and a vision. And animation is a very programmatic visual art, complete with reusable chunks of action that branch off into separate scenes. Today, there are Flash artist/programmers responsible for both the artwork and the programming code in their projects. There are also large teams producing Flash projects where artists create the objects that the programmers animate.

ActionScript 3

Each version of Flash has introduced new more sophisticated features, like better video handling à la YouTube. As mentioned in Chapter 3, Flash CS4 introduces a powerful new Motion Editor for creating and adjusting tweens. All along, ActionScript has kept pace. The box on page 378 details some of the history. With ActionScript 3, Flash's programming language has matured quite a bit, adopting the latest and best programming concepts. As a result, ActionScript is more powerful, more consistent and a better tool for team-based projects. If you're a lone artist/programmer, does that mean ActionScript 3 doesn't have any benefits for you? Not at all. You'll benefit from ActionScript 3's consistency and power. New tools like the Display List and the Event Listener system will help you write better programs and keep your sanity in the process.

ActionScript vs. JavaScript and Other Languages

ActionScript and JavaScript have a lot in common. They're both *scripting* languages, meaning that they're programming languages that run inside of other programs. Specifically, ActionScript runs inside Flash, and JavaScript runs inside HTML, the code that Internet browsers use to display Web pages. On top of that, ActionScript and JavaScript sprouted from the same programming language specification, ECMA-262.

Note: Since you're just dying to know, ECMA stands for European Computer Manufacturers Association, the standards group that established the spec.

Initially, programmers used both ActionScript and JavaScript in snippets to perform quick and easy chores. For example, in ActionScript, you'd write something like the following:

```
on (press) {
    startDrag(this);
}
```

CHAPTER 11: INTRODUCTION TO ACTIONSCRIPT 3

About ActionScript 1, 2, and 3

ActionScript 1 (2000). Flash 5 was the first version to introduce the term ActionScript, and for the first time animators could type in code like a real programmer. Before that, Flash kept track of commands chosen from drop-down menus and dialog boxes.

The ActionScript language was based on ECMAScript, which was a great move, since the popular JavaScript also has the same roots. Web programmers who know JavaScript can easily pick up ActionScript.

ActionScript 2 (2003). Flash MX 2004 introduced Action-Script 2 a few months prior to the date implied by its moniker. ActionScript 2 adopted additional object-oriented programming concepts, making it a better tool for larger projects and projects developed by teams of programmers. Some concessions were made so that both ActionScript 1 and ActionScript 2 animations would run in the same Flash Player that was installed on so many computers.

ActionScript 3 (2006). Adobe introduced ActionScript 3 with Adobe Flex 2.0 (a Programming system that makes use of the Flash Player, but doesn't use the Flash Authoring program)—a sure sign that the language had matured beyond a simple macro language for controlling Flash animations. ActionScript 3 follows established object-oriented programming concepts very closely, bringing benefits as well as changes from the previous versions. Adobe Flash CS3 was the first version to include ActionScript 3 as an option.

Today's Adobe Flash Player can run programs written with any version of ActionScript (1, 2, or 3), but it uses an entirely different engine to run the ActionScript 3 programs. More important, ActionScript 3 programs run faster. ActionScript 3 programs also work better with XML, a popular, nearly universal way to store data, and with CSS (Cascading Style Sheets) used to format Web pages.

You would literally attach to a drawn object on Flash's stage. JavaScript uses similar chunks of code to control the behavior of buttons and rollover images. However, JavaScript is often interspersed throughout the HTML code that describes Web pages. From a technical point of view, ActionScript and JavaScript are considered high-level languages because they're closer to human language than the 1's and 0's of machine language.

As human nature kicked in and Flash animations became more elaborate, Action-Script snippets got tucked in all over the place. As a result, if an animation didn't work as expected, it was hard to find the misbehaving code. It could be almost anywhere. ActionScript script writers started to use more disciplined programming techniques, and new versions of ActionScript encouraged better programming practices. The idea of attaching ActionScript code to any old object became frowned upon. Instead, programmers tried to keep all their code in one place, usually a single layer in the timeline. At the same time, *object-oriented programming* was becoming more popular and better defined in programming circles from the Visual Basic coders to the C programming crowd. ActionScript added object-oriented concepts in version 2 and even more in ActionScript 3.

ActionScript 3 Spoken Here

The following ActionScript chapters in this book focus entirely on ActionScript 3. If you're already versed in one of the earlier versions, you may be pleased to know that's Flash CS4 still supports ActionScript 1 and 2, but you can't *mix* code from

Diving Deeper into ActionScript

This book introduces ActionScript 3 and covers many of the commonly used elements of ActionScript programming. The object is to make you comfortable writing ActionScript code to the point that you can use it to control your Flash animations. Ideally, you'll be able to experiment with ActionScript code and branch out from the examples in this book. If you find yourself in the midst of a project and have an Action-Script question, try Flash's help (Help → Flash Help). In the upper-left corner of the Help window (Figure 11-1, left), choose ActionScript 3.0 and Components for help with programming concepts. When a new page opens, you'll notice, there are a couple of ActionScript 3 categories as shown in Figure 11-1, middle. *Programming ActionScript 3.0* is the place to look for explanations to more general programming concepts. When you're working with ActionScript 3.0 components, you'll find all the details you need in *Using Action-Script 3.0 Components*. Turn to *ActionScript 3.0 Language*

and Components for the nitty-gritty on particular elements in the ActionScript elements, like classes, functions and operators (Figure 11-1, right). If you do a lot of ActionScript 3.0 coding, this last reference is probably the one you'll use the most.

In an effort to get you up and programming quickly, this book doesn't cover everything you'd learn in an advanced computer science course. There are great books that go into more detail on ActionScript topics. *Learning ActionScript 3.0* by Rich Shupe and Zevan Rosser (O'Reilly) is a clearly written guide for beginners. For a more advanced reference, *Essential ActionScript 3.0* by Colin Moock (O'Reilly) is ideal. If you're an old hand with ActionScript 2 and want to make the move to ActionScript 3, consider *ActionScript 3.0 Quick Reference Guide* (O'Reilly) to ease you through the transition.

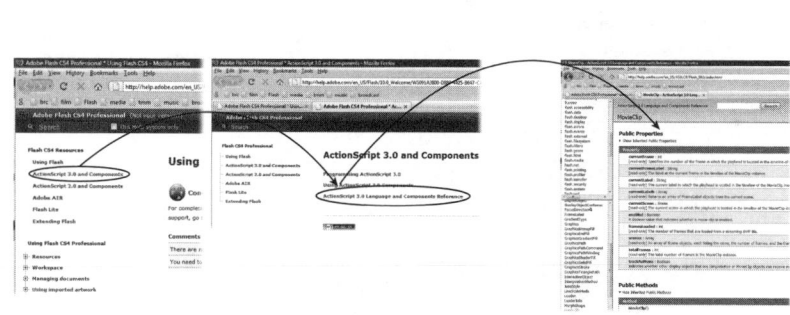

Figure 11-1:
It takes a few steps to reach the ActionScript 3.0 Language and Components *Reference, but it's worth the trip. This is where you look for details on the properties and methods for* ActionScript 3.0 classes.

ActionScript 3 with code from earlier versions. The reason is that the Flash Player now includes two completely separate *virtual machines* (the software that interprets ActionScript code and turns it into actions). The original one runs Action-Script versions 1 and 2. A completely new virtual machine handles ActionScript 3 code, which tends to run faster.

Note: If you're interested in learning more about ActionScript 2, you'll find a brief introduction in *Flash CS3: The Missing Manual*. For a complete intermediate to advanced education, find a copy of *Essential ActionScript 2.0* by Colin Moock.

If you're new to ActionScript, no problem. As the language of the future, Action-Script 3 is the version to learn. If you're an experienced ActionScript programmer, it's worth a little relearning to gain the advantages that ActionScript 3 gives you.

Beginning Your ActionScript Project

When your Flash project includes ActionScript programming, you have some decisions to make at the outset. As explained in the previous section, you need to decide whether you're using ActionScript 2 or ActionScript 3, since you can't mix version 3 with earlier versions. (The exercises in this book all use ActionScript 3). Once you've made that decision, you choose the type of Flash file you want to create in the intro screen or the File → New dialog box (Figure 11-2).

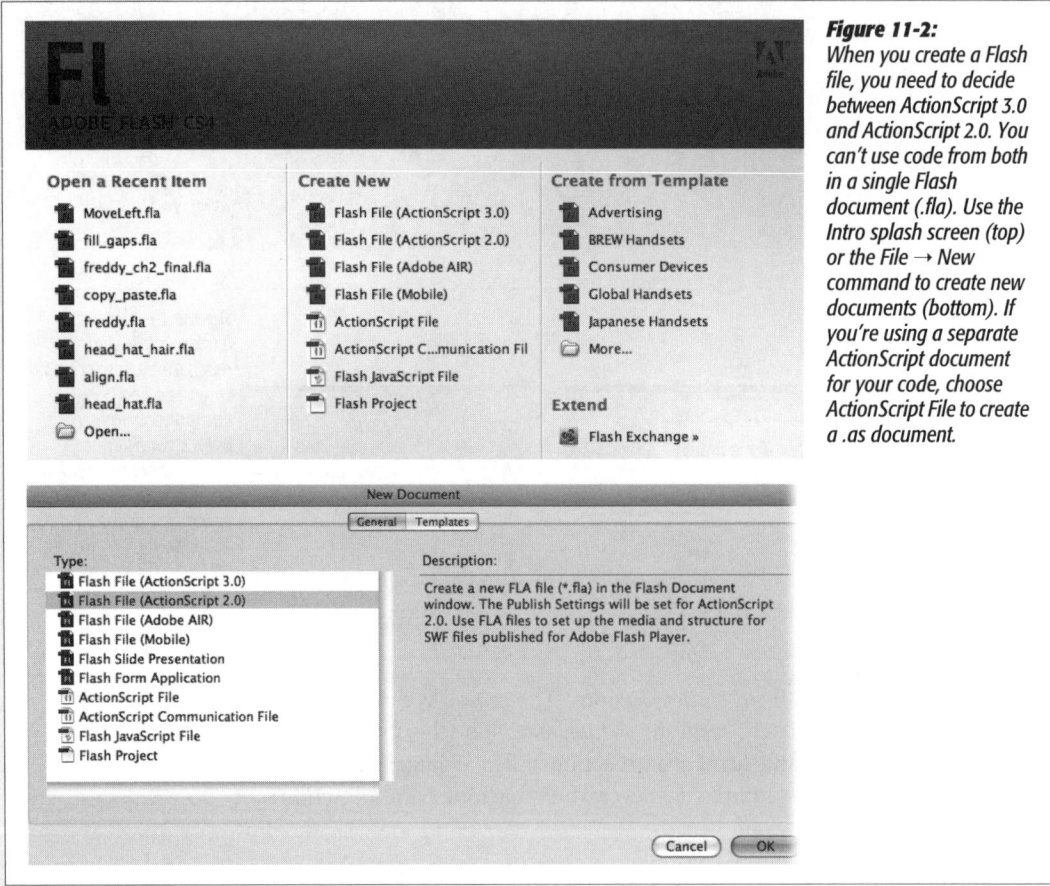

Figure 11-2:
When you create a Flash file, you need to decide between ActionScript 3.0 and ActionScript 2.0. You can't use code from both in a single Flash document (.fla). Use the Intro splash screen (top) or the File → New command to create new documents (bottom). If you're using a separate ActionScript document for your code, choose ActionScript File to create a .as document.

CODERS' CLINIC

Timeline Programming: Pros and Cons

Ask more than one script writer where it's best to place code—Flash timeline or ActionScript file—and you're likely to start an energetic debate. If you plan on a long ActionScript career, it's worth learning both techniques.

Originally, ActionScript was considered a helper tool for animations. If you wanted the moon to rise at a certain point in an animation, you'd attach a snippet of ActionScript code to the moon or to a specific frame in an animation. Before you knew it, you had bits and pieces of code tucked in every nook and cranny of your timeline and Flash file. That situation is bad enough if you're the only one working on the project, but it was really a problem for team projects. Eventually, it became a common practice to keep one timeline layer devoted to ActionScript code. That way, at least most code was in one place. In recent years, the growing trend is to store ActionScript code in a separate file, making it easier for teams to work on the same project. Artists can work on the drawing in a .fla document, and programmers can write code in .as documents.

If you're working on a team project, chances are your team leaders will tell you exactly where and how to add Action-Script to the project. If you're working on your own, you can choose the method that's best for you. In some cases, particularly with smaller projects or projects that need to be hammered out quickly, it may make perfect sense to attach code to the Flash timeline. Here are more details about both methods:

Timeline programming is the way everyone used to write ActionScript. You attach scripts to individual frames in the Flash timeline. Quick and easy, this method gives a certain amount of instant gratification. If you want to quickly test an idea, the tendency is to attach some code to the timeline. The problem is that you may end up with snippets of Action-Script code in many different places, which makes it more difficult to troubleshoot the code if something goes wrong. It's even worse if you (or someone else) return to a project years later to make some changes.

ActionScript file programming is the preferred method for large projects and true object-oriented programming. One of the goals of object-oriented programming is to create code that's easily reusable. First of all, it has to be readable and understandable. Second, the chunks of code have to be somewhat independent. Placing all your code in a separate .as file forces you to provide more thorough definitions of the objects in your Flash project. As a result, you write more lines of code, but there's a better chance that you can reuse that code for other projects. When teams of programmers work on the same project, it's much easier to update the code and keep track of each updated version.

In the end, it comes down to the needs of your project and, if you're the project boss, your personal preference.

Next, you need to decide where you're going to place your ActionScript code. You have two choices. You can place your ActionScript code in frames in the Flash timeline, or you can place your code in a completely separate ActionScript (.as) file:

- **To place ActionScript code in the timeline of your Flash file, create a Flash document (.fla)** *File → New → Flash File (ActionScript 3).* You have a choice between creating a Flash document based on ActionScript 2 or ActionScript 3. When Flash creates a new .fla file, it includes information that (ultimately through the .swf file) tells the Flash Player what flavor of ActionScript to use. You can use timeline programming for smaller projects and when you're not working with a team of other programmers. It's more difficult to reuse your ActionScript code if it's embedded in a Flash document's timeline.

- To place ActionScript code in a separate ActionScript file, create an Action-Script document (.as) *File → New → ActionScript File*. When you work with teams of programmers and artists, it's likely the team manager will tell you to keep ActionScript code in a separate file. Even if you're working alone, you may want to keep code in a separate *.as* file so that your work can be reused with other Flash projects. There's a bit more programming overhead when you keep your ActionScript code in a separate file. On the plus side, that overhead leads to better object-oriented practices, making your code easier to reuse.

For more details on making the choice between timeline programming and keeping your code in a separate ActionScript file, see the box on page 381.

Note: Most of the examples in this book use timeline programming to show ActionScript programming principles.

Writing ActionScript Code in the Timeline

If you've got a Flash document open, you're ready to begin adding ActionScript code to the timeline. Here are the steps to get you started:

1. **Click a keyframe where you want to add your code. Create a new layer in the timeline to store your code.**

   To make your life easier later, keep your ActionScript code in one place—a single layer at the top of the timeline that holds only ActionScript code. You can use any name you want for this layer, but for clarity's sake call it *actions* or *scripts*.

2. **Open the Actions panel (Window → Actions).**

   The Actions panel is divided into three main parts, as shown in Figure 11-3. The Script pane is where you type your ActionScript code. The Actions toolbox holds a list of ActionScript objects, properties, methods, and events. The Script navigator shows a list of objects that have ActionScript code attached.

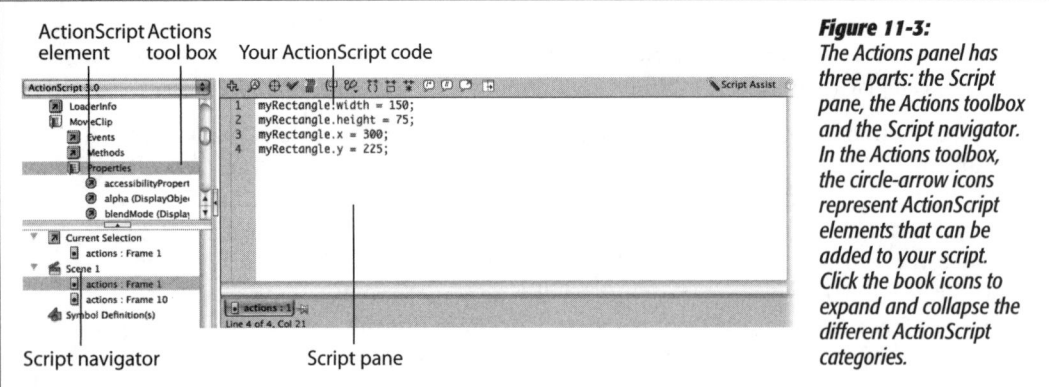

ActionScript   Actions
element   tool box   Your ActionScript code

Script navigator   Script pane

Figure 11-3:
The Actions panel has three parts: the Script pane, the Actions toolbox and the Script navigator. In the Actions toolbox, the circle-arrow icons represent ActionScript elements that can be added to your script. Click the book icons to expand and collapse the different ActionScript categories.

3. **Type your statements in Script pane, or choose statements from the Actions toolbox.**

   You can type code directly into the Script pane, or you can double-click or drag the ActionScript elements in the Actions toolbox. As you add code to individual frames, you see them listed in the Script navigator (in the toolbox, located on the left side of the Actions panel), giving you a running list of the objects that have code attached. To view or edit code for a particular object, click the object in the Script navigator, and you see the code in the Script pane.

Tip: You can collapse and expand the Actions toolbox and its panels. If you don't see the item you're looking for, click the rectangular buttons with the triangles to open and close the panels.

Using the Script Pane Toolbar

The toolbar above the Script pane provides helpful tools for working with your ActionScript code (Figure 11-4). The buttons aren't labeled, but you can see their names when you mouse over them. From left to right, the buttons are:

- **Add a new item to script.** Provides access to the same elements as the Actions toolbox. Useful if you've hidden the toolbox using the Show/Hide Toolbox command (last in this list of buttons).

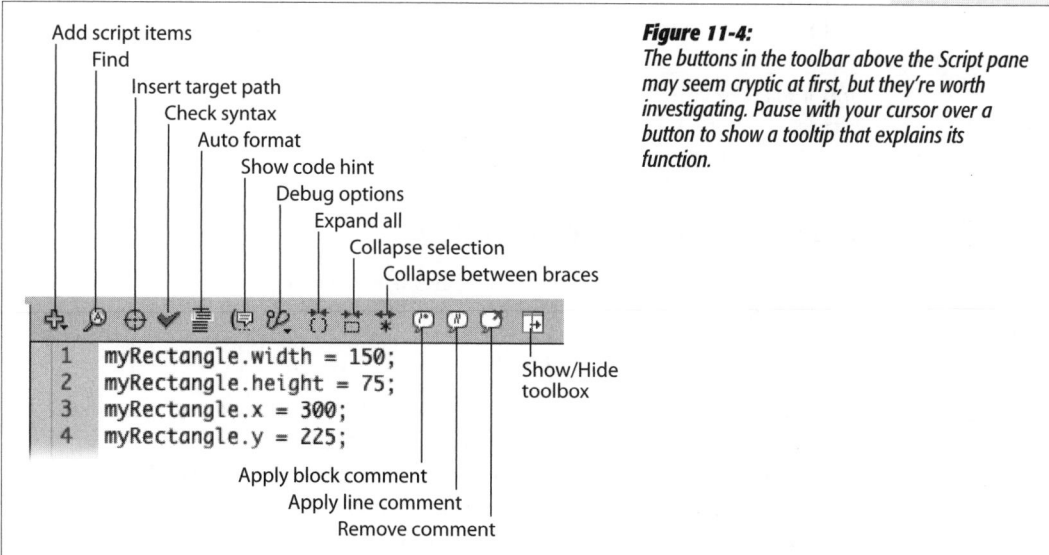

Figure 11-4:
The buttons in the toolbar above the Script pane may seem cryptic at first, but they're worth investigating. Pause with your cursor over a button to show a tooltip that explains its function.

- **Find.** Searches your script for words and characters.

- **Insert a target path.** Click this button, and then choose your target object from a list, and this tool writes the proper code identifying it.

- **Check syntax.** Inspects your code for obvious errors.

- **Autoformat.** Formats your script, making it easier to read, by using colors and indents. To set formatting options, go to Edit → Preferences → ActionScript (Flash → Preferences → ActionScript on a Mac).

- **Show code hint.** Displays tooltips with suggestions for your script.

- **Debug options.** Inserts and removes breakpoints in your code. Breakpoints stop your program from running, giving you an opportunity to examine your program.

- **Collapse between braces.** Hides the text between a set of curly braces {} making it easier to read and understand your code. Similar to collapsing an outline in a word processor.

- **Collapse selection.** Select the text you want to hide, and then click this button to hide it.

- **Expand all.** Expands collapsed portions of your script after you've used one of the two previous commands.

- **Apply block comment.** Inserts the /* and */ used to create a block comment.

- **Apply inline comment.** Inserts the // used to create an inline comment.

- **Remove comment.** Removes the comment characters from a comment.

- **Show/Hide Toolbox.** If you need more room to see your Script pane, use this button to hide the Actions toolbox. When the toolbox is hidden, you can use the "Add a new item to script" button to insert elements.

Tip: If you need more room to see your script, use the Show/Hide Toolbox button on the far right to temporarily hide the Actions toolbox. When the toolbox is hidden, you can use the "Add a new item to script" button (far left) to insert ActionScript elements.

Writing Code in an ActionScript File

When you want to store all your code in an ActionScript (.as) file, the first thing you need to do is create the file:

1. **Create a new ActionScript file (File → New → ActionScript File).**

   A new window opens, as shown in Figure 11-5. Initially, the window has a tab that reads Script-1 or something similar. When you save the ActionScript file with a name of your choice, that name appears on the tab. The Script window has two sections a Script pane and the Actions toolbox. The toolbar above the Script pane is identical to the one described on page 382.

2. **Save your ActionScript file in the same directory as your Flash file (File → Save).**

   A dialog box opens where you can select a folder, and then name your document. You want to save your file in the same directory as your Flash file. This way, Flash's compiler can find it when it creates a .swf file for distribution. Another option is to save your file in a directory that's designated as the Action-Script class directory. Steps to do that are described in the box on page 385.

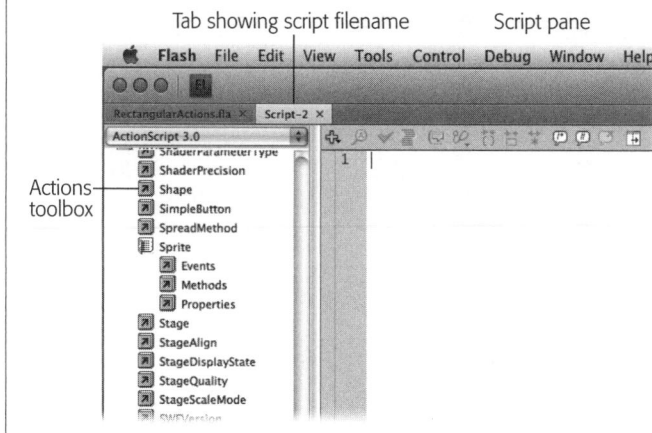

Tab showing script filename   Script pane

Actions
toolbox

Figure 11-5:
The Script window used to write code in an
ActionScript (.as) file looks very similar to
the Actions panel of a Flash document.
There's no Script navigator, because the
ActionScript code is linked to particular
objects by statements within the code itself.

3. **Type your statements in Script pane or choose statements from the Actions toolbox.**

You can type code directly into the Script pane or you can double-click or drag the ActionScript elements in the Actions toolbox.

When you separate your ActionScript code from a Flash document, it's up to you to establish links between your code and the objects in a Flash document. Because this chapter focuses on the basics, the following examples use timeline programming.

CODERS' CLINIC

Creating an ActionScript Class Folder

If you're working on several ActionScript projects over time, you want to reuse as much of your ActionScript code as possible. So you may create objects that work with a variety of Flash projects.

Perhaps you have some great shopping cart code that you can use for several different clients. You can put your shopping cart code in one ActionScript file (.as), and then put code for each of your clients in separate files. Your client files need to reach out and use that shopping cart code, but it's probably in a different file folder. The solution is to create one or more ActionScript class folders, where you store code that's used by many different Flash projects. Then you need to tell Flash and ActionScript where to find those class folders.

You do that through Flash preferences. Go to Edit → Preferences → ActionScript → ActionScript 3.0 Settings (on a Mac, go to Flash → Preferences → ActionScript → ActionScript 3.0 Settings).

Figure 11-6 shows the box that opens where you can set file paths for three different types of ActionScript files. Use the middle tool labeled "Folders containing ActionScript class files." Click the + button to add a new path to the list; you may have more than one library path. Click the folder icon to browse to the directory that holds the class files.

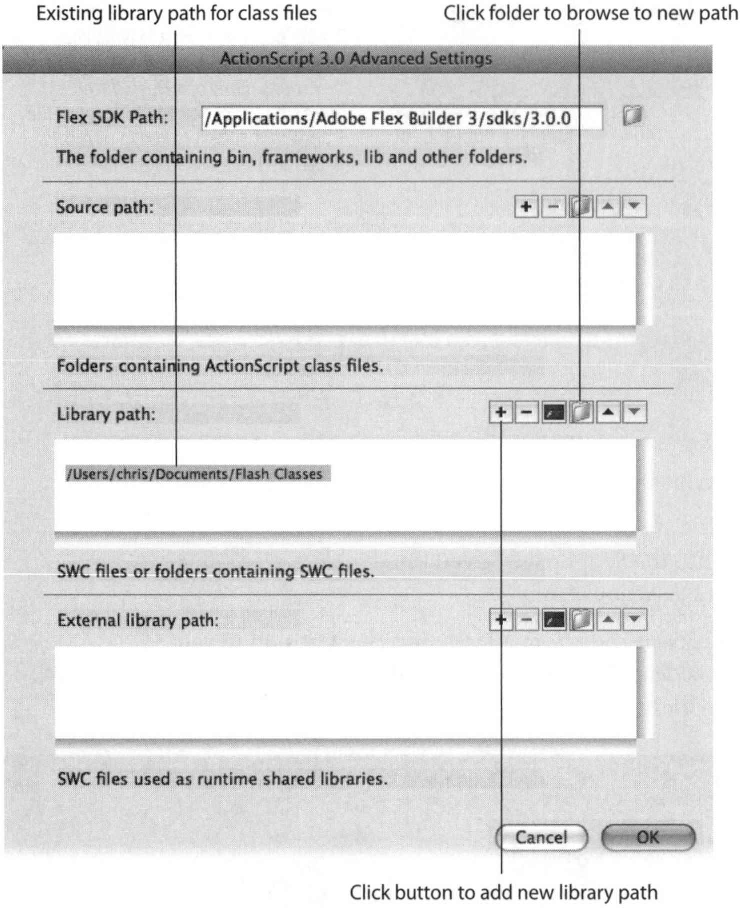

Existing library path for class files   Click folder to browse to new path

Figure 11-6:
Use the Preferences box to
change the basic settings for
ActionScript. Here the path to
a folder holding ActionScript
is specified so the Flash
compiler can find it when it
builds .swf files.

ActionScript 3.0 Advanced Settings

Flex SDK Path: /Applications/Adobe Flex Builder 3/sdks/3.0.0

The folder containing bin, frameworks, lib and other folders.

Source path:

Folders containing ActionScript class files.

Library path:

/Users/chris/Documents/Flash Classes

SWC files or folders containing SWC files.

External library path:

SWC files used as runtime shared libraries.

Cancel   OK

Click button to add new library path

Object-Oriented Thinking

When programmers talk about object-oriented programming, they're referring to specific programming techniques—a way of looking at the parts of a program and the overall design. The idea is to create chunks of programming code that do a specific job. If you design them all, those chunks can fit together with other pieces of code. Think for a second about a typical home theater system that has an amplifier/receiver, a DVD player, a TV screen, and maybe a cable box. Each unit is an object. The folks who designed the DVD player don't have to know how to build a TV screen, they just have to make a DVD player that can plug into a TV. You can plug the same DVD player into another home theater system, and it'll work perfectly well. Programmers strive for that kind of modularity when they build objects.

**Object-Oriented
Thinking**

The benefits are obvious. As long as the objects have an agreed-upon method for interacting, different programmers can work on different objects. When they all come together, they'll play well with each other. If the objects are truly useful and flexible, you can reuse them in future projects. Future programmers won't have to understand how the DVD player works, all they need to know is how to plug it in and how to send and receive signals from it.

In addition to reusability, there are a handful of other concepts that define object-oriented programming. Some of them don't make a lot of sense until you understand the basics of ActionScript, but here are a few of the basics for reference:

- **Classes.** A class describes an object in the abstract, like the concept of DVD players. A class is like a generalized blueprint for building an object.

- **Instances.** An instance is a specific object, like a Sony DVD player model N55.

- **Properties.** Characteristics that define an object. For example, color may be a property of the Sony DVD player; that property may be set to black or silver. Properties are part of an object's definition, so they're called *members* of the object.

- **Methods.** Methods are actions that an object can perform. To continue the DVD player example, play, pause, and fast-forward are methods of the DVD player class. These methods also belong to the Sony N55 instance of the DVD player class. Methods are part of an object's definition so, like properties, they're members of the object.

- **Events.** Events act as triggers. Someone presses the Play button on the DVD player—the event—and the play method runs. Events are also part of an object's definition.

- **Encapsulation.** It's not necessary or wise to expose all the inner workings of an object. It's important for people to be able to play, pause, and eject discs in the DVD player, but they don't need to control the rotation speed or the intensity of the laser that reads the discs. In object-oriented programming, encapsulated features are those your audience can't mess with.

CODERS' CLINIC

Is ActionScript a True Object-Oriented Language?

If you use the strictest definition for object-oriented programming languages, ActionScript doesn't make the cut. In true object-oriented programming everything is an object and derives from objects. Even ActionScript 3, with its enhanced object-oriented features, has a few loopholes that you won't find in a language like Java (not to be confused with JavaScript). For example, timeline programming in Flash breaks some of the accepted rules of object-oriented

programming. ActionScript permits functions that exist outside of an object, referred to as *function closures*.

ActionScript doesn't force you to always use object-oriented programming techniques. Instead, it takes advantage of many object-oriented concepts and lets you choose how strictly you want to use them.

Flash itself gives you a good head start toward object-oriented thinking. Consider the lowly rectangle you draw on the Flash stage. That's an *object*. All rectangles share some of the same properties. For example, they have four sides defined by four points, and they have a surface or face between those sides. All the corners of a rectangle are right angles.

Once you understand the basics, you can describe a Flash rectangle using a few properties:

- Width

- Height

- Stroke thickness

- Stroke color

- Fill color

Taking it a step farther, you can place that rectangle anywhere on the stage by placing its upper-right corner on a particular point. That location is another property of a Flash rectangle.

ActionScript Classes

If you're working in Flash, chances are you're going to use more than one rectangle, and you don't have to build every rectangle from the ground up. You can take certain rectangular characteristics for granted—four sides, right-angled corners. Other properties, you need to define separately for each rectangle—width, height, color, location on the stage. So you need a class that defines rectangles in general, and you can then create specific instances of rectangles by defining their individual properties. And that's exactly how Flash works. *Class, instance,* and *property* are all fundamental terms for object-oriented programming and thinking.

Changing an Object's Properties

In Flash, you change a rectangle's height or width using the Modify → Transform → Scale command. To change its location, you drag it to a new place. In Action-Script, by contrast, you change the height, width and location by changing the properties in your ActionScript code:

```
myRectangle.width = 150;
myRectangle.height = 75;
myRectangle.x = 300;
myRectangle.y = 225;
```

Note: It's common practice to refer to locations on a computer screen as *x/y* coordinates. The *x* refers to the horizontal position and the *y* refers to the vertical position. If you need something to help you remember which is which, remember that a lower case *y* extends further in a vertical direction.

Want to put some of these programming concepts to work? Try this:

1. **In a new document, draw a rectangle of any size and shape.**

   You can think of this step as defining an object.

2. **Select the rectangle, and then convert it to a symbol (Modify → "Convert to Symbol"), choosing Movie Clip as the type.**

   Movie clip is a great catch-all symbol for ActionScript programming. Movie clips can be as simple or complicated as you want.

3. **Create a new layer, double-click the layer name, and then type *actions*.**

   It's good programming practice to create a separate layer in the timeline for your ActionScript code. Naming it *actions* or *scripts* makes it clear that the layer is reserved for code.

4. **For consistency, rename the rectangle layer *drawings*.**

   Your timeline now has two layers with descriptive names.

5. **Make sure the instance on stage is selected, and then in the Properties panel, type *myRectangle* in the "Instance name" box, as shown in Figure 11-7.**

   This step is important. If you don't give objects on the stage a name, there's no way to tell ActionScript exactly which object you're talking about.

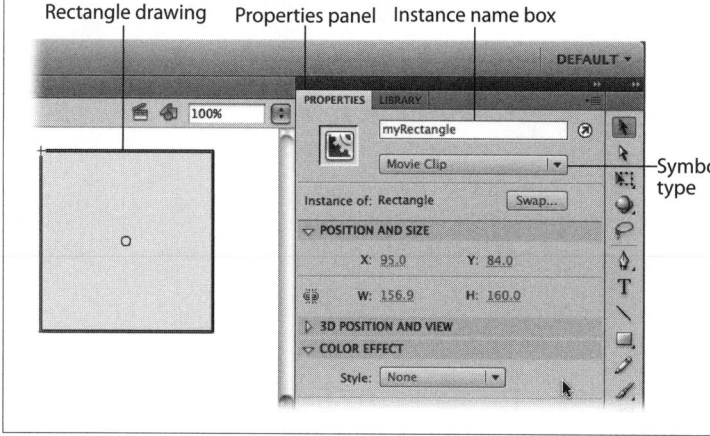

Figure 11-7:
Before you can control objects on the Flash stage with ActionScript, you have to convert them to Movie Clip or Button symbols, and then name them in the "Instance name" box on the Properties panel.

Tip: Uppercase and lowercase spelling make a difference to ActionScript. Objects named myRectangle, MyRectangle, and myrectangle are completely different things to ActionScript. ActionScript programmers use certain typographic conventions that make it easier to read and understand code. One of those conventions is to use *camel case* for instances of objects. Camel case uses an initial lowercase letter and then uppercase for the first letter of additional words. For example: thisIsCamelCase.

---

6. **Open the Actions panel.**

The Actions panel looks pretty busy when you first see it, as shown in Figure 11-3. All the details are described on page 382. For now, focus on the big blank area in the middle, where you type ActionScript code.

7. **Select the first frame of the actions layer in the timeline, and then type the following lines in the Actions panel:**

```
myRectangle.width = 150;
myRectangle.height = 75;
myRectangle.x = 300;
myRectangle.y = 225;
```

When you're done, the Script pane should look like Figure 11-8.

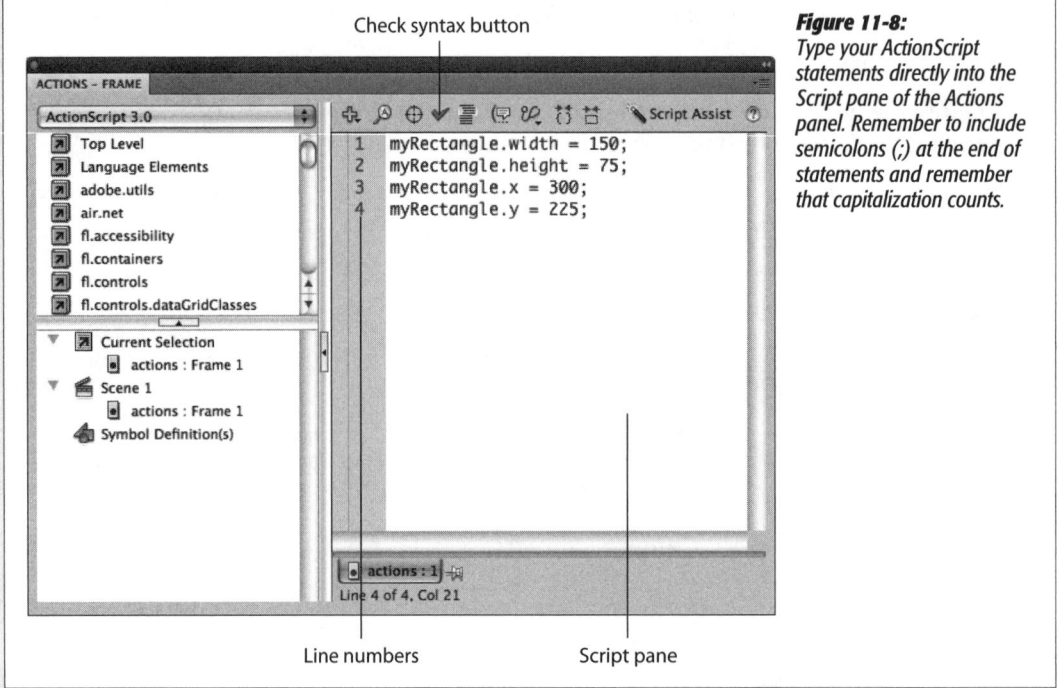

Check syntax button

Line numbers   Script pane

Figure 11-8:
Type your ActionScript statements directly into the Script pane of the Actions panel. Remember to include semicolons (;) at the end of statements and remember that capitalization counts.

8. **Click the Check Syntax button (the checkmark) at the top of the Actions panel to check for typos in your code.**

The check syntax feature in ActionScript 3 isn't as picky as it could be. Still, it helps you find major bloopers in your code, so it's worth using, especially when you're just starting out.

9. **Test your movie.**

After a little churning, the Flash Player or your browser appears on your screen. If everything's working right, your rectangle changes its shape and size. No matter what dimensions and location your rectangle had to begin with, it takes on the properties you defined in your ActionScript code. It's 150 pixels wide and 75 pixels high, and it's located 300 pixels from the left (x) of your screen and 225 pixels from the top (y).

You can probably guess what you need to do to animate this baby. Just add new frames, including a keyframe, to your timeline, and then type some instructions similar to the ones in step 7 above. Here are the specific steps:

1. **Click the 40th frame in both layers of your timeline, and then press F5 to insert frames.**

   You've just added 39 new blank frames to each layer of the timeline. Blank frames show whatever is on the stage in the previous keyframe without changing anything.

2. **Click the 20th frame in the timeline's "actions" layer, and then press F6 to insert a keyframe.**

   Pressing F6 here places a second keyframe in the middle of the timeline, where you can change the look of myRectangle using another snippet of ActionScript. When you're done, the timeline should look similar to Figure 11-9.

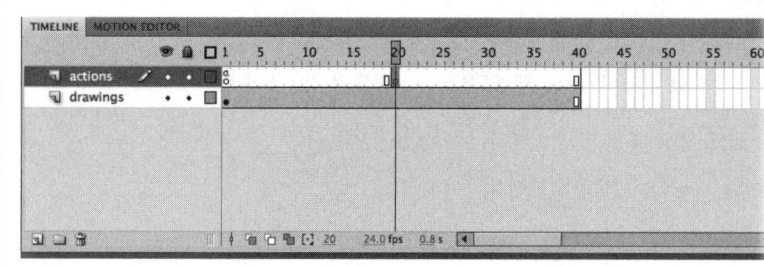

Figure 11-9:
The timeline shows where ActionScript is attached to frames with a small "a" icon. To prevent confusion, keep your ActionScript code on a layer of its own at the top of the timeline.

3. **In the Actions panel, type the following lines:**

   ```
   myRectangle.width = 200;
   myRectangle.height = 200;
   myRectangle.x = 100;
   myRectangle.y = 225;
   ```

   Or, to avoid duplicate effort, use the Copy (Ctrl+C for PCs; ⌘-C for Macs) and Paste (Ctrl+V for PCs; ⌘-V for Macs) commands to steal the code from keyframe 1 to keyframe 20. Just copy, paste, and then change the numbers. It's faster than typing in new code, and you're less likely to create a typo.

4. **Click the Check Syntax button.**

   You never know!

5. **Test your movie.**

Halfway through your animation, the rectangle turns square and moves to the left. Exactly as you programmed it. Not terribly exciting, but you can use these same methods to dress it up a bit more, which you'll do in the next section.

Tip: When you're starting out in any programming language, the most common error is misspelling. Computers are worse than your second-grade teacher. They want everything spelled and punctuated perfectly. If something goes wrong, double-check your spelling and punctuation first. You can save yourself some grief by copying and pasting words, like myRectangle, to avoid typos.

Functions and Methods Put the Action in ActionScript

As explained on page 387, properties define the characteristics of objects. Methods are the actions. Methods explain how a particular object can do something. If you, as a human being, are an object, and your height, hair color, and gender are your properties. Walking, talking, and keyboarding are your functions and methods.

Note: In ActionScript, methods are actions that are a defined part of an object, just like its properties. Functions are actions that are independent of any particular object.

In the exercise in the previous section, your code moved myRectangle to the left 200 pixels. What if you want to move to the left by 5 pixels at several different points along the timeline? The script writer's way to do that is to write a *moveLeft( )* function, and then run that function anytime you want to move your object. Here's the code for a function that handles the move:

```
function moveLeft(anyMovieClip:MovieClip):void
{
    anyMovieClip.x = anyMovieClip.x -5;
}
```

Go ahead and type the function below the ActionScript code on the first frame of your document. Start on line 6, so that there's a little room between the different parts of your code. Click the Check Syntax button and double-check your spelling and punctuation. When you're done, it should look like Figure 11-10.

Your function *moveLeft( )* is an *action*, and as such it needs an *actor*. Something's gotta move, and that something is named inside the parentheses. You're moving anyMovieClip. That's probably a clear enough explanation for you, but it's not for your computer. To your computer, the word "anyMovieClip" might as well be "joeJones." They're both names it's never heard of. Your computer needs to know exactly what kind of object it is that you're moving. So, on the other side of the colon (:) you explain that anyMovieClip is in fact a MovieClip object. With that explanation, ActionScript can look up the definition for MovieClips, and it knows exactly what anyMovieClip can and can't do. Your computer also knows how much memory it needs to devote to anyMovieClip—an issue that becomes more important as your programs grow bigger.

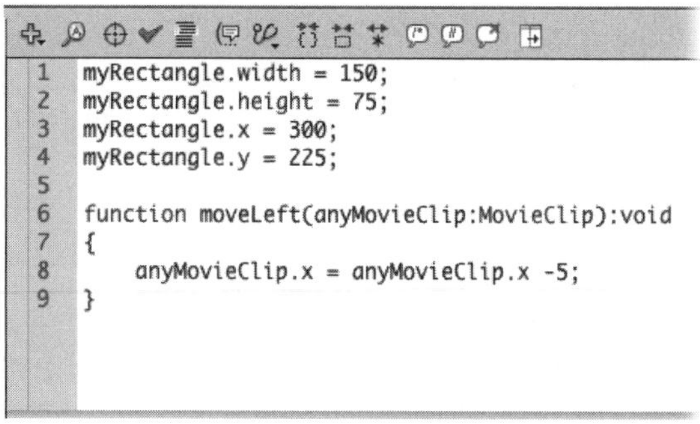

```
1   myRectangle.width = 150;
2   myRectangle.height = 75;
3   myRectangle.x = 300;
4   myRectangle.y = 225;
5
6   function moveLeft(anyMovieClip:MovieClip):void
7   {
8       anyMovieClip.x = anyMovieClip.x -5;
9   }
```

Figure 11-10:
Compared to the object's properties, a function is just a tad more geeky and complicated. The first word, function, explains that the code that follows defines a function. The next word is the name of the function, moveLeft( ). You'll use this name every time you want to run the function.

Following the parentheses is the mysterious *:void*—another bit of ActionScript housekeeping. This code tells ActionScript that *moveLeft( )* doesn't perform a calculation and provide a value in return. Suppose you created a function to find the area of a rectangle; *getArea( )* would do its calculation, and the result would be a number. Instead of expecting the ominous-sounding *:void*, you'd tell Action-Script to expect *:Number*.

The actual instructions for your *moveLeft( )* function has to be between curly brackets *{...}*, like the ones you see on second and fourth lines. The brackets don't have to be on lines by themselves, but sometimes it's easier to read your code when it's written that way.

The action in your code is all on one line, everything else was just the necessary ActionScript overhead used to create every function.

```
anyMovieClip.x = anyMovieClip.x -5;
```

Remember how myRectangle.x was shorthand for "the horizontal position of myRectangle"? You're using the same shorthand here with anyMovieClip. Action-Script knows what you mean by *x*, because it's one of the built-in properties of the MovieClip class. What's more, if you change the value of *x,* the movie clip changes position. You saw that in the example on page 390. Changing a value is also called *assigning a new value*. And while you may know the = symbol as *equals*, in Action-Script it's called the *assignment operand*, because it assigns the value on the right side to the property or variable on the left.

When you wrote:

```
myRectangle.x = 100;
```

you were assigning the value *100* to the *x* property of myRectangle. Your *moveLeft( )* function's code is just a little bit more complicated. You're saying "take the value that's currently assigned to anyMovieClip.x, subtract 5, and then put the result back in the anyMovieClip.x property." This method of reassigning a value is very common in ActionScript and almost any programming language.

So you may be wondering why your function used the word *anyMovieClip* instead of using *myRectangle* as the object of this *moveLeft( )* action. The function is literally for moving *any* movie clip. The name in the parentheses is a parameter of the function, so when you run *moveLeft( )*, you tell ActionScript specifically which movie clip you want to move. Here's how it's done:

```
moveLeft(myRectangle);
```

It's that simple to run a function, or as the fellow with the pocket protector and tape on his glasses would say, "to call a function and pass it a parameter." To put your function into action, go back to your timeline. Add keyframes (press F6) every fifth frame from Frame 5 to Frame 25. Delete all the code that's on Frame 20. In the keyframes from 5 onward, type your function:

```
moveLeft(myRectangle);
```

With the code inserted, your timeline looks like the one in Figure 11-11.

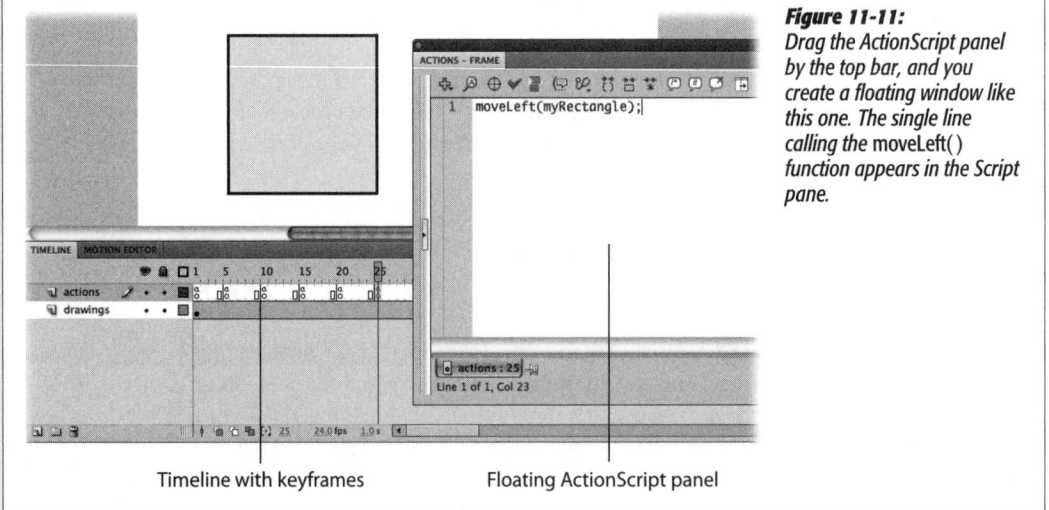

Figure 11-11:
Drag the ActionScript panel by the top bar, and you create a floating window like this one. The single line calling the moveLeft( ) function appears in the Script pane.

Timeline with keyframes   Floating ActionScript panel

Check syntax, spelling, punctuation, and then test your movie by pressing Ctrl+Enter (PC) or ⌘-Return (Mac). If the scripting deities smile upon you, myRectangle should move left in 5-pixel increments, and then pause for a bit.

Here's another great thing about using functions instead of *hard-coding* everything. Suppose you decide that 5-pixel steps isn't quite the grand sweeping motion you had in mind. All you have to do is change one number in the original function. Change the code:

```
anyMovieClip.x = anyMovieClip.x -5;
```

to the following:

```
anyMovieClip.x = anyMovieClip.x -25;
```

and then test the results.

The complete geeky moniker for *moveLeft( )* in this example is *function closure*. In ActionScript, functions that are part of an object definition are called *methods*. Functions that aren't part of an object definition are called function closures. (Often, in other languages, they're referred to simply as functions.) If *moveLeft( )* was part of the definition for a rectangle object, it would be called a method of *myRectangle*.

Events

In the olden days of programming, programs simply ran through a series of statements. The experience was similar to watching an animation with no way to change it. All you could do was watch it run from beginning to end. The concept of events helped change all that. When a person clicks a button in a Flash animation, that's an event. The response to that event might be a number of things: perhaps a new shape appears on the stage, or maybe the animation jumps to a new scene or frame.

ActionScript programmers create routines that *listen* for a particular event, like that mouse click, and then *handle it* with a particular action, like jumping to a new scene. It's a great tried and true method of interaction that lots of programming languages use.

When you write an ActionScript program, you decide what *events* your program will listen for. Those events can include:

• Mouse events, like mouse clicks or mouse movements.

• Keyboard events, like pressed keys.

• Frame events, like the Flash playhead moving into or out of specific frames.

• Load events, which report on the progress when loading external files.

Once you've identified the events you want your ActionScript program to respond to, you write *event handlers* to spring into action. Your event handlers will run through a series of ActionScript statements, which may be made up of functions like the *moveLeft( )* function from the previous section. Your event handlers can also change an object's properties.

You can use events to hand the controls over to the folks watching your Flash animations, which makes events an important tool in your Flash/ActionScript toolbox. Events are so important they have their own chapter (Chapter 12).

Note: Previous versions of ActionScript handled events in a few different ways, including the well-known *on* statements. ActionScript 3 has only one method for handling events—*event listeners* as introduced here and in covered in more detail on page 409.

Using Data Types, Variables, and Constants

Flash animations are made up of different elements, like drawings, text, frames, timelines, and MovieClips. Some of these elements serve as containers for the others. For example, frames can hold drawings and text, and timelines hold frames. ActionScript is similar. A few basic elements, like *Numbers* and *Strings* are the building blocks for more complicated data containers. Many programming languages use similar data types, but have slightly different rules about the way they're used.

This section introduces the most common data types that you use in ActionScript and explains how they're used. If you've worked your way through this chapter, you've used some of these already. In examples in the following chapters, you'll have an opportunity to give these data types a workout.

Tip: This book isn't an exhaustive reference on ActionScript. It gives you a solid introduction to the language and shows you how to put it to work right away. If you're hungry for more details on the subject, check out the recommendations in the box on page 379.

Numbers

Numbers are one of the data building blocks ActionScript uses. For example, you may want to tell Flash to play the same movie clip three times. As you saw earlier, Flash uses numbers to identify positions on the stage; to identify certain frames in a timeline, and to identify colors. Numbers are so important, that Flash has three different data types for numbers. Why have more than one? Well, numbers that include fractions like 2.5 or 3.14159 require more computing power than integers like 3 or -1. Choose the right type of number for the job, and you can make your computer do less work so that your programs run faster.

Number

In ActionScript, a *Number* can be any type of number, including fractions. In many programming languages integer data types, like int and uint, described next, are preferred over numbers when fractions aren't needed. That's not necessarily the case in ActionScript. For some fairly technical reasons having to do with how ActionScript is designed, many programmers use the Number data type most of the time.

int

The *int* (think *integer*) data type can represent any number from -2,147,483,648 to 2,147,483,647. The int type can't represent fractions. If you need a fraction or a number outside of this range, use the Number data type.

uint

The *uint* (think *unsigned integer*) data type can represent numbers from 0 to 4,294,967,295. If you need a negative number, use the *int* data type. If you need a

---

fraction, use the Number data type. The *uint* is particularly useful to identify colors, since colors are always positive whole numbers.

Numbers and Operators

When you work in ActionScript, you can and probably will perform mathematical operations with numbers. To perform these feats, you use *operators,* the characters that indicate addition, subtraction, multiplication, and so on. The following table shows the operators you can use in ActionScript:

Operator	Function	Example
+	Adds two numbers	2+3
–	Subtracts number on right from number on left	3–2
*	Multiplies two numbers	2*3
/	Divides number on left by number on right	6/2
>	Expresses greater than (which may make a statement true or false)	6>2
<	Expresses less than (which may make a statement true or false)	2<6
>=	Expresses greater than or equal to (which may make a statement true or false)	6>=2
<=	Express less than or equal to (which may make a statement true or false)	2<=6
==	Expresses equality (which may make a statement true or false)	12==6*2
!=	Expresses inequality (which may make a statement true or false)	3!=2
=	Assignment operator	myNumber = 6*2

Notice the difference between the equality operator and the assignment operator. The equality operator is used to make a statement: the data on the right side of the equality operator is equal to the data on the left. That statement may be true or false. The assignment operator has a different job. The assignment operator changes the value of the *variable* on the left. (There's more on variables on page 401.)

Precedence and parentheses

Some statements are simple and unambiguous, like this one:

```
myNumber = 3 + 12
```

But a statement can include more than one operator:

```
myNumber = 3 + 12 / 3
```

When there's more than one operator, it's a little harder to anticipate the value. In general, ActionScript multiplies and divides before it adds and subtracts. But you can make things easier for yourself (and others) to read and understand your work by using parentheses to dictate the order of operations. So the following statement forces ActionScript to perform the addition before it performs the division:

```
myNumber = (3 + 12) / 3
```

Strings

In geek-speak, Strings are sequential lists of letters, numbers, and symbols—strings of characters. For example, this very sentence is a string. "Foo" is a string with three characters. You identify strings by placing them inside of either single or double quotes:

```
myCar = "Stutz Bearcat";
visitorName = "Erwin Baker";
```

If you want to include quotes within your string, you have a couple of options. For example, you can use single quotes to enclose your string when you want to use double quotes *in* the string, like so:

```
famousQuote = 'He said "My name is Erwin Baker."'
```

Strings and operators

You can't do math with Strings, not even if some of the characters are numbers. But there are other types of operations that work with Strings. One very common operation is to build up longer strings by adding words or characters. Usually this is called *concatenation*, and it looks a lot like string addition.

```
carModel = "Stutz" + " " +"Bearcat";
```

The previous statement adds three strings together. First, it adds a *space* character (between the two empty quotes) to the word *Stutz*. Spaces, punctuation, and numbers are all part of the String data type. Then it adds *Bearcat* onto the string. So, the value of the stored variable carModel reads *Stutz Bearcat*.

Just to prove the point that you can't do math with strings, consider these two statements:

```
parkingTicket = 50 + 25;
parkingTicket = "50" + "25";
```

In the first example, parkingTicket is an unpleasant but reasonable number, *75*. In the second example where two strings are concatenated, you end up with a string value in parkingTicket of *5025*.

It's also fairly common to compare two strings to see if they're the same, which you have to do every time someone types in a password. To do that type of comparison, you use the equality operator (==), not the assignment operator (=). Here's an example:

```
visitorPassword == textFieldPassword;
```

You can use a statement like that to test whether a password typed into a Flash text field matches the password the visitor previously supplied.

These aren't the only operations you can perform with strings, just two of the most common. You'll see examples using strings throughout the rest of the book. Chapter 16 covers several common string programming techniques beginning on page 549.

Boolean

A *Boolean* is a data type that has one of two values: true or false. The *Boolean* is very handy because programs often test conditions, and then report on the results. For example, parkingMeterExpired could be a Boolean data type. In that case, you might see an expression:

```
If (parkingMeterExpired == true)
{
ticketVehicle( );
}
```

In human-ese, this translates to "If the value of parkingMeterExpired equals *true*, then run the function *ticketVehicle( )*." The equality operator creates a statement that's either true or false. You're not assigning a value to parkingMeterExpired; you're creating a statement that ActionScript can test.

Booleans and operators

The most common Boolean operator has been used several times in this chapter; that's the equal (==) operator that's used to test if two statements are equivalent. So, if parkingMeterExpired is a Boolean data type, it has one of two values: *true* or *false*. That makes the statement:

```
parkingMeterExpired==true
```

either true or false.

For the times when it's more convenient to test for a false statement, use the inequality operator (!=) as shown in this example:

```
parkingMeterExpired!=true
```

Arrays

Unlike the simple data types, *Arrays* are containers that can hold more than one item. Those items don't even need to be the same data type. For example, a single Array can hold Numbers and Strings, which makes them a great way to keep related information together. Imagine you want to collect different tidbits of information about people who belong to your Stutz Bearcat auto club. For example, you might want to record their first name, last name, age, number of speeding tickets, and whether their club dues are paid up:

```
memberDetailsArray = ["Erwin", "Baker", 38, 12, true]
```

Each tidbit of data is called an *element*, so the above Array has five elements. In the example, the first two elements of the array are Strings. The following two are Numbers. The last item is a Boolean, so it can only have two values: true or false. An Array can even hold another array as one of its elements. Individual elements are separated by commas, and the entire Array is enclosed in square brackets. You can access individual elements in the array by number; but there's one "gotcha" to remember. The first element in an array is referred to as number *0*. So, if you want to change the last name "Baker" to "Paxton" you assign a new value, like so:

```
memberDetailsArray[1] = "Paxton";
```

In ActionScript, Arrays are a type of object and there are a whole crop of methods (functions) you can use to work with them. For example, there are methods to:

- Add a new element to an Array
- Remove an element from an Array
- Report the number of items in an Array
- Sort and reorder the elements in an Array

Earlier in this chapter (page 392), you saw examples of ActionScript *functions*. Methods are also functions—they're actions, they do something. What makes methods special is that they're part of the definition of an object. For example, the method that adds a new element to an Array is called *push*. You can think of it as pushing another plate on a stack of dishes. You use the dot (.) nomenclature to connect it to the function. Suppose you want to add a new element to your memberDetailsArray that represents the year a member's car was built. Here's the statement that does the job:

```
memberDetailArray.push(1937);
```

The dot (.) nomenclature looks familiar because ActionScript also uses it to access an object's properties. Arrays are used in examples in the following chapters.

ActionScript Built-in Data Types

ActionScript has a number of built-in data types that are made up of some of the simple data types. Some examples include familiar Flash objects, like the following:

MovieClip

A symbol (from the Flash Library) that's a movie clip.

TextField

A field (or box) that holds text. You can set and change the contents, or your audience can type them when your program is running.

SimpleButton

A special type of graphic that's preprogrammed to behave like a button. Click it, and your program does something.

Date

The Date data type represents a specific moment in time. ActionScript code can access the month, day, hour, and second.

Variables

If you followed some of the exercises earlier in this chapter, you may have noticed that programming is the fine art of swapping one value for another. Move an object, change a color, start playing a movie clip at a certain point—those actions require providing a new value for a color, stage position, and timeline position.

Like buckets or baskets, variables are the containers that hold these changing values.

Declaring variables

Before you can use a variable, you have to tell ActionScript 3 what to expect. You introduce the name you're planning on using and you explain whether it's a Number, String, or some other data type. It's called *declaring a variable,* and here are some examples:

```
var minutesOnMeter : Number;
var carModel    : String;
var licensePlate  : String;
var meterExpired  : Boolean;
```

If you want, you can assign a value to your variable when you declare it.

```
var minutesOnMeter : Number = 60;
var carModel    : "Stutz Bearcat";
var meterExired  : Boolean = False;
```

Tip: In general, ActionScript isn't fussy about white space. If you want to include extra spaces to line things up as shown in previous examples, that's fine. Just don't make mistakes with your spelling and punctuation or you'll get a virtual ruler to the back of your hand.

Once you've declared that the variable *minutesOnMeter* is a Number, you can't store a different type of data in it. For example, if you try to assign a String to minutesOnMeter, an error message appears in the Compiler Error panel, like the one in Figure 11-12: "Implicit coercion of a Value of type Number to an unrelated type String." Sentences like that may make you feel like you should call a lawyer, but you can usually figure out the problem. Double-click the error message, and Flash takes you directly to the line in your code that caused the error.

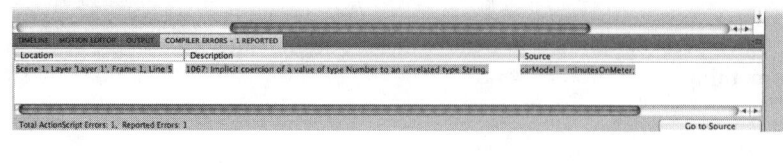

Figure 11-12:
ActionScript's Compiler Error panel provides three bits of help. From left to right, Location tells you where the error is, Description names the type of error, and Source shows you the offending code.

Constants

A constant is a value that never changes through the course of the program. It might be the color of a stop light (red) or the boiling point of water (100° C). Use constants when it's easier or more readable to refer to something by name (Stop, BoilingPoint) rather than value. ActionScript programs use variables more often than constants.

Declaring constants

As with variables, you have to declare constants, and it makes sense to provide their value at the same time:

```
const PARKING_TICKET : Number = 50;
```

Most programmers use all caps for constants to differentiate them from variables. If you accidentally try to assign a value to a constant, you get one of those nasty compiler error messages.

Conditionals and Loops

Using conditions and loops, you can teach your Flash animations how to make decisions, and viewers will think both you and your animations are very smart. ActionScript provides a few different decision-making statements that you can use depending on your needs. In human-ese, they work like this:

• If (this condition exists) do (these actions)

• While (this condition exists) do (these actions)

• For (X number of times) do (these actions)

Those three forms of decision-making may seem very similar, but as you'll see in the following explanations and examples, there are some important basic differences. You'll hear programmers refer to these decision-making statements using different terms, like program flow controls, conditionals, and loops. These tools have one thing in common: they all help you dictate whether or not ActionScript runs some specific lines of code.

Conditionals: *if()* and *switch()* Statements

Two of ActionScript's statements tackle the "If (this condition exists) do (these actions)" situations. The first and simplest state is appropriately called an *if* statement.

if( ) *statements test a condition*

The most basic *if* statements are built like this:

```
if (this is true) {do this}
```

So, if you're writing an ActionScript statement for a parking meter cop, it might look like this:

```
if (parkingMeterExpired==true) {writeTicket( );}
```

It works like this: if the condition within the parentheses is true, then your code performs the statements within the curly brackets. If the expression in the parentheses is false, then your code ignores the statements within the curly brackets. In this example, if the parking meter has expired, the cop writes a ticket. If the parking meter hasn't expired, the cop doesn't do anything. (Well, maybe she goes for donuts.)

Note: The parentheses *( )* after *writeTicket* are part of any function including the *writeTicket( )* function. The following semi-colon is the proper way to end a statement. So, those punctuation marks aren't officially part of the *if( )* statement.

In some cases, you may want to provide some additional alternatives. Suppose you're sending your assistant to the auto store. You want him to buy a Stutz Bearcat, but in the unlikely event that the store doesn't have any Bearcats, you want him to buy a Packard Roadster. In ActionScript, that instruction takes the form of an *if..else* statement.

```
if (storeHasStutzBearcat==true) {
 buyStutzBearcat( );
} else {
 buyPackardRoadster( );
}
```

if..else if *statements choose from many options*

You can string *if..else* statements together to handle several different conditions. The result looks like this:

```
if (storeHasStutzBearCat=true) {
buyStutzBearcat( );
} else if (storeHasPackardRoadster=true) {
 buyPackardRoadster( );
}
 else if(storeHasHudson=true) {
 buyHudson( );
}
```

There's a statement that should resolve any out of stock issues at the car store. ActionScript works through the statements from top to bottom. When it finds a car in stock, it buys the car. Using this *if..else if* structure, your assistant will purchase only one car. For example, you won't end up with both a Packard Roadster and a Hudson. If the Packard is in stock, the function *buyPackardRoadster( )* runs and the *else if(storeHasHudson...)* portion is ignored. If none of the conditions are met, your assistant buys no car.

switch( ) *statements choose from many options*

You can string together as many *if..else if* conditions as you want, but at some point the code gets a little awkward and hard to read. The *switch( )* statement makes a good alternative when you have more than three conditions to check. Suppose you want to create a system where a parking ticket costs more depending on the number of tickets the scofflaw has received. The variable numberOfTickets holds a Number value. A s*witch( )* statement might look like this:

```
switch (numberOfTickets) {
    case 1 :
    parkingTicket = 25;
    break;
    case 2 :
    parkingTicket = 50;
    break;
    case 3 :
    parkingTicket = 75;
    break;
    case 4 :
    parkingTicket = 100;
    break;
    case 5 :
    parkingTicket = 125;
    break;
    default :
    parkingTicket = 0;
}
```

The switch statement takes the variable numberOfTickets and, starting at the top, compares it to the first *case*. If the offender has a single parking ticket the value of parkingTicket is set to 25. When ActionScript gets to the word *break*, it jumps to the end of the *switch( )* statement and doesn't run any of the other cases. The original case is used when none of the other cases match.

Loops: *while()* and *for()* Statements

There's a good rule of thumb to remember with computers. If *you're* doing the same chore over and over again, there's probably some way your computer can to do it more efficiently. Computers are great at repetitive tasks, and that's certainly true of ActionScript, which has two great ways to repeat statements in your programs. Using the *while( )* statement you can have your computer repeat a task as long as a certain condition exists. Using the *for( )* statement, you can tell your computer exactly how many times to repeat a task.

while( ) *statements repeat tasks when a condition is met*

The *while( )* statement checks to see if a condition is met. If it is, then the code within the curly brackets runs. If the condition isn't met, then ActionScript moves on to the next statement. It's very common to use the *while( )* statement with a variable that's incremented. So, if you want your assistant to pop down to the auto store and buy six Stutz Bearcats (enough for you and a few close friends), you'd put together a statement like this.

```
while (myStutzBearcats < 6) {
    buyStutzBearcat();
    myStutzBearcats = myStutzBearcats + 1;
}
```

Like the *if( )* statement, the condition for the *while( )* statement is inside of parentheses and if the condition is met, the statements inside of curly brackets *{}* run. In this example, the second line runs a function that buys a Bearcat. The third line *increments* the variable that keeps track of how many Bearcats you own. As long as that number is less than 6, the program loops; you buy another and add 1 to the number of Bearcats you own.

The whole idea of incrementing a value, like myStutzBearcats, is so common, there's even a shorthand way of adding one to a variable. The third line could also read:

```
myBearCats++;
```

There's no assignment operator (=), but the statement is assigning a new value to myBearcats. When you want to count down, you can use the decrement operator (--). Here's a statement that sells off your Stutz Bearcats until you only have three left.

```
while (myStutzBearcats > 3 {
    sellStutzBearcat();
    myStutzBearcats--;
}
```

Note: If, as you're reading ActionScript code for pleasure, you come across *i++*, don't be surprised. The *i* usually stands for *iterator* or *integer*. It's the programmers' way of saying, "I need an integer to operate this loop, but it can be any old integer, it doesn't need a fancy variable name." Using the lowercase *i* as a stand-in isn't a rule, just a programmers' tradition.

---

for( ) *statements repeat tasks a specific number of times*

The *for( )* loop gives you a very compact way to repeat a portion of your program. The mechanics that make a *for( )* statement run are all packed in the first line. It's so compact and down to business, that it reads a little more like machine talk than human talk. Here's an example:

```
for (var myStutzBearcats:Number = 0; myStutzBearcats < 6; myStutzBearcats++)
{
    buyStutzBearcat( );
}
```

Like the earlier statement, this loop buys six Stutz Bearcats. A lot goes on in that very first line of code. From left to right, here's what happens:

- The word *for* indicates a *for( )* statement.

- The beginning parenthesis is your clue that the condition follows.

- The word *var* means that a variable is being declared.

- *myStutzBearcats:Number* is the name of that variable and its data type.

- The assignment operator (=) immediately gives the variable a value of zero.

- Following the semicolon, you finally arrive at the condition that's being tested: Are there fewer than six Bearcats?

- The semicolon ends that statement, and in the next *myStutzBearcats* is *incremented.*

The *for( )* statement is very compact, and it puts everything you need to know right up front. Script writers often create *for( )* statements using the variable *i* for the condition (see the note on page 405). You'll often see something like:

```
for (var i = 0; i < 6; i++) {
    buyStutzBearcat;
}
```

Just like the earlier *for* statement, this one purchases six of those beautiful Bearcats.

Combining ActionScript's Building Blocks

This chapter covered a lot of ActionScript theory, and you may be itching to put some of these concepts into real action. In the following chapters, there are many examples that show you how to do just that.

Here's a recap of the topics covered in this chapter:

- *Classes* are blueprints for objects.

- *Instances* are specific objects, in use.

- ActionScript objects may have *properties, methods,* and *events.*

- Properties are the characteristics of objects; by changing values, your programs can change those characteristics.

- *Methods* and *functions* are the actions in ActionScript.

- *Methods* are included in the definition of an object.

- *Functions* (technically called function closures) are independent of objects.

- *Events* are used to make Flash projects interactive.

- *Events* have two parts: 1) *event listeners* that wait for events like mouse clicks; and 2) *event handlers* that run ActionScript statements in response to the event.

- *Variables* are containers for values.

- *Constants* are named values that never change.

- Variables can be one of several different data types: *Numbers, int, uint, String, Boolean,* and *Array.*

- *Arrays* can hold several different types of data.

- *Operators* are used to perform math functions, assign values, and compare values.

- *Conditional* statements, like (*if, if..else if,* and *switch*) test to see if a condition exists, and then, based on the result, run or ignore portions of ActionScript code.

- *Loop* statements (like *while* and *for*) run portions of ActionScript code either a specified number or times, or while a condition exits.

Controlling Actions with Events

In the previous chapter, you learned how to use ActionScript to move, transform, and change parts of your animation. But *when* something happens is just as important as the action itself. For example, you may want a movie object to start playing as soon as the Web page opens, or you may want to let your viewer decide when to watch it. You use *events* to control the actions in your animation. It's as if your ActionScript program tells Flash: "When this (event) happens, do this (action)." The classic example is a button on the stage. The action statement says something like: "When this button gets clicked, go to Frame 25 of the movie clip, and then start playing." You provide the programming that puts the people who view your Flash creations in the driver's seat. Using events and event handlers, you can send your programs off into the world on their own, confident that they'll behave.

This chapter explains how to use ActionScript to detect events when they happen and how to get your animations to perform specific actions as a result. Unlike previous versions, ActionScript 3.0 has one single way of handling all kinds of events. So, once you learn the basics, you're all set to handle any event.

How Events Work

There are many different types of events. Some events—like a mouse click—are triggered by the people viewing your animation. Other events are simply occurrences in a Flash animation—like a movie clip reaching the last frame. The button is one of the easiest events to understand, and, not surprisingly, it's one of the most common. Someone clicks a button, and then an action takes place. To the person clicking, it appears that the button makes something happen. That's true to some extent, but there are some additional gears and levers behind the scenes.

The object related to the event is called the *event target*. So in the button example, the button is the event target. When an event like a button click happens, an *event object* is created. The job of this new event object is to deliver information to an *event listener*, which has instructions about what to do when that event happens. So, how does the event target know where to deliver the information carried within the event object? That detail is handled by *registering* the event. In effect, the code that registers an event says, "When this event happens, send that event object to this location." Figure 12-1 shows the major elements involved in event handling.

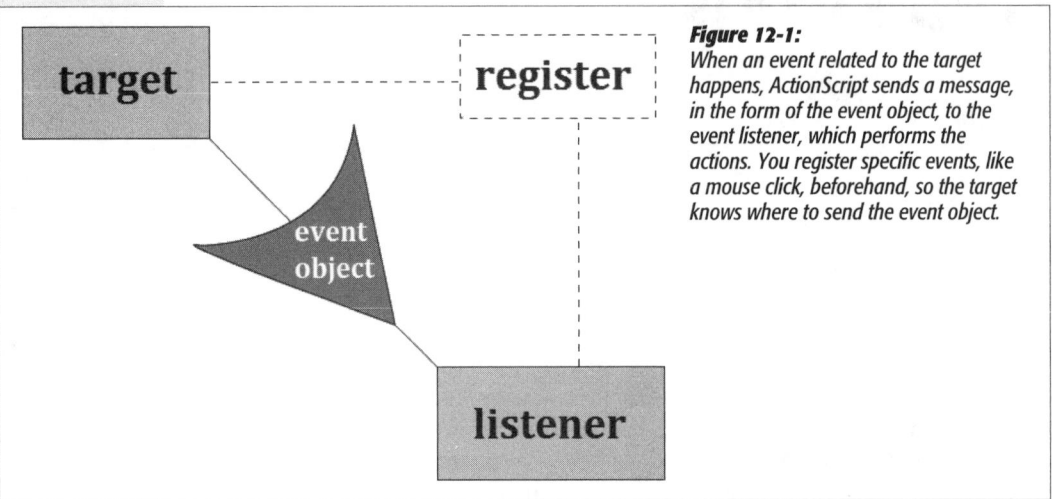

Figure 12-1:
When an event related to the target happens, ActionScript sends a message, in the form of the event object, to the event listener, which performs the actions. You register specific events, like a mouse click, beforehand, so the target knows where to send the event object.

Like most things in ActionScript, an event is considered an object. Obviously, it's not an object in the sense that a rectangle or a circle on your stage is an object. It's an object by the strict ActionScript definition of an object because it has properties where it stores information about the event, and it has methods (functions) that let you perform actions related to the event. The Event class is the definition of events in a very general sense—similar to the class definition of a rectangle as a four-sided object. The Event class is the basis for other more specific Event objects. Different types of events, such mouse events, keyboard events and error events, have properties and methods that serve their specific needs.

Mouse Events

The mouse is the most common way your audience interacts with your Flash creation, so a lot of events center around the mouse. The MouseEvent class detects all sorts of mouse events, including a variety of clicks and mouse movements, like mouse over (when the cursor moves over an object) and mouse out (when the cursor moves away from an object). Such events are the stuff that buttons and other smart objects are made of. So, roll up your sleeves, and get ready to create a mouse event listener.

Note: A mouse event refers to an event generated by *any* kind of pointer device, whether it's a mouse, a trackpad on a laptop, or a drawing pad.

This first example uses two movie clip objects: a circle and some text. The goal is to create an event listener that recognizes when the mouse is over the circle and when it's not—your basic rollover action. When the mouse moves over the circle, the text changes to say "mouse over." When the mouse moves out of the circle, the text changes back to the original message "mouse out." Not an earth-shaking event, but you have to start somewhere.

Note: You can create your own movie clip as described in the steps below, or you can download *mouse_event_begin.fla* from the "Missing CD" page at *http://missingmanuals.com/cds*. If you want to see how the final project works, download and test *mouse_event_finished.fla*.

Here are the steps to set up a Flash document with the necessary symbols for the mouse event experiment.

1. **In a new Flash document, draw a circle, and then create some static text that reads "mouse out."**

    When you're done, you have two objects in Frame 1 of your movie, as shown in Figure 12-2.

2. **Convert both the circle and the text to movie clip symbols (Modify → "Convert to Symbol").**

    This creates a symbol in the Library and leaves instances of the symbols on your desktop. As you create the symbols, use whatever name seems appropriate, like *Circle* and *Text*. The symbol names in the Library aren't as critical as the *instance* names described in the next step. Your ActionScript code will use these instance names.

3. **Select the circle movie clip instance on the stage, and then, using the Properties panel, name it *mcCircle* as shown in Figure 12-2. Select, and then name the text movie clip instance *mcText*.**

    You can use any name you want for instances on your desktop, but it's helpful to add something to the name that identifies the type. Here, *mc* indicates that the symbol instances are movie clips.

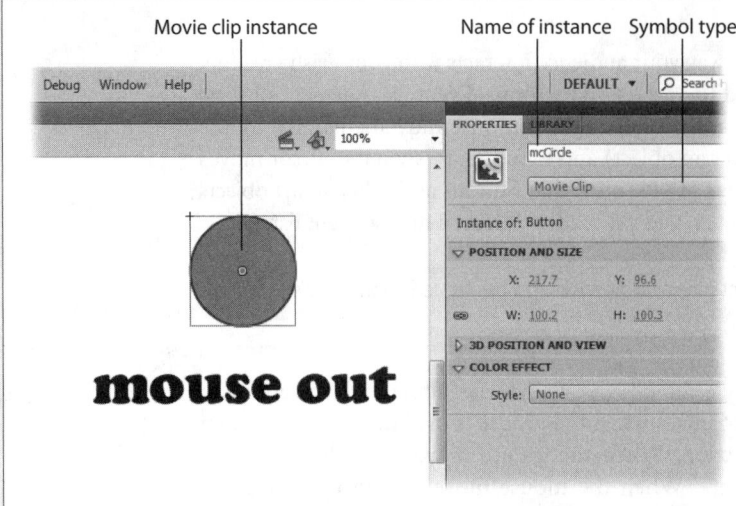

Figure 12-2:
Before you can program the instances of the symbols on the stage, you need to give them names. Here the circle is a movie clip symbol named mcCircle. The text is a movie clip symbol named mcText.

4. **Double-click mcText to open the movie clip symbol for editing.**

   As shown in Figure 12-3, the Text movie clip opens, showing you a new tab with the Library symbol name (not the instance name). The text remains boldly colored to indicate that it's part of the symbol that you're editing. The circle is faded to indicate it's not part of the symbol you're editing.

5. **Click Frame 2 in the timeline, and then press F6 to add a keyframe that includes content from the previous frame.**

   A new keyframe appears containing your text.

6. **Use the text tool to change the text in Frame 2 to read "mouse over."**

   Click anywhere in the text to begin editing. When you're done, just click outside of the text or choose another tool from the Tools palette.

7. **Use the Properties panel to label Frame 1 *out*, and then label Frame 2 *over*.**

   You can use either labels or frame numbers as references in ActionScript programming. In many ways, labels are the best choice because they make your code easier to understand when you read it. A good label explains more than a number any day. Also, if you insert new frames in the timeline, the frame numbers in your ActionScript will no longer be valid.

8. **Click Scene 1 to exit the mcText movie clip and go back to your main movie clip.**

   The symbol closes and the Text tab disappears.

9. **Add a new layer to your main movie clip, and then name it *actions*.**

   It's always best to create a special, well-labeled layer to hold your ActionScript code.

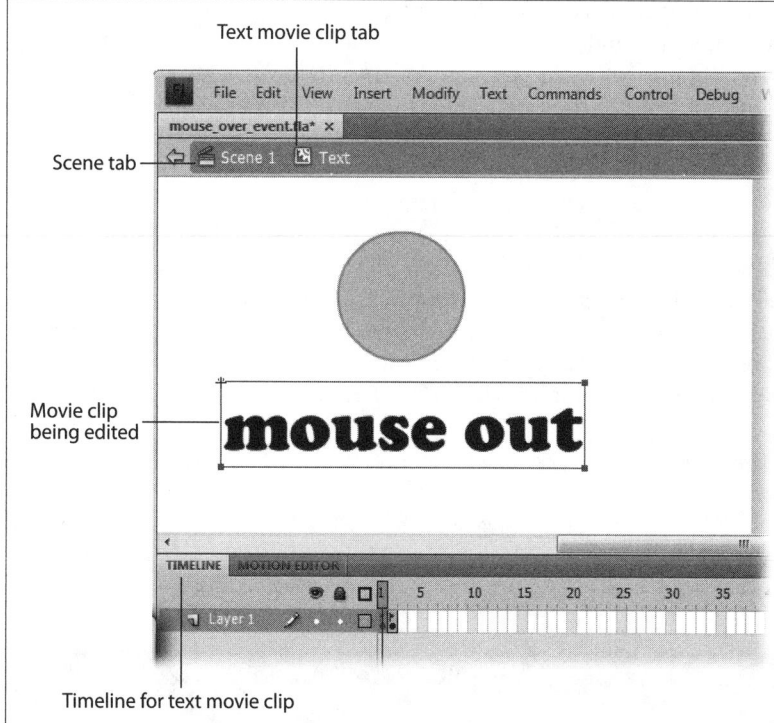

Text movie clip tab

Scene tab

Movie clip being edited

TIMELINE · MOTION EDITOR

Timeline for text movie clip

Figure 12-3:
When you double-click a movie clip symbol on the stage, Flash changes to symbol edit mode and the symbol's name appears in the edit bar. Any changes you make to a symbol change all the instances based on that symbol.

Getting Help for Events and Event Listeners

Now that the Flash document is ready to go, it's time to write and register an event listener, but where do you start? Computers are fussy beasts and won't work properly unless everything is done their way. ActionScript is the same. Event handling uses specific words, punctuation, and even capitalization. Everything has to be just so, or your event will be a non-event. For beginner ActionScript coders, one of the challenges is learning the right words to use to define and register particular events. This section explains what questions you need to ask as you're coding and where to find the answers.

The first question to ask is: What type of event is going to serve as the trigger to set your actions in motion? In this case, the event is the movement of the mouse over an object named mcCircle, so this is a mouse-related event. With that bit of knowledge, you can consult ActionScript reference tools that list different types of events. You're looking for one that sounds like it deals with mouse events.

The best reference tool that's close at hand while you're ActionScripting is the *ActionScript 3.0 Language and Components Reference*. Open it through the help menu: Help → Flash Help. Flash opens the Help pages in your web browser. In the upper-left corner of the page, click the link ActionScript 3.0 and Components. Another page opens. In the middle of that page, click ActionScript 3.0 Language and Components Reference. This electronic reference book provides details on every object, function, and element of ActionScript. Click the names on the left to open up descriptions and examples in the main window. Events are in the list of "packages" in the upper-left corner. The packages that begin with "fl." are related to Flash components, video, multi-language tools, motion classes, tweens, and transitions. Some of these, you can't use unless you've added the related components to your Flash document. The packages that begin with "flash." are built into Flash Player and work in any Flash document. Scroll down and click "flash.events." The main window fills with classes and descriptions. Under the heading Classes, you see all the different types of event classes. Some may seem a little mysterious, like AsyncErrorEvent. But other names—like KeyboardEvent and MouseEvent—sound more helpful. One click on MouseEvent, and your journey is over. The window fills with all the programmer's details you need to handle a MouseEvent.

Tip: It's kind of a lengthy trip to hunt down the help details on a specific event type, but it's worth remembering. If you end up writing a lot of event listeners, you'll probably remember the details for the events you use all the time. Occasionally, though, you'll need to look up the details for some oddball and unfamiliar event type. So leave some breadcrumbs (or fold down the corner of this page) to remind yourself how to look up events in the *ActionScript 3.0 Language and Components Reference*.

CODER'S CLINIC

Mouse Events: Public Constants

Here's the complete list of constants used by MouseEvent, as shown in *ActionScript 3.0 Language and Components Reference*. The first word, in capital letters, is the constant you use to identify the event. The word after the colon, *String*, indicates that the constant is of the String type. The word in quotes is the constant's actual value. The most important part of this definition is the word in caps, because that's the word you use to register listeners for a particular mouse event, as explained on page 415. You can think of these constants as the specific triggers for a MouseEvent.

CLICK : String = "click"

DOUBLE_CLICK : String = "doubleClick"

MOUSE_DOWN : String = "mouseDown"

MOUSE_MOVE : String = "mouseMove"

MOUSE_OUT : String = "mouseOut"

MOUSE_OVER : String = "mouseOver"

MOUSE_UP : String = "mouseUp"

MOUSE_WHEEL : String = "mouseWheel"

ROLL_OUT : String = "rollOut"

ROLL_OVER : String = "rollOver"

The reason for mucking through all this programming gobbledegook is about to become apparent. Scroll down and look at the items under Public Constants. These are the names of the actual events that MouseEvent can recognize: CLICK, DOUBLE_CLICK, and so on, including MOUSE_OUT and MOUSE_OVER—the two events that you need for your script. Each event type (MouseEvent, KeyboardEvent, ErrorEvent) has related *constants* that you use when you create event listeners. You have to type these constants exactly as they're defined (including capital letters, underscores, and so on) for your event listener to work. In addition to the constants, the events have properties you can use in your programs. For example, MouseEvent has properties called altKey, ctrlKey, and shiftKey. These are Booleans, and they can tell you whether a particular key is being pressed during a mouse event. You can use them to define, say, a special action for Shift-click and a different one for Alt-click.

Tip: You can ignore the items with the red triangles next to their names unless you're planning on doing some AIR (Adobe Integrated Runtime) programming. The triangles indicate that these classes, properties and methods are available only in AIR.

Creating a Rollover with a Mouse Event

So, you know you want to listen for a mouse event; specifically, you want to trigger some actions when the mouse is over the mcCircle movie clip. That makes mcCircle the *event target*, because it's the object where the event takes place. As described earlier and shown in Figure 12-1, the event target creates an event object, and then sends it to an event listener. The event object delivers information about the event that happened. Often, all that's necessary is notification that the event took place. As programmer, it's your job to tell the event target the name of the event that serves as a trigger and where to deliver the event object. This process is called *registering* an event, and it's done with a line of code like this:

```
mcCircle.addEventListener(MouseEvent.MOUSE_OVER, mouseOverListener);
```

In ActionScript-speak, this statement "registers an event listener." Almost all events use a similar method to register event listeners, so it's worthwhile to examine the statement completely. The first chunk of code, *mcCircle.addEventListener,* is nearly recognizable. The dot syntax indicates that mcCircle is an object, and that makes addEventListener either a property or method of the object. The action verb "add" in the name hints that it's a method, because methods are actions, while properties are characteristics. In fact, addEventListener is a method that's included with just about every object in Flash. That means you can use nearly any object to register an event listener. The details in the parentheses are the *parameters* for the method.

The first parameter is the event the listener is listening for. In this case, it's a MouseEvent, and the specific type of event is named by the constant MOUSE_OVER. As you know from your extensive research in the Flash Help files, those capital-lettered constants *are* the specific triggers for a MouseEvent. A comma separates the parameters of the method. In this statement, there are two parameters. The second parameter, *mouseOverListener,* is the name of the event listener. An *event listener* is simply a function—a series of statements or actions—that run when the event happens. You get to name (and write all the code for) the event listener. It's helpful to use a name that shows that this is an event listener and that describes the event that triggers the actions; hence the name mouseOverListener.

The event listener is a function, much like the functions described on page 392. The most significant detail is that the function has to list the event object in its parameters. You can think of the event object as the message sent from the event target to the event listener. Here's the code for mouseOverListener:

```
function mouseOverListener (evt:MouseEvent):void {
    mcText.gotoAndStop("over");
}
```

The first line begins with the keyword *function,* indicating that what follows defines a function—a list of actions. Next comes the name of the function: *mouseOverListener.* The function's parameter is the event object; in this case, the event object's name is *evt.* That's followed by a colon (:) and the object class *MouseEvent.* The name doesn't matter, it can be *evt, e,* or *george.* As always, it's helpful to choose a name that means something to you now, and will still make sense 5 years from now when you're trying to remember how the code works. You do have to accurately define the class or type of event, which in this case is MouseEvent. The term *:void* indicates that this function doesn't return a value. If you need to brush up on how to build a function, see page 392.

Once the curly brackets begin, you know that they contain the list of statements or actions that the function performs. In this case, there's simply one line that tells the movie clip mcText to go to the frame labeled "over" and stop there. All in all, here's the complete code so far, with accompanying line numbers:

```
1   mcCircle.addEventListener(MouseEvent.MOUSE_OVER, mouseOverListener);
2
3   function mouseOverListener (evt:MouseEvent):void {
4       mcText.gotoAndStop("over");
5   }
```

What you have at this point is one complete and registered event listener. Line 1 identifies mcCircle as the event target for a MOUSE_OVER event. It also registers the event listener as mouseOverListener. Beginning on line 3, you have the code for mouseOverListener. Any actions you place between those curly brackets will happen when the mouse cursor is over mcCircle.

You can go ahead and test your movie if you want, but it's not going to behave all that well. It needs a few more lines of code to make it presentable. If you test your movie at this point, you'll see a lot of movie clip flickering. If you mouse over the circle, the flickering stops and the text changes to "mouse over." That much works well. When you move the mouse out of the circle…nothing happens. The text still reads "mouse over." That's because you haven't written the mouse-out event. Fortunately, it's very similar to the mouse-over code. In fact, all you have to do is copy and paste the mouse-over code, and then make changes where needed, as shown in bold text in this example:

```
1   mcCircle.addEventListener(MouseEvent.MOUSE_OUT, mouseOutListener);
2
3   function mouseOutListener (evt:MouseEvent):void {
4       mcText.gotoAndStop("out");
5   }
```

By now, you should be able to read and understand most of the code. Like the first example, the event is registered using the mcCircle object. The event in this case is MOUSE_OUT, and the event listener is named accordingly: mouseOutListener. The action part of the event listener sends the timeline playhead to the frame labeled "out," which displays the text "mouse out"; back where it was when the program started. Perfect.

Well, almost perfect. If you test the movie now, you'll find that it behaves well when you mouse over the circle and when you mouse out of the circle. At the beginning though, there's still a bunch of movie clip flickering. Time for a little Flash troubleshooting. Unless they're told otherwise, movie clips play one frame, and then the next, and so on, until they reach the last frame, and then they play over again. And again. And again. Your main movie has only one frame, so it's not causing the flickering. mcCircle only has one frame, so it's not causing the flickering either. The mcText clip has two frames, and those are the ones doing the dance when you start your animation. You need a line of code that stops the movie clip on Frame 1. Then it will be up to the mouse events to control which frame is shown. All you need is one line that says:

```
mcText.gotoAndStop(1);
```

CODER'S CLINIC

Getting Help for ActionScript Classes

On page 413, the section "Getting Help for Events and Event Listeners" explained how to find an event and all its programming details in the *ActionScript 3.0 Language and Components Reference*. You can use the same reference to look up the properties and methods of particular classes and objects. For example, if you can't remember the exact spelling for the "goto and stop" method, you can look up the MovieClip class and you see all the methods associated with the class.

After opening the *ActionScript 3.0 Language and Components Reference* (page 413) look for MovieClip in the

scrolling box at the bottom-left under All Classes. Click the word MovieClip, and you see the complete and formal definition of the class, including the Public Properties that you can change through ActionScript programming. Below that, you see the Public methods including *gotoAndStop()*. There's a short description that describes what the method does, and the type of parameters it requires. Scroll down far enough, and you'll see examples of how to use the MovieClip class, along with its properties and methods.

The method *gotoAndStop( )* is part of every movie clip. This bit of code tells mcText to go to Frame 1 and stop. The parameter inside the parentheses has to refer to a specific frame. You can do that with a frame number, as shown here, or you can do it with a frame label as you did in your event listeners. If you're wondering how you can find out about the properties and methods for particular classes and objects, see the box on page 417.

As a statement on the first frame of your main movie clip, *mcText.gotoAndStop(1)* runs when the animation begins. It doesn't really matter whether it comes before or after the other lines of code. Those other bits of code don't do anything until an event happens. Not so with the statement above. There's nothing to prevent it from running as soon as Frame 1 of the main movie clip loads.

In ActionScript programming, the order in which different functions and statements appear isn't always important. It doesn't matter which event listener appears first in your code. The order in which the event listeners *run* is determined by the order in which someone mouses over or out of mcCircle. So whenever possible you may as well arrange your code so it's easy to read and understand. In this case, it's probably best to register all of your event listeners in the same spot, and then put the event listener functions together. You may also want to put the code that isn't dependent on a listener at the very top. So here, with a little rearranging for readability, is the code up to this point:

```
1   mcText.gotoAndStop(1);
2
3   mcCircle.addEventListener(MouseEvent.MOUSE_OVER, mouseOverListener);
4   mcCircle.addEventListener(MouseEvent.MOUSE_OUT, mouseOutListener);
5
6   function mouseOverListener (evt:MouseEvent):void {
7       mcText.gotoAndStop("over");
8   }
9
10  function mouseOutListener(evt:MouseEvent) :void {
11      mcText.gotoAndStop("out");
12  }
```

Line 1 stops mcText in its tracks before it has a chance to start flickering between its two frames. Lines 3 and 4 register event listeners. Beginning on line 6 are the functions that make up the event listeners. At this point, you can test your program, and it should behave pretty well. If something unexpected happens, double-check your spelling and make sure you have semicolons at the end of the statements.

Adding Statements to an Event Listener

So far in this example you've seen how an event listener attached to one object (mcCircle) can effect a change in another object (mcText). A single event listener can change any number of objects, including the object that registers the listener. After all, any statements you put between the curly brackets of an event listener will run when the event happens.

So, the next steps change the mcCircle object to give it a rollover style behavior. Once you make these changes, both the text and the circle will change in response to MOUSE_OVER and MOUSE_OUT events. Before you can indulge in Action-Script programming fun, you need to create a new keyframe in the mcCircle movie clip with a different image. Then you get to add statements to the two event listeners, mouseOverListener and mouseOutListener, to describe the actions.

Here are the steps to setup mcCircle's timeline:

1. **On the stage, double-click mcCircle to open it for editing.**

   The Circle symbol opens, showing a single frame in the timeline.

2. **Click Frame 2 in the timeline, and then press F7 to add a blank keyframe.**

   A new empty keyframe appears in Frame 2 of the Circle timeline.

3. **Draw a star in Frame 2 using the Polystar tool.**

   The Circle timeline now has a circle on Frame 1 and a star on Frame 2.

4. **In the Properties panel, label Frame 2 *over*, and then label Frame 1 *out*.**

   It's good to get in the habit of labeling frames you refer to in ActionScript code.

5. **In the Edit bar above the stage, click Scene 1 to close the movie clip.**

   The Circle movie clip symbol closes, and you're back at the main movie clip's timeline.

In your ActionScript, you need to add the lines that control the behavior of the mcCircle movie clip. They're all of the *gotoAndStop( )* variety. Start off with a line that stops the movie clip from flickering when the animation begins.

```
mcCircle.gotoAndStop(1);
```

Then, between the curly brackets of mouseOverListener, add code to change the circle to a star when a MOUSE_OVER event happens.

```
mcCircle.gotoAndStop("over");
```

Last but not least, between the curly brackets of the mouseOutListener, add code to change the star back to a circle when the mouse moves away from mcCircle.

```
mcCircle.gotoAndStop("out");
```

When you're done, the complete code should look like this:

```
1   mcText.gotoAndStop(1);
2   mcCircle.gotoAndStop(1);
3
4   mcCircle.addEventListener(MouseEvent.MOUSE_OVER, mouseOverListener);
5   mcCircle.addEventListener(MouseEvent.MOUSE_OUT, mouseOutListener);
```

```
 6
 7    function mouseOverListener (evt:MouseEvent):void {
 8        mcText.gotoAndStop("over");
 9        mcCircle.gotoAndStop("over");
10    }
11
12    function mouseOutListener(evt:MouseEvent):void {
13        mcText.gotoAndStop("out");
14        mcCircle.gotoAndStop("out");
15    }
```

This is a good time to test your movie. If everything runs as it should, you'll enjoy a high-quality mouse over and mouse out experience. Both the graphic and the text change with the mouse events. On the other hand, if you're getting somewhat different results, you may want to download *mouse_event_finished.fla* from the "Missing CD" page at *http://missingmanuals.com/cds*, and look for places where your code doesn't match the downloaded file.

Applying mouse events to other projects

As it stands now, your mouse event project isn't the flashiest thing on the block (pun intended). Still, it's worth considering how you can take the same rollover style behaviors and create larger, more impressive projects. For example, using the same mouse events, it would be easy to create a photo gallery that has half a dozen or more photo thumbnails and one large "feature" image like the one in Figure 12-4. When the mouse moves over one of the thumbnails, the thumbnail changes to display a highlight, and the feature image changes to match the thumbnail. You can even add a text caption that changes for each picture. Once you've created one photo gallery, it's easy to reuse your code by simply swapping in new photos.

Figure 12-4:
Using the mouse event techniques described so far, you can create a photo gallery like this one. When the mouse is over a thumbnail, a large version of the picture is shown to the right.

Creating a Tabbed Window with Mouse Events

So far this chapter covered two types of mouse events: MOUSE_OVER and MOUSE_OUT. The technique for using other events is nearly identical. The most frequently used mouse event is probably the CLICK event. If you understand the previous examples with MOUSE_OVER and MOUSE_OUT, you'll have no problem putting CLICK to work. Suppose you want to create a Flash project that's organized with tabs? You've seen a similar system on Web sites and in programs including Flash. You click a tab, and it reveals different information or a panel of tools.

Using the ActionScript programming tools that have been introduced in this chapter and the preceding one, you can create a tabbed window like the one shown in Figure 12-5. Here are the tools that you need in your Flash and ActionScript toolbox:

- Three mouse events: MOUSE_OVER, MOUSE_OUT, and CLICK

- A few IF..ELSE conditional statements to control tab behavior

- Four movie clips to serve as tabs

- One movie clip that holds the "content" shown under each tab

Setting the Stage for Tabbed Windows

The tabbed bar in Figure 12-5 is made up of four movie clips, one for each tab subject: dog, cat, flower, and Porsche. You can make the graphic part of the tab any shape you want. In this example, the tabs are created with a rectangle primitive. The top corners are rounded to give it that old-fashioned, tabbed folder look. The static text was created with the text tool. The important thing is that each tab is a separate movie clip, and each movie clip has three frames: over, out, and selected. In the example, the tabs are 137.5 pixels wide, so that four tabs fit snugly in a 550-pixel horizontal space.

Note: You can follow the instructions in this section to set up your tabbed folder document, or you can download *tabbed_folders_begin.fla* from the "Missing CD" page (*http://missingmanuals.com/cds*). If you want to see a finished and working copy of the project, download *tabbed_folders_finished.fla*.

As the mouse moves and clicks, you want to change the tabs' appearance to provide some interactive feedback for your audience. In this example, when the mouse is "out," the tab contrasts in color with the color of the content's folder. It looks as if the tab is behind another open folder. When the mouse moves over the tab, it changes size and color and the text is bold, providing a highlight effect.

Figure 12-5:
*You can make a tabbed window
interface using three simple mouse
events.*

*Top: The dog tab is selected and
the content area below shows a
dog.*

*Bottom: Clicking the cat tab
changes the tab's appearance
and the content below.*

When the tab is selected and its content is showing, the color of the tab matches the background color of the folder, giving it the appearance of an open folder. The frames are labeled *out*, *over*, and *selected* as shown in Figure 12-6. The ActionScript code uses the labels to identify particular frames.

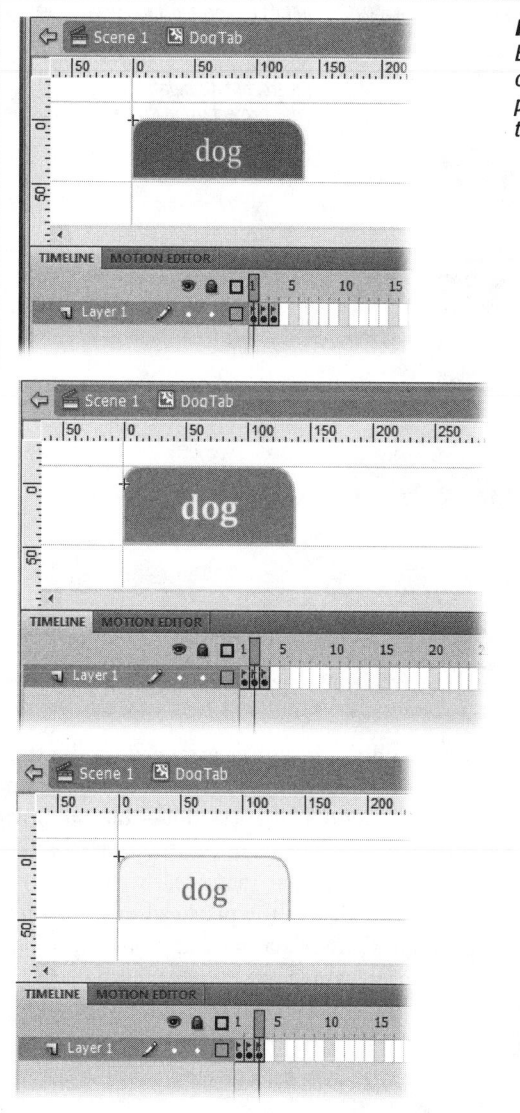

Figure 12-6:
Each tab is a movie clip with three frames, one for each state of the tab. Shown here in the symbol editing view, the top picture shows the "out" state, the middle shows "over," and the bottom shows "selected."

The main movie clip has only one frame, but it organizes the actions, tabs, and content into three layers as shown in Figure 12-7.

Each tab is a separate movie clip symbol, and the instances arranged on the stage are named: mcDogTab, mcCatTab, mcFlowerTab, and mcPorscheTab. There's one other movie clip in this project, called mcContent. You guessed it—that's a movie clip that covers most of the stage and shows the contents for each of the tabs. The mcContent movie clip has four frames with labels that match each tab: dog, cat, flower, and Porsche. So, when the "cat" tab is clicked, the playhead in mcContent moves to the "cat" frame. In the example file, there's a matching photo for each mcContent frame. If you don't have photos of your favorite dog, cat, flower, and Porsche, a static text word will do.

Tip: It's easy to line up and arrange the tabs on the stage using the align commands. Use Modify → Align → Bottom to line up all the bottom edges. Then use Modify → Align → Distribute Widths to space them evenly.

Planning Before Coding

As projects become more complicated, you can save a lot of time by thinking things through before you start writing code. It's a lot like doing a rough pencil sketch or storyboard (page 48) before you draw. With programming, it helps to list the actions that need to take place for your program to work. You can put these down in the human language of your choice, but it certainly helps to keep in mind the ActionScript tools you'll be using to build your project. Here's an example of planning notes for the tabbed window project:

- On startup, the *dog tab* should be selected and *dog content* should be showing. The other tabs should show the "out" frame.

- If the mouse rolls over or out of the *dog tab*, it shouldn't change its appearance, it should stay "selected."

- If the mouse rolls over any of the *non-selected tabs*, they should highlight, showing the "over" image when the mouse is over and they should change back to "out" when the mouse moves away.

- When the mouse clicks *any tab*, the clicked tab should change to "selected" and all the *other tabs* should change to "out." The *content* should change to match the selected tab.

These points present a pretty good sketch of how the tabbed window should behave, and it gives you some programming goals. To help grapple with the elements in your program, the words indicating movie clips are in italics, and the words indicating frames are in quotes. In your sketch, use any tools (typographic effects, colors, circles, and arrows) you want that help you understand the project.

The first bullet point in the sketch is easy to tackle, especially if you warmed up by completing the rollover project outlined earlier in this chapter (page 415). Here's the code you need to start with the dog tab selected and the other tabs set to the "out" frame:

```
1    // Start with the Dog tab selected and Dog content showing
2    mcDogTab.gotoAndStop("selected");
3    mcContent.gotoAndStop("dog");
4    // Stop the other tab movie clips from playing on start up
5    mcCatTab.gotoAndStop("out");
6    mcFlowerTab.gotoAndStop("out");
7    mcPorscheTab.gotoAndStop("out");
```

Because this project involves more lines of code and is a bit more complicated, it's good programming practice to use line numbers and to add comments to the code. If you don't have line numbers in your Actions window, click the Options button in the upper-right corner of the Actions window, and then choose Line Numbers near the bottom of the menu. In the code shown, the lines that begin with two slashes (//) are comments. ActionScript ignores anything from the slashes to the end of the line, so you're free to put whatever words will help you and others understand the logic behind your program.

Looking over the "sketch" of your program, you can see that each tab needs to react to three different mouse events: MOUSE_OVER, MOUSE_OUT, and CLICK. So, each tab needs to register event listeners for those mouse events. (If you need a refresher on registering an event listener, the details are on page 409.) It may look like a lot of code, but each line uses the same form, or as programmers like to say, *syntax*, to register an event listener.

```
8
9    // Register mouse event listeners for mcDogTab
10   mcDogTab.addEventListener(MouseEvent.MOUSE_OVER, dogOverListener);
11   mcDogTab.addEventListener(MouseEvent.MOUSE_OUT, dogOutListener);
12   mcDogTab.addEventListener(MouseEvent.CLICK, dogClickListener);
13
14   // Register mouse event listeners for mcCatTab
15   mcCatTab.addEventListener(MouseEvent.MOUSE_OVER, catOverListener);
16   mcCatTab.addEventListener(MouseEvent.MOUSE_OUT, catOutListener);
17   mcCatTab.addEventListener(MouseEvent.CLICK, catClickListener);
18
19   // Register mouse event listeners for mcFlowerTab
20   mcFlowerTab.addEventListener(MouseEvent.MOUSE_OVER, flowerOverListener);
21   mcFlowerTab.addEventListener(MouseEvent.MOUSE_OUT, flowerOutListener);
22   mcFlowerTab.addEventListener(MouseEvent.CLICK, flowerClickListener);
23
24   // Register mouse event listeners for mcPorscheTab
25   mcPorscheTab.addEventListener(MouseEvent.MOUSE_OVER, porscheOverListener);
26   mcPorscheTab.addEventListener(MouseEvent.MOUSE_OUT, porscheOutListener);
27   mcPorscheTab.addEventListener(MouseEvent.CLICK, porscheClickListener);
```

Note: Some lines in this script are left empty on purpose. ActionScript doesn't mind, and a little white space makes the code easier to read and understand, especially when viewed in the Actions panel.

Now that the event listeners are registered, you have a roadmap for the action part of your code. The last word in each of those statements—like dogOverListener, catOutListener, and porscheClickListener—is a reference to an event listener, and it's up to you to write the code that defines the actions. For example, lines 10, 11, and 12 show that mcDogTab needs three listeners, so that's a good place to start.

Looking back at the sketch, you have a rough outline of how the dog tab is supposed to behave. Those two middle bullet points from page 425 describe what's supposed to happen:

• If the mouse rolls over or out of the *dog tab*, it shouldn't change its appearance, it should stay selected.

- If the mouse rolls over any of the *non-selected tabs*, they should be highlighted, showing the "over" image when the mouse is over, and they should change back to "out" when the mouse moves away.

The word "if" is a good clue that you've got an *if..else* situation here. At this point, it may help to refine your human language describing the actions; however, if you're feeling confident, you can jump in and start to code. Here's a refined version of what should happen when the mouse moves over the dog tab:

- If the movie clip *mcDogTab* is selected, the movie clip *mcDogTab* should remain on the frame labeled "selected."

- Else if the movie clip *mcDogTab* isn't selected, movie clip *mcDogTab* should change to the frame labeled "over."

With the refined description, it's just a hop, skip, and a jump to the ActionScript code for the mouse-over event listener. Remember, the lines with double slashes (//) are just comments, not statements:

```
28
29   // Event listeners for mcDogTab
30   function dogOverListener(evt:MouseEvent):void {
31       // if the tab is selected, leave it selected on mouse over
32       if (mcDogTab.currentLabel == "selected") {
33           mcDogTab.gotoAndStop("selected");
34       }
35       // else if the tab isn't selected, change it on mouse over
36       else {
37           mcDogTab.gotoAndStop("over");
38       }
39   }
```

The *if..else* conditional statement for mcDogTab follows this form:

```
if (condition) {
      do these statements;
}
else {
      do these statements;
}
```

The *if..else* structure works well for the tabs because it helps you manage the possibility that the tab may already be selected when the mouse moves over it. (There are more details on conditional statements like *if..else* on page 403.)

Note: When you write the *(condition)* part of the statement (line 32), you want to use ActionScript's equality operator, which is two equal signs (==). You use the equality operator (==) to test whether a statement is true or false. A single equals symbol (=) is the *assignment operator* in ActionScript and is used to change values.

The next event listener for mcDogTab handles the MOUSE_OUT event. Similar to the MOUSE_OVER event, you want the tab to do nothing if the tab is selected. If it's not selected, than you want the tab to change back to the "out" state. Another job for *if..else*, and the form for the listener is very similar:

```
40    function dogOutListener(evt:MouseEvent):void {
41        // if the tab is selected, leave the tab selected
42        if (mcDogTab.currentLabel == "selected") {
43            mcDogTab.gotoAndStop("selected");
44        }
45        // else if the tab isn't selected, change it to show the "out" frame
46        else {
47            mcDogTab.gotoAndStop("out");
48        }
49    }
```

The actions that need to be performed for the CLICK event were listed in the sketch as follows:

• When the mouse clicks *any tab*, the clicked tab should change to "selected" and all the *other tabs* should change to "out." The *content* should change to match the selected tab.

There's no *if..else* situation here. There's simply a series of actions that need to take place when a tab is clicked. Those actions position the playhead on specific frames of the "tab" and "content" movie clips. Here's the dogClickListener code:

```
50    function dogClickListener(evt:MouseEvent):void {
51        // when clicked change the tab to selected
52        mcDogTab.gotoAndStop("selected");
53        // when clicked change the mcContent to show related frame
54        mcContent.gotoAndStop("dog");
55        // Set all the other tabs to the "out" frame
56        mcCatTab.gotoAndStop("out");
57        mcFlowerTab.gotoAndStop("out");
58        mcPorscheTab.gotoAndStop("out");
59    }
60
```

When the dog tab is clicked, line 52 changes the dog tab to "selected", and line 54 displays dog stuff in the content movie clip. The other three lines of code, 56–58, change the other tabs to the "out" state.

Testing your work so far

You've finished writing the event listeners for the dog tab. You've got three more tabs to go; however, if you use the "copy and tweak" coding technique described in this section, the last three tabs will go quickly. Before you copy and reuse code, you want to make sure it's working properly. There's no benefit in copying mistakes, so this is a good time to test the code for the dog tab.

The first thing to do is check for typos and obvious errors with the Check Syntax tool. At the top of the Actions window, click Check Syntax, as shown in Figure 12-8. A box appears, telling you whether or not there are errors in the code. If there are errors, you'll see them listed by line number in the Compiler Errors tab next to the timeline. Double-click an error, and Flash highlights the offending line of code. The explanations of errors may seem a little cryptic. If you don't understand what Flash is saying, compare your code to the code in this book. Check spelling, capitalization, and punctuation carefully. Punctuation errors can include missing semicolons at the end of statements or missing parentheses and brackets. Sometimes, bracket confusion includes using an opening bracket ({) when you should use a closing bracket (}).

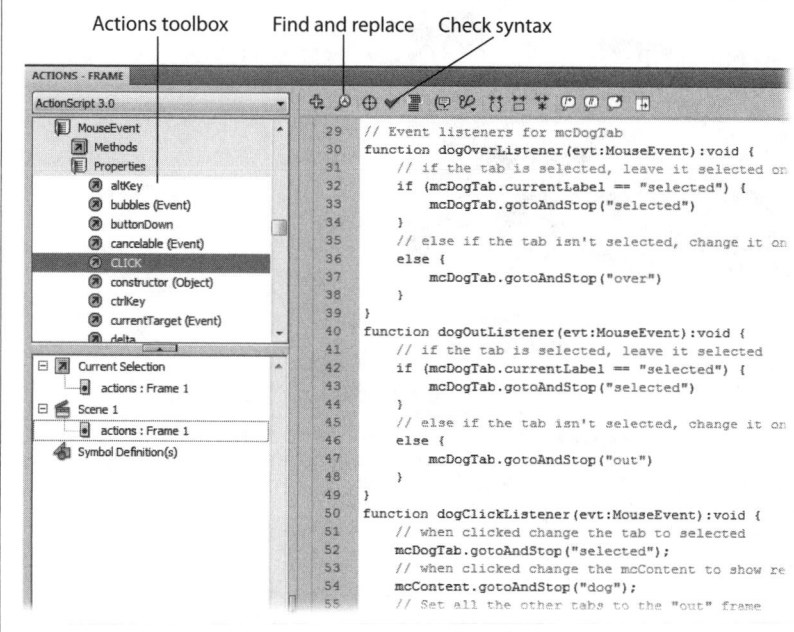

Figure 12-8:
The Actions window has tools to help you find typos (Check Syntax), find and replace words, and insert prebuilt chunks of code (Actions toolbox).

It takes a little extra effort to test part of your code before your program is complete, but the process gives you a better understanding of how it works. If you're copying and reusing code, testing is worth the effort, and it's likely to save you time in the long run.

If you test your movie at this point, you just get a lot of flickering, and the Compiler Errors panel fills up with errors with descriptions like the ones in Figure 12-9: "Access of undefined property catOverListener." In the Compiler Errors panel, double-click the error, and Flash highlights line 15 in your code. The problem is this line (and others) register event listeners and point to functions that you haven't written yet. This confuses ActionScript. Often, if one part of your code doesn't work (or isn't complete), the rest of the code doesn't run properly. Hence the flickering when you test your program.

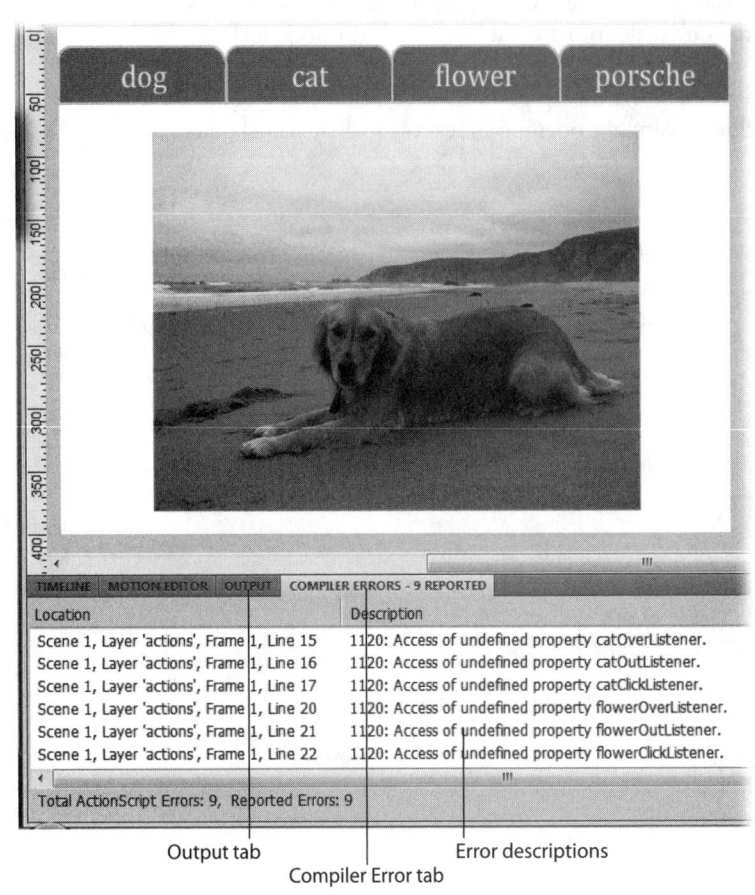

Figure 12-9:
When testing your ActionScript programs, errors appear in the Compiler Errors window. Double-click an error, and ActionScript highlights the line of code that created the problem.

The solution is to temporarily remove these lines from your program while you test the dog tab. You don't want to delete lines you've already written—that would be a waste of time. Instead you can *comment them out*. In other words, when you place double slash lines in front of the code, ActionScript ignores the lines because they look like comments. After testing, you remove the comment marks and turn your code back into legitimate statements.

So, to comment out line 15, which registers the catOverListener, place two slash marks at the beginning so that it looks like this:

```
// mcCatTab.addEventListener(MouseEvent.MOUSE_OVER, catOverListener);
```

Problem solved. Place comment marks in front of the lines for the mcCatTab: 15, 16, and 17. For the mcFlowerTab: 20, 21, and 22. For the mcPorscheTab: 25, 26, and 27.

Note: When you want to comment out more than one line of code, you can use the block comment characters. Put /* at the front, and then put */ at the end. Everything between those markers is considered a comment, not matter how many characters, words or lines there are.

Now, you can test the dog tab part of your movie; press Ctrl+Enter (⌘-Return). If everything is working properly, there shouldn't be any flickering when the animation runs, because all the movie clips are told to *gotoAndStop( )* at a specific frame. The dog tab should be selected, and the other tabs should be showing the "out" movie clip frame. When you mouse over any of the tabs, nothing should happen. The dog tab doesn't change when you mouse over and out of it, because that's what you programmed it to do. The other tabs don't change because you haven't programmed their actions yet.

It would be nice to test the MOUSE_OVER and MOUSE_OUT events on the dog tab before you copy the code and use it for the other tabs. To do that, you have to tweak your code so that mcDogTab isn't "selected" when you test the program. Change line 2 to read:

```
mcDogTab.gotoAndStop("out");
```

And then, change the mcCatTab so that it is selected by changing line 5 to:

```
mcCatTab.gotoAndStop("selected");
```

Now, when you test your movie, the dog tab should change when you mouse over it. If everything works as expected, great. If not, you need to search and destroy any typos that appear in your code. You can download the file *tabbed_folders_test.fla* from the "Missing CD" page (*http://missingmanuals.com/cds*) to compare coding. Open the Actions window in the downloaded file, and you see the tabbed folders statements with the proper lines commented out and tweaked for testing. If you compare the code line by line to your project, you should be able to identify any errors.

Once your code has passed the testing phase, you need to undo the changes you made. So, change line 2 back to its original form:

```
mcDogTab.gotoAndStop("selected");
```

And, likewise, change line 5 back to:

```
mcCatTab.gotoAndStop("out");
```

Remove the comment marks from the lines that register event listeners for the mcCatTab: 15, 16, and 17; for the mcFlowerTab: 20, 21, and 22; for the mcPorscheTab: 25, 26, and 27.

With your code tested and working properly, you can copy and tweak with confidence, as described in the next section.

Copy and Tweak Coding

If you've typed all of the 60 lines of code shown so far in this example, you probably agree that writing and testing code can be a little tedious. The good news is, if you've gotten this far, you can use the copy and tweak technique to develop code for the other three tabs. When you have some code that works properly, and you need to write nearly identical code for another part of your program, it makes sense to copy the code and then change a name or word here and there. In this example, all of the tabs have very similar behavior. You can copy the event listeners for mcDogTab, and then paste that code to the bottom of your script. Then, all you need to do is swap a few names. For example, where it says *mcDogTab*, change it to *mcCatTab*.

First copy and paste the code you want to modify:

1. Select and copy the code between line 29 and line 59.

2. Click in line 61, and then paste the code back into your script.

At this point, you need to rewrite the code for mcCatTab. You can do so in a couple of ways, but for learning purposes, this exercise will walk you through the changes one at a time to reinforce your ActionScript reading comprehension.

Table 12-1. This table shows how to convert the code for the event listener dogOverListener to catOverListener. Elements in bold were changed.

Line #	Code as written for mcDogTab	Code Revised for mcCatTab
61	// Event listeners for **mcDogTab**	// Event listeners for **mcCatTab**
62	function **dogOverListener**(evt:MouseEvent):void {	function **catOverListener**(evt:MouseEvent):void {
63	// if the tab is selected, leave it selected on mouse over	// if the tab is selected, leave it selected on mouse over
64	if (**mcDogTab**.currentLabel == "selected") {	if (**mcCatTab**.currentLabel == "selected") {
65	**mcDogTab**.gotoAndStop("selected")	**mcCatTab**.gotoAndStop("selected")
66	}	}
67	// else if the tab isn't selected, change it on mouse over	// else if the tab isn't selected, change it on mouse over
68	else {	else {
69	**mcDogTab**.gotoAndStop("over")	**mcCatTab**.gotoAndStop("over")
70	}	}
71	}	}

Tip: Reading your code line-by-line, thinking through the actions that the code performs, and then making changes is the safest way to rewrite your code. You can also employ ActionScript's find-and-replace tool; however, it's awfully easy to get carried away and make bad changes. To use find and replace, click the magnifying glass at the top of the Actions window as shown in Figure 12-9.

The event listener, catOverListener, is very similar to the previous example. You need to change "dog" to "cat" in the function name and everywhere the tab movie clip symbol appears. When you're finished, the code should look like this example:

```
72    function catOutListener(evt:MouseEvent):void {
73        // if the tab is selected, leave the tab selected
74        if (mcCatTab.currentLabel == "selected") {
75            mcCatTab.gotoAndStop("selected");
76        }
77        // else if the tab isn't selected, change it to show the "out" frame
78        else {
79            mcCatTab.gotoAndStop("out");
80        }
81    }
```

To rewrite the code for the CLICK event, think back to the tasks the code has to perform. When *any* tab is clicked, it should change to "selected" and all the *other* tabs should change to "out." The content needs to be changed to match the selected tab. With those concepts clearly in mind, it's fairly easy to adapt the dog-ClickListener code to work for catClickListener. Below is the code as it should read after you've made changes. The bolded words have been changed.

```
1     function catClickListener(evt:MouseEvent):void {
2         // when clicked change the tab to selected
3         mcCatTab.gotoAndStop("selected");
4         // when clicked change the mcContent to show related image
5         mcContent.gotoAndStop("cat");
6         // Set all the other tabs to the "out" frame
7         mcDogTab.gotoAndStop("out");
8         mcFlowerTab.gotoAndStop("out");
9         mcPorscheTab.gotoAndStop("out");
10    }
11
```

That finishes the changes that transform the dog tab code to work for the cat tab. Now you need to repeat the process for the remaining two tabs: flower and porsche. When you've done that, your code should look like this:

```
12    // Event listeners for mcFlowerTab
13    function flowerOverListener(evt:MouseEvent):void {
14        // if the tab is selected, leave it selected on mouse over
```

```
15      if (mcFlowerTab.currentLabel == "selected") {
16          mcFlowerTab.gotoAndStop("selected");
17      }
18      // else if the tab isn't selected, change it on mouse over
19      else {
20          mcFlowerTab.gotoAndStop("over");
21      }
22  }
23  function flowerOutListener(evt:MouseEvent):void {
24      // if the tab is selected, leave it selected
25      if (mcFlowerTab.currentLabel == "selected") {
26          mcFlowerTab.gotoAndStop("selected");
27      }
28      // else if the tab isn't selected, change it on mouse out
29      else {
30          mcFlowerTab.gotoAndStop("out");
31      }
32  }
33  function flowerClickListener(evt:MouseEvent):void {
34      // when clicked change the tab to selected
35      mcFlowerTab.gotoAndStop("selected");
36      // when clicked change the mcContent to show related image
37      mcContent.gotoAndStop("flower");
38      // Set all the other tabs to the "out" frame
39      mcDogTab.gotoAndStop("out");
40      mcCatTab.gotoAndStop("out");
41      mcPorscheTab.gotoAndStop("out");
42  }
43
44  // Event listeners for mcPorscheTab
45  function porscheOverListener(evt:MouseEvent):void {
46      // if the tab is selected, leave it selected on mouse over
47      if (mcPorscheTab.currentLabel == "selected") {
48          mcPorscheTab.gotoAndStop("selected");
49      }
50      // else if the tab isn't selected, change it on mouse over
51      else {
52          mcPorscheTab.gotoAndStop("over");
53      }
54  }
55  function porscheOutListener(evt:MouseEvent):void {
56      // if the tab is selected, leave it selected
57      if (mcPorscheTab.currentLabel == "selected") {
58          mcPorscheTab.gotoAndStop("selected");
59      }
```

```
60      // else if the tab isn't selected, change it on mouse out
61      else {
62          mcPorscheTab.gotoAndStop("out");
63      }
64  }
65  function porscheClickListener(evt:MouseEvent):void {
66      // when clicked change the tab to selected
67      mcPorscheTab.gotoAndStop("selected");
68      // when clicked change the mcContent to show related image
69      mcContent.gotoAndStop("porsche");
70      // Set all the other tabs to the "out" frame
71      mcDogTab.gotoAndStop("out");
72      mcCatTab.gotoAndStop("out");
73      mcFlowerTab.gotoAndStop("out");
74  }
```

When you test the code, using Ctrl+Enter on a PC or ⌘-Return on a Mac, it should work as advertised. On startup the dog tab is selected. Mouse over any of the other tabs and they should show a highlight. Click a tab, and it becomes the selected tab, showing related content in the main part of the window.

Modifying tabbed windows for projects

The tabbed window project creates a container. You can rename the tabs and put anything you want in the "content" movie clip. The example in this chapter holds a single picture, but each tab could hold an entire photo collection or a collection of widgets that work with a database. The tabs simply provide a way to organize elements of a project.

You can easily change the tabs themselves for a different look. Metallic hi-tech tabs, perhaps? All you have to do is change the shape or the color of the graphics in the tab movie clips. For example, if you'd like a look that emulates colored file folders, you can coordinate the color of the tabs with the background of the content movie clip. If it works better for your project, you can use the same ActionScript code to manage tabs that run vertically along the edge of the content area.

Keyboard Events and Text Events

ActionScript 3.0 uses a single technique for handling events, so if you know how to register an event listener for a mouse event, it's not difficult to handle events for keyboards or other objects. All events use the same event register and event listener duo. For example, the keyboard event has two constants: KEY_DOWN and KEY_UP. You can use the Flash stage itself to register keyboard events.

Note: You can download the Flash document for this example *keyboard_events.fla* from the "Missing CD" page at *http://missingmanuals.com/cds*.

Here's a simple example that shows you how to start and stop a movie clip from running using the KEY_DOWN and KEY_UP events. The movie clip simply shows a number for each frame as it's running. This example references an instance of the Stage class. The stage represents the drawing area in a Flash animation. As a result the stage has properties, like width and height; and like other objects, it has an addEventListener method.

Start a new document. Add a layer, and then name one layer *actions* and the other layer *counter*. At the first frame of the counter layer, add a movie clip symbol to the stage. Open the movie clip and put a big number 1 on the stage. Add four more keyframes with numbers 2 thru 5 on the stage. In the Properties panel, name the movie clip mcCounter. Click the first frame in the actions layer, open the Actions window, and then type this short script:

```
stage.addEventListener(KeyboardEvent.KEY_DOWN, keyDownListener);
stage.addEventListener(KeyboardEvent.KEY_UP, keyUpListener);

function keyDownListener(evt:KeyboardEvent):void {
    mcCounter.stop();
}

function keyUpListener(evt:KeyboardEvent):void {
    mcCounter.play();
}
```

When you test the animation (Control → Test Movie), it quickly runs through the frames showing the numbers 1 through 5 on the stage. Press and hold the Space bar, and the numbers stop. Release the Space bar, and the numbers start again.

Note: When you test keyboard events inside of Flash, you may notice some odd behavior. That's because Flash itself is trapping some keyboard events, and it tends to catch the letter keys. If you actually publish your Flash project, and then run the SWF in Flash Player or a browser, you get a more accurate experience.

Using Event Properties

Like most things in ActionScript, an event is actually an object. The event object is passed to the event listener as a parameter inside of parentheses. Take this line of code:

```
function keyDownListener(evt:KeyboardEvent):void {
```

The *evt* is an instance of the keyboard event that was created when a key was pressed. You can use any name you want in place of *evt*. The colon and word KeyboardEvent indicate the type of event.

The KEY_DOWN and KEY_UP constants are parts of the KeyboardEvent class. Keyboard events also have properties that store changeable values. Properties can be passed to the event listener and used in the event listener's actions. For example, the charCode property holds a value that identifies the specific keyboard character of KEY_DOWN and KEY_UP events. Programs use character codes to identify the characters shown on a screen or sent to a printer. By adding a couple of lines to your keyboard event listeners, you can view character codes as you press keys.

```
stage.addEventListener(KeyboardEvent.KEY_DOWN, keyDownListener);
stage.addEventListener(KeyboardEvent.KEY_UP, keyUpListener);

function keyDownListener(evt:KeyboardEvent):void {
    mcCounter.stop();
    trace("Key Down");
    trace(evt.charCode);
}

function keyUpListener(evt:KeyboardEvent):void {
    mcCounter.play();
    trace("Key Up");
    trace(evt.charCode);
}
```

The *trace( )* statement is a remarkably handy programmer's tool that's used to display values in the Output panel as shown in Figure 12-10. If your Output panel is closed, you can open it with Window → Output or the F2 key. Like any function, you pass values to the *trace( )* statement by placing them inside of the parentheses. If you put a string inside of the parentheses, like *"Key Down"*, Flash shows that string in the Output panel when it reaches the *trace( )* statement in your code. The two strings "Key Down" and "Key Up" are called *string literals* by programmers, because the value of the string is defined. It's not a variable or a property that changes.

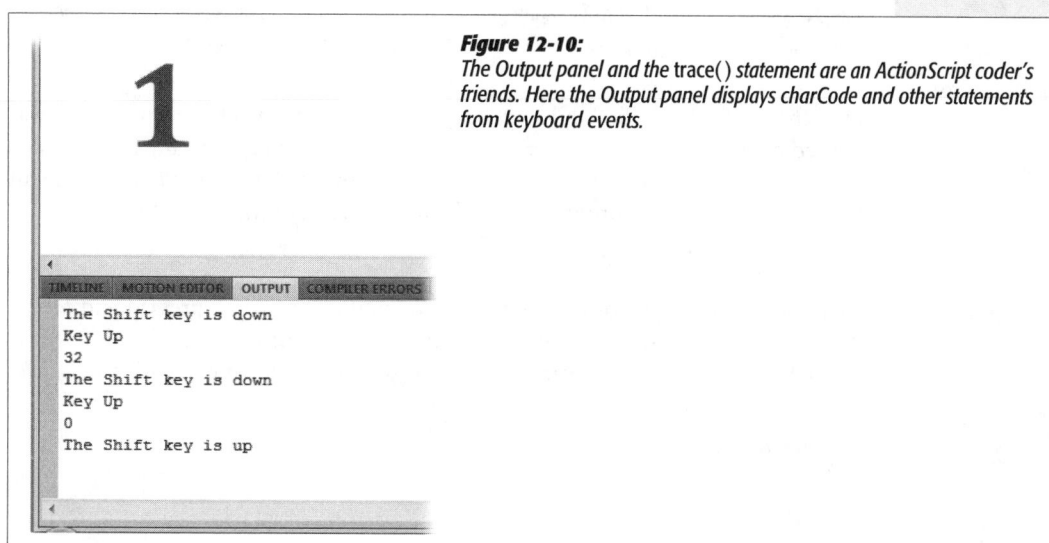

Figure 12-10:
The Output panel and the trace() *statement are an ActionScript coder's friends. Here the Output panel displays charCode and other statements from keyboard events.*

Note: The *trace( )* statement doesn't have any use in final Flash animations. The most common use of *trace( )* is to examine the value of variables while testing a program. Sometimes a *trace( )* statement is used to simply determine whether a program reaches a certain point in the script.

The second *trace( )* statement shows the value of a property in the Output window. As explained previously, *evt* is the event object that's passed to the event listener, and charCode is a property of *evt*. Like all good properties, it's shown with dot syntax as *evt.charCode*. So, the second *trace( )* statement shows the value of *evt*'s char-Code property. Each time a key is pressed, a new instance of the KeyboardEvent is created and passed to the listener keyDownListener. Each instance holds a single value in the charCode property that corresponds to the key that was pressed.

When you test the program, as you press keys, string literals (Key Down and Key Up) and numbers appear in the Output panel. If you press the Space bar, the key-DownListener sends the Key Down string, and then the value 32. Because keyboards repeatedly send character codes when a key is held down, you may see multiple 32s while you hold the key down and one final 32 on KEY_UP.

Keyboard events have six properties called *public* properties, because you can access them from your ActionScript program, see Table 12-2.

***Table 12-2.** Public Properties of KeyboardEvent*

Public Property	Data type	Description
altKey	Boolean	True if the Alt key is pressed
charCode	uint (unsigned integer)	Value of the character code for key up or key down
ctrlKey	Boolean	True if the Control key is pressed
keyCode	uint (unsigned integer)	Value of the key code for key up or key down
keyLocation	uint (unsigned integer)	Indicates the location of the key on the keyboard
shiftKey	Boolean	True if the Shift key is pressed

Like charCode, keyCode, and keyLocation are used to determine what key was pressed on a keyboard. The other three properties are used specifically to determine whether the Alt, Control, or Shift keys are down or up. Add this *trace( )* statement to your keyboard event program to see how the shiftKey property works:

```
trace(evt.shiftKey);
```

As a Boolean, the value of shiftKey is *true* when the Shift key is pressed and *false* if it's not pressed. You can use an *if* conditional statement to test if the Shift key is pressed. For example, you can replace the preceding statement with this *if..else* statement:

```
if (evt.shiftKey==true) {
    trace("The Shift key is down");
}
```

```
else {
    trace("The Shift key is up");
}
```

The result is a more complete description than the bare bones *true* and *false* reports.

Capturing Text Input with TextEvent

KeyboardEvent works fine for detecting whether or not keys are pressed on the keyboard, but it's not very good at capturing the actual text or characters that are typed into a program. The best tool for that job is the *TextEvent*. You use the TextEvent with an object like an Input Text box.

1. **Open a new document.**

2. **Click the Text tool in the Tools palette, and then choose Input Text from the drop-down list, as shown in Figure 12-11.**

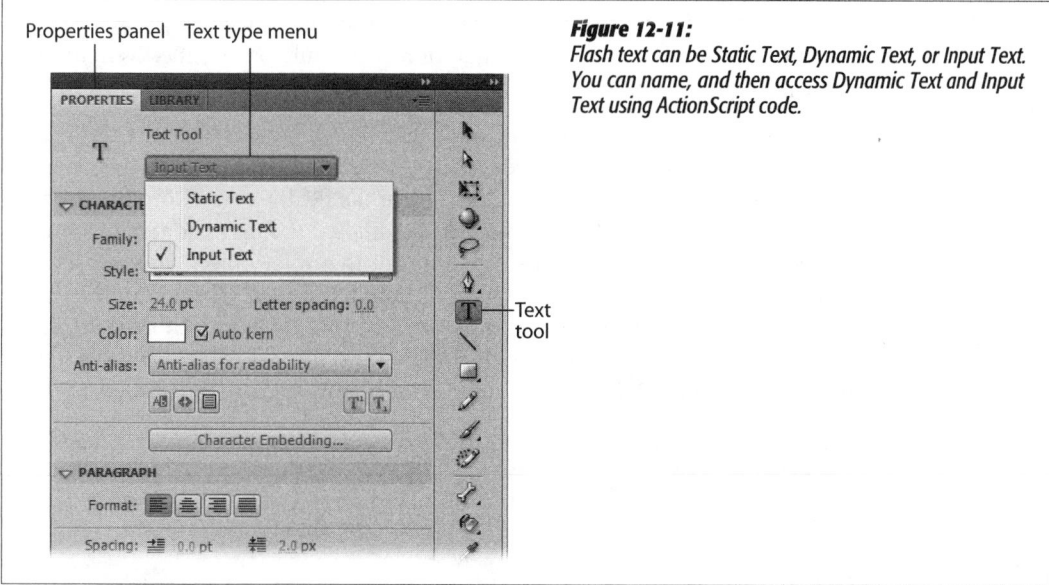

Properties panel   Text type menu

Figure 12-11:
Flash text can be Static Text, Dynamic Text, or Input Text. You can name, and then access Dynamic Text and Input Text using ActionScript code.

Text tool

3. **Draw a text box on the stage, and then add some preliminary text to the text box, like *Your name here.***

4. **In the Properties panel, name the Input Text box *txtfldName.***

5. **Open the Actions window, and then type in this code:**

```
txtfldName.addEventListener(TextEvent.TEXT_INPUT, textInputListener);

function textInputListener(evt:TextEvent):void {
    trace(evt.text);
}
```

When you test the Flash program, you see a text box on the stage with the words "Your name here". Select the text, and then type your own name in its place; the characters you type appear in the Output panel. Any key you press while the text box is *in focus* appears in the Output panel. The text box captures each letter and stores it in the *text* property of the TextEvent object *evt*. The TextEvent is passed to textInputListener, which uses the *text* property in the statement:

```
trace(evt.text);
```

> **Note:** You can download the Flash document for this example *input_text.fla* from the "Missing CD" page at *http://missingmanuals.com/cds*.

Keeping Time with TimerEvent

All the events explored in this chapter so far rely on audience input. There are other types of events that occur as part of a process and don't involve audience input. A good example is the TimerEvent, which triggers an event when a specified amount of time has passed. Suppose you're developing a quiz and you want to give students 30 seconds to answer each question. You could use a TimerEvent to move to the next question every 30 seconds. Sounds merciless, doesn't it?

Here's an example that's not quite so cruel. All it does is change the text on the screen after a certain interval. Open a new document, and then add a dynamic text field to the stage. Put some placeholder text in the field, like the word *blank*. In the Properties panel, name the dynamic text field *dText*. Using ActionScript, you can create a Timer object. Using the properties of the timer object, you can set it to trigger an event after a certain amount of time has passed. This example uses the event to change the text in the dynamic text box. Initially, it says "It's not yet time." The color of the type is blue. After the timer event, the text reads "Now, it's time!", as shown in Figure 12-12, and the color of the type changes to red.

Figure 12-12:
In this example a timer event is used to change the text displayed in a dynamic text field.

```
1    var timer:Timer = new Timer(1000,3);
2
3    dText.text = "It's not yet time.";
4    dText.textColor = 0x0066FF;
```

```
5
6    timer.addEventListener(TimerEvent.TIMER_COMPLETE, timerCompleteListener);
7    timer.start();
8
9    function timerCompleteListener(evt:TimerEvent):void {
10       dText.text = "Now it's time!";
11       dText.textColor = 0xFF0000;
12   }
```

You can't just drag a timer out of the Tools palette like a circle or a text box, so you have to use ActionScript code to create a new object. That's exactly what the code in line 1 does. From left to right it creates a variable called *timer* (lowercase *t*) which is of the data type Timer (uppercase *T*). The = *new Timer* portion of the line creates the timer object. The numbers inside of the parentheses are the parameters you use to set the timer. The first number sets the *delay* property, and the second number sets the *repeatCount* property. The ActionScript Timer measures time in milliseconds, so 1000 equals a second. With repeatCount set to 3, the timer waits 3 seconds before triggering the TIMER_COMPLETE event. Setting these two numbers is sort of like winding up a kitchen timer to a specified interval.

In line 3, a new string of characters is displayed in the text box: "It's not yet time." The following line sets the color of the text to blue. If you've read from the beginning of this chapter, line 6 probably looks familiar. It registers the event listener called timerCompleteListener. As you can probably guess, line 7 starts the countdown. Lines 9 through 12 are the event listener for TIMER_COMPLETE. The function displays the new message in the text box "Now it's time!" And, it changes the type to red for added dramatic effect.

Note: You can download the Flash document for this example *timer_event.fla* from the "Missing CD" page at *http://missingmanuals.com/cds*.

Removing Event Listeners

When you create an event listener, it sits there constantly waiting for the event to happen. You may forget it's even there; but still, it sits patiently, waiting, listening, and using up computer resources in the process. There are a couple of good reasons why you should specifically remove event listeners when they're no longer needed. One is the computer resource issue. It's also possible for a forgotten event listener to foul up some other process when you least expect it.

Ideally, you should remove an event listener whenever your program no longer needs it. For example, in the preceding TimerEvent, you can remove the listener after the TIMER_COMPLETE event triggers. You can place the code to unregister the timer within timerCompleteListener:

```
timer.removeEventListener(TimerEvent.TIMER_COMPLETE, timerCompleteListener);
```

The code to remove an event listener is very similar to the code used to register it in the first place. The *removeEventListener( )* function is a method of any object that has a method to *addEventListener( )*. The same parameters that define the event type and the event handler identify the event listener being removed.

In Case of Other Events

The events covered in this chapter are just a few of the many events defined in Flash and ActionScript. There are events to handle error messages and events to track the process of a file or Web page loading. There are events specific to components like scroll bars, sliders, context menus, text lists and color pickers. The good news is that you use the same statements to register an event listener and to specify the actions that are to take place when an event happens.

Here's a partial list of some of the event classes recognized by the Flash Player:

Class	Description
Activity Event	Used by cameras and microphones to indicate they're active.
AsyncErrorEvent	Used to indicate an error in network communication.
ContextMenuEvent	Indicates a change when the audience interacts with a context menu.
DataEvent	Indicates raw data has completed loading.
ErrorEvent	Used to indicate a network error or failure.
Event	The base class for all other events classes.
FocusEvent	Triggers an event when the audience changes focus from one object to another.
FullScreenEvent	Indicates a change from or to full-screen display mode.
HTTPStatusEvent	Creates an event object when a network request returns an HTTP status code.
IOErrorEvent	Indicates an error when trying to load a file.
KeyboardEvent	Indicates keyboard activity.
MouseEvent	Indicates mouse activity.
NetStatusEvent	Reports on the status of a NetConnection, NetStream, or SharedObject.
ProgressEvent	Reports on the progress while a file loads.
SampleDataEvent	Used when the Flash Player requests audio data.
SecurityErrorEvent	Reports a security error.
ShaderEvent	Indicates the completion of a shader operation.
StatusEvent	Used by cameras and microphones to report on their status and connection.
SyncEvent	Used by SharedObjects to indicate a change.
TextEvent	Indicates a change when the audience enters text.
TimerEvent	Indicates the passing of a timing interval.

Organizing Objects with the Display List

When you create your animation using the Flash authoring tool, you draw objects on the stage or drag them from the Library. Often, you put one object inside of another. For example, you might place a shape and some text inside of a movie clip that's on the stage. Then you can move or transform the movie clip and its content as a whole. When you want one displayed object to appear in front of or behind another, you use Flash's Modify → Arrange commands. To a designer, it all seems pretty natural. But what happens when you put on your ActionScript programmer's hat and want do those same display-related chores using only ActionScript? The key is the Display List, and that's the sole topic of this chapter.

The Display List is exactly what its name implies. It's a running list of the objects displayed on the stage during a Flash animation. You make things visible by adding them to the Display List and make them disappear by removing them from the list. The Display List keeps track of the stacking order of objects on the stage, managing the way they overlap one another. This chapter shows you how to add and remove items from the Display List and how to mange the stacking order. You'll learn a lot about the DisplayObject and DisplayObjectContainer classes. At the end of the chapter, there's a handy reference table for some of the most common properties and methods related to Display List tasks.

The Display List: Everything in Its Place

Simply put, anything that appears on the stage in Flash Player is a *display object*. That includes shapes, lines, text fields, and movie clips. Because they're displayable, these objects have a lot of similar properties, including x/y coordinates that mark their position on the stage. They have width and height properties, which you can see in the Properties panel whenever you select them. If you're following the ActionScript discussion that began in Chapter 11, it's probably clear that displayable objects inherit these similar properties from some ancestor class (page 386). In fact, they're all descendants of a class called, appropriately enough, *DisplayObject*. As you work in ActionScript, you'll find lots of objects that get important, much-used properties and methods from DisplayObject.

When Display Objects are Display Object Containers

Suppose you create a new Flash document, with nothing on the stage and you publish it or test it with Ctrl+Enter (⌘-Return on a Mac). From Flash Player's point of view, that empty .swf has two display objects: the stage itself (yep, it's a display object) and the animation's main timeline. Even if there's only a single frame, the main timeline is considered a display object that's placed on the stage. It works like this: though the Flash Player's stage looks empty, it still has a couple of displayable features, like a background color and the width and height of the stage. Equally, important, the stage is a container. When you put display objects on the stage, they become visible. Along the same lines, the main timeline is also a display object. Anything that you put in a frame of that main timeline is displayed in the Flash animation. So it, too, is a container for other display objects. So, before you even start the process of building your animation, Flash always starts out with two display objects, which are also containers, as shown in Figure 13-1.

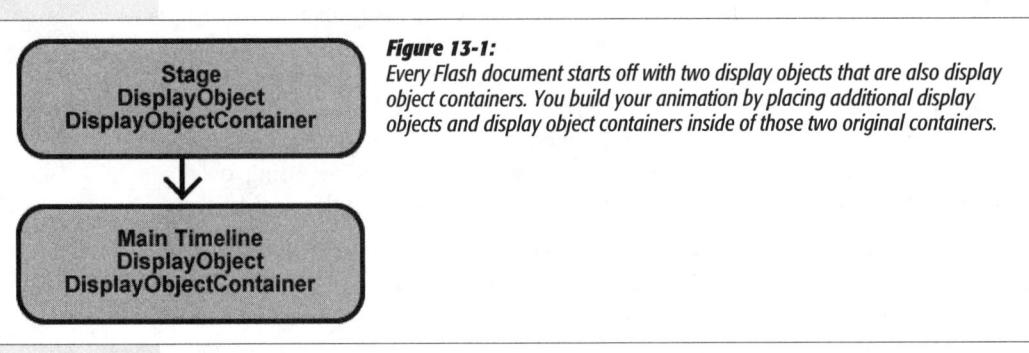

Figure 13-1:
Every Flash document starts off with two display objects that are also display object containers. You build your animation by placing additional display objects and display object containers inside of those two original containers.

Note: Technically, the main timeline for any .swf is referred to as the .swf's *main class instance*, but it's easier to think of it as the main timeline and that's what it's called in this chapter.

Now, suppose you place something on that stage. Perhaps you've already drawn a playing card and saved it as a movie clip in the Library. Drag that card from the Library onto the stage, and now you've got three display objects. The stage is a container holding the main timeline and the timeline is a container holding the playing card movie clip. Everything that appears in a Flash animation has to be in a container and ultimately, those containers are held in the main timeline, which is held in the stage. Objects that can hold or contain other objects are a special type of display object—they're *display object containers*. Objects that descend from the DisplayObjectContainer class have special properties and methods that are uniquely suited to acting as containers for display objects.

Note: If you're eager to see a list of some of DisplayObjectContainer's special properties and methods, go ahead and flip to page 468. If you'd like a gradual introduction, just keep on reading.

All display object containers are also display objects, but there are display objects that don't have the special properties of a display object container. For example a rectangle can't contain another object. You can group a rectangle with another object, but technically it doesn't contain another object. Table 13-1 shows which objects inherit properties from the DisplayObjectContainer class and which don't.

Table 13-1. Display objects that can hold or contain other objects inherit the special properties of the DisplayObjectContainer class.

DisplayObject and DisplayObjectContainer class	DisplayObject class only
Stage	Shape
Sprite	TextField
MovieClip	SimpleButton
Loader	Bitmap
	Video
	StaticText
	MorphShape (tween)

In practical terms, you won't spend a lot of time fretting over the stage and the main timeline as display objects or display object containers. They're always there. You can count on them being there. And there aren't many ways you can change them. If you're approaching ActionScript 3.0 with a Flash designer's background, you probably consider the act of placing something in the main timeline as "placing an object on the stage." On the other hand, you need to be aware of the properties and methods available when you're working with the movie clips, buttons, shapes, and text that you place on that stage.

Adding Objects to the Display List

Enough theory! It's time to back get to that empty stage and the task of displaying an object. The following exercises use a file called *playing_cards_begin.fla* that's available *on* the "Missing CD" page at *http://missingmanuals.com/cds*. Several of the examples in this chapter gradually add ActionScript code to this Flash document.

1. Select File → Open, and then browse to *playing_cards.fla.*

    When you open this document, there's nothing on the stage.

---

2. **If the Library isn't visible, go Window → Library to display it.**

   The Library holds seven movie clips. Five of the movie clips look like simple playing cards, and are named PlayingCard1 through PlayingCard5. No suits, just numbers. There are two simple rectangles that represent card tables: Green-CardTable and BlueCardTable.

3. **Open the Actions window (Window → Actions).**

   The Actions window appears without any code. If the Line Number option is turned on, you see the number 1 in the left margin. If line numbering isn't turned on, click the Options button in the upper-right corner, and then choose Line Numbers from the menu.

4. **In the ActionScript window, type in the following code:**

```
1    var card1:PlayingCard1 = new(PlayingCard1);
2    addChild(card1);
```

   The first line creates a new instance of the *PlayingCard1 class* and stores it in the variable *card1*. (If you want to learn more about how PlayingCard1 became a class, see "Making Library Objects Available to ActionScript" on page 447.) The second line adds card1 to the Display List.

5. **Press Ctrl+Enter (⌘-Return) to test your ActionScript code.**

   When the Flash Player runs, a single card with the number 1, appears in the upper left corner of the stage.

The second line of code shown in step 5 adds card1 to the Display List, making it visible on the stage, as shown in Figure 13-2. It's almost as if you dragged the card out of the Library. You may be wondering why the method for adding an object to the Display List is called "addChild." It has to do with the hierarchical relationship of displayed objects. (ActionScript just loves hierarchical relationships.) In the case of the Display List, an object contained in another object is considered a child of the container. The *addChild()* statement adds the card1 as a child to the main timeline DisplayObjectContainer.

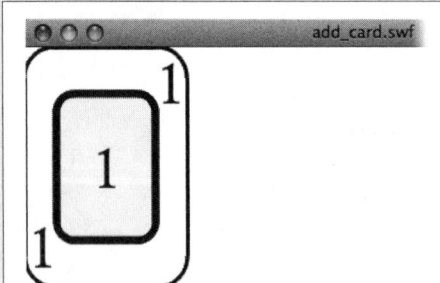

Figure 13-2:
When you add this playing card to the Display List using ActionScript, you'll see it on the stage when you preview the Flash document (Ctrl+Enter or ⌘-Return).

CODERS' CLINIC

Making Library Objects Available to ActionScript

In the exercises in this chapter, you use ActionScript to display instances of objects in the Library on the stage using ActionScript code. When you drag a symbol out of the Library, and then place it on the stage, Flash knows what object you're referring to because, well, you dragged it. ActionScript 3.0, on the other hand, only knows classes and objects. Every object has to derive from a class. In this chapter, the objects in your Library are movie clips, but that's not specific enough to distinguish one from the other. So, in the Flash documents created for this chapter, each of the movie clips in the Library are *classes* that *extend* the MovieClip class. In other words, they're custom classes derived from ActionScript's built-in MovieClip class.

It's not that hard to turn a movie clip symbol in the Library into a custom class that's accessible to ActionScript. In the Library, right-click the symbol's name, and then choose Properties

from the pop-up menu. The Symbol Properties dialog box opens with details about that particular symbol, as shown in Figure 13-3. Turn on the appropriately named Export for ActionScript checkbox, and then type in a class name for the new class you're creating in the Class text box. Immediately below the Class text box is the name of the base class. In the example shown in Figure 13-3, the PlayingCard1 class *extends* the MovieClip class. When you click OK, the Symbol Properties dialog box closes. Flash can't find an existing definition for the PlayingCard1 class, so it displays an alert mentioning the fact, but because a de facto definition exists in the Library, Flash can create a definition and place it in the *.swf*, which is what it does.

In the document *playing_cards.fla*, each of the cards and the card tables are custom classes created using this same technique.

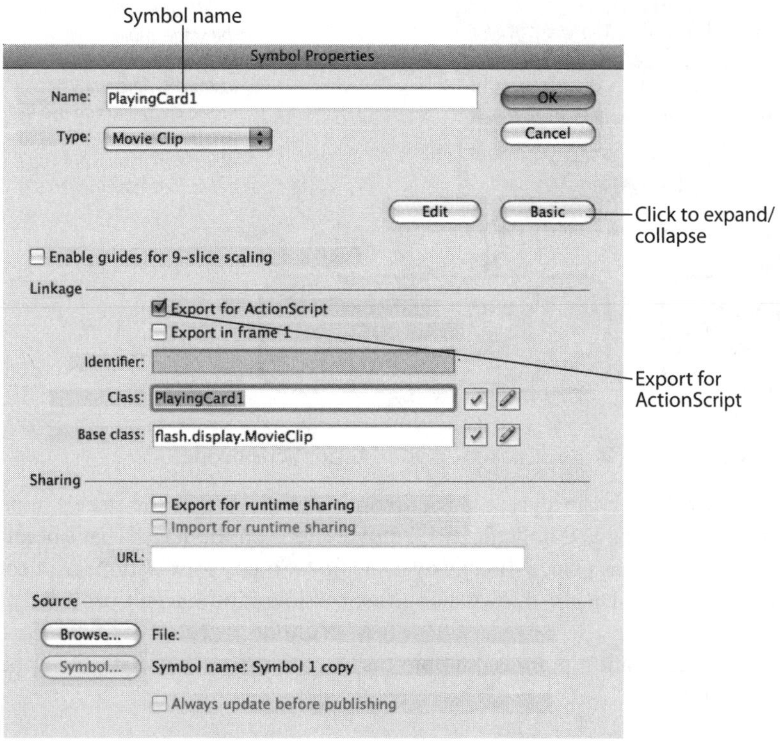

Figure 13-3:
Use the Symbol Properties dialog box to turn symbols into classes that you can access with ActionScript code. After turning on the Export for ActionScript checkbox, provide a name for the new class in the Class text box.

Adding a Second Object to the Display List

You can add a second card using the same two steps in your code. First create an instance of PlayingCard2 using the variable name card2. Then add card2 to the Display List using the *addChild( )* method. Here are the steps:

1. **Click at the end of line 1, and then press Enter or Return.**

   A blank line appears at line 2, pushing the previous contents of that line down to line 3.

2. **Type the following code into line 2:**

   ```
   var card2:PlayingCard2 = new(PlayingCard2);
   ```

3. **Click at the end of line 3, and then press Enter or Return.**

   An empty line appears at line 4.

4. **Type the following code into line 4:**

   ```
   addChild(card2);
   ```

   The main timeline now has two children, as shown in Figure 13-4.

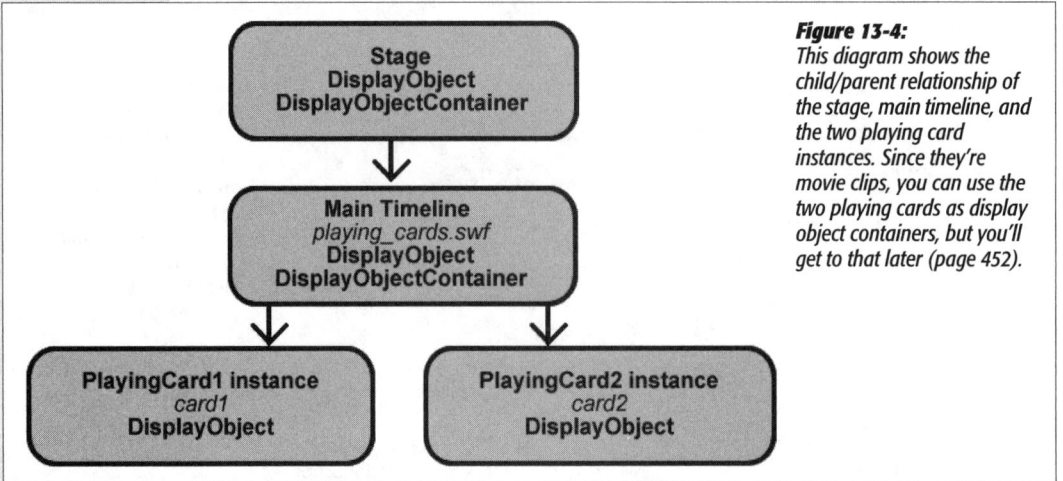

Figure 13-4:
This diagram shows the child/parent relationship of the stage, main timeline, and the two playing card instances. Since they're movie clips, you can use the two playing cards as display object containers, but you'll get to that later (page 452).

5. **Press Ctrl+Enter (⌘-Return) to test your ActionScript code.**

   When Flash Player runs, you see the second playing card in the stage's upper-left corner. It looks as if only the card2 movie clip is on the stage. That's because the second card was placed directly over the first. So far, your ActionScript code adds cards to the Display List, making them visible. You haven't provided any instructions about where to place the cards. Without instructions, ActionScript places the registration point of an object at 0, 0 on the stage—that's the upper-left corner.

6. **Click at the end of Line 2, and then press Enter or Return twice. Type the following code beginning on line 4:**

```
card2.x = 50;
card2.y = 50;
```

These lines reposition the card2 movie clip so it appears 50 pixels from the top and left margin.

7. **Press Ctrl+Enter (⌘-Return) to test your ActionScript code.**

This time when Flash Player shows your document, you see both cards (Figure 13-5). The first card movie clip you placed, card1, appears to be underneath card2.

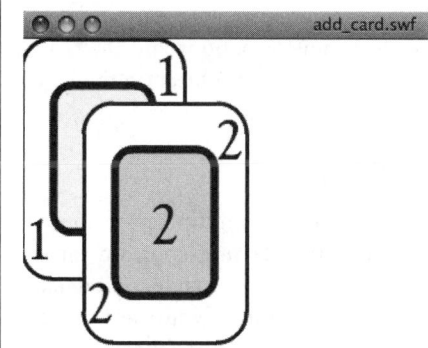

Figure 13-5:
The card2 movie clip is positioned using x/y coordinates. Because card1 was added to the Display List first, it appears beneath card2.

At this point the complete code for your project looks like this:

```
1    var card1:Card1 = new(Card1);
2    var card2:Card2 = new(Card2);
3
4    card2.x = 50;
5    card2.y = 50;
6
7    addChild(card1);
8    addChild(card2);
```

The empty lines at line 3 and 6 aren't necessary, they're there for housekeeping purposes only, making the code a little easier to read. The two middle lines (4 and 5) position the card2 movie clip on the stage. It's just as if you typed coordinates into the Properties panel. Now, when you test the animation, you see card1 peeking out from behind card2.

You can make a couple of interesting conclusions from the code. Display List factoids so far include:

- **Objects added to the Display List are placed on top of each other.** Just like cards dealt onto a card table, the second object you add to the Display List covers the first.

• **You can apply properties to an object before you display it.** In lines 4 and 5, you define the x/y coordinates for card2 before you display the card using the *addChild( )* method in line 8.

You can use both points to your advantage when you develop projects using ActionScript. Every visible object has a position index number (sometimes called the Z-order) that tracks its position (or depth) in the stack. No two objects in a container share the same position index number. When the way objects overlap is important, you can control their appearance by adding them to the Display List in a specific sequence. If you're thinking that's not always possible, don't worry—this chapter shows plenty of other ways to shuffle cards. Also, you can change the properties of objects before they're displayed. For example, you can set the x/y coordinates prior to displaying the card2 movie clip on the stage. You can work with an object in code without showing the object to your audience. You can set its position, change its dimensions and colors, and add transformations and filters without adding it to the Display List. When you finally place that object on the Display List, it's essentially preformatted.

Using *trace( )* to Report on the Display List

As mentioned on page 437, the *trace( )* statement is a multipurpose tool that ActionScript programmers use to double check their code and report on variables and objects. It never hurts to trace some of the objects in your code to understand how ActionScript sees them. A good first step is to place one of your cards inside of the trace statement's parentheses and see what shows up in the Output panel, as shown in Figure 13-6. Trace shows the following text: [object PlayingCard1]. From this you can deduce that the variable card1 is an object of the PlayingCard1 class.

```
trace(card1);
```

Helpful, but what happens if you check the name property for card1?

```
trace(card1.name);
```

The message that appears in the Output panel is: *instance1*. Not so helpful. If you don't specifically give names to objects as you add them to your ActionScript code, Flash names them for you, and you end up with names of the instance1 variety. So, the next step for the *playing_cards.fla* project is to modify your code a little and add names for both card1 and card2. (If you find the differences between class names, variable names, and the name property of an object a little confusing, see the box on page 451.) You can assign any string you want to the name property of card1 and card2, but there's no need to be *too* creative. Something like the following works just fine. Create a new line on line 2, and then add:

```
card1.name = "Card 1";
```

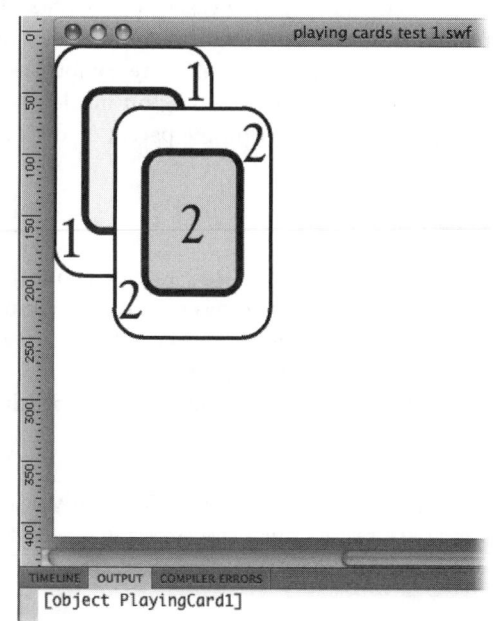

Figure 13-6:
Using the trace( ) *statement you can learn how ActionScript
views the objects and variables in your code. Here* trace( )
*reports that the variable card1 is an object of the PlayingCard1
class.*

CODERS' CLINIC

Naming Conventions and Your Sanity

In ActionScript, everything gets named. There are class
names, object names, variable names, and more. Sometimes, when you're up to your neck in code, you have one
of those can't see the forest for the trees moments. One of
the ways experienced coders tell class names apart from variable names is by the way they spell the names.

Flash gives you a fair amount of freedom in how you name
the classes that you create; however, it's a convention to use
an initial uppercase letter for class names like PlayingCard1.

It's also a convention to use an initial lowercase letter for
a variable name like card1. In this example, the names for
instances of cards are: Card 1, Card 2 and so on. (Class
names and variable names don't permit a space in the name,
but instance names do.) This makes the *trace( )* statements
a little more readable; plus it's different from the class and
variable names. Obviously, once you decide on a naming
convention, stick to it. It'll make your code easier to read and
understand.

Now the trace statements show the names of the objects in the Output panel.
Instead of getting "instance1" and so forth, you get "Card 1" and "Card 2." Much
better, but you can fashion your *trace( )* statements into something even more
helpful by adding some more explanatory text. Anything that appears in quotes in
a *trace( )* statement is displayed literally in the Output panel. If you write a statement like *trace("dog")* you see the word *dog* displayed in the Output panel. So you
can modify your *trace( )* statement a bit to make a descriptive sentence about your
card variables:

```
trace(card1.name, " is ", card1);
```

CHAPTER 13: ORGANIZING OBJECTS WITH THE DISPLAY LIST

This statement displays an "almost sentence" that's a little easier to understand: *Card 1 is [object PlayingCard1]*. Creating this statement might seem like a lot of unnecessary work at this point, but as your ActionScript becomes more complicated, statements like this are a big help in understanding what's going on inside your code. The next section, uses *trace( )* statements to report on the parent or display object containers that hold the cards.

Placing Objects Inside of Display Containers

So far, the code that adds the two cards to the Display List isn't specific about the container that holds the objects. When no specific container is identified, Action-Script places the object in the main timeline. As you might expect, if your card is referred to as a "child," the display object container holding the card is referred to as a parent. You can use the trace statement to show the name of the parent (the display object container) that holds your cards.

Note: If you look up the class description for DisplayObject in the ActionScript 3.0 Reference, you find that it has a property called *parent*. Every display object is held in a display object container, so every display object has a parent.

Add these lines to the end of the code in the Actions panel:

```
trace(card1.name, " is ", card1);
trace("The parent of ", card1.name," is ", card1.parent);
trace(card2.name, " is ", card2);
trace("The parent of ", card2.name," is ", card2.parent);
```

Placing *card1.parent* inside of the trace statement parentheses causes Flash to show the object class of the parent in the Output panel—in this case, MainTimeline. The Output panel displays the words in the quotation marks verbatim. You can include these words to make the output a little clearer for humans. As shown in Figure 13-7, both of the cards have the same parent, meaning they're both held in the same display object container.

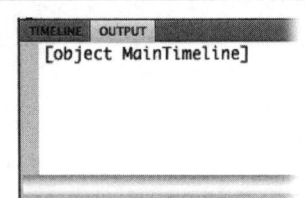

Figure 13-7:
The trace( ) *statement shows that the main timeline is the parent of both cards.* Trace( ) *is often used by programmers to make sure code is behaving as expected.*

Once your animations get more populated, you're likely to place display objects inside of other display object containers. To show that point, the next example adds a card table to the Display List. The card table is a movie clip, so it has all the properties and methods of the DisplayObjectContainer class. Using the *addChild( )*

---

method, you can move one of the cards into the card table display object container. Finally, you'll add some additional trace statements at the end of the code to gain more understanding about how the code works:

Follow these steps to update *playing_cards.fla.*

1. **Click at the end of line 4, and press Enter or Return.**

   A new empty line appears on line 5.

2. **Beginning on Line 5, type the following two lines of code:**

   ```
   var greenTable:GreenCardTable = new(GreenCardTable);
   greenTable.name = "Green Table";
   ```

   The first line creates a new variable, *greenTable*. It's an instance of the Green-CardTable symbol in the Library. (Think of it as one of those professional green felt card tables.) Press Enter or Return at the end of the first line to create a new line for the second. The second line changes the name property of this instance to "Green Table."

3. **Click at the end of line 10, and then press Enter or Return again.**

   A new empty line appears at line 11.

4. **At line 11, type the following line of code:**

   ```
   greenTable.x = 250;
   ```

   This code positions greenTable so that it's 250 pixels from the left margin. That way, it won't cover up the other items on the stage. You may want to add another empty line, just to keep things organized.

5. **Click the end of line 14, and then press Enter or Return.**

   A new empty line appears at line 15.

6. **Beginning on line 15, type the following two lines of code.**

   ```
   addChild(greenTable);
   greenTable.addChild(card2);
   ```

   The *addChild( )* method in the first line adds greenTable to the Display List. No parent is designated, so greenTable is in the main timeline. In the second line, you're using the *addChild( )* method a little differently than in the previous examples. Since you're running it specifically as a method of greenTable, *addChild( )* adds card2 to the Display List as a child of greenTable. In other words, greenTable is a display object container that holds card2. Figure 13-8 shows a diagram of the relationships between the objects on the stage.

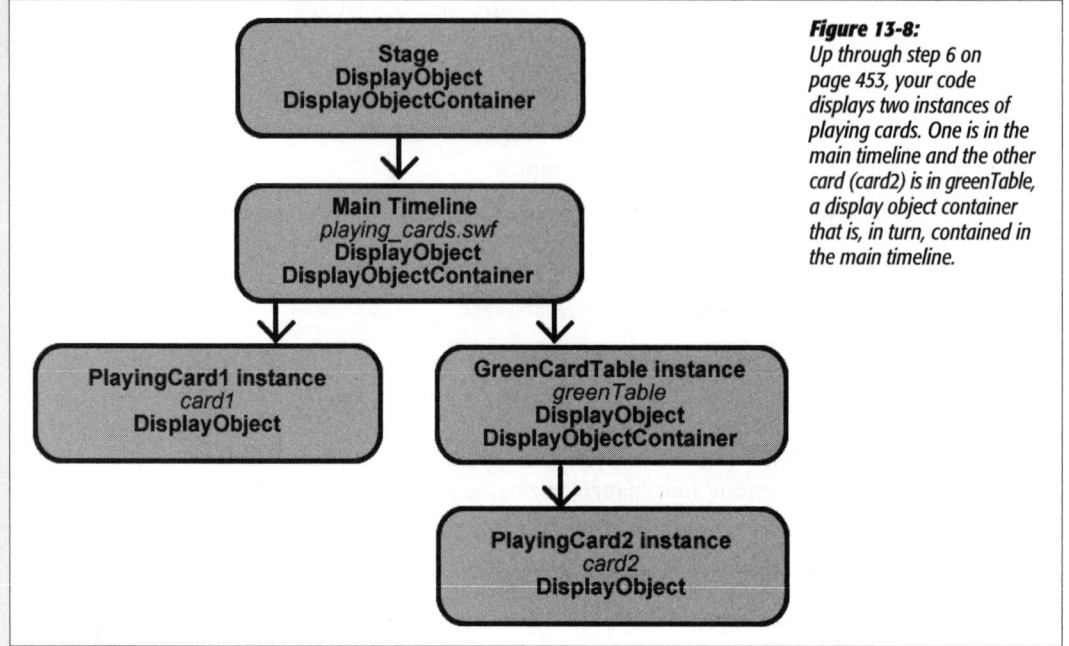

Figure 13-8:
*Up through step 6 on
page 453, your code
displays two instances of
playing cards. One is in the
main timeline and the other
card (card2) is in greenTable,
a display object container
that is, in turn, contained in
the main timeline.*

7. Beginning on line 18, update the trace statements to match the following code:

```
trace(card1.name, "is", card1);
trace("The parent of", card1.name,"is", card1.parent);
trace(card2.name, "is", card2);
trace("The parent of", card2.name,"is", card2.parent.name);
trace(greenTable.name, "is", greenTable);
trace("The parent of", greenTable.name, "is", greenTable.parent);
```

8. Press Ctrl+Enter (⌘-Return) to test your animation.

   When you test the code, the display looks like Figure 13-9. In the Output tab,
   you see that now the parent of card2 is of the Green Table. The parent of Green
   Table is an object of the MainTimeline class.

   The complete text in the Output panel reads:

   Card 1 is [object PlayingCard1]

   The parent of Card 1 is [object MainTimeline]

   Card 2 is [object PlayingCard2]

   The parent of Card 2 is Green Table

   Green Table is [object GreenCardTable]

   The parent of Green Table is [object MainTimeline]

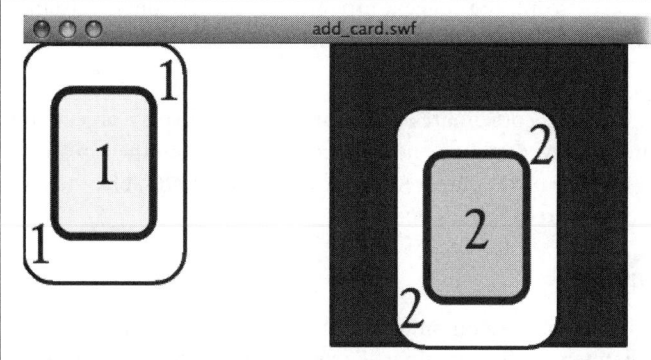

Figure 13-9:
After you add card2 to the Display List as a child of greenTable, it appears in its container. Now that it's a container, card2's x/y coordinates use greenTable (not the stage) as a reference point. The card is placed 50 pixels from the left edge and 50 pixels from the top of greenTable's borders.

If you've been following the examples in this chapter and adding code along with the step-by-step instructions, your code looks like this:

```
1    var card1:PlayingCard1 = new(PlayingCard1);
2    card1.name = "Card 1";
3    var card2:PlayingCard2 = new(PlayingCard2);
4    card2.name = "Card 2";
5    var greenTable:GreenCardTable = new(GreenCardTable);
6    greenTable.name = "Green Table";
7
8    card2.x = 50;
9    card2.y = 50;
10
11   greenTable.x = 250;
12
13   addChild(card1);
14   addChild(card2);
15   addChild(greenTable);
16   greenTable.addChild(card2);
17
18   trace(card1.name, "is", card1);
19   trace("The parent of", card1.name,"is", card1.parent);
20   trace(card2.name, "is", card2);
21   trace("The parent of", card2.name,"is", card2.parent.name);
22   trace(greenTable.name, "is", greenTable);
23   trace("The parent of", greenTable.name, "is", greenTable.parent);
```

The main thing the new code does is create and display a new display object container—the greenTable movie clip instance. A new *addChild( )* statement places card2 inside greenTable. If you're keeping track of interesting Display List factoids, here are some more for you:

- **You can move display objects from one display object container to another with the *addChild( )* statement.** There are two *addChild( )* statements related to card2 in the code on lines 14 and 16. The second *addChild(card2)* statement (line 16) moves card2 from the stage onto greenTable. A single instance, like card2, can only appear in one place at a time, so the latter statement takes precedence.

- **A display object's position coordinates are relative to the display object container that holds it.** Initially, card2 was positioned 50 pixels from the top and 50 pixels from the left border of the stage. After moving it to greenTable, the code displays card2 relative to greenTable's borders.

Modifying display containers

The objects inside a display object container are pretty much at the mercy of any transformations that happen to the container. For example, suppose you move or scale the width of greenTable, while card2 is contained within it? Those changes and transformations affect card2, since it's a child of greenTable. You can test this process by inserting these lines into your code beginning on line 12.

```
greenTable.y = 75;
greenTable.scaleX = 1.5;
```

The first line moves greenTable down from the top margin 75 pixels. The second line scales the display object container, greenTable, making it one and one half its original width. When you test the code after these changes, you see that both the move and the transformation affect card2 as well as greenTable (Figure 13-10). It's interesting to note that it doesn't matter whether the code places card2 in the greenTable container before or after transforming the table: card2 is transformed in either case.

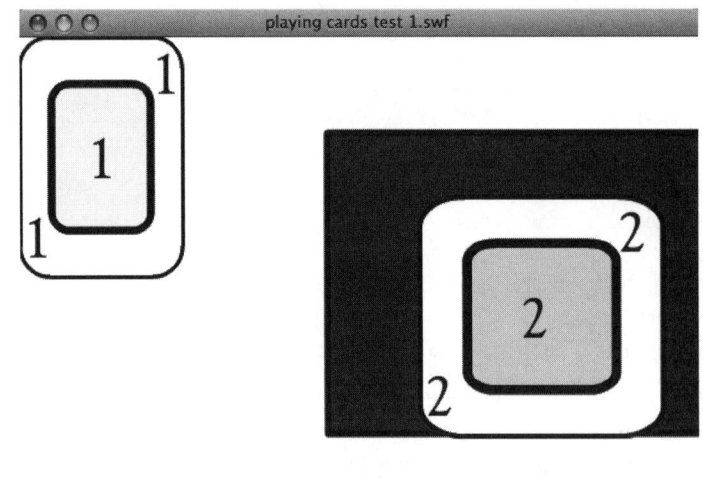

Figure 13-10:
As discussed in "Modifying display containers" on page 456, the transform statement that scales greenTable also scales the card inside it.

Moving Objects from One Container to Another

It's not unusual for a Flash animation to have more than one container, and you'll often want to move display objects from one container to another, just as you'd move a document from one folder to another on your computer. The following updated ActionScript code expands on the cards and card table theme. It adds a second table to the stage (blue this time). It then places card1 on the new, blue table. *Trace( )* statements at the end of the code report on Blue Table.

```
1    var card1:PlayingCard1 = new(PlayingCard1);
2    card1.name = "Card 1";
3    var card2:PlayingCard2 = new(PlayingCard2);
4    card2.name = "Card 2";
5    var greenTable:GreenCardTable = new(GreenCardTable);
6    greenTable.name = "Green Table";
7    var blueTable:BlueCardTable = new(BlueCardTable);
8    blueTable.name = "Blue Table";
9
10   card2.x = 50;
11   card2.y = 50;
12
13   greenTable.x = 250;
14   greenTable.y = 75;
15   greenTable.scaleX = 1.5;
16
17   addChild(card1);
18   addChild(card2);
19   addChild(greenTable);
20   addChild(blueTable);
21   greenTable.addChild(card2);
22   blueTable.addChild(card1);
23
24   trace(card1.name, "is", card1);
25   trace("The parent of", card1.name,"is", card1.parent);
26   trace(card2.name, "is", card2);
27   trace("The parent of", card2.name,"is", card2.parent.name);
28   trace(greenTable.name, "is", greenTable);
29   trace("The parent of", greenTable.name, "is", greenTable.parent);
30   trace(blueTable.name, "is", blueTable);
31   trace("The parent of", blueTable.name, "is", blueTable.parent);
```

The lines that add blueTable (lines 7-8), and then place card1 inside of the blueTable display object container (line 22) are nearly identical to the code used for greenTable (page 453). When you test the code, Flash Player displays it, as shown in Figure 13-11.

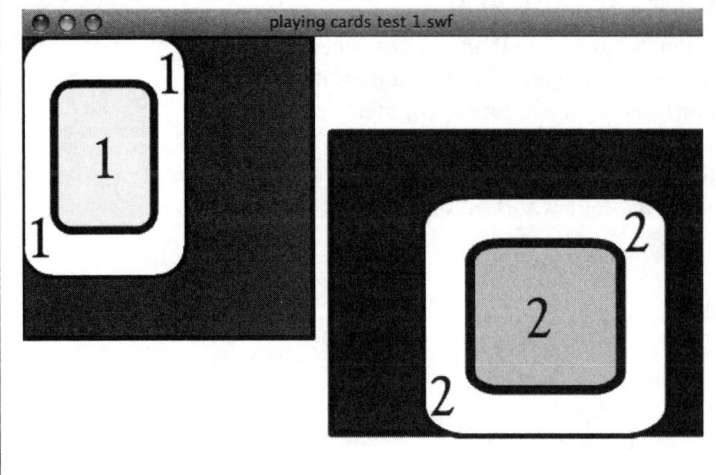

Figure 13-11:
In the code on page 457, there are two display object containers representing tables, with cards in them. A scaleX( ) method transforms the green table (right). The transformation affects both the table and the card in the table.

So, at this point you have two tables and two cards. One of the tables is distorted a bit by scaling. Suppose you want to move a card from one table to another. That would be a good job for a mouse click. You can add an event listener to the blue table that waits for a mouse click, and then moves card2 from the green table to the blue table. Here's the code for the event listener and the function that runs on a mouse click. You can insert this code so it begins on line 24:

```
blueTable.addEventListener(MouseEvent.CLICK, clickTableListener);

function clickTableListener(evt:MouseEvent):void {
    blueTable.addChild(card2);
}
```

Now when you test *playing_cards.fla*, you first see the blue table with card1 and the green table with card2. If you click the blue table, card2 moves to the green table. It works as planned, but it's kind of a one shot deal and pretty dull. One click, and the fun is over. It would be more exciting if you could click either table to make card2 jump over to that table. It's not hard to modify the event listener to do the job. In fact, the MouseEvent class has a special property—called *target*—that identifies the object that's clicked.

As explained in Chapter 12, this process involves a listened-for event and an event object. Like any object, the event object has properties, one of which is *target*. This property stores the name of the object that initiates the event. In this case, blueTable initiated the event, so it's the target. To modify the code so card2 jumps to whichever table is clicked, you need to modify the *clickTableListener( )* function so it identifies the clicked target object. Then you need to add an event listener to greenTable.

Here are the changes you need to make to the code:

```
blueTable.addEventListener(MouseEvent.CLICK, clickTableListener);
greenTable.addEventListener(MouseEvent.CLICK, clickTableListener);

function clickTableListener(evt:MouseEvent):void {
    evt.target.addChild(card2);
}
```

Remember, *evt* is the variable name that identifies the MouseEvent in *clickTableListerner( )*. Like any variable, the actual name is up to you. It could be *event* or simply the letter *e*. The property *target* identifies the object that triggered the event. With the modified code, either of the tables can listen for the click event. There's nothing in the *clickTableListener( )* function that's specific to either the blue or the green table, so it behaves relative to the container that's clicked. When you test the animation, card2 moves to the table you click. If it's already on the table you're clicking, nothing happens.

Now that a display object (card2) is shuffling around between display object containers (greenTable and blueTable) it makes the *trace( )* statements that report on parent and child relationships a little more interesting. Unfortunately, the trace statements only run once, and they don't provide any updates when the *clickTableListener( )* function runs. One solution would be to copy and paste all the *trace( )* statements so they're inside the *clickTableListener( )* function's brackets, but that adds a lot of extra lines to your code. For a more elegant solution, you can turn all of the trace statements into a single function, and then simply call that function whenever you need it.

Turning the *trace( )* statements into a single function is relatively easy. Create a line that defines the function with the keyword *function*, and a name you supply, like *traceDisplayList*. Place all the trace statements inside the curly brackets that hold the function's code. When you're done, it looks like the following. The bold line at the top and the bold curly bracket at the bottom are the only changes:

```
function traceDisplayList( ):void {
trace(card1.name, "is", card1);
trace("The parent of", card1.name,"is", card1.parent);
trace(card2.name, "is", card2);
trace("The parent of", card2.name,"is", card2.parent.name);
trace(greenTable.name, "is", greenTable);
trace("The parent of", greenTable.name, "is", greenTable.parent);
trace(blueTable.name, "is", blueTable);
trace("The parent of", blueTable.name, "is", blueTable.parent);
}
```

Throughout this chapter, you've added *trace( )* statements as the code developed and grew. If, as you're working, you want to add more *trace( )* statements, just place the new lines inside the curly brackets. They'll run with the other statements whenever you code calls *traceDisplayList( )*.

Note: There are more details about creating functions and methods on page 392.

Now, to show the results of the *trace( )* statements in the Output window you need only one line of code:

```
traceDisplayList();
```

For example, if you add this line to the *clickTableListener( )*, every time someone clicks one of the tables, the Output panel shows all of the *trace( )* statements. Here's the *clickTableListener( )* code with the call to *traceDisplayList( )* included:

```
function clickTableListener(evt:MouseEvent):void {
    evt.target.addChild(card2);
    traceDisplayList();
}
```

Test *playing_cards.fla* now with Ctrl+Enter (⌘-Return), and card2 jumps to whichever table you click. Keep an eye on the Output panel, and you see that the card2's parent is updated with each click.

Removing Objects from the Display List

The statement that removes a display object from the Display List is pleasingly consistent with the statement that adds objects. It looks like this:

```
displayObjectContainer.removeChild(child);
```

So, if you want to remove card1 from the blue table, you write:

```
blueTable.removeChild(card1);
```

If you don't specifically define the display object container, Flash assumes that you're referring to the main timeline. That's the same assumption it makes with the *addChild( )* statement. For example, if you want to remove the blue table, you write:

```
removeChild(blueTable);
```

That removes blueTable from the main timeline. If blueTable is a display object container holding other objects, those contained objects also get removed. Everything from the container on down disappears from view. If blueTable isn't contained in the main timeline—if it's contained in another display object container, for example—the code won't find it and won't remove it.

The previous section explained how to use a MouseEvent to move a card from one table to another. That code used the *target* property to identify the table that was clicked. To remove a card from the Display List when it's clicked, you need to identify both the target (card1) and the target's parent (blueTable). It may look a little convoluted, but the code that does the trick looks like this:

```
evt.target.parent.removeChild(evt.target);
```

Here's how that statement works, moving from left to right. As explained in the previous section, *evt.target* identifies the object that was clicked, initiating the event. By tacking the *.parent* on to that, you identify the container of the object that was clicked. That's all you need to invoke the *removeChild( )* method. Remember, *removeChild( )* is a method of the display object container. Because the child you want to remove is the object that was clicked, you can place *evt.target* inside of the parentheses of the *removeChild( )* statement.

Here's the event listener for card1, with a call to run *traceDisplayList( )* at the end of the function:

```
card1.addEventListener(MouseEvent.CLICK, clickCardListener);

function clickCardListener(evt:MouseEvent): void {
    evt.target.parent.removeChild(evt.target);
    traceDisplayList( );
}
```

As you see, there's nothing in the function *clickCardListener( )* that mentions card1. It simply identifies the target that was clicked and the container of that target. So, it's easy to add an event listener to card2, so that it works in exactly the same manner and removes card2 from the Display List.

Note: Removing display objects from the Display List, removes them from the main timeline and the stage, but it doesn't remove them from memory. As your programs increase in both size and their demands on computer resources, it becomes important to remove them from memory when they're no longer needed.

It may not be the most entertaining card game in the world, but at this point when you test *playing_cards.fla,* it performs two basic card tricks.

- Click one of the tables, and card2 jumps to that table, if it's not there already.

- Clicking card1 removes the card from the Display List.

In the next section, you'll learn how to stack the deck the ActionScript way.

Managing the Stacking Order

As mentioned earlier, when you add display objects to the Display List, it's like laying cards on a card table. The first card appears on the table, and the next card is placed on top of it (Figure 13-12). Each card placed on the table is at a specific position in the stack. Like a lot of programming lists, the Display List position index begins at 0. So the first object placed in a display object container is at position 0. The second object is placed at position 1, and so forth. The position is known as the *index,* and it's represented by a number that's an *int* type (integer). As the display objects in your Flash animation become more numerous, it's harder to keep track of them. There are times where it might be easier for you, the ActionScripter,

---

to identify an object by its position in the stack rather than by its instance name. For example, you might have a card game where you want to deal the top five cards in the deck. In this case, the cards' names don't matter as much as their position in the deck.

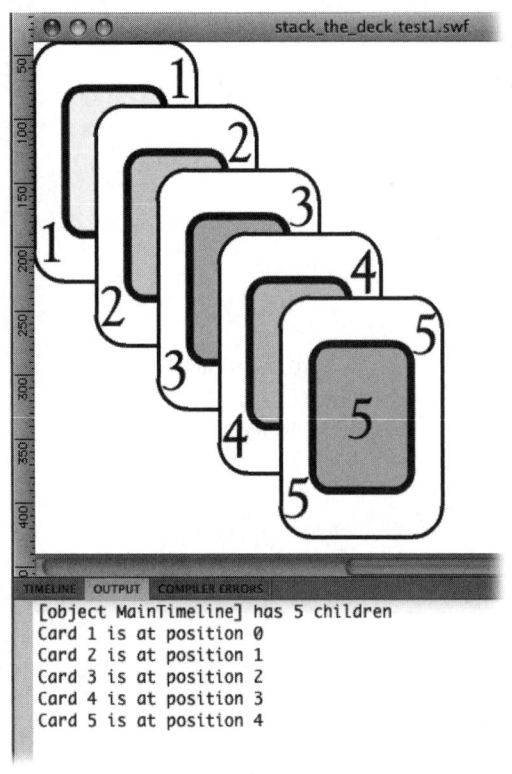

Figure 13-12:
The code in the box on page 467 places cards on the main timeline display object container. Card 1 was placed first, then Card 2 and so forth. Trace statements show that Card 1 is at position 0, Card 2 is at position 1 and so forth.

```
[object MainTimeline] has 5 children
Card 1 is at position 0
Card 2 is at position 1
Card 3 is at position 2
Card 4 is at position 3
Card 5 is at position 4
```

Adding Display Objects by Index Position

Just as display object containers have methods for working with child display objects by name, they have other methods for working with them by their index. For example, when you used the *addChild( )* method earlier in this chapter, it looked like this:

```
greenTable.addChild(card1);
```

This statement adds the display object *card1* to the display object container *greenTable*. Suppose there were already five cards on greenTable, and you want to place card1 in the second from the bottom position. You use the *addChildAt( )* method:

```
greenTable.addChildAt(card1, 1);
```

The *addChildAt( )* method needs two parameters to work: the variable name of the display object (card1) and the index position (1). Because the position index starts with 0 at the bottom, you use the *int* 1 to place the card in the second position from the bottom.

The Flash document *stack_the_deck.fla* (on the "Missing CD" page at *http://missingmanuals.com/cds*) shows this example. The code below is similar to the previous examples in this chapter. Here's a rundown on how the code works:

- The lines with double slashes (//) are comments; they have no effect on the way the program runs.

- Lines 3 through 12 create and name instances of playing cards that were previously drawn and stored in the Library.

- Lines 15 through 22 set the x/y properties (on the stage) for card2 through card5. You can set properties for display objects before they're added to the Display List. The cards overlap each other, so that their stacking order is easily understood.

- Lines 25 through 28 add card2 through card5 to the Display List using the *addChild( )* method. This way, each new display object gets placed on top of the previous one. As the code adds them, it gives each card a position index: card2 index = 0, card3 index = 1, card4 index = 2, card5 index = 3. Because no display object container is explicitly defined, it places the display objects in the main timeline.

- Line 31 adds card1 to the Display List at index position 1, using the *addChildAt( )* method. No x/y coordinates are used to position card1 on the stage, so it's automatically positioned at 0,0. When card1 is added at index position 1, any card at or above that index gets bumped up by one, to make room for the new card. No two cards (DisplayObjects) can have the same index in the main timeline (DisplayObjectContainer).

- Lines 36 through 43 make up the *traceDisplayList( )* function.

- Line 37 uses *card1.parent* to identify the display object container holding card1; that is the main timeline. The statement also uses the numChildren property to display a value showing the number of children held in the display object container.

- Lines 38 through 42 report on the index value for each of the cards displayed using the *getChildIndex( )* method of the DisplayPropertyContainer.

```
1    // Create and name instances of PlayingCard symbols
2    // Previously drawn, PlayingCard symbols are stored in the Library
3    var card1:PlayingCard1 = new(PlayingCard1);
4    card1.name = "Card 1";
5    var card2:PlayingCard2 = new(PlayingCard2);
6    card2.name = "Card 2";
7    var card3:PlayingCard3 = new(PlayingCard3);
8    card3.name = "Card 3";
```

```
9    var card4:PlayingCard4 = new(PlayingCard4);
10   card4.name = "Card 4";
11   var card5:PlayingCard5 = new(PlayingCard5);
12   card5.name = "Card 5";
13
14   // Places cards on the screen so an added card shows its index position
15   card2.x = 50;
16   card2.y = 0;
17   card3.x = 50;
18   card3.y = 50;
19   card4.x = 50;
20   card4.y = 100;
21   card5.x = 50;
22   card5.y = 150;
23
24   // Place card2 through card5 on the stage
25   addChild(card2);
26   addChild(card3);
27   addChild(card4);
28   addChild(card5);
29
30   // Insert card1 at a specific index position
31   addChildAt(card1,1);
32
33   traceDisplayList();
34
35   // Function used to show Display List details in Flash's Output panel
36   function traceDisplayList() {
37       trace(card1.parent,"has", numChildren,"children");
38       trace(card1.name, "is at index position",getChildIndex(card1));
39       trace(card2.name, "is at index position",getChildIndex(card2));
40       trace(card3.name, "is at index position",getChildIndex(card3));
41       trace(card4.name, "is at index position",getChildIndex(card4));
42       trace(card5.name, "is at index position",getChildIndex(card5));
43   }
```

Test *stack_the_deck.fla,* and you see a Flash stage that looks like Figure 13-13. The
Output panel shows a report on the number of display objects in the main timeline and the index position of each card:

> [object MainTimeline] has 5 children
>
> Card 1 is at index position 1
>
> Card 2 is at index position 0
>
> Card 3 is at index position 2
>
> Card 4 is at index position 3
>
> Card 5 is at index position 4

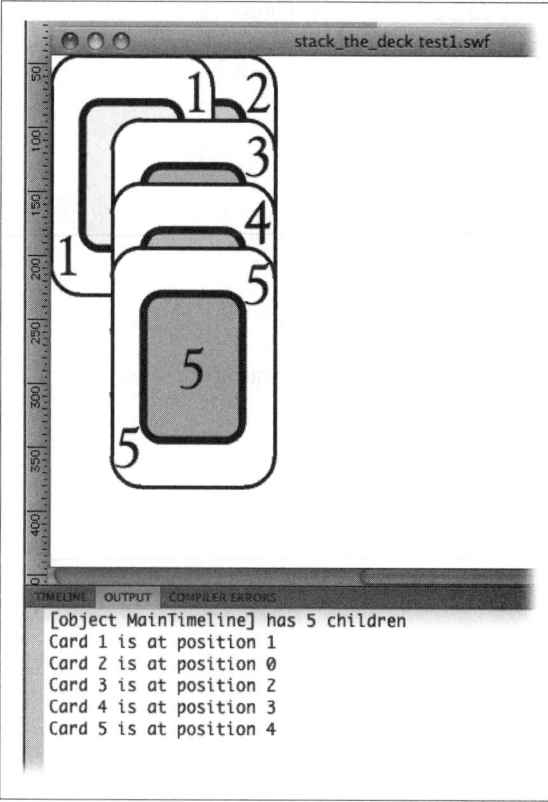

Figure 13-13:
Using the method addChildAt(card1,1) *places card1 at
the second index position, because the position index
begins counting at 0. For the full code that creates this
stack_the_deck.fla animation, see page 463.*

```
[object MainTimeline] has 5 children
Card 1 is at position 1
Card 2 is at position 0
Card 3 is at position 2
Card 4 is at position 3
Card 5 is at position 4
```

You can experiment with the code by changing the index number in line 31. As a
result, you see card1 at different levels in the pile and the Output panel reports a
different index position.

Removing Display Objects by Index Position

Display object containers have a method for removing the display objects they
hold by referencing their index position. You don't need to mention the variable
name, just identify the index position by number. You can give the method a try-
out in *stack_the_deck.fla*. At line 32, insert a line with this statement:

```
removeChildAt(0);
```

This statement removes card2, the first card that was placed in the main timeline.
Comment out the line with the *trace( )* statements for card2, so it won't produce
an error by placing two slashes in front of the front of the line so that it looks like
this:

```
//trace(card2.name, "is at index position",getChildIndex(card2));
```

Test the code, and you find that card2 isn't displayed (Figure 13-14), and the index position numbers for all of the cards have changed:

[object MainTimeline] has 4 children

Card 1 is at index position 0

Card 3 is at index position 1

Card 4 is at index position 2

Card 5 is at index position 3

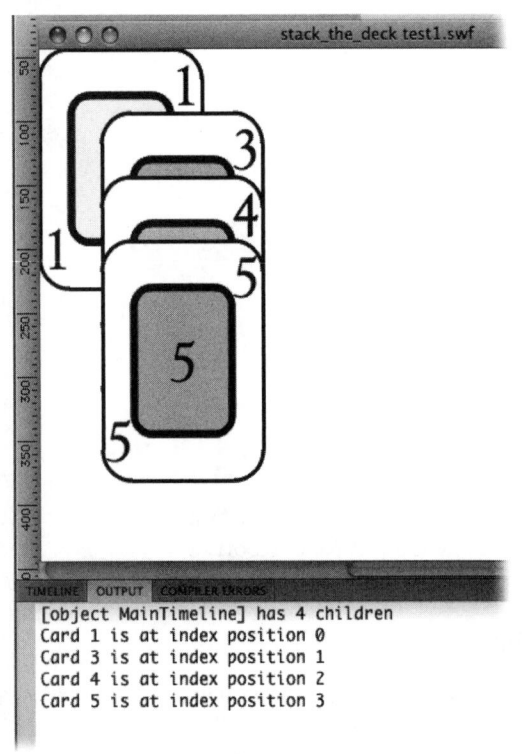

Figure 13-14:
In this example, card2 was removed from the display, so only four cards are displayed.

```
[object MainTimeline] has 4 children
Card 1 is at index position 0
Card 3 is at index position 1
Card 4 is at index position 2
Card 5 is at index position 3
```

Getting the Name or Index Position of a Display Object

A major part of the battle in writing ActionScript code is identifying a particular object that you want to change or manipulate. Display object containers give you two ways to identify the objects that they hold: You can identify them either by their variable name or by the index position. If you have either the name or the index, the DisplayObjectContainer will provide the other descriptor. For example, greenTable is a display object container holding several cards. You can get the index for card1 with a statement like this:

```
greenTable.getChildIndex(card1);
```

Attacking it from the other direction, if greenTable is a display object container holding several cards and you want to know the name of a card at a specific index position, you can use a command like this:

```
greenTable.getChildAt(2).name;
```

In *stack_the_deck.fla*, the *getChildIndex( )* method is used in the *trace( )* statements to report on the index position of the various cards. It may be a little redundant, but you can add statements using the *getChildAt( )* method to display the names of display objects at different index levels. To do so, add these lines before the last curly brace of the traceDisplayList function:

```
trace("The name of the object at index position 0 is",getChildAt(0).name);
trace("The name of the object at index position 1 is",getChildAt(1).name);
trace("The name of the object at index position 2 is",getChildAt(2).name);
trace("The name of the object at index position 3 is",getChildAt(3).name);
```

CODERS' CLINIC

Using a While Loop to Eliminate Repetitive Code

In this chapter, you see lots of nearly identical statements grouped together, like the *trace( )* statements in the example above. The examples in this book use this method to clarify how the code works. There's nothing wrong with these statements and they produce fine results. But, when you see repetitive code like that, it's important to know that there's almost always a more elegant way to handle the job. Usually a *while* or a *for* loop (page 404) will do the trick. For example, you can replace the code above with the following:

```
var positionIndex:int = 0;
while (positionIndex < numChildren) {
    trace("The name of the object at
index position", positionIndex, "is",
getChildAt(positionIndex).name);
    positionIndex++;
}
```

The first line creates a variable named *positionIndex* of type *int* and stores the value 0 in it. The next line starts a *while* loop. It says "while positionIndex is less than the number of children in the display object container, run the code between the curly brackets." There are two statements in between the curly brackets. The first is a *trace( )* statement that uses

positionIndex to identify a child of the display object container. The first time positionIndex is used, it displays a number and the second time it's the index for a *getChildAt( )* method. The second and last statement before the curly bracket increments the positionIndex. So, on the first trip through the loop, positionIndex starts with a value of 0 and ends with a value of 1. The loop continues to run until the value of positionIndex is greater than or equal to the number of children in the display object container. If you replace the *trace( )* statements above with this *while* loop, the lines displayed in the Output panel are identical. They look like this:

```
The name of the object at index position
0 is Card 1
The name of the object at index position
1 is Card 3
The name of the object at index position
2 is Card 4
The name of the object at index position
3 is Card 5
```

One major advantage that this *while* loop has over the more literal code is that it works no matter how many children are held in the display object container. You don't have to know in advance (and write specific code) for each child.

Swapping the Position of Two Children

If you're into multitasking, you'll be glad to know can reposition two display objects at once using the *swapChildren( )* or the *swapChildrenAt( )* methods. As you might anticipate at this point, the *swapChildren( )* method uses the variable names of the child display objects, while the *swapChildrenAt( )* method uses the index positions.

Going back to the tried and true green card table, here are a couple of examples that show how to swap the positions of two child display objects. The following code swaps positions using variable names of the children:

```
greenTable.swapChildren(card1, card4);
```

To swap children by referencing their position index, you provide an *int* value, like this:

```
greenTable.swapChildrenAt(0,3);
```

Swapping children makes a pretty good mouse click event. You can try it by adding the following lines to the code in *stack_the_deck.fla*. Adding the *traceDisplayList( )* function to *clickSwapListener( )* updates the Output panel after the swap has taken place:

```
card1.addEventListener(MouseEvent.CLICK, clickSwapListener);

function clickSwapListener(evt:MouseEvent):void {
    swapChildrenAt(0,3);
     traceDisplayList( );
}
```

Test *stack_the_deck.fla* after you've added the event listener, and you find a little interactivity in the animation. Click card1, and it swaps position with the card at index position 3. (If there are four cards in your deck, that means the card at the top and the card at the bottom swap positions.) Click card1 again, and they move back to their original positions. The *trace( )* statements send updated reports to the Output panel.

Summary of Properties and Methods

This section gives you a summary of the properties and methods covered in this chapter. This list isn't exhaustive, but it includes some of the handiest and most frequently used tools. You can find a complete list in the Flash CS4 help files: Help → Flash Help → ActionScript 3.0 and Components → ActionScript 3.0 Language and Components Reference. Look for the DisplayObjectContainer class, and then scroll down to find the properties and methods. If you see a method and want more details about it, click its name.

DisplayObjectContainer Properties

All display object containers are also descendants of the DisplayObject type. They have all the properties you'd expect in a displayable object, like x/y position coordinates, height, and width. In addition, they have a few properties that are particularly useful in their role as containers. The summary below lists the name of the property in bold, followed by a description, explaining the characteristics of the property and a few details about its use. The formal description is the description found in Adobe's ActionScript 3.0 Reference. It lists the property name, and then on the right side of the colon it shows the data type that's stored in the property. The formal description is helpful, but a little abstract, so this list also has an example, which is a little more concrete and follows the card table and card theme used throughout this chapter. The examples show how you'd use the property assuming that the display object container is an instance of a movie clip named greenTable.

- **name.** You can assign a name to a display object container using the *name* property. You can use just about anything for a name. In the examples in this book, the *name* property was used with the *trace( )* statement. Be careful not to confuse the *name* property with variable names or class names. See page 451 for more details about the *name* property.

  Formal Description: name: String

  Example: greenTable.name

- **numChildren.** A property that keeps track of the number of children in a display object container. The value is an *int* data type. This value is helpful when you're writing routines that identify specific child objects in a container. If you use numChildren along with the position index of the children, keep in mind that the index begins its count a 0, while numChildren starts its count at 1. See page 463, for an example that uses the numChildren property.

  Formal Description: numChildren: int

  Example: greenTable.numChildren

- **parent.** Display object containers can have parents, too. Use the parent property to show the parent of the display object container, which has to also be a DisplayObjectContainer type. When you work with the Display List, the methods used most are those that belong to the display object container. Often the easiest way to identify the display object container is with the *parent* property. See page 452, for more details about the *parent* property.

  Formal Description: parent: DisplayObjectContainer

  Example: card1.parent In this example, if *card1* is a display object held in the display object container *greenTable*, the result identifies *greenTable* as the parent.

DisplayObjectContainer Methods

When you work with the Display List, you're working with the methods of display object containers. Methods like *addChild( )* and *removeChild( )* are indispensable. The summary list below is made up of three parts. The first part shows the name of the method in bold, and then gives a description, explaining what the method does, and the result or value that comes from the method. There may also be a page reference pointing you to a place in this chapter that provides more details about the method and related issues.

The second part of the summary shows the formal description of the method as provided by Adobe in the help system's *ActionScript 3.0 Language and Components Reference.* From left to right, the formal description begins with the method name, and then in parentheses shows the parameters required by the method. Parameters include a descriptive word on one side of the colon and the data type on the other side of the colon. Some methods have more than one parameter. On the right side of the parentheses is another colon and a word that describes the data type or class that the method returns. The formal description is somewhat abstract. The examples at the end of each summary are more concrete, showing you how you'd write a statement using the method. The examples continue using the card table and card theme used in this chapter. The assumption is that the display object container in the example is an instance of a movie clip named greenTable. The display object is an instance of a movie clip named "card1." Where a *name* property is used, card1 has a *name* property of "Card 1."

- **addChild( ).** Adds a display object to the Display List using the variable name of the display object. Adding a display object to the Display List makes it visible in the animation. The display object is added as a child of the display object container, and then placed on the top of the visual stack, giving it the highest position index number. See page 446 for more details about the *addChild( )* method.

  Formal description: addChild(child:DisplayObject): DisplayObject

  Example: greenTable.addChild(card1);

- **addChildAt( ).** Adds a display object to the Display List using the variable name of the child and a specified index position. The child is positioned at the exact index included in the method parameters. Objects already on the Display List at that index level or above are bumped up by one. The position index doesn't permit empty spots. So, for example, if a display object container only has four children and you attempt to add a new child at position index 7, your animation won't run and you see an error message with the words "The supplied index is out of bounds." For more examples using the *addChildAt* method, see page 462.

  Formal description: addChildAt(child:DisplayObject, index:int)

  Example: greenTable.addChildAt(card1,3);

- **contains( ).** Determines whether a display object is held in a DisplayContainer-Object. The result is true if the display object is in the display object container.

  Formal description: contains(child:DisplayObject):Boolean

  Example: greenTable.contains(card1);

- **getChildAt( ).** Returns the child display object instance at a particular position index. After identifying the instance you can use the properties and methods of the object. See page 466 for more details.

  Formal description: getChildAt(index:int):DisplayObject

  Example: greenTable.getChildAt(3);

- **getChildByName( ).** Returns the child display object by identifying the *name* property. After identifying the instance, you can use the properties and methods of the object.

  Formal description: getChildByName(name:String):DisplayObject

  Example: greenTable.getChildByName("Card 1");

- **getChildIndex( ).** Returns the position index of a display object using the variable name. The result is a value of type *int*. See page 466 for more examples using the *getChildIndex( )* method.

  Formal description: getChildIndex(child:DisplayObject):int

  Example: greenTable.getChildIndex(card1);

- **removeChild( ).** Removes a display object from the Display List and from its display object container. A child removed from the Display List is no loner visible in the animation. The object is referenced by its variable name. If the object is itself a display object container, the display objects it holds are also removed. For more details see page 460.

  Formal description: removeChild(child:DisplayObject):DisplayObject

  Example: greenTable.removeChild(card1);

- **removeChildAt( ).** Removes a display object from the Display List and from its display object container. The object is referenced by its positionIndex; its name or variable name isn't required. If the object is itself a display object container, the display objects it holds are also removed. For another example of the *removeChildAt( )* method, see page 465.

  Formal description: removeChildAt(index:int):DisplayObject

  Example: greenTable.removeChildAt(2);

- **swapChildren( ).** Swaps the position of two display objects in their display object container. This also changes the visual stacking order—the way objects appear to overlap each other as well as other display objects in the container. For more on *swapChildren( )*, see page 468.

Formal description: swapChildren(child1:DisplayObject, child2:DisplayObject): void

Example: greenTable.swapChildren(card1, card2);

- **swapChildrenAt( ).** Swaps the position of two display objects in their display object container. This also changes the visual stacking order—the way the objects appear to overlap each other as well as other display objects in the container. There are more details on the *swapChildrenAt( )* method on page 468.

Formal description: swapChildrenAt(index1:int, index2:int):void

Example: greenTable.swapChildrenAt(1,3);

Controlling Animation

Ordinarily, Flash assumes you want to play your animation in sequential order from the first frame in your timeline to the last. But sometimes start-at-the-beginning-and-quit-at-the-end isn't exactly what you want. Fortunately, by using a combination of scenes, frame labels, and ActionScript (Chapter 11), you can control your animation virtually any way you like.

For example, say you're putting together an instructional animation. You want to start with an introductory section, move on to the meat of your topic, and then wrap up with a question-and-answer section. If you organize these sections into separately named scenes, then you can play with the order of your animation quickly and easily. If you decide to reposition the question-and-answer scene directly after the introduction as a kind of pretest, for example, you can do that with a simple drag of your mouse. You can even add buttons that the trainee can click to replay the question-and-answer scene over and over, as many times as she likes.

In this chapter, you'll see how to stop and start playback using ActionScript code. You'll see how to use Flash labels, scenes and ActionScript to make the most common types of nonsequential playback effects, including *looping* (replaying a section of your animation over and over again). To make these effects easy to test, you'll also see how to add interactive buttons to your animations. To start it off, this chapter describes how to control the overall speed at which Flash plays your animation on your audience's computers.

Slowing Down (or Speeding Up) Animation

As you saw in Chapter 1, animations are nothing more than a series of content-containing frames that Flash plays one after another so quickly that your eyes interpret the overall effect as continuous movement.

You get a pretty good idea of how your animation will appear to your audience when you test your animation on your own computer. But the speed at which Flash actually displays your frames on *someone else's* computer depends on several factors, many of which you can't control:

- **Your audience's computer hardware.** Both processor speed and memory affect animation playback, especially if the animation's very long or includes multimedia, like bitmaps, sound, or video clips (Chapter 10). You have no control over this factor unless you're developing an animation for playback on a specific set of machines: for example, if you're creating a tutorial in Flash that you know will be played only on the computers in your company's training room.

- **Your audience's Internet connection.** If you've added your animation to a Web page, the speed of your audience's Internet connection affects how quickly your animation downloads and plays on their computers. You have little or no control over this factor (beyond *preloading*, which you can learn about in Chapter 18) because, even if you're targeting your animation for specific machines with, say, 56 kbps connections, Internet congestion may force download speeds of much less than that.

- **The delivery option you've chosen (if you've added video).** If you've incorporated a video clip into your animation (Chapter 10), you've had to tell Flash whether you want to:

  — **Embed the video into your Flash document.** If you've chosen this option, your animation won't begin to play until the person has downloaded the entire (enormous) Flash document, video clip and all. When the animation *does* begin to play, however, neither his Internet connection speed nor overall Internet traffic affect playback.

  — **Stream the video at runtime.** If you've chosen not to embed the video clip into your Flash document, the person's Flash Player begins playing the animation as soon as a few frames' worth of the animation file has finished downloading to his computer. When the animation *does* begin to play, however, it might run in fits and starts, depending on his computer hardware, Internet connection speed, Internet traffic, and the size of your animation and video files.

- **The size and configuration of your finished animation file.** Large animation files—files containing complex animated effects, lots of gradients and transparent images, video clips, and so on—take longer than small files to download or stream over the Internet. They can also take longer to play because large files tend to suck up all the memory on a computer. You can control this factor by optimizing your animation to keep the file size as small as possible and by *preloading* sections of your animation. (Chapter 19 shows you how.)

- **The frame rate you've applied to your animation.** In your animation's time-line, you can tell Flash the maximum frame rate you want it to shoot for, in frames per second (fps).

The easiest factor to control—and the only one covered in this chapter—is the last one: the frame rate. The following section shows you how to set a new frame rate for an animation.

Setting a Document Frame Rate

When you create a new animation, Flash assumes a maximum frame rate of 24 *fps* (frames per second). In other words, given the constraints listed in the previous section, Flash tries its best to display one frame every 1/24th of a second. Here's another way to look at frame rate: If your animation spans 240 frames, you're looking at roughly 10 seconds of screen time.

Note: Previous versions of Flash started out using 12 fps because most people had slower Internet connections. At 24 fps, Flash matches the frame rate used for years by motion pictures.

In many cases, the standard 24 fps works just fine, but if you're planning to put your animation up on a Web site you may want to consider a slower rate, like 12 fps. Your rule of thumb should be to use the lowest frame rate that still provides smooth action for your animation. Usually, you decide on a frame rate when you create a new Flash document, as shown in Figure 14-1. But you can change the frame rate at any time using the document properties or using ActionScript. Changing the frame rate has some pretty significant side effects. First and most important, higher frame rates speed up your document. If you have a 4-minute animation with a 12 fps frame rate and you change it to 24 fps, your animation now finishes in 2 minutes. Too high a frame rate can make animation look blurry and adds considerably to the file size. Too slow a frame rate creates herky-jerky movements and may cause audio-sync problems.

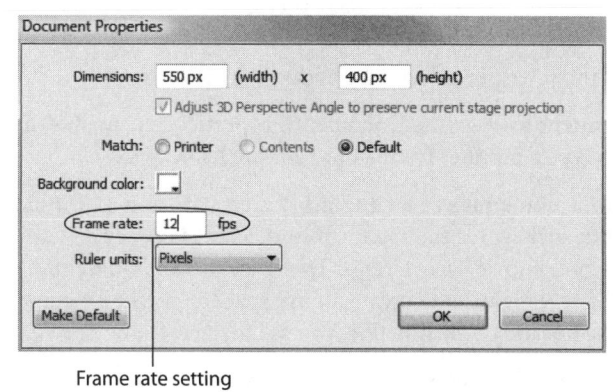

Frame rate setting

Figure 14-1:
Flash can play your movies at frame rates from 0.01 frames per second (that is, a super-slow 100 seconds per frame) to a blistering 120 frames per second. Going with a super-low or super-high frame rate, though, can cause audio synchronization problems. Also, setting a frame rate doesn't ensure that your animation will actually play at that frame rate; it's just a suggested maximum. Several other factors (page 474) affect playback, regardless of the frame rate you set.

The next few examples use a Flash document, *stop_go_begin.fla,* which you can find on the "Missing CD" page at *http://missingmanuals.com/cds.*

To see the effects of different frame rates, follow these steps and feel free to add some of your own experiments:

1. **Open** *stop_go_begin.fla,* **and then press Ctrl+Enter (⌘-Return on a Mac) to test the animation.**

   The Stutz Bearcat auto races across your screen at a blazing 12 frames per second (FPS). The car is the only animated object in the movie and uses a motion tween to move from left to right across the screen.

2. **Below the timeline, click the Frame Rate setting, and then type 8 (Figure 14-2).**

   You can click the Frame Rate, and then type a new number, or you can drag to change the setting.

Frame rate setting

Figure 14-2:
In addition to clicking the Frame Rate setting (circled) in the timeline, Flash gives you two additional ways to set your animation's frame rate. You can select Modify → Document (which pops up the window in Figure 14-1) or click the stage, and then change the frame rate directly in the Properties panel (Properties → Properties → fps). Flash doesn't prevent you from changing your frame rate in the middle of building an animation, but it's such a basic characteristic that you typically want to set it once up front and only change it later if you absolutely have to.

3. **Test the animation by pressing Ctrl+Enter (⌘-Return).**

   The car moves across the screen in a decidedly herky-jerky fashion.

4. **Click Modify → Document to open the Document Properties box, as shown in Figure 14-1, and then type a number from 24 to 120. Click OK.**

   Flash lets you type in a frame rate of anything between 0.01 and 120. But in most cases, you want to stick with a frame rate of somewhere between 12 and 24 (the standard Hollywood movie frame rate). Every animation's different, of course, and you might actually *want* to create an unusual effect. The Document Properties window disappears. In the timeline, you see the new frame rate.

5. **Test your new frame rate by choosing Control → Test Movie.**

   If you type in a frame rate greater that 24, the car moves noticeably faster and may even look a bit blurry.

Note: Frame rate affects the playback speed of the entire animation. Base your frame rate decisions on how smooth you want the animation to be and the capabilities of your intended audience, as explained on page 474. If you want to speed up (or slow down) only certain sections of your animation, change the rates by removing (or adding) frames, as described on page 97.

Setting a Frame Rate with ActionScript

ActionScript gives you the tools to change the frame rate for your animation, too, since the stage has a frameRate property. (If you need more basics on ActionScript and properties, see page 386.) When you use ActionScript to set the frameRate property for the stage, it has the same effect as setting a new frame rate in the timeline when you're designing your animation.

1. **Add a new layer for actions to the timeline.**

   If you're going to add code to the timeline, it's good practice to add a special layer at the top just for code and name it something like "actions." That way, it's much easier later if you have to hunt down and debug your code.

2. **In the actions layer, click the first frame, and then open the Actions panel (Window → Actions).**

   The Actions panel opens, as shown in Figure 14-3. For more details about the tools available in the Actions panel, see page 382.

3. **In the Actions panel, type the following line of code:**

   ```
   stage.frameRate=60;
   ```

   Even though you're changing the frameRate in ActionScript, the rate showing below the time line still shows a frame rate of 24 fps (or whatever you used in the last setting). In fact, the frameRate doesn't officially change until the actions on Frame 1 of the timeline are processed.

4. **Click the 25th frame in the actions layer of the timeline, and then press F7.**

   Flash inserts a blank keyframe is inserted in the timeline.

5. **In the Actions panel, type the following code:**

   ```
   stage.frameRate=6;
   ```

   Make sure that the 25th frame in the timeline is selected when you type in the code, because you want the frame rate to change at that point in the animation. The Current Selection tab should change to show a frame symbol and the words *actions : Frame 25.*

6. **Test your animation using Ctrl+Enter (⌘-Return on a Mac).**

   The Stutz Bearcat races up to the stop sign and performs a Hollywood stop, slowing down and rolling through the intersection, and then off the stage.

Tip: Though you can change the frame rate of a timeline mid-stream as shown in this example, in most cases, it's better to keep your frame rate a single speed. Instead, to speed up action, remove frames from the sequence; if you want to slow things down, add frames. If you want to slow down or speed up a tweened motion, that's easy to do using the Motion Editor as described on page 282.

Click to open/close panels   ActionScript code

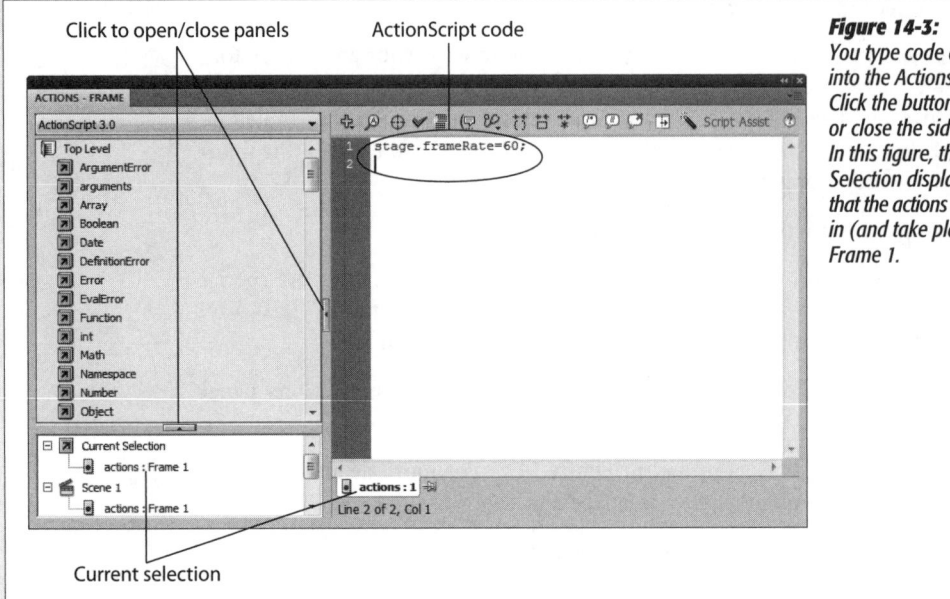

Figure 14-3:
You type code directly into the Actions panel. Click the button to open or close the side panels. In this figure, the Current Selection display shows that the actions are stored in (and take place at) Frame 1.

Current selection

Timeline Stop and Go

Starting and stopping an animation is similar to hitting the pause and play buttons on a DVD player. If your audience is viewing your animation in the desktop version of Flash Player, they can pause and play the animation by pressing Enter or Return, just as when you start and stop the playback when you're working in the Flash authoring environment. ActionScript gives you the tools to start and stop animations programmatically. There are all sorts of ways you can put this feature to use. Suppose you want the Stutz Bearcat to make a real stop at that Stop sign, instead of the kind of stop that'll get you a ticket. You can place a *stop( )* command in the timeline at the frame where you want the animation to stop.

Note: The *stop()* and *go()* examples in this section use the same Flash document *stop_go_begin.fla* from the previous exercises. If you don't have a copy of the file, you can find it on the "Missing CD" page at *http://missingmanuals.com/cds*.

Here's how to tell your animation when to stop using ActionScript:

1. **In the timeline's actions layer, click the 25th frame. In the Actions panel, delete (or comment out) any other code that may be present.**

   Use two slashes // to comment out code, as described on page 425.

2. **Type the following code:**

   ```
   stop( );
   ```

   This line of code is a little more complex than it may appear. In essence, it tells the main timeline of the animation to stop playing. A more complete version of this statement would read *this.stop( )*. In that case, this refers to the main timeline. If you don't explicitly reference the timeline that you're stopping, ActionScript assumes you mean the main timeline.

3. **Test your animation using Ctrl+Enter (⌘-Return).**

   When the main timeline reaches the 25th frame, it stops. Oddly, the wheels of the Stutz Bearcat keep on spinning (Figure 14-4). (That's got to be hard on the tires!) The car on the stage is an instance of the StutzBearcat symbol in the Library. The symbol is a movie clip made up of two frames that make the car's wheels spin. To stop the wheels from turning, you need to stop the StutzBearcat animation, too.

Figure 14-4:
In this scene, the animation of the main timeline stops, but the animation in the car's movie clip keeps running, so the wheels appear to spin even when the car is stopped. To restore the laws of physics, you have to stop both the main timeline and the car's movie clip using ActionScript statements.

4. **In the Actions panel, add the following line of code:**

   ```
   stutzBearcat.stop( );
   ```

   Now, Frame 25 has two *stop( )* statements. The first stops the main timeline and the second stops the instance of the stutzBearcat movie clip.

5. **Test your animation using Ctrl+Enter (⌘-Return).**

   When the animation runs, the car *and* the car's wheels make a legal stop in front of the Stop sign.

Using ActionScript to Start a Timeline

As you saw in the previous steps, the *stop( )* command stops an animation nicely. But what about getting that Bearcat rolling again? You stopped the animation by putting the *stop( )* statement in the frame where you wanted to stop, but putting a *play( )* statement in the following frame, as logical as it sounds, will do you no good. The Flash Player will never reach the next frame—it's stopped. So you have a couple of choices, depending on what you want to trigger the starting and stopping. If you want your audience to control it, you can give them clickable buttons or controls. If you want the animation to resume on its own, a TimerEvent is the best tool in your toolbox. You can add a TimerEvent to the same frame where the *stop( )* happened, as shown in Figure 14-5. When the timer is complete, it can trigger a *play( )* statement for both the main timeline and the stutzBearcat movie clip. Modify the code on Frame 25 of the actions layer to read as follows:

```
1   stop( );
2   stutzBearcat.stop( );
3
4   var carTimer = new Timer(400, 1);
5   carTimer.start( );
6
7   carTimer.addEventListener(TimerEvent.TIMER_COMPLETE, timerCompleteListener);
8
9   function timerCompleteListener(evt:TimerEvent):void {
10      play( );
11      stutzBearcat.play( );
12  }
```

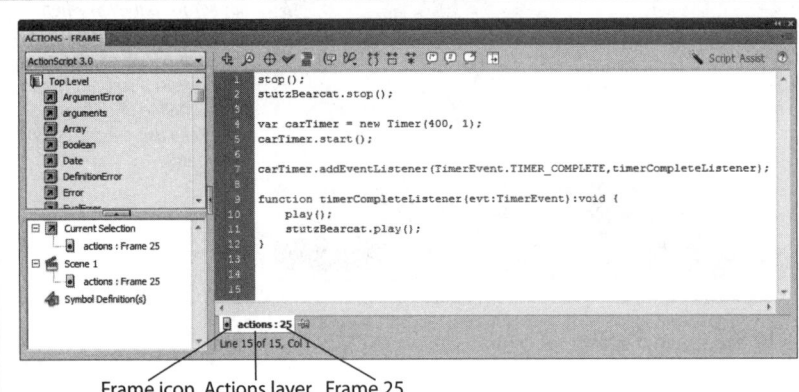

Frame icon   Actions layer   Frame 25

Figure 14-5:
The tab at the bottom of the Actions panel provides details about the location of the code shown. In this case, the code resides on the 25th frame of the actions layer.

The first two lines were already in the code. Line 4 creates a new timer called *carTimer*. The first number in parentheses (400) sets the timer to wait a little less than half a second (400/1000s of a second). The second number (1), sets the timer to run once. Line 5, starts the timer. The remainder of the code sets up the event handler.

Line 7 registers the event listener to run the function *timerCompleteListener( )* when the timer runs out. (For more details on events and event listeners, see page 409.) The code between the curly brackets (line 10 and line 11) are the statements that start the main timeline and the stutzBearcat movie clip.

Note: In 1915, Erwin "Cannon Ball" Baker set a record driving from Los Angeles to New York in 11 days, 7 hours, and 15 minutes in a Stutz Bearcat.

Organizing an Animation

As you see in a lot of the examples earlier in this book, you don't have to do a thing to your standard timeline, organization-wise. You can let Flash play your animation sequentially, from Frame 1 right through to Frame 500 (or whatever number your last frame is) with no problems.

If you need your animation to jump around and play out of sequence, though, there are a few ways you can do it. The best method depends on what you're trying to do. Here are three methods along with their pros and cons:

- Use *labels* to create bookmarks in the timeline. If you break an animation into named chunks with frame labels, then you give your animations the potential to be flexible and more interactive, because you can write ActionScript actions that *target* (act on) each individual chunk. For example, you can let your audience decide whether to play the ralph_reacts scene first, last, or skip it altogether. This method is one of the most popular, especially with the ActionScript crowd. It's easy to create labels and easy to use them in ActionScript. In short, wherever you use a frame number to refer to a specific frame in a timeline, you can also use a frame label.

- Divide your animation into *separate .swf files* and load them as needed. This method is great if you have different teams working on a long animation. Team members can create movie clips independently, and then a master movie clip can load the other movie clips as needed. One of the advantages of this method is that it's faster, especially if you're sending .swf files over the Internet. Your audience needs to download only the .swf files they actually want to view.

- Create *scenes* within your Flash document. In some ways, scenes may have more benefits for the Flash designer than they do either the Flash coder or the Flash audience. If you break an animation into scenes, then you can find what you're looking for quickly; you can also easily rearrange your animation, using the Scene panel. Scenes make it easy to focus on a small section of your animation, while you're creating and previewing it. You don't have to preview an entire animation, when all you want to see is one small section. All of the scenes are stored in a single .swf file, so your audience has to download the complete file, even if they're only viewing one or two of the scenes.

Tip: Both scenes and labeled frames are a natural fit for creating a Web site in Flash because they let you organize your content nonsequentially. Page 421 shows you an example of linking content to navigation buttons.

Working with Labeled Frames

Labeled frames are like named bookmarks. Once you label a frame, you can jump to that specific point in the timeline using the label's name. Labeled frames are great tools to use when you want to give your audience an opportunity to interact with the animation. For example, if you're creating a series of lessons, you can create a label for each lesson. You can then give your students a table of contents, where they can jump to any lesson with the click of a button. Or, suppose you're using Flash to build an animated Web site and you want to display a different Web page when someone clicks a button on your navigation bar. If she clicks the Contact Us button, for instance, you want to display a Web page showing your company's contact information.

Technically, you don't have to label your frames in order to do this. You can create an *event listener* for your Contact page button that uses code like this:

```
gotoAndPlay(15);
```

The problem with this approach is that if you go back and add frames to the beginning of your timeline, it muffs up your code. If you add 10 frames to the beginning of your animation, for example, the old Frame 15 is now the new Frame 25. So, to make your button work again, you'd have to change the ActionScript code to this:

```
gotoAndPlay(25);
```

A much better approach is to give Frame 15 a meaningful label, like *contact*, and write the ActionScript code this way:

```
gotoAndPlay("contact");
```

When you label a frame like this, Flash always associates the same frame with the label—no matter what number that frame ends up being. So you can edit your timeline to your heart's content without ever having to worry that you're breaking your actions. As a side benefit, using words rather than numbers makes your code easier to read and understand.

The following sections show you how to label frames, and how to reference those labels in ActionScript code. This exercise uses a file called *label_begin.fla*, which you can find at the "Missing CD" page at *http://missingmanuals.com/cds*. The completed project is in a file named *label_finished.fla*.

Labeling a frame

Labeling a frame is easy. All you have to do is select a frame, and then, in the Properties panel, type a name for the label.

Note: As with all content (images, sounds, actions, and so on), the label you attach to a keyframe stays in force until the next keyframe.

To label a frame:

1. **Open *label_begin.fla* in Flash, and then press Enter to play the animation.**

   This rather abbreviated movie is made up of three words: Intro, Main, and Credits. Each word is animated using Classic tweens. There are new words at Frame 1, Frame 16, and Frame 46. The animation has three layers: "words," "buttons," and "labels." You can label any keyframe in a timeline, but if you place all your labels in a single layer, they're easier to find.

2. **In the timeline, in the labels layer, click the first frame.**

   Flash highlights the selected frame, and the Properties panel shows properties associated with Frame 1. (If the Properties panel isn't showing, go Window → Properties.)

3. **In the Properties panel, click the Label → Name box (Figure 14-6), and then type *intro*.**

   Your first label is complete. In the timeline, Flash displays a little red flag in the frame you attached the label to, followed by the label itself. You may need to click the triangle button next to Label to expand the Label panel.

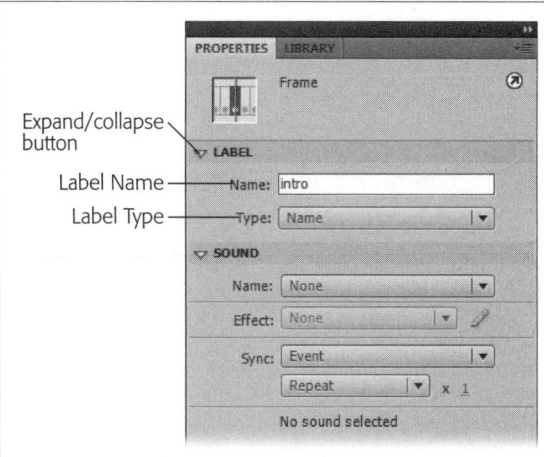

Figure 14-6:
Flash assumes a label type of Name, and that's exactly what you want in most circumstances. (The other label types Flash has are Comment, which displays your label in the timeline but doesn't let you access it using ActionScript, and Anchor, which lets you designate the frame as a separate HTML anchor page that your audience can return to using the browser's Back button.)

4. **In the labels layer, click Frame 16, and then press F6.**

   A new keyframe appears at Frame 16. Only keyframes can have labels. So to attach a new label to Frame 16, you need to create a keyframe first.

5. **In the Properties panel, click the Label → Name box, and then type *main*.**

   The second label named *main* appears in the labels layer.

FREQUENTLY ASKED QUESTION

The Difference Between Scenes and Labeled Frames

It sounds like scenes and frame labels do the same thing: Both let me break up my animation into chunks and make the chunks interactive, and both let me target a frame using a name instead of just the frame number. So if they both do the same thing, when do I use one over the other?

Using labeled frames *is* very similar to using scenes. But there are three big differences between the two:

- **Simply dragging scenes around in the Scene panel rearranges the way Flash plays your animation**. You can't drag-and-drop to rearrange labeled frames. (You can rearrange the way your animation plays using labeled frames, but you have to write the ActionScript code to do it.)

- **It's harder to break up scenes than to add labels**. When you use scenes, you need to either add new content for each scene as you build your animation, or—if you've already created your animation and want to break it into scenes after the fact—you need to cut and paste frames from the original Scene 1 into your new scenes. Hardly rocket science, but it is extra work. Adding or changing frame labels is much quicker.

- **You work with scenes in separate timelines; you work with labeled frames in one big timeline**. This difference is usually the deal breaker: Some people love working with content in separate timelines; some people hate it.

6. **In the labels layer, click Frame 46, and then press F6.**

   A new keyframe appears at Frame 46.

7. **In the Properties panel, click the Label → Name box, and then type** *credits.*

   The third label named *credits* appears in the labels layer

Targeting a labeled frame

After you've labeled a frame, you can reference that label in an ActionScript action. This section shows you how to program three buttons that jump to a specific frame label in the timeline.

This example continues from the previous exercise on page 482. If you want to start fresh, you can use the Flash file *label_no_action.fla from* the "Missing CD" page at *http://missingmanuals.com/cds.*

Note: The example in this section is identical to the one on page 488 except for two differences: This example shows ActionScript targeting labeled frames in a single timeline, while the one on page 488 shows ActionScript targeting separate scenes.

To target a labeled frame:

1. **Open the Flash file, and then move the playhead to Frame 1.**

   On the stage you see the word "Intro" and three buttons with the text Play Intro, Play Main, and Play Credits.

2. **Test the animation by selecting Control → Test movie.**

In the Test window, you see the word "Intro" recede; the word "Main" approach and recede; and the word "Credits" approach. Clicking the Play Intro, Play Main, and Play Credits buttons turns the buttons from red to yellow but has no other effect on the animation.

3. **Below Flash's timeline, click the New Layer button. Then click the name and type actions, as shown in Figure 14-7.**

A new layer named *actions* appears in the timeline. You'll use this layer to hold all of your ActionScript code. As a rule of thumb, it's best to keep your Action-Script code as close together as possible. When snippets of code are tucked away in different layers or movie clips, it's harder to troubleshoot.

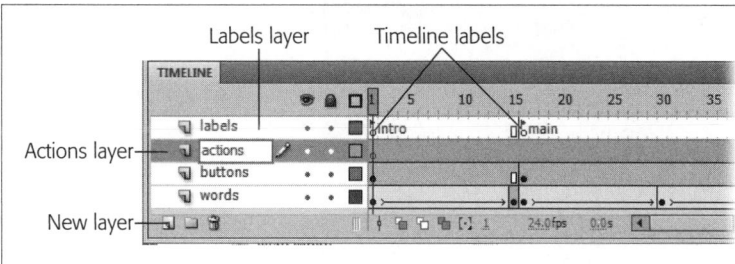

Figure 14-7:
When you place ActionScript code in the timeline, it's always best to devote a specific layer to the code, which makes it easier to find and debug your code later. It's also a good idea to keep both the labels layer and the actions layer at the top of the timeline.

4. **In the actions layer, create a keyframe at Frame 15 by selecting the frame, and then pressing F6.**

An empty circle appears in Frame 15, indicating a keyframe.

5. **With Frame 15, still selected type the following ActionScript statement in the Actions panel:**

```
stop( );
```

This statement stops the animation from playing when it reaches Frame 15. This marks the end of the "intro" segment of the animation.

6. **Create keyframes and *stop( )* statements for frames 44 and 60, similar to what you did in steps 4 and 5.**

At this point, each of the three animation segments (intro, main, credits) has a *stop( )* statement at the end. If you test your animation now, it will stop at the end of the intro. In the following steps, you write code for each of the three Play buttons.

7. **Click the outside edge of the Play Intro button.**

The button shows a selection box, and a button icon appears in the Properties panel, as shown in Figure 14-8. If you see the letter T in the Properties panel, it means you selected the Play Intro text, not the Play Intro button, so try again.

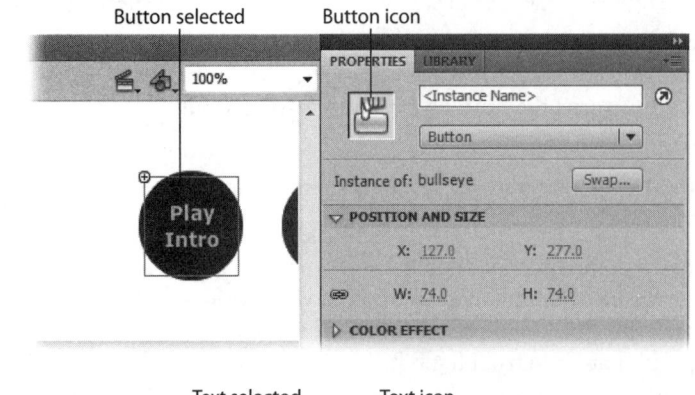

Button selected   Button icon

Figure 14-8:
These buttons are made up of two parts: a button symbol, plus text placed over the symbol. To select just the button, click the edges outside of the text. You can tell whether you've selected the button symbol or the text by the icon that shows in the Properties panel.

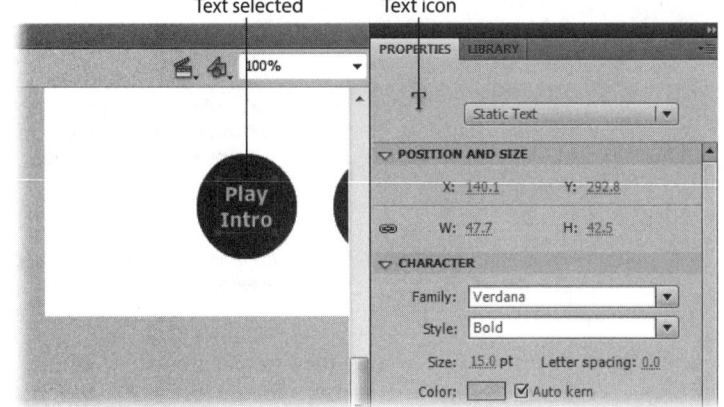

Text selected   Text icon

8. **In the Properties panel, name the button instance btnIntro.**

There are three instances of buttons on the stage: Play Intro, Play Main, and Play Credits. They're all instances of the BullsEye button in the Library. Before you can write ActionScript code for each button, you have to name them.

9. **Repeat steps 7 and 8 to name the remaining two buttons.**

Using a consistent naming convention, name the Play Main button *btnMain*, and the Play Credits button *btnCredits*.

10. **Click Frame 1 in the actions layer, and then type in the following code to create an event listener for btnIntro.**

```
1    btnIntro.addEventListener(MouseEvent.CLICK, clickIntroListener);
2
3    function clickIntroListener(evt:MouseEvent) {
4        gotoAndPlay("intro");
5    }
```

Line 1 registers a MouseEvent listener for btnIntro. Lines 3 through 5 comprise the function *clickIntroListener( )*. It holds the code that runs when someone clicks the btnIntro button. (For more details on handling events and event listeners, see page 409.) Line 4 holds the important action for the function. The *gotoAndPlay( )* statement tells the Flash Player to jump to the frame labeled "intro" and to begin playing from that point forward. You can place either a label, like "intro," or a specific frame number like *16* inside of the *gotoAndPlay( )* parentheses. As explained on page 482, labels are much more flexible than specific frame numbers.

11. **Add event listener code for the remaining two buttons. When you're through it should look like this:**

```
btnIntro.addEventListener(MouseEvent.CLICK, clickIntroListener);
btnMain.addEventListener(MouseEvent.CLICK, clickMainListener);
btnCredits.addEventListener(MouseEvent.CLICK, clickCreditsListener);

function clickIntroListener(evt:MouseEvent) {
    gotoAndPlay("intro");
}

function clickMainListener(evt:MouseEvent) {
    gotoAndPlay("main");
}

function clickCreditsListener(evt:MouseEvent) {
    gotoAndPlay("credits");
}
```

When you have several similar statements, like these mouse event listeners, you can save time by writing and testing one statement. Then, with a little copy, paste, and modify magic, you can quickly create the similar statements. If things don't work as planned, double-check the way you modified the code. In this case, you'd carefully examine all the code where "intro," "main," and "credits" appear.

12. **Test your animation using Ctrl+Enter (⌘-Return).**

If your code is working properly, the animation plays the "intro" and then stops. When you click any of the Play buttons, Flash player plays that segment and then stops.

As this example shows, frame labels and *gotoAndPlay( )* statements are powerful tools for animations that play out of sequence. Labels give you an easy and convenient way to mark off segments in a timeline, and you can add as many of them as you want. There's another related statement, *gotoAndStop( )*, which does exactly what you imagine. It jumps to a specific frame and stops Flash Player from moving on to the next frame. The next section of this chapter explains how to use scenes to accomplish the same tasks.

Working with Scenes

A *scene* in Flash is a series of frames to which you assign a name of your choosing. Each scene has its own timeline. In the preceding example using labels, a single timeline was marked off into three parts: intro, main, and credits. Each segment occupied frames in the same timeline. The first 15 frames made up the "intro," the next 30 frames were labeled "main," and the final 15 frames were labeled "credits." You can use scenes to break a larger animation into smaller chunks that can be targeted with ActionScript.

Each time you create a new scene, Flash displays a brand new timeline for you to fill with content. Then, when you play your animation, Flash plays each scene in top-down order, beginning with the first scene listed in the Scene panel (Figure 14-9), and ending with the last.

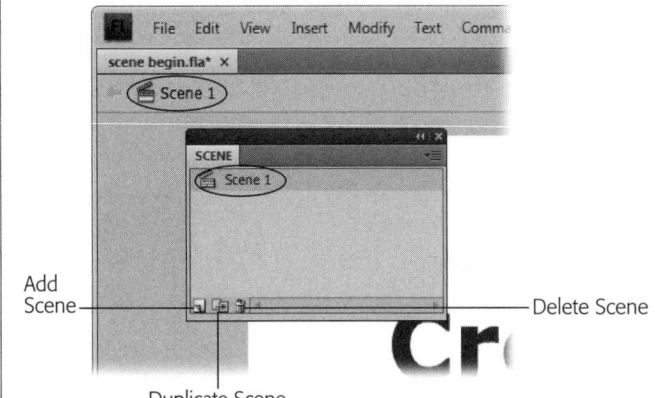

Add Scene

Duplicate Scene

Delete Scene

Figure 14-9:
Every animation you create has at least one scene (named Scene 1, unless you tell Flash differently). By using the Scene panel to create and name new scenes, you can organize long animations into manageable chunks. Flash displays the timeline for each scene separately, so it can be easy to forget which scene you're in at any given time. In fact, your only cue is the scene name Flash displays in the Edit bar. If you don't see it (along with the little clapper icon), choose Window → Toolbars → Edit Bar.

As the following sections show, after you create scenes, you can rename them and reorganize them with the click of a button.

Tip: As an alternative to using scenes, you may want to consider publishing separate .swf files and loading them into your main animation as needed. This method can be helpful when teams of animators produce a long animation. Each team works with separate Flash documents and publishes their own .swf files.

Creating a scene

Flash automatically starts you out with one scene (cleverly named Scene 1) each time you create a new Flash document.

To create additional scenes:

1. **In the timeline, create content for the frames you want in your first scene.**

   If you're using the example file *scenes_start.fla*, you see two layers, buttons and words, each of which extends from Frame 1 through Frame 15. (You can download this example file from the "Missing CD" page at *http://.missingmanuals.com/cds.*)

---

2. **Choose Window → Other Panels → Scene.**

   The Scene panel appears.

3. **Click the "Add scene" icon.**

   In the Scene panel, Flash creates a new scene, and then places it directly below Scene 1. Flash also displays a brand new timeline and a clean, fresh stage (Figure 14-10).

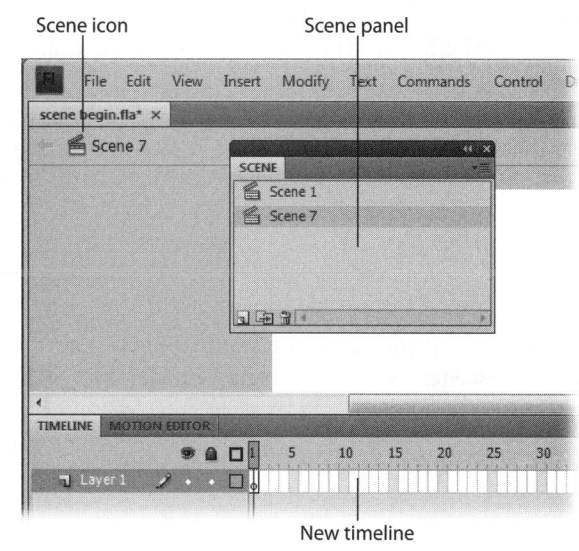

Scene icon   Scene panel

New timeline

Figure 14-10:
Each time you create a new scene, Flash hides the timeline for the previous scene and displays a brand-new workspace. At this point, Flash associates everything you add to the stage and the timeline to the newly created scene—here, Scene 7. (Flash names scenes sequentially; in this figure, Scenes 2 through 6 were created and then deleted.)

4. **In the timeline, create content for the frames you want in your new scene.**

   When you're done, you may want to rename the scene (as discussed in the next section), and then test it by choosing Control → Test Scene. Or, to create additional scenes, simply repeat steps 3 and 4.

Renaming a scene

The names Flash gives each scene you create—Scene 1, Scene 2, Scene 3, and so on, as you see in Figure 14-10—aren't particularly useful if you're using scenes as a way to find the frames you need quickly. Fortunately, Flash makes it easy for you to rename scenes. Here are the steps:

1. **Choose Window → Other Panels → Scene.**

   The Scene panel appears.

2. **In the Scene panel, double-click the name of the scene you want to change.**

   Flash displays the scene name in an editable text box.

3. **Type the new name.**

You'll need to refer to this name in ActionScript code if you're planning to make your animation interactive, so short and meaningful is best. For example, you might choose *intro* for an introductory scene, *main* for the meat of your animation, and *credits* for the last few wrap-up frames that display your company's name and contact info.

Reorganizing scenes

Flash always plays scenes in order from the scene that appears at the top of the Scene panel down to the scene that appears in the bottom. To change the order in which Flash plays your scenes:

Note: Another way to change the order in which Flash plays your scenes and frames is by using Action-Script (page 481).

---

1. **Choose Window → Other Panels → Scene.**

The Scene panel appears.

2. **In the Scene panel, click the name of the scene you want to move, and then drag it above or below the other scenes, as shown in Figure 14-11.**

The instant you let up on your mouse, Flash reorders the scenes in the Scene panel. The new order is the order in which Flash plays your animation when you choose Control → Test Movie.

Changing scene sequence

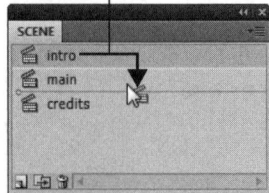

Figure 14-11:
Dragging a scene to a new location in the Scene panel automatically reorganizes the sequence in which Flash plays your animation—no ActionScript necessary. The line that appears as you drag a scene lets you know where Flash will put the scene when you let up on your mouse.

Tip: To play just the scene currently on the stage, select Control → Test Scene (instead of Control → Test Movie).

Scripting (targeting) a scene

In Flash-speak, *targeting* a scene means writing ActionScript code that performs some action on a scene. The example in this section shows how to program the buttons to jump to a new scene and begin playing the animation at that point. The tools you use are similar to those used with labels: event listeners and the *gotoAndPlay( )* statement. Figure 14-12 gives you a quick overview of how the finished example looks.

Figure 14-12:
You'll often want to break an animation into scenes so that you can give your audience the ability to play the scenes independently. Here, pressing the Play Credits button plays the credits scene, pressing the Play Main button plays the main scene, and pressing the Play Intro button plays the (you guessed it) intro scene. To put together an interactive animation, you have to first create named scenes, and then tie those scenes to buttons using ActionScript code.

Note: For more information on creating button symbols, see page 252.

---

1. **Open the file *scenes_no_action.fla.***

   In the Scene panel (Window → Other Panels → Scene), notice that the animation contains three scenes (intro, main, and credits). The stage has three buttons labeled Play Intro, Play Main, and Play Credits, respectively.

Note: You can download the example files for this section from the "Missing CD" page at *http://missingmanuals.com/cds*. The file *scenes_no_action.fla* is the starting point, and *scenes_finished.fla* is the completed animation with ActionScript.

---

2. **Test the animation by selecting Control → Test movie.**

   In the test window, the word "Intro" recedes; the word "Main" approaches and recedes; and the word "Credits" approaches. Clicking the Play Intro, Play Main, and Play Credits buttons—which only appear while the intro scene's playing—turns the buttons from red to yellow but has no other effect on the animation.

3. **Click the Edit Scene icon (Figure 14-13), and then choose "intro" if it's not already chosen.**

   The Edit bar displays "intro" to let you know you're about to edit the intro scene. On the stage, you see the three buttons shown in Figure 14-13.

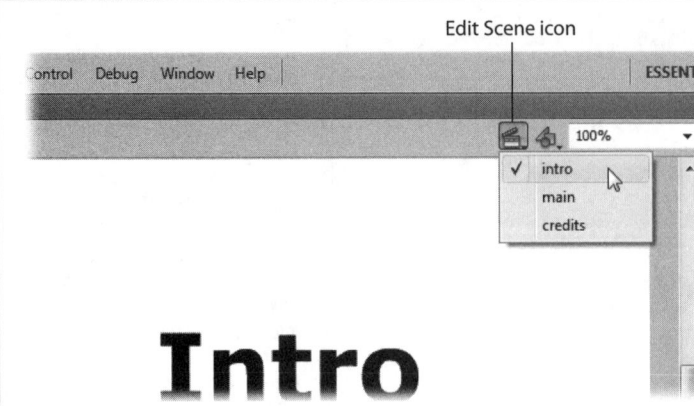

Edit Scene icon

Figure 14-13:
You can switch from scene to scene in your animation using the Scene panel, but you'll probably find clicking the Edit Scene icon much handier, because the Edit Scene icon doesn't disappear while you're working.

4. **Below Flash's timeline, click the New Layer button. Then click the name and type actions, as shown in Figure 14-7.**

   A new layer named *actions* appears in the timeline. You use this layer to hold all of your ActionScript code. As a rule of thumb, it's best to keep your Action-Script code as close together as possible. When snippets of code are tucked away in different layers or movie clips, it makes it hard to troubleshoot.

5. **In the actions layer, create a keyframe at Frame 15 by selecting the frame, and then pressing F6.**

   An empty circle appears in Frame 15, indicating a keyframe.

6. **With Frame 15, still selected, type the following ActionScript statement in the Actions panel:**

   ```
   stop();
   ```

   This statement stops the animation from playing when it reaches Frame 15. Without a *stop( )* statement here, the Flash Player automatically plays the next scene.

7. **Repeat steps 3 through 6, to create keyframes and *stop( )* statements on the last frames of the "main" scene and the "credits" scene.**

   Use the Edit Scene icon to move from one scene to another

8. **Go back to the "intro" scene, and then click the first frame in the actions layer.**

   Flash displays the timeline for the intro scene.

9. **In the Actions window, type in the following code:**

   ```
   1    btnIntro.addEventListener(MouseEvent.CLICK, clickIntroListener);
   2    btnMain.addEventListener(MouseEvent.CLICK, clickMainListener);
   3    btnCredits.addEventListener(MouseEvent.CLICK, clickCreditsListener);
   4
   ```

```
5    function clickIntroListener(evt:MouseEvent):void {
6        gotoAndPlay(1,"intro");
7    }
8    function clickMainListener(evt:MouseEvent):void {
9        gotoAndPlay(1,"main");
10   }
11   function clickCreditsListener(evt:MouseEvent):void {
12       gotoAndPlay(1,"credits");
13   }
```

If you've been following the ActionScript code sections in this and previous chapters, the event listeners used in this code should look pretty familiar. If you need to brush up on event listeners, check out page 409. The only differences between this code and the code used to target labels is in the way the *gotoAndPlay( )* method is used. In this example, *gotoAndPlay( )* has two parameters inside of the parentheses. The first parameter is a frame number, but it could just as easily be a label like "start" or "intro." The second parameter is the name of a scene. Like labels, the name of the scene has to be inside of quotes. Each of the statements on lines 6, 9, and 12, tell Flash Player to go to a scene and begin playing the animation at the first frame of that scene.

10. Select lines 1 through 3 in the Actions panel, and then press Ctrl+C (⌘-C).

    The three statements that register event listeners for the buttons are copied and stored on your computers clipboard.

11. Go back to the "main" scene, and click the first frame in the actions layer.

    Flash displays the timeline for the main scene.

12. Click the first line in the Actions panel, and then press Ctrl+V (⌘-V).

    You've just copied the three statements that register event listeners into the Actions panel. Each scene is shown on a new timeline beginning with key-frames at frame one for each layer. The statements that register event listeners in the "intro" scene don't register event listeners for the other scenes. Note, you don't need to (and shouldn't) copy the functions, just the code with that uses the *addEventListener( )* method.

13. Go back to the "credits" scene, and click the first frame in the actions layer.

    Flash displays the timeline for the main scene.

14. Click the first line in the Actions panel, and then press Ctrl+V (⌘-V).

    The three statements that register event listeners are copied into the Actions panel.

15. Test your animation using Ctrl+Enter (⌘-Return on a Mac).

    If your code is working properly, the animation plays the Intro, and then stops. When you click any of the "play" buttons, Flash player plays that segment, and then stops.

Note: With a long exercise like this, it's super-easy to miss a step. To see a working example, check out the finished file *scenes_finished.fla*.

Looping a Series of Frames

Looping—replaying a section of your animation over and over again—is an efficient way to create long-playing effects for a modest investment of effort and file size.

Say, for example, you want to create a repetitive background effect like sunlight glinting off water, palm fronds waving in the breeze, or flickering lights. You can create the frames necessary to show the effect briefly (a couple seconds' worth or so), save the frames as a movie clip, and place an instance of that movie clip in one of the layers of your animation so that the effect spans your entire animation. Flash automatically replays the movie clip until you tell it otherwise, so you get an extended effect for a just a few frames' worth of work—and just a few frames' worth of file size, too. What a deal! (For a more in-depth look at movie clip symbols, check out Chapter 6.)

Note: You've seen this kind of looping background effect in action if you've ever watched *The Flintstones*—or just about any other production cartoon, for that matter. Remember seeing the same two caves shoot past in the background over and over again as Fred chased Barney around Bedrock?

To loop a series of frames using a movie clip symbol:

1. **Open the file** *loop_begin.fla,* **which you can download from the "Missing CD" page at** *http://missingmanuals.com/cds.*

   On the stage, you see a sprinkling of white stars on a blue background. In the Library, you see four symbols, including the blink_lights movie clip symbol (Figure 14-14).

   Since you've never seen this movie clip before, take a look at the preview.

Note: To loop a section of your *main* timeline, all you have to do is attach the following action to the last frame of the section you want to loop: *gotoAndPlay(1).* (If you want your loop to begin at a frame other than Frame 1, replace the 1 in the preceding ActionScript code with the number of the frame at which you want Flash to begin looping.)

2. **In the Library, select the blink_lights movie clip. Then, in the Library's preview window, click the Play icon.**

   You see the lights on the cactus change from red to yellow, pink, and blue in rapid succession.

3. **Preview the main animation by selecting Control → Test Movie.**

   In the Test window, you see a lone shooting star streak across the background.

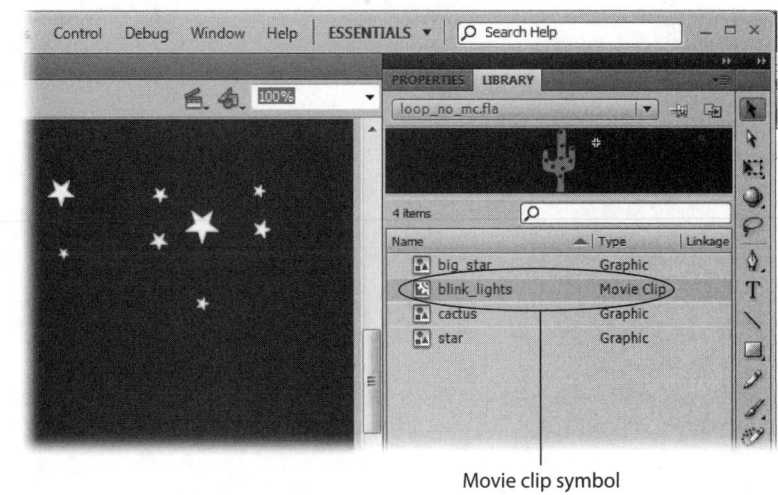

Figure 14-14:
Looping a series of frames using a movie clip is super-easy because Flash does all the work. In fact, Flash always assumes you want to loop the movie clips you add to your animations. (If you don't want to loop them, you can tell Flash to stop playing a movie clip after the first time through by attaching the stop( ) *action to the last frame of your movie clip symbol.)*

Movie clip symbol

4. Click the X in the upper-left corner of the Test window to go back to the workspace.

   First stop: Add an instance of the xmas_cactus movie clip to the animation.

5. In the xmas_cactus layer, click the first keyframe (Frame 1) to select it. Then, drag the blink_lights movie clip from the Library to the stage.

   Choose Control → Test Movie again to see the results. In the Test window that appears, you see the lights on the cactus blink repeatedly as the shooting star moves across the screen.

Note: If you *don't* want your movie clip to loop, you need to tell Flash to stop playing the movie clip after the first time through. To so instruct it, attach the *stop( )* action to the last frame of your movie clip symbol (*not* the movie clip instance).

Reversing a Series of Frames

Reversing a series of frames is a useful effect. A basketball bouncing up and down, a flag waving side to side, or a boomerang advancing and receding: These things are all examples of reversing a single series of frames.

Instead of creating the two complete series of frames by hand—one showing a ball falling, for example, and another showing the same ball bouncing back up—you can copy the frame series, paste it, and use Modify → Timeline → Reverse Frames to reverse the pasted frames.

Power to the People

Early on, one of the beefs people had with Flash advertising and splash screens (intro pages) was the inability to control the animations. It wasn't easy to stop, start, bypass, or control the sound on some of those pages. It gave Flash a bad name.

Things have changed. You can use Flash to create entire Web-based environments with ingenious and creative navigation systems. If you don't, even though your audience can right-click (or Control-click) your animation to view a context menu that lets them interact with your animation, context menus aren't particularly useful when it comes to providing consistent playback control. For one thing, few audience members know about them. Also, Flash gurus who also happen to be expert ActionScript coders can modify, rearrange, add to, and delete menu options.

Don't be one of them. Consider the Flash experience from your audience's point of view. You won't go wrong by giving power to the people. Giving your audience as much control as possible is always a good idea, but it's crucial if you're planning to put your Flash animation on the Web. You can't possibly know your Web audience's hardware configuration.

Say, for example, you create a splash page animation with a stage size of 550 × 400 pixels, and a file size of 10 MB. Someone accessing your animation on a handheld, over a slow connection, or on a machine that's already maxed out running 10 other resource-hogging programs won't be able to see the animation you see on *your* machine.

But even if everyone on the planet had a high-speed connection and the latest computer hardware, giving your audience control would still be important. Why? Because no matter how kick-butt your animation is, by the 23rd time through, it's going to wear a little thin. If you don't offer at least one of the options listed below, you risk turning away repeat visitors:

- The ability to bypass intro splash screens and advertising and go straight to the site's home page
- The ability to stop and restart the animation
- The ability to choose which sections of your animation to play
- The ability to choose a low-bandwidth, reduced length, or small-screen version of your animation

To add buttons, hotspots, text fields, and other controls that let your audience control the way they interact with your animation, you use *object-based scripts*. (Object-based scripts are so called because you attach the scripts directly to the objects, like buttons, with which you want your audience to interact.)

To create automatic effects, like reversing a movie clip or loading a Web page when your animation reaches Frame 12, you attach a script to a frame to create a frame-based script. Page 484 has an example of a frame-based script.

Using Modify → Timeline → Reverse Frames

When you use Modify → Timeline → Reverse Frames in conjunction with Flash's copy-and-paste function, you can create the reverse of a series of frames quickly, right in the timeline.

To create a reversed series of frames using Modify → Timeline → Reverse Frames:

1. **Click the first frame in the series you want to reverse. Then Shift-click the last frame in the series you want to reverse.**

   Flash highlights every frame in the series, from first to last.

2. **Select Edit → Timeline → Copy Frames. In the timeline, click the first frame where you want to insert the reversed series of frames.**

    Flash highlights the selected frame.

3. **Select Edit → Timeline → Paste Frames.**

    Flash pastes the copied frames onto the timeline, beginning at the selected frame.

4. **If the pasted frame series isn't highlighted, select it (Figure 14-15, top).**

5. **Choose Modify → Timeline → Reverse Frames (Figure 14-15, bottom).**

    Flash reverses the frames in the timeline.

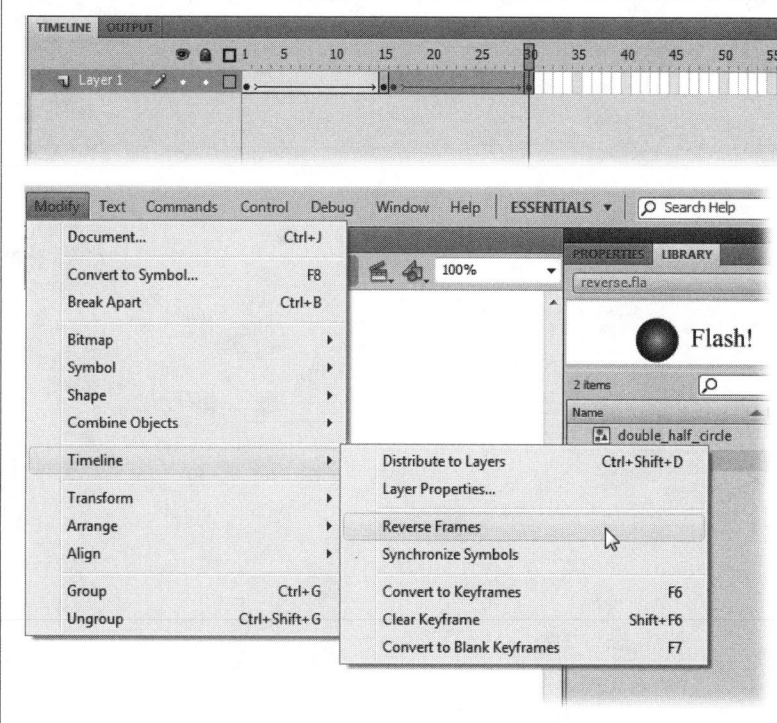

Figure 14-15:
Top: You don't have to begin a reverse series directly after the original series, but in most cases— where you want a seamless transition—you do. After you paste the series, make sure you select the pasted frames if Flash hasn't done it for you.

Bottom: The Reverse Frames option here appears grayed out if the pasted frame series isn't highlighted.

Components for Interactivity

Creating common Flash elements like playback controls (Play and Pause buttons), text fields, checkboxes, and buttons can add up to a lot of grunt work. Since they pretty much look the same in every animation, some kind Flash developers did the grunt work for you and put ready-made versions of these Flash bits and pieces—called *components*—right into the program.

A component is a compiled, prebuilt movie clip that you can drag onto the stage and customize. Flash CS4 comes with dozens of components (Figure 15-1). If you do a lot of work in Flash, you'll appreciate the time that components can save you. But another great thing about components is the consistency they give. For example, the User Interface Components discussed in this chapter all look like they belong together. If you don't like their style, Flash gives you some convenient ways to change their appearance. So, if you're working in a design shop, you can add time-test components to your projects and still give each client a look that matches its image and brand.

There's a consistency in the way you work with components, which also makes them easy to use. This chapter starts off showing you how to add, modify, and write code for the Button and ColorPicker components. By the time you're done, you'll not only know how to work with Button components, you'll be 90% of the way to knowing how to use the other Flash components.

After you learn how to add, modify, and program a couple of components, you'll learn about the different types of components available and what they can do for you. To wrap it all up, you'll learn how to find and install components that come from sources other than Adobe.

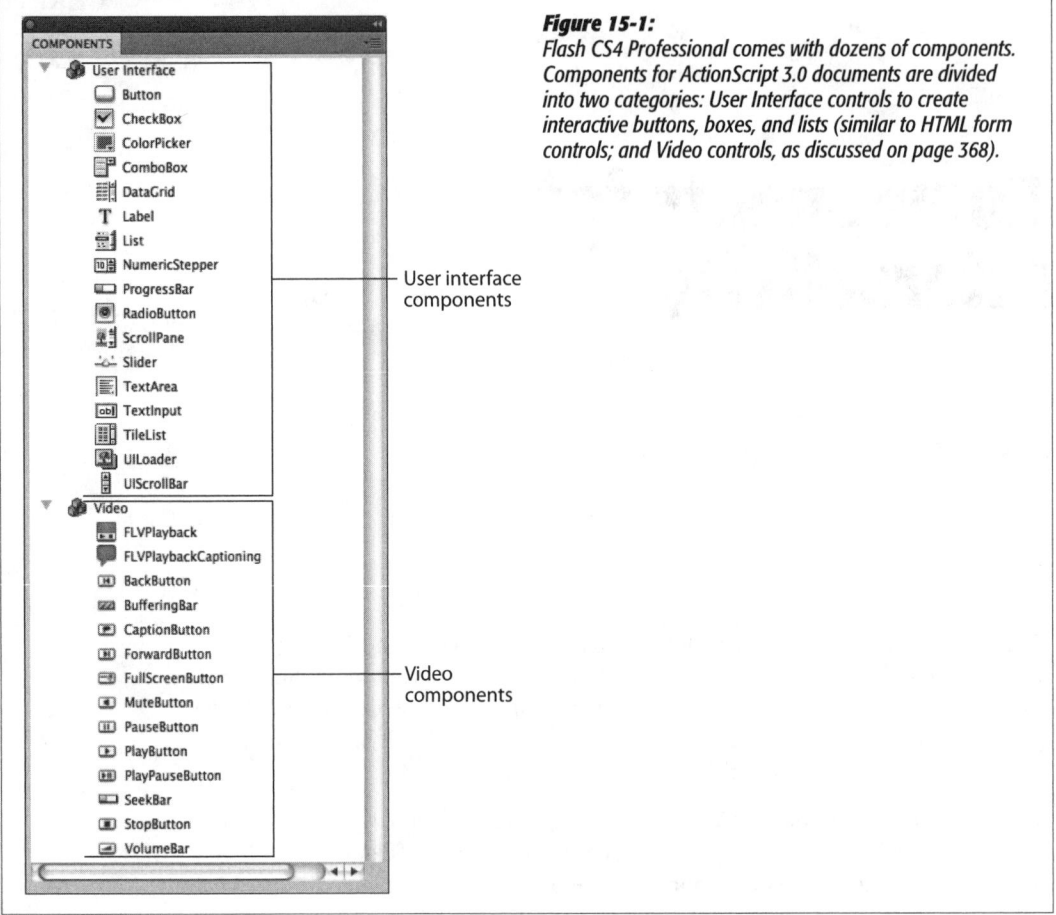

Figure 15-1:
Flash CS4 Professional comes with dozens of components. Components for ActionScript 3.0 documents are divided into two categories: User Interface controls to create interactive buttons, boxes, and lists (similar to HTML form controls; and Video controls, as discussed on page 368).

Note: Using components requires a fair amount of ActionScript knowledge. But *creating* your own components is an even more ActionScript-intensive proposition. If you'd like to explore creating your own components, check out both the ActionScript 3.0 Language and Components Reference you find in Flash Help (see page 413), and a good book that covers both ActionScript and object-oriented design. Colin Moock's *Essential Action-Script 2.0* and *Essential ActionScript 3.0* (O'Reilly) are two of the best on the market.

Adding Components

Adding a component to your animation is the first step in using that component. As you'll see in the following sections, adding an instance of a component to the stage is similar to adding an instance of a symbol: all you have to do is drag and drop. But instead of dragging a component from the Library panel, you drag components from the Components panel.

To add a component to your animation:

1. **Select Window → Components.**

   The Components panel appears.

2. **In the Components panel, click to a select the component you want, and then drag it to the stage.**

   As Figure 15-2 shows, Flash displays an instance of the component on the stage. It also places a copy of the component in the Library (Window → Library).

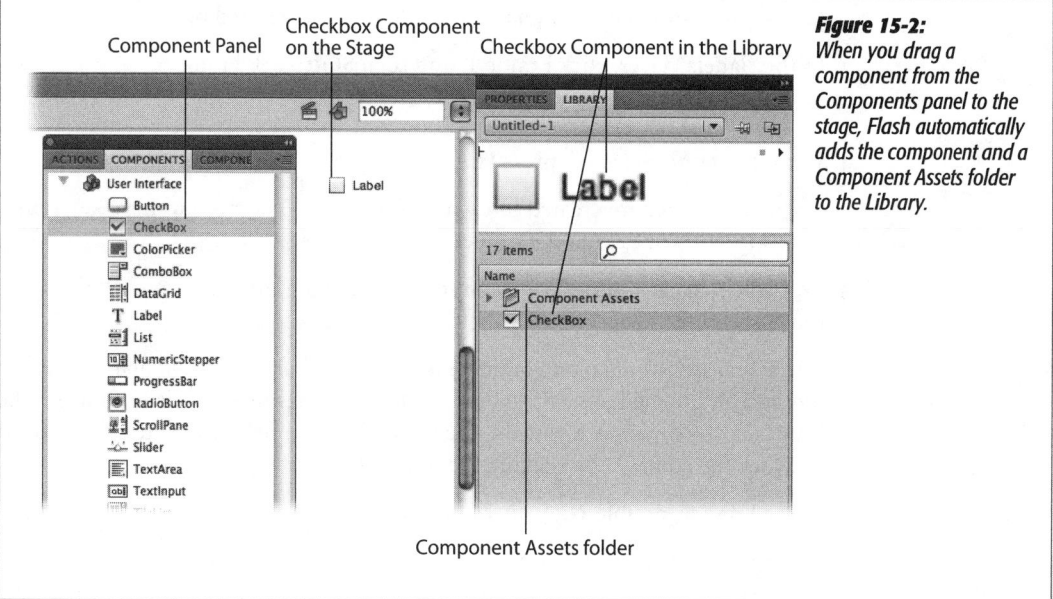

Figure 15-2:
When you drag a component from the Components panel to the stage, Flash automatically adds the component and a Component Assets folder to the Library.

Tip: Flash gives you another way to add a component: In the Components panel, double-click the component. When you do, Flash immediately places an instance of the component on the center of your stage.

In most cases, adding a component to the stage is just part of the process. After you add the component, you still need to customize it and—depending on the component you choose—add ActionScript code to make it work with the other parts of your animation. That's exactly what you'll do in the following steps. In this example, you'll learn how to add buttons to an animation, and then use those buttons to control both the main timeline and the timeline of a movie clip that's added to the main timeline.

This project uses a file *button_component_begin.fla* that you can download from the "Missing CD" page (*http://missingmanuals.com/cds*). If you'd like to see the completed project, you can download *button_component_finished.fla*. The first steps in this example set up the Flash document so it works with Button components and the ActionScript code that makes the buttons work. That involves creating new layers for actions, labels, and buttons.

1. **In Flash, open *button_component_begin.fla.***

   There's a layer named "words" containing five keyframes. In the last four keyframes are the names of famous cities. There's a second empty layer called "maps." In the Library, there's a folder called "map jpgs" and a movie clip called Maps.

2. **Click the New Layer button in the lower-left corner of the timeline to add three layers. From top to bottom, name them actions, labels and buttons.**

3. **In the "labels" layer, click Frame 1, and then Shift-click Frame 5.**

   You've selected all five frames.

4. **With the frames selected, press F6.**

   Empty keyframes are created in each of the frames. You need to have keyframes to create labels in each of the frames.

5. **Add labels to each of the five keyframes by clicking the frame, and then typing the name in the Properties → Label → Name box.**

   Name Frame 1 *world*; name Frame 2 *paris*; name Frame 3 *london*; name Frame 4 *moscow*; and name Frame 5 *beijing*. ActionScript uses these labels to find specific frames in the timeline. You won't be using this layer again, so you can go ahead and lock the contents by clicking the button under the padlock.

6. **In the Library, double-click the Maps movie clip.**

   The movie clip opens in Flash.

7. **Drag the playhead to inspect the individual frames in the movie clip, and then click the Scene 1 button.**

   As you move the playhead, each frame shows a different map. The labels in the timeline name the map. When you click the Scene 1 button, the movie clip closes and brings you back to the main timeline

8. **Click the "maps" layer in the main timeline, and then drag the Maps movie clip to the stage.**

   The Maps movie clip appears in all five frames of the main timeline because there's only one keyframe in the "maps" layer.

   You don't have to sweat positioning the movie clip by hand; you can do the job with the Properties panel, as shown in Figure 15-3.

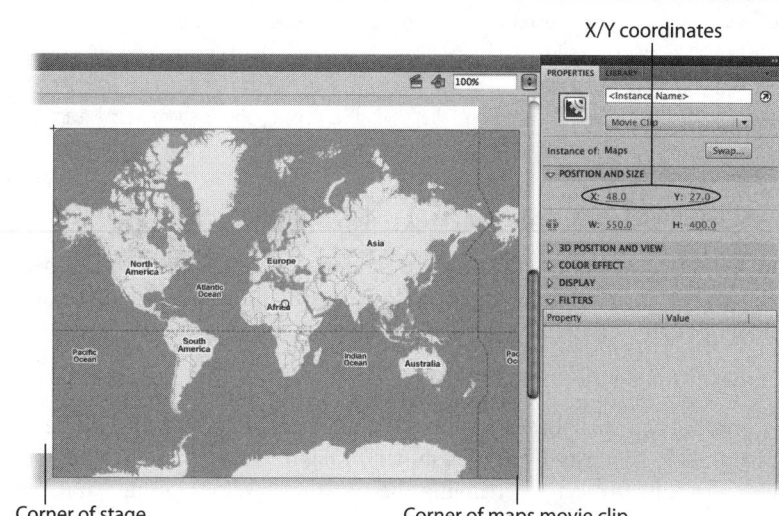

X/Y coordinates

Figure 15-3:
The Maps movie clip is exactly the same size as the Flash document, 550 × 400 pixels. Here, the Maps movie clip isn't lined up with the stage, but, setting the x/y coordinates in Properties to 0,0 positions it perfectly to cover the entire stage.

©2008 Google Maps

Corner of stage   Corner of maps movie clip

9. **With the Maps movie clip selected, in the Properties panel type the instance name maps.**

   You have to name the instance of the Maps movie clip before you can control it with ActionScript.

   Once the Maps movie clip is positioned and named, lock the "maps" layer, so you don't accidentally move it when you're repositioning other elements on the stage.

   If you test your animation at this point (Ctrl+Enter or ⌘-Return on a Mac), you'll see the maps and city names flash by rapidly. So far, your steps have set up a sort of a slideshow with labels that you can use as bookmarks for your buttons and ActionScript code. In the next steps, you'll add buttons and use ActionScript to control both the main timeline and the Maps movie clip timeline.

10. **In the timeline, click the "buttons" layer.**

   You want to place all the new buttons in the button layer of the timeline.

11. **Select Window → Components to open the components panel, and then drag the Button component to the stage.**

   The button appears on the stage and two items appear in the Library: a Button symbol and a folder named Component Assets.

Note: When you add your first component to a Flash project, it increases the file size of the published .swf file by about 20 kilobytes. This isn't a whopping leap in file size by today's standards, but it's good to know that if you add more components, they won't increase your file size by the same amount. They'll only add a couple kilobytes for each component. That's because all components share a certain amount of underlying code. Once the basic code is added to the .swf file it's available to any components that need it.

12. **With the button selected, in the Properties panel, type the instance name btnParis.**

When you select the button, the Instance Name box is at the top of the Properties panel. As with other symbols, you have to name the Button components before ActionScript can work with them.

13. **Select the button on the stage, and then select Window → Component Inspector.**

The Component Inspector shows the Parameters tab, showing the two parts of each parameter: name and value, as shown in Figure 15-4. You customize components for your project by changing the parameter values. Some parameters, like those with true/false values, have drop-down menus. Other parameters, like the Label parameter for buttons, have text boxes where you can type a new label.

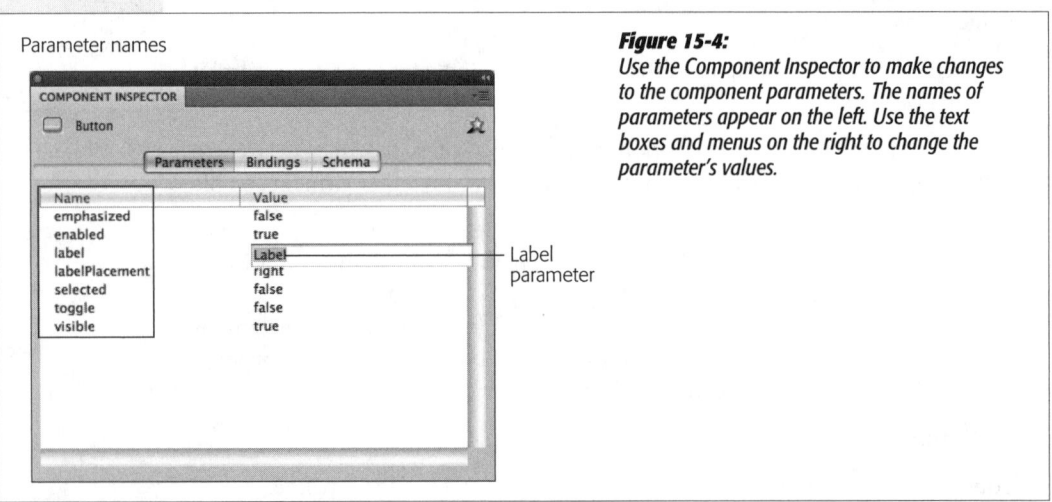

Parameter names

Label parameter

Figure 15-4:
Use the Component Inspector to make changes to the component parameters. The names of parameters appear on the left. Use the text boxes and menus on the right to change the parameter's values.

Note: The Bindings and Schema tabs work with ActionScript 2.0 documents, which aren't covered in this book.

14. **Click the text box for the Label parameter, and then type *Paris*.**

What you type in this text box changes the word that appears on the button. You don't need to change any of the other parameters right now, but here's a rundown on their uses:

• **emphasized.** If this value is *true*, it changes the button's appearance. Use it when you want to make one button stand out from a group of buttons.

- **enabled.** If this value is, *false* the button won't work. It's helpful in situations where you don't want your audience to use a button, but you still want it to be visible.

- **labelPlacement.** As it sounds, this parameter gives you several choices for the way a label is positioned: left, right, top, or bottom.

- **selected.** Like emphasized, this parameter changes the button's appearance to show that it's selected.

- **toggle.** If this value is *true*, the button works like a toggle and its appearance changes to reflect that.

- **visible.** You can hide a button by making setting the visible parameter to *false.* You can use this feature when you want to prevent your audience from using the button.

Note: Components are sometimes called *black boxes* because you can't inspect their inner workings. The only things you can look at or change are the characteristics that the developer *exposes* (lets you access) through the Properties panel, the Component Inspector, or ActionScript classes.

---

15. Drag three more buttons from the Library to the stage. Give them the instance names: btnLondon, btnMoscow, and btnBeijing, and then label them London, Moscow, and Beijing.

    As shown in Figure 15-5, you don't have worry too much about how the buttons are arranged. In the next steps, you'll use the Align tool to position them precisely.

16. Select all the buttons, and then select Modify → Align → Distribute Widths.

    The Distribute Widths command evenly lines the buttons up end to end.

17. Select Modify → Align → To Stage, and then Select Modify → Align → Bottom.

    A checkmark appears next to To Stage on the menu, meaning that subsequent align commands will be relative to the stage; the Bottom command pushes all the buttons to the bottom of the stage.

18. Press Ctrl+G (⌘-G on a Mac) to group the buttons, and then select Modify → Align → Horizontal Center.

    This command centers the buttons at the bottom of the stage. You won't be doing anything immediately with single buttons, but you may as well ungroup them now with a Ctrl+Shift+G (⌘-Shift-G).

At this point, you've got everything positioned on the stage and labeled all the necessary frames. The only thing that's missing is the ActionScript code that glues it all together. If you test the animation at this point, it's pretty clear what that code needs to do. The first thing it needs to do is stop the movie clips from playing when the animation starts. The second thing the code needs to do is program the buttons to jump to specific frames in the main timeline and the "maps" timeline.

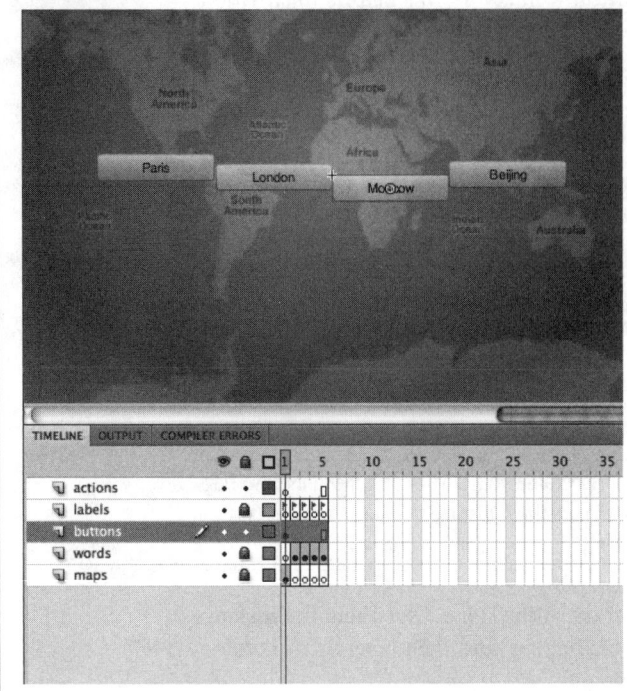

Figure 15-5:
Arrange the buttons so that they're roughly, end to end, in a left to right order: Paris, London, Moscow, and Beijing. Then use Flash's Modify → Align tools to tidy them up.

©2008 Google Maps

Making Button Components Work with ActionScript

If you've followed the ActionScript code exercises earlier in this book, chances are you've been introduced to ActionScript 3.0's event listeners. Unlike previous versions, ActionScript 3.0 uses a single method for recognizing and reacting to events. The following example uses event listeners to react to clicks on the Button components. If you need to brush up on using event listeners, see page 409.

1. **In the "actions" layer, click Frame 1, and the press F9.**

   The Actions panel opens.

2. **Type the following code to stop the main timeline and the Maps movie clip.**

   ```
   stop( );

   maps.stop( );
   ```

   The first line stops the main timeline. The second line stops the Maps movie clip from playing.

3. **Type the following code to register an event listener for the Button component with the variable name btnParis, as shown in Figure 15-6.**

   ```
   btnParis.addEventListener(MouseEvent.CLICK, clickParisListener);
   ```

   Event listeners come in two parts. This first part registers an event listener. In other words, it tells ActionScript to wait for a mouse click on btnParis. When there's a click, the *clickParisListener( )* function runs.

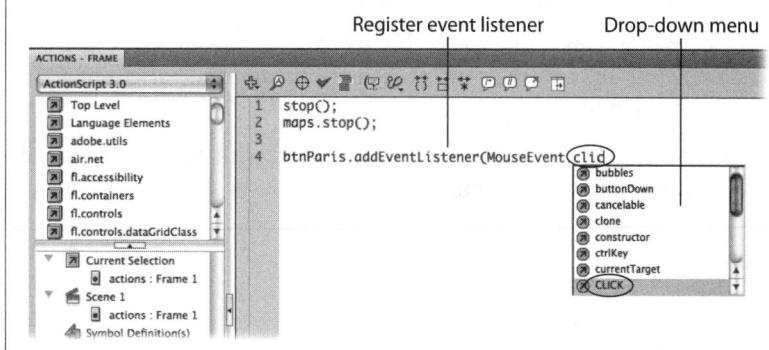

Register event listener   Drop-down menu

Figure 15-6:
As you type code, the Actions panel provides help. For example, after you enter MouseEvent and a period (.), a drop-down menu displays the properties and methods for MouseEvent. You can keep on typing, or you can make a selection from the list.

4. Type the code for the *clickParisListener( )* function:

```
function clickParisListener(evt:MouseEvent):void {
    gotoAndStop("paris");
    maps.gotoAndStop("paris");
}
```

The *clickParisListener( )* function has two lines of code that control movie clip timelines. As you might guess, the *gotoAndStop( )* method moves to a specific frame, and then prevents the playhead from moving beyond that frame. The first line inside the curly brackets moves the playhead on the main timeline to the frame labeled "paris," which displays the word "Paris" on the stage. The second line inside the curly brackets moves the playhead on the Maps movie clip to a frame also labeled "paris." This displays the map of Paris background, as shown in Figure 15-7.

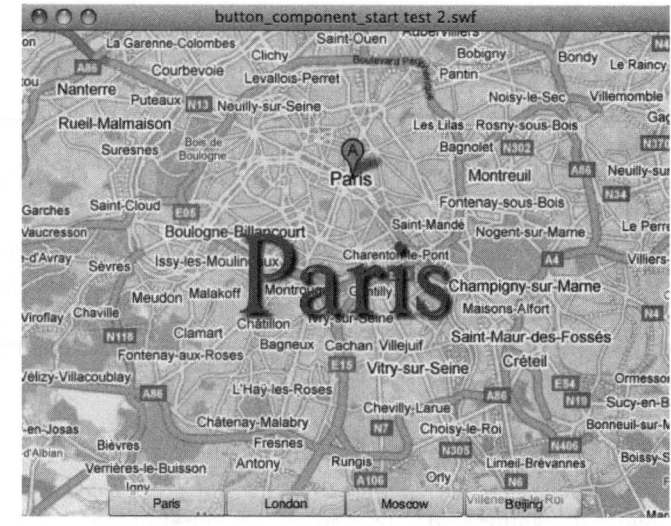

Figure 15-7:
ActionScript code controls the main timeline, which displays the word "Paris," and the Maps movie clip, which displays the Paris city map background.

©2008 Google Maps

5. **Press Ctrl+Enter (⌘-Return) to test the animation.**

When the animation runs, it stops on the first frame showing the world map. Click the Paris button, and the word Paris appears and the background map changes to a city map of Paris.

6. **Add event listeners for the remaining three buttons with the following code. When you're done, the code in Frame 1 in the actions layer should look like this:**

```
stop( );
maps.stop( );

btnParis.addEventListener(MouseEvent.CLICK,clickParisListener);
btnLondon.addEventListener(MouseEvent.CLICK,clickLondonListener);
btnMoscow.addEventListener(MouseEvent.CLICK,clickMoscowListener);
btnBeijing.addEventListener(MouseEvent.CLICK,clickBeijingListener);

function clickParisListener(evt:MouseEvent):void {
    gotoAndStop("paris");
    maps.gotoAndStop("paris");
}
function clickLondonListener(evt:MouseEvent):void {
    gotoAndStop("london");
    maps.gotoAndStop("london");
}
function clickMoscowListener(evt:MouseEvent):void {
    gotoAndStop("moscow");
    maps.gotoAndStop("moscow");
}
function clickBeijingListener(evt:MouseEvent):void {
    gotoAndStop("beijing");
    maps.gotoAndStop("beijing");
}
```

7. **Test the animation again.**

When you test the animation, button clicks display the city name and a matching background map.

In this example, it would have been easier to use a single timeline for both the words and the background maps, but the point is to show you to use how buttons and other events to control multiple timelines. For example, the "maps" timeline could include dozens of different maps, and you could use the same code to jump to any labeled frame.

Modifying Components in the Properties Panel

There are several ways you can modify components after you've added them to your project. The most straightforward way is to change the properties of the component in the Properties panel. Suppose you'd like to make the buttons in the previous example wider, so they run all the way across the bottom of the stage. Select btnParis, and in the Properties panel's Position and Size section, change the width setting to 137.5 (a fourth of the width of the stage). The width of btnParis changes, but all the other properties (position, height, and color) remain the same, as shown in Figure 15-8.

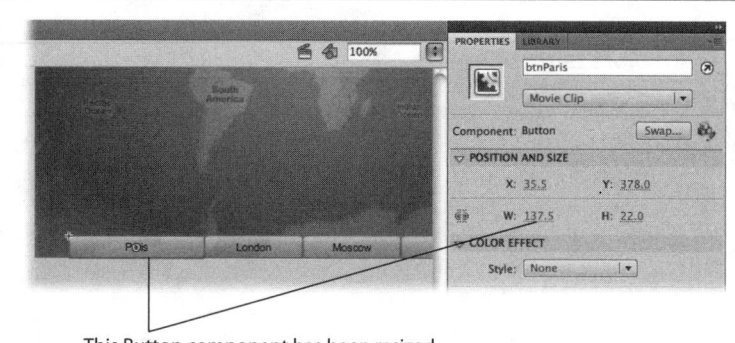

Figure 15-8:
Changing the properties of an instance of a component changes that single instance. Notice that the other buttons, btnLondon, btnMoscow, and btnBeijing remain the same width.

©2008 Google Maps

This Button component has been resized

For this example, go ahead and make all the instances of the Button component the same width: 137.5. Then use the Align commands to align them along the bottom of the stage, so it looks like Figure 15-9.

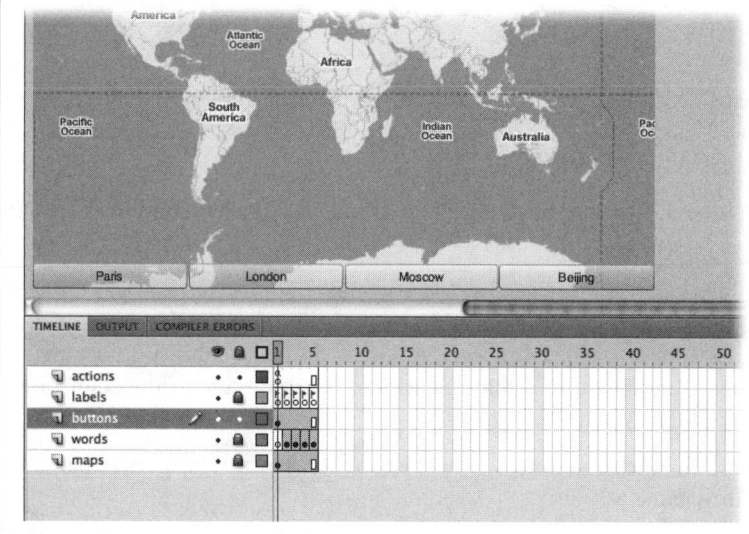

Figure 15-9:
Using the Properties panel, you can change properties of the instances on the stage. Here the width of the Button components has been changed.

©2008 Google Maps

Adding a ColorPicker Component

One of the great things about Flash components is their consistency. Once you know how to add and customize one component, like the Button component, it's easy to apply that knowledge to other components. For example, the ColorPicker tool appears in an animation as a little color swatch. When your audience clicks the swatch, it displays a palette of colors to choose from, as shown in Figure 15-10. Using this handy tool, you can give your audience the power to change the colors of elements in your animation. Even though components like buttons and color pickers have very different purposes, the steps for adding them to the stage, setting their parameters, and creating event listeners to react to them is very similar.

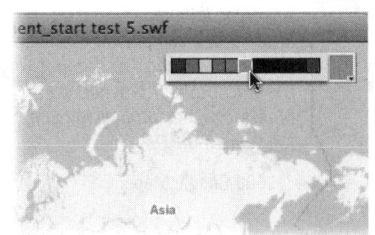

Figure 15-10:
The ColorPicker is one of those components that's fun for your audience. It gives them a way to customize elements in your animation to suit their own taste.

©2008 Google Maps

In this example, you'll add a ColorPicker component to the animation so your audience can choose a background color for the main timeline.

Note: This example continues exercises that started at the beginning of this chapter. If you didn't work on those examples, but would like to jump in at this point, download the file *begin.fla* from the "Missing CD" page at *http://missingmanuals.com/cds*. To see the final version, get *colorpicker_component_finished.fla*.

1. **In the timeline, unlock the "maps" layer.**

   The "maps" layer is a good place to put the ColorPicker because there are no keyframes. Placing the ColorPicker in the "maps" layer makes it available in every frame in the animation.

2. **Select Window → Component, and then drag a ColorPicker component on the stage.**

   You can place the ColorPicker any place you like, but the upper-right corner is a good spot if you can't decide. In addition to the instance on the stage, a Color-Picker gets added to the Library. If you delve into the Library folder named Component Assets, you find that folders and items specific to the color picker have been added as well.

3. **With the ColorPicker selected, type *cpBackground* in the Properties panel for the instance name.**

   It's good to identify object types as you create instance names. In this case *cp* is used to identify the object as a ColorPicker. Background indicates what the ColorPicker is changing.

4. **Press F9 to open the Actions window, and then type the following code to import the ColorPickerEvent.**

   ```
   import fl.events.ColorPickerEvent;
   ```

   When you create documents with Flash, you automatically have access to the most commonly used ActionScript classes, like the MovieClip class, the Shape class, and so on. The ColorPickerEvent isn't included, so you need to import the packages that define those classes. If you try to run your program without importing the package, you'll see an error that says "Error 1046: Type was not found…"

5. **Continue your code by registering an event listener for the ColorPicker and a function that runs when the ColorPicker changes:**

   ```
   cpBackground.addEventListener(ColorPickerEvent.CHANGE,changeColorPicker);

   function changeColorPicker(evt:ColorPickerEvent):void {
       opaqueBackground = evt.color;
   }
   ```

   This code follows the standard event listener format. One statement registers the event listener for an object, and the function explains what to do when the event happens. If you're already familiar with event listeners, the juicy bit of this example is the line that says: *opaqueBackground = evt.color;*. This line changes the background color of the main timeline. The opaqueBackground property is inherited by all DisplayObjects. The ColorPicker event has a property, appropriately called *color,* that holds the value of the color that was selected. (If you need to brush up on events and event handling, see page 409.)

6. **With the ColorPicker selected, choose Window → Component Inspector, and then change the selectedColor and the showTextField parameters.**

   At first the selectedColor parameter is set to *black.* If you want folks to notice that they can change the color, it's best to set this to something more colorful. Note that this command only changes the color displayed in the ColorPicker. It doesn't actually change the background color at this point; that's done by the code within the event listener.

   The showTextField parameter gives the audience a text box where they can type a color's hexadecimal value. You can assume that your audience would rather click a color swatch, so set this parameter to *false.*

7. **Select the Maps movie clip on the stage, and then select Properties → Color Effect → Alpha and type 50.**

   The Maps movie clip becomes semi-transparent, letting the background color show through, as explained in Figure 15-11.

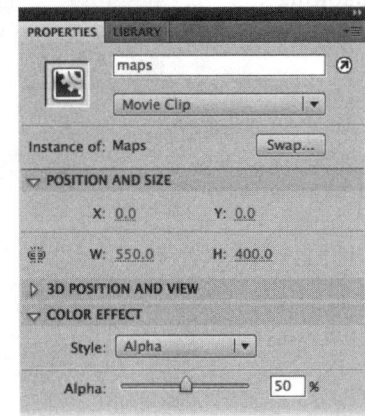

Figure 15-11:
The background color won't show through if there's a completely opaque movie clip covering the stage. Setting the movie clip's alpha value to 50% lets the background color show through, giving the image on top a pleasing color effect.

8. **Press Ctrl+Enter (⌘-Return) to test the animation.**

   When the animation first runs, there's no background color, since the code that sets the background color is inside of the ColorPicker event. The color changes when you select a new color in the ColorPicker. If you use the buttons to jump from city to city, the background color remains constant until a new color is selected.

As this example shows, the steps for putting the ColorPicker component into action are similar to those for using the Button component. Adding an instance of the component to the stage, creating an event listener, and changing the component parameters are much the same. The only differences are related to the components purpose and behavior.

Modifying the ColorPicker with ActionScript

Components have properties just like any other objects. When you change the parameters of a component, you're changing properties that the author of the component has made available to designers. (Other component properties are hidden, where you can't mess with them.) You can change those properties using ActionScript, too. Specifically, you can change a component's properties while an animation is running, or as coders like to say, "You can change the properties at runtime."

Here's an example that changes the ColorPicker using ActionScript code. The ColorPicker's palette shows bunches of colors, many of them very similar. There may be times when you don't want to offer so many color choices. For example, if you're letting customers choose the color for their new Stutz Bearcat automobile, you may offer only a handful of color options. Using ActionScript, you can specify each color shown on the palette, as long as you know the hexadecimal code that identifies the color.

Add this to the code for your ColorPicker project (page 509). You can place it following the line that begins with the word "import":

```
cpBackground.colors =
[0xFF0000,0xFF7700,0xFFFF00,0x00FF00,0x000044,0x0000FF,0x0066FF];
```

The colors property of the ColorPicker is an array. The values held inside of an array are enclosed in square brackets and separated by commas. Each of the odd looking numbers, like 0xFF7700 are hexadecimal values. Now when you test the animation, the ColorPicker shows a palette of only seven colors, as shown in Figure 15-10.

Tip: Use Flash's color panel Window → Color to look up the hexadecimal numbers for the colors you need. Select a color and the hexadecimal value appears in the text box, as shown in Figure 15-12. Replace the # with ActionScript's identifier for hex values *0x*.

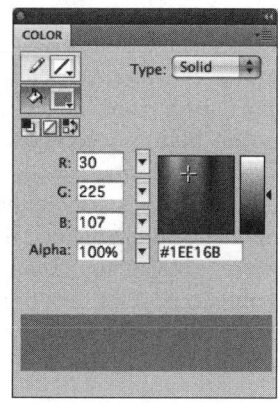

Figure 15-12:
Drag the crosshairs to choose a hue, and then adjust the brightness of the color using the vertical slider on the right. When you're happy with the color previewed at the bottom, select and copy the hexadecimal number that appears in the box. To use the number in ActionScript, replace the # with 0x (ActionScript's identifier for hex values).

You can use similar code to change the properties of the ColorPicker (or other components). In step 6 on page 511, you used the Component Inspector to change the ColorPicker's showTextField property. To change that setting using ActionScript, use a statement like this:

```
cpBackground.showTextField = false;
```

The Built-in Components

Choose Window → Components and you see a panel full of built-in components that you can drag and drop into your Flash document. Well, it's almost that easy. You see different components depending on whether your document is based in ActionScript 2.0 or ActionScript 3.0. Like any ActionScript code, you can't mix version 2 components and version 3 components in the same document. This

---

forward-looking chapter focuses on the ActionScript 3.0 components. The Action-Script 3.0 built-in components fall into two main categories:

- **User Interface components.** Similar to HTML components, Flash User Interface components include buttons, checkboxes, lists, text fields, and windows—everything you need to create a Flash form and collect data from your audience.

- **Video components.** Similar to the earlier version media components used to play, pause, and mute animations, these components give you more sophisticated tools to work with video clips. For example, they work with streaming video (where a movie begins to play before the entire file is downloaded). These components are an indication of Flash's growing role as a tool to provide Web-based video.

Note: This chapter focuses on the User Interface components, because they're by far the most popular Flash components. For an introduction to the video components, see Incorporating Video on page 350.

User Interface Components

Similar to HTML form components, Flash's popular *user interface components* (Figure 15-1) let you interact with your audience, display information, and gather information. Examples of user interface components include buttons, checkboxes, text fields, and drop-down lists. In this section, you'll find details about Action-Script 3.0 user interface components. For each component, there's a table that details the parameters you see when you select the component, and then open the Component Inspector (Window → Component Inspector). If you use components a lot, some of the parameters will become very familiar, because they work with several different components. Other parameters are specific to the purpose of a particular component, and you may need to refer to this section for the full explanation. See the box on page 516.

Note: There's a companion Flash document for this section. It's called *component_index.fla,* and you can see it in Figure 15-13 and download it from the "Missing CD" page (*http://missingmanuals.com/cds*). Test the document with Ctrl+Enter (⌘-Return), and you'll see all the components do their things. If you explore the .fla document, you'll find that each component is contained on its own, labeled frame in the timeline. Interested in checking out the ActionScript code behind the component? Just click the related frame in the actions layer, and then open the Actions panel (Window → Actions). The code includes lots of explanatory comments.

Button

The Button hardly needs introduction. It's a multipurpose component you can use to receive input from your animation's audience. The process of using a Button component is covered in detail beginning on page 500, and you see an example of the clickable Button component in Figure 15-14.

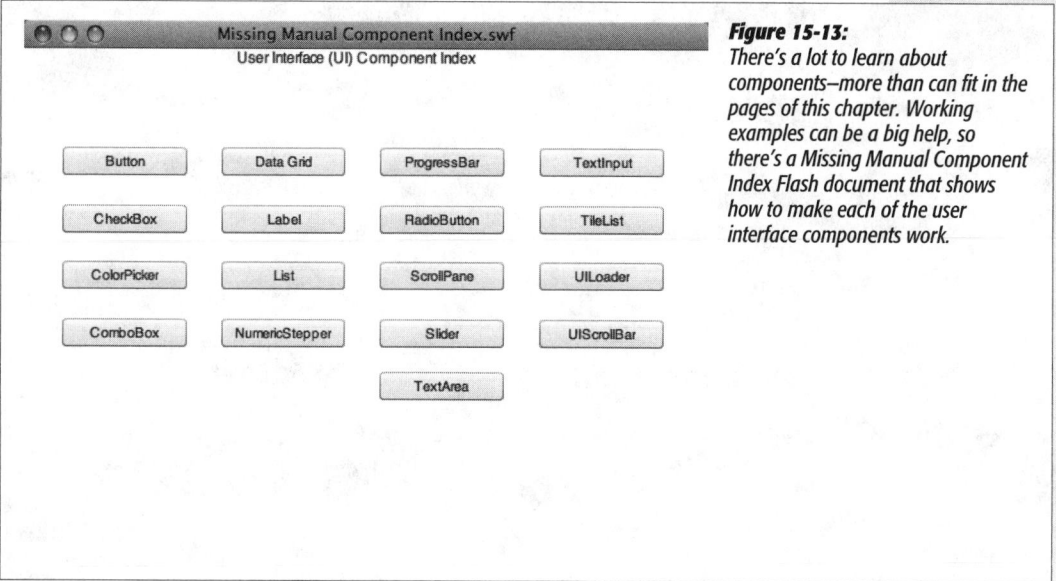

Figure 15-13:
There's a lot to learn about components—more than can fit in the pages of this chapter. Working examples can be a big help, so there's a Missing Manual Component Index Flash document that shows how to make each of the user interface components work.

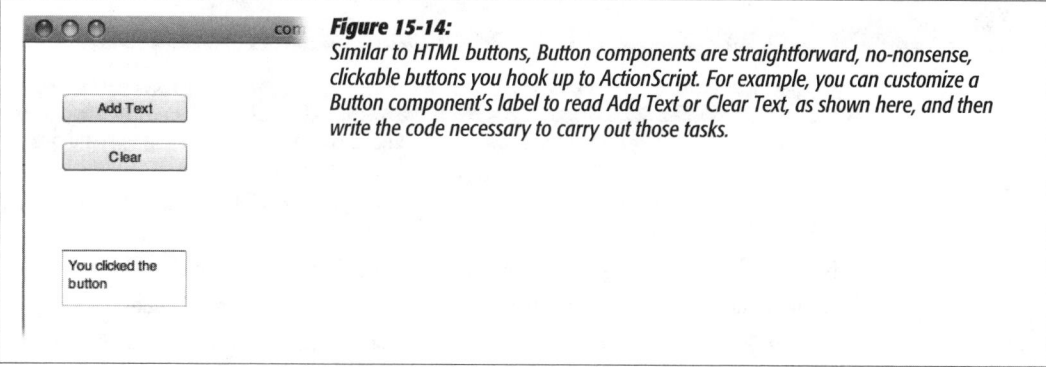

Figure 15-14:
Similar to HTML buttons, Button components are straightforward, no-nonsense, clickable buttons you hook up to ActionScript. For example, you can customize a Button component's label to read Add Text or Clear Text, as shown here, and then write the code necessary to carry out those tasks.

You may be wondering when it's best to use a Button component and when it's best to use Flash's button symbol from the Library. If you're into customizing a button with, say, animations and other snazzy effects, go for the button symbol from the Library. The symbol gives you a movie clip timeline where you can do your magic—for all the details see page 252. The Button component is a predesigned button that you don't have to fiddle with too much to make it useful. The button's a good alternative if you're using other components, because they'll all have a similar look. As you see in the Button Parameters table, one handy built-in feature of the Button component is the toggle parameter. When you set this parameter to true, the button displays on/off characteristics. Clicking the button turns it on, and it stays down. Click it again, and it pops back up into position.

FREQUENTLY ASKED QUESTION

Knowing What to Type for a Parameter

I understand the concept of parameters and values, but if I don't know what a parameter does. And frankly, the Parameters panel doesn't give me much in the way of clues. How do I know what to type for the parameter's value?

The parameters Flash lets you set in the Component Inspector panels vary from component to component. In some cases, you can figure out the value you're supposed to type by looking at the parameter's name. For example, it doesn't take a rocket scientist to guess what you're supposed to type for the TextArea component's *text* parameter. But you can't always so easily decipher the values Flash expects for other parameters. This section of the chapter is designed to help.

In the upper-right corner of the Component Inspector, there's a wizard icon. (It looks like a little magic wand.) The hope is that Adobe will eventually make wizards available for each component that comes with Flash. As this book goes to

press, however, clicking the wizard icon has no effect (unless you count the pop-up message "No wizards for this component").

Until that wonderful day when Flash comes with a full set of component wizards, you need to select Help → Flash Help → ActionScript 3.0 Language and Components Reference, and then search for the name of the component you're customizing to get the skinny on parameters. When you do, you see a somewhat brief explanation of the component's purpose, the properties and methods for the component, and an example or two.

Unfortunately, if you're working with a third-party component you've found on the Internet (see page 531), Flash Help doesn't help: You need to contact the component author and ask for documentation.

Button Parameters	Expected Value	Purpose
emphasized	true or false	Changes appearance of button to stand out from other buttons.
enabled	true or false	If false, the button doesn't accept audience input.
label	a string of characters	Explanatory text label for button.
labelPlacement	left, right, top, bottom	Positions label relative to button.
selected	true or false	Changes appearance of button to show it's selected.
toggle	true or false	Give the button on/off functions.
visible	true or false	If false, the component is hidden.

CheckBox

The CheckBox is another familiar friend to anyone who has completed an online survey or filled out a questionnaire. The CheckBox component lets you offer your audience an easy way to choose multiple options, as shown in Figure 15-15. With checkboxes, folks can make several selections in a group of options. If you want to limit your audience to a single choice, use the RadioButton component. CheckBoxes are common in computer programs, on the Web, and in print, so your audience will easily understand how to use them. You can customize the CheckBox component at design time using the following parameters. For example, if you set the "selected" parameter to *true* at design time, a checkmark appears in the CheckBox when your animation first runs.

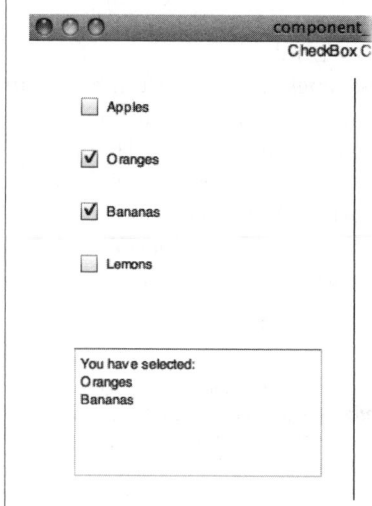

Figure 15-15:
Unlike RadioButtons (page 525), CheckBoxes let your audience make multiple selections.

Note: For ActionScript coders there are two distinct categories for time: *design time* and *runtime*. Design time is where you are now, when you have Flash open on your computer and you can control events, drawings, and all details in Flash. Runtime is when your Flash project is out there in the world, where your audience is viewing it and controlling it.

Using ActionScript, you can change components' properties while the animation is running. For example, examine the following code, which could appear at any time within your animation:

```
cbApples.enabled = false;
cbOranges.visible = false;
cbBananas.selected = true;
```

This code turns off the CheckBox *cbApples*, making it appear grayed out and unclickable. The CheckBox *cbOranges* is hidden entirely and *cbBananas* is selected so it sports a handsome checkmark.

CheckBox Parameters	Expected Value	Purpose
enabled	true or false	If false, CheckBox doesn't accept audience input.
label	a stringy of characters	Explanatory text for CheckBox.
labelPlacement	left, right, top, bottom	Positions label relative to component.
selected	true or false	Makes a checkmark appear in the CheckBox.
visible	true or false	If false, the component is hidden.

ColorPicker

The ColorPicker component (shown in Figure 15-16) displays a palette of colors, giving your audience an opportunity to select a single color. You can give your audience a way to customize, say, text, background colors, and just about any other elements in the display. For example, suppose you're selling laptop computer cases. You can limit the colors shown in the ColorPicker to just those you have available. You can learn how to use the ColorPicker tool in detail on page 509. Select a ColorPicker, and then open the Component Inspector (Window → Component Inspector), and you see the parameters shown in the following table.

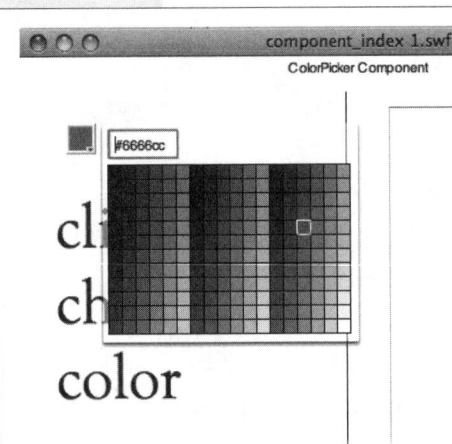

Figure 15-16:
The ColorPicker makes it easy for your audience to select a single color from an entire palette of options. Using ActionScript code, you can limit the colors shown in the palette.

ColorPicker Parameters	Expected Value	Purpose
enabled	true or false	If false, ColorPicker doesn't respond when clicked.
selectedColor	hexadecimal color value	The currently selected color that's displayed when the palette is closed. ActionScript code can work with the hexadecimal value of this color.
showTextField	true or false	If set true, a text field displays the hexadecimal value of the selectedColor, and your visitors can type a new hexadecimal value.
visible	true or false	If false, the component is hidden.

ComboBox

As Figure 15-17 shows, the ComboBox component lets you display a drop-down list of options. Use this component when you want to offer people an easy way to choose a single option (like which animation they want to play, or which Web page they want to hop to) from a predefined list. You can customize the ComboBox component at design time using the Component Inspector to change the parameter values. Flash automatically adds a scrollbar to your ComboBox component if you create a long list (over five options). Short list or long, the ComboBox lets your audience choose only one option. If you want to offer people a list from which they can Shift-click or Control-click multiple options, use the List component (page 522). The ComboBox uses a DataProvider as the source for its list. You can point to an external file or create the DataProvider in ActionScript within your document. For more details, see the box on page 521.

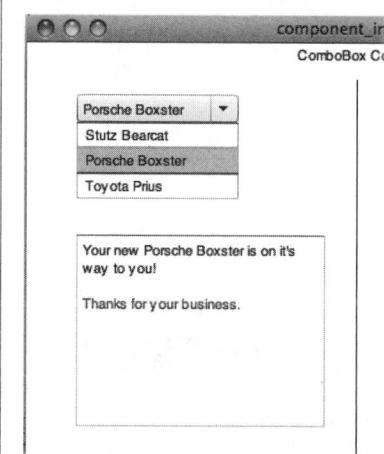

Figure 15-17:
Use the ComboBox component to give your audience a single choice from a list of items.

ComboBox Parameters	Expected Value	Purpose
dataProvider	a DataProvider object (for more details see the box on page 521.)	Points to a data source to provide the items in the list. The DataProvider object can come from an external source, or you can create one using ActionScript code. You can also manually add values by clicking the Value box in the Component Inspector.
editable	true or false	If false, your audience can't make changes to the ComboBox.
enabled	true or false	If false, your audience can't use the ComboBox.
prompt	a string of characters	The words that appear before your visitor uses the ComboBox.
restrict	a string of characters	Limits the characters that a visitor can enter in the text field.
rowCount	a number value	Sets the number of items displayed in the list. If the list has more items, a scroll bar appears. If the list has few items, the list is sized to fit.
visible	true or false	If false, the component is hidden

DataGrid

The DataGrid component lets you display a table containing multiple rows and columns of data, similar to a spreadsheet, as shown in Figure 15-18.

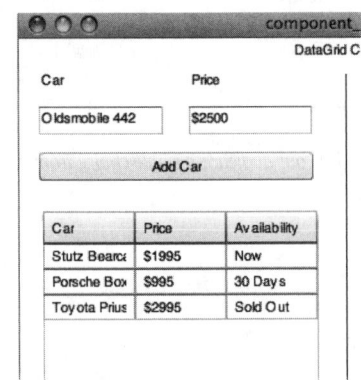

Figure 15-18:
The DataGrid component displays information in a spreadsheet-style format with rows and columns.

DataGrid Parameters	Expected Value	Purpose
allowMultipleSelection	true or false	If true, allows the selection of more than one list item in the data grid.
editable	true or false	If false, your audience can't change the DataGrid.
headerHeight	a number value	Sets header height in pixels.
horizontalLineScrollSize	a number value	The amount of content to be scrolled, horizontally, when your audience clicks a scroll arrow.
horizontalPageScrollSize	a number value	The number of pixels the scroll marker moves when your audience clicks the scroll bar track. Similar to a page up or page down command.
horizontalScrollPolicy	ON, OFF, AUTO	Controls whether a scroll bar appears in the component.
resizableColumns	true or false	If false your audience can't change column widths.
rowHeight	a number value	Sets the height of the rows in pixels.
showHeaders	true or false	If false, the DataGrid doesn't display headers.
sortableColumns	true or false	If false, your audience can't sort the data in the columns.
verticalLineScrollSize	a number value	The amount of content to be scrolled, vertically, when a scroll arrow is clicked.
verticalPageScrollSize	a number value	The number of pixels the scroll marker moves when your audience clicks the scroll bar track. Similar to a page up or page down command.
verticalScrollPolicy	ON, OFF, AUTO	Controls whether a scroll bar appears in the component.

FREQUENTLY ASKED QUESTION

Providing Data

What's a DataProvider?

Several Flash components—notably List, DataGrid, TileList, and ComboBox—use DataProvider objects to fill in the blanks. The DataProvider class is like any other ActionScript class; it has properties and methods, all of which relate to storing and retrieving data. You can use methods like AddItem and AddItemAt to fill a DataProvider with a list of items. When it's time to use a component, you can assign your prefilled DataProvider to the dataProvider parameter (or property) of a component. For example, here's the code that adds fine wines to a DataProvider named wineList:

```
wineList.addItem({label:"Chateau Thames
Embankment", data:24});
wineList.addItem({label:"Domaine Dogtown
Reserve", data:18});
wineList.addItem({label:"Cuvee Cuyahoga",
data:21});
```

In this example, each item consists of two parts: label and data. Label stores a text string representing the name of the wine, while data stores a number value representing the wine's quality rating. (Yes, that's 24 out of a possible 100.) If you're familiar with XML, the paired format consisting of a name and a value may look familiar.

In this format, you can add the items to a List component. The List component expects to receive a name and a data element for each item. To make these fine wines appear in a list component, you assign the *wineList* DataProvider to the *lstFineWine* List component:

```
lstFineWine.dataProvider = wineList;
```

The DataProvider is one more way that Flash Components achieve consistency even though their purposes and functions are different.

Typically, you use this component when you want to transfer data from your server (for example, product names, descriptions, and prices) and display it in Flash in table form. But you can also use it to display the data you collect (or create) in your Flash animation. You can populate the cells in the data grid from an external source, or you can create a DataProvider and store values in it, using ActionScript (see the box above).

Label

A Label component lets you add noneditable, nonclickable text to your Flash creation. To use the Label component, add the text you want displayed to the *text* parameter in the Component Inspector. If you're using ActionScript code, assign a string to the *text* property of the label. As an alternative, you can display HTML-encoded text using the *htmlText* parameter or property.

Tip: For most Flash designers, using Flash's Text tool is easier and keeps .swf files smaller. Even if you want to change text during runtime with ActionScript, you can do that with a Dynamic text field.

Parameters	Expected Value	Purpose
autoSize	true or false	If true, the label shows all of its text, regardless of the W and H properties.
condenseWhite	true or false	The value true removes extra white space from HTML text.
enabled	true or false	If false, your audience can't access the component.
htmlText	HTML-encoded text	Displays HTML encoded text, showing formatting, hyperlinks, and other features.
selectable	true or false	
text	a string of characters	The text shown in the display.
visible	true or false	If false, the component is hidden.
wordWrap	true or false	Controls line breaks in large chunks of text.

List

You use the List component (Figure 15-19) to create a clickable, scrollable list from which your audience can Shift-click to select multiple options. The List uses a DataProvider as the source. You can point to an external file or you can create the DataProvider in ActionScript within your document. For more details, see the box on page 521. The items that make up each row in a list consist of a label and data. The label appears in the list display; the data is the part that's invisible to your audience, but accessible to ActionScript. So, for example, you can create a list where someone can choose an employee by name; that selection can then pass the employee's ID number to another part of your program.

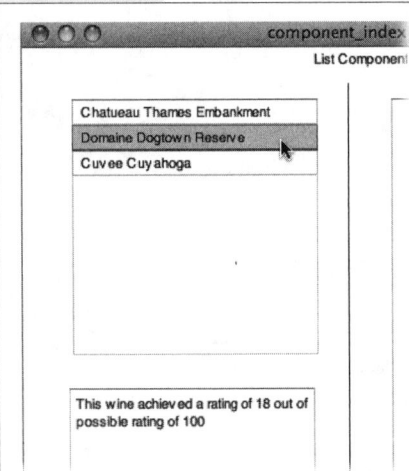

Figure 15-19:
The List component is similar to multiple checkboxes (see page 516) in that both let your audience select multiple options (once you customize the List component by setting allowMultipleSelection to true in the Component Inspector). But because List components are scrollable, they tend to take up less screen real estate than checkboxes, and so they're helpful when your stage is already packed with graphics and other components.

List Parameters	Expected Value	Purpose
allowMultipleSelection	true or false	If false, your audience can only select one item from the list at a time.
dataProvider	a DataProvider object (for more details see the box on page 521.)	Points to a data source to provide the items in the list. The DataProvider object can be an external source, or you can create one using ActionScript.
enabled	true or false	If false, your audience can't use the ComboBox.
horizontalLineScrollSize	a number value	The amount of content to be scrolled, horizontally, when your audience clicks a scroll arrow.
horizontalPageScrollSize	a number value	The number of pixels the scroll marker moves when your audience clicks the scroll bar track. Similar to a page up or page down command.
horizontalScrollPolicy	ON, OFF, AUTO	Controls whether a scroll bar appears in the component.
verticalLineScrollSize	a number value	The amount of content to be scrolled, vertically, when a scroll arrow is clicked.
verticalPageScrollSize	a number value	The number of pixels the scroll marker moves when your audience clicks the scroll bar track. Similar to a page up or page down command.
verticalScrollPolicy	ON, OFF, AUTO	Controls whether a scroll bar appears in the component.
visible	true or false	If false, the component is hidden.

NumericStepper

You use the NumericStepper component to create the clickable list of numbers, as shown in Figure 15-20. Simpler for people to use than a type-in-your-own-number text field, this component makes it easy for you to limit your audience's choices to a predefined set of valid numbers.

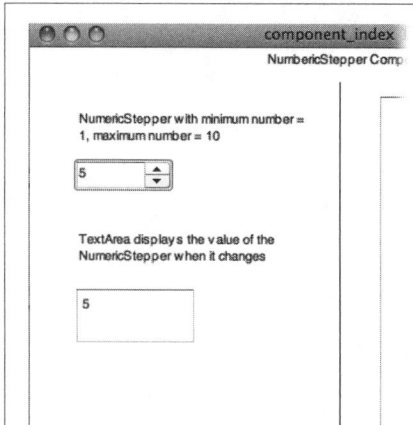

Figure 15-20:
When you use the NumericStepper component, your audience gets an easy way to specify a number, and you don't have to use ActionScript to examine the number and see whether it's valid (the way you would if you let them type any number they want).

Parameters	Expected Value	Purpose
enabled	true or false	If false, your audience can't use the component.
maximum	a number value	Sets the highest number the component can display.
minimum	a number value	Sets the lowest number the component can display.
stepSize	a number value	Sets the amount the value changes with each click.
value	a number value	The current value selected by the NumericStepper.
visible	true or false	If false, the component is hidden.

ProgressBar

The ProgressBar component, shown in Figure 15-21, is a visual indicator that a file—like a Flash .swf file—is loading. There are two ways a ProgressBar can work. If you're loading a file and have no way of knowing how big the file is, then you can't very well say the file is, for example, 50% loaded. In that case, the progress bar is considered *indeterminate*. In other words, it provides some motion, kind of like a barber's pole, to show that something's going on. On the other hand, if you know how big the file is, you can give your audience more detail on the process. You've probably seen the ProgressBar in action when Flash animations are loading from Web pages. To have the ProgressBar report on the progress of loading a file, type the name and path of the file in the *source* parameter. In ActionScript, you assign the name to the source property of the ProgressBar. You can also use ActionScript to access the percentComplete property, giving you a way to create a companion line of text.

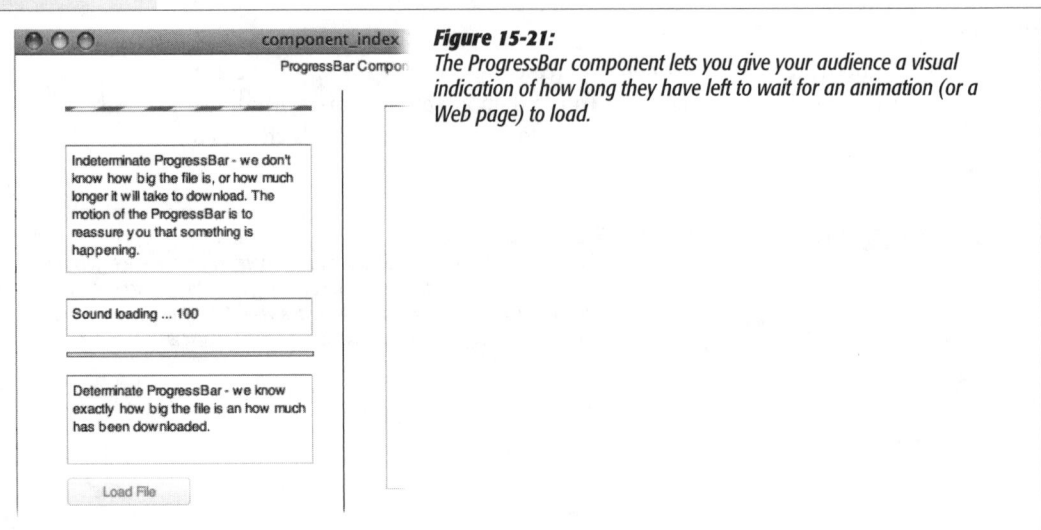

Figure 15-21:
The ProgressBar component lets you give your audience a visual indication of how long they have left to wait for an animation (or a Web page) to load.

Parameters	Expected Value	Purpose
direction	left or right	Sets whether the bar fills from the left or from the right.
enabled	true or false	If false, your audience can't access the component.
mode	event, polled, manual,	Selects different methods for providing progress information. Event and polled are the most common modes.
source	an object that's being loaded; for example. a Loader instance	Sets the source for the object that's being loaded.
visible	true or false	If false, the component is hidden.

RadioButton

When you want to make sure your audience chooses just one of several mutually exclusive options, use a group of RadioButton components (Figure 15-22). RadioButtons are frequently used in programs and on the Internet, so it's likely your audience will be familiar with them.

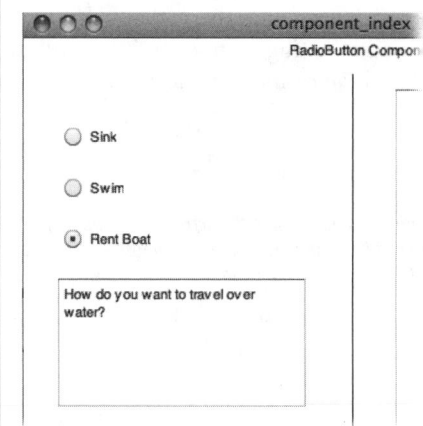

Figure 15-22:
RadioButton components let you offer your audience mutually exclusive options, so you never use just one. You always use RadioButton components in groups of two or more. (If you think you want a single RadioButton, you probably want to use a CheckBox.) Turning on one radio button tells Flash to turn off all the other radio buttons with the same groupName.

RadioButton Parameters	Expected Value	Purpose
enabled	True or false	If false, your audience can't use the component.
groupName	RadioButtonGroup	Identifies the group of buttons from which your audience can make a single selection.
label	a string of characters	Explanatory text for the RadioButton component.
labelPlacement	left, right, top, bottom	Positions label relative to button.

RadioButton Parameters	Expected Value	Purpose
selected	True or false	Changes the appearance of the RadioButton to show it's selected.
value	An object like a string or a number	You the designer define the values represented by radio buttons.
visible	True or false	If false, the component is hidden.

ScrollPane

The ScrollPane component helps you include an image that's too big to fit into your animation. Think about some of those map programs that let you move a map image inside of a frame. You can let your audience position an image using scroll bars or by dragging in the image. Figure 15-23 shows you the ScrollPane in action, and the table on page 527 lists the multitude of parameters you find in the Component Inspector. There are two parameters for each type of scroll bar: horizontal and vertical. These parameters determine how far the window scrolls when you click the scroll bar's arrows and when you click the body or track of the scroll bar. A ScrollPolicy lets you define scrolling behavior and assign that behavior to many objects and components. The ScrollPolicy settings can get a little involved, but in most cases, you can leave *horizontalScrollPolicy* and *verticalScrollPolicy* set to AUTO without adverse effects.

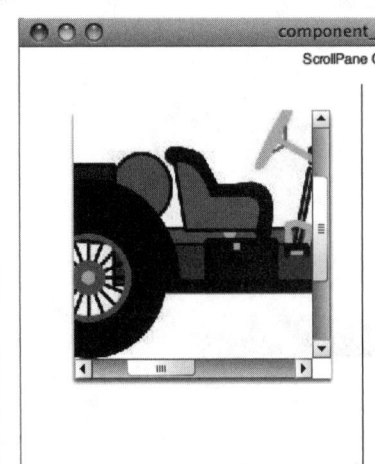

Figure 15-23:
When you display an animation or image using the ScrollPane component, Flash automatically tacks on scrollbars people can use to choose which part of the animation they want to see through the window.

ScrollPane Parameters	Expected Value	Purpose
enabled	true or false	If false, your audience can't use the component.
horizontalLineScrollSize	a number value	The amount of content to be scrolled, horizontally, when your audience clicks a scroll arrow is clicked.
horizontalPageScrollSize	a number value	The number of pixels by which to move the scroll marker on the horizontal scroll bar when your audience clicks the scroll bar track.
horizontalScrollPolicy	ON, OFF, AUTO	Controls whether a scroll bar appears in the component.
scrollDrag	true or false	If true, your audience can drag an image within the ScrollPane.
source	name and path to the file to be displayed; this can be an internet address	Sets the source for the file to be displayed in the ScrollPane.
verticalLineScrollSize	a number value	The amount of content to be scrolled, vertically, when a scroll arrow is clicked.
verticalPageScrollSize	a number value	The number of pixels by which to move the scroll marker on the vertical scroll bar when your audience clicks the scroll bar track.
verticalScrollPolicy	ON, OFF, AUTO	Controls whether a scroll bar appears in the component.
visible	true or false	If false, the component is hidden.

Slider

The Slider component gives your audience an easy way to select a value. Better still, it helps you prevent them from choosing a useless value. (Ever had someone type his name into a box where you expected a number?) Sliders are a natural for controlling volume or sizing an image, and there are lots of creative ways to use them. Use the maximum and minimum parameters to set the range. Use the snapInterval to count by fives or twos if you want. The tickInterval refers to a visual scale that appears above the slider, as shown in Figure 15-24.

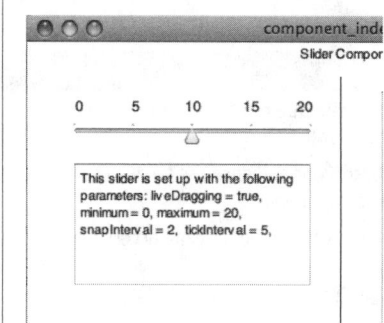

Figure 15-24:
The slider component doesn't automatically provide numbers for its scale. Here the numbers were added using Flash text.

Slider Parameters	Expected Value	Purpose
direction	horizontal or vertical	Sets the slider's orientation.
enabled	true or false	If false, your audience can't access the component.
liveDragging	true or false	The setting true lets your audience drag to change the slider value. If you set the value to false, it's up to you to move the slider through ActionScript to display a value.
maximum	a number value	The high number on the Slider's scale.
minimum	a number value	The low number on the Slider's scale.
snapInterval	a number value	Sets the precision available on the Slider's scale.
tickInterval	a number value	Shows visual tick marks above the Slider.
value	a number value	The value represented by the Slider's position.
visible	true or false	If false, the component is hidden.

TextArea

The TextArea component (Figure 15-25) is an all-purpose, multiline, scrollable text field that's useful when you want your audience to be able to type a long comment, or any other information longer than a few words. You can also modify the text property through ActionScript, which means you can change the text that appears in a text field while you're animation is running.

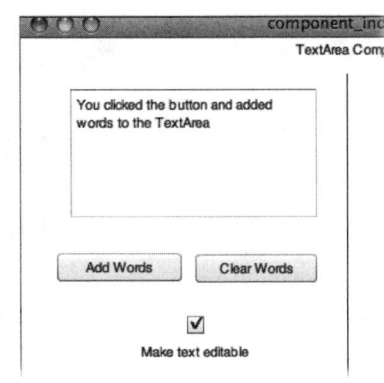

Figure 15-25:
The TextArea and TextInput components both let your audience type text, but the TextArea component (shown here) lets them type multiple lines of text. Flash automatically adds scrollbars if someone types in more text than the TextArea component's dimensions can display.

TextArea Parameters	Expected Value	Purpose
condenseWhite	true or false	The value true removes extra white space from HTML text.
editable	true or false	If false, your audience can't make changes to the component.
enabled	true or false	If false, your audience can't access the component.
horizontalScrollPolicy	ON, OFF, AUTO	Controls whether a scroll bar appears in the component.

TextArea Parameters	Expected Value	Purpose
htmlText	HTML-encoded text	Displays HTML encoded text, showing formatting, hyperlinks, and other features.
maxChars	a number value	Limits the number of characters that the TextArea component can contain. The setting 0 means there's no limit.
restrict	a string of characters	Lets you specify which characters your audience can type into the TextArea component. For example, you can limit input to the numbers 0–9 if you expect a phone number.
text	a string of characters	The text to be displayed in the TextArea
verticalScrollPolicy	ON, OFF, AUTO	Controls whether a scroll bar appears in the component.
visible	true or false	If false, the component is hidden.
wordWrap	true or false	Controls line breaks in large chunks of text.

TextInput

The TextInput component lets you create a single-line text field, used mostly as a field in a form. Using this component lets you give your audience a freeform text field just long enough to type what you want them to type (for example, a name, phone number, or email address).

TextInput Parameters	Expected Value	Purpose
displayAsPassword	True or false	The value true disguises the actual characters in the display.
editable	True or false	If false, your audience can't change the text.
enabled	True or false	If false, the component can't be accessed by the audience.
maxChars	a number value	Limits the number of characters that can be contained in a TextArea component. If it's set to 0, there's no limit.
restrict	a string of characters	Used to limit the characters that can be typed into the TextArea; for example you can limit input to numbers if you expect a phone number.
text	a string of characters	The text shown on the display.
visible	True or false	If false, the component is hidden.

TileList

The TileList is used to display several images in a grid (Figure 15-26). For example, you may want to show several thumbnail images in a row. When your audience clicks a thumbnail, a larger version of the image is displayed.

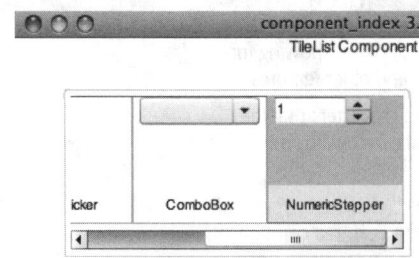

Figure 15-26:
Usually TileList components are filled with images and captions. In honor of this chapter's topic, this TileList is filled with other components.

TitleList Parameters	Expected Value	Purpose
allowMultipleSelection	true or false	If true, your audience can select more than one image.
columnCount	a number value	Sets the number of columns in the grid.
columnWidth	a number value	Sets the width of the column in pixels.
dataProvider	a DataProvider object (for more details see "What's a Data Provider?" on page 521.	Points to a data source to provide the items in the list. The DataProvider object can come from an external source, or you can create one using ActionScript code.
direction	horizontal or vertical	Sets whether the TileList scrolls horizontally or vertically.
enabled	true or false	If false, your audience can't use the component.
horizontalLineScrollSize	a number value	The amount of content to be scrolled, horizontally, when your audience clicks a scroll arrow.
horizontalPageScrollSize	a number value	The number of pixels by which to move the scroll marker on the horizontal scroll bar when your audience clicks the scroll bar track.
rowCount	a number value	Sets the number of rows in the grid.
rowHeight	a number value	Sets the height of the rows in pixels.
scrollPolicy	ON, OFF, AUTO	Controls whether a scroll bar appears in the component.
verticalLineScrollSize	a number value	The amount of content to be scrolled, vertically, when a scroll arrow is clicked.
verticalPageScrollSize	a number value	The number of pixels by which to move the scroll marker on the vertical scroll bar when your audience clicks the scroll bar track.
visible	true or false	If false, the component is hidden.

UILoader

Think of the UILoader (user interface loader) as a container for images (.jpg, .gif, and .png) and Flash animations (.swf). You provide the name and path of the file you want to load into the source parameter. If you're ActionScripting, you can assign the name to the source property of the UILoader. Through ActionScript, you can also access the percentLoaded property.

UILoader Parameters	Expected Value	Purpose
autoLoad	true or false	If false, the UILoader waits until it receives a *load( )* statement.
enabled	true or false	If false, your audience can't access the component.
maintainAspectRatio	true or false	Determines whether an image maintains its proportions; usually left set to true.
scaleContent	true or false	If set to true, the UILoader automatically scales the image to fit the loader's dimensions.
source	name and path to the file to be displayed; this can be an internet address	Sets the source for the file to be loaded.
visible	true or false	If false, the component is hidden.

UIScrollBar

The UIScrollBar component is a fancy, color-customizable scrollbar you can add to a TextInput or TextArea field to make your text fields match your overall color scheme.

UIScrollBar Parameters	Expected Value	Purpose
direction	horizontal or vertical	Sets the orientation of the scroll bar.
scrollTargetName	instance name of a textArea or textInput component	Identifies the text field to be scrolled.
visible	true or false	If false, the component is hidden.

Finding Additional Components

In addition to the components that ship with Flash, you can also find components on the Web (try searching the Web for "Flash components" using your favorite search engine).

Below are a few of the most popular sources for Flash components as this book goes to press:

- **Flash Exchange** (*www.adobe.com/cfusion/exchange/index.cfm*). Adobe hosts a Web site called Flash Exchange (see Figure 15-27). Adobe itself doesn't create the components on the Flash Exchange; instead, regular folks and third-party software companies submit the components, and the site categorizes and rates them. To visit the Flash Exchange, select Help → Flash Exchange.

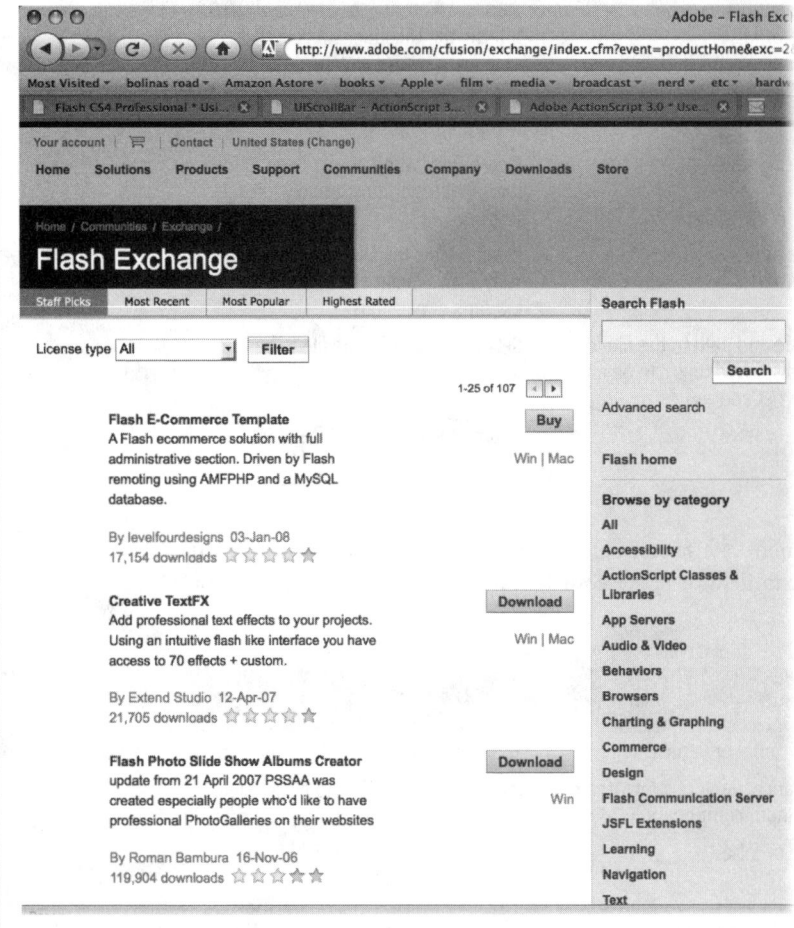

Figure 15-27:
The Flash Exchange Web site (which you can surf to by selecting Help → Flash Exchange) lists hundreds of components in nearly a dozen different categories, from Navigation to Commerce and Accessibility. Some you pay for; others you can download for free. Use the component specifications, number of downloads, and rating associated with each component to help you decide which ones to try.

- **The Flash components network** (*www.flashcomponents.net*). Similar to Adobe's Flash Exchange, this site lists and rates Flash components submitted by a variety of Flash enthusiasts and software companies.

- **ActionScript.org** (*www.actionscript.org*). This everything-Flash site lists dozens of freely downloadable components.

Note: Because anyone with the time, inclination, and ActionScript experience can create a Flash component, Flash enthusiasts (as opposed to established software companies) create most of the Flash components on the Web. Many of the components are free, but there's a downside: Components don't always come with the documentation you need to customize them, and they virtually never come with a guarantee. They may *not* work as promised, and they *may* harbor viruses that can damage your computer. Don't be afraid to try out useful components, but do exercise the same care and caution you use when you download and install any other software program.

Installing Third-Party Components

After you find and download a component (page 532 lists several online component resources), you need to install the component so that you can use it in Flash.

1. First, exit Flash if you've got it running.

2. Place the .swc or .fla file containing the component in the folder where you keep components.

For PCs, use C:\Program Files\Adobe\Adobe Flash CS4\language\Configuration\Components. For Macs, use Macintosh HD:Applications:Adobe Flash CS4:Configuration: Components.

1. Start Flash.

2. Open the Components panel (Window → Components) and check to make sure that the new component is available.

Getting a Component's Version Number

Like programs, components get updates from time to time. Perhaps the folks who designed the component added new features, or maybe they needed to make changes so that the component is compatible with an updated version of Flash. In any case, there may come a time when you'll want to find out the version number of a component that you're using in your Flash project. Fortunately, every component has a version property, so there's a consistent way to check. All you need to do to check a version number is drag an instance of the component onto the stage, and then add this Action-Script code to the timeline:

    trace(component_instance_name.version);

Replace "component_instance_name" with the actual instance name of the component you added to the stage. Press Ctrl+Enter (⌘-Return) to test your document. The component's version number appears in the Output panel (Figure 15-28).

```
TIMELINE  OUTPUT  COMPILER ERRORS
3.0.0.16
```

Figure 15-28:
You can display the version number of a component in the Output panel by simply placing a snippet of code in the Actions panel.

Choosing, Using, and Animating Text

Flash isn't just about moving pictures. Text is a big part of many projects, and with Flash you can do some remarkable things with text and type. You can label buttons, boxes, and widgets with small, helpful text, and make page headlines pop with big, bold type. When you use large blocks of text—as in newspaper articles or how-to instructions—you can add scroll bars so your readers can see all the text in one place, or you can create hyperlinks that lead to other pages. And of course, Flash can do things to type that wouldn't enter Microsoft Word's wildest dreams: morphing paragraphs as they move across the screen; exploding words and letters into dozens of pieces. You can also create the same kind of effects that you see in the opening credits of TV shows. To handle all this variety, Flash provides different text tools. As with any craft, it's important to choose the right tool for the job. This chapter will guide you to the right tool and share some of the tricks of the trade along the way.

About Typefaces and Fonts

Choosing a typeface for your project should be, fun—just not too much fun. Text should communicate, not distract. Make your decisions with that in mind, and you can't go wrong. Consider the job you expect your type to do, and then help it do that job by choosing the right typeface, size, container, and background. Beginning designers often treat text as yet another design element and let the desire for a cool look override more practical concerns. Designers sometimes talk about a text block like just another shape on the page. But cool type effects can torture your readers' eyes with hard-to-read backgrounds, weird letter spacing, or hopelessly small font sizes. (For more advice on readability, see the box on page 536.)

Note: If you want to be technical in a Gutenbergian fashion, typefaces are *families* of fonts. Times Roman is a typeface, while "Times Roman, bold, 12 point" is a font. Somewhere along the line, as type moved from traditional typesetters to computer desktops, the meaning of the word "font" came to be synonymous with "typeface." That's okay, but knowing how the terms originated makes great cocktail party banter.

Small Is Beautiful

How can I use small type and make sure it stays readable?

For most people, reading text on a computer screen is more difficult than reading it off a piece of paper. If your Flash project includes text with small font sizes (12 points or less), there are a few things that you can do to keep your audience from straining their eyes. Actually, the fact of the matter is, people simply won't read text if it's too hard to see.

- **If possible, bump the type up to a larger size** (Properties → Character → Size). At small sizes, a point or even half a point makes a big difference.

- **It's easiest to read black text on a white background.** If you don't want to use that combination, opt for very dark text on a very light background. If you have to use light text on a dark background, make sure there's a great deal of contrast between the colors.

- **Use sans-serif type, like Helvetica or Arial for small sizes.** Sans-serif type looks like the text in this box, it doesn't have the tiny end bars (serifs) you find in type like the body text in this book. Computer screens have a hard time creating sharp serif type at very small sizes.

- **Use both upper and lowercase type for anything other than a headline.** Even though all uppercase type looks bigger, it's actually less readable. The height differences in lowercase type make it more readable. Besides, too much uppercase type makes it look like you're shouting.

- **Avoid bold and italic type.** Often bold and italic type is hard to read at small font sizes. It varies with different typefaces, so it doesn't hurt to experiment.

- **If your text isn't going to be animated, turn on Anti-aliasing for readability** (Properties → Character → Anti-alias → Anti-alias for readability). Anti-aliasing is a bit of computer magic and fool-the-eye trickery that gives small type nice smooth edges.

- **Choose Anti-aliasing for animation** (Properties → Character → Anti-alias → Anti-alias for animation) if you're going to be pushing that text around the screen, with tweens or ActionScript.

It never hurts to get second and third opinions. If you've got eyes like an eagle, you may want to get some opinions from your less gifted colleagues when it comes to readability. You want your Flash project to be accessible to as wide an audience as possible.

What Font Does your Audience Have?

It's not always possible to anticipate the fonts your audience will have. (Heck, these days it's hard to guess whether your audience will be watching on a computer, a telephone, an iPod, or a television screen.) But it's important to at least make an educated guess, since Flash handles fonts in two different ways when it publishes the .swf animation that you distribute to your audience:

- **Embedded fonts.** When fonts are embedded, the outlines of the fonts are stored in the .swf file. That means your .swf file is larger, but Flash Player can display the typeface image exactly as it appeared when you created your animation. Static text is embedded. (With the Text tool selected, choose Properties → Static Text).

• **Named fonts.** In other cases, Flash records the name of the fonts used, and then, when the animation runs on your audience's computer, it looks for the font on that computer. If Flash Player finds the font, great. If the program can't find the font, it tries to find the best match it can. More obscure typefaces can lead to hit or miss results. Dynamic text and input text stores font names. (With the Text tool selected, choose Properties → Dynamic Text or Properties → Input Text).

You don't need to worry too much about embedded fonts, because they'll look the same on your audience's computer as they do on yours. The main concern about embedded fonts is the additional heft they add to your .swf file. It's a different story with named fonts. If your audience doesn't have exactly the same font on their computer, they'll be seeing something else. That means there'll be differences in the overall shapes, the line breaks and the type sizes. These are the same issues that Web designers wrestle with on a regular basis. When you have choices like those shown in Figure 16-1, nobody wants to limit their type choices to Helvetica, Arial, Times, and Times New Roman. But they're the safe choices, since you can count on your audience having them or something that makes a close match.

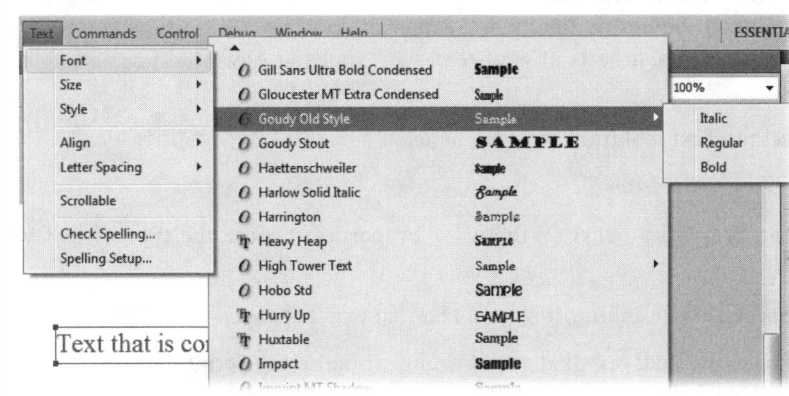

Figure 16-1:
Most likely, you've got a bewildering number of typefaces on your computer. Many of the typefaces include style variations, like bold, italic, and so on. Choose carefully, making sure that your text performs its intended job—communication.

Flash helps a bit with this problem, because it uses embedded fonts for static text and uses named fonts for dynamic text and input text. That way, you can use static text for those big beautiful headings where fancier, unique fonts can be appreciated. Then for forms and larger blocks of text, you can use dynamic text or input text.

If you need to use dynamic or input text and want to make sure your audience has a specific font, you can manually embed the necessary fonts in the .swf file. With your dynamic or input text field selected, go to Properties → Character → Character Embedding to open the Character Embedding dialog box. Once there, you can tell Flash which letters and other characters appear in your text, as shown in Figure 16-2. To include an entire font in your Flash file, choose "All" at the top of the list. If you have a text field selected, hit the Auto Fill button and Flash automatically puts the need characters in the "Include these characters:" box.

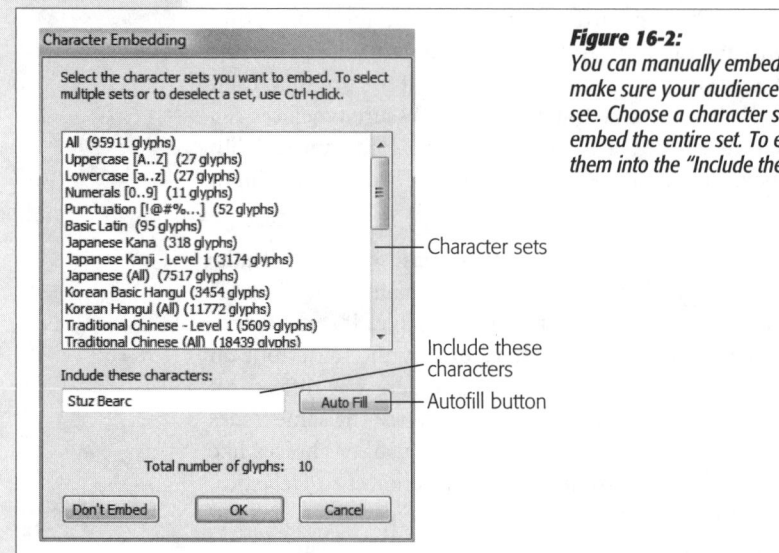

Figure 16-2:
You can manually embed characters in your .swf files to make sure your audience sees the same typefaces you see. Choose a character set from the scrolling list to embed the entire set. To embed specific characters, type them into the "Include these characters:" box.

Here are the quick steps for creating text for your Flash Document. You'll use these standard steps every time you create text. For those cases where you want to fine-tune the visual aspects of your text, see "Applying Advanced Formatting" on page 542.

1. **Select the Text tool from the Tool panel.**

   It looks like the letter T.

2. **In the Properties panel (Window → Properties) choose the type of text you need:**

   • **Static Text:** headlines, blocks of text that won't change.

   • **Dynamic Text:** text that you'll change using ActionScript, like stock quotes and baseball scores.

   • **Input Text:** text used with forms that accept audience input.

3. **Choose a typeface (Properties → Character → Family) that suits the job at hand.**

   If you're creating static text, Flash will embed your fonts in your .swf file, which increases the file size but accurately displays the typeface. If you're creating Dynamic or Input Text, Flash stores the name of the font, and then looks for that font on your audience's computer when the .swf file runs. If it can't find the font, it finds the best match. The safest choices are the fonts found on all Macs and PCs, like Arial, Helvetica, Times, and Times New Roman.

4. **In the Properties → Character panel (Figure 16-3), choose a font size, a style (bold, italic), and a color.**

If you're creating a text field with a smaller type size, see the box on page 536 for tips. There are other options available in the Character panel, but size, style, and color are the main features that you specify each time you create text. See page 542 for the more advanced details.

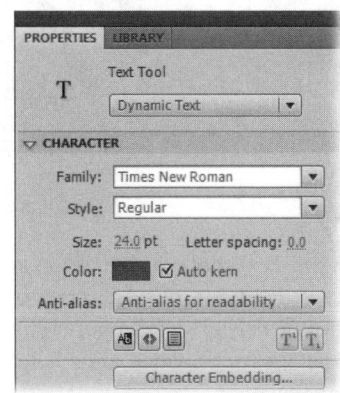

Figure 16-3:
The Character panel puts all your type specifications in one place. It's much easier and faster to use than multiple menus and dialog boxes.

5. **In the Properties → Paragraph panel, click a Format button that matches your need.**

You see paragraph formatting choices similar to those found in word processers: left, center, right, and justified.

6. **If you chose dynamic or input text, select Properties → Paragraph → Behavior.**

Choose from Single Line, Multiline and Multiline No Wrap. Use **Single Line** for form text fields. **Multiline** is appropriate for book and newspaper type text fields. **Multiline No Wrap** is a good choice if the text is computer code or other text that shouldn't have line breaks.

7. **Drag to create a text field on the stage.**

A rectangle appears on the stage as you drag. You don't have to worry too much about the text box's dimensions because you can always modify them later.

8. **Click inside of the box, and then type the text.**

It's best to put some placeholder text inside of your text box even if it's going to be changed by ActionScript code or your audience at a later time. While you're designing other elements in your animation, it's surprisingly easy to misplace or delete a text box that has no text.

You're not locked into the choices you make when you create a text field. You can always go back and change any of the properties. If you find you have more room than you thought, you can bump up the font size. If the color combinations seem wrong, no problem, click that swatch in the Character panel and make the change.

Choosing and Using Text Containers

At design time, when you click in a text field with the Text tool, you can select and edit the existing text. You may also notice that the handles around the text box change. One of the handles on the right or bottom of the text box appears larger than the rest, as shown in Figure 16-4. This handle always provides some helpful information about the text box's characteristics and behavior.

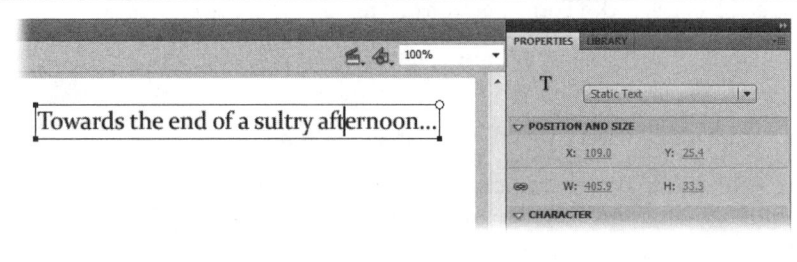

Figure 16-4:
The handles on a text box provide details about the type of text field and the way it's sized. The hollow, round handle shown in the upper-right corner of this text field shows that it's static text that expands with the text.

Here's your secret text field handle decoder ring for horizontal text:

- Handle in upper-right corner means it's static text.

- Handle in lower-right corner means it's dynamic or input text.

- Hollow circle means the text field expands as text is added.

- Hollow square indicates that the text has a fixed width (as shown in Figure 16-5).

- Solid square means the dynamic text is scrollable.

The codes for vertical text are similar, except that the handle providing information is always at the bottom of the text box. It appears bottom-left for static text and bottom-right for dynamic and input text.

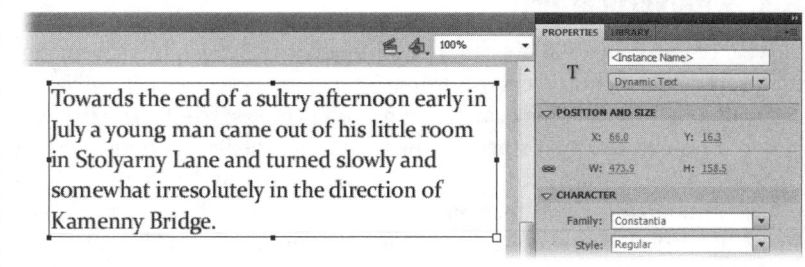

Figure 16-5:
*The handle shown in the
lower-right corner of this
text box indicates that
this dynamic text has a
fixed width.*

Resizing and Transforming Text Fields

You can resize a text field by dragging any of the handles. There are always at least four handles at the corners. You can drag whether you're using the Text tool or the Selection tool (solid arrow). The container holds the text and changes size, but the text itself remains the same size. When you resize a text field that's set to automatically expand, it changes it to a fixed-width field. To change a fixed-width text field to one that automatically resizes to fit the text, double-click the hollow square handle.

Using the Transform tool to make changes to a text field can produce interesting and sometimes unexpected results: transformations of static text fields are much different from those with dynamic or input text—with good reason. In the case of static text fields, Flash has embedded the font description, giving it all the information it needs to create fancy visual effects, so Flash can skew and rotate static text with gusto (Figure 16-6). Not so with dynamic or input text (unless the fonts are embedded in the .swf file; see page 536). You can stretch the text box by dragging the handle vertically or horizontally, but if you try to rotate or skew the text, Flash gives up and the text simply disappears from the display. Don't panic; the text is still there, and you can restore it with Ctl+Z, or Command-Z on your Mac.

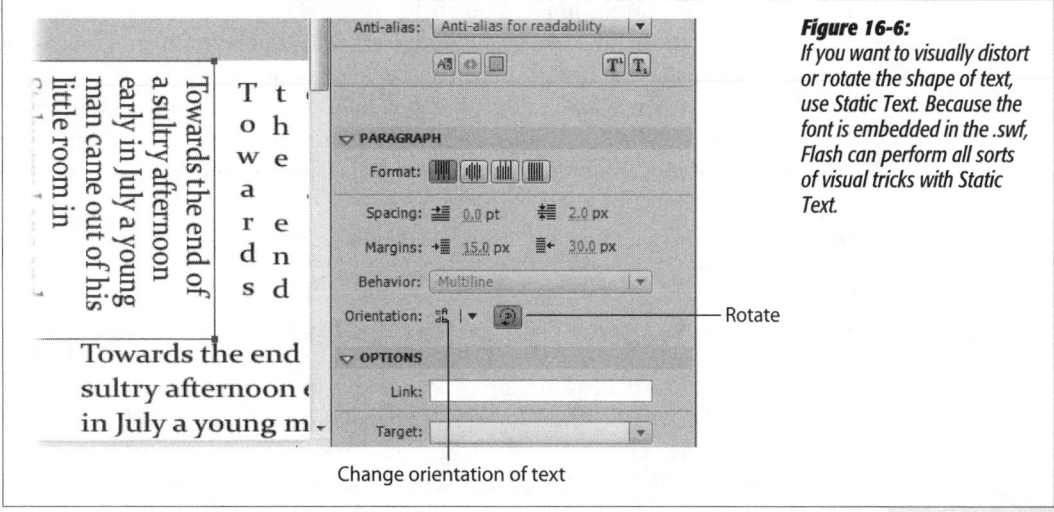

Figure 16-6:
*If you want to visually distort
or rotate the shape of text,
use Static Text. Because the
font is embedded in the .swf,
Flash can perform all sorts
of visual tricks with Static
Text.*

Rotate

Change orientation of text

Working with Vertical Text

You can change the orientation of Static Text (Properties → Paragraph → Orientation). Use the drop-down menu to choose from: Horizontal; Vertical, left to right; or Vertical, right to left. Next to the drop-down menu is a button that toggles the letter's orientation. You edit text that's been turned with the orientation options as with any other text. Choose the Text tool from the Tools panel, and click the text field. It may take a moment or two for you to get your bearings if you're not used to working with vertical text; see Figure 16-7 for guidance. But you'll soon find it's easy to drag to select text. The arrow keys help you navigate back and forth. When you type, text appears vertically and follows the paragraph's orientation properties.

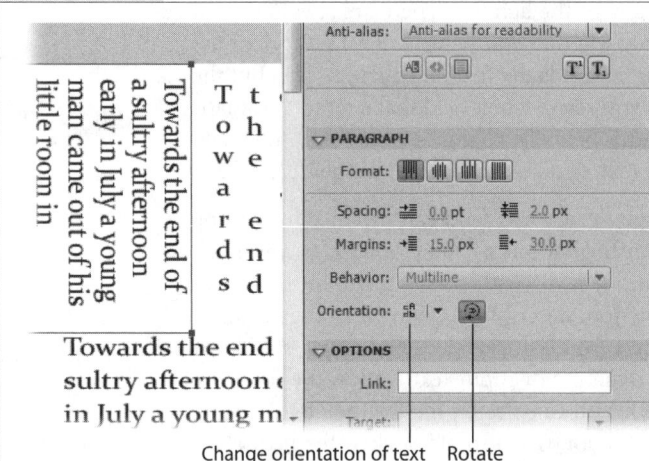

Figure 16-7:
Use the Change orientation of text button to create vertical text. Then, use the Rotate button to change the direction the vertical text points.

Creating Line Breaks

You can create line breaks in Flash text fields as you do in your word processor, by pressing Enter (Return on a Mac). The Static Text field requires no special settings; it automatically creates the needed line breaks when you change the width of the text box by resizing it. To create multiple line text fields with Dynamic Text and Input Text, select the text field, and then, in the Properties panel, choose Paragraph → Behavior → Multiline. This creates a text box that allows line breaks.

Tip: When you're using ActionScript to create text for a text field, use \n to create a new line.

Applying Advanced Formatting to Text

Typographers and art directors are as particular about text as winemakers are about wine. With Adobe, the Ministry of Fonts, as its publisher, Flash has lots of tools to keep type connoisseurs smiling. You can delve into these features if you like, but right out of the box, Flash has some pretty good settings.

- **Letter spacing** (Properties → Character → Letter spacing). This setting increases or decreases the space between individual letters. Used moderately, it can give text a distinctive appearance. Too much letter spacing affects text's readability, so use it carefully.

- **Auto kern** (Properties → Character → Auto kern). Kerning also affects the space between characters, but its purpose is different. Some letters, like A and V, look better when they're tucked a little closer together, to eliminate the awkward gaps that are especially noticeable at larger type sizes. Flash's Auto kern feature is on when you first begin using Flash. If you want to turn it off, click to turn off the "Auto kern" checkbox.

- **Line Spacing** (Properties → Paragraph → Line Spacing). You can change the distance between lines with Line Spacing. Click and enter a new number or drag to scrub in a number. As with other type features, too much line spacing may give text a unique appearance but make it harder to read. Experiment with line spacing to find the right balance.

Adding Hyperlinks to Text

You can add hyperlinks to your text with or without using ActionScript to generate the code. As is often the case, static text behaves one way and non-static text (dynamic text and input text) behaves differently. If you want to highlight a couple of words inside of a paragraph of text, you need to use static text, as shown in Figure 16-8. When you add a hyperlink to dynamic text Flash applies a link to the entire text field. You can get around this behavior by selecting the text, and then, in the Properties → Character panel, clicking the "Render text as HTML button". (There's no text label for the button, which looks like HTML angle brackets: < >.)

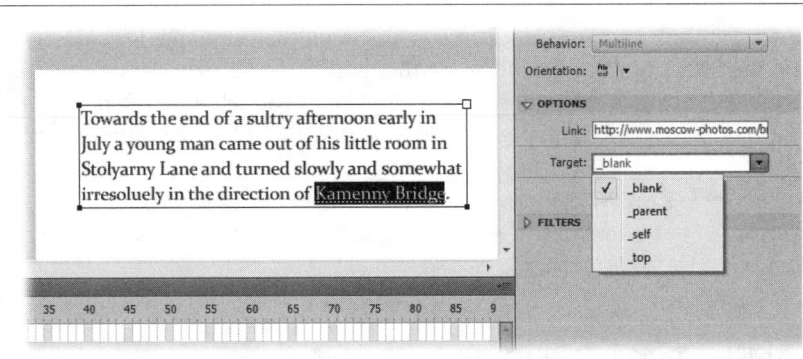

Figure 16-8:
If you want to add a hyperlink to a couple of words within a block of text, you need to use Static Text or you need to use ActionScript to create a link in HTML text as explained on page 562.

Note: The techie term for a link is *URL*, which stands for Universal Resource Locator. You usually hear this term in relation to the Internet, but a URL can just as well point to a file on your computer. The key is in the prefix. Instead of beginning with *http://*, a link that points to a file on your computer begins with *file:///*.

Here are the steps for applying a link to static text:

1. **With the Text tool, drag to select the words within the static text that you want to link.**

   If you prefer to navigate by keyboard, you can use the Shift and arrow keys to select text, too—just as in a word processor.

2. **In Properties → Options → Link, type in the link details.**

   You need to include the path for the file, unless you're certain that it's going to be in the same folder as the .swf tile when the animation runs. A complete link to a file on the Internet might look like this:

   http://www.missingmanual.com/cds/flashcs4tmm/text_scram_finished.fla

3. **If you want your link to open in a new browser window or tab, select Properties → Options → Target → _blank.**

   If you don't change the target setting, the new page replaces your animation in your audience's browser. The other Target settings let you open documents in different sections of an HTML page using frames—a Web design technique that's fallen out of fashion.

4. **Highlight the hyperlinked text so your audience knows it's a link.**

   If you want the linked words highlighted, you'll have to do it yourself by changing the text color or underlining the words. Don't be fooled. When you create a link, you see a line beneath the linked words in the Flash authoring program, but when your animation runs in Flash Player, there's no line, no highlight, no indication that the words are linked. The only clue your audience has that the words are linked is the changing cursor if they chance to move the mouse over the words.

If you want to link an entire block of dynamic text, the technique is similar. You can use the Select tool (arrow) to select the text field, and then provide the link details in the Properties → Options → Link box. Unless you select the "Render text as HTML" option as described on page 543, Flash applies the link to the entire text field.

Tip: You can create a link that opens and addresses an email message—great for a "contact us" link. Instead of *http://*, type *mailto:*, and then add your email address to the end. For example, a complete address might look like this: *mailto:harry@stutzmotors.com*.

Animating Text without ActionScript

You can animate text in the Flash authoring environment, or you can animate text using ActionScript. Which technique you choose depends on your own skills and inclinations. This section explains how to create some interesting animation effects for text using only the Flash authoring environment.

Note: If you'd like to see the finished animation before you begin, you can download *text_scram_ finished.fla* at *http://missingmanuals.com/cds*.

1. **Select File → New → Flash File (ActionScript 3.0).**

   Make the document size 550×400 pixels, the frame rate 12 fps, and choose a light colored background.

2. **Use the Text tool to create a line of static text with a font size of about 36 and a darker color that complements the document background color.**

   You can use any word or phrase you want. If you don't have anything in mind "Make this text scram" would be appropriate for this exercise. If you need help creating static text, see page 538.

3. **Click Frame 12 in the text layer, and then press F5 to insert a frame.**

   The text layer now has 12 frames. Equally important, when you create new layers, they'll automatically be 12 frames long, saving you a click or two of work.

4. **With the text selected, choose Modify → Break Apart.**

   The Break Apart command comes in very handy when you want to animate text. It puts each letter in its own text field, which gives you an opportunity to move the letters independently.

5. **While the text is still selected, choose Modify → Timeline → Distribute to Layers.**

   Flash places each letter in its own layer in the timeline, and thoughtfully names each layer by the letter, saving you a lot of cut, paste, and layer creation work. Layer 1 is empty at this point, and you can remove it, if you want to tidy things up. Click the layer, and then click the Delete icon (trash can) below the layer names.

6. **Click the M layer (the capital M in "Make"), right-click anywhere in the timeline, and then choose Create Motion Tween.**

   The 12 frames of the M layer take on the blue hue that indicates a motion tween.

7. **Click Frame 12, and then drag the letter M off the right edge of the stage.**

   Press the Shift key down as you drag to create a perfectly straight motion path. The letter M displays a motion path. If you scrub the playhead, you see that it moves from the left side of the stage until it exits stage right.

8. **With the letter M still selected and the playhead still at Frame 12, select the Transform tool, and then scale the letter so it's about five times its original size.**

   If, after you resize it, part of the letter is still visible on the stage, go ahead and pull it a little more to the right. If you want to accurately resize the letter, use the Motion Editor to handle the scaling (Window → Motion Editor → Transformation → Scale X).

9. With the letter M still selected in Frame 12, open the Properties → Filters panel.

   Click the small triangle next to the word Filters to open the panel. Initially the panel is empty.

10. Click the Add filter button in the lower-left corner, and then choose Blur from the pop-up menu.

    The menu lists all the available filters that you can apply to the selected object—in this case, the over-sized letter M. When you click Blur, the properties for the filter appear in the Filter panel, as shown in Figure 16-9.

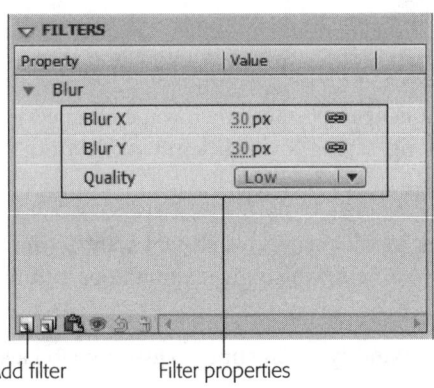

Figure 16-9:
You apply filters to selected objects. Each filter has different properties. Here the Blur filter shows three different properties to control the direction and the quality of the blurring effect.

Add filter   Filter properties

11. Click the Blur X setting and type *30*.

    Doing so changes both the Blur X and Blur Y settings, which initially are linked together. Sometimes, you can create a better speeding blur effect by limiting the blur to one axis. If you want to unlink one of the settings, click the link icon to the right of the setting; the icon changes to a broken link. Then you can enter a separate value in each property.

12. Move the playhead to Frame 0, and then with the letter M selected, type *0* in the Blur X and Blur Y filter settings.

    You need to re-select the letter M after scrubbing the Playhead. Setting the Blur filter in Frame 12, also affects the letter in Frame 1. Setting Blur X and Blur Y to 0 creates a nice sharp letter again.

13. Move the playhead to Frame 6, and with the letter M still selected, type *0* in the Blur X and Blur Y filter settings.

    As explained in the chapter on Motion Tweens (page 127), you can change just about any property, at any point, along a motion path. In this case, you're changing the Blur filter so that the letter stays focused for the first part of its trip and then becomes blurry as it leaves the stage.

You're done with the motion tween effect. If you test your animation at this point (Ctrl+Enter or ⌘-Return on a Mac) you see the letter M move from left to right becoming larger and blurry as it makes its journey. In the next steps, you'll copy the motion tween from the letter M and paste that motion into the layers with the other letters. (Admit it—you were worried you were going to have to create all those tweens by hand.)

14. **Right-click the motion tween in the M layer, and then choose Copy Motion.**

    Flash stores a copy of the tween on its clipboard. It includes that carefully constructed motion and all its property changes.

15. **Click the first frame of the "a" layer, and then Shift-click the first frame of the m layer in the word "scram."**

    The first frame of each layer (except for M in the word "Make") is selected.

16. **Right-click one of the selected frames, and then choose Paste Motion from the shortcut menu.**

    Flash pastes the tween into the each of the selected layers. Obediently, the letters now follow the same motion, scale and blurring changes as dictated by the tween.

17. **Press Ctrl+Enter (⌘-Return on a Mac) to test your animation.**

    The letters rush off the right side of the stage in a large blurry clump. Kinda cool, but your audience will appreciate the effect even more if the letters peel off one by one across the stage. You can do that by staggering the frames on each layer, as detailed in the next steps.

18. **In the "a" layer, click the motion tween, and then drag all 12 of the selected frames down the timeline a distance of six frames.**

    The motion tween for "a" begins its action on Frame 7. This creates about a half-second gap between the time when the M starts moving and when the "a" starts moving. After the move, there are six blank frames at the beginning of the "a" layer.

19. **Select the letter "a" in Frame 7, and then paste it into Frame 1 using the Edit → Paste in Place (Ctrl+Shift+V on a PC or ⌘-Shift-V on a Mac).**

    After you move the tween, you need to put a copy of each letter back in the first frame of the animation. Using the Paste in Place positions displays the letter in the right position in the frames before the tween takes effect.

20. **Repeat steps 18 and 19 to create a six-frame offset between each of the letters.**

    When you're done, the timeline looks something like Figure 16-10.

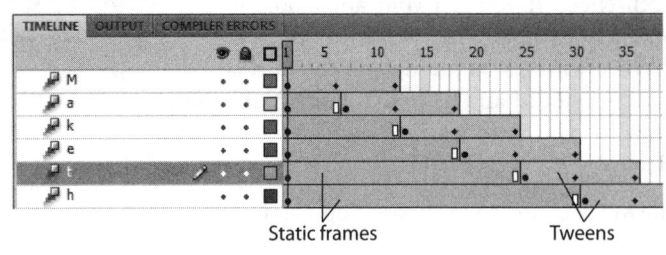

Figure 16-10:
Staggering the tween action in the timeline creates an interesting effect as the letters make their move, one after the other.

Static frames   Tweens

21. **Test the animation.**

The individual letters of the phrase chase each other across the stage growing larger and blurrier as they disappear from the right side of the stage. At 108 frames, the animation runs about 9 seconds.

Experimenting with Animated Text

By applying motion tweens to text, you can capture the attention of your audience. It works great for headlines, intros and transitions, but like anything else, it's possible to have too much of a good thing. No one likes to wait these days, so be careful not to strain your audience's patience. That said, you can pack more effects into the previous animation without making it run longer. You can add other moving objects to the animation, like more text or shapes. If you turn each of the letters into a movie clip, you can take advantage of Flash's new 3-D capabilities. Then your tweens can twist and flip the letters as they move through three dimensional space. Experiment; let your imagination run wild! If you're looking for inspiration, study the techniques used by some of the network and cable news programs. They love to use moving text and other visuals to make the news seem more exciting than it really is.

Store the techniques that work in your Flash toolkit and remember the lessons you learn from the ones that flop. As with any craft, you're likely to learn as much by your mistakes as your successes.

Controlling Text with ActionScript

If you're used to using a word processor, it probably seems pretty natural to format your text with menus and the Properties panel. After all, they aren't that much different from Microsoft Word menus and dialog boxes. On the other hand, if you want to make major changes to text on the fly, or if you want to format text with HTML (hypertext markup language) or CSS (cascading style sheets), you have to use ActionScript to produce your text. You saw some text and ActionScript examples in Chapter 11 (page 398). You'll find more here. First, the elementary basics, which begin with string theory.

ActionScript Text: String Theory

Flash has lots of text containers—Static Text, Dynamic Text, and Input Text—and then there are the components: Label, TextArea, and TextInput. All of these text-displaying tools use the String data type (page 398). As far as ActionScript is concerned a string is similar to an array, in that it's a list of characters. The list can be a single character or hundreds of characters. Each character is in a specific position in the list—its index number (page 399). Arrays and strings both begin counting at position zero (0). So if the string is "Stutz Modern Motorcars" that capital S is at position 0.

Note: Strings are common to most programming languages, and there are loads of books that explain how to perform string manipulation magic. Most Flash programs don't require such trickery. This chapter explains some of the most common techniques used by Flash designers. However, if you're an aspiring string magician, you may want to start out with *ActionScript 3.0 Cookbook* or *Essential ActionScript 3.0*, both published by O'Reilly.

Creating a New String

You want to use the name of your company, "Stutz Modern Motorcars," in an ActionScript program. The typical way to do so is to create a variable with the data type String, and then store the name of your company inside of that variable. Whenever you need the company name to appear in your program, you can provide the name of the variable. Here's the way you'd create a string variable for your company name:

```
var strCompanyName:String = "Stutz Modern Motorcars";
```

This statement does a few things in a single line. It creates and names a string variable strCompanyName, and then assigns a string value to the variable. You only have to create the variable with the *var* statement once, and then you can use it as many times as you want. In this case, the variable name begins with the three letters "str" to indicate that it's a string, but that's not necessary. The variable name could be a single letter.

Note: String values, like "Stutz Modern Motorcars" are always shown within either double or single quotes (page 398). One of the reasons you can use either type of quotes is that it provides an easy way to include quotes within your string. So here are examples of valid strings:

```
strDont = "don't";
strQuote = 'Ed said, "I love my Stutz Bearcat. I drive it everywhere."';
```

The important rule is that you have to begin and end the string with the same type of quotes.

Because you assign your strings to variables, you can change the string's value. For example, if the boss changes the name of Stutz Modern Motorcars to the simpler (and even more modern) Stutz Motor Company, you can update your Action-Script code by assigning the new name to the strCompanyName variable, like so:

```
strCompanyName = "Stutz Motor Company";
```

Joining Strings

One of the most common ways to modify a string is to add more text to it. In geek-speak that's called concatenation, but you can think of it as joining strings. Suppose your boss finally gets around to filling out those incorporation papers and your company has yet another new name. If you want to add the word "Incorporated" to the existing strCompanyName, here's how you'd do it:

```
strCompanyName = strCompanyName + ", Incorporated";
```

As you can see, you're adding a new string value to the end of the existing string. The end result is a complete name "Stutz Motor Company, Incorporated." Joining strings is such a common and popular task there's a shortcut to help you do so with few keystrokes. It looks like this:

```
strCompanyName += ", Incorporated";
```

That line of code does exactly the same thing as the preceding example, just with fewer keystrokes. Make sure you keep the + sign to the left of the = sign. When you do it the other way around, the code has an entirely different meaning to Action-Script.

When you have a string inside of quotes like the ", Incorporated", it's known as a *string literal*. The string is *literally* what's inside the quotes, similar to a constant. When a string is represented by a variable, like strCompanyName, it's a *string variable*. In most situations, you can use either representation. For example, here's another way you can construct the new company name:

```
var strCompanyName:String = "Stutz Motor Company";
var strInc:String = ", Incorporated";
strCompanyName += strInc;
```

You can use a combination of string literals and string variables when you're joining a string. You see this technique in use when Web sites greet you by name. An ActionScript example looks like this:

```
var strVisitorName = "Chris Grover";
strGreeting = "Hello " + strVisitorName + ". What can I do to put you in a
Stutz Bearcat today?";
```

When you join strings with the concatenation operator (+ or +=), everything inside of the quotes has to be on a single line. That's one of the reasons you see multiple assignment statements when an ActionScripter is creating a long paragraph of text.

```
strSalesPitch = "The legendary Stutz Bearcat.";
strSalesPitch += "It's your best value in high performance ";
strSalesPitch += "sport cars today.";
strSalesPicth += "At the Stutz Motor Company we want to know.";
strSalesPitch += "What can we do to put you in a Stutz Bearcat today?";
```

This block of text produces a single long string. Even though there were line breaks in the ActionScript code, those have no effect on the string when it is displayed. The line breaks are dictated by the properties and size of the text container. To see how you specifically place line breaks in a string, see the next section.

Using TextField's *appendText( )* Method

When you're using objects of the TextField class, you can use the *appendText( )* method. In fact, *appendText( )* is preferred because it runs faster that the concatenation operator. Here's some code that shows *appendText( )* in action:

```
1    var txtBearcatBanner:TextField = new TextField();
2    var strSalesPitch:String = new String();
3    strSalesPitch = "Stutz Motor Company\nHome of the legendary Stutz Bearcat\n";
4    txtBearcatBanner.text = strSalesPitch;
5    txtBearcatBanner.appendText("What can we do to put you in a Bearcat today?");
6
7    txtBearcatBanner.x = 40;
8    txtBearcatBanner.y = 40;
9    txtBearcatBanner.width = 280;
10   txtBearcatBanner.height = 160;
11
12   addChild(txtBearcatBanner);
```

The first two lines create a text field and a string. The third line puts some text in the string strSalesPitch. Line 4 assigns that string to the text property of the text field. Line 5 is where the *appendText( )* method comes in. The text in the parentheses is a string literal, but it could just as easily be a variable. Lines 7 through 10 position and size the text field on the stage. The last line, adds the text field to the display list, which makes it visible on the stage. When you run this bit of code, Flash Player displays the text as shown in Figure 16-11.

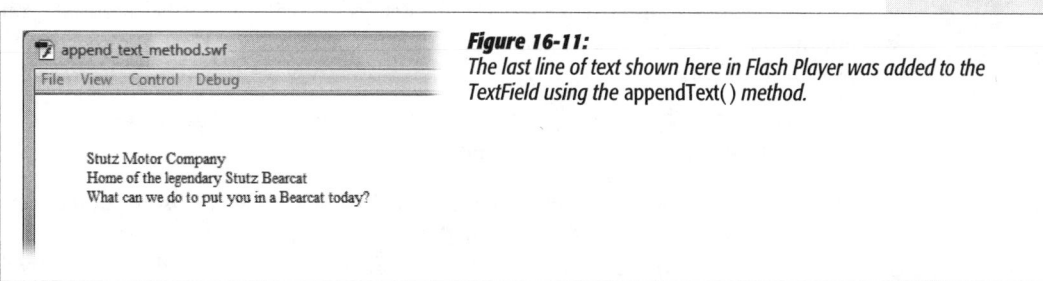

Figure 16-11:
The last line of text shown here in Flash Player was added to the TextField using the appendText( ) *method.*

Adding Line Breaks to a String

When you're typing text into a text field, you hit the Enter (or Return) key to begin a new line, but that doesn't work when you're creating a string in ActionScript.

You need to insert a special signal within the string. It's a backslash with a lower-case n, which stands for new line. Here's an example:

```
strSalesPitch = "Stutz Motor Cars \n Home of the legendary Stutz Bearcat.";
```

If placed in a multiline text field and given enough room to display, this string appears as two lines:

Stutz Motor Cars

 Home of the legendary Stutz Bearcat

There's a space after the word "Cars" and before the word "Home," because, after all, strings are literal. To avoid the extra space at the beginning of the second line, you have to eliminate the space characters on both sides of \n. It looks strange to us humans, because we see individual words, but that's not the way ActionScript sees a string. ActionScript just sees a long line of characters: letters, numbers, spaces, and punctuation. The only thing that really grabs its attention is the sequence \n. When ActionScript sees that back slash followed by a lowercase n, it knows that's the signal for a new line.

Finding a String within a String

Suppose your Flash animation is more like a computer program. It's so complex that you've provided 200 pages of Help text to help your audience learn how to use it. You want to create some sort of search function so folks can zero in on the help they need. A string that's inside of another string is often called a *substring*, and ActionScript provides some methods to help you find a substring inside of a larger string.

To make it simple, this example is going to search for the word "legendary" within the longer string "Home of the legendary Stutz Bearcat." Not quite hundreds of pages, but you get the idea. All strings inherit the same properties and methods from the String class. Two of those methods are *indexOf( )* and *lastIndexOf( )*, and they're specifically used to search for substrings. As with any good method, you put them to work by tacking them onto the end of an object. Here's some code to show how it works:

```
var strSalesPitch:String = "Home of the legendary Stutz Bearcat.";
strSalesPitch.indexOf("legendary");
```

The first line creates the string variable named strSalesPitch. The second line runs the String method *indexOf( )*. The method needs to know what substring you're searching for, so you provide that as a parameter. You can put the string literal right inside the parentheses, as shown here with "legendary," or you can provide a string variable, which, of course, wouldn't include the quotes.

So, what does the *indexOf( )* method do? It gives you back a number. Specifically, it gives you the index number where the searched-for string begins. In the case above, *strSalesPitch.indexOf("legendary")* is equal to 12, because if you start counting at zero, and you count the letters and spaces, you find that the letter "l" is at index 12. The *lastIndexOf( )* method works in a similar manner, except that it starts searching from the end of the string rather than the beginning. If either method is unable to find the substring, it gives back the number -1. That result is actually helpful, since you can use it with conditional statements. For example, this code would work:

```
if (strSalesPitch.indexOf("legendary ") == -1) strComment = "Not legendary.";
```

The *if( )* statement tests to see if the string "legendary" is part of strSalesPitch. If the statement doesn't find that string, the *indexOf( )* method returns -1. When that condition exists, the words "Not legendary" are assigned to strComment. It's also useful to partner the "does not equal" (!=) operator with *indexOf( )* and *lastIndexOf( )*. So you can write code that says something like the following:

```
if (strSalesPitch.indexOf("legendary") != -1) strComment = "This is a
legendary automobile.";;
```

In other words, if the code finds the substring, it assigns the string "This is a legendary automobile." to strComment.

Replacing Words or Characters in a String

Search and replace go hand in hand in the computer world. Suppose there were changes at the car dealership and you need to make changes to your sales pitch: "Home of the legendary Stutz Bearcat." You can use the replace method. It works like this:

```
strSalesPitch.replace("Stutz Bearcat","Toyota Prius");
```

As usual with methods, you tack *replace( )* onto the end of the object, in this case, a string. For parameters, you provide the search words or letters then you provide the replace words or letters. Also, as usual, you use a comma to separate parameters when there's more than one. The *replace( )* method works with both string literals, like the ones shown here or string variables. If you assigned the line above as the text for a text field or the parameter of a *trace( )* statement, the result you'd see would be:

Home of the legendary Toyota Prius.

Converting Strings to Uppercase or Lowercase

You can change the case of a string using the *toUpperCase( )* or *toLowerCase( )* methods. Part of the String class, you use these the same way as the other methods. Continuing with the car dealership theme, here are some examples that use *trace( )* to display the strings in the Output panel:

```
var strSalesPitch = "Home of the legendary Stutz Bearcat";
trace("This is the initial string: \n" + strSalesPitch);
trace("\nThis is toUpperCase: \n" + strSalesPitch.toUpperCase());
trace("\nThis is toLowerCase: \n" + strSalesPitch.toLowerCase());
```

The first line creates the strSalesPitch variable and assigns the words "Home of the legendary Stutz Bearcat" to the variable. The next line uses *trace( )* to send the string to the Output panel. (As mentioned on page 437, the *trace( )* statement is a favorite debugging tool of ActionScripters.) The first string inside the *trace( )* statement's parentheses is a string literal that explains what's to follow: "This is the initial string:". The \n is the new line character that forces the following text to start on a new line. It works in the output panel the same way it works in a text field. The + (concatenation operator) joins the two strings. The last string is the variable strSalesPitch. The final two lines are nearly identical to the second line. They add one more \n to provide some additional, helpful white space. Finally, the methods are applied to the strings. What appears in the Output panel comes as little surprise:

> This is the initial string:
>
> Home of the legendary Stutz Bearcat
>
>
> This is toUpperCase:
>
> HOME OF THE LEGENDARY STUTZ BEARCAT
>
>
> This is toLowerCase:
>
> home of the legendary stutz bearcat

Enough with the string theory. The next sections show how to create text on the fly using ActionScript and how to format that text using a few different tools.

Creating Text Fields with ActionScript

You've seen how to create, and then display objects using ActionScript (page 443), and text and text fields are no different. You create, and if needed, format the object, and then you use the *addChild( )* method to add the text to the Display List. Objects added to the display list are on the stage and they're visible unless you've programmed them otherwise.

ActionScript has a class called TextField that's the basis for Static Text, Dynamic Text, and Input Text. The properties and methods related to text are defined by the TextField class. That means if you ever have a question, or you're ever digging deeper for details about text, you can look up "TextField" in the *ActionScript 3.0 Language and Components Reference* (page 663), where you'll find a listing of all the properties, methods and events that are part of the TextField class. This section will familiarize you with quite a few of these features.

Note: In this chapter you see the terms *text field* and TextField used frequently. When you see TextField, it's a reference to the ActionScript class by that name. When you see *text field*, it's a more generic reference to one of the many tools that contain text in a Flash animation.

You create a new text field like you create an instance of any ActionScript class, using its constructor method. Here's some code that creates a text field and displays it. To try this demonstration yourself, create a new Flash 3.0 document (File → New → Flash File (ActionScript 3.0). Open the Actions panel, and then type the code shown here:

```
var txtBanner:TextField = new TextField( );
var strSalesPitch:String = new String( );
strSalesPitch = "Stutz Motor Company\nHome of the legendary Stutz Bearcat";
txtBanner.text = strSalesPitch;
addChild(txtBanner);
```

When you test this little snippet of code, it looks like Figure 16-12. If you've followed the earlier ActionScript examples in this book, the code may seem pretty familiar. The first line creates a variable called txtBanner that's an instance of TextField. The second line creates a variable called strSalesPitch that's a String. The third line assigns a string value to the string. The \n in the middle of the string creates a new line. The fourth line assigns strSalesPitch to the text property of the text field. The last line adds the text field to the display list making the text field visible on the stage. Without a single Flash tool touching the stage, you made text, albeit a bit dull and truncated, appear in a Flash animation. In the next few steps, you'll spruce it up.

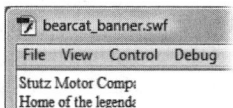

Figure 16-12:
Text created in ActionScript usually requires some formatting before it's ready for prime time. Here the typeface is small and a bit blah. The text doesn't fit in the 100 × 100 pixel text field that ActionScript provides unless you specify different dimensions.

Positioning, Sizing and Formatting a Text Field

You position and size your text field on the stage as you do other visual elements. In fact, because text fields are rectangular, it's very similar to working with a rectangle. You use the *x* and *y* properties to put the text field in a certain spot on the stage, and then you use the *width* and *height* properties to size the text field. So, the first step for the Bearcat Banner is to move away from that upper-left corner, and then give it enough width to show all the text. Here's the code you add before the *addChild( )* statement.

```
txtBanner.x = 40;
txtBanner.y = 40;
txtBanner.width = 220;
txtBanner.height = 160;
```

In addition to positioning and sizing, text fields have some other properties that come in handy. For example, you can add colored background and borders for text fields. You can also set some of the same behavior properties that appear in the property panel. These include whether the text field displays a single line or multiline. If it's a multiline text field, you can turn wordWrap on or off. With the autoSize property, you can determine whether a text field changes size to accommodate the text it holds and which direction it grows when needed. Here are some examples:

```
txtBanner.border = true;
txtBanner.borderColor = 0x00CDCD;
txtBanner.background = true;
txtBanner.backgroundColor = 0xCDFFFF;
```

Autosizing a Text Field

It's hard to set the dimensions for a text field when you don't know how much text it's going to hold. The ideal solution to this common dilemma is to pin one or more of the edges of the text field down to the stage and let other edges shrink and grow to accommodate the text. ActionScript lets you do just that with the help of two tools: the TextField's autoSize property and the TextFieldAutoSize class. First, you use the value of one of the TextFieldAutoSize constants to define the edge of the text field you want to pin down. Then you pass that value to your TextField's autoSize property. It sounds more complicated than it is: the good news is you can take care of the whole job with a single line code.

```
txtBanner.autoSize = TextFieldAutoSize.LEFT;
```

On the right side of the assignment operator (=), TextFieldAutoSize is set to the constant LEFT. Then, the value is assigned to txtBanner's autoSize property. The autoSize property expects this value to come packaged with the TextFieldAutoSize object. It won't work if you just try to assign the LEFT constant by itself. There are four constants that control the sizing behavior of a text field:

- **TextFieldAutoSize.NONE** is what you use if you don't want to set autosizing in your code. The text field doesn't resize at all. If there's more text than can be displayed in the text field, it simply doesn't show.

- **TextFieldAutoSize.LEFT** is one of the most common settings. In this case, the left edge of the text field stays anchored. The right edge can resize to accommodate text see Figure 16-13. If it's a multiline text field and there are line breaks, the bottom can resize too. When wordWrap is used, only the bottom is resized. The left, right, and top edges stay put.

- **TextFieldAutoSize.RIGHT** is used less frequently, because it behaves as if the text is right-justified and flowing to the left. The right edge stays anchored. When a single line runs long, the left edge resizes. If it's a multiline text field and there are line breaks, the bottom resizes, too. When wordWrap is used, only the bottom is resized.

- **TextFieldAutoSize.CENTER** comes in handy for headers or other cases where you want your text right in the middle. Resizing is equally distributed to both the left and right edges. For multiline text fields with line breaks, the bottom resizes to accommodate the new lines. If wordWrap is set to *true*, the bottom resizes and the left, right and top edges stay put.

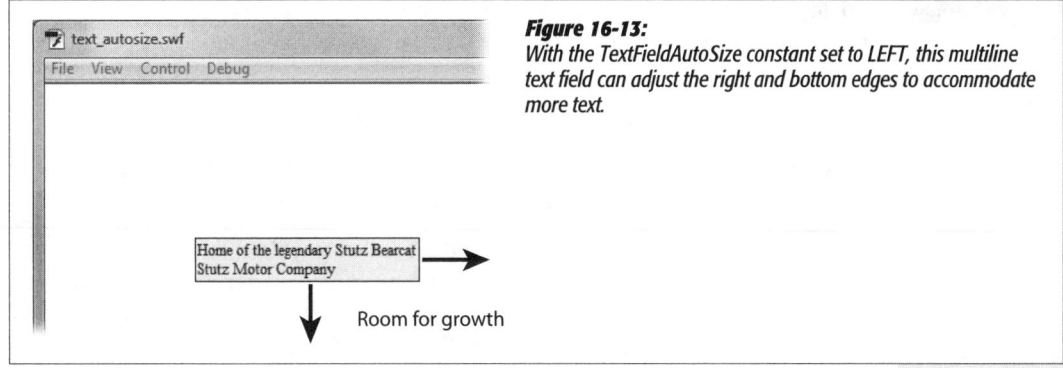

Figure 16-13:
*With the TextFieldAutoSize constant set to LEFT, this multiline
text field can adjust the right and bottom edges to accommodate
more text.*

Formatting Characters and Paragraphs

Formatting text is such a noble endeavor that ActionScript has an entire class devoted to the job. Once you learn the ins and outs of the TextFormat class, you can do it all. It works the same for static and dynamic text fields. You can apply a single format to an entire text field, and then fine-tune specific words or phrases with special formatting like bold, italic, or color-highlights. Some of the formatting properties you apply specific characters while others you apply to entire paragraphs.

Most of the action takes place using the properties of the TextFormat class. As you'd expect, the TextFormat class has character-level properties that set font names, size, style, and color. It also includes paragraph-level properties that control the alignment, margins, indents, kerning and leading (line spacing), and bullets.

TextFormat is an object itself, so you need to create an instance of the TextFormat class to use in your program. Here's an example of code that does that:

```
var txtFormat:TextFormat = new TextFormat();
```

The next step is to choose the format options you want to include in this specific instance of the class. For example, you can choose the typeface and font size using the TextFormat's properties:

```
txtFormat.font = "Constantia";
txtFormat.size = 20;
```

As explained earlier, it's best to choose fonts that you know are on your audience's computers because some fonts are embedded in Flash animations, while others are just referenced by name. If the font isn't available, the Flash Player finds a substitute. The number in the size property refers to points, the traditional typographic measurement also used in programs like Microsoft Word. The actual size and readability of typefaces at the same size can vary, so it's good to review and experiment when choosing a typeface and size.

To format a text field, you use the *setTextFormat( )* method and provide your newly created format as the parameter. That means you put it inside the parentheses, like this:

```
txtBanner.setTextFormat(txtFormat);
```

This statement registers the format for the entire txtBanner text field. A TextFormat object can include as many or as few properties as you want.

You can use more than one instance of the TextFormat class. Suppose you want to apply special formatting to a word or two. You can create formats that make type bold, italic, or change its color. Here's code that creates two new TextFormat objects, one for bold text and one for italic text.

```
var txtFormatBold:TextFormat = new TextFormat( );
txtFormatBold.bold = true;

var txtFormatItalic:TextFormat = new TextFormat( );
txtFormatItalic.italic = true;
```

If you want to apply formatting to a word or phrase inside of a text field, you need to tell ActionScript exactly which characters to format, which you do using the index numbers in the string. For example, if you want to italicize the word "legendary" in the text "Home of the legendary Stutz Bearcat," you need to count characters. Don't forget to start that count at 0. Then, when you use the *setTextFormat( )* method, you also provide a starting point and ending point for the formatting. It looks like this:

```
txtBanner.setTextFormat(txtFormatItalic,12,20);
```

Formatting with ActionScript is similar to setting properties in the Properties panel. When you apply the txtFormatItalic format, it doesn't mess with any of the other formatting properties. It leaves the font and size settings as they were, changing only the properties that it specifically defines.

Tip: When you format text with the *setTextFormat( )* method, the text has to already be assigned to the text field and the formatting applies to then entire text field. If you assign the text after running *setTextFormat( )*, it won't be as "dressed up" as you expect.

Here's a chunk of ActionScript code that uses all the TextField coding tricks covered so far:

```
1    var txtBanner:TextField = new TextField( );
2    txtBanner.text = "Home of the legendary Stutz Bearcat"
3
4    var txtFormat:TextFormat = new TextFormat( );
5    txtFormat.font = "Constantia";
```

```
6    txtFormat.size = 20;

7

8    var txtFormatBold:TextFormat = new TextFormat( );
9    txtFormatBold.bold = true;

10

11   var txtFormatItalic:TextFormat = new TextFormat( );
12   txtFormatItalic.italic = true;

13

14   txtBanner.x = txtBanner.y = 120;
15   txtBanner.width = 200;
16   txtBanner.height = 120;
17   txtBanner.autoSize = TextFieldAutoSize.LEFT;
18   txtBanner.background = true;
19   txtBanner.backgroundColor = 0xCDFFFF;
20   txtBanner.border = true;
21   txtBanner.setTextFormat(txtFormat);
22   txtBanner.setTextFormat(txtFormatItalic,12,20);
23   txtBanner.setTextFormat(txtFormatBold,22,35);

24

25   addChild(txtBanner);
```

Line 1 creates the text field called txtBanner, and line two assigns a string literal to its text property. Lines 4 through 6 create a TextFormat object that sets the font name and size. The next two blocks, lines 8 through 12, create two more TextFormat objects, that, respectively, set the bold and italic properties of text. The next block goes to business setting the properties of the txtBanner text field. Line 14 uses a little ActionScript trickery to set both the x and y properties at the same time. You can do this when you're assigning the same value to two properties. Line 17 sets the autoSize property using TextFieldAutoSize.LEFT. Lines 18 through 20 create a text field with a colored background and a border. Because there's no explicit setting for borderColor, Flash will use a black border. Lines 21 through 23 go about the business of applying the TextFormat objects to txtBanner. Line 21 applies a typeface and size to the entire text field, while lines 22 and 23 apply italic and bold formatting to specific characters. Finally, the *addChild( )* method adds txtBanner to the display list, which makes the text field visible on the stage.

When all is said and done, the text field looks like Figure 16-14 (shown in Flash Player).

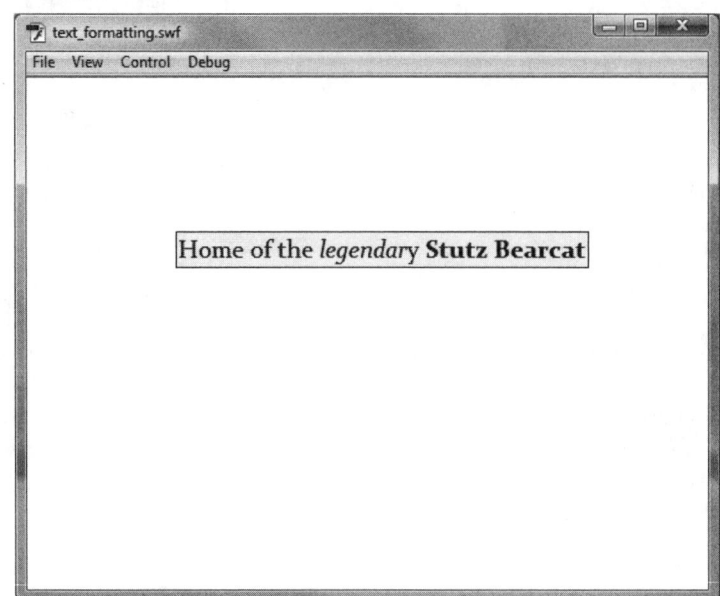

Figure 16-14:
This text was created and formatted entirely by ActionScript. Using the TextFormat object, you can apply formatting to an entire block of text or to specific characters as shown in the italic and bold words in this example.

Formatting with HTML and CSS

When you're working in ActionScript, there's more than one way to format text. The previous technique using ActionScript's TextFormat object works well when you're working on a project on your own. The properties and methods are familiar if you're used to working with Flash's Properties panel. Flash also lets you use the same formatting tools used by Web designers: HTML (hypertext markup language) and CSS (cascading style sheets). There are a few reasons why you might want to go this route for a project. Perhaps your project uses lots of text and it's already formatted using HTML. In some cases, you may be working on a large project where some people are responsible for generating the text and others are responsible for presenting it on the Web or in a Flash-based program.

HTML and CSS Philosophical Differences

Before you make a decision about using either HTML or CSS for your Flash formatting chores, it helps to understand their approaches to formatting text. HTML embeds formatting codes inside of the text. For example, the text in the txtBanner text field of the previous example might look like this if you formatted in HTML:

```
<font face="Constantia" size="3"> Home of the <i>legendary</i> <b>Stutz
Bearcat</b></font>
```

When a Web browser like Internet Explorer, Safari, or Chrome reads this text, it knows how to display the text in the browser window. It applies the formatting instructions and shows the text. So HTML coding works fine from the audience point of view. For designers, it can be a bit of a pain. One of the problems of HTML coding is that the message gets a bit lost in the formatting tags. Complicated HTML coding is hard for human eyes to read, and that makes it easy to foul up. When you want to make changes, it's a lot of work to go in there and tweak all those bits of embedded code.

These days, the fashionable technique is to use CSS (cascading style sheets) to format Web pages. The underlying philosophy is that it's best to separate the formatting from the content. You create styles (type specs) for body text, major headlines, sub heads, captions, and so forth. You store those definitions in a style sheet. Then, in the text, you tag different portions, indicating the styles they should use. In effect, you say: this is a major headline, this is body text, and this is a caption. When the browser goes to display your Web page, it comes to the text tagged as a headline, and then it looks up the type specs in the style sheet. It does the same thing for the body text and the captions. From a designer's point of view, this system is a tremendous timesaver. If you want to change the caption style for a Web site that has 400 captioned pictures, all you need to do is edit one definition in the style sheet. If all those type specs were embedded HTML code, you'd need to make 400 separate edits.

Note: Most Web pages designed today use a combination of HTML and CSS to format pages. HTML is still the basic, underlying code for Web pages. CSS, JavaScript and Flash are technologies built on top of the HTML foundation.

Using HTML Text in Flash

There are two steps to using HTML encoded text in Flash. First, you need to create strings with the HTML codes embedded. Then you need to assign those strings to the htmlText property of the text field that will display the formatted text.

When you want to use HTML with its embedded codes in a Flash project, you need to build strings of text that include all the HTML codes. That means you end up with a lot of angle brackets, equal signs, and quotes inside your strings. The quotes present a small challenge, because your string needs to be wrapped in quotes when it's assigned to a variable or a text field (page 398). Fortunately, Flash accepts either single or double quotes. So if the HTML you're embedding looks like this line:

```
<p><font face="Constantia" size="3"> Home of the <i>legendary</i> <b>Stutz
Bearcat</b></font></p>
```

You can place it inside of single quotes when you use it in Flash. For example, this statement that assigns the HTML coded string to the txtBanner text field. It uses single quotes to define the string:

```
txtBanner.htmlText = '<p><font face="Constantia" size="3"> Home of the <i>
legendary</i> <b>Stutz Bearcat</b></font></p>';
```

HTML is like Flash in that it can use either single or double quotes in most places. Most of the time, you'll use double quotes, but be aware that you may sometimes see single quotes used to assign values in HTML code. In that case, you'd use double quotes to define your string in Flash.

Once you've stored your text in a string, you need to assign that string to a text field. Lucky for you, all TextField objects have an htmlText property, as shown in the code example above. It works just like the regular text property except it understands how to read and then display text with HTML codes.

Creating a Hyperlink with HTML

If there's one thing that made HTML king of the World Wide Web, it's the hyperlink. Hyperlinks are the threads that form that web. Click a linked word, and suddenly you're in a different part of the universe (or at least, the Web). Earlier in this chapter (page 543), you saw how to create hyperlinks using the standard Flash authoring tools. The ability of text fields to use HTML encoded text, also enables them to use HTML links. You create the links using the usual HTML codes: <a> anchor tags. Here's an example of an HTML hyperlink:

```
<a href="http://www.stutzbearcat.net">click me</a>
```

Like most HTML tags, the anchor tag comes in pairs: *<a>in between stuff</a>*. The slash is the defining mark of an end tag. In HTML, you stuff that first tag with any necessary parameters. In this case, the parameter is a Web address. The *href* stands for hypertext reference; the equals sign assigns a value to the reference inside double quotes. The specific value here is a Web address. The words in between the two <a> tags "click me" are visible in the browser window. Depending on the tag's formatting, they may appear underlined or highlighted in some way to show that they're a link.

Beyond that there's no magic to adding and using HTML hyperlinks in Flash. Here's an example of the same link included in a string that's passed to the html-Text property of a text field:

```
txtBanner.htmlText = '<p>To visit our website <a href="http://www.
stutzbearcat.net">click me</a> </p>';
```

Flash Player isn't a Web browser, so when your audience clicks the link, their browser opens, and then loads the Web page that specified in the link. The link can just as easily point to a file on the local computer. In that case, instead of the *http://* reference you'd use a *file:///* reference.

Using CSS to Format Text in Flash

CSS is the acronym for *cascading style sheets*—an ingenious system for formatting HTML and XML text. If you want to read up on how CSS works, you can get an excellent introduction in David Sawyer McFarland's *CSS: The Missing Manual*. You need to have a basic understanding of CSS to use it Flash. This book provides a quick overview of CSS, and an example or two to get you started.

CSS style sheets are a little like those wooden Russian dolls where one object is inside of another. Starting from the outside and working in, here's what you find in a CSS style sheet. A style sheet is a list of formatting specifications. Each formatting spec has a selector that identifies the HTML tag that it formats. That tag could be the paragraph tag <p>, or the heading tag <h1>, or an anchor tag <a>. In CSS lingo, the formatting spec is called a *declaration block*. The declaration block is contained inside of curly braces {}. Within those curly braces are specific declarations that define fonts, styles, colors, sizes, and all the other properties that can be defined in CSS. (Flash works with only some of these properties.) The declarations have two parts: a property and a value. So, in CSS if that property is *font-size*, then the value is a number representing point size. A CSS definition to format an <h1> heading tag might look like this:

```
h1 {

font-family: Arial;

font-size:18;

font-weight: bold;

color: red;

}
```

The first line has the selector for *h1* headings, usually the biggest, boldest heading on a Web page. The next four lines show pairs of properties and values. On the left side of the colon is the property, which is hyphenated if it's made up of more than one word. On the right side is the value assigned to that property.

In Flash, you can recreate the function of a CSS style sheet using the StyleSheet object. It gives you a way to create selectors, and then assign values to the properties that Flash recognizes. Here's Flash's version of the specification shown above.

```
1    var txtBanner:TextField = new TextField( );
2    var styleSheet:StyleSheet = new StyleSheet( );
3    var h1Style:Object = new Object( );
4    var pStyle:Object = new Object( );
5
6    h1Style.fontFamily = "Arial";
7    h1Style.fontSize = "24";
8    h1Style.fontWeight = "bold";
9    h1Style.color = 0x00FF00;
10
11   pStyle.fontFamily = "Arial";
12   pStyle.fontSize = "12";
13   pStyle.fontWeight = "normal";
14
15   styleSheet.setStyle("h1", h1Style);
16   styleSheet.setStyle("p", pStyle);
17   txtBanner.styleSheet = styleSheet;
```

```
18
19   txtBanner.x = 60;
20   txtBanner.y = 120;
21   txtBanner.width = 200;
22   txtBanner.height = 120;
23   txtBanner.autoSize = TextFieldAutoSize.LEFT;
24   txtBanner.background = true;
25   txtBanner.backgroundColor = 0xCDFFFF;
26   txtBanner.border = true;
27
28   txtBanner.htmlText = '<h1>Home of the legendary Stutz Bearcat</h1> <p>What
     can we do to put you into a Bearcat today?</p>';
29   addChild(txtBanner);
```

Here's a line-by-line rundown on the ActionScript. As in the other examples, line 1 creates the TextField object called txtBanner. The next three lines also create objects. Line 2 creates an instance of the StyleSheet class and lines 3 and 4 create instances of the more generic Object class. You use this object to hold the CSS declarations. That's exactly what's going on in lines 6 through 13. Values are being assigned to the h1Style object, and then the pStyle object.

Note that the property names have been changed slightly. That's because Action-Script jumps into action when it sees a minus sign (–). Instead, these properties eliminate the hyphen and use an uppercase letter for the word following the hyphen. So where the CSS property is named font-family, the ActionScript property is named fontFamily. Lines 15 and 16 use styleSheet's *setStyle( )* method. The first parameter in the parentheses defines the selector; *h1*, the heading style in line 15 and *p*, the paragraph style in line 16. The second parameter in each case is the object that was created to hold the declarations. These are ActionScript's substitute for a declaration block with those paired sets of properties and values.

The styleSheet Object now has formatting instructions for two tags that it's likely to encounter in an HTML document. Line 17 assigns the styleSheet object to txt-Banner's styleSheet property. Lines 19 through 26 are the ActionScript code that formats the text field. There's no CSS here, it's just straight ActionScript. Line 28 gets back into the CSS business. When you format with CSS, you pass the string to the text field using the htmlText property. The string itself is formatted like HTML, but instead of embedding formatting specs, it uses style tags. This little snippet uses two tags, first the <h1> tag for the heading, and then the <p> tag for its rather skimpy paragraph. With CSS, you need to assign the StyleSheet property before you put text in the text field. The last line adds the txtBanner to the display list for the world to see. Figure 16-15 shows how the CSS-formatted text looks.

Note: Flash is very fussy about its style sheets. If it's unable to read or use any of the styles, it tends to ignore the entire style sheet. The result is that no formatting is applied.

Home of the legendary Stutz Bearcat
What can we do to put you into a Bearcat today?

<p> tag   <h1> tag

Figure 16-15:
This text is formatted with CSS. Styles are applied to the paragraph <p> tag and to the heading 1 <h1> tag. You can create CSS styles within your ActionScript code or you can load an external CSS file.

There are quite a few things missing from Flash's version of CSS. First of all, you can only assign one StyleSheet at a time to a text field's styleSheet property. One of the handy things about CSS is the way you use multiple style sheets for the formatting chores. Another feature missing from Flash's HTML capabilities is tables, causing moans among Web-savvy designers. Web designers like to use tables to format and organize text and pictures.

Formatting Text with an External CSS File

One of the great features of CSS for designing Web pages is that you can use a single external file (called a CSS style sheet) to format many Web pages. Want change the color of a heading? Simply change the definition in the style sheet, and that changes the look of all the Web pages. You can use external CSS style sheets with Flash projects too—just keep in mind the limitations of HTML and CSS in Flash mentioned in the previous section.

Note: There are two files for this project *flash_text.css* and *text_external_css.fla*. You can find both at *http://missingmanuals.com/cds*.

To start this exercise, you need a file that defines CSS styles. You can download *flash_text.css* from the "Missing CD" site or create your own using a text editor. It's short and sweet:

```
p {
    font-family: Arial;
    font-size: 12px;
    font-weight: normal;
}
h1 {
    font-family: Arial;
    font-size: 24px;
    font-weight: bold;
    color: #00FF00;
}
```

This external CSS file defines the same CSS styles that were used in the previous example—the paragraph <p> tag and the heading 1 <h1> tag. Most CSS style sheets are more complicated than this, but as an example, this works just fine.

The ActionScript code that uses this external file needs to do a few things:

- Load the external CSS file.

- Read (parse) and store the CSS style instructions.

- Apply the CSS styles to a text field rendered as HTML.

- Display the text field.

- Assign text with HTML tags to the htmlText property of the text field.

Here are the steps to load an external CSS style sheet and use the styles with code created in ActionScript:

1. **Create an instance of the URLLoader class.**

   ```
   var loader:URLLoader = new URLLoader();
   ```

   The URLLoader class is used to load external files that reside on a computer or on the Internet.

2. **Register an event listener that triggers when the CSS file has completed loading.**

   ```
   loader.addEventListener(Event.COMPLETE, loadCSSListener);
   ```

   The URLLoader class triggers an event when a file has loaded. When that event triggers, the function *loadCSSListener( )* will run.

3. **Create an instance of the URLRequest class to identify the CSS file to be loaded.**

   ```
   var request:URLRequest = new URLRequest("flash_text.css");
   ```

   The URLRequest class is used to identify files by filename and if needed a path. In this case, just the filename is used because *flash_text.css* is to be stored in the same folder as the Flash project.

4. **Use the load( ) method of *loader* to load the CSS file. Use *request* as the parameter for the load method.**

   ```
   loader.load(request);
   ```

   Adding an extra blank line here sets the function for the event listener off from the rest of the code.

5. **Create the function that runs when the loader event is complete.**

   ```
   function loadCSSListener(evt:Event):void {
   ```

   The rest of the statements in this exercise are part of this function, which ends with the closing curly bracket.

6. **Create an instance of the StyleSheet class.**

```
var cssFlashStyles:StyleSheet = new StyleSheet( );
```

The StyleSheet class holds CSS style definitions.

7. **Read the data in the external CSS file (*flash_text.css*) and store the data in the style sheet cssFlashStyles.**

```
cssFlashStyles.parseCSS(URLLoader(evt.target).data);
```

The process of reading and processing the CSS definitions is called *parsing*. The method parseCSS is part of the StyleSheet class.

8. **Create an instance of the TextField class with the variable name txtBanner.**

```
var txtBanner:TextField = new TextField( );
```

The text field txtBanner displays text stored in one of two properties—the *text* property or the htmlText property.

9. **Position and size the txtBanner, and then format the background and border.**

```
txtBanner.x = 60;
txtBanner.y = 120;
txtBanner.width = 200;
txtBanner.height = 120;
txtBanner.autoSize = TextFieldAutoSize.LEFT;
txtBanner.background = true;
txtBanner.backgroundColor = 0xCDFFFF;
txtBanner.border = true;
```

These statements aren't related to CSS and their formatting applies to the entire text field.

10. **Add txtBanner to the Display List.**

```
addChild(txtBanner);
```

Adding txtBanner to the Display list makes it visible on the stage.

11. **Assign the cssFlashStyles to the styleSheet property of txtBanner.**

```
txtBanner.styleSheet = cssFlashStyles;
```

It may seem a little backward, but the style sheet needs to be applied before the text is assigned to txtBanner.

12. **Assign a string of text to txtBanner's htmlText property.**

```
txtBanner.htmlText = '<h1>Home of the legendary Stutz Bearcat</h1> <p>
What can we do to put you into a Bearcat today?</p>';
}
```

The text assigned to the htmlText property of txtBanner is a string literal. The HTML tags <p> and <h1> are embedded within the string.

---

13. Save your Flash file *text_external_css.fla* in the same folder as the CSS file *flash_text.css*.

If you don't store the two files in the same folder, you need to provide complete path information in the URLRequest, step 3.

When you test the movie, Control → Test Movie, you see text formatted as shown in Figure 16-15. The style definitions are identical in this example and the previous example, where CSS styles were written into the ActionScript code, so the results look the same.

In general, using external CSS style sheets gives you more flexibility, because you can change the appearance of text inside of your Flash project by simply editing the style sheet. As long as the name and location of the external CSS file stay the same, you don't even need to fire up Flash or ActionScript or republish your .swf files. How cool is that?

Choosing the Right Text Formatting System

So far this chapter has described four different ways to format text in Flash animations. How do you choose the right technique for your project? Here are some general guidelines about when to use Flash's Properties panel, ActionScript's TextFormat object, HTML, or CSS to format text in your Flash projects:

- Use the Properties panel for its ease of use and when you make all your formatting decisions as you design the animation.

- Use ActionScript's TextFormat object when you need to make changes to your text while the animation is running.

- Use ActionScript's TextFormat object when you want to work quickly and your project creates TextField objects on the fly.

- Use HTML if you have lots of text already formatted in HTML or your workgroup requires it.

- Use HTML or CSS when you want to embed hyperlinks in dynamic text.

- Use CSS if you're working on a large Web-based project that already has established CSS type specs.

- Use CSS if you're working with lots of text and there are timesaving benefits to be gained by separating formatting from content.

Note: When you use HTML and CSS in Flash, you can only use a few of the most common tags and properties. It's not surprising that these are the tags and properties that are matched by TextFormat object. If you're choosing HTML or CSS for a specific feature, make sure that you can use that feature in Flash and ActionScript. You can find a complete list in the ActionScript 3.0 Language and Components Reference in Flash's Help system. Look under flash.text, and then choose the TextField class. Then choose htmlText property, and you see a table that lists the tags Flash supports. For CSS, look under flash.text for the StyleSheet class. In its Help pages, you see a table listing the CSS properties supported in Flash and ActionScript.

Drawing with ActionScript

If you were one of those kids who loved their Etch-A-Sketch, then you're probably going to love this chapter. With ActionScript, you can draw lines and shapes in your Flash animations. The great advantage of drawing with ActionScript is your animations can draw new objects on the fly.

This chapter will introduce the Graphics class and all the power it puts at your fingertips. To start with, you'll learn how ActionScript works with points and lines. You'll learn about the virtual pen and how, as it moves from one spot to another, you can tell it to draw lines (or not). Then you'll learn how to draw and display Flash's built-in shapes: including ellipses, rectangles, and rounded rectangles. There are times when prebuilt shapes won't do the job, so you'll see how to draw more complex and irregular shapes using nothing but ActionScript code. To wrap things up, this chapter shows how to move the shapes you've drawn about the stage using ActionScript's TimerEvent to trigger the motion.

What's the Point?

It all comes down to the point. Flash's stage is a mass of points measured by X/Y coordinates. In the upper-left corner, there's a point that referenced by 0, 0, which means it's at the 0 point on the horizontal axis and the 0 point of vertical axis. ActionScript describes the point as: $X = 0$ and $Y = 0$. If you put something on the stage and don't tell Flash or ActionScript where you want to place it, chances are that something will end up at 0, 0. If your stage is one of Flash's standard sizes, say 540×400 pixels, the lower-right corner is 540, 400 or $X = 540$ and $Y = 400$. When drawing with ActionScript, you can bet that you'll be dealing with a lot of X/Y coordinates and a lot of points. If you want to draw a line from one place to another, you need to define two points. If you want to draw a trapezoid, you need to define, at least by inference the four corner points.

Since the point is a building block for all the lines and shapes and drawings to follow, ActionScript has a special Point class. Not only does the class give you a place to store information about specific points, it also provides some helpful methods that you can use when you're working with points and their relationships. For reference, the Point class is part of the *flash.geom* package. You create instances of the Point class the same way you create other objects in ActionScript, like so:

```
var ptNear:Point = new Point();
```

When you enter this line of code, you're doing a couple of things at once. First, of all, you're creating a new variable and providing a variable name ptNear. The word after the colon declares the data type; in this case, Point. Then, after the assignment operator (=), you use the reserved word *new* to explain that you're creating a new instance of an object. The word *Point( )* with its parentheses is the constructor for the Point class. When all is said and done, you've got yourself a new instance of the Point class that's addressed by the name ptNear.

As you might guess, Point objects have two properties, *x* and *y*. You can assign values to these properties to set a point's location, and if you have the name of a point but you don't know where it is, you can read these properties to learn its location.

```
ptNear.x = 20;
ptNear.y = 20;
trace("The location of ptNear is:",ptNear);
```

The first two lines assign values to ptNear, an instance of the Point class. The third line uses that handy *trace( )* statement to place information in the Output panel. In this case, the *trace( )* statement reports:

The location of ptNear is: (x=20, y=20)

The Point class has just one other property, oddly called *length*. Thankfully, it's not referring to the length of the point. That would confuse everyone, including Euclid. In this case, *length* refers to the length of a line from 0, 0 to the point. It's a *read-only* property, meaning you can't assign a new value to length; all it does is report on its value.

Most of the interesting and useful features of the point class are the methods. These include:

- *distance( )*. Calculates the distance between two points. Example:

```
distanceBetweenPoints = Point.distance(ptNear,ptFar);
```

- *add( )*. Adds the coordinates of two points and returns another point in X, Y values.

```
sumOfPoints = ptNear.add(ptFar);
```

- *subtract( )*. Subtracts the coordinates of two points and returns another point in X, Y values.

```
differnceOfPoints = ptFar.subtract(ptNear);
```

- *equals( )*. Tests to see if two points are equal. Useful for creating conditional statements, like *if ptBall* equals *ptGround* then bounce.

```
if (ptBall.equals(ptGround)) bounce( ); //run the function Bounce( )
```

- *interpolate( )*. Calculates a point between two end points. You use a third parameter, with a value between 0 and 1, to find a point and to determine how close that point is to one or the other of the end points. Think of it as a percentage.

```
ptHalfWay = Point.interpolate(ptNear, ptFar, 0.5);
ptQuarterWay = Point.interpolate(ptNear, ptFar, 0.75);
```

The *interpolate( )* method uses three parameters, which as usual make their appearance inside of the parentheses. The first two parameters have to be points. The third parameter is a number between 0 and 1; that's common ActionScript technique for indicating a percentage. In this case, the closer the number is to 1, the closer the point is to the first point. The closer the number is to zero, the closer it is to the second point. So, in the examples above, the value 0.5, finds the midpoint between ptNear and ptFar. The value 0.75 is closer to the first point, so it finds a point a quarter of the way between the two points.

The best way to understand how these methods work is to use them in ActionScript. Follow these steps to see how to run the Point class through some of its paces:

1. **Select File → New and choose Flash File (ActionScript 3.0). Select the first frame on the timeline, and then press F9.**

   The Actions panel opens. Figure 17-1 shows the Actions panel with some code entered.

2. **Type the following code (but not the line numbers at left):**

```
1    var ptNear:Point = new Point( );
2    var ptFar:Point = new Point( );
3    var distanceBetweenPoints:Number = new Number( );
4    var sumOfPoints:Point = new Point( );
5    var differenceOfPoints:Point = new Point( );
6    var pointBetweenPoints:Point = new Point( );
7    var ptHalfWay:Point = new Point( );
8    var ptQuarterWay:Point = new Point( );
9    var ptBall:Point = new Point( );
10   var ptGround:Point = new Point( );
11
12   ptNear.x = 0;
13   ptNear.y = 20;
14   ptFar.x = 100;
15   ptFar.y = 20;
```

```
16
17   distanceBetweenPoints = Point.distance(ptNear, ptFar);
18   sumOfPoints = ptNear.add(ptFar);
19   differenceOfPoints = ptFar.subtract(ptNear);
20   ptBall.x = 200;
21   ptBall.y = 350;
22   ptGround.x = 200;
23   ptGround.y = 350;
24   ptHalfWay = Point.interpolate(ptNear, ptFar, 0.5);
25   ptQuarterWay = Point.interpolate(ptNear, ptFar, 0.75);
26
27   trace("The location of ptNear is:",ptNear);
28   trace("The location of ptFar is:",ptFar);
29   trace();
30   trace("A line from 0, 0 to ptNear is",ptNear.length, "long.");
31   trace("The distance between ptNear and ptFar is:",distanceBetweenPoints);
32   trace("If you add ptNear to ptFar you get:", sumOfPoints);
33   trace("If you subtract ptNear from ptFar you get:",differenceOfPoints);
34   trace("This point is half the way between ptNear and ptFar:", ptHalfWay);
35   trace("This point is a quarter of the way between ptNear and ptFar:",
     ptQuarterWay);
36   trace();
37   trace("The location of ptBall is:",ptBall);
38   trace("The location of ptGround is:",ptGround);
39   if (ptBall.equals(ptGround)) bounce();
40
41   function bounce():void {
42       trace("I'm bouncing");
43   }
```

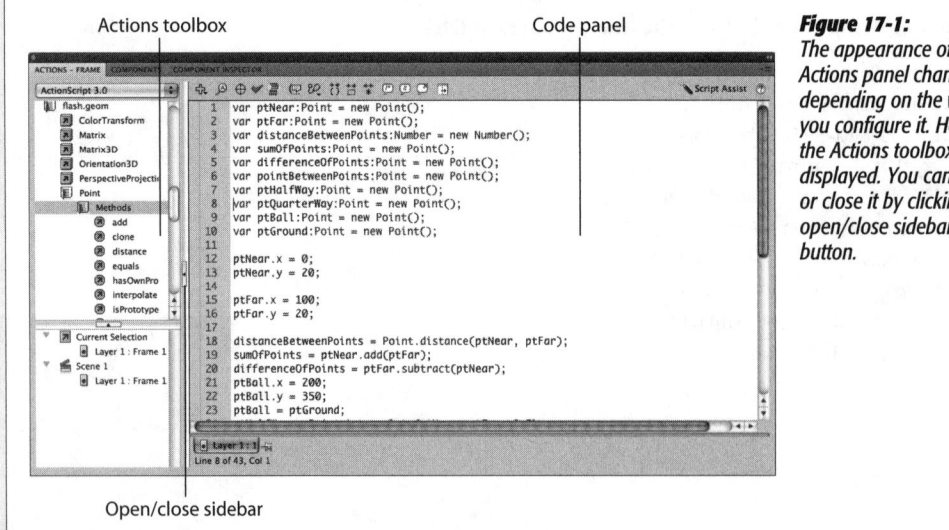

Actions toolbox   Code panel

Open/close sidebar

Figure 17-1:
The appearance of the Actions panel changes depending on the way you configure it. Here the Actions toolbox is displayed. You can open or close it by clicking the open/close sidebar button.

The first 10 lines in the code create instances of objects. All except one are Point class objects. The data type for distanceBetweenPoints is *Number*. Lines 12 through 15, assign values to the X and Y properties to ptNear and ptFar. The next block of statements (lines 17 through 25) show the Point methods discussed in this section. If you want to experiment with these methods, you can use these examples as a model. From line 27 to line 38 there are *trace( )* statements that send text to the Output panel. The text inside of quotes is displayed literally; the items outside of the quotes are the variable names. Most of the variables refer to points, so the Output panel lists the values of their X and Y properties. In some cases the output is a distance, which is a number. Line 39 is a conditional *if( )* statement that demonstrates the Points class's *equals* property. The two points are equal, because they have the same values for the X and Y properties, so the value of the statement *ptBall.equals(ptGround)* is *true*. With the condition *true*, the if statement calls the *bounce( )* function, which is written on lines 41 through 43. The bounce function sends the words "I'm bouncing" to the Output panel, as shown in Figure 17-2.

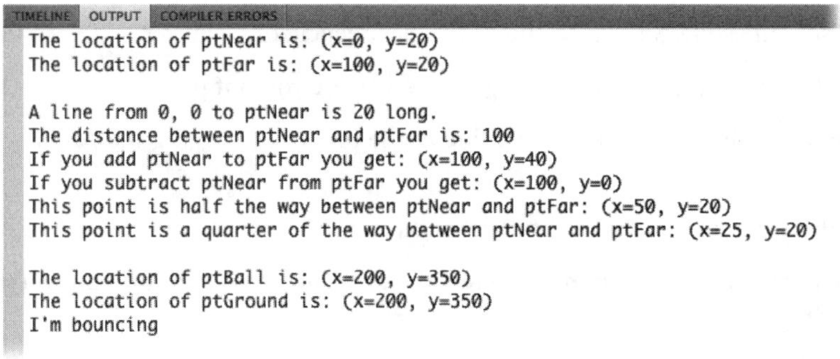

```
TIMELINE   OUTPUT   COMPILER ERRORS
  The location of ptNear is: (x=0, y=20)
  The location of ptFar is: (x=100, y=20)

  A line from 0, 0 to ptNear is 20 long.
  The distance between ptNear and ptFar is: 100
  If you add ptNear to ptFar you get: (x=100, y=40)
  If you subtract ptNear from ptFar you get: (x=100, y=0)
  This point is half the way between ptNear and ptFar: (x=50, y=20)
  This point is a quarter of the way between ptNear and ptFar: (x=25, y=20)

  The location of ptBall is: (x=200, y=350)
  The location of ptGround is: (x=200, y=350)
  I'm bouncing
```

Figure 17-2:
When you put a reference to a point in a trace( ) *statement, Flash automatically shows the values of the X and Y properties. This Output panel shows the results of several Point class methods.*

Working with points is a little abstract, because you can't really draw points on the stage in Flash. It's good to understand how points work in ActionScript and to be aware of the methods of the Point class, but the fun really begins when you start drawing lines and shapes.

Beginning with the Graphics Class

With ActionScript, you can draw lines, curves, shapes, fills, and gradients. As with most ActionScript features, this ability comes to you courtesy of a class—in this case, the flash.display.Graphics class. Using the Graphics class, you can draw on instances of these three classes: Shape, Sprite, and MovieClip. Each of these classes has a graphics property, which, in turn, provides all the properties and methods of the Graphics class. So, for example, if you want to define how a line looks, you use the *graphics.lineStyle( )* method. It looks like this:

```
spriteLine.graphics.lineStyle(3,0x00FF00);
```

Or, if you want to actually draw a line, it looks like this:

```
spriteLine.graphics.lineTo(20,150);
```

The important point to notice about the Graphics class is that it's a property of the Shape, Sprite, or MovieClip classes. You reference it by naming an instance of one of those classes, then the graphics class itself, and then the property or method of the Graphics class that you want to use.

Drawing Lines

Think about the steps you take when you draw a line in the real world. You probably have your piece of paper in front of you. You pick up a pen, pencil, or marker. You place the writing instrument down on a specific point on the paper and drag it to another point. If you don't want to continue with another line, you pick up your pen and the job is done. You pretty much follow those same steps when you draw a line using ActionScript. Here's a list of the ActionScript steps:

- **Open a Flash document and the Actions panel.** The stage is your paper.

- **Choose a line style.** Similar to choosing a pen, pencil, or whatever.

- **Move to a specific point on the stage.** Here's where you put pen to paper.

- **Move to another point, drawing a line in the process.** Dragging the pen across the paper.

- **Stop drawing lines.** Lifting the pen from the paper.

With those generalizations in mind, here are the specific steps to draw a line on the Flash stage:

1. **Select File → New and choose Flash File (ActionScript 3.0).**

   A new, empty Flash document appears.

2. **Press F9 (Option-F9 on a Mac).**

   The Actions window opens, where you can enter ActionScript code.

3. **In the Actions panel, create an instance of the Sprite class by typing the following.**

   ```
   var sprtLine:Sprite = new Sprite();
   ```

   A Sprite is a container like a MovieClip, except it doesn't have a timeline. Using a Sprite instead of a MovieClip when you don't need a timeline keeps the size of your .swf smaller.

4. **Use the *lineStyle( )* method to set the style for the line you want to draw.**

   ```
   sprtLine.graphics.lineStyle(16,0x00FF00);
   ```

   The first parameter inside of the parentheses sets the thickness of the line. In this case, setting the value to 16 draws a monster line 16 pixels thick. It's just as if you typed *16* in the Properties → "Fill and Stroke" → Stroke box. The second number is a color value shown in hexadecimal format. (For more on colors and the hexadecimal format, see page 213.)

The *lineStyle( )* method has other parameters that define properties like the opacity of the line or how lines meet at the corners. Often, all you need are the first two parameters, and if that's the case you don't need to worry about the *lineStyle( )* parameters. But in case you do, here's a rundown on all the *lineStyle( )* parameters:

- **thickness.** Provides a number for the thickness of the stroke in pixels.

- **color.** Provides a color value in hexadecimal format

- **alpha.** Provides a number from *1* to *0* that indicates a percentage of transparency.

- **pixelHinting.** Provides *true* or *false* to change the way Flash Player displays corners. Flash usually has this option set to *false*, and you seldom need to change it.

- **scaleMode.** Provides one of the following constants to determine how a stroke changes when an object is scaled. *NORMAL* means the line is scaled with the object. *NONE* means the line keeps its thickness when scaled. *VERTICAL* means the line keeps its thickness if the object is scaled vertically only. *HORIZONTAL* means the line keeps it thickness if the object is scaled horizontally only.

- **caps.** Provides the constants *NONE, ROUND,* or *SQUARE* to set the way the ends of lines appear.

- **joints.** Provides the constants *MITER, ROUND,* or *BEVEL* to set the way lines appear when they meet at endpoints and corners.

- **miterLimit.** Provides a number from *1* to *255* to indicate the limit at which a miter is cut off. The miter in effect trims off the point of a corner when two lines meet.

The *lineStyle( )* method does expect to receive these values in a particular order so, for example, you'd get a confused result if you swapped the color value for the stroke thickness. Or, for example, if you want to provide a *NONE* constant for scaleMode you need to provide values for the alpha and pixelHinting parameters, too. It looks like this:

```
sprtLine.graphics.lineStyle(3,0x00FF00,1,false,"NONE");
```

5. **Move the virtual pen to the line's starting point:**

```
sprtLine.graphics.moveTo(20,50);
```

Think of this statement as moving your pen to a position on the page without drawing a line. Flash expects a value for X and Y for parameters for the *moveTo( )* method. Unlike the *lineTo( )* method, *moveTo( )* is similar to picking the pen up from the paper and moving it to a new location. This action doesn't draw a line.

---

6. **Draw a line to another point.**

   ```
   sprtLine.graphics.lineTo(500,380);
   ```

   Think of this move as dragging your pen across the paper. The *lineTo( )* method draws a line from the current point to the point specified in the parentheses.

7. **Add the sprtLine Sprite to the display list.**

   ```
   addChild(sprtLine);
   ```

   Until you use the *addChild( )* method to add sprtLine to the display list, nothing actually appears in the Flash Player.

8. **Use the *moveTo( )* method to pick up the virtual pen.**

   This step isn't mandatory, but it's sort of like putting your crayons away when you're done. The *moveTo( )* method moves the virtual pen without drawing a line. If you want to draw a line that's connected to the end point 500, 380, you can use another *lineTo( )* method.

9. **Test the animation.**

   You see a Flash Player stage with a big fat green line running diagonally across the stage, as shown in Figure 17-3.

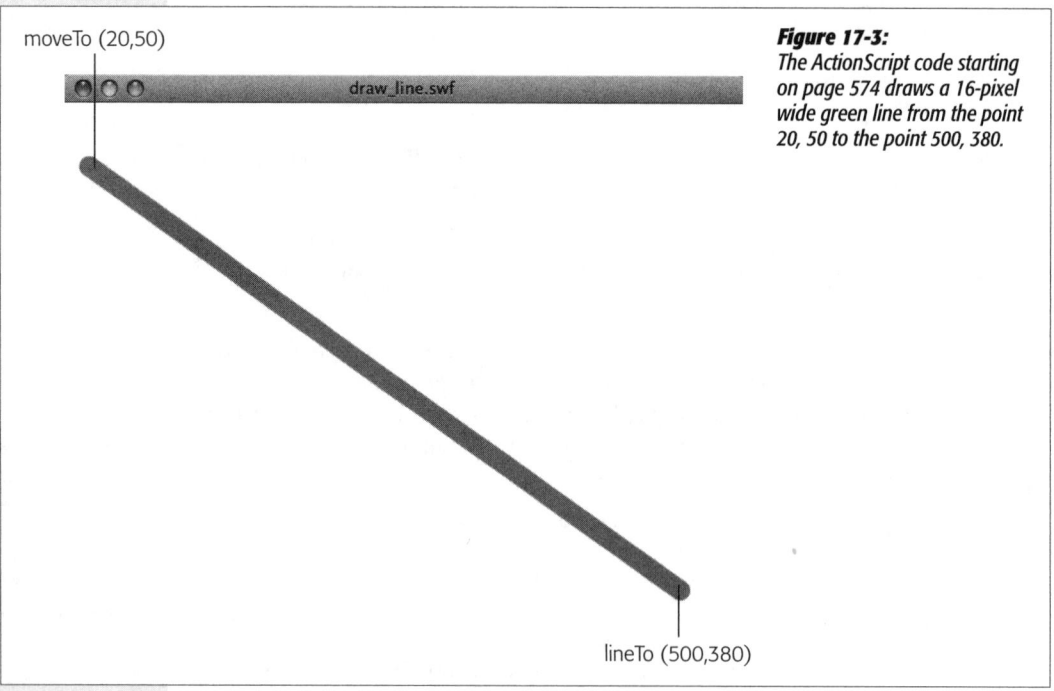

moveTo (20,50)

draw_line.swf

lineTo (500,380)

Figure 17-3:
The ActionScript code starting on page 574 draws a 16-pixel wide green line from the point 20, 50 to the point 500, 380.

While you might not draw lines as frequently as you draw rectangles and other shapes, it's still good to have a thorough understanding of lines and the *lineStyle( )*

---

property, because the stroke outline for other shapes works the same way. If you want to draw an irregular shape as described on page 582, then you need to draw a series of connected lines.

Drawing Curves

When you draw a curve using ActionScript, you need to add one more point to the mix. Think about the way you draw curves in Flash or Adobe Illustrator. You have a line with two anchor points, and you drag control handles from the anchors to create a curve. The line doesn't travel through the control handles, it's just geometrically influenced by the position of the handles. ActionScript uses a similar method to create curves, but you have to imagine that there's a single control point connected to both endpoints. Figure 17-4 shows the concept. By repositioning that control point, you change the shape of the curve. The *curveTo( )* method is similar to the *lineTo( )* method described in the previous section. You are creating a line from the current position of the virtual pen (one anchor point) to the end point of the curve (another anchor point). The shape of that line is influenced by a control point.

When you draw a curve in ActionScript, the control point isn't usually visible; it's defined but it doesn't get displayed on the stage. In the code example here, the control point is marked with an X, and it's displayed in a text field. It shares the control point's X and Y values.

```
1    var shpLine:Shape = new Shape( );
2    var ptAnchor1:Point = new Point( );
3    var ptAnchor2:Point = new Point( );
4    var ptControl:Point = new Point( );
5    var txtControl:TextField = new TextField( );
6
7    ptAnchor1.x = 100;
8    ptAnchor1.y = 180;
9    ptAnchor2.x = 500;
10   ptAnchor2.y = 180;
11   ptControl.x = 500;
12   ptControl.y = 350;
13
14   txtControl.text = "X";
15   txtControl.x = ptControl.x;
16   txtControl.y = ptControl.y;
17   addChild(txtControl);
18
19   shpLine.graphics.lineStyle(16,0x00FF00);
20   shpLine.graphics.moveTo(ptAnchor1.x,ptAnchor1.y);
21   shpLine.graphics.curveTo(ptControl.x,ptControl.y,ptAnchor2.x,ptAnchor2.y);
22   addChild(shpLine);
23
24   shpLine.graphics.moveTo(0,0);
```

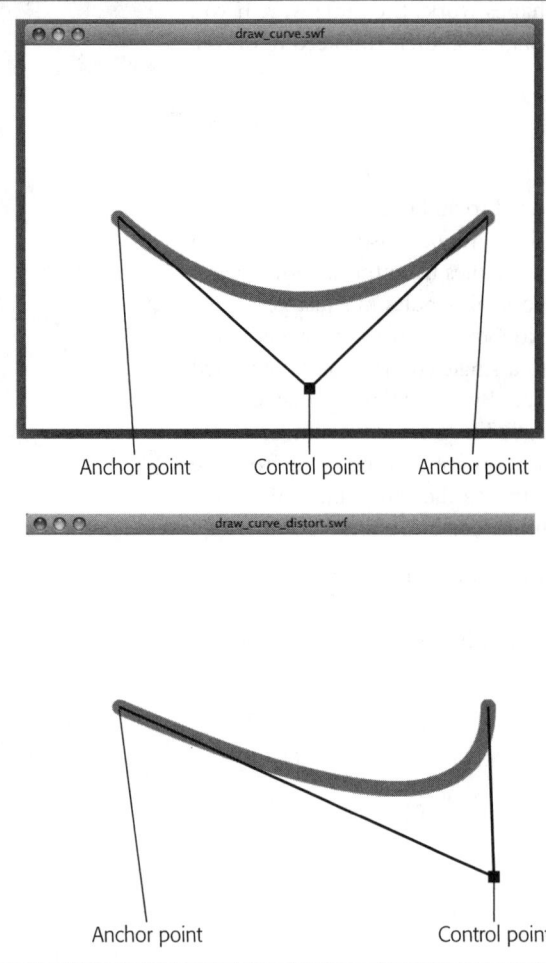

Figure 17-4:
ActionScript's curveTo( ) method draws curves using a quadratic Bezier equation, but you don't have to remember that. Just keep in mind there are two anchor points and one control point. You change the shape of the curve by repositioning the control point, using ActionScript code, naturally.

The first line in this example creates a shape. You can create vector drawings in Sprites, Shapes, and MovieClips. Shapes use even less space than Sprites in your Flash animation. The three lines from 2 through 4 create points. The names could be anything, but in this example there's a hint that two of them are going to serve as anchor points and one will serve as a control point. Line 5 creates a text field that's named txtControl. Lines 7 through 12 position the three points. You can tell from their Y values that ptAnchor1 and ptAnchor2 appear on the same horizontal axis. The ptControl Y value is quite a bit below that axis. Line 14 stores an X in the text property of txtControl. (Think *X* marks the spot.) Then, the code assigns *x* and *y* values of the text box the same values that are in ptControl.x and ptControl.y. Line 17 displays the txtControl text field when it's added to the display list using the *addChild( )* method. Line 19 defines a *lineStyle( )*. The *moveTo( )* method on line 20 positions the virtual pen at the first anchor point for the line. Then the *curveTo( )* method is used. The first anchor point was already established by the preceding *moveTo( )* method, so the *curveTo( )* method needs two points. The X and Y values of the control point come first, and then come the X and Y values of the second anchor point. The *addChild( )* method in line 22 displays the curve. The last line moves the virtual pen back to 0, 0.

When you test the curve code, it draws a curve similar to the one bottom Figure 17-4. If you want to experiment, you can go ahead and change the *x* and *y* values of ptControl in lines 11 and 12. That changes the shape of the curve, and it also moves the X in the text field to mark the new position of the control point.

Drawing Built-in Shapes

When you graduate from lines to shapes, you get to fill your shapes with a color. The *lineStyle( )* method becomes optional, because shapes don't have to have an outline stroke. You can draw simple shapes using ActionScript's built-in methods. The technique is very similar to drawing lines and curves with the addition of the *beginFill( )* method that lets you choose a color and transparency percentage for the fill color. Here's the step-by-step for drawing a rectangle and a circle in a MovieClip:

1. **Select File → New and choose Flash File (ActionScript 3.0).**

   A new, empty Flash document appears.

2. **Press F9 (Option-F9 on a Mac).**

   The Actions panel opens where you can enter ActionScript code.

3. **Type this line into the Actions panel to create an instance of the mcShapes MovieClip class:**

   ```
   var mcShapes:MovieClip = new MovieClip( );
   ```

   MovieClip is one of three data types that let you draw vector graphics. The other two classes are Sprite and Shape.

4. **Define a *lineStyle( )* for your first shape:**

   ```
   mcShapes.graphics.lineStyle(4,0x003300,.75);
   ```

   This statement uses the Graphics class, which is a property of the MovieClip class. As explained on page 574, the *lineStyle( )* method can accept several parameters. This code uses three parameters, and the remaining ones are left unchanged from their original values. The first parameter sets the line or stroke thickness to 4 pixels. The second parameter provides a hexadecimal color value (dark green) for the line color. The third and last parameter sets the transparency for the line to 75%.

5. **Define a fill style for your shape:**

   ```
   mcShapes.graphics.beginFill(0x339933, .75);
   ```

The method to fill a shape is *beginFill( )*. There's also an *endFill( )* method, but you don't need to use it when you work with the ActionScript's built-in shape methods. The *beginFill( )* method uses only two parameters. The first sets the fill color, a lighter green, and the second sets the transparency to 75%.

6. **Position the mcShapes movie clip on the stage:**

   ```
   mcShapes.x=mcShapes.y=50;
   ```

   This line sets both the X and Y properties of mcShapes to 50 in one statement. You can use this form or use separate statements for each property.

7. **Use the built-in *drawRect( )* method to define a rectangle.**

   ```
   mcShapes.graphics.drawRect(0,0,300,250);
   ```

   The first two parameters for *drawRect( )* set the X and Y values for the rectangle. Set at 0,0, the rectangle is positioned in the upper-left corner of the mcShapes movie clip; but keep in mind that the movie clip is positioned at 50, 50 on the stage. The next two parameters set the rectangle's X and Y values. In this case, the rectangle is 300 pixels wide and 250 pixels high. As with the other vector drawings, even though you've defined the object, it won't be visible until you add it to the display list.

8. **Use the addChild method to display the movie clip mcShapes:**

   ```
   addChild(mcShapes);
   ```

   The addChild method adds the movie clip to the display list, which makes its contents visible.

9. **Test the animation.**

   When the animation runs, the rectangle appears with its registration point (upper-left corner) at 50, 50 on the stage. Even though you gave the stroke and fill some transparency, the rectangle looks pretty solid because it's on a plain white background.

10. **Set new colors for the stroke and fill for a second shape, the circle:**

    ```
    mcShapes.graphics.lineStyle(4,0x0033CC,.5);
    mcShapes.graphics.beginFill(0x003333,.5);
    ```

    These are the same methods used in steps 4 and 5, but you're changing the color values to shades of blue and set the transparency to 50%.

11. **Use the built-in *drawCircle( )* method to define a circle.**

    ```
    mcShapes.graphics.drawCircle(275,100,75);
    ```

    To define a circle, you need to provide the *drawCircle( )* method with a center point and a radius. The first two parameters are the X and Y values of the center point. The third parameter is the radius, which means this circle will be 150 pixels in diameter.

12. **Test the animation.**

When the animation runs, the circle appears overlapping the rectangle as shown in Figure 17-5. The rectangle (the first shape you defined) appears on the bottom. Both the rectangle and the circle are positioned relative to their container mcShapes, not the stage.

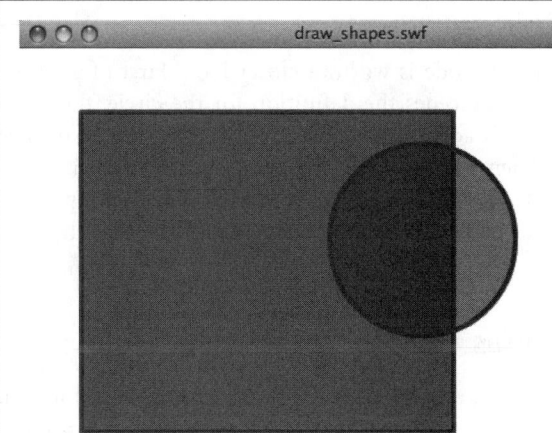

Figure 17-5:
These two shapes are drawn on a movie clip that's positioned at 50,50 on the stage. The rectangle was defined first, so it appears underneath the circle.

ActionScript includes two other built-in shapes, and you use them the same way: Define the stroke and fill, use one of the draw methods to create the shape, and then use the *addChild( )* method to display the shape. All that varies from shape to shape are the parameters you use to describe them. Here are definitions and a brief explanation for each built-in shape:

• **drawEllipse(x:Number, y:Number, width:Number, height:Number).** The first two parameters position the center of the ellipse. The next two parameters set the dimensions for the ellipse.

• **drawRoundRect(x:Number, y:Number, width:Number, height:Number, ellipseWidth:Number, ellipseHeight:Number).** The first two parameters are numbers that position the rectangle using its registration point. The next two parameters set the rectangle's width and height. The last two parameters, ellipseWidth and ellipseHeight, define the curve for the rounded corners. If the curves are equal, you can set just the first number, ellipseWidth, and ignore the second value. If the curve isn't equal use both parameters to set different width and height values.

If you entered the statements in this exercise line-by-line, following the instructions, the code in your Actions panel looks something like this:

```
var mcShapes:MovieClip = new MovieClip( );

mcShapes.graphics.lineStyle(4,0x003300,.75);
mcShapes.graphics.beginFill(0x339933, .75);
```

```
mcShapes.x=mcShapes.y=50;
mcShapes.graphics.drawRect(0,0,300,250);

addChild(mcShapes);

mcShapes.graphics.lineStyle(4,0x0033CC,.5);
mcShapes.graphics.beginFill(0x003333,.5);
mcShapes.graphics.drawCircle(275,100,75);
```

The order of the statements in this code is worth a closer look. First of all, even though the *addChild( )* statement precedes the definition for the circle, the circle appears in the movie clip when it's added to the display list. Also, the first shape defined, the rectangle, appears beneath the circle. You can change its position by changing its position in the code. If you want the rectangle to appear on top of the circle in the movie clip, move the code that defines the rectangle to follow the code that defines the circle.

Drawing Irregular Shapes

When you draw the built-in shapes, ActionScript does a lot of the work for you, but you're limited to the shapes that ActionScript offers. Sometimes, you need to draw irregular shapes. For example, suppose you needed to draw a floor plan for a modern home with a number of odd angles and curves. In that case, you need to draw each line and curve separately. To fill the shape with a color, use the *beginFill( )* method when you begin drawing lines. Then, when you're finished with the shape, use *endFill( )*.

For example, here's some code that draws a very irregular shape that includes a variety of angles and one curved edge (see Figure 17-6). Open a new document and type the following into the Actions panel:

```
1    var mcShapes:MovieClip = new MovieClip( );
2
3    mcShapes.graphics.lineStyle(4,0x330000,.5);
4    mcShapes.graphics.beginFill(0xFF3300,.5);
5    mcShapes.graphics.moveTo(200,50);
6    mcShapes.graphics.lineTo(300,150);
7    mcShapes.graphics.lineTo(400,150);
8    mcShapes.graphics.curveTo(425,175,400,200);
9    mcShapes.graphics.lineTo(200,200);
10   mcShapes.graphics.lineTo(200,150);
11   mcShapes.graphics.lineTo(100,150);
12   mcShapes.graphics.lineTo(200,50);
13   mcShapes.graphics.endFill( );
14
15   addChild(mcShapes);
```

If you worked your way through the previous sections in this chapter, most of this will look familiar. The first two lines set the line style and the fill color. The third line moves the virtual pen to point 200, 50. Following that are several *lineTo( )* methods with one *curveTo( )* method added for good measure. If you want to match up the code with the lines in the shape, see Figure 17-6. These lines form a closed path when the last *lineTo( )* method ends up back at the beginning: 200, 50. The final line runs the *endFill( )* method.

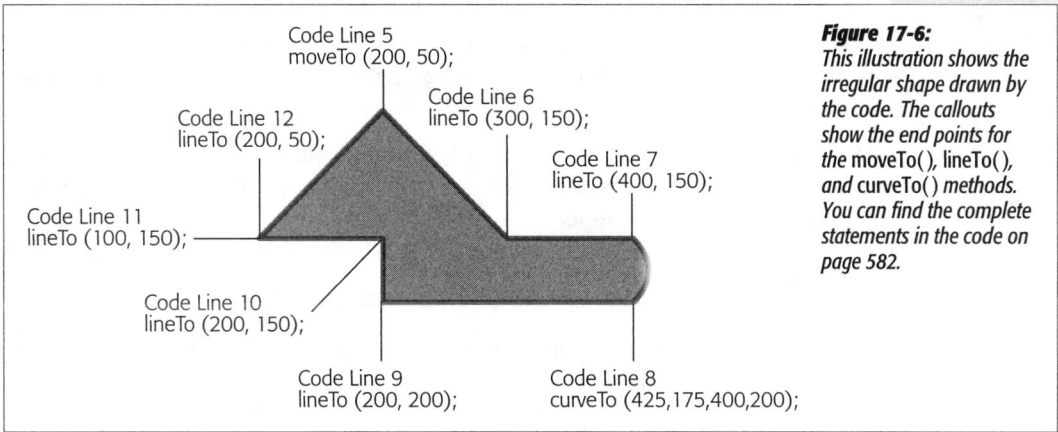

Code Line 5
moveTo (200, 50);

Code Line 12
lineTo (200, 50);

Code Line 6
lineTo (300, 150);

Code Line 7
lineTo (400, 150);

Code Line 11
lineTo (100, 150);

Code Line 10
lineTo (200, 150);

Code Line 9
lineTo (200, 200);

Code Line 8
curveTo (425,175,400,200);

Figure 17-6:
This illustration shows the irregular shape drawn by the code. The callouts show the end points for the moveTo( )*,* lineTo( )*, and* curveTo( ) *methods. You can find the complete statements in the code on page 582.*

Note: Flash fills shapes even if they aren't entirely enclosed. So, even if line12 (the line that closes the shape) was missing in the example above, Flash would still apply a fill to the shape that's defined by the rest of the lines.

When you test your animation (Ctrl+Enter on a PC or ⌘-Return on a Mac) you see an image like Figure 17-6.

Making Drawings Move

As shown earlier in this chapter, you draw lines and shapes on three classes of objects: Shape, Sprite, and MovieClip. In effect, these objects are canvases for the drawings. To make drawings move from one location to another, you move the canvas. You can think of the Shape, Sprite, and MovieClip containers as transparent sheets of film with the drawings inked on top. You place the film on the stage. Then to create motion you reposition the film on the stage. If you want to move objects together, you can place them on the same piece of film. If you want to move them independently, you have to place them on separate pieces of film.

To make Shapes, Sprites, and MovieClips move, you change those good old friends, the X and Y properties. You can make them move in response to mouse clicks or other input from your audience. If you want them to move without prompting, you need to set up the mechanism.

Using ActionScript's TimerEvent to Animate Drawings

One popular animation technique makes use of Flash's TimerEvent. It's sort of like setting one of those kitchen minute timers, and each time it goes "ding!" you move the drawing. ActionScript's Timer class uses two constants: *TIMER_COMPLETE* and *TIMER*. In earlier examples (page 480) you saw *TIMER_COMPLETE* in action. It triggers an event when the time has completely run out. You use the *TIMER* constant when you want to trigger repeated events at regular intervals.

Here's how it works: When you create an instance of the Timer class, you provide two parameters. The first parameter is called the *delay*. Think of it as the time in milliseconds before the timer goes "ding." The second parameter is the repeat-Count. Think of it as the number of times you want to reset the timer to run again.

So, suppose you want a drawing every half second and you want it to move across the stage in 12 steps, you can set a timer with a delay of *500* and a repeatCount of *12*. Then every time the timer sends a TIMER event (ding!), you move the drawing by changing its X and/or Y properties. Follow these steps to perform this feat of animation in code:

> **Note:** You can find a copy of this code in the Flash file *animating_shapes_finished.fla* on the "Missing CD" page at *http://missingmanuals.com/cds*.

1. **Select File → New and choose Flash File (ActionScript 3.0).**

   A new, empty Flash document appears.

2. **Press F9 (Option-F9).**

   The Actions panel opens, where you can enter ActionScript code.

3. **Type this line into the Actions panel to create an instance of the MovieClip class named mcShapes:**

   ```
   var mcShapes:MovieClip = new MovieClip( );
   ```

   MovieClip is one of three data types that let you draw vector graphics.

4. **Create an instance of the Timer class.**

   ```
   var tmrMover:Timer=new Timer(500,12);
   ```

   The parameters set the timer's delay value to 500 milliseconds and the repeat-Count to 12.

5. **Define the line and fill style for the circle.**

   ```
   mcShapes.graphics.lineStyle(4,0x000033);
   mcShapes.graphics.beginFill(0x0099FF,.5);
   ```

   You've set the line and fill colors to shades of blue. The code sets no alpha value (transparency) in the line style, so ActionScript assumes it should be 100%; that is, opaque. The fill has an alpha value of .5, making its transparency 50%.

6. **Draw the circle with the *drawCircle( )* method.**

   ```
   mcShapes.graphics.drawCircle(250,100,75);
   ```

   The first two parameters place the center of the circle at 250, 100 in the movie clip. (You haven't positioned the movie clip, so Flash automatically positions it at 0, 0.)

7. **Add the movie clip to the display list.**

   ```
   addChild(mcShapes);
   ```

   This code adds the movie clip to the display list, making it visible.

8. **Start the timer.**

   ```
   tmrMover.start( );
   ```

   The timer starts.

9. **Register a TimerEvent listener.**

   ```
   tmrMover.addEventListener(TimerEvent.TIMER,timerMoverListener);
   ```

10. **Write the function for the TimerEvent listener.**

    ```
    function timerMoverListener(evt:TimerEvent):void {
        mcShapes.x=mcShapes.x+10;
    }
    ```

    The *timerMoverListener( )* function assigns a new value to the *x* property of the mcShapes movie clip, which makes it move horizontally. To calculate the new value for *x*, the function takes the current value of *x* and adds 10 to it. Each time the *TIMER* event triggers, the movie clip moves.

11. **Test the animation.**

    When the animation runs, the blue circle moves across the stage 10 pixels at a time. It moves 12 times, and then stops as shown in Figure 17-7.

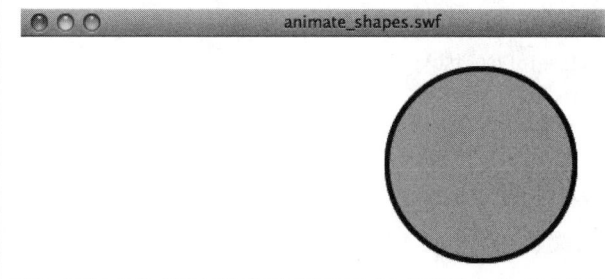

Figure 17-7:
This circle is animated to move across the stage through the use of a TimerEvent and the x property of the object that contains the circle—a movie clip.

In the example above, if you want to move another object along with the circle, all you need to do is add that object to the movie clip. Suppose you want to move a small square along at the same speed. All you need to do is add one line to step 6 to define the position and size of the square.

```
mcShapes.graphics.drawRect(100,300,75,75);
```

Now, if you test the animation, both the circle and the square move across the stage in sync.

Moving Objects Independently

The world and your animations don't always move in lockstep. So to make objects move independently, you can place them in different containers. Here's a variation on the previous example that places a circle, a rectangle, and a triangle in separate containers. The code uses the Shape class as a container because it keeps the size of the published .swf file at a minimum, but you can do the same thing with Sprites, MovieClips, or any combination.

Note: You can find a copy of this code in the Flash file *move_three_shapes.fla* on the "Missing CD" page at *http://missingmanuals.com/cds*.

```
1    var shpCircle:Shape = new Shape();
2    var shpRectangle:Shape = new Shape();
3    var shpTriangle:Shape = new Shape();
4
5    shpCircle.graphics.beginFill(0x000077,1);
6    shpCircle.graphics.drawCircle(250,100,75);
7    shpCircle.graphics.endFill();
8
9    shpRectangle.graphics.beginFill(0x009900,1);
10   shpRectangle.graphics.drawRect(200,100,150,100);
11   shpRectangle.graphics.endFill();
12
13   shpTriangle.graphics.moveTo(200,150);
14   shpTriangle.graphics.beginFill(0x880000)
15   shpTriangle.graphics.lineTo(300,250);
16   shpTriangle.graphics.lineTo(100,250);
17   shpTriangle.graphics.lineTo(200,150);
18   shpTriangle.graphics.endFill();
19
20   addChild(shpRectangle);
21   addChild(shpTriangle);
22   addChild(shpCircle);
23
24   var tmrMover:Timer = new Timer(250,30);
25   tmrMover.start();
26
27   tmrMover.addEventListener(TimerEvent.TIMER,timerMoverListener);
```

```
28
29    function timerMoverListener(evt:TimerEvent) : void {
30        shpCircle.x += 3;
31        shpRectangle.x -= 3;
32        shpTriangle.y += 3;
33    }
```

What distinguishes this example from the previous one is that the first three lines create three instances of the Shape class, appropriately named shpCircle, shpRectangle, and shpTriangle. Lines 5 through 18 define the objects. None of them have a *lineStyle( )* definition, so they're all fill and no stroke. The alpha value is set to 1, so they're completely opaque. The circle and the rectangle are drawn using built-in shapes, but the triangle is drawn line-by-line. Lines 20 through 22 use the *addChild( )* method to place each shape on the stage.

The TIMER portion of the code is similar to the previous example. On line 24 when the tmrMover is created, the delay is set to 250 and the repeatCount is set to 30. This means this timer will tick off events twice as quickly as the earlier example, where the delay was set to 500. Line 27 registers the event listener *timerMoverListener( )*. By using the *TIMER* constant instead of the *TIMER_COMPLETE* constant, this timer will trigger 30 events, instead of just one. (For more details, see page 480.) The function *timerMoverListener( )* from line 29 through the last line of the code runs each time the event triggers.

To move the circle 3 pixels from left to right, the line:

```
shpCircle.x += 3;
```

increments the value of the shpCircle's x property by three. It's simply an abbreviated way of saying:

```
shpCircle.x = shpCircle.x + 3;
```

The other two lines in the function work similarly, except that by decrementing the *x* property, line 31 moves the rectangle from right to left. Line 32 operates on the *y* property of shpTriangle, so it moves down the stage.

Each time the clock ticks, the objects move. There are a couple of ways to make them move at different rates of speed. Make the values smaller and the objects will move less distance in the same time period. Or, for the most versatility, you can create separate timers for each object. That way, you can change the delay and the intervals, as well as the distance that the objects move.

Shape, Sprite, and MovieClip for Drawings

When you create drawings on Shapes, Sprites and MovieClips, it's tempting to think you're placing the drawings inside of containers—but you're not. At least, not in the true ActionScript sense of the word "container." Back in Chapter 13 (page 444), Sprite and MovieClip objects are DisplayObjectContainers, meaning that by using the *addChild( )* method, you can put objects inside of a Sprite or MovieClip and the objects will be displayed. Shape, on the other hand, isn't a DisplayObjectContainer, so how can it show the drawn objects as shown in this chapter?

The fact of the matter is, when you draw, as described in this chapter you're drawing lines and shapes on the canvas or the background of the Shape, Sprite, or MovieClip. It's not the same thing as using the *addChild( )* method, which adds an object to a DisplayObjectContainer. For example, you can't position a drawing to appear in front of an object that's added to a MovieClip using the *addChild( )* method. Here's an example:

```
1    var txtBlahBlahtxtPoem:TextField = new TextField();
2    var mcCanvas:MovieClip = new MovieClip();
3
4    txtBlahBlahtxtPoem.text = "Twas brillig, and the slithy toves";
5    txtBlahBlahtxtPoem.x = 110;
6    txtBlahBlahtxtPoem.y = 110;
7    txtBlahBlahtxtPoem.autoSize=TextFieldAutoSize.LEFT;
8    mcCanvas.addChild(txtBlahBlahtxtPoem);
9
10   mcCanvas.graphics.beginFill(0x99FFFF);
11   mcCanvas.graphics.drawRect(100,100,200,150);
12
13   addChild(mcCanvas);
```

This example has only two objects: a TextField called txtPoem and a MovieClip called mcCanvas. Note that the rectangle isn't an object in its own right. Lines 4 through 7 define the text field, adding text, positioning it, and setting its autoSize property to accommodate the text. Line 8 places the txtField inside of mcCanvas. The text field is now contained in the movie clip, a DisplayObjectContainer. The technique for creating and displaying the drawing is different, though. The rectangle is defined in lines 10 and 11, but that's done through the graphics property of mcCanvas. It never uses the *addChild( )* method in mcCanvas. This means the rectangle has no index value, and you can't reposition it in the display list using a command like *addChild( )* or *addChildAt( )*.

The last line of the code adds mcCanvas to the main timeline. When mcCanvas is placed in the main timeline (also a DisplayObjectContainer), then both the rectangle drawn on mcCanvas and the text field that's contained by mcCanvas are displayed.

Removing Lines and Shapes

So far, this chapter has shown several ways to draw lines and shapes. This section tells how to make them disappear. The Graphics class has a *clear( )* method. When you use this method, it erases the drawings that were created in the object, resets the line and fill style settings, and moves the virtual pen back to the 0,0 position. The *clear( )* method is a multipurpose cleanup tool. Here's an example of the *clear( )* method in action. A text field is added to the code that begins on page 588. This text field serves as kind of a button that, when clicked, triggers the *clear( )* method to remove the drawings on the mcCanvas movie clip.

```
1    var txtBlahBlahtxtPoem:TextField = new TextField();
2    var mcCanvas:MovieClip = new MovieClip();
3
4    txtBlahBlahtxtPoem.text = "Twas brillig, and the slithy toves";
5    txtBlahBlahtxtPoem.x = 110;
6    txtBlahBlahtxtPoem.y = 110;
7    txtBlahBlahtxtPoem.autoSize=TextFieldAutoSize.LEFT;
8    mcCanvas.addChild(txtBlahBlahtxtPoem);
9
10   mcCanvas.graphics.beginFill(0x99FFFF);
11   mcCanvas.graphics.drawRect(100,100,200,150);
12
13   addChild(mcCanvas);
14
15   var txtRemoveRectangle = new TextField();
16   txtRemoveRectangle.text = "Click here to remove the rectangle";
17   txtRemoveRectangle.x = 110;
18   txtRemoveRectangle.y = 250;
19   txtRemoveRectangle.autoSize=TextFieldAutoSize.LEFT;
20   addChild(txtRemoveRectangle);
21
22   txtRemoveRectangle.addEventListener(MouseEvent.CLICK,clickListener);
23   function clickListener(evt:MouseEvent): void {
24       mcCanvas.graphics.clear();
25   }
```

There are no changes to the code until line 15. A new text field, txtRemoveRectangle, is created, and on the following line text is assigned to the text property. The text field is positioned on the stage, and the autoSize property is set. On line 20, the *addChild( )* method adds the txtField to the main timeline. Lines 22 through 25 create and register an event listener.

When you test this code, it looks like Figure 17-8.

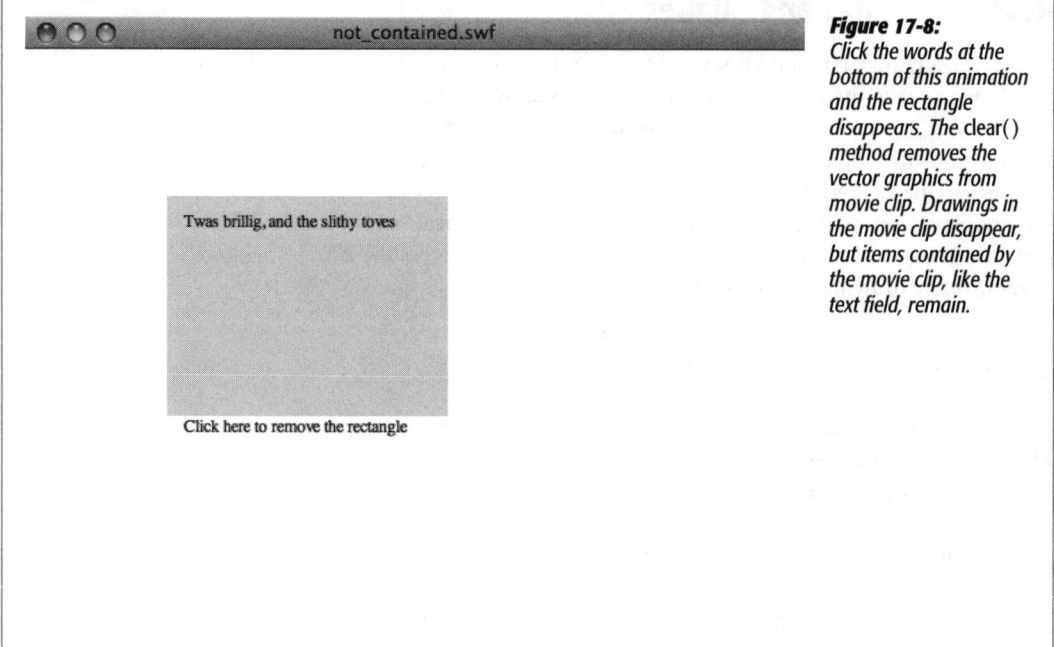

Figure 17-8:
Click the words at the bottom of this animation and the rectangle disappears. The clear() method removes the vector graphics from movie clip. Drawings in the movie clip disappear, but items contained by the movie clip, like the text field, remain.

Part Four: Delivering Your Animation to Its Audience

4

Testing and Debugging

Testing your animation is a lot like filing your income taxes. Both can be tedious, time-consuming, and frustrating—but they've got to be done. Even if your animation is short, straightforward, and you've whipped out 700 exactly like it over the past 2 years, you still need to test it before you release it into the world. Why? Murphy's Law: Anything that *can* go wrong *will* go wrong. Choosing a motion tween when you meant to choose a shape tween, adding content to a frame instead of a keyframe, tying actions to the wrong frame or object, or mistyping an ActionScript keyword are just a few of the ways a slip of your fingers can translate into a broken animation. And it's far better that you find out about these problems *before* your audience sees your handiwork rather than after.

Throughout this book, you've seen examples of testing an animation using the Control → Test Movie option (for example, Figure 18-5). This chapter expands on that simple test option, plus it shows you how to test animation playback at a variety of connection speeds. And if you've added ActionScript to your animation, this chapter shows you how to unsnarl uncooperative ActionScript code using Flash's debugging tools.

Testing Strategies

All your audience ever sees is the finished product, not your intentions. So no matter how sophisticated your animation or how cleverly constructed your ActionScript code, if you don't test your animation and make sure it works the way you want it to, all your hard work will have been in vain.

The following section shows you how to prepare for testing from the very beginning by following good Flash development policies. Also, you find out the differences between testing on the stage and testing in Flash Player, along with tips for testing your animation in a Web browser.

Planning Ahead

The more complex your animation, the more you need a thorough plan for testing it. Few of the guidelines in the next two sections are specific to testing in Flash. Instead, they're tried-and-true suggestions culled from all walks of programming life. Following them pays off in higher-quality animations and reduced time spent chasing bugs.

Ideally, you should begin thinking about testing before you've created a single frame of your animation. Here are some pre-animation strategies that pay off big:

Separate potentially troublesome elements

ActionScript actions are very powerful, but they can also cause a lot of grief. Get into the habit of putting them into a separate layer named "actions", at the top of your list of layers, so that you'll always know where to find it. Putting all your labels into a separate layer (named "layers") and all your sounds into a layer (named "sounds") is a good idea, too.

Reuse as much as possible

Instead of cutting and pasting an image or a series of frames, create a graphic symbol and reuse it. That way, if a bug raises its ugly head, you'll have fewer places to go hunting. You can cut down on bugs by reusing ActionScript code, too. Instead of attaching four similar ActionScript actions to four different frames or buttons, create a single ActionScript method (also called *function*; see page 392) and call it four times.

Be generous with comments

Before you know it, you'll forget which layers contain which images, why you added certain actions to certain objects, or even why you ordered your Action-Script statements the way you did. In addition to adding descriptive comments to all of the actions you create, get in the habit of adding an overall comment to the first frame of your animation. Make it as long as you want and be sure to mention your name, the date, and anything else pertinent you can think of. You create a comment in ActionScript two different ways, as shown below.

```
// This is an example of a single-line ActionScript comment.

/* This type of ActionScript comment can span more than one line. All you
have to remember is to begin your multi-line comment with a slash-asterisk
and end it with an asterisk-slash, as you see here. */
```

Stick with consistent names

Referring to a background image in one animation as "bg," in another animation as "back_ground," and in still another as "Background" is just asking for trouble. Even if you don't have trouble remembering which is which, odds are your office teammates will—and referring to an incorrectly spelled variable in ActionScript causes your animation to misbehave quietly. In other words, type *Backgruond* instead of *Background*, and Flash doesn't pop up an error message; your animation just looks or acts odd for no apparent reason. Devise a naming convention you're comfortable with and stick with it. For example, you might decide always to use uppercase, lowercase, or mixed case. You might decide always to spell words out, or always to abbreviate them the same way. The particulars don't matter as much as your consistency in applying them.

Note: Capitalization counts. Because Flash is case-sensitive, it treats background, Background, and BACKGROUND as three different names.

Techniques for Better Testing

The following strategies are crucial if you're creating complex animations as part of a development team. But they're also helpful if it's just you creating a short, simple animation by your lonesome.

- **Test early, test often.** Don't wait until you've attached actions to 16 different objects to begin testing. Test the first action, and then test each additional action as you go along. This iterative approach helps you identify problems while they're still small and manageable.

- **Test everything.** Instead of assuming the best-case scenario, see what happens when you access your animation over a slow connection or using an older version of Flash Player. What happens when you type the wrong kind of data into an input text field or click buttons in the wrong order? (Believe this: Your audience will do all of these things, and more.)

- **Test blind.** In other words, let someone who's unfamiliar with how your animation's supposed to work test it. In programming circles, this type of testing is known as *usability testing*, and it can flush out problems you never dreamed existed.

- **Test in "real world" mode.** Begin your testing in the Flash authoring environment, as you see on page 596, but don't end there. Always test your animation in a production environment before you go live. For example, if you're planning to publish your animation to a Web site, upload your files (including your .swf file and any external files your animation depends on) to a Web server, and then test it there, using a computer running the operating system, connection speed, browser, and Flash Player plug-in version you expect your audience to be running. (Sure, transferring a few files isn't *supposed* to make a difference—but it often does.) Chapter 19 covers publishing to the Web, as well as other publishing options.

Testing on the Stage vs. Testing in Flash Player

Flash gives you two options for testing your animation: on the stage and in the built-in Flash Player. Testing on the stage is faster, and it's good for checking your work as you go along, but in order to try out your animation exactly as your audience will see it, you have to eventually fire it up in Flash Player. Here's some more advice on when to choose each:

Testing on the stage is the quick and easy option, using the Controller toolbar and the associated menu options (Control → Play, Control → Stop, Control → Rewind, Control → Step Forward One Frame, Control → Step Backward One Frame, and Control → Go to End). Testing on the stage is quicker than testing in Flash Player, because you don't have to wait for Flash to compile (*export*) your Flash document, and then load it into the Player. Instead, when you test on the stage, Flash immediately resets the playhead and moves it along the timeline frame by frame. For simple animations, testing on the stage can be easier as well as quicker than testing in Flash Player because you can position the Controller toolbar on your workspace where it's handy—no need to wait for Flash Player's menu options to appear.

The downside to testing on the stage is that it doesn't always test what you think it's testing. For example, if you test a frame containing a movie clip instance, you don't see the movie clip playing; you have to switch to symbol editing mode, and then test the symbol there to see the movie clip in action. And if your animation contains a button instance and you forget to turn on the checkbox next to Control → Enable Simple Buttons, the button doesn't work on the stage—even though it may work perfectly well when you test it in Flash Player.

Testing in the built-in Flash Player (Control → Test Movie, and Control → Test Scene) is the more accurate option. When you test an animation by selecting Control → Test Movie or Control → Test Scene, Flash generates a .swf file. For example, if you're testing a Flash document named *myDocument.fla*, Flash generates a file called *myDocument.swf* (or *myDocument_myScene.swf*, if you're testing a scene) and automatically loads that .swf file into Flash Player (test window) that's part and parcel of the Flash development environment. This testing option shows you exactly what your audience will see, not counting computer hardware and connection differences (page 602).

Testing on the Stage

If all you want to do is check out a few simple frames' worth of action, this is the option to use. It's also the best choice if you want to see your motion path or *not* see the layers you've marked as hidden. (For the skinny on hiding and showing layers, check out page 153.)

To test your animation on the stage:

1. **Select Window → Toolbars → Controller.**

   The Controller toolbar you see in Figure 18-1 appears.

2. **Turn on the checkbox next to one or more of the following options:**

   • **Control → Loop Playback.** Tells Flash to loop playback over and over again after you click Play on the Controller. Flash keeps looping your animation until you click Stop. If you don't turn on this option, Flash just plays the animation once.

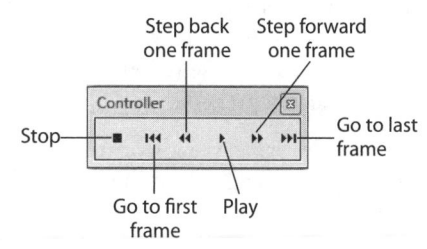

Figure 18-1:
You can reposition the Controller by dragging it to wherever it's most convenient for you. Or, if you prefer, you can skip the Controller altogether and use the button-equivalent menu options: Control → Stop, Control → Rewind, Control → Step Forward One Frame, Control → Play, Control → Step Backward One Frame, and Control → Go to End.

- **Control → Play All Scenes.** Tells Flash to play all the scenes in your animation, not just the scene currently visible on the stage.

- **Control → Enable Simple Frame Actions.** Tells Flash to play the actions you've added to frames in the timeline. If you don't turn on this option, Flash ignores all frame actions.

- **Control → Enable Simple Buttons.** Tells Flash to make your buttons work on the stage. (If you don't turn on the checkbox next to this option, mousing over a button or clicking it on the stage has no effect.)

- **Control → Enable Live Preview.** Tells Flash to display any components you've added to the stage the way they'll appear in Flash Player. (The components don't work on the stage, but you see how they're supposed to look.) If you have components on the stage and you don't choose this option, only the outlines of your components appear.

- **Control → Mute Sounds.** Tells Flash not to play any of the sound clips you've added to your animation.

3. **Make sure that what you want to test is at least partially visible in the timeline.**

   If you want to test a particular scene, for example, click the Edit Scene icon in the Edit bar, and then choose a scene to display the timeline for that scene. If you want to test a movie clip symbol, select Edit Symbols to display the timeline for that movie clip.

4. **In the Controller toolbar, click Play to begin testing.**

   Your other options include:

   - **Stop.** Clicking this square icon stops playback.

   - **Go to first frame.** Clicking this icon rewinds your animation. That is, it moves the playhead back to Frame 1.

   - **Step back one frame.** Clicking this double-left-arrow icon moves the playhead back one frame. If the playhead is already at Frame 1, this button has no effect.

- **Play.** Clicking this right-arrow toggle button alternately runs your animation on the stage, and pauses it. Playback begins at the playhead. In other words, playback begins with the frame you selected in the timeline and runs either until the end of your animation, or until you press the Stop button.

- **Step forward one frame.** Clicking this double-right-arrow icon moves the playhead forward one frame (unless the playhead is already at the last frame, in which case clicking this icon has no effect).

- **Go to last frame.** Clicking this icon fast-forwards your animation to the very end. That is, it sets the playhead to the last frame in your animation.

Note: You can also drag the playhead back and forth along the timeline to test your animation on the stage (a technique called *scrubbing*).

Flash plays your animation on the stage based on the options you chose in step 2.

Testing in Flash Player

Flash's Test mode shows you a closer approximation of how your animation will actually appear to your audience than testing on the stage. When you fire up the Test Movie command, your animation plays in the Flash Player that comes with Flash CS4. Test mode is your best bet if your animation contains movie clips, buttons, scenes, hidden layers, or actions, since it shows you *all* the parts of your animation—not just the parts currently visible on the stage.

Note: Motion paths (the lines) don't appear when you test your animation in Flash Player, for good reason: Flash designed them to be invisible at runtime. If you want to see your motion paths in action, you need to test your animation on the stage.

To test your animation in Flash Player:

1. **Select Control → Test Movie.**

   The Exporting Flash Movie dialog box in Figure 18-2 appears, followed by your animation running in Flash Player (test window) similar to the one in Figure 18-3.

Figure 18-2:
When you see this dialog box, you know Flash is exporting your animation and creating a .swf file. If you've tested this particular animation before, Flash erases the .swf file it previously created and replaces it with the new one. Finishing an export can be fast or slow depending on the size and complexity of your animation and your computer's processing speed and memory.

Figure 18-3:
Normally, when you select Control → Test Movie or Control → Test Scene, Flash opens up Flash Player in its own window. To control playback, you have a couple of choices: You can choose options from the File, View, Control, and Debug menus, or you can right-click the window if you're running Windows (Control-click if you're running Mac), and then choose options from the shortcut menus that appear.

2. **To control playback—to stop the animation, and then rewind it, for example—choose options from the Control menu.**

   In you're running Windows, the Control menu appears in Flash Player; on a Mac, you get the Control menu in Flash itself. (In Windows you can also see the Control menu in Flash itself if you turn on tabbed viewing in Preferences. See the box on page 600 for details.)

3. **To close Flash Player, select File → Close or click the X in the upper-right (Windows) or upper-left (Mac) corner of the window.**

Note: Testing your animation in Flash Player gives you a great sense of what your audience will see. But factors like connection speed and hardware differences come into play when you actually publish your animation, so you'll want to test your animation in a real-life production setting (using the same kind of computer, same connection speed, and same version browser as you expect your audience to use) before you go live (see page 595).

Testing Inside a Web Page

In addition to letting you test your animation in Flash Player, Flash lets you test your animation embedded in a Web page. This option lets you see how your animation looks in a Web browser based on the animation alignment, scale, and size options Flash lets you set.

Here's how it works. You tell Flash in the Formats tab of the Publish Settings window (Figure 18-4, left) that you want to embed your animation in a Web page. Then, in the HTML tab, you tell Flash how you want your animation to appear in the Web page (Figure 18-4, right). When you choose File → Publish Preview → HTML, Flash constructs an HTML file containing your animation, and then loads it automatically into the Web browser on your computer.

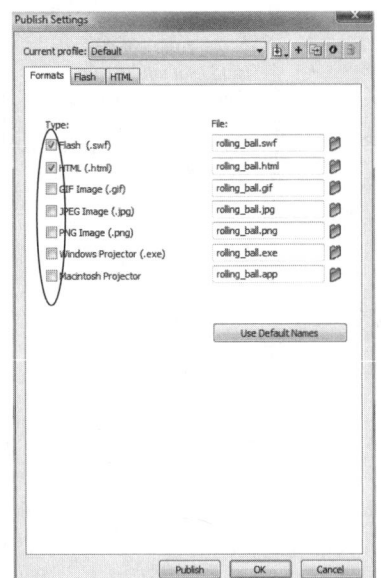 

Figure 18-4:
Left: Flash gives you several publishing options, one of which is embedding your animation into an HTML file.

Right: Flash constructs an animation-containing HTML file based on the options you choose in this tab. The name Flash uses for your HTML file is the name of your Flash document, but with a .html extension.

Note: Tucking your animation into a Web page is the most popular publishing option, but it's not the only one Flash has. You got acquainted with the other publishing options, including publishing your animation as a QuickTime movie and a standalone Flash projector file, in Chapter 19.

Testing Multiple Animations

Some folks find a tabbed page—like the tabs in some Web browsers—easier to pop back to, especially if they're trying to test several different animations at once. If you'd rather Flash Player appear in a tabbed page, select Edit → Preferences (Windows) or Flash → Preferences (Mac).

In the Preferences window that appears, click the General category. Turn on the checkbox next to "Open test movie in

tabs." Then choose Control → Test Movie. This time, Flash Player appears as a tab. When you click the tab, the Flash Developer menu options change to the Flash Player options. If you're using Windows, the window with the stage has to be maximized to use tabs.

To test your animation inside a Web page:

1. **Choose File → Publish Settings.**

   The Publish Settings dialog box in Figure 18-4 (left) appears.

2. **Make sure the "HTML (.html)" checkbox is turned on, and then click the HTML tab.**

   Flash displays the contents of the HTML tab shown in Figure 18-4 (right).

3. **Click the Template drop-down menu, and then choose "Flash only." Click OK.**

   Flash accepts your changes and closes the Publish Settings dialog box.

Note: For a description of each of the settings on this tab, see page 640.

---

4. **Choose File → Publish Preview → HTML.**

   The Publishing dialog box appears briefly to let you know Flash is creating an HTML file. When the dialog box disappears, Flash loads the completed HTML, including your embedded animation, into the Web browser on your computer (Figure 18-5).

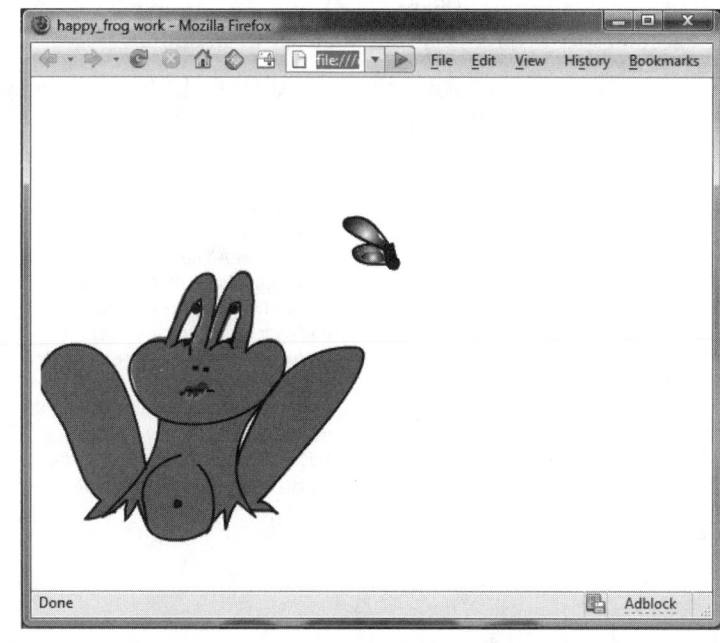

Figure 18-5:
In addition to creating an HTML file, choosing File → Publish Preview → HTML launches your Web browser preloaded with that file.

Right-clicking (Windows) or Control-clicking (Mac) the running animation shows you standard menu options you can use to control playback inside the browser, although how many options you see depends on whether you turned off the checkbox next to "Display menu" in the Publish Settings dialog box.

CHAPTER 18: TESTING AND DEBUGGING

Testing Download Time

If you're planning to publish your animation on the Web, you need to know how long it takes your animation to download from a Web server to somebody's computer. Chapter 19 gives you several optimization techniques, including tips for preloading content and reducing your animation's file size; but before you begin to optimize your animation, you need to know just how bad the situation is and where the bottlenecks are. The following sections show you how.

Simulating Downloads

You *could* set up a bank of test machines, each connected to the Internet at a different transfer speed, to determine the average download time your audience will eventually have to sit through. But Flash gives you an easier option: simulating downloads at a variety of transfer speeds with the click of a button. The simulation takes into consideration any additional, non-Flash media files that you've included in your animation, like sound and video clips.

To simulate different download speeds:

1. **Choose Control → Test Movie.**

   The Flash Player (test window) appears.

2. **Select View → Download Settings (Figure 18-6), and then, from the submenu, select the connection speed you expect your audience to be running.**

   Your choices range from 14.4 (1.2 KB/s) to T1 speed (131.2 KB/s). If you need to simulate a faster speed, check out Figure 18-7.

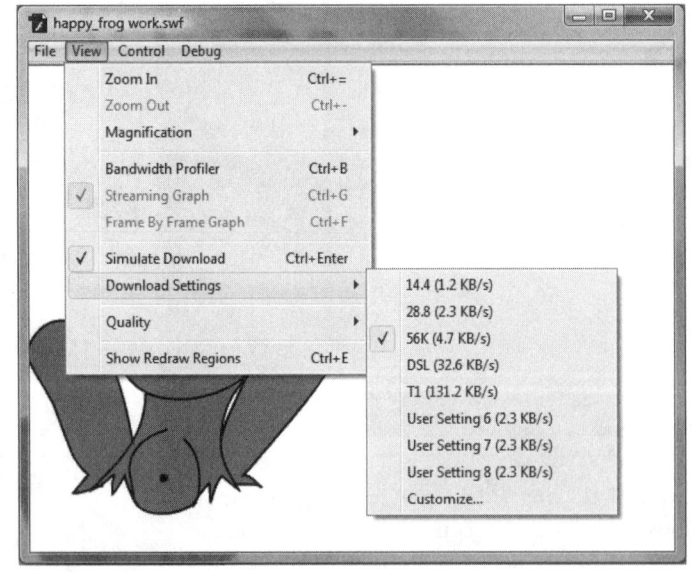

Figure 18-6:
If you're used to testing your animation inside the Flash development environment, you'll be shocked when you see how long it takes to download and play your animation over the Web. Flash automatically adjusts for standard line congestion to give you a more realistic picture. So, for example, when you choose the 14.4 kbps setting, Flash actually simulates the transfer at the slightly lower rate of 12.0 kbps.

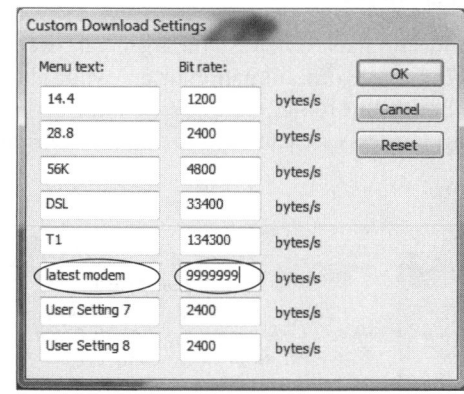

Figure 18-7:
To keep up with the latest advances in transfer technology, you can select a faster transfer rate than any of the options Flash has. To do so, select View → Download Settings → Customize, and then type a label and the new transfer speed you want to test (from 1 byte per second to 10,000,000).

Note: Unless you're planning to let only certain folks to view your animation (for example, students in your company's training classes), you can't possibly know for sure what connection rates your audience will be using. The best approach is to test a likely range. If the animation plays excruciatingly slowly at the lowest connection speed in your test range, consider either optimizing or offering a low-bandwidth version. Chapter 19 (page 624) tells you how.

---

3. **Choose View → Simulate Download.**

   The test window clears, and Flash plays your animation at the rate it would play it if it had to download your file from a Web server at the connection speed you chose in step 2.

4. **Repeat steps 2 and 3 for each connection speed you want to test.**

If you're like most folks, you'll find that your animation takes too long to play at one—or even all—of the simulated connection speeds you test. Fortunately, Flash gives you additional tools to help you pinpoint which frames take longest to download (so that you know which frames to optimize). Read on for details.

CODERS' CLINIC

Size Reports

Flash has a second statistical report called a *size report*. To create a size report, choose File → Publish Settings → Flash, and then turn the "Generate size report" checkbox. Make sure you can see the Output window (Window → Output). Then, when you choose File → Publish, Flash displays the size report in the Output window. It also automatically generates a text file named *yourFlashFile Report.txt* that you can pull into a text editor or word processor.

This report provides detailed information about the elements that add to the size of the published .swf file. It thoroughly

breaks down the details frame by frame, giving a running total of the file size in bytes. A summary lists scenes, symbols, and fonts and shows how the shapes, text, and ActionScript code adds to the heft of your published file. If you're suffering from file bloat, generate a report to see which images, symbols, sounds, or other elements are causing the problem.

Pinpointing bottlenecks with a bandwidth profiler report

Simulating downloads at different connection speeds gives you a general, overall feel for whether or not you'll need to optimize your animation or give your audience a low-bandwidth alternative (or both). But to get more precise information, like which frames represent the greatest bottlenecks, you need to run a *bandwidth profiler report* (Figure 18-8).

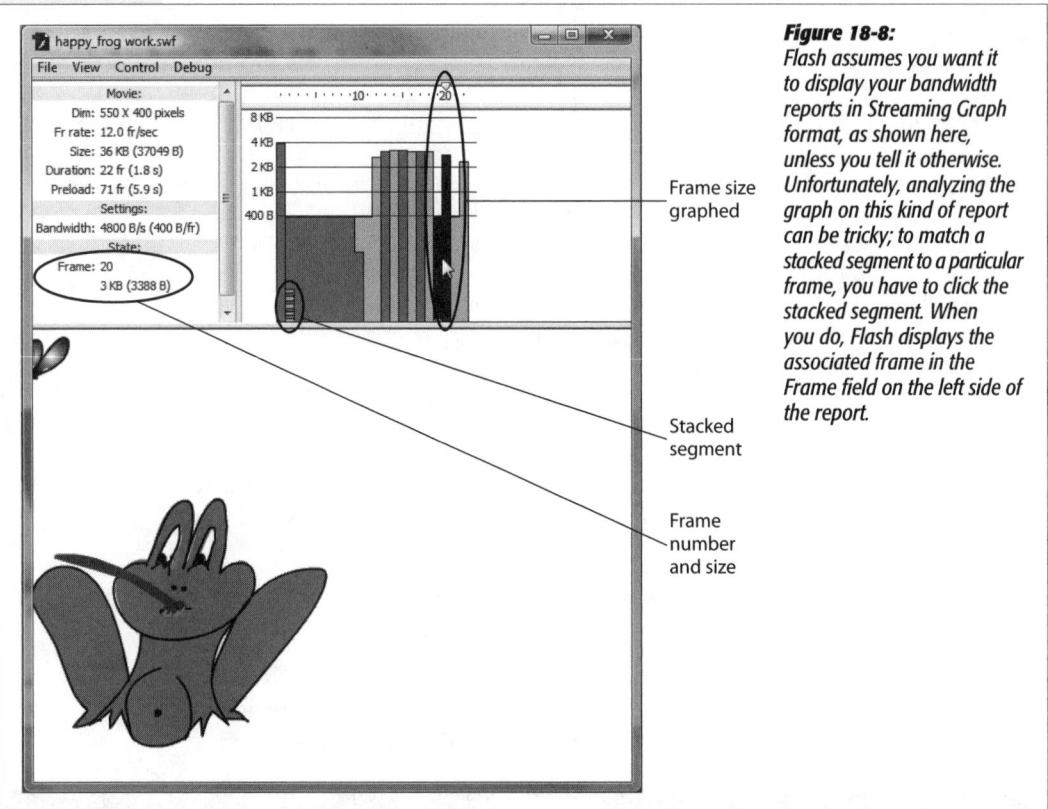

Figure 18-8:
Flash assumes you want it to display your bandwidth reports in Streaming Graph format, as shown here, unless you tell it otherwise. Unfortunately, analyzing the graph on this kind of report can be tricky; to match a stacked segment to a particular frame, you have to click the stacked segment. When you do, Flash displays the associated frame in the Frame field on the left side of the report.

The report gives you information you can use to figure out which frames of your animation are hogging all the bandwidth. There are a timeline and a playhead at the top of the report. As your animation plays, the playhead moves along the timeline to help you see at a glance which frames are causing Flash to display those tall bandwidth-hogging frame bars. *Preload*, the most useful number, tells you how long your audience will have to sit and wait before your animation begins playing. Additional download details in the bandwidth profiler report include:

- **Dimensions(Dim).** The width and height of the stage in pixels (page 41).

- **Frame rate(Fr rate).** The frame rate you set for this animation (page 475).

- **Size.** The size of the .swf file Flash created when you exported (began testing) the movie.

- **Duration**. The number of frames in this animation, followed by the number of seconds the frames take to play based on the frame rate you set.

- **Preload**. The total number of seconds it takes Flash to begin playing the animation at the bandwidth setting you chose (see page 632).

- **Bandwidth**. The connection simulation speed you chose by selecting View → Download Settings.

- **Frame**. The frame Flash is currently loading.

To generate a bandwidth profiler report:

1. **Choose Control → Test Movie.**

   The Flash Player (test window) appears containing your running animation.

2. **In the test window, select View → Bandwidth Profiler.**

   In the top half of the window, Flash displays a report similar to the one in Figure 18-8.

3. **Select View → Frame By Frame Graph.**

   The graph Flash displays when you choose the Frame By Frame option makes detecting rogue frames much easier than if you stick with Flash's suggested View → Streaming Graph option shown in Figure 18-8. Figure 18-9 has an example of a Frame By Frame graph.

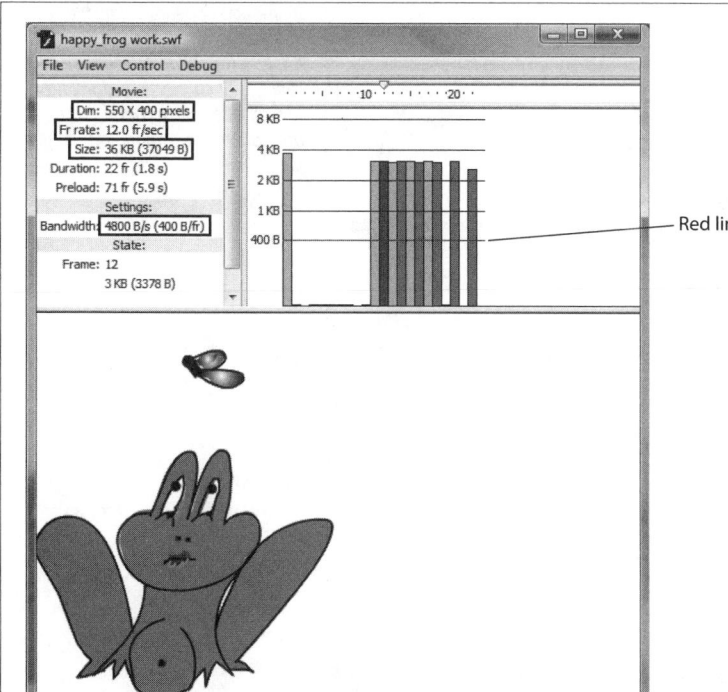

Figure 18-9:
On the left side of this Frame By Frame bandwidth profiler report, you see animation properties pertinent to playback, including the .swf file size and the stage dimensions and frame rate you set in Flash. The right side of the report shows you a frame-by-frame picture of the download process. Frame bars that appear above the red line (here, Flash has drawn the red line at 400B) mean a wait for data. So Frame 1, along with most of the frames between Frame 10 and Frame 22, are the culprits in this slow-playing animation; at a connection speed of 56 kbps, they make Flash pause the animation while they're being downloaded.

4. **Select View → Simulate Download.**

The progress bar at the top of the bandwidth profiler report moves as Flash simulates a download.

If your animation played just fine, try testing it using a slower simulated connection. (Your goal is to make sure as much of your potential audience can enjoy your animation as possible—even folks running over slow connections and congested networks.) To do this test, redisplay the bandwidth profiler report, this time using a different connection simulation speed:

1. **Choose View → Download Settings.**

A submenu menu appears, showing a list of possible connection simulation speeds, like 28.8, 56K, and T1.

2. **Choose the new simulation speed you want to test. Then choose View → Simulate Download again.**

A new bandwidth profiler report appears, based on the new connection speed (Figure 18-10).

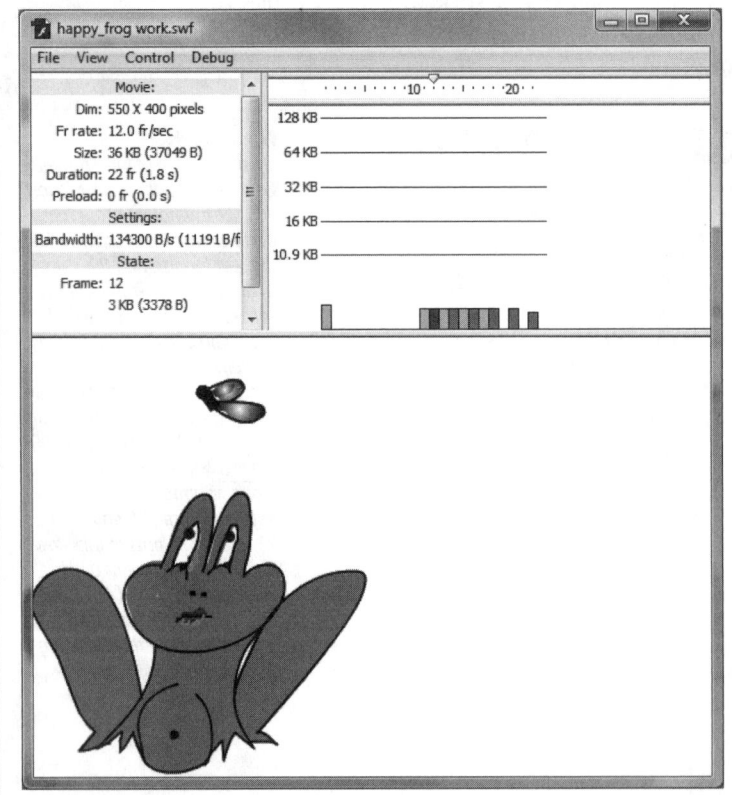

Figure 18-10:
Oh, what a difference a faster connection speed makes! Here, every last one of the frames in the animation appears below the red line that Flash has drawn at 10.9 KB, meaning that audiences running T1 connections don't have to wait one split second for the animation to download and begin playing.

The Flash Player View Menu Options

Flash Player has several menu options that you can use to change the way your animation appears as it's playing. If you turn on the checkbox next to *Display menu* in the Publish Settings → HTML dialog box (coming up in Figure 18-1), your audience can see some of these same options, by right-clicking (Windows) or Control-clicking (Mac).

Note: If you're running a Mac, the following menu options don't appear directly in Flash Player; instead, they appear in the Flash menu.

- **View → Zoom In**. Tells Flash to enlarge your animation. This option's useful if you want to examine your artwork close-up.

- **View → Zoom Out**. Tells Flash to shrink your animation.

- **View → Magnification**. Displays a menu of percentage options you can choose from to tell Flash to enlarge or shrink your animation.

- **View → Bandwidth Profiler**. Creates a bandwidth profiler report.

- **View → Streaming Graph**. Tells Flash to display download data in stacked bars when it creates a bandwidth profiler report (Figure 18-8).

- **View → Frame By Frame Graph**. Tells Flash to display the download time for each frame separately when it creates a bandwidth profiler report (Figure 18-9).

- **View → Simulate Download**. Tells Flash to pretend to download your animation from a Web server based on the download settings you select using View → Download Settings.

- **View → Download Settings**. Displays a list of connection speeds, from 14.4 to T1, to test the download speed of your animation on a variety of different computers.

- **View → Quality**. Tells Flash to display your animation's artwork in one of three different quality modes: low, medium, or high. Flash assumes you want high quality unless you tell it differently. (Choosing low or medium quality doesn't reduce simulation download time, but reducing image quality in the Flash authoring environment does reduce your animation's file size, which in turn speeds up download time.)

- **View → Show Redraw Regions**. Displays borders around the moving images in your animation.

The Art of Debugging

Imagine, for an instant, that your animation isn't behaving the way you think it should. Testing it on the stage or in Flash Player, and then eyeballing the results, as described in the previous section, is a good place to start tracking down the problem. But if you've added ActionScript to your animation, chances are you need more firepower. You need to be able to examine the inner workings of your ActionScript code—the variables, instance names, methods, and so on—to help you figure out what's wrong. Debugging is one of those activities that's part art, part craft, and part science. Flash and ActionScript provide several tools that help you track down and eliminate those pesky bugs of all types. The tools at your disposal include:

- The **Check syntax** button catches the most obvious typos. If you've got too many parentheses in a line or you misplaced a comma or semi-colon, the syntax checker is likely to notice. Still, it lets lots of the bad guys through.

• The **Compiler Errors** panel is the next layer of defense against bugs. If there's a flaw in your code's logic (for example, a reference to some object that doesn't exist or is misnamed), a message is likely to appear in the Compiler Errors panel. Sometimes your animation will run anyway; other times it won't.

• The **Output** panel displays messages. Using the *trace( )* statement, you can display the values of variable and object properties in the Output panel. So, you get to tell ActionScript what to report on.

• The **Debugger** is your debugging power tool. It's kind of like the diagnostic machine your mechanic connects to your car to see what's going on inside. The debugger combines the usefulness of the other tools with the all-important ability to stop your animation and code in its tracks. That gives you an opportunity to examine the critical variable and object values.

Note: The debugger for ActionScript 3.0 is different in a few ways from the debugger for ActionScript 2.0 and 1.0 code. For details on the older debugger, see *Flash CS3: The Missing Manual*.

You're likely to use the first three tools as you're writing and testing your animation. As your code gets more complex, with multiple timelines, multiple objects, and multiple functions and methods, you'll turn to the debugger. This section starts off with the quick and easy bug squashers, and then moves on to the more complex. The troublesome program attached to that diagnostic machine is called *draw_random_lines_begin.fla* and you can find download it from the "Missing CD" page at *http://missingmanuals.com/cds*. If you'd like to see how the program is supposed to behave, check out *draw_random_lines_finished.fla*.

UP TO SPEED

Deciphering the Actions Panel's Color Code

One quick way to spot problems in your ActionScript code is to examine the colors Flash uses to display your code in the Actions panel.

Right out of the box, Flash displays ActionScript keywords in blue, comments in light gray, text strings (text surrounded by quotes) in green, and stuff it doesn't recognize in black. So if you notice a function call or a property that appears black, you know there's a problem. A properly spelled function call or property should appear blue (unless it's a custom function), so if it's black, chances are your finger slipped.

If Flash's ActionScript coloring scheme is too subtle for your tastes, you can change the colors it uses.

To change colors:

1. Select Edit → Preferences (Windows) or Flash → Preferences (Mac).

2. In the Preferences panel that appears, select the ActionScript category. Make sure the checkbox next to "Code coloring" is turned on.

3. Click the color pickers next to Foreground, Key-words, Identifiers, Background, Comments, and Strings to choose different colors for each of these ActionScript code elements.

For example, if you have trouble making out the text strings in your scripts due to red-green color-blindness, you can change Strings to a different hue.

Using the Syntax Checker

The animation *draw_random_lines_begin.fla* isn't behaving the way it should—pretty ornery for a snippet of code that's only 16 lines long. It's supposed to draw lines on the screen from one random point to another. The lines are supposed to randomly vary in thickness, color, and transparency. There are four text fields in the display that are supposed to flash the X/Y coordinates of the points used to draw the lines. If you try to test the program Ctrl+Enter (⌘-Return on a Mac), a little text appears on the screen, but nothing much happens. The first step to putting things on track is to use the "Check syntax" button in the Actions panel, as shown in Figure 18-11.

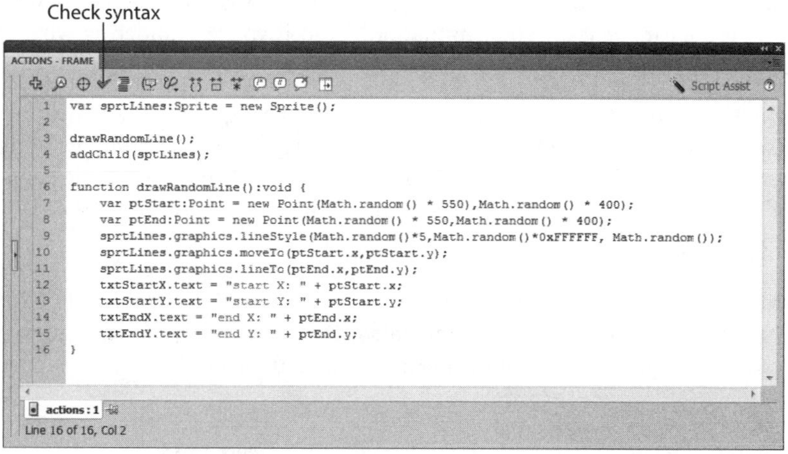

Check syntax

```
1   var sprtLines:Sprite = new Sprite();
2
3   drawRandomLine();
4   addChild(sptLines);
5
6   function drawRandomLine():void {
7       var ptStart:Point = new Point(Math.random() * 550),Math.random() * 400);
8       var ptEnd:Point = new Point(Math.random() * 550,Math.random() * 400);
9       sprtLines.graphics.lineStyle(Math.random()*5,Math.random()*0xFFFFFF, Math.random());
10      sprtLines.graphics.moveTo(ptStart.x,ptStart.y);
11      sprtLines.graphics.lineTo(ptEnd.x,ptEnd.y);
12      txtStartX.text = "start X: " + ptStart.x;
13      txtStartY.text = "start Y: " + ptStart.y;
14      txtEndX.text = "end X: " + ptEnd.x;
15      txtEndY.text = "end Y: " + ptEnd.y;
16  }
```

actions : 1

Line 16 of 16, Col 2

Figure 18-11:
The Check syntax button looks like a check. One click, and Flash proofreads your code to find typo and punctuation errors.

1. **With *draw_random_lines_begin.fla* open in Flash, select Window → Actions.**

   The Actions panel opens. The Actions panel can look different depending on how you've set up your workspace. It also remembers some of the settings, like which panels are open and closed, from the last time you used it.

2. **If you don't see code in the Actions panel, in the animation's timeline, click Frame 1 in the "actions" layer.**

   The Actions panel shows the code associated with particular frames in the timeline. It's not a problem with this little snippet, but with larger animations, if you don't see the actions you want to debug, make sure you've selected frame that holds the code.

3. **In the Actions panel, click the "Check syntax" button.**

   The "Check syntax" button looks like a checkmark. After a little deep thinking, ActionScript sends you a message like the one in Figure 18-12. If there's an error in your code, you're referred to the Complier Errors panel.

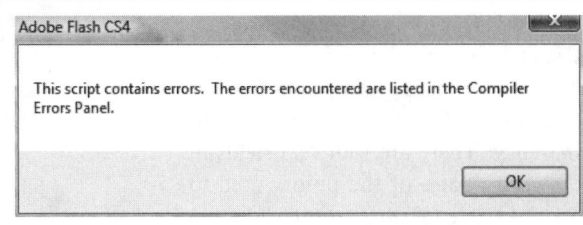

This script contains errors. The errors encountered are listed in the Compiler
Errors Panel.

OK

Figure 18-12:
*When the Check syntax button uncovers a typo in
your code, it sends you this message, which refers
you to another message in the Compiler Errors
panel.*

4. **In the Compiler Errors panel, double-click the error message.**

   If the Compiler Errors panel was closed or hidden, it opens when "Check syntax"
   finds an error. The Compiler Errors panel's location may vary depending on
   how you've organized your workspace. If you're using the Essentials workspace, it appears beneath your animation. (And if you're wondering what the
   heck a compiler is, see the box on page 611.)

   The message in the Compiler Errors panel looks like Figure 18-13. As helpful as
   these details are, sometimes your view of the issue and the compiler's view
   aren't coming from the same direction, so the messages may seem a bit cryptic.
   In this case, you're told the error is on Line 7. The error's description is:

   1086: Syntax error: expecting semicolon before dot.

   That's a little on the cryptic side, but it means there's probably something
   wrong with the way the line is punctuated. Double-clicking the error message
   puts your cursor in the offending line in the Actions panel.

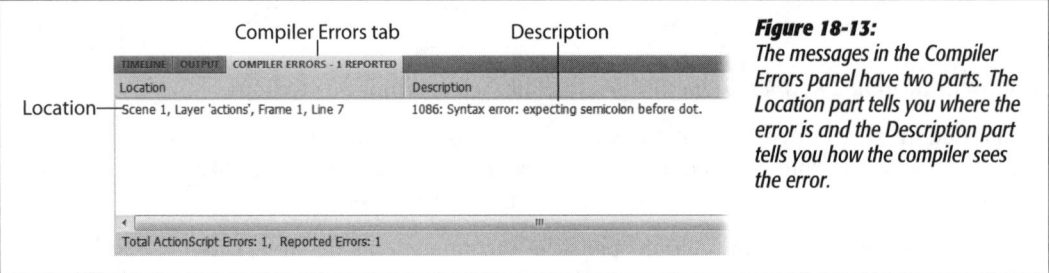

Compiler Errors tab   Description

TIMELINE OUTPUT   COMPILER ERRORS - 1 REPORTED

Location   Description

Location—Scene 1, Layer 'actions', Frame 1, Line 7   1086: Syntax error: expecting semicolon before dot.

Total ActionScript Errors: 1, Reported Errors: 1

Figure 18-13:
*The messages in the Compiler
Errors panel have two parts. The
Location part tells you where the
error is and the Description part
tells you how the compiler sees
the error.*

5. **Examine the highlighted line for a syntax error.**

   Here's where you get into the grunt work of debugging, looking through your
   code to find out where there might be a problem. Flash is a lot fussier than your
   third grade teacher about punctuation, so double-check to make sure there are
   commas between parameters and a semicolon at the end of the line. Parentheses are another place where it's easy to make a mistake. In any statement (from
   the beginning of the line to the semicolon), there should be an equal number of
   left parentheses and right parentheses. And yes, they all need to be in the right

spots, too. But it's so easy to mess up on parentheses that counting is a legitimate debugging technique. In the code in line 7, there's one extra closing parenthesis before the comma.

```
var ptStart:Point = new Point(Math.random( ) * 550),Math.random( ) * 400);
```

6. **Delete the error, and then click "Check syntax" again.**

This time, a little box appears that happily says, "This script contains no syntax errors." That's fine as far as it goes. With ActionScript 3.0 code, all the syntax checker does is check the punctuation and a few other details of your code. The Syntax checker works quickly because it doesn't actually compile your code. That means it doesn't catch nearly as many errors as you find when you test your animation using Ctrl+Enter (⌘-Return on a Mac).

What's a Compiler and Why Does It Err?

When you write ActionScript code, you name objects and write statements in a language that's relatively understandable by humans. Your computer, however, speaks a different language altogether. When Flash compiles your ActionScript code, it translates the code from your human language to the computer's machine language. When Flash comes across statements that don't make sense, it says "Aha! A compiler error!" For example, one very common compiler error is the simple misspelling of an object's name.

Flash and ActionScript are very literal. If there's a misplaced letter or even an error in capitalization in a word, that's an error. For example, if your program has a variable named *myBall* and you mistakenly type in *myball*, ActionScript sees that second reference as an undefined object and a compiler error. Anything that prevents the compiler from successfully identifying all the objects and values and performing all the methods in your program results in an error.

Using the Compiler Errors Panel

When you test your animation using Control → Test Movie or by pressing Ctrl+Enter (⌘-Return on a Mac), Flash creates a .swf file. That's the same as the finished file you distribute or put on a Web site so the world can see your animation. In the process, your ActionScript code is translated into a computer language that's smaller and faster than your ActionScript. The process of compiling your code is likely to catch mistakes that the "Check syntax" button misses. (See the box above for more details.)

Note: This example continues debugging the file *draw_random_lines_begin.fla*. The entire process began on page 608.

---

1. **Test your animation using Ctrl+Enter (⌘-Return on a Mac).**

An error appears in the Compiler Errors panel, as shown in Figure 18-14. (It could be worse; sometimes you see seven or eight errors stacked up in the panel.) This error didn't appear when you clicked the "Check syntax" button in the previous exercise, because "Check syntax" doesn't compile the code. Obviously, the compiler choked on something you're trying to feed it. The Compiler Errors panel reports that the location of the error is "Scene 1, Layer 'actions', Frame 1, Line 4." That's very helpful information, and what's more, when you double-click the error message in the panel, Flash zips you to the Actions panel and finds that point in your code. But before you double-click, read the description of the error:

> 1120: Access of undefined property sptLines.

That's also a good clue; explaining the problem, at least as far as the compiler sees it. The compiler thinks you're trying to make a change to a property that doesn't exist. That property is called sptLines.

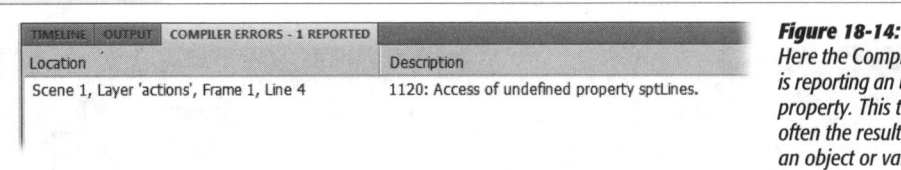

Figure 18-14:
Here the Compiler Errors pane is reporting an undefined property. This type of error is often the result of misspelling an object or variable's name.

2. **Double-click the error message in the Compiler Errors panel.**

Flash zips you to the Actions panel and highlights line 4, which reads:

```
addChild(sptLines);
```

3. **Examine the highlighted line for a syntax error.**

At first this might seem a little puzzling. It's a simple statement that adds sptLines to the display list which should make its contents visible on the stage. The compiler error said something about a property, but this line doesn't seem to be changing a property. You know, however, that the compiler sees something it can't identify, and that's *sptLines*. It makes sense to check the code that precedes the error for previous references to *sptLines*. There aren't any, and that's exactly the problem. The variable sprtLines is defined in the first line of the code, and the reference to sptLines is a typo.

4. **In line 4, correct the spelling of sprtLines, and then test the animation.**

This time, *draw_random_lines_begin.fla* is a little more entertaining. The animation draws random lines on the stage. The lines vary in thickness, color, and transparency. But the text boxes, like the one that reads *start X*, don't change or provide any other information. Sounds like there's more debugging to do.

Note: The animation *draw_random_lines_begin.fla* uses a very slow frame rate of 2 fps so that each line appears slowly on the screen. If you want to speed up the action, go to Modify → Document and change the frame rate.

Note: Stop the *draw_random_lines_begin.fla* when you're sufficiently entertained. Because there's no automatic end to the animation, Flash can conceivably draw so many lines that your computer will run out of memory trying to display them.

Using the Output Panel and *trace()* Statement

The ActionScript *trace()* statement is one of the easiest ways to debug your programs—and it delivers a lot of bang for your debugging buck. You get to tell ActionScript exactly what variable value or object you want to keep track of, and Flash obligingly sends the details to the Output panel. *Trace()* is such an important code writing tool that it's used throughout the ActionScript examples in this book. Here's another good example of the way you can use *trace()* to understand why your program isn't behaving as expected.

Note: This example continues debugging the file *draw_random_lines_begin.fla.* The entire process begins on page 608.

When you tested *draw_random_lines_begin.fla* in the last step on page 612, the drawing lines part of the program worked, but the text fields didn't display information about the points used to start and end the lines. Text fields display strings of text in your animation. There are a few different types of text fields and you can format them in a number of ways. (For all the details, see page 538.) In this case, the text fields show some of the information that you want displayed, but not all of it.

The *trace()* statement works kind of like a text field. You put the information that you want displayed inside of the *trace()* statement's parentheses. If you want to display a string of text, put it inside of quotes, like this:

```
trace("show this text");
```

When your ActionScript code gets to that line, the words "show this text" appear in the Output panel (without the quotes). If you have a variable named strMsg, and its value is "show this text", then you can write a *trace()* statement like this:

```
trace(strMsg);
```

This statement would also send the words "show this text" to the Output panel. The Output panel isn't at all fussy about the data types. Put the name of a variable, an instance of an object, or just about anything inside of a *trace()* statement, and something is bound to appear in the Output panel. If the value is a number, that's what you see. If it's a reference to an object, you'll see the object's name.

Following are some steps to gain a little insight into the problem with the text fields in the file *draw_random_lines_begin.fla.*

1. **Test the animation as it worked at the end of the previous section.**

   When you test the animation, you see the random lines drawn properly, but you see only part of the text that should be displayed in text fields, as shown in Figure 18-15. Don't forget to stop the animation (Control → Stop) or close the window (File → Close).

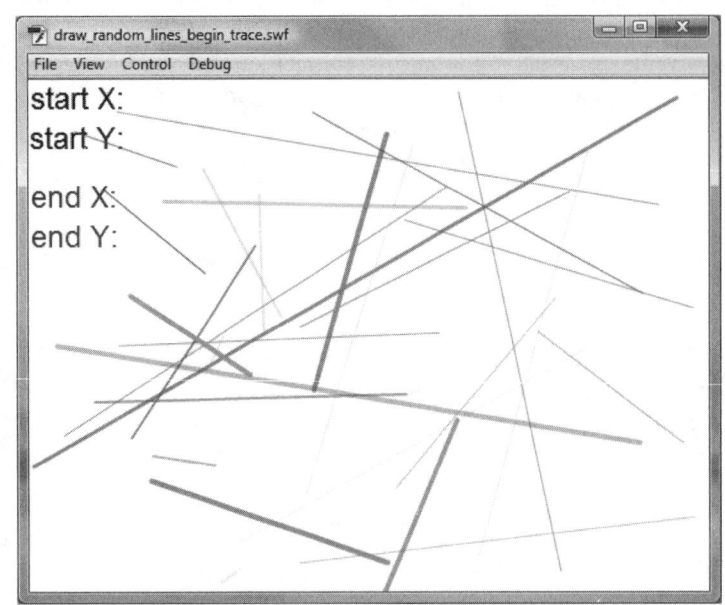

Figure 18-15:
When you test the animation draw_random_lines_begin.fla, it displays lines on the stage, but it doesn't display the point coordinates for the lines as it should.

2. **On the stage, click the text fields, and then, in the Properties panel, check the names of the text fields.**

   In your Flash document, the text fields on the stage show text, like "start X" and "start Y." When you select a text field, you see its name at the top of the Properties panel. For example, the text field with the text "start X" is named txtStartX. The others are named txtStartY, txtEndX, and txtEndY. These are the names of misbehaving text fields, so you'll look for references to them in your code.

3. **Select Window → Actions to open the Actions panel.**

   The Actions panel displays this code, which amounts to only 16 lines:

```
1    var sprtLines:Sprite = new Sprite();
2
3    drawRandomLine();
4    addChild(sprtLines);
5
6    function drawRandomLine():void {
7        var ptStart:Point = new Point(Math.random() * 550,Math.random() * 400);
```

```
8        var ptEnd:Point = new Point(Math.random( ) * 550,Math.random( ) * 400);
9        sprtLines.graphics.lineStyle(Math.random( )*5,Math.random( )*0xFFFFFF,
     Math.random( ));
10       sprtLines.graphics.moveTo(ptStart.x,ptStart.y);
11       sprtLines.graphics.lineTo(ptEnd.x,ptEnd.y);
12       txtStartX.text = "start X: " + ptStart.x;
13       txtStartY.text = "start Y: " + ptStart.y;
14       txtEndX.text = "end X: " + ptEnd.x;
15       txtEndY.text = "end Y: " + ptEnd.y;
16   }
```

4. **Search for lines with references to the misbehaving text fields: txtStartX, txt-StartY, txtEndX, and txtEndY.**

   In lines 12 through 15, values are assigned to the text fields' properties. Each value is made of two parts, a string literal with text like "start X:", and then the string concatenation operator (+) and a reference to an object's property, like *ptStart.x.* Looking back up in the code, you see on line 7 that the data type for ptStart is Point. The reference ptStart.x is a reference to the X property of a point. That value is a number. Still, there's nothing apparently wrong with the code.

5. **Insert a line at line 13, and then type the following** *trace( )* **statement:**

   ```
   trace("start X: " + ptStart.x);
   ```

   The text inside the parentheses is exactly the text that's supposed to appear in the text field. In fact, you can copy and paste to create the line. Using copy and paste is a good technique for an operation like this, because you'll be sure the text in the two statements is identical.

Tip: If you don't see your *trace( )* statement in the Output panel, select File → Publish Settings → Flash, and make sure the "Omit trace actions" checkbox is turned off.

---

6. **Test your animation using Ctrl+Enter (⌘-Return on a Mac) and examine the Output panel.**

   When you run your animation, the Output window starts to fill up with lines like:

   start X: 549.6419722447172

   start X: 499.13692246191204

   start X: 239.57312640268356

   start X: 64.5334855420515

   Comparing the Output panel details, you see that your text fields display the string literals, like *start X:,* but they aren't displaying the numbers with all those decimal places. Those long numbers are generated by the *random( )* method used earlier in the code. For example, the value for ptStart.x is created in line 7 with the statement:

```
var ptStart:Point = new Point(Math.random( ) * 550,Math.random( ) * 400);
```

This line creates a new variable called *ptStart*. Its data type is Point, which includes x and y properties. At the same time that the new instance of Point is being created, values are assigned to those *x* and *y* properties. Instead of providing specific numbers, you want to provide random numbers that change every time the *drawRandomLine( )* method runs. So the statement uses a method that's provided by the Math class. The section of the statement that reads *Math. random( ) * 550* is in effect saying, give me a random number between zero and 550 (the width of the stage). Likewise, the next bit of code is providing a number for the y property that matches the height of the stage. *Math.random( )* is providing a number with a little more precision than is necessary for this snippet of a program. In fact, the number is too long to fit in the text field.

7. **Select the txtStartX text field on the stage and change the width property to 550.**

    The width of the text field expands so it's the length of the stage.

8. **Test your animation using Ctrl+Enter (⌘-Return on a Mac).**

    When the animation runs, the entire number is displayed in the txtStartX text field, as shown in Figure 18-16. The *x* and *y* properties aren't displayed in the other text fields.

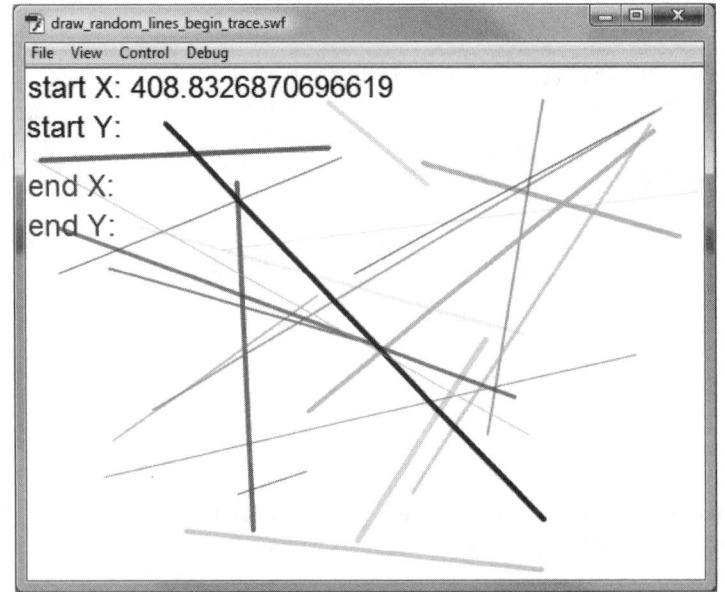

Figure 18-16:
After changing the width of the text field, Flash displays the very long number that represents the x property for your line's starting point.

Mystery solved. You figured out what's gone wrong with the code. The solution is a little less than satisfactory—you don't really need a number that long for this animation. Fortunately, that gives you an opportunity to explore the Debugger in action, as you'll see in the next section.

You can delete the *trace( )* statement from your code or you can leave it in. It doesn't change the appearance of the animation in any way. A third alternative is to use a handy programmer's trick called *commenting out*; see the box below.

TRICK OF THE TRADE

Comment Me Out

If you're planning to keep working on your ActionScript code and think you'll need to reuse these *trace( )* statements at some point down the road, you don't have to delete them, and then type them in again later. Instead, you can "comment them out" by placing two slashes in front of each line, like this:

    // trace("start X: " + ptStart.x);

When you stick two slashes at the beginning of a line of ActionScript code, Flash ignores everything it finds on the line

after those slashes. In other words, it treats the code as if it were a plain old comment. Later, when you want to use that *trace( )* statement again, all you have to do is remove the slashes and you're back in business.

It's a good idea to remove or comment out *trace( )* statements when you no longer need them. Not only will you avoid cluttering up your Output panel, there's a performance boost, too.

Using the Debugger

When you need as much debugging muscle as Flash can provide, click Debug → Debug Movie. You may think you've fired up a different program, but actually, Flash has merely closed some panels, opened others, and rearranged your view of your animation (Figure 18-18). It also automatically compiles and runs your animation. Your first visit to the debugger can be a little intimidating, but don't worry. Look around for familiar landmarks, and you soon figure out the purposes of the multiple panels and the messages within.

- The **Debug Console** in the upper-left corner shows DVD-like Play and Stop buttons (Figure 18-17) and that's exactly what you do with the buttons in the debug console. You use them to move forward and backward through your code. You can also open the Debug Console using menus: Window → Debug Panels → Debug Console.

- The **Variables** panel below the Debug Console is where you really learn what's going on in your program. You see variable and object names on the left and their related values on the right. There are probably a lot of unfamiliar words in there, because this panel keeps track of every property for every object in your animation. You don't need to worry about many of these, because Flash takes care of them perfectly well . But when something goes wrong, look up the name of the offending text box, variable name, or object in this list, and you'll be on your way to a solution. You can also open the Variables panel using menus: Window → Debug Panels → Variables.

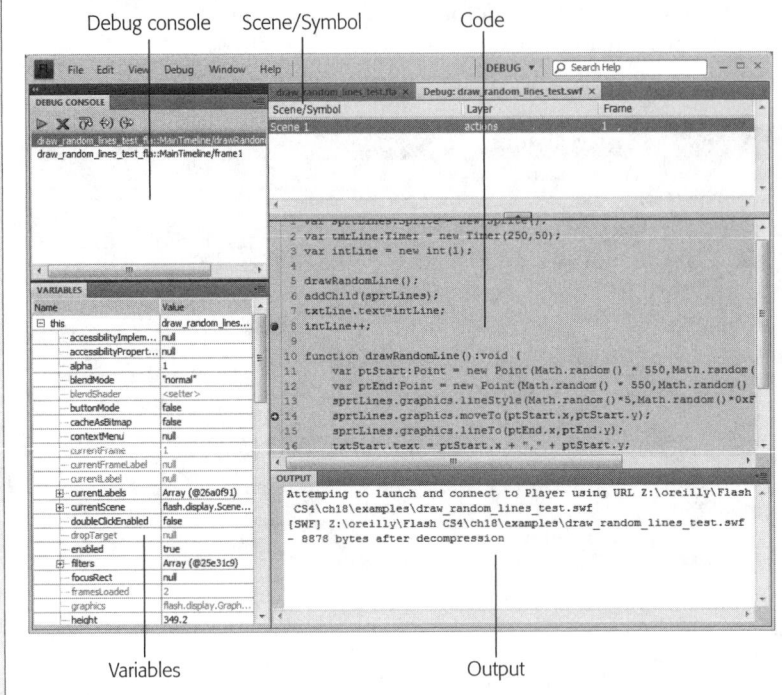

Figure 18-17:
The Debugger shows you what Flash is thinking behind the scenes. This panel shows the instance names, property values, variable names and values, and other ActionScript keywords and statements that either you (or Flash) added to your animation.

- In the upper-right corner, the **Scene/Symbol** panel is pretty straightforward. It tracks your animation's current position in the main timeline, scene, or symbol timeline. You see the name of the scene or symbol, the layer that contains code, and the frame number.

- The middle panel shows the **ActionScript code** you wrote, similar to the Actions panel. You can force your program to stop at certain places in your code to give you a chance to inspect the inner workings of the objects. More on that in the next section: Setting and Using Breakpoints.

- At the bottom is the **Output** panel, covered earlier in this chapter (page 613). If you've used the *trace( )* statement while you were writing code and experimenting with ActionScript, you know how helpful the Output panel can be.

Setting and Using Breakpoints

One of the most important debugging tools in any well-stocked ActionScript programmer's arsenal is the *breakpoint*. A breakpoint is an artificial stopping point—sort of a roadblock—that you can insert into your ActionScript code to stop Flash Player in its tracks. Setting breakpoints lets you examine your animation at different points during playback so that you can pinpoint where a bug first happens.

Flash lets you set breakpoints at specific lines in your ActionScript code. Setting a breakpoint lets you play the animation only up until Flash encounters that breakpoint. The instant Flash encounters a line with a breakpoint, it immediately stops the animation so that you can either examine object property values (as described in the previous section) or step through the remaining code in your action slowly, line by line, watching what happens as you go.

Setting breakpoints is a great way to track down logic errors in your ActionScript code. For example, say you've created a chunk of code containing a lot of *if* and *switch* conditionals or *while* and *for* looping statements. Stopping playback just before you enter that long stretch of code lets you follow Flash as it works through the statements one at a time. By stepping through statements in the order Flash actually executes them (as opposed to the order you thought Flash was supposed to execute them), you may find, for example, the cause of your problem is that Flash never reaches the *else* section of your *if...else* statement, or never performs any of the statements inside your *while* block because the *while* condition is never met.

Note: For more information on using *if...else, do...while,* and other logical statements in ActionScript, check out Colin Moock's *Essential ActionScript 2.0* (O'Reilly) or *Essential ActionScript 3.0* (O'Reilly). Both books have detailed coverage of more advanced ActionScript topics that are beyond the scope of this book.

So far, this chapter has shown how to clean up the buggy code in the file *draw_random_lines_begin.fla*. In this section, you can make further improvements to the animation while learning how to stop your animation and code in its tracks and examine individual properties using the debugger.

Note: This example continues debugging the file *draw_random_lines_begin.fla*. The entire process began on page 608.

To get started, follow these steps:

1. **With *draw_random_lines_begin.fla* open in Flash, click Debug → Debug Movie.**

   A Flash Player window opens and begins playing your animation. The panels in Flash change to show the Debug Console, the Variables panel, the Scene/Symbol panel, your code, and the Output panel. There's no information showing in either the Debug Console or the Variables panel at this point. If you followed the steps in the previous example, some information appears in the Output panel.

2. **In the Flash Player window, select the toggle Ctrl+Enter (⌘-P on a Mac).**

   The animation stops playing.

3. **In the panel with the ActionScript code, click to the left of the line numbers 7 and 8.**

   A red dot appears next to the line number, indicating a breakpoint.

4. **In the Flash Player window, press Ctrl+Enter (⌘-P on a Mac).**

   The Flash Player may be hidden by the debugger. If necessary, use Alt+Tab (or ⌘-Tab on a Mac) to bring it to the front. When you press Ctrl+Enter, the animation runs for a moment, and then stops. A small arrow appears in the breakpoint next to line 7, indicating that the animation is at this point in the ActionScript code. You see more details in both the Debug Console (Figure 18-18) and the Variables panel.

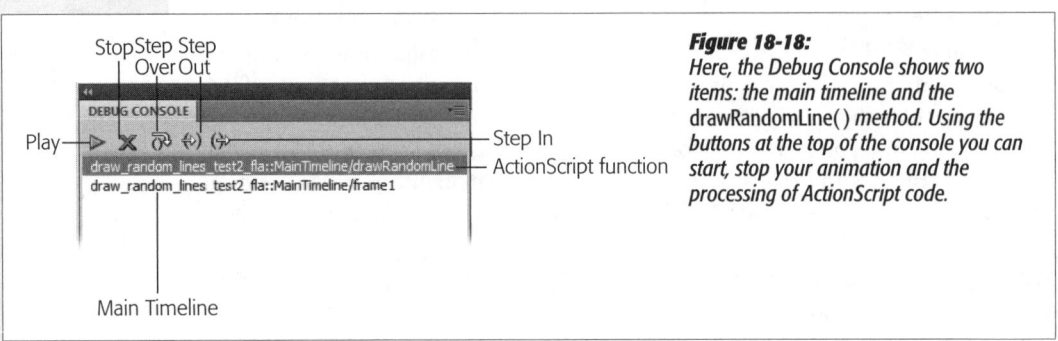

Figure 18-18:
Here, the Debug Console shows two items: the main timeline and the drawRandomLine( ) method. Using the buttons at the top of the console you can start, stop your animation and the processing of ActionScript code.

   There are two items displayed in the Debug Console. You may need to drag the right edge of the panel to read the entire lines. The line at the top references the *drawRandomLine( )* method in your code. The bottom line references the main timeline in the animation. When you click different items in the Debug Console, the items listed in the Variables panel change. Click the top line before examining the Variables panel in the next step.

5. **In the Variables panel, click the plus sign next to the word "this", and then scroll the panel to view all the variables.**

   Initially, there are three items in the variables panel: *this, ptStart,* and *ptEnd. This* refers to the main timeline; *ptStart* and *ptEnd* are variables inside of the *drawRandomLine( )* function. At this point, the value for both variables is undefined. When you click the + button next to *this,* a list expands beneath showing all the properties and variables related to the main timeline. Some of the items are familiar, like alpha, height, and width. Others may be a bit mysterious, especially if they're properties you haven't yet used in ActionScript: in Flash, there are a lot of preset values, which you may never need to worry about. If you look carefully in the list, you find the names of the text fields in your animation: txtStartX, txtStartY, txtEndX, and txtEndY.

6. **Click a second time to close the list.**

   The lists closes, leaving just the three items showing: *this, ptStart,* and *ptEnd.*

7. **Click the green Continue button in the Debug Console.**

   Flash moves ahead just one step in the code because there's a breakpoint at line 8. In the Variables panel, you see that the ptStart item has changed. The value is no longer undefined; there's some weird-looking number there. And there's a + button next to the name.

When you place a breakpoint in your code, the debugger stops before that line is executed. That's why, with a breakpoint at line 8, ptStart has newly assigned values, but ptEnd is still undefined.

8. **Click the + button next to ptStart and examine its properties.**

As explained on page 570, the Point class has three properties: *length, x,* and *y.* Now that ptStart is defined, the variables panel shows values for each. More of those are really long decimal numbers.

9. **Double-click the x value for ptStart and type** *300.* **Then, double-click the y value and type** *200.*

One of the extremely handy features of the Debugger is that you can change values of properties when the animation is stopped at a break point.

10. **Click the green Continue button.**

The animation movies through its two frames, and then it runs the *drawRandomLine( )* method again. It stops again at line 7 in the code.

11. **Examine the animation in the Flash Player window.**

The two text fields at the top of the animation show the values you entered in the Variables panel: 300 and 200 as shown in Figure 18-19. This small test proves that if you round the numbers to whole numbers, they'll fit in the text fields.

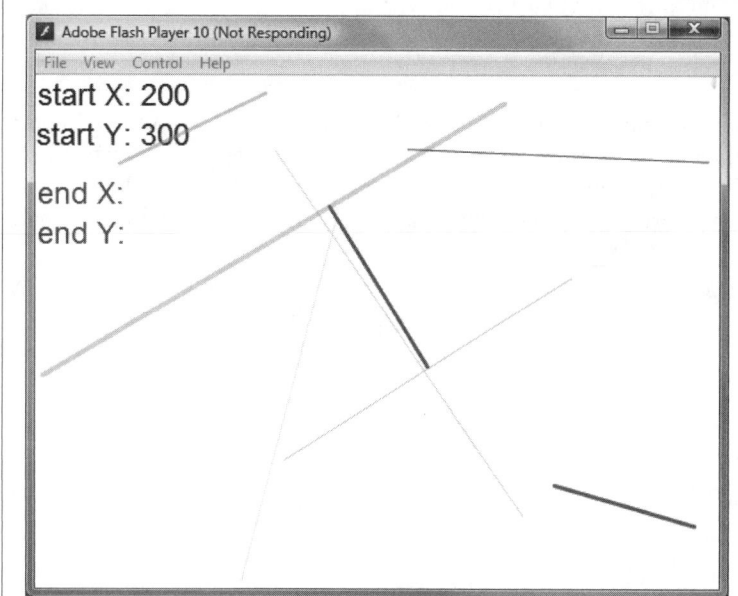

Figure 18-19:
When you change values in the Debugger, you can see the results in your animation. Here, the values for two of the text fields have been changed. Before the change, the numbers were too long to be displayed by the text fields.

12. **In the Debug Console, click the red X, also known as the End Debug Session button.**

Flash restores your project to its appearance before you entered the debugger.

So, one solution to making the numbers fit in the text fields is to round them off to whole numbers. You can do that with another method that's part of the Math class. Here's what the finished code looks like. The two bold lines show the changes using the *Math.round( )* method.

```
var sprtLines:Sprite = new Sprite( );

drawRandomLine( );
addChild(sprtLines);

function drawRandomLine( ):void {
    var ptStart:Point = new Point(Math.round(Math.random( ) * 550),Math.
round(Math.random( ) * 400));
    var ptEnd:Point = new Point(Math.round(Math.random( ) * 550),Math.
round(Math.random( ) * 400));
    sprtLines.graphics.lineStyle(Math.random( )*5,Math.random( )*0xFFFFFF,
Math.random( ));
    sprtLines.graphics.moveTo(ptStart.x,ptStart.y);
    sprtLines.graphics.lineTo(ptEnd.x,ptEnd.y);
    txtStartX.text = "start X: " + ptStart.x;
    trace("start X: " + ptStart.x);
    txtStartY.text = "start Y: " + ptStart.y;
    txtEndX.text = "end X: " + ptEnd.x;
    txtEndY.text = "end Y: " + ptEnd.y;
}
```

Now the animation runs as it was intended. It draws lines that are random in position, color, thickness, and transparency. The X/Y coordinates for the start and end of the lines is shown in upper-left corner of the animation. Not only do the whole numbers fit in the text fields, they're a little easier to discern than the monster decimals.

Note: Flash lets you debug your animations remotely after you've uploaded them to a Web server. This book doesn't cover remote debugging, but you can find out more about it in Flash's help files.

Publishing and Exporting

When you're finished creating an animation in Flash, you want to do one of two things with it: *Publish* it, which means packaging it in a form your audience can play using the Flash Player they've installed on their computers; or *export* it, which means packaging it in a form you can edit using another graphics or animation program (like Adobe Illustrator or Adobe Fireworks).

Note: Note: *Publishing* means something different in Flash (where it means "creating an executable Flash file") from what it means in the larger world of Web development (where it means "transferring files to a Web server").

In this chapter, you'll learn how to do both.

Using Flash's publishing settings (Figure 19-1), you'll see how to tell Flash to publish your animation as part of a Web page, and as a standalone *projector*. You'll also see how to export the artwork in your animation as editable image files. But before you publish or export, you need to learn how to *optimize* your animation (reduce your animation's file size) so that it runs as quickly and efficiently as possible—a real concern if you're planning to publish your animation on the Web (see the box on page 623).

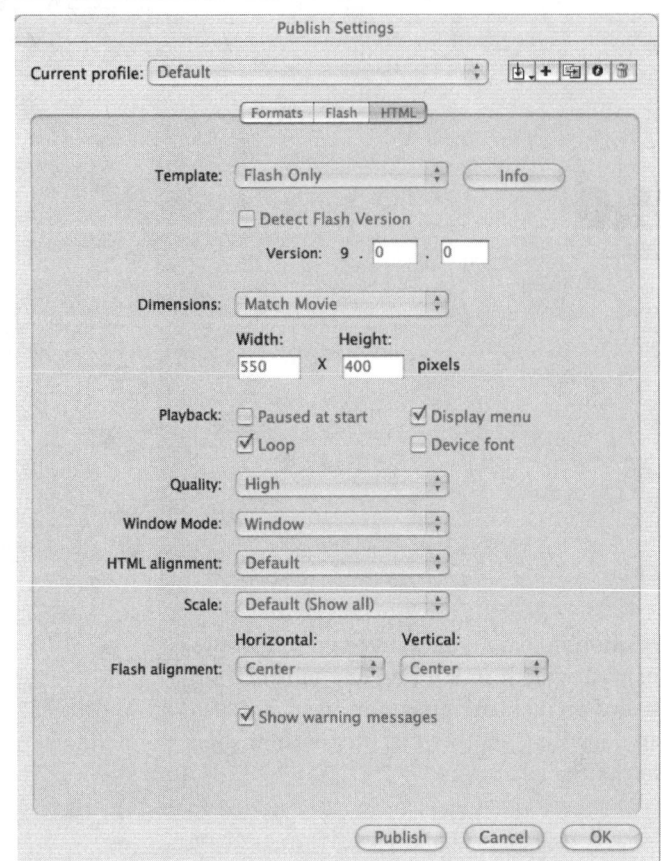

Figure 19-1:
Flash lets you choose how to deliver your
compiled animation. The options shown
here produces a plain .swf that plays in
most browsers. You can also publish it
as a standalone projector file (a self-
contained executable file you double-
click to run, with no need for a Web
browser or a separate Flash Player), an
image file, or embedded in a Web page.

Optimizing Flash Documents

The larger your published Flash animation file size, the longer it takes for your audience to download it from the Web, and the more stress it puts on their computers when it does begin to play. (Find out more about the difference between an editable .fla Flash document and a published, ready-to-roll .swf document on page 631.) A large file size can cause someone to stare at a blank screen for seconds or even minutes at a time, while she waits for your animation to download and begin playing. A large file size can also cause your animation (including any sound files it contains) to play in fits and starts once it *does* begin.

Optimizing your animation means paring down its file size by making various changes to your images, text, and other elements—all while making sure your animation continues to play the way you want it to. You can think of optimization as low-fat cooking for the animation set: The goal is to get rid of the fat without getting rid of the flavor. And, as with low-fat cooking, Flash doesn't have a single approach to optimization; instead—because every animation and target audience is different—you need to experiment, tweak, and retest using the strategies outlined next.

The Importance of Being Optimized

In an era where lightning-fast connections, high-speed processors, and multimegabyte memory cards abound, why should I bother optimizing my Flash documents?

Here's why: Not everyone has access to the latest, greatest equipment and Internet service. In many parts of the world, people don't have access to affordable T1 connections, for example. Also, folks relying on the computers at their schools or jobs don't have control over their equipment. And, of course, not everyone has the time, money, or patience necessary to upgrade every time a new "revolution" in hardware or software technology hits the market.

There's a tendency among some animators (especially those who don't have a background in building non-Flash software programs) to resist the extra effort that optimizing their animations (as you see on page 624) requires. But here's the fact: If people can't see your animation, nothing else matters. Not the beauty or cleverness of your artwork, nor the sophistication of your animated sequences, nor the appropriateness of your perfectly synchronized background music.

Here's a short list of the most common excuses some animators give for not optimizing their animations (and the reasons why these excuses don't fly):

- **It looks great on my machine. If my audience doesn't have a fast enough connection, they need to upgrade.** Animators and others using Flash tend to be running high-end equipment—much faster and more powerful than the equipment their audiences are running. That's why testing your animation at a variety of connection speeds (as discussed on page 602) and even on a variety of machines, if possible, is so important. As noted above, not everyone *can*

upgrade, and not everyone *wants* to. But even if they do, chances are they're not going to do it just to see your animation.

- **So what if it takes 5 minutes to download my animation file? My animation is so fantastic it's worth waiting for.** It doesn't matter if your animation is in line for the next Webby Award: If your audience can't run it (or surfs away impatiently instead of waiting for it to download and stutter across their screens), you haven't communicated effectively—and communicating effectively is, or should be, the goal of every animation you create in Flash.

- **The big boys (Hollywood trailer-makers, high-end advertisers, and super-sophisticated, high-traffic sites) don't worry about optimization. Why should I?** It's true that some folks would still check out the latest Hollywood teaser even if it took all day to download. But they don't have to because the big boys pay an army of professional testers and software designers to optimize their animations using the techniques in this chapter.

The bottom line, as you've read over and over in this book, is to determine the needs of your target audience *first,* and then construct your animation to meet those needs. If you're delivering your animation as a standalone file on DVD, you're absolutely sure that your audience will be running high-end equipment, and you know for a fact they're highly motivated to run your animation (for example, they have to work through the Flash training tutorial you created in order to keep their jobs), then by all means take optimization with a grain of salt. But if your audience fits any other profile, ignore optimization at your own risk.

Tip: As you check out the optimization strategies in this section, keep in mind that effective optimization is always a balancing act. You may decide some effects are worth the bloated file size they require, and some aren't. In still other cases, you'll want to compromise. For example, you might choose to remove half of the gradient effects you've applied to your images so that you reduce file size, but keep the other half. In Flash, you're the director, so you get to decide how much is enough.

Ten Optimization Strategies

Below you'll find 10 strategies for reducing file size by tweaking the images you draw, the bitmaps you import, the graphic effects you apply, and more. Apply as many of the strategies as you can. You can use any of these techniques to trim down a completed animation. Better yet, keep them in mind as you create your next animation. That way, you'll end up with a streamlined animation without a lot of extra, after-the-fact work.

Choose tweens over frame-by-frame animations

Every time you add a keyframe to your timeline, the size of your file goes up dramatically. In contrast, when you use a motion or shape tween (Chapter 3), Flash only has to keep track of the beginning and ending keyframes; for the in-between frames it generates, it has to save only a few calculations. (Obviously, there are times you need to use frame-by-frame animation to create the effect you're after; but for those times when tweening will do the job, use it.)

Choose the Pencil tool over the Brush tool

Brush tool fills are more complex than the lines you create with the Pencil tool, so brush strokes take up more file space. When you feel both strokes are equally acceptable, choose the Pencil.

Choose solid over dashed or dotted lines

Through the Property Inspector, Flash lets you apply a handful of dash-and-dot effects to the lines you draw on stage using the Pencil, Pen, Line, and Shape tools (page 64). But do so sparingly, because these line effects increase file size.

Simplify curves

The less points that make up your lined curves and fill outlines, the less information Flash has to keep track of—and the smaller your file size. Flash even gives you a special Optimize command to remove superfluous points from your shapes. Here's how to use it:

1. Select the curved line or fill outline you want to optimize, and then choose Modify → Shape → Optimize.

   The Optimize Curves dialog box you see in Figure 19-2 (top) appears.

2. Drag the smoothing slider to tell Flash how much optimization to apply, from none to maximum, and then click OK.

   Flash displays a message (Figure 19-2, bottom) letting you know what percentage of the selected line or outline it was able to dispense with.

3. Click OK.

   On the stage, you see the (subtle) results of the optimization.

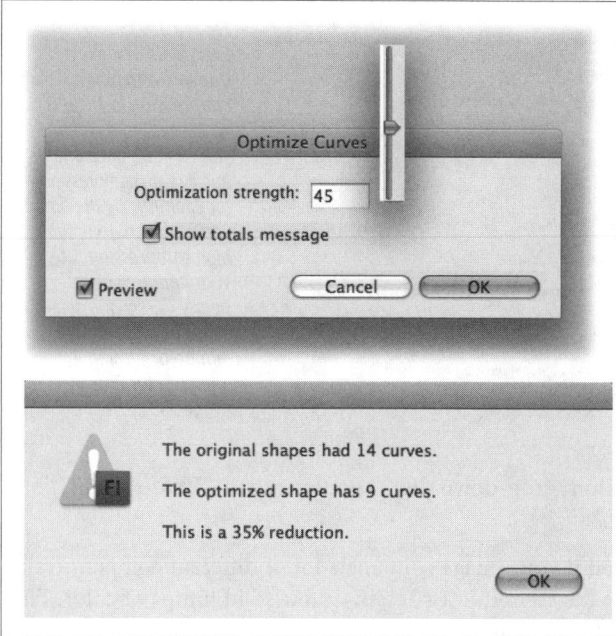

Figure 19-2:
Top: Optimizing a line doesn't straighten it out or even smooth it the way that Modify → Shape → Advanced Straighten and Modify → Shape → Advanced Smooth do; instead, it ever-so-subtly shifts the points that make up the line. If you want to see how successful the optimization is, make sure you leave the "Show totals" message checkbox turned on.

Bottom: Because optimization is a final tweak meant for you to do after your image already looks the way you want it to look, you don't see a huge reduction in size here. Still, depending on the number of curved lines and fill outlines your animation contains, the saved bytes can add up fast.

Use symbols

Creating a reusable symbol (Chapter 6) lets you add multiple instances of a shape or drawing to your animation without dramatically increasing file size. Even shrinking, rotating, or recoloring your instances costs less in file size than creating separate images.

Avoid bitmaps (or optimize them)

Bitmaps are expensive in terms of file size. If you can do without them, do so; if not, crop them (so that you use as little of them as possible) or optimize them by choosing a higher-than-standard compression option, as described below. However, in some cases, overly complicated vector graphics also use a lot of space. If in doubt, test both options and compare the sizes by generating a size report (page 603).

Note: You can also optimize bitmaps in the Publish settings dialog box (page 632).

To optimize a bitmap:

1. **Import the bitmap into your document's Library panel.**

   The steps, if you need a refresher, are in Chapter 9 (page 328).

   In the Library, double-click the icon next to the imported bitmap's file name. (Or select the bitmap, and then, from the Options menu in the upper-right corner of the Library, choose Properties.)

   Either way, the Bitmap Properties window you see in Figure 19-3 appears.

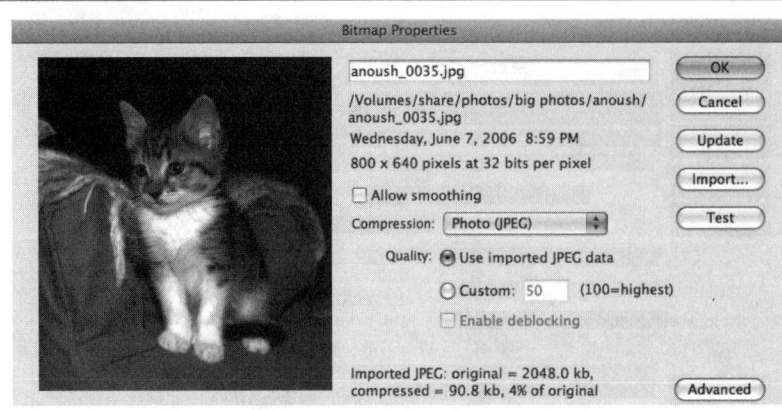

Figure 19-3:
Everything in life is a tradeoff, and bitmap optimization in Flash is no exception. If you find you can't balance image quality with compression— for example, by the time you reach an acceptably high compression rate, your image appears nearly unrecognizable— consider cropping the bitmap or turning it into a vector drawing (page 333).

2. **From the Compression drop-down list, choose either "Photo (JPEG)" or "Lossless (PNG/GIF)."**

   Choose the first option if your image contains a lot of different colors or transparent effects; choose the second if it contains a few solid lumps of color. Find out more about JPEGs, PNGs, and GIFs beginning on page 327.

   Flash calculates a percent compression rate and displays it near the bottom of the Bitmap Properties window.

   If you chose "Photo (JPEG)", you can compress the image further. Click the Custom radio button, and then type a number into the box (Figure 19-3). A value of 100 is the highest quality and the least compression.

Tip: Flash starts you out with a quality rate of 50. You need to experiment to find out the lowest number that gives you an acceptable tradeoff between file size and quality, but one way to begin is to jot down the current file size (Flash displays it just below the Quality field), type 25, and then click OK. When you open the Bitmap Properties window again, Flash displays the new file size for the bitmap based on a file quality of 25. If the image looks OK, type a lower number; if not, type a higher number. The higher the number, the larger the file size; the lower the number, the lower the file size.

---

3. **Take a look at your newly optimized image by clicking the Test button.**

   The preview area shows the way the image looks using the optimization settings you chose. Near the bottom of the Bitmap Properties window, you see the percent compression rate Flash has calculated based on the Quality setting you typed in. If the image quality looks horrible, repeat step 2 with a higher quality setting; if the quality looks okay but the compression rate doesn't seem low enough, try again with a lower quality setting. (Sometimes, depending on your image, a lower quality setting will look practically identical to a slightly higher quality setting.)

4. When you're satisfied with the quality-vs.-file size tradeoff, click OK.

Flash hides the Bitmap Properties window and brings you back to your workspace.

Note: The image doesn't appear optimized in the Library preview area. But you can preview the effects of different optimization settings when you drag the image to the stage.

Keep sound clips to a minimum; when you do use them, optimize them.

Sound clips can quickly swell your animation size. Always use the shortest clips you can get by with (page 351 shows you how to shorten sound clips) and optimize them by compressing them as much as possible without sacrificing too much sound quality.

To optimize a sound file:

1. **Import the sound file into your document's Library panel.**

"Importing Sound Files on page 342 has the full detail on importing audio files.

2. **In the Library, double-click the icon next to the imported sound file's name.**

Alternatively, select the sound file, and then, from the Options menu in the upper-right corner of the Library, choose Properties.

Either way, the Sound Properties dialog box you see in Figure 19-4 appears.

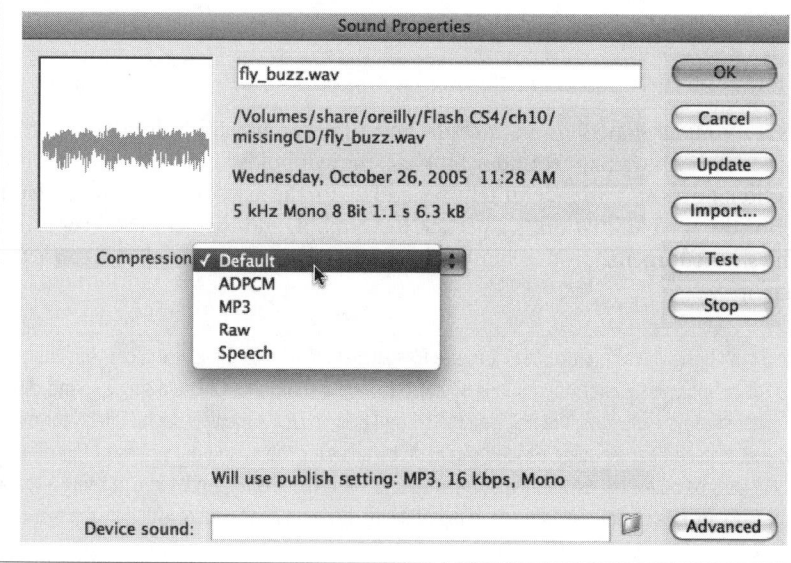

Figure 19-4:
If you leave compression set to Default, Flash uses the Compression option you set in the Publish Settings dialog box (page 632) to figure out how to compress this sound clip. Otherwise, Flash applies the Compression option you set here (unless you've told Flash to override this compression setting; see page 635 for details).

3. From the Compression drop-down list, choose a compression scheme.

Page 636 describes the different schemes.

4. When you're satisfied with the quality-vs.-file size tradeoff, click OK.

Flash hides the Sound Properties dialog box and brings you back to your workspace.

Note: To make sure Flash uses the Compression option you set in the Sound Properties dialog box, turn off the "Override sound settings" checkbox in the Publish Settings dialog box. Page 636 has details.

Group elements

Grouping shapes, lines, and other portions of your drawings (by selecting them, and then choosing Modify → Group) cuts down on file size because Flash can streamline in the information it needs to store. Chapter 5 (page 195) has full instructions.

Avoid the extraneous

The more you add to your animation, the larger your file size. If you absolutely, positively need to pare down your file, consider removing or simplifying some (or all) of your drawings, multimedia files, and graphic effects, paying particular attention to these space hogs:

• Sound files, embedded video clips, and bitmaps

• Gradient effects

• Alpha (transparency) effects

• Custom colors

Make sure your .swf files don't include any unnecessary symbols. Look in the Library panel. If it says Export under Linkage, the symbol is being exported for use with ActionScript and will definitely be added to the .swf. If the symbol isn't needed for the final animation, right-click the symbol, and then choose Properties from the shortcut menu. In the Symbol Properties dialog box, deselect Export for ActionScript.

Tip: If you can't bring yourself to do without media files altogether, go ahead and use them—but abbreviate them. For example, instead of using a long sound clip, loop a short one. Or use a single sound clip a bunch of different ways (soft, loud, the first half, the second half) to create multiple sound effects for minimal overhead. Instead of embedding a video clip as is, try adjusting the in and out points to clip off any nonessential intro or outro frames when you import it into Flash (page 356). And if you're using a mask layer (page 118), make sure you clip off every scrap of the background image not revealed by the mask.

Tell Flash to keep your file size down

One of the options you want to make sure you set when you're ready to publish your animation is the "Compress movie" option in the Publish Settings dialog box

---

(page 632). (Out of the box, Flash turns on this option, but do double-check that you haven't inadvertently turned it off.) Choosing this option tells Flash to squeeze your animation file as much as it can without sacrificing content. How much Flash compresses your file depends on the specific elements and effects you've included in your animation; the more text and ActionScript code your animation contains, for example, the more "bloat" Flash can squeeze out of your file.

Publishing Your Animations

Publishing your animation is Flash shorthand for "using the editable .fla file you work with in Flash to generate a noneditable file your audience can play."

The kind of noneditable file Flash produces depends on how you decide to publish your animation. Your choices include:

- **A compiled Flash file (.swf).** Flash Players, including the Flash Player plug-in that comes with most browsers, play .swf files. If you plan to include your Flash animation in a hand-coded HTML file (or to import it into a Web site creation program like Adobe Dreamweaver), you want this option.

- **A Web page (.html, .swf).** Choose this option if you want Flash to put together a simple Web page for you that includes your animation. (You can always tweak the HTML file later, either by hand or using another Web site creation program.)

- **An image file (.jpg, .gif, or .png).** This option lets you display one of the frames of your animation as an image file or as an animated GIF file—useful for those times when your audience doesn't have a Flash Player installed because at least they can see *part* of your animation. (For more advice on using ActionScript to detect your audience's Flash Player at runtime and offer alternatives, see the box on page 645.)

Note: Flash gives you another way to turn your artwork into an image file: by *exporting* it (page 654).

- **A standalone projector file (.exe, .hqx).** A *projector* file is a self-contained Flash-player-plus-your-animation file. Your audience can run a projector file to play your animation even if they don't have a copy of Flash Player installed. Typically, you choose this option if you plan to deliver your animation to your audience on CD or DVD (as opposed to over the Web). Projector files for Windows carry the .exe extension. If you create a Mac projector file in Windows, the projector extension that Flash creates is .hqx.

You can choose more than one publishing option at a time, simply by turning on as many checkboxes as you like in the Publish Settings dialog box. For example, you can publish your animation as a compiled Flash file, a Web page, and a stand-alone projector file all at once when you click Publish.

The following sections show you each of these five publishing options in detail.

Preloading

If you drop in on Flash user groups, you may hear talk of *preloading*, which is a strategy related to optimization. Preloading means that you use a frame-based script (Chapter 11) to download as much of your animation as you can before you actually need it. For example, to keep your audience entertained—in other words, to keep them from getting so bored waiting for your animation to download that they surf away in frustration—you might want to display a quick-to-download scene and loop it a few times while your real, byte-intensive animation quietly downloads in the background.

The ActionScript required to create your own preloader script is beyond the scope of this book, but Flash Help has details. Simply choose Help → Flash Help and search for "about loading and working with external media." (See Appendix A for more tips on using Flash Help.)

Publishing as a Compiled Flash (.swf) File

When you publish your animation as a .swf file, your audience can run it using a Flash Player—either a standalone version of Flash Player, or a Web browser plug-in version. Publishing as a .swf file gives you the flexibility of including your animation in a from-scratch Web page.

Note: If you've worked through any of the examples in this book, you're already familiar with .swf files. Each time you test your animation using Control → Test Movie, Flash automatically generates a .swf file and plays it in the Flash Player that comes with Flash.

To publish your animation as a compiled Flash (.swf) file:

1. **Choose File → Publish Settings.**

   A Publish Settings dialog box, similar to the one in Figure 19-5 appears. Here's where you tell Flash what kind of files to publish, and you can choose as few or as many as you like. When you turn on a checkbox, Flash shows you a panel where you can choose settings specific to that file type.

2. **Turn on the checkbox next to "Flash (.swf)", and then turn off all the other checkboxes.**

   The Flash tab appears next to the Formats tab.

3. **Click the Flash tab.**

   The Flash settings in Figure 19-6 appear.

4. **Change one or more of the following settings:**

   • **Player.** Lets you select the version of Flash Player you want to be able to run your animation. Choose the latest version (Flash Player 10) if you've included any of the new-in-Flash-10 features (page 5) or if you're not sure whether or not you've included any new features. If you know your audience is running an earlier version of Flash Player (for example, Flash Player 7) and you know you won't be using any new-in-Flash-10 features, you can choose the earlier version.

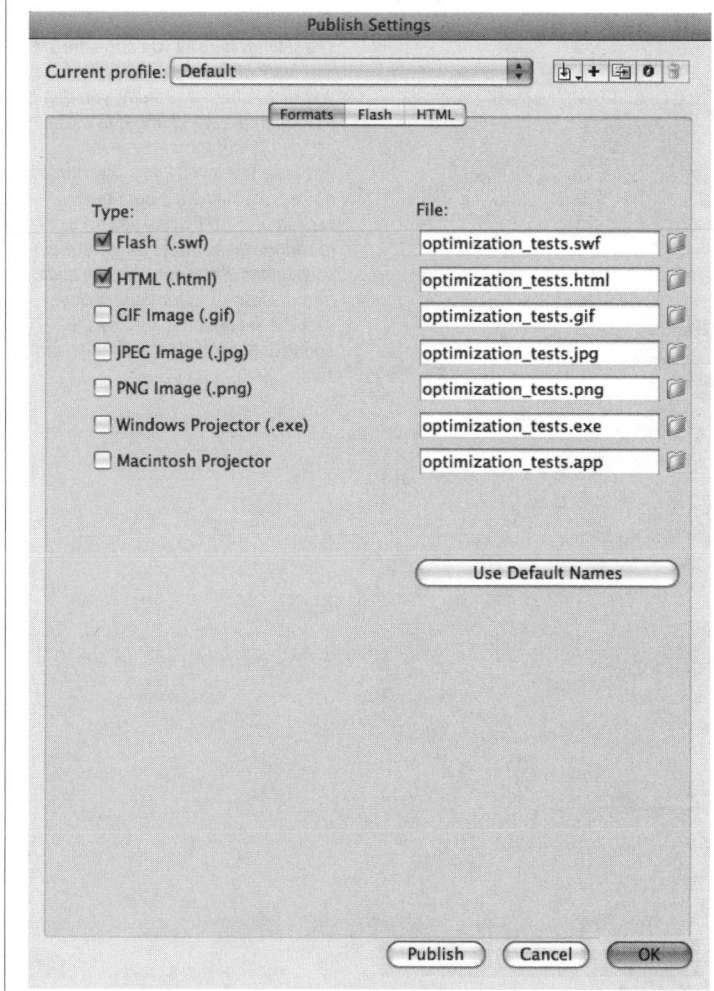

Flash activates the relatively unhelpful *Info* button only when you choose one of the Flash Lite versions. Flash Lite is a special Flash Player designed for handhelds, like handheld PCs and devices. (This book doesn't cover Flash Lite, but you can find out more about it by visiting the online sources listed in Appendix A: Installation and Help.)

Note: If you choose Flash Player 10 and it turns out your audience is running an earlier version of the player, like Flash Player 7, they may need to download and install Flash Player 10 in order to play your animation (depending on the features you included in your animation). Adobe makes a free downloadable copy of the latest Flash Player available at *www.adobe.com/products/flashplayer*, but it's your responsibility to let your audience know when (or if) they need to surf there and download a new player. For more information, see the box on page 645.

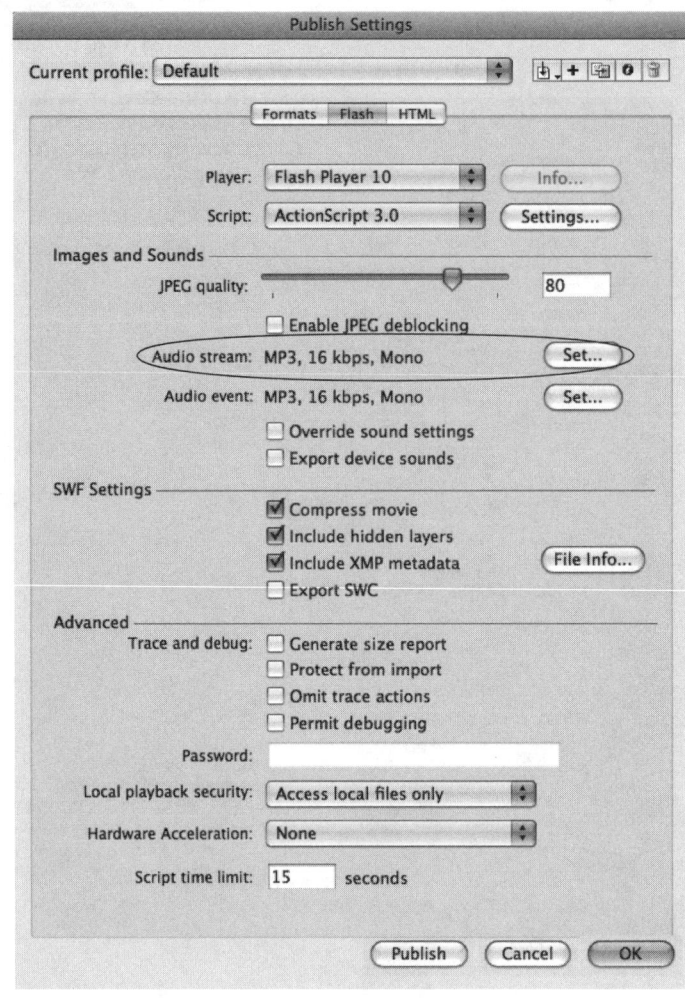

Figure 19-6:
The settings here let you fine-tune the .swf file that Flash generates when you click Publish. Normally, you don't have to make any changes to these settings. But in some cases—for example, when you know your target audience is running a backlevel version of Flash Player—you do want to change them. These pages explain each setting. If you don't like the audio format Flash picks for you (circled), click the Set button to display the Sound Settings dialog box shown in Figure 19-8.

- **Script.** Tells Flash which version of ActionScript to use. For the examples in this book, leave ActionScript 3.0 selected. If you venture into ActionScript 2.0, change this setting to match.

Note: If you're an ActionScript programmer and know for sure that your audience is running Flash Player 6 or earlier (or the Flash Lite player) and that you haven't included any ActionScript 2.0 or 3.0 statements in your actions, go ahead and choose ActionScript 1.0.

- **JPEG quality.** Lets you set the quality (and therefore the size) of the bitmaps you've added to your animation—but only for those bitmaps for which you've turned on the "Use document default quality" checkbox in the Bitmap Properties dialog box (Figure 19-7, top). To set JPEG quality, either drag the slider or, in the box, type a number from 1 to 100 (Figure 19-7, bottom).

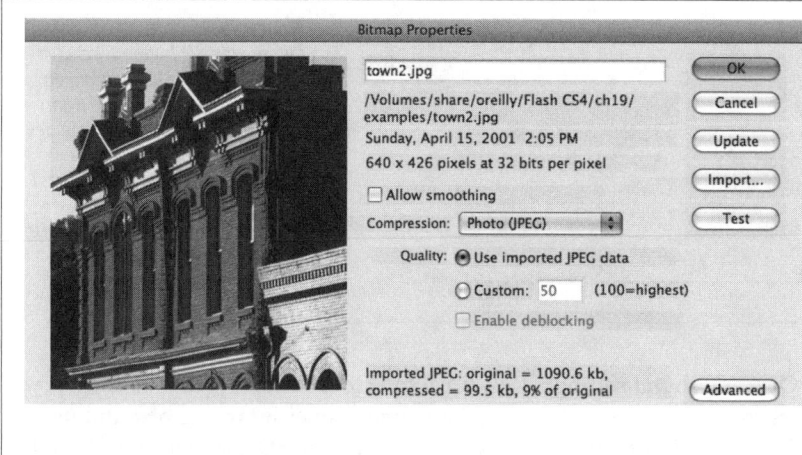

Figure 19-7:
If you turn on the checkbox next to "Use imported JPEG data", as shown here, Flash lets you set bitmap quality using the JPEG quality checkbox in the Publish Settings window's Flash tab. If you set the quality of your bitmap using the Bitmap Properties dialog box, however, Flash ignores the JPEG quality checkbox in the Publish Settings window. In other words, you can't tell Flash to compress the same image twice.

- **Enable JPEG deblocking.** Makes JPEG images that are highly compressed look better. As the term implies, it smoothes that blocky look you sometimes see in compressed photos.

- **Audio stream.** Tells Flash which compression scheme to use for streaming audio clips for which you haven't already specified a compression scheme (page 636). Flash displays the compression scheme it assumes you want. To specify another one, click the Set button, and then, in the Sound Settings dialog box that appears (Figure 19-8), choose the compression scheme you want.

- **Audio event.** Tells Flash which compression scheme to use for audio events for which you haven't already specified a compression scheme, using the Sound Properties dialog box. Flash displays the compression scheme it assumes you want. To specify another one, click the Set button next to "Audio event," and then, in the Sound Settings dialog box that appears, choose another compression scheme. Your options are identical to the options Flash gives you for setting "Audio stream" (see Figure 19-8), and they don't override individual sound properties unless you turn on "Override sound settings."

Note: Flash gives you two ways to specify a compression scheme for your sound clips. You can specify a compression scheme for individual sound clips using the Sound Properties dialog box (page 629) or you can specify one for all of the sound clips in your animation using the Audio Stream and Audio Event options you find in the Publish Settings window. (See this page and the next for more detail on the difference between audio streams and audio events.)

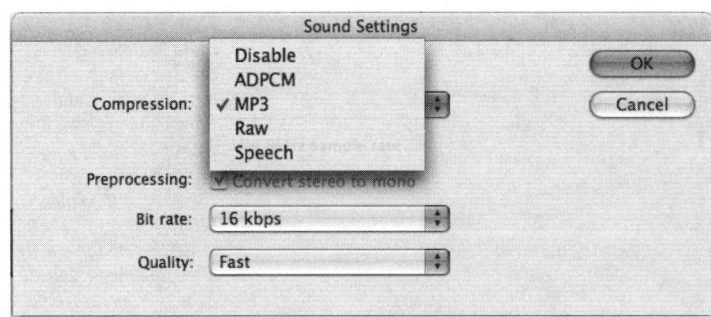

Figure 19-8:
Clicking the Set button (circled in
opens the Sound Settings dialog
box. Here, you can choose from
high-quality compression schemes
(like MP3, suitable for long,
continuous clips like soundtracks)
and lower-quality, byte-saving
schemes (like Speech or ADPCM).
Choosing Raw tells Flash not to
compress your sounds at all.

- **Override sound settings.** Tells Flash to ignore the compression schemes you set for your sound clips using the Sound Properties dialog box and use the compression schemes (both streaming and event) you set in the Publish Settings window instead. If you *don't* turn on this checkbox, Flash uses the compression settings you set in the Publish Settings window only for those sound clips assigned a Default setting in Sound Properties dialog box.

Note: Flash can only work with what you give it. Specifying a high-quality compression scheme doesn't improve a low-quality sound clip.

- **Export device sounds.** Tells Flash to include MIDI and other device sound files with the .swf file. Turn on this option only if you're targeting mobile devices.

- **Compress movie.** Tells Flash to reduce .swf file size as much as possible without sacrificing your animation's quality. Make sure this option is turned on. (Flash can't compress animations targeting pre-6 versions of Flash Player, but odds are you aren't doing that anyway.)

- **Include Hidden Layers.** Flash's factory settings export all the layers in your animation, even those that are hidden or nested in movie clips. Uncheck this option if you want to test or create different versions of your animation by hiding layers in the Flash file.

- **Include XMP metadata.** Publishes all the details about your animation included in the File Info box. Metadata is a standard method for storing details about a media file. To create metadata in the first place, choose File → File Info, and then fill in whatever information you want your audience to see.

- **Export SWC.** Lets ActionScript programmers distribute Flash components. Typically, .swc files contain a compiled clip, including the component's ActionScript class file and documentation that explains how to use the component.

- **Generate size report**. Tells Flash to list the bytes in your .fla file by frame, scene, action, object, and so on. This report is also useful for keeping track of the content you've added to your animation.

- **Protect from import**. Theoretically, this option tells Flash to encode your .swf file so that other folks can't import it into Flash and edit (steal!) your animation. Unfortunately, human nature being what it is, you can find programs floating around the Web to bypass this encoding. So if you need to reference sensitive information in your Flash animation (like passwords or confidential company info) don't store that information in Flash; instead, store it safely on a protected server and get it at runtime.

- **Omit trace actions**. Tells Flash to ignore any *trace( )* statements you've added to your ActionScript actions (page 437). It's best to turn this on before publishing a .swf that's going out in public. You don't need other folks with a Flash debugger seeing your trace details and trace statements can slow down playback.

Note: Flash Player won't display the Output panel or any *trace( )* actions even if you *don't* turn on the "Omit trace actions" checkbox. The only time you need to turn on this checkbox is if you plan to debug your animation remotely, using the special Flash Debug Player, but for some reason don't want to see your *trace( )* statements.

- **Permit Debugging**. Tells Flash to let you debug your animation remotely (over the Web) using the special Flash Debug Player browser plug-in. This book doesn't cover remote debugging, but you can find out more about it using Flash Help (see Appendix A).

- **Password**. If you've chosen "Protect from import" or "Debugging permitted," type a password in this box. Typing a password lets anyone with the password import the compiled .swf file into Flash at a later date, and then edit it—a potential security risk if your ActionScript code contains confidential company information. Typing a password also lets anyone with the password debug the .swf file remotely. (This book doesn't cover remote debugging.)

- **Local playback security**. Lets you tell Flash whether you want your .swf to be able to exchange information with *local files* (files located on your audience's computers) or *network files* (files located elsewhere on the Web).

- **Hardware Acceleration**. These settings let your animation take advantage of any advanced video hardware capabilities your audience's computers may have. The Direct option bypasses the computer browser and draws directly to the screen. The GPU option uses advanced graphics processing units if they're available.

- **Script time limit**. Sets the maximum time that scripts can take to run in a .swf file. If a script runs longer, Flash Player stops the script from running.

---

5. Click Publish.

The Publish Settings window disappears, and Flash generates a Flash file based on the name you set in the Formats tab. If you didn't type a name of your own choosing, Flash names the file similar to your .fla file. For example, if the name of your Flash document is *myAnimation.fla*, Flash generates a file named *myAnimation.swf*. If you click OK, Flash saves your settings and uses them later when you're ready to publish.

Tip: You don't have to go through the Publish Settings window every time you want to publish your animation. Once you've got the settings the way you want them, all you have to do is select File → Publish.

Publishing as a Web Page

If you want to put your animation on a Web page, a .swf file by itself isn't sufficient: You also have to create an HTML file (a Web page) that embeds that .swf file. You can create the HTML file either by using your favorite HTML editor or by telling Flash to generate a simple HTML file for you.

At a minimum, the HTML file needs to tell the Web browser how to display the .swf file: at the top of the page or in the middle, whether you want the animation to begin playing immediately or wait until the audience clicks a button, and so on.

Because most people who use Flash want to put their animations on the Web, Flash simplifies the process by letting you create a .swf in addition to a simple Web page (.html) in one fell swoop, using the Publish Settings dialog box.

POWER USERS' CLINIC

Creating a Publish Profile

Customizing all the different publishing settings Flash has can be time-consuming. If you suspect you'll want to reuse a batch of options—because, for example, your boss wants you to publish each animation both for Web pages and a Flash projector—you can save each batch of settings as a named profile: say, myWebPageProfile and myFlashProjectorProfile.

That way, when you want to publish a Web page version of your animation, for example, all you have to do is specify myWebPageProfile. When you want to change gears and publish a Flash Projector version, you can switch to myFlash-ProjectorProfile (instead of having to hunt through all the options, figure out which ones to change, and change them…again…and again…and again).

To create a publish profile:

1. In the Publish Settings dialog box, click the "Create new profile icon." (It looks like a + sign.)

2. In the Create New Profile dialog box that appears, type a name for your profile, and then click OK.

3. Flash saves all your current settings to that profile. As you continue to make changes in the Publish Settings window, Flash continues to save those changes to your profile.

4. You can create as many profiles as you like. To change profiles, click Current Profile, and then select a profile from the drop-down list.

To publish your animation as a Web page (.html and .swf):

1. **Choose File → Publish Settings.**

   The Publish Settings dialog box appears.

2. **Make sure the checkboxes next to "Flash (.swf)" and "HTML (.html)" are turned on; if they're not, turn them both on now.**

   The Flash and HTML tabs appear next to the Formats tab, as shown in Figure 19-9.

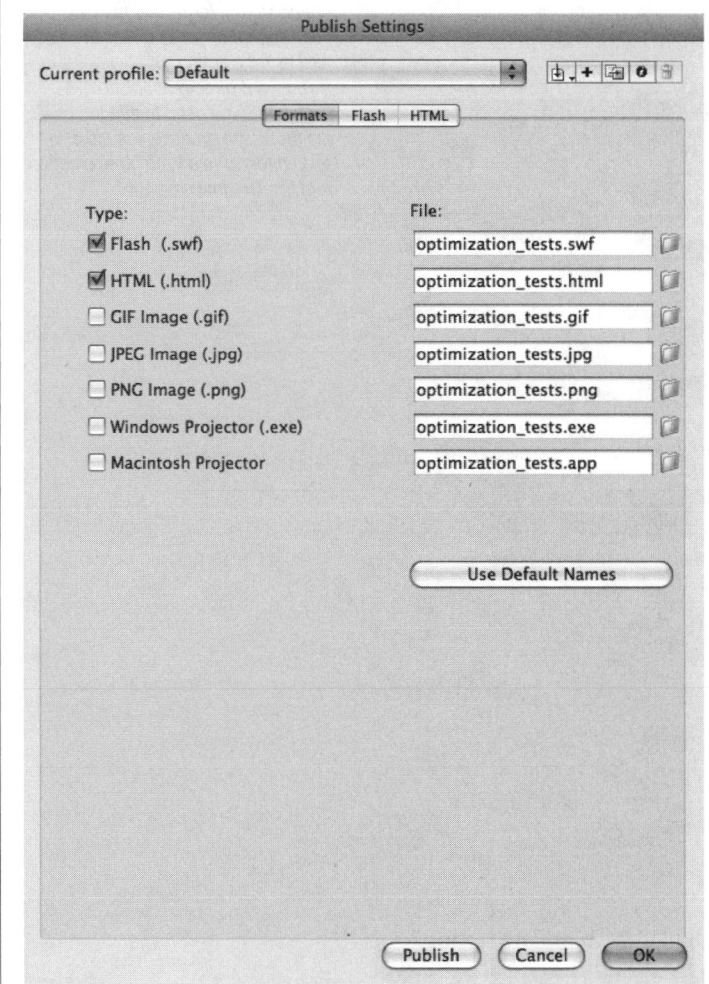

Figure 19-9:
Flash assumes you want to publish your animation on the Web–for which you need both a .swf file and a .html file–unless you tell it otherwise. You can change the suggested file names, all of which begin with the name of your Flash document (here, optimization_tests).

---

3. **Click the Flash tab, and then set up your .swf file.**

   For the details, see step 4 on on page 632.

4. **Click the HTML tab.**

   The HTML publish settings you see in Figure 19-10 appear.

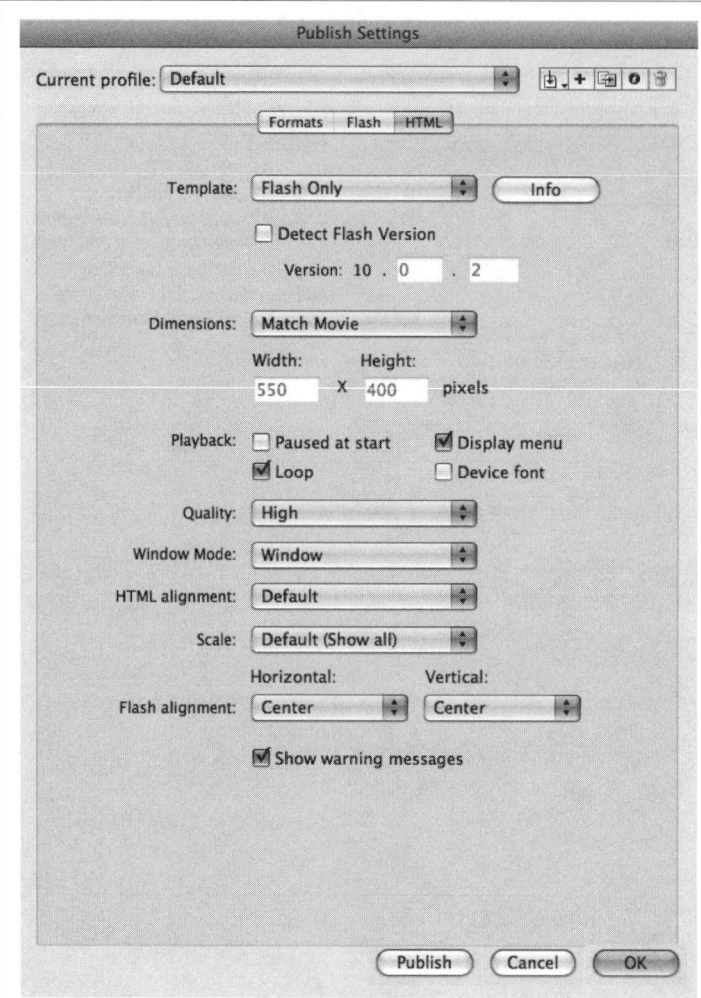

Figure 19-10:
These settings let you tell Flash how you want your animation to be included in your Web page. This option's great for testing the way your animation looks on the Web as well as for creating simple pages. But if you want a really sophisticated Web page, you need to edit the HTML file that Flash produces—in either a text editor, or in a Web page creation tool like Dreamweaver.

5. **If you like, change the template setting.**

   Most of the time, you want to stick with the "Flash only" template that Flash assumes you want. But if you've added certain elements to your animation, or if you want to target a specific Web browser, Flash needs to insert special HTML tags into the template it uses. In that case, you may need one of the following options:

- **Flash for Pocket PC 2003.** Creates an HTML file that runs on Pocket PC 2003.

- **Flash HTTPS.** Choose this option if you plan to upload your HTML and .swf file to a secure Web server (https://).

- **Flash Only.** Creates a basic HTML file that runs in any Web browser.

- **Flash Only—Allow Full Screen.** Used only with Flash Player 9 or later. This option adds a parameter to the HTML code that lets Flash content run in Full Screen mode. The animation fills an entire monitor without menus, borders, or the other usual computer paraphernalia.

- **Flash with AICC Tracking.** Choose this option if you've added Learning Interaction components (Window → Common Libraries → Learning Interactions) to your animation and plan to have these components interact with an AICC learning management system. (AICC stands for Aviation Industry CBT Committee.)

- **Flash with FSCommand.** Choose this option if you've included the Action-Script *fscommand( )* statement in your animation. (*fscommand( )* lets your Flash animation call a JavaScript statement. JavaScript is the scripting language supported by most Web browsers.)

- **Flash with Named Anchors.** Choose this option if you've organized your animation into named scenes (Chapter 14). Flash generates the tags necessary to let people surf directly from scene to scene using their browsers' Back buttons.

- **Flash with SCORM 1.2 Tracking** and **Flash with SCORM 2004 Tracking.** Choose one of these options if you've added Learning Interaction components (Window → Common Libraries → Learning Interactions) to your animation, and plan to have these components interact with a SCORM learning management system. (SCORM stands for Shareable Content Object Reference Model.)

- **Image Map.** Choosing this option tells Flash to create an HTML image map (which an HTML-savvy person can turn into hotspots). For this option to work, you need to have added the frame label *#map* to the frame you want Flash to turn into an image map, and you have to have chosen GIF Image (.gif), JPEG Image (.jpg) or PNG Image (.png) in addition to HTML (.html) in the Formats tab of the Publish Settings window. (Chapter 14 explains how to add frame labels.)

6. **If you chose "Flash Only" or "Flash HTTPS" in the previous step, you can now turn on Detect Flash Version/Version to help make sure your audience has the correct version of Flash Player to view your animation.**

When you turn on the checkbox for this option, your audience sees a Web page telling them where to download the latest Flash Player (but only if the version of Flash Player they have installed doesn't match the version of Flash Player you

---

specify in the Version box). For example, if you type a Version of 10.0.0, someone trying to run your animation with version 7.0 Flash Player sees a Web page
similar to the one shown in Figure 19-11. When you turn on Detect Flash Version, anyone who doesn't have the version of Flash Player you specify sees this
Web page (instead of the Web page containing your animation). Clicking the
Get Flash link whisks your audience to Adobe, where they can download a free
copy of the correct Flash Player. You can edit this HTML file if you'd like to
reword the message, and of course you have to upload it to your Web server
along with the .swf file in order for your audience to see its contents. (See the
box on on page 645 for further advice.)

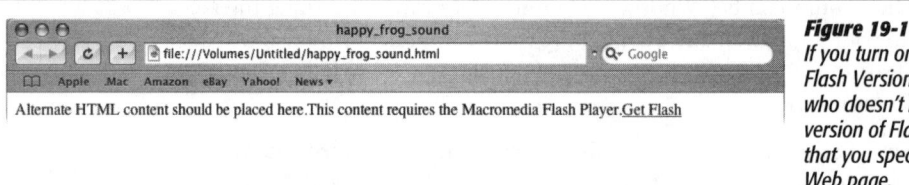

Figure 19-11:
*If you turn on Detect
Flash Version, anyone
who doesn't have the
version of Flash Player
that you specify sees this
Web page.*

7. **Turn on any of the following settings if you'd like you tweak how your animation appears in the Web page—which may be different from how it appears in
Flash on the stage:**

- **Dimensions.** Lets you tell Flash how large you want your animation to
appear in the Web page. Your options are *Match Movie*, which tells Flash to
use the dimensions of the stage you specified in the Document Properties
window (page 42); Pixels, which tells Flash you want to specify new height
and width dimensions in pixels (see below); and *Percent*, which tells Flash
you want to specify new height and width dimensions as a percentage of the
Web page display (see below).

- **Width/Height.** Lets you specify your animation's width and height in the
Web page in pixels or in a percentage of the Web page.

- **Paused at start.** Tells Flash *not* to begin playing your animation as soon as
your audience loads your Web page into their browser. If you choose this
option, make sure you either turn on Display menu (see below) or—a better
solution—make sure you've included an obvious visible Play button in your
animation. Otherwise, your audience won't be able to play your masterpiece.

- **Display menu.** Tells Flash to include a shortcut menu for your animation so
that when your audience right-clicks (Windows) or Control-clicks (Mac),
they see animation controller options like Zoom In, Zoom Out, Play, Loop,
Rewind, Forward, and Back.

- **Loop.** Tells Flash to automatically play your animation over and over again.

- **Device font.** Tells Flash to check your audience's Windows computer for fonts that match the fonts in your animation. If Flash doesn't find any matching fonts, it substitutes the closest system fonts it can find on your audience's computer. (This option only applies to Windows computers.)

- **Quality.** Tells Flash how precisely (and how processor-intensively) you want it to *render*, or draw, your animation on your audience's computer. Your options range from Low to Best.

8. **Choose one of the following Window Mode settings to tell Flash how you want your animation to appear with respect to HTML/DHTML content that you add to your .html file:**

   - **Window.** This standard mode tells Flash to place your animation in a rectangular area on the Web page. HTML content can appear around the animation.

   - **Opaque Windowless.** Tells Flash to place your animation on top of HTML content.

   - **Transparent Windowless.** Tells Flash to erase the background of your animation (the blank parts of the stage) so that HTML and DHTML content can show through.

   - **HTML alignment.** Tells Flash how you want it to align your animation with respect to the rest of your Web page—the text, images, and so on you plan to add to your HTML file. Your options include *Default* (center), *Left, Right, Top,* or *Bottom.*

9. **Choose one of the following Scale options to tell Flash whether to stretch or crop your animation in those cases where your stage size doesn't match the height/width dimensions you set in the Publish Settings window (page 646).**

   - **Default (Show All).** Fits as much of the animation into the height/width dimensions you set as possible without stretching or distorting the animation. If there's extra room left over, Flash fills in the empty spaces with black bands, letterbox style.

   - **No border.** Fits as much of the animation into the height/width dimensions you set as possible without stretching or distorting the animation. If there's extra room left over, Flash crops it.

   - **Exact fit.** Stretches (or squishes) the animation to fit the height/width dimensions you set.

   - **No scale.** Tells Flash to preserve the stage height/width dimensions you set in the Document Properties dialog box.

   - **Flash alignment: Horizontal.** Tells Flash how you want to align your animation with respect to the dimensions you set in the Publish Settings dialog box —in other words, how you want to position your animation horizontally inside the width-and-height box you're adding to your Web page. Your options include *Left, Center,* and *Right.*

Note: See "HTML alignment" in the previous step if you want to align the width-and-height box with respect to your Web page (as opposed to aligning your animation with respect to the width-and-height box, which you do using "Flash alignment," as described on page 643).

- **Flash alignment: Vertical.** Tells Flash how you want to align your animation with respect to the dimensions you set in the Publish Settings dialog box s; in other words, how you want to position your animation vertically inside the width-and-height box you're adding to your Web page. Your options include Top, Center, and Bottom.

Note: You need to know when Flash encounters problems so that you can fix them, so make sure the "Show warning messages" option is always turned on. Turning on this option tells Flash to pop up any errors that happen during the publishing process.

10. **Click Publish.**

The Publish Settings window disappears, and Flash generates both an HTML file and a Flash file based on the names you set in the Formats tab. If you didn't type names of your own choosing, Flash names both files similar to your .fla file. For example, if the name of your Flash document is *myAnimation.fla*, Flash generates a file named *myAnimation.html* and *myAnimation.swf.* To make your HTML file and Flash animation available on the Web, you'll need to upload both of these files to your Web server.

Tip: Sometimes, after you've published your .html and .swf files, you may want to change the name of your Web page (.html) to match the other pages on your Web site. You can do that without a problem, as long as you don't change the extension (.html). On the other hand, if you change the name of your animation (.swf), say from *myAnimation.swf* to *thatAnimation.swf*, the HTML code won't know how to find it and it won't run in the Web page.

Publishing a Frame as a Static Image File

It may seem odd that Flash lets you publish a frame of your animation as a single, static image—after all, the point of using Flash is creating animations, not images. But publishing your animation as an image file (in addition to publishing it as a Flash file) can be a savvy design choice: If some people don't have a Flash Player installed on their machines and so can't see your animation, at least they can see your opening frame. Also, sometimes Web designers use static images produced by Flash as graphic links to the animation.

Note: When you *do* choose to publish an image file, you're the one who needs to create the HTML to display that image file; Flash doesn't do it for you when you select the "HTML (.html)" option in the Formats tab of the Publish Settings window.

DESIGN TIME

The Problem with Detecting Your Audience's Flash Version

If you create an animation that uses only Flash 10 features, your audience won't be able to play it in an earlier version of Flash Player. But how do you know which version of Flash Player your audience has installed? And if it turns out they *are* running an earlier version, how can they see your animation?

The easiest approach to this dilemma is the one most Flash-ionados opt for: using the Detect Flash Version publishing option described on page 641.

But making people jump through hoops before they can see your animation isn't always the best design choice. For one thing, not everyone wants to stop what they're doing and download yet another plug-in. For another, folks in many corporate settings aren't allowed to download and install software of any kind, even a free Flash Player.

Fortunately, hoop-jumping isn't necessary: Computers excel at this kind of automatic detect-this-and-do-that process. With a little bit of elbow grease, you can devise a more seamless, professional approach, like:

- Detecting your audience's installed Flash Player and automatically displaying a version of your animation that runs in that player

- Having your HTML file substitute a static image or animated GIF file if it doesn't find the correct Flash Player

- Having your animation download and install the correct version of Flash Player for your audience so they don't have to

Adobe maintains several TechNote Web pages devoted to this oh-so-common design problem. You'll find descriptions, examples and sample code at *www.adobe.com/products/ flashplayer/download/detection_kit/*.

Many Flash programming folks use another option, called SWFObject, to detect the presence of a Flash Player in their audience's browsers. A small chunk of JavaScript code—SWFObject—is easy to use and works with both HTML and XHTML. You can find SWFObject and more details at: *www. adobe.com/devnet/flash/articles/swfobject.html*.

Publishing a static GIF

GIF (Graphic Interchange Format) files are super-small, thanks in part to the fact that they limit your image to 256 colors. GIF files are the best choice for vector images containing just a few areas of solid color.

Note: Another way to create static images is to export them by choosing File → Export → Export Image (page 654).

To publish a frame of your animation as a static GIF file:

1. **In the timeline, click to select the frame you want to publish.**

   Flash highlights the selected frame. On the stage, you see the image you're about to publish.

Note: Another way to tell Flash which frame you want to publish is to add the frame label #*Static* to the frame you want to publish. Make sure you've selected a file type (like GIF, JPG or PNG) for the image as described in step 3. Chapter 14 (page 482) shows you how to label a frame.

---

2. **Choose File → Publish Settings.**

   The Publish Settings dialog box appears.

3. **Turn on the checkbox next to "GIF Image (.gif)."**

   The GIF tab appears next to the Formats tab.

4. **Click the GIF tab.**

   The GIF publishing options shown in Figure 19-12 appear.

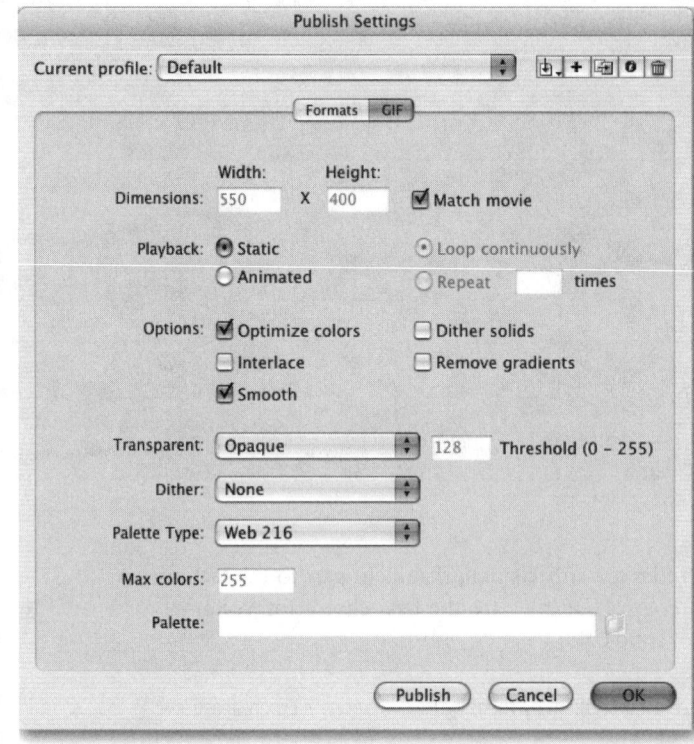

Figure 19-12:
GIFs are generally the most compact of the three static image file formats, but they're also the most restrictive: They can display only 256 colors. (If the image you're exporting contains a bunch of custom colors, your GIF may look slightly off.) Two different types of GIFs exist: static and animated. In this section, you see how to publish frame content to a static GIF.

5. **Choose one or more of the following publishing options:**

   • **Dimensions (Width/Height).** Tells Flash how large you want the GIF file to be, in pixels. These options are available only if you haven't turned on "Match movie" (see below).

   • **Match movie.** Tells Flash to create a GIF image the same size as the stage.

   • **Static/Animated.** Tells Flash whether to create a static GIF file or an animated GIF file. Make sure you turn on Static. (Page 652 shows you how to create an animated GIF file.)

- **Optimize colors**. Lowers file size as much as possible without sacrificing image quality. Always make sure you turn this option on.

- **Interlace**. Tells Flash to create a GIF that downloads in several passes, so that a fuzzy version appears first, then a clearer version, then a still clearer version, and so on. Turning on this option doesn't reduce download time, but it does give your audience quick successive "tastes" of the image while they're waiting—useful for very large images.

- **Smooth**. Tells Flash to smooth (anti-alias) your image. Turning on this option may improve the look of any text your image contains; it can also save a few bytes.

- **Dither solids**. Tells Flash to attempt to match any solid custom colors you've used as closely as it can by combining two colors. If you don't turn on this option, Flash chooses the nearest-in-shade solid color in its palette.

- **Remove gradients**. Tells Flash to convert the gradients in your image to solid colors. (Gradient effects don't translate well to the GIF format anyway, so if your image contains gradient effects, you probably want to turn on this option.)

- **Transparent**. Lets you specify the transparency of your image background (the blank area of the stage). Your options include *Opaque* (a regular, solid background), *Transparent* (no background), or *Alpha* and *Threshold* (lets you choose how transparent you want the background to appear).

- **Dither**. Tells Flash to *dither* (mix two colors) to try to match all the non-solid areas of your image as closely as possible. Your options include *None* (no dithering), *Ordered* (minimal dithering, minimal file size increase), and *Diffusion* (maximum dithering, maximum file size increase).

- **Palette Type**. Lets you tell Flash which 256 colors to use to create the GIF image. (GIFs are limited to 256 colors, but you get to pick which 256.) Your options include *Web 216* (Web-safe colors), *Adaptive* (non-Web-safe colors), *Web Snap Adaptive* (a mix of Web-safe and non-Web-safe colors), and *Custom* (lets you specify a color palette you've saved as an .act file, using a program like Fireworks). Depending on the image you're publishing, one of these options may yield better-looking results—although in most cases, you want to leave this option set to Web 216.

- **Max colors**. Available only if you've selected a Palette Type of Adaptive or Web Snap Adaptive (see above), this option lets you specify a maximum number of colors lower than 256 to save on file size.

- **Palette**. Available only if you've selected a Palette Type of Custom (see above), this option lets you type the file name of your own custom color palette. The palette has to have been created using another program, like Fireworks, and saved with the .act file extension. If you prefer, you can click the file icon to browse your computer for the palette file name.

---

6. **Click Publish.**

The Publish Settings window disappears, and Flash generates a GIF file based on the name you set in the Formats tab. If you didn't type a name, Flash names the GIF file similar to your .fla file. For example, if the name of your Flash document is *myAnimation.fla*, Flash generates a file named *myAnimation.gif*.

Publishing a JPEG

JPEG (Joint Photographic Experts Group) files typically don't end up being as small as GIF files, but they can contain many more colors. Sometimes referred to as the "photo format," JPEG is the best choice if your image, like a scanned-in photograph, contains lots of colors, subtle shading, or gradient effects.

To publish a frame of your animation as a JPEG file:

1. **In the timeline, click to select the frame you want to publish.**

   Flash highlights the selected frame. On the stage, you see the image you're about to publish.

2. **Choose File → Publish Settings.**

   The Publish Settings dialog box appears.

3. **Turn on the checkbox next to "JPEG Image (.jpg)."**

   The JPEG tab appears next to the Formats tab.

4. **Click the JPEG tab.**

   The JPEG publishing options shown in Figure 19-13 appear.

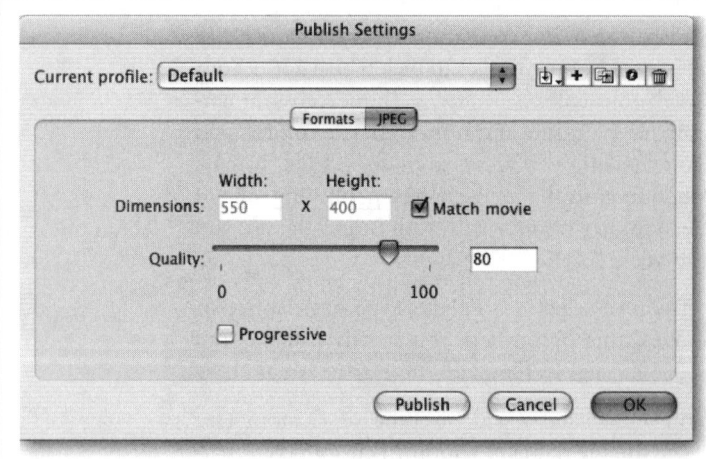

Figure 19-13:
Publishing a frame of your animation as a JPEG file is a pretty cut-and-dried process. As you can see here, the only options Flash gives you are to specify your image's JPEG version's size and quality.

5. **Choose one or more of the following publishing options:**

- **Dimensions (Width/Height)**. Tells Flash how large you want the JPEG file to be, in pixels. These options are available only if you haven't turned on "Match movie," described next.

- **Match movie**. Tells Flash to create a JPEG image the same size as the stage.

- **Quality**. Tells Flash how much detail you want it to include. The larger the number you type (or specify by dragging the slider), the better your JPEG image will look, and the larger your JPEG file size will be. (Depending on your particular image, the image quality may appear similar enough at different quality levels that you can get away with a lower number, thereby whittling away at your animation's finished file size. See page 624 for more on optimization.)

- **Progressive**. Similar to the GIF's Interlace option (page 647), turning on this option tells Flash to create a JPEG that downloads in several passes, so that a fuzzy version appears first, then a clearer version, then a still clearer version, and so on. Turning on this option doesn't reduce download time, but it does give your audience quick successive "tastes" of the image while they're waiting, which some audiences appreciate.

6. **Click Publish.**

The Publish Settings window disappears, and Flash generates a JPEG file based on the name you set in the Formats tab. If you didn't type a name, Flash names the JPEG file similar to your .fla file. For example, if the name of your Flash document is *myAnimation.fla*, Flash generates a file named *myAnimation.jpg*.

Publishing a PNG

Developed to replace and improve on the GIF file format (back when it looked like Web developers would have to pay royalties for every GIF they produced), the PNG (Portable Network Graphics) file format offers the best of both worlds: the tiny file size of a static GIF with the support for 24-bit color of a JPEG. PNG files can include transparent (alpha) effects, too.

To publish a frame of your animation as a PNG file:

1. **In the timeline, click to select the frame you want to publish.**

Flash highlights the selected frame. On the stage, you see the image you're about to publish.

2. **Choose File → Publish Settings.**

The Publish Settings dialog box appears.

3. **Turn on the checkbox next to "PNG Image (.png)."**

   The PNG tab appears next to the Formats tab.

4. **Click the PNG tab.**

   The PNG publishing options shown in Figure 19-14 appear.

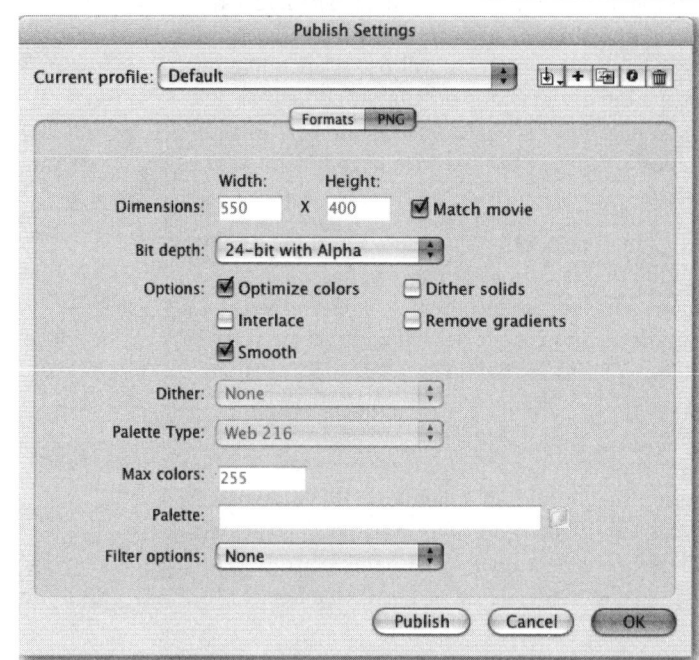

Figure 19-14:
*Some older Web browsers—for
example, Internet Explorer versions
6 and earlier—don't completely
support PNG files. If you want to
publish a static image but you're
not sure which browser your
audience has installed, you may
want to opt for GIF or JPEG instead.*

5. **Choose one or more of the following publishing options:**

   • **Dimensions (Width/Height).** Tells Flash how large you want the PNG file to
     be, in pixels. These options are available only if you haven't turned on
     "Match movie," described next.

   • **Match movie.** Tells Flash to create a PNG image the same size as the stage.

   • **Bit depth.** Tells Flash how many colors you want the PNG to be able to render.
     Your options include 8-bit (256 colors, the same as GIF), 24-bit (16.7 mil-
     lion colors), and 24-bit with Alpha (16.7 million colors plus the ability to
     render your image background as transparent). The more colors, the larger
     the file size.

   • **Optimize colors.** Reduces file size without sacrificing the quality of your
     image. You always want to turn this option on.

- **Interlace.** Tells Flash to create a PNG that downloads in several passes, so that a fuzzy version appears first, then a clearer version, then a still clearer version, and so on. Turning on this option doesn't reduce download time, but it does give your audience quick successive "tastes" of the image while they're waiting—useful for very large images.

- **Smooth.** Tells Flash to smooth (anti-alias) your image. Turning on this option may improve the look of any text your image contains; it can also save a few bytes of file size.

- **Dither solids.** Tells Flash to attempt to match any solid custom colors you've used as closely as it can by combining two colors (only necessary if you choose a Bit depth of 8-bit as described above). If you don't turn on this option, Flash chooses the nearest-in-shade solid color in its palette.

- **Remove gradients.** Tells Flash to convert the gradients in your image to solid colors to save on file size.

- **Dither.** Tells Flash to *dither* (mix two colors) to try to match all the nonsolid areas of your image as closely as possible (only necessary if you've chosen a Bit depth of 8-bit). Your options include None (no dithering), Ordered (minimal dithering, minimal file size increase), and Diffusion (maximum dithering, maximum file size increase).

- **Palette Type.** Available only if you choose a bit depth of 8-bit (see above), this option lets you tell Flash which 256 colors to use to create the PNG image. Your options include *Web 216* (Web-safe colors), *Adaptive* (non-Web-safe colors), *Web Snap Adaptive* (a mix of Web-safe and non-Web-safe colors), and *Custom* (lets you specify a color palette you've saved as an .act file, using a program like Fireworks). Depending on the image you're publishing, one of these options may yield better-looking results—although in most cases, you want to leave this option set to Web 216.

- **Max colors.** Available only if you've selected a Palette Type of Adaptive or Web Snap Adaptive (see above), this option lets you specify a maximum number of colors lower than 256.

- **Palette.** Available only if you've selected a Palette Type of Custom (see above), this option lets you type the file name of your own custom color palette. The palette has to have been created using another program, like Fireworks, and saved with the .act file extension. If you prefer, you can click the file icon to browse your computer for the palette file name.

- **Filter options.** This option lets you tell Flash to apply an additional compression algorithm when it's creating your PNG file. Normally, you don't use this option unless you're trying to pare down your PNG file by a few bytes. Your options include *None, Sub, Up, Average, Paeth*, and *Adaptive*.

6. **Click Publish.**

The Publish Settings window disappears, and Flash generates a PNG file based on the name you set in the Formats tab. If you didn't type a name, Flash names the PNG file similar to your .fla file. For example, if the name of your Flash document is *myAnimation.fla*, Flash generates a file named *myAnimation.png*.

Publishing as an Animated GIF

In addition to static images, the GIF file format lets you create animated images. Animated GIFs are mini-animations that play right in the Web browser, with no need for a Flash browser. The quality isn't always stellar and your audience can't interact with them (which is why Flash was invented). But depending on how long your animation is, and what quality of playback you're shooting for, they can be an impressive alternative.

To publish your animation as an animated GIF file:

1. **Choose File → Publish Settings.**

The Publish Settings dialog box appears.

2. **Turn on the checkbox next to GIF Image (.gif).**

The GIF tab appears next to the Formats tab.

3. **Click the GIF tab.**

The GIF publishing options shown in Figure 19-15 appear.

4. **Set the publishing options you see in Figure 19-15 just as you would for a static GIF file (page 645) except for the following:**

   • **Static/Animated.** This option tells Flash whether to create a static or animated GIF file. Make sure you turn on Animated.

   • **Loop continuously.** Turn on this option to tell Flash to replay the animated GIF over and over again.

   • **Repeat.** Tells Flash to create an animated GIF that automatically plays the number of times you type into the times box.

5. **Click Publish.**

The Publish Settings window disappears, and Flash generates a GIF file based on the name you set in the Formats tab. If you didn't type a name, Flash names the GIF file similar to your .fla file. For example, if the name of your Flash document is *myAnimation.fla*, Flash generates a file named *myAnimation.gif*.

Publishing as a Standalone Projector

A *projector* is the equivalent of a .swf file and a copy of Flash Player all rolled up into a single executable file. When you create a projector, your audience doesn't need to have either a Web browser or a Flash Player installed on their computers: All they need to do to play your animation is run the projector file.

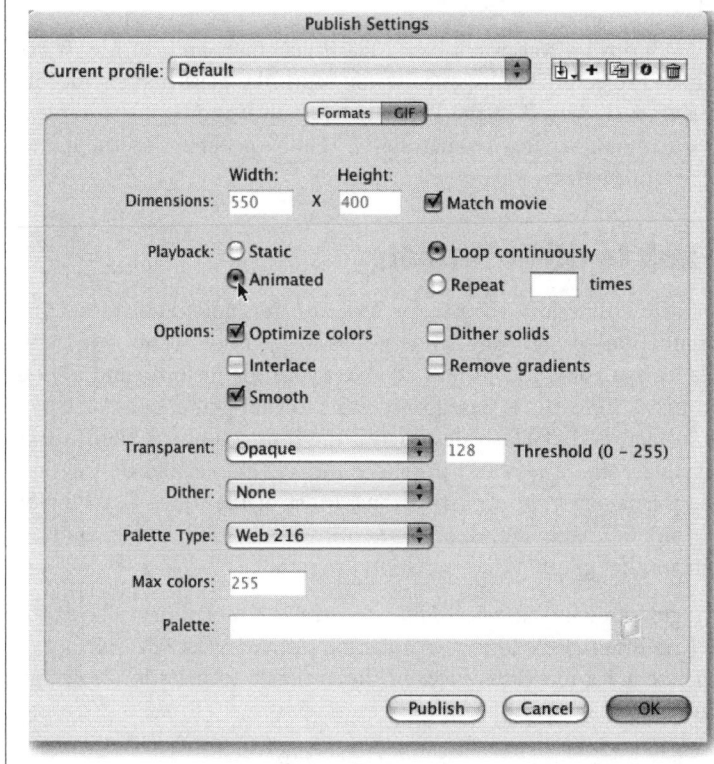

Figure 19-15:
*Animated GIFs are amazing
creatures: small, decent quality
(especially if you're only talking
about a few frames), and as easy to
include in an HTML file as a static
GIF file (the basic line of HTML code
you need is <img src="yourGIF.gif"/
>). The only extra settings you have
to specify for an animated GIF, as
opposed to a static GIF, are whether
you want the animated GIF to loop
continuously, loop a few times, or
not loop at all.*

You'll want to choose this option if you want to deliver your animation on a CD or DVD (as opposed to over the Web). Tutorials, product demonstrations, and program mock-ups (as well as the programs themselves) are all examples of the kinds of animations you might want to publish as projectors.

Note: If you plan to distribute a Flash projector to folks outside your company, take a look at the Adobe Player Distribution License, a legal-ese description of what you can and can't do with your projector files. Adobe may change the location of this document, but the time of this writing, you can find a copy online at *www.adobe.com/products/players/fpsh_distribution1.html*.

To publish your animation as a standalone projector:

1. **Choose File → Publish Settings.**

   The Publish Settings dialog box appears.

2. **Turn on the checkbox next to one or both of the following, depending on the operating system you expect your audience to be running:**

   • **Windows Projector (.exe)** to create a projector that runs on Windows.

   • **Macintosh Projector** to create a projector that runs on the Mac.

3. Click Publish.

If you chose "Windows Projector (.exe)", Flash generates an .exe file. If you chose Macintosh Projector, Flash generates an .app file. Flash names the files based on the names displayed in the Formats tab. For example, if the name of your Flash document is myAnimation.fla, Flash generates files named *myAnimation.exe* or *myAnimation.app*.

Exporting Flash to Other Formats

Exporting your entire animation—or one or more of the individual frames that make up your animation—is very similar to publishing. In both cases, you get to specify which file format you'd like Flash to convert your .fla file into, and in both cases, you get to tweak file settings based on the file format you choose. The only real difference, in fact, is that Flash designated the most common file formats (.html, .swf, .gif, .jpg, .png, .mov, and projector files) as publishing destinations and all other file formats as export destinations. Most of the time, you'll export (rather than publish) an image, sound, or your entire animation because you want to work with it in another graphics or animation program.

To export to a single frame image, select File → Export → Export Image. To export to an animation (multiframe) file format or an audio format, select File → Export → Export Movie. There are a few differences in the available formats for Macs and PCs, as shown in Table 19-1.

Table 19-1. File formats to which you can export your Flash animation

Format	Extension	Platform	Note
SWF Movie	.swf	Windows, Mac	Single Frame Image
PICT file	.pct	Mac	Single Frame Image
Enhanced Metafile	.emf	Windows	Single Frame Image
Windows Metafile	.wmf	Windows	Single Frame Image
Adobe Illustrator	.ai	Windows, Mac	Single Frame Image
Bitmap	.bmp	Windows	Single Frame Image
JPEG Image	.jpg	Windows, Mac	Single Frame Image
GIF Image	.gif	Windows, Mac	Single Frame Image
PNG Image	.png	Windows, Mac	Single Frame Image
SWF Movie	.swf	Windows, Mac	Animation
Windows AVI	.avi	Windows	Animation
QuickTime	.mov	Windows, Mac	Animation
Animated GIF	.gif	Windows, Mac	Animation
Pict Sequence	.pct	Mac	Animation
WAV Audio	.wav	Windows	Audio
EMF Sequence	.emf	Windows	Animation

Table 19-1. *File formats to which you can export your Flash animation (continued)*

Format	Extension	Platform	Note
WMF Sequence	.wmf	Windows	Animation
Bitmap Sequence	.bmp	Windows	Animation
JPEG Sequence	.jpg	Windows, Mac	Animation
GIF Sequence	.gif	Windows, Mac	Animation
PNG Sequence	.png	Windows, Mac	Animation

Exporting the Contents of a Single Frame

Exporting the contents of a single frame of your animation lets you create a one-frame animation or (more commonly) an image file you can edit with another image-editing program.

Note: Exporting an image from one animation, and then importing the image into another animation is one way to share images between Flash documents. You can also share by saving the image as a graphic symbol in one animation, and then using the Library panel's drop-down list to add the symbol to another animation, as described in Chapter 6.

1. **On the stage, click to select the frame you want to export.**

   Flash highlights the selected frame.

2. **Choose File → Export → Export Image.**

   The Export Image dialog box you see in Figure 19-16 appears.

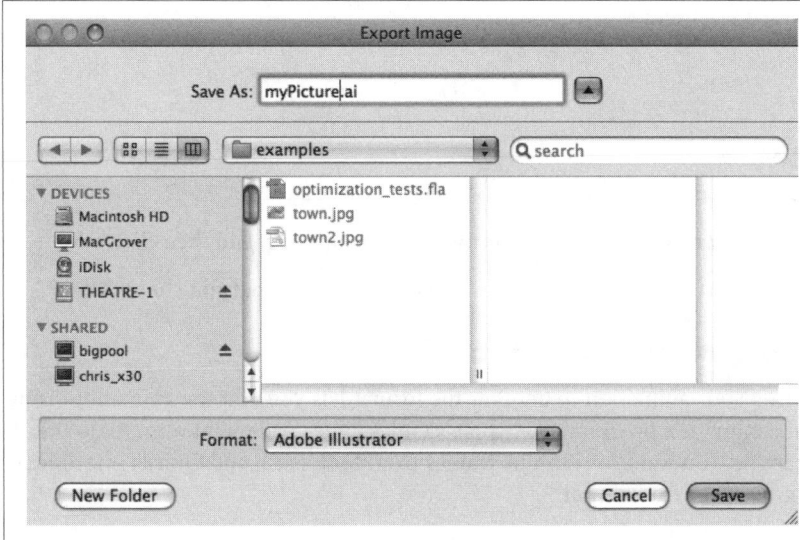

Figure 19-16:
The Export Image dialog box lets you export a frame to any of the following image formats: SWF movie, PICT, Adobe Illustrator, JPEG, GIF, or PNG file.

3. From the pop-up menu, choose the file format to which you want to export.

In Windows, this menu is called "Save as type"; on the Mac, it's called Format.

4. In the Save As box, type a name for your exported file.

Leave the file extension Flash suggests.

5. Click Save.

Flash displays an Export window containing format-specific settings, as shown in Figure 19-17.

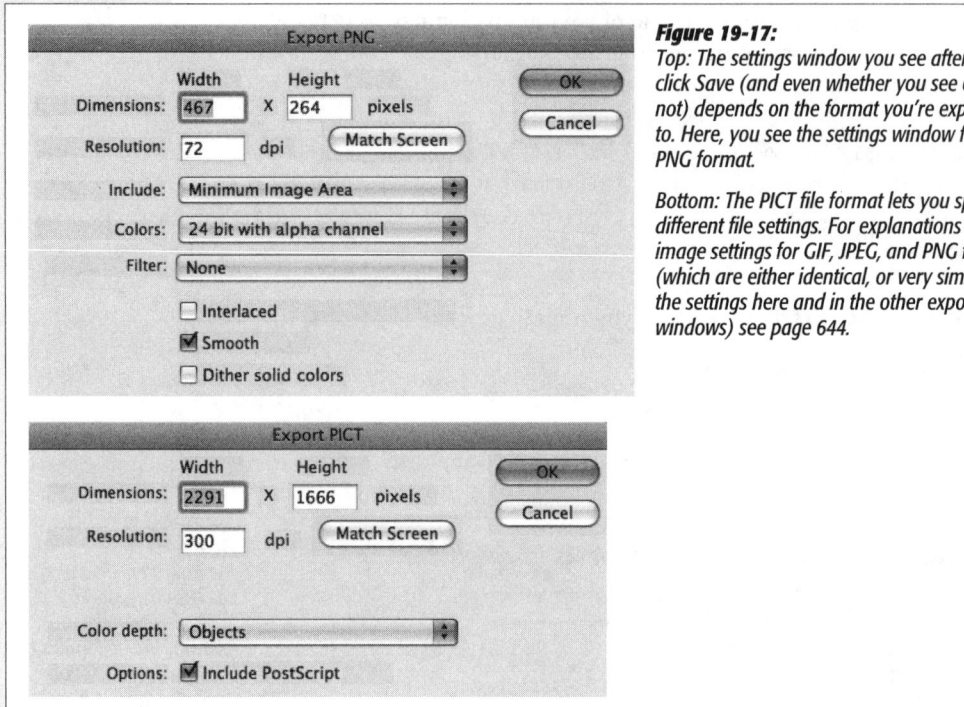

Figure 19-17:
Top: The settings window you see after you click Save (and even whether you see one or not) depends on the format you're exporting to. Here, you see the settings window for the PNG format.

Bottom: The PICT file format lets you specify different file settings. For explanations of the image settings for GIF, JPEG, and PNG formats (which are either identical, or very similar, to the settings here and in the other export windows) see page 644.

6. In the Export window, set one or more export options, and then click OK.

Flash exports the contents of your frame to the file format you chose in step 3.

Exporting an Entire Animation

Exporting your animation to another file format lets you edit the animation using another animation program, like Apple's QuickTime. You might want to do this if, for example, you want to combine frames from both Flash and QuickTime animations into a single animation.

1. Choose File → Export → Export Movie.

   The Export Movie dialog box you see in Figure 19-18 appears.

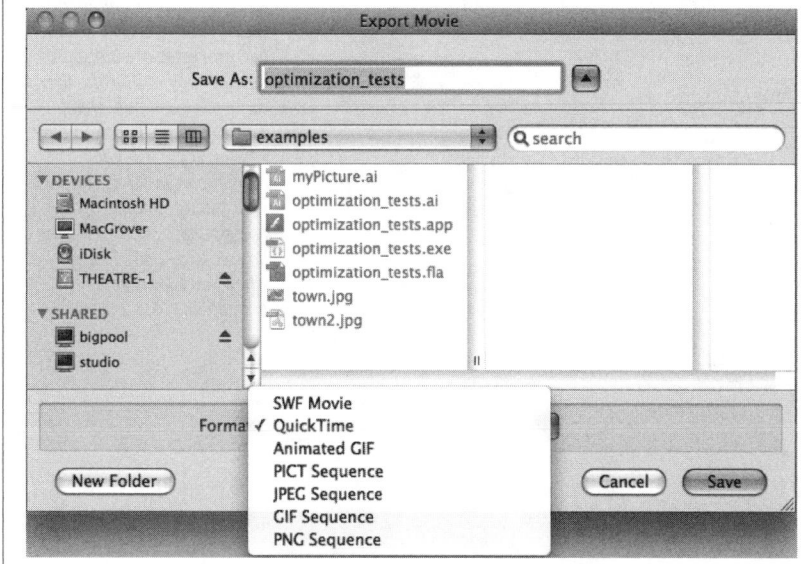

Figure 19-18:
*The Export Movie dialog
box lets you export your
animation to a variety of
formats, several of which
will be familiar to you if
you've had a chance to
check out the section on
publishing (page 631).*

2. From the pop-up menu, choose the file format to which you want to export.

   In Windows, this menu is called "Save as type;" on the Mac, it's called Format.

3. In the Save As box, type a name for your exported file.

   Leave the file extension Flash suggests.

4. Click Save.

   Flash displays an Export window containing format-specific settings, as shown in Figure 19-19.

5. In the Export window, set one or more export options, and then click OK.

   Flash exports the contents of your frame to the file format you chose in step 2.

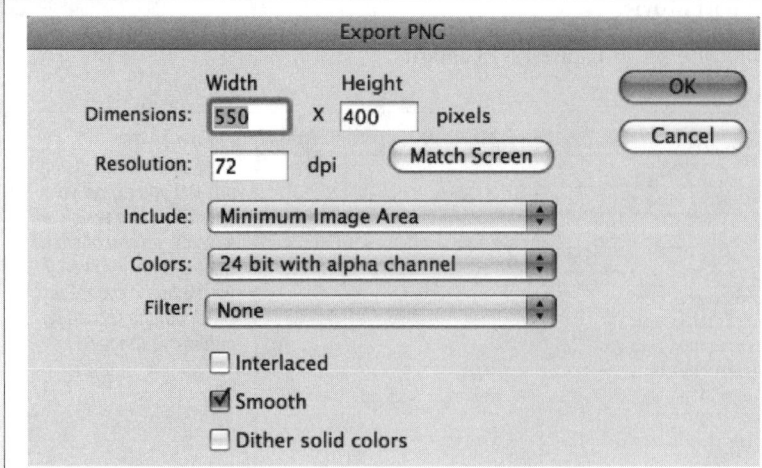

Figure 19-19:
When you export your animation, Flash displays the same settings you see when you publish your animation. From Flash's perspective, the two processes are the same, but you may appreciate the convenience of publishing over exporting. For example, when you publish your animation, Flash lets you save your settings in an easy-to-reuse publish profile (see the box on page 638). Not so when you export your animation.

Part Five:
Appendixes

5

Installation and Help

It's 2:00 a.m., you're *this close* to finishing your animation, and you run into a snag. If you can't find the answer to your question in the pages of this book, you have plenty of other possibilities. First of all, Flash has its own built-in Help system, which may give you the answer you need on the spot. For more complex problems, you can seek technical support from the developer (Adobe, as mentioned on page 666) or from fellow Flash fans via the Web. This appendix outlines all these options.

First, in case you need help getting Flash installed on your computer, some basic instructions follow.

Flash CS4 Minimum System Requirements

While the Flash box lists minimum requirements, *minimum* is the operative word. You'll want at least 20 GB free on your hard disk—not just for the program installation, but to give you room to create and store your Flash masterpieces and import additional files (like previously created images, sound files, and movies) from elsewhere.

Adobe lists the minimum amount of computer memory as 1 GB for both Macs and PCs, but as usual, you won't be sorry if you have twice that amount. The same is true of processor speed. For a PC, the minimum requirement is a 1 GHz processor (not much of a stress for today's new computers). If you have a PC that's 4 or 5 years old, you may want to double-check the processor speed. For Macs, the requirement is a PowerPC G5 or one of the newer Macs with a multicore Intel processor. Last, and certainly not least, is screen size. The minimum is listed as

1024×768 pixels. Again, most of today's PCs and Macs, even laptops, meet this requirement. Flash has so many windows and panels, it's great to have a system with more than one monitor or one very large display. It's great to be able to display multiple panels, the Flash stage, and the Actions window without having to open, close, and then reopen them all of the time.

Installing and Activating Flash CS4

As with most programs, before you can use Flash, you need to install it on your computer and activate it. Fortunately, this one-time process is fairly painless. To get started, grab your Flash installation DVD and the jacket that it comes in. (You need the jacket because it contains the serial number you need to activate Flash.)

Then follow these steps:

1. **Close any other programs you have open.**

   Flash demands all your computer's attention during the installation and configuration process, so you don't want any other files or programs open when it installs.

2. **Insert the Flash installation disc into your CD/DVD drive.**

   If you're in Windows, the installation screen appears automatically.

   If you're on a Mac, you have an extra step: On the desktop, double-click the CD/DVD icon; then double-click the name of installation program (for example, FL_Client_Installer). The installation screen appears.

Note: If the installation screen doesn't appear when you insert your Flash installation disk (and you're running Windows), click Start → My Computer, and then double-click the drive letter for your CD or DVD drive. The installation disc's contents—including something called a Setup file—appear in your My Computer window. Double-click the Setup file to start the installation.

---

3. **Follow the onscreen installation instructions on the next few screens, telling Flash that you accept its license agreement (you can't install the program unless you do), and confirming that you want to install the free Flash Player plug-in.**

   When you finish, a message appears to let you know you've successfully installed Flash.

4. **Launch your newly installed copy of Flash.**

   You can use any of the methods described on page 18, like the Start menu (Windows) or the Dock (Mac).

   The first time you launch the program, it asks you for your serial number.

5. Type your serial number, and then click Next to activate your copy of Flash.

   An optional registration screen appears.

6. **If you wish to register, type your name, your email address, and the country where you're located.**

   Registering your copy of Flash gives Adobe a record of your purchase in case you run into any snags down the line.

7. Click Finish.

   You're good to go.

Getting Help from Flash

In the olden days of computing, software companies provided nice thick paperback manuals with their programs. They weren't always well-written, and sometimes they were downright wrong, but at least you could read them on the bus or train on the way to work or school. These days, companies, including Adobe, provide book-length help files either in the program or online. If you want printed pages, crank up your printer and load up a ream or two of paper. The descriptions are more up to date and accurate than they were in those old printed volumes, but they're often a bit cryptic, as if the software engineers who designed the programs wrote them. Funny, that.

On the positive side, electronic help documents let you use your computer's search capabilities to hunt down an answer. Flash stores some help files on your computer when you install the program. However, if your computer is connected to the Internet, Flash automatically shows you Web-based help files, since they're likely to be the most current.

Flash Documentation: The Help Page

The Help page lets you search the Flash and ActionScript documentation you automatically installed on your computer when you installed Flash.

To use the Help page:

1. **Select Help → Flash Help or press F1.**

   The Help page in Figure A-1 appears. This first help page provides links to several different help resources. In the upper-left corner, you see several help resources listed, including:

   • **Using Flash.** The help system for using the Flash authoring system.

   • **ActionScript 3.0 and Components.** Two different help systems with specific information about ActionScript and the prebuilt components supplied with Flash. Use this reference when you're writing ActionScript code and need to look up the properties and methods for specific ActionScript classes.

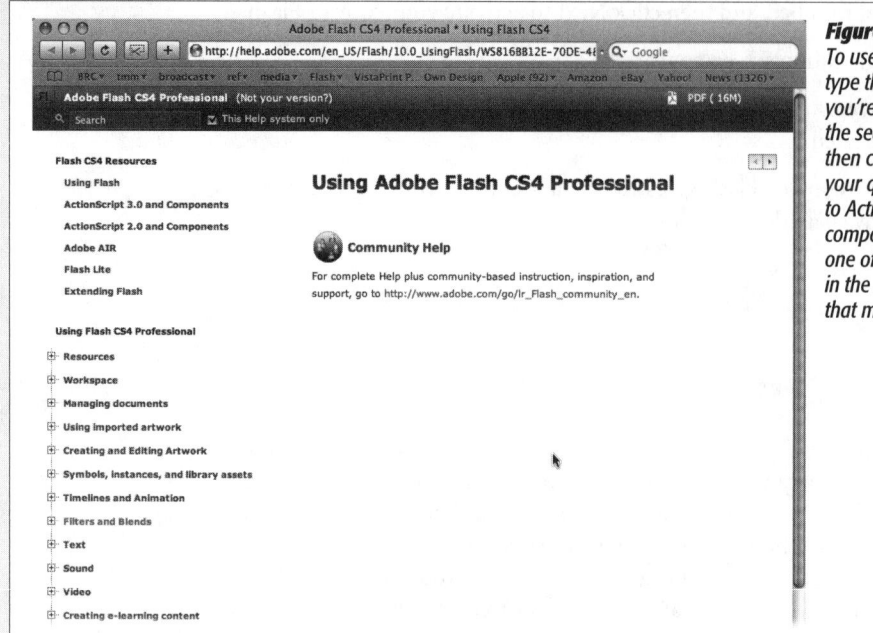

Figure A-1:
To use Flash's Help page, type the word or phrase you're looking for in the search box, and then click Search. If your question pertains to ActionScript or components, choose one of the books listed in the upper-left corner that matches your quest.

- **ActionScript 2.0 and Components.** Help systems devoted to these earlier Flash tools.

- **Adobe AIR.** A help system focusing on the needs of Adobe Air developers.

- **Flash Lite.** A help system for developers building animations and programs to be used with handheld computers and devices.

- **Extending Flash.** Help materials for folks writing and developing Flash components.

Below the links to the resources, you see the chapter outline for Using Flash. Click the + buttons to expand the chapter outline to see the subsections.

In the middle of the screen, you see a link and a logo for Community Help. Click here, and you can search the forums where other Flash developers discuss problems and solutions, which may not be your best bet for immediate answers to a question. You should probably check Using Flash first. Then if you can't find an answer or you need more details, go ahead and turn to Community's Help.

2. **In the search box, type the word or phrase with which you need help.**

Flash displays a list of topics in the left-hand side of the Help page.

3. **Click the topic that looks like the closest match to what you're searching for.**

Flash displays the text for that topic in the Help page's right-hand side. You may have to repeat this step several times to zero in on the information you want. The word or phrase you typed in the search box is highlighted in the Flash text, which makes it easier to find the pertinent details in the longer help articles.

Tip: To view Flash documentation online, choose Help → Help Resources Online.

ActionScript 3.0 Reference

When you're writing ActionScript code, it's not just helpful to have a reference close at hand, it's necessary. Even experienced ActionScripters need to look up the class definitions for new objects. You'll often come across a class, property, or method that you haven't used before.

1. **Select Help → Flash Help or press F1.**

Flash opens your Web browser and displays the help page shown in Figure A-1.

2. **Select ActionScript 3.0 and Components.**

A new page appears in your browser listing a three ActionScript help resources. The first two references are written in paragraph form. While you can't call them verbose, they do provide some helpful descriptions about certain Action-Script techniques. The third book is a dictionary-style reference book:

- *Programming ActionScript 3.0.* A general help reference for ActionScript 3.0 that explains in prose how to work with ActionScript.

- *Using ActionScript 3.0 Components.* A general help reference for components that explains in prose how to add components to your Flash animations.

- *ActionScript 3.0 Language and Component Reference,* A dictionary-style reference book listing every class along with the properties and methods. If you're looking for a quick answer about a specific class, this is the help system to search.

3. **Choose ActionScript 3.0 Language and Component Reference.**

The ActionScript 3.0 reference opens in your Web browser (Figure A-2).

4. **If you know the name of the "package" that holds the class you're researching, click its name in the upper-left cover. Otherwise, type the name of the class, property, or method in the search box at the top of the page.**

The details about ActionScript classes appear in main part of your browser window. Hyperlinks abound, so don't be afraid to click words to jump to other parts of this reference. You can always use the Back button in your browser to backtrack to previous pages.

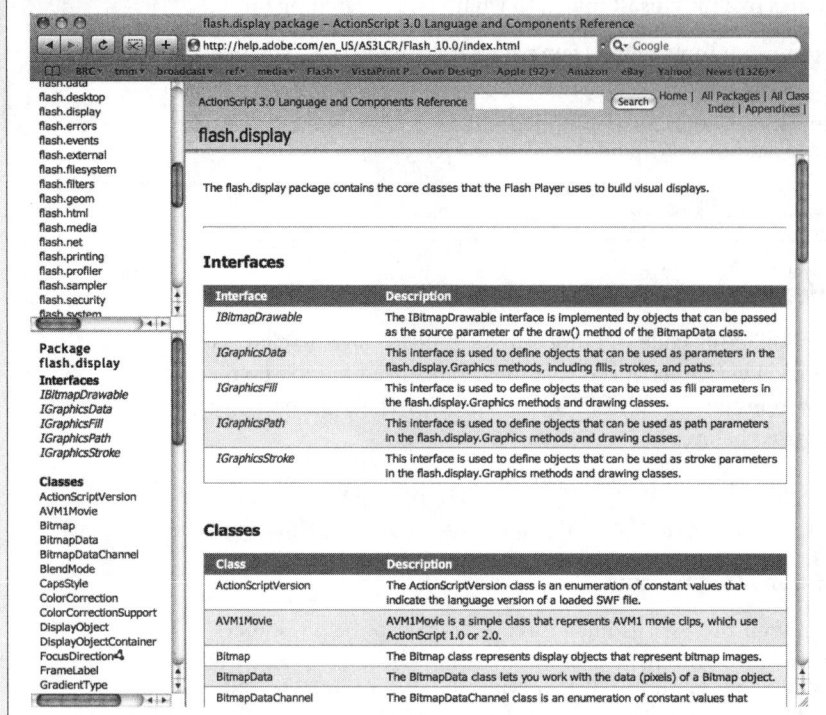

Figure A-2:
To look up the definition for an ActionScript class, click a package in the upper-left corner.

Flash Video Workshop Tutorials

Making good use of their own tools, Adobe serves up AdobeTV, where you can find video tutorials for Flash and other Creative Suite 4 programs. The company seems to be adding new programs, tutorials, and demonstrations all the time. Go to *http://tv.adobe.com*, and you'll see a page like Figure A-3. You can use the search box to hunt down videos on a particular topic, or you can select an index based on specific Adobe products. For beginners, the series "Flash in a Flash" is a good place to start.

Getting Help from Adobe

Adobe offers a variety of technical support options, from free to for-a-fee.

Online Articles, FAQs, and Sample Code

Adobe maintains a Web site containing articles on Flash, as well as sample code and answers to frequently asked Flash-related questions. You can get there quickly through the Help menu: Help → Flash Support Center. You'll find lots of articles and tutorials. If you're looking for more advanced help, check out the Developer Centers listed in the column on the right side of the page. There are Developer Centers for Adobe AIR for Flash, Flash, Flash Lite, Flash Media Server, and Flash Player.

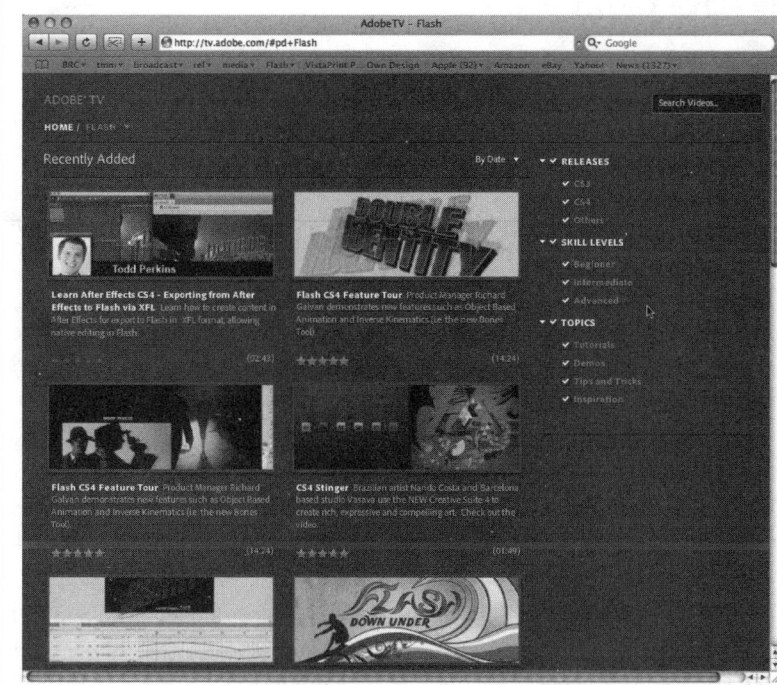

Figure A-3:
Go to AdobeTV (http://tv.
adobe.com) for
demonstrations and
tutorials on Adobe
products.

If you're interested in creating animations that folks can play on mobile devices like mobile phones and PDAs, check out the Mobile and Devices Developer Center at *www.adobe.com/devnet/devices/flashlite.html*.

Forums

Adobe hosts online forums, where anyone can ask a question about Flash, and anyone can answer. User-to-user means that Adobe employees don't officially monitor the forums or answer any questions, so the feedback you get has no official sanction or guarantee of accuracy. Still, the best and fastest answers and advice often come from other folks in the trenches, so if you've worked your way through Adobe's Tech Notes, Knowledgebase (online articles), FAQs, and documentation, these forums (Help → Adobe Online Forums) are definitely worth a look.

Direct Person-to-Person Help

Sometimes, nothing will do but asking a real live technical support person for help. Adobe sells several different pay-to-play support plans. For example, single-incident support costs $39, or you can purchase a 5-Incident Pack for $175. If you'd like a years worth of unlimited support it costs $1200. Go to *www.adobe.com/support/ programs/flash* for the details.

Finding Flash Gurus

Flash is one of those programs that people tend to get passionate about, so it's not surprising that there are hundreds of great resources on the Web offering everything from example code to free components, articles, tutorials, and more.

Here are a few that are definitely worth checking out:

- **FlashGuru** (*www.flashguru.co.uk*). With its professional-quality articles and tutorials, this wondrous Flash blog would be useful enough by itself; but it also lists dozens of other Flash blogs maintained by heavy-hitters in the Flash world.

- **Flash Kit** (*www.flashkit.com*). Surprisingly badly designed for a site that focuses on a design program, Flash Kit nevertheless offers a wealth of sound effects, fonts, components, and movie clips. It also hosts a well-attended online forum.

- **Best Flash Animation Site** (*www.bestflashanimationsite.com*) and **Webby Awards** (*www.webbyawards.com*). There's nothing like watching a beautifully constructed Flash animation to get you thinking about good design. On these two sites you can nominate the coolest Flash animation you've ever seen (including your own) or simply visit the sites others have nominated.

- **Boston Adobe Mobile and Devices User Group** (*www.flashmobilegroup.org*). If you're interested in creating Flash content for mobile devices (like mobile phones), you'll want to check out this site, which offers Flash Lite–specific articles, seminars, links, and live chats.

- **FlashPro Mailing list** (*www.muinar.org*). FlashPro is an open and nonmoderated email list "for professional Flash designers and ActionScript coders." This is where the big dogs run, so you may want to exhaust some of the resources listed above (and comb through FlashPro's archived posts) before posting a question.

- **ActionScript dot Org** (*www.actionscript.org*). If you're interested in all things ActionScript, this site offers tutorials, articles, and forums populated by ActionScript programmers. Once you've earned your stripes there are even job listings where you can put your newfound skills to work.

Flash CS4, Menu by Menu

Flash CS4: The Missing Manual is full of details, explanations, and examples. This appendix provides quick thumbnail descriptions of every command in every menu.

File

The File menu commands work on your Flash document as a whole. Use the File menu for major events, like starting a new project, opening a file you created previously, and adjusting Flash's Publish and Preview settings.

New

Windows: Ctrl+N

Mac: ⌘-N

The New command opens the New Document dialog box, where you can create many different types of Flash documents. For Web pages, choose Flash File (ActionScript 2.0 or ActionScript 3.0). To create Flash files that will run on phones, organizers, or other small handheld devices, use Flash File (Mobile).

Open

Windows: Ctrl+O

Mac: ⌘-O

Opens the standard dialog box where you can navigate through your folders and open Flash files. Use the Open command to quickly find, and then open files in Flash. Consider using the Browse command (described next) if you need to organize your files and perform other housekeeping chores.

Browse in Bridge

Windows: Ctrl+Alt+O

Mac: Option-⌘-O

Opens Adobe Bridge where you can organize, preview, import, and work with all different types of graphic files. Bridge shows thumbnail animations of SWF files and previews of JPEGs and other image files. Use Bridge to edit and search through the metadata and keywords attached to your graphic files.

Open Recent

Leads to a submenu that shows a list of the last 10 Flash (.fla or .as) files that you opened and saved. Click a file name to open the Flash animation.

Close

Windows: Ctrl+W

Mac: ⌘-W

Closes the active Flash document. If you made changes to the document, Flash asks if you want to save it before closing.

Close All

Windows: Ctrl+Alt+W

Mac: Option-⌘-W

Closes all open Flash documents. If you made changes to the documents, Flash asks if you want to save them before closing.

Save

Windows: Ctrl+S

Mac: ⌘-S

Saves the changes that you've made to your Flash document. If you haven't made any changes since opening the document, the Save command is dimmed.

Save and Compact

Saves your Flash document and reduces the file size by removing deleted items from the Flash file. Once you Save and Compact your document, you won't be able to restore deleted items using the Undo or History commands.

Save As

Windows: Shift+Ctrl+S

Mac: Shift-⌘-S

Use Save As to save the active Flash document with a new name or as a different file type. For example, you can save your Flash CS4 file in the Flash 8 file format.

Save as Template

Saves your document as a Flash template. Templates provide easy-to-use starting points for Flash projects. When you save a Flash file as a template, you provide a category and description of the template. You see templates listed when you use the File → New command and click the Templates button at the top of the New Document dialog box.

Check In

Flash can use Adobe's Version Cue program to make it easier track changes in your project and work collaboratively with others. After making changes to a file on your local computer, use Check In to post those changes on the Version Cue server.

Save All

Saves all open Flash documents.

Revert

Discards any changes you've made to your document and reverts to the last saved version.

Import

Adds graphics, sound, video, and other media files to your Flash animation. Sub-commands on this menu let you import files to the stage or to the Library of your active Flash animation. You can also import files to an External Library, where they're available to all Flash animations.

Export

Lets you save images and movies in a variety of different file formats so you can use them in other programs. Some of the Image options include: JPEG, GIF, PNG, Illustrator, and AutoCAD. Some of the Movie options include: SWF Movie, QuickTime, Animated GIF, and JPEG Sequence.

Publish Settings

Windows: Shift+Ctrl+F12

Mac: Shift-Option-F12

Opens the extensive Publish Settings dialog box, where you can fine-tune the production of your Flash animations. Use Publish Settings to create Web pages (HTML files) complete with commands to show your Flash animations and position them on the page. With Publish Settings, you can choose to create Flash *projectors* (standalone programs that run your animation for Windows or Mac computers).

Publish Preview

Windows: F12

Mac: ⌘-F12

Publish Preview runs your Flash animation in the format of your choice. Using the factory setting for Publish Preview, you see your animation embedded in a Web page. With the submenus, you can choose to see your animation in a projector file or other formats, like an animated GIF, JPEG, or PNG file.

Publish

Windows: Shift+F12

Mac: Shift-F12

Produces the finished files that make up your Flash animation. Flash uses the Publish Settings dialog box (see page 632) to create the files of your choosing. These may include: Flash movies (SWF), Web pages (HTML), projector files (EXE for Windows, APP for Mac), and the whole spectrum of graphic files (JPEG, GIF, PICT, and PNG).

AIR Settings

AIR stands for Adobe Integrated Runtime, which is a system for creating desktop programs that run on PCs, Macs, and other systems using Flash Player and other Web technologies, like HTML, JavaScript, and CSS. The benefits to programmers are that they can use familiar programming tools and don't have to rewrite programs for different computer systems. Once you create a new AIR file by selecting File → New → Flash File (Adobe AIR), use the options on this submenu to set metadata and link to supporting files. For more detail on Adobe AIR go to *www.adobe.com/products/air/*.

File Info

Stores metadata for your Flash file. Metadata can include details like the date you created a file, the name of the file's author, and the copyright information. Programs like Adobe Bridge read the metadata stored in files, and provide database-type features. For example, in Bridge you can search through all your media files for ones that were created or modified on certain dates.

Share My Screen

Adobe ConnectNow lets you share your screen with up to three other people online. Click the Share My Screen option to open the ConnectNow panel and have live online meetings with others. Adobe IDs are required, but it's free to register for one.

Page Setup

Flash documents are meant to be viewed on a computer, but you can print frames of your document on paper. Page Setup opens the dialog box where you can choose a printer, page size, and orientation before you print from your Flash document.

Print Margins (Mac only)

Opens the Print Margins dialog box, where you can position Flash frames on your page before printing. The settings include margin measurements and options for centering the document horizontally and vertically on the page. (To set margins for Windows computers, use the Page Setup command.)

Print

Windows: Ctrl+P

Mac: ⌘-P

Prints a frame or a sequence of frames from your Flash document using the settings from Page Setup and Print Margins.

Send (Windows only)

Opens your email program and attaches the current .fla file to a blank email message. All you need to do is type an address and message.

Exit (Mac: Flash → Quit Flash)

Windows: Ctrl+Q

Mac: ⌘-Q

Stops the program, and then closes the Flash window. If there are open documents, Flash closes them. If there are unsaved documents, the program prompts you to save them before quitting.

Edit

Use this menu to cut, copy, paste, and change items you've selected on Flash's stage.

Undo

Windows: Ctrl+Z

Mac: ⌘-Z

This command undoes the last command you applied. So, if you accidentally deleted a drawing from your stage, the Undo command brings it back like magic. Remember the Undo command for those moments when you smack your forehead and say, "Oh no! Why'd I do that?" For extensive undoing, consider using the History panel: Window → Other Panels → History (Windows: Ctrl+F10; Mac: ⌘-F10).

Redo

Windows: Ctrl+Y

Mac: ⌘-Y

Repeats the last command you used. So if the last thing you did was paste a circle on the stage, Redo pastes another circle on the stage. If you've just used the Undo command, Redo restores the change. Thus, you can use Undo to step backward through your recent commands and Redo to step forward again.

Cut

Windows: Ctrl+X

Mac: ⌘-X

Removes the selected object from the stage and places a copy of it on your computer's clipboard. Once it's on the clipboard, you can paste it to a new location or a new document.

Copy

Windows: Ctrl+C

Mac: ⌘-C

Makes a copy of any selected objects and places the copy on the clipboard. The original objects remain on the stage. Once you've copied an object or group of objects to the clipboard, you can paste them to a new location or a new document.

Paste in Center

Windows: Ctrl+V

Mac: ⌘-V

Tells Flash to paste the cut (or copied) object right smack in the middle of the stage's visible area, on top of any other image that happens to be there.

Paste in Place

Windows: Shift+Ctrl+V

Mac: Shift-⌘-V

Tells Flash to paste the cut or copied object in its original position on the stage. Useful for copying objects from one frame to another, this command ensures the objects are positioned in exactly the same location in both frames.

Clear

Windows: Backspace

Mac: Backspace

Removes any selected objects from the stage. Flash doesn't store cleared objects on the clipboard, so you can't use the Paste command to put them back on the stage.

Duplicate

Windows: Ctrl+D

Mac: ⌘-D

Copies any selected objects, and then immediately pastes a duplicate on the stage. This one command combines the Copy and Paste commands.

Select All

Windows: Ctrl+A

Mac: ⌘-A

Selects all the objects on the stage and work area.

Deselect All

Windows: Shift+Ctrl+A

Mac: Shift-⌘-A

Removes the selection from any currently selected objects.

Find and Replace

Windows: Ctrl+F

Mac: ⌘-F

Opens the Find and Replace panel, where you search your document or scene for text, symbols, graphics, and media that you specify. You can then, if you wish, replace those items with something else.

Find Next

Windows: F3

Mac: F3

Searches for the next occurrence of the items identified in the Find and Replace panel.

Timeline

Leads to a submenu that shows Edit commands specific to Flash's timeline. The submenu commands include the following:

Remove Frames

Windows: Shift+F5

Mac: Shift-F5

Removes frames from the timeline, shortening the length of the timeline.

Cut Frames

Windows: Ctrl+Alt+X

Mac: Option-⌘-X

Cuts the contents of the frames, placing that content on the clipboard, where you can paste it into other frames. Cut Frames doesn't reduce the number of frames in the timeline.

Copy Frames

Windows: Ctrl+Alt+C

Mac: Option-⌘-C

Copies the selected frames and places them on the clipboard, so you can paste them to a different location in the timeline.

Paste Frames

Windows: Ctrl+Alt+V

Mac: Option-⌘-V

Pastes copied or cut frames into the timeline after the selected frame. Pasting frames increases the overall length of the timeline.

Clear Frames

Windows: Alt+Backspace

Mac: Option-Backspace

Removes the contents of the selected frames, leaving empty frames in place. (Unlike Cut, Clear Frames *doesn't* place the frames on the clipboard.)

Select All Frames

Windows: Ctrl+Alt+A

Mac: Option-⌘-A

Selects all the frames in all the layers in the visible timeline so you can make changes to the entire timeline at once.

Copy Motion

Copies the properties of a motion tween so you can paste them onto another object.

Copy Motion as ActionScript 3.0

Copies the properties of a motion tween and creates ActionScript 3.0 code, which you can then use in the Actions panel.

Paste Motion

Used after Copy Motion to paste the properties of a motion tween onto another object.

Paste Motion Special

Lets you choose specific tween properties you want to paste onto another object. For example, your choices include: X and Y positions, horizontal, and vertical scales, rotation, skew, colors, and filters.

Edit Symbols/Document

Windows: Ctrl+E

Mac: ⌘-E

When you edit symbols, you change every instance of the symbol in your document. Edit Symbols opens the selected Flash symbol so you can edit it in its own timeline. (When you're in Edit Symbols mode, this command changes to Edit Document, and brings you back to the document timeline.)

Edit Selected

Lets you edit a selected group or object within a group. Other objects on the stage that aren't part of the group are dimmed and inaccessible. Use Edit All (below) to return to the normal stage.

Edit in Place

Use Edit in Place to edit symbols within the context of the stage. Other objects on the stage are dimmed and inaccessible. When you edit a symbol, you change all instances of that symbol in your document.

Edit All

Restore the normal stages after you use the Edit Selected command.

Preferences (Mac: Flash → Preferences)

Windows: Ctrl+U

Opens the extensive Flash Preferences panel, where you can tweak dozens of settings to make Flash work the way you like to work. You can set Preferences in the following groups: General, ActionScript, AutoFormat, Clipboard, Drawing, Text, Warnings, PSD File Importer, and AI File Importer. For example, General settings include: Flash's startup options, how many levels of undo to save, and whether or not to display tooltips when the cursor is over a command or object.

Customize Tools Panel (Mac: Flash → Customize Tools Panel)

Opens the Customize Tools Panel, where you can set up the Tools panel with just the tools you want and arrange them any way you like.

Font Mapping (Mac: Flash → Font Mapping)

Opens the Font Mapping panel, where you can choose substitute fonts for fonts that are missing on your system. For example, you can choose Times Roman to substitute for Times.

Keyboard Shortcuts (Mac: Flash → Keyboard Shortcuts)

Use Keyboard Shortcuts to add or change the keys used to invoke specific commands.

View

Go To

Lets you navigate Flash animations that are broken up into multiple scenes. The Go To command leads to a submenu where you can select scenes by name or choose First, Last, Previous, and Next options.

Zoom In

Windows: Ctrl+=

Mac: ⌘-=

Changes the view of the stage by zooming in twice as much. So, if the view is at 500%, zooming in changes the view to 1000%.

Zoom Out

Windows: Ctrl+−

Mac: ⌘-−

Changes the view of the stage by zooming out twice as much. So, if the view is at 500%, zooming out changes the view to 250%.

Magnification

Leads to a submenu where you can choose from several preset Zoom levels that range from 25% to 800%. In addition, there are options to Show All (zoom to show all the contents of the current frame), Show Frame (shows the entire stage), and Fit in Window (scale the entire stage to fit in the program window).

Preview Mode

Leads to a submenu with several options related to previewing your animation with the Control → Play command. The options include the following:

Outlines

Windows: Shift+Ctrl+Alt+O

Mac: Shift-⌘-Option-O

Displays shapes in the animation as outlines or wireframe representations. With older, slower computers this mode can help speed up previews, although most of today's machines can keep pace with even the most complex Flash animations.

Fast

Windows: Shift+Ctrl+Alt+F

Mac: Shift-Option-⌘-F

Turns off anti-aliasing and other settings that slow down Flash previews.

Anti-Alias

Windows: Shift+Ctrl+Alt+A

Mac: Shift-Option-⌘-A

Turns on anti-aliasing, a computer graphic technique that makes shapes and lines appear smoother on computer screens.

Anti-Alias Text

Windows: Shift+Ctrl+Alt+T

Mac: Shift-Option-⌘-T

Uses anti-aliasing on text to create a smoother appearance. These settings change the appearance of text while you're working inside of Flash; to adjust anti-alias settings for your published files, use the Properties panel settings for the Text tool.

Full

Renders your Flash animation fully, providing a close approximation of the published animation.

Pasteboard

Windows: Shift+Ctrl+W

Mac: Shift-⌘-W

Shows the workspace around the stage. Works in conjunction with the Magnification commands (page 679). A checkmark appears in the menu when this option is in force.

Rulers

Windows: Shift+Ctrl+Alt+R

Mac: Shift-Option-⌘-R

Shows or Hides the rulers that appear at the top and left of the program window. With rulers visible, you can drag guidelines to place on the stage. (Guides don't appear in your final animation; they're just visual aids to help you position items on the stage.) A checkmark appears in the menu when this option is turned on.

Grid

The Grid is another visual aid to help you position and align objects on your stage. The grid appears as horizontal and vertical lines, similar to graph paper. The Grid command leads to a submenu where you can show or hide the grid and change the color and spacing of the lines. You can turn the grid's "snapping" behavior on and off (see page 681).

Guides

Show, hide, and lock guides using the submenu under the Guides command. Use the Edit Guides command to adjust the appearance and behavior of your guides. The Clear Guides command removes all guides from the stage.

Snapping

When Snapping is turned on, objects automatically line up with other objects. So, for example, if you turn on Snapping for Guides, objects you drag snap into alignment with the nearest guide. You can turn Snapping on or off for: the grid, guides, and objects. The Snapping submenu displays the following commands:

Snap Align

When Snap Align is turned on, dotted lines appear on the stage when you drag an object near another object or the edge of the stage.

Snap to Grid

Windows: Shift+Ctrl+'

Mac: Shift-⌘-'

Toggles the snapping behavior of the grid on or off.

Snap to Guide

Windows: Shift+Ctrl+;

Mac: Shift-⌘-;

Toggles the snapping behavior of guides on or off.

Snap to Pixels

Use Snap to Pixels for super-accurate alignment. With Snap to Pixels on, a grid appears when the zoom level is 400% or greater. This grid represents individual pixels on your Flash stage.

Snap to Objects

Windows: Shift+Ctrl+/

Mac: Shift-⌘-U

Toggles the snapping behavior of objects on or off.

Edit Snapping

Windows: Ctrl+/

Mac: ⌘-/

Opens the Edit Snapping panel, where you can adjust the settings for snapping behaviors, including *tolerance* (how close objects need to be before snapping behavior kicks in).

Hide Edges

Windows: Ctrl+H

Mac: Shift-⌘-E

Toggles the highlight that appears on objects when you select them. If you want to see the object without the highlight, click Hide Edges; a checkmark appears on the menu.

Show Shape Hints

Windows: Ctrl+Alt+H

Mac: Option-⌘-H

Shows and hides shape hints on the stage. Shape hints are used to control shapes that are being tweened. By positioning shape hints, you control the appearance of an object as it changes shape during a tween. Turn Show Shape Hints on to make adjustments, and then turn them off to see your objects as they'll appear in your animation.

Show Tab Order

Tab Order establishes keyboard navigation in forms and Web pages. For example, if you create a form with the tab order Name = 1, Address = 2, and Phone number = 3, your visitors can fill in their name, press Tab key to move on to the Address field, and so on. Use Show Tab Order to see a visual representation of the Tab Order of items on your stage.

Insert

Use the Insert menu to add objects to your animation and make changes to the timeline.

New Symbol

Windows: Ctrl+F8

Mac: ⌘-F8

Opens the Create Symbol dialog box, where you name and select the symbol type (movie clip, button, or graphic).

Motion Tween

Applies a motion tween to an object, which is great for animating movement and changing properties over time—like color, transparency and dimensions. You can use the new Motion Editor to fine-tune every aspect of a motion tween.

Shape Tween

Creates a shape tween between adjacent keyframes. Shape tweens work only on editable shapes (not text or symbols). They're great for morphing objects from one form to another—an acorn to an oak, for example.

Classic Tween

Creates a motion tween between adjacent keyframes (represented by an arrow on a blue background). Use motion tweens to create nonlinear motions. Motion tweens work only on symbols, grouped objects, and text blocks. While Adobe still makes classic tweens available in Flash CS4 for compatibility reasons, it's replaced them with the more versatile and powerful motion tween

Timeline

The Timeline command leads to a submenu with commands for adding layers and frames to your timeline.

Layer

Inserts a new layer in your timeline. You use layers to organize objects on the stage. For example, layers can hold elements like shapes and text. You can also create keyframes and tweens on individual layers.

Layer Folder

Creates a layer folder. Layer folders are used to organize and group layers. By opening and closing layer folders, you can simplify the appearance of your timeline.

Frame

Windows: F5

Mac: F5

Inserts frames into your timeline. If no frame is selected, this command inserts one frame in every layer after the current position of the playhead. If one or more frames are selected, then an equal number of frames are inserted following the selection. If a position is selected on the right, outside the range of the current timeline, Flash adds new frames up to the selected point.

Keyframe

Inserts new keyframes into the timeline (represented by a solid circle), similar to the Frame command. Keyframes are different from ordinary frames in that the changes and repositioning of objects in keyframes represent significant changes in the action of your animation. When you use the Insert Keyframe command, objects on the stage become part of the new keyframe.

Blank Keyframe

Inserts blank keyframes into your timeline (represented by a hollow circle). Similar to the Keyframe command, except there are no objects in a blank keyframe—you've got a clean slate where you can add new objects to the stage.

Scene

Adds a new scene to your Flash animation. Scenes let you divide long animations into smaller, more manageable parts and create nonlinear animations or animations that repeat certain segments.

Modify

The commands in the Modify menu let you change the properties of your document, your timeline, and the objects in your animation. For example, you use commands in this menu to rotate, scale, and distort the shapes on the stage.

Document

Windows: Ctrl+J

Mac: ⌘-J

Opens the Document window, where you set the width, height, and background color of the stage. Document settings also control the speed (frames per second) of your animation and the measurement units used by rulers.

Convert to Symbol

Windows: F8

Mac: F8

Converts selected objects to a symbol, which can be a movie clip, a graphic, or a button. Symbols are key to many aspects of Flash animations. Among other things, symbols help to reduce the overall file size of Flash animations.

Break Apart

Windows: Ctrl+B

Mac: ⌘-B

Used to break an imported bitmap into separate pixels that can be selected and edited. (When you first import a bitmap, Flash treats it as a single discrete element.) This command also separates grouped objects and symbols into their component parts.

Bitmap

Flash has two Modify commands to help you work with imported bitmap (raster) images:

Swap Bitmap

Replace the selected instance of a bitmap with another bitmap.

Trace Bitmap

Converts the selected bitmap into a vector image, by converting areas of color into editable vector shapes. In some cases, this can reduce the Flash file size, but it's worth testing to see whether that's the case and that you're OK with the changes it makes to the image.

Symbol

Flash has two Modify commands to help you work with symbols.

Swap Symbol

Replace the selected instance of a symbol with another symbol from the Library.

Duplicate Symbol

Creates a new instance of a symbol you've selected on the stage.

Shape

Flash has several commands to help you modify shapes in your animation.

Advanced Smooth

Windows: Ctrl+Alt+Shift+N

Mac: Shift-Option-⌘-N

Removes the hard angles and bumps from shapes and lines. Applying this command repeatedly creates smoother and smoother shapes.

Advanced Straighten

Windows: Ctrl+Alt+Shift+N

Mac: Shift-Option-⌘-M

Removes the curves from lines and line segments. You can apply this command repeatedly, creating straighter lines each time.

Optimize

Windows: Shift+Ctrl+Alt+C

Mac: Shift-Option-⌘-C

Reduces the number of anchor points (control points) in a shape or line by removing unneeded anchor points. This doesn't change the shape, but it does reduce the file size and helps make shapes more manageable.

Convert Lines to Fills

Changes lines into fills, in effect giving them the properties of fills. For example, once a line is changed to a fill, you can apply gradients to the line or erase a portion of it.

Expand Fill

Opens the Expand Fill window where you can expand (enlarge) or inset (shrink) the fill portion of a shape. This is similar to scaling a shape and works best on simple objects.

Soften Fill Edges

Softens the edges of the selected shape giving it the appearance of fading away. In the Soften Fill Edges window you can choose the distance and the steps (gradations) for the effect.

Add Shape Hint

Windows: Ctrl+Shift+H

Mac: Shift-⌘-H

When you're creating a shape tween, you can use hints to control the appearance of objects as they change from one shape to another. By adding hints, you can highlight important parts of the shape that should be defined during the transition.

Remove All Hints

If you've applies hints to a shape tween (see the previous command), this command removes them.

Combine Objects

The Combine Objects submenu lets you create more complex objects by combining multiple objects and altering their features.

Delete Envelope

Removes the Envelope modifier from the selected object.

Union

Combines two or more shapes to create a new object by deleting unseen overlapping sections. The new object consists of the visible portions of the joined shapes.

Intersect

Creates an object from the intersection of two or more objects. The new object shape consists of the overlapping portions of the combined shapes.

Punch

Removes portions of an object as defined by the overlapping portions of another object placed on top of it. Areas where the top object overlaps the lower object are removed, and the top object is deleted entirely.

Crop

Uses the shape of one object to crop another object. The front or topmost object defines the shape to be retained. Any part of an underlying shape that overlaps the top shape remains, while the visible portions of the underlying shapes are removed, and the topmost shape is deleted entirely.

Timeline

The Timeline submenu's commands help you organize and manipulate the parts that comprise your animation, notably layers and frames.

Distribute to Layers

Windows: Shift+Ctrl+D

Mac: Shift-⌘-D

Distributes the selected objects so that each object is on its own layer. Useful for making sure different shapes are on separate layers before applying a tween.

Layer Properties

Opens the Layer Properties window, where you name layers and adjust settings like: layer type, layer colors, layer height, layer visibility, and layer locking.

Reverse Frames

Rearranges the selected frames in reverse order. In effect, this arranges the frames so that the animation runs in reverse.

Synchronize Symbols

Synchronizes the animation of a graphic symbol instance to match the timeline. It also recalculates the number of frames in a tween to match the number of frames allotted to it in the timeline.

Convert to Keyframes

Windows: F6

Mac: F6

Converts the selected frames in the timeline into keyframes. This command retains the contents of the preceding keyframe. Keyframes are represented by a solid circle.

Clear Keyframe

Windows: Shift+F6

Mac: Shift-F6

Converts a keyframe to a standard frame.

Convert to Blank Keyframes

Windows: F7

Mac: F7

Converts the selected frame to a blank keyframe. Represented in the timeline by a hollow circle, blank keyframes have no content.

Transform

Leads to a submenu with the following Transform commands:

Free Transform

Puts the selected object in Free Transform mode where you can perform scale, rotate, and skew transformations.

Distort

Puts the selected object in Distort mode. You can change the shape of the object using handles on the bounding box.

Envelope

The Envelope modifier lets you distort the shape of an object using handles on the bounding box.

Scale

Scale lets you change the height and width of an object by dragging the handles on the bounding box. Press Shift to resize the object proportionally.

Rotate and Skew

Places a bounding box around the selected object. Using the handles, you can freely rotate and skew the object.

Scale and Rotate

Windows: Ctrl+Alt+S

Mac: Option-⌘-S

Opens the Scale and Rotate window where you can resize and rotate the selected object by typing numbers into text boxes.

Rotate 90 degrees CW

Windows: Shift+Ctrl+9

Mac: Shift-⌘-9

Rotates the selected object by 90 degrees in a clockwise direction.

Rotate 90 degrees CCW

Windows: Shift+Ctrl+7

Mac: Shift-⌘-7

Rotates the selected object by 90 degrees in a counter-clockwise direction.

Flip Vertical

Flips the selected object vertically, putting the top of the object at the bottom.

Flip Horizontal

Flips the selected object horizontally, putting the left side of the object on the right.

Remove Transform

Windows: Shift+Ctrl+Z

Mac: Shift-⌘-Z

Removes the previously applied transformations from the selected object.

Arrange

The Arrange submenu's commands act on the objects in your animation's layers.

Bring to Front

Windows: Shift+Ctrl+Up Arrow

Mac: Shift-Option-Up Arrow

Brings the selected object to the top level in the frame so that the object appears to be in front of all other objects in the same frame. This action pertains only to objects in the same layer in the timeline, it doesn't reposition layers or move objects from one layer to another.

Bring Forward

Windows: Ctrl+Up Arrow

Mac: ⌘-Up Arrow

Brings selected objects forward one step in front of other objects in the same frame. This action pertains only to objects in the same layer in the timeline; it doesn't reposition layers or move objects from layer to another.

Send Backward

Windows: Ctrl+Down Arrow

Mac: ⌘-Down Arrow

Sends the selected object backward one step behind other objects in the same frame. This action pertains only to objects in the same layer in the timeline; it doesn't reposition layers or move objects from one layer to another.

Send to Back

Windows: Shift+Ctrl+Down Arrow

Mac: Shift-Option-Down Arrow

Sends the selected object to the bottom level in the frame, so that the object appears to be behind every other object in the same frame. This action pertains only to objects in the same layer in the timeline; it doesn't reposition layers or move objects from one layer to another.

Lock

Windows: Ctrl+Alt+L

Mac: Option-⌘-L

Locks selected objects in their current position on the stage. Locked objects can't be selected to be moved or transformed in any other way.

Unlock All

Windows: Shift+Ctrl+Alt+L

Mac: Shift-Option-⌘-L

Unlocks objects that have been locked in position using the Lock command.

Align

The Align submenu's commands help you position your animation's objects neatly in relation to the edges of the stage or to each other.

Left

Windows: Ctrl+Alt+1

Mac: Option-⌘-1

Aligns selected objects along the left edge.

Horizontal Center

Windows: Ctrl+Alt+2

Mac: Option-⌘-2

Aligns the center of the selected objects to the same horizontal position.

Right

Windows: Ctrl+Alt+3

Mac: Option-⌘-3

Aligns selected objects along the right edge.

Top

Windows: Ctrl+Alt+4

Mac: Option-⌘-4

Aligns selected objects along the top edge.

Vertical Center

Windows: Ctrl+Alt+5

Mac: Option-⌘-5

Aligns the center of the selected objects to the same vertical position.

Bottom

Windows: Ctrl+Alt+6

Mac: Option-⌘-6

Aligns selected objects along the bottom edge.

Distribute Widths

Windows: Ctrl+Alt+7

Mac: Option-⌘-7

Spaces selected objects evenly on the stage from left to right.

Distribute Heights

Windows: Ctrl+Alt+9

Mac: Option-⌘-9

Spaces selected objects evenly on the stage from top to bottom.

Make Same Width

Windows: Shift+Ctrl+Alt+7

Mac: Shift-Option-⌘-7

Makes the width property of selected objects equal.

Make Same Height

Windows: Shift+Ctrl+Alt+9

Mac: Shift-Option-⌘-9

Makes the height property of selected objects equal.

To Stage

Windows: Ctrl+Alt+8

Mac: Option-⌘-8

Toggles the To Stage behavior of alignment tools. For example, with To Stage selected, the Align Bottom command aligns selected objects with the bottom of the stage. A checkmark appears on the menu when this option is selected.

Group

Windows: Ctrl+G

Mac: ⌘-G

Combines selected objects into a group. Grouped objects behave as if they're a single object. They can be selected with a single click, and modified and transformed with a single command.

Ungroup

Windows: Shift+Ctrl+G

Mac: Shift-⌘-G

Breaks grouped objects (see above) apart into their individual elements.

Text

Use the commands on the Text menu to modify the appearance of text on the stage.

Font

Choose a typestyle from a list of fonts available on your computer.

Size

Apply a new size to the selected text. Sizes range from 8 point to 120 point.

Style

Available type styles include: Plain, Bold, Italic, Subscript, and Superscript.

Align

Use this command to set the text alignment to: Left, Centered, Right, or Justified.

Letter Spacing

Letter spacing is a typographic effect sometimes used in headings and logos to increase or decrease the space between all letters by the same fixed amount.

Scrollable

Use the Scrollable command to make dynamic text or input text fields scrollable, so the text can be longer than the available space in the text box.

Check Spelling

Runs Flash's spell checker on the text in the Spelling Setup window (see below).

Spelling Setup

Use the Spelling Setup command to identify the text that needs to be spell-checked, select your language, choose a personal dictionary, and set options for words you want the spell checker to ignore.

Commands

The Commands menu helps you automate tasks in Flash. You can create commands for tasks that you perform repeatedly and download prebuilt commands from the Adobe Exchange Web site.

Manage Saved Commands

Opens the Manage Saved Commands panel where you can rename and delete commands.

Get More Commands

Opens your Web browser to the Adobe Exchange page, where you can find commands others have created. Some are for sale and some are free.

Run Command

Use Run Commands to run a JavaScript command. An Open File dialog box opens where you can navigate to the script you wish to run.

Copy Motion as XML

Records an XML description of your animation that you can reuse in other projects.

Export Motion XML

Exports a copied motion as an XML file so you can import and reuse it in other animations.

Import Motion XML

Imports an XML file that defines a Flash motion so you can apply it to objects in your animation.

Control

Control menu commands provide playback controls to test your animation in the program window, the Flash Player, and HTML pages.

Play

Windows: Enter

Mac: Return

Plays the timeline in the Flash window, showing the contents of each frame on the stage.

Rewind

Windows: Shift+, (comma)

Mac: Shift-, (comma)

Moves the playhead in the timeline back to the first frame.

Go To End

Windows: Shift+. (period)

Mac: Shift-. (period)

Moves the playhead in the timeline to the last frame.

Step Forward One Frame

Windows: . (period)

Mac: . (period)

Moves the playhead in the timeline ahead one frame.

Step Backward One Frame

Windows: , (comma)

Mac: , (comma)

Moves the playhead in the timeline back one frame.

Test Movie

Windows: Ctrl+Enter

Mac: ⌘-Return

Compiles the animation, and then runs it in the Flash Player. If your movie has more than one scene, this command plays all the scenes in order.

Test Scene

Windows: Ctrl+Alt+Enter

Mac: Option-⌘-Return

Compiles and tests the scene in the timeline. If you want to test and view all the scenes in your movie, use Test Movie (above).

Delete ASO Files

Flash sometimes creates ASO (ActionScript Object) files when it compiles your movie; this command deletes those files. (Sometimes, Flash doesn't update these files properly and it creates undesirable results.) If necessary, Flash creates new ASO files if they're needed the next time you compile.

Delete ASO Files and Test Movie

ASO files are temporary files Flash uses when compiling and previewing animations (see above). This command deletes the files, forcing Flash to create new ASO files (if needed), and then tests the movie.

Loop Playback

Repeats the playback of your movie or scene when testing. When the movie reaches the end, it starts playing from the beginning again.

Play All Scenes

Tells Flash to play all the scenes in your animation, not just the currently selected scene.

Enable Simple Frame Actions

Windows: Ctrl+Alt+F

Mac: Option-⌘-F

Tells Flash to play the actions you've added to frames in the timeline. (These are basic actions like Play and Stop commands.) If you don't turn on Enable Simple Frame Actions, Flash ignores frame actions.

Enable Simple Buttons

Windows: Ctrl+Alt+B

Mac: Option-⌘-B

Makes your buttons work on the stage. If you turn off this menu item, mousing over and clicking buttons have no effect.

Enable Live Preview

Displays components you've added to the stage as they'll appear in the Flash Player. If you turn this item off, Flash displays components as outlines.

Mute Sounds

Windows: Ctrl+Alt+M

Mac: Option-⌘-M

Prevents Flash from playing sound clips during playback.

Debug

Debug commands give you tools to play back your movie and, at the same time, examine the inner workings of the timeline, object properties, and ActionScript code.

Debug Movie

Windows: Shift+Ctrl+Enter

Mac: Shift-⌘-Return

Plays your animation while displaying information in the Debugger window, where you can monitor the list of objects and variables your animation and ActionScript are using.

Continue

Windows: Alt+F5

Mac: Option-F5

Continues playback after being stopped by the debugger.

End Debug Session

Windows: Alt+F12

Mac: Option-F12

Stops the debugging session and stops playback of the animation.

Step In

Windows: Alt+F6

Mac: Option-F6

Used during debugging in combination with breakpoints, the Step In command runs ActionScript functions step-by-step.

Step Over

Windows: Alt+F7

Mac: Option-F7

Use Step Over during debugging in combination with breakpoints to step through your ActionScript code a line at a time. Stepping over a line of code tells Flash to execute the code even if the line contains a function call.

Step Out

Windows: Alt+F8

Mac: Option-F8

Use Step Out during debugging in combination with breakpoints. You use this command to return from examining a function in your ActionScript code (see Step In above).

Remove All Breakpoints

Windows: Ctrl+Shift+B

Mac: Shift-⌘-B

Breakpoints are used in debugging as a way to stop the animation and Action-Script program running, which gives you the opportunity to examine the code, variables, and properties. This command removes all the breakpoints that you previously placed in your ActionScript program.

Begin Remote Debug Session

Remote debugging is the programmer's art of debugging a .swf file on a remote server. Use this command to begin remote debugging after you've done the necessary setup chores of choosing your ActionScript version, creating a remote debugging file (.swd), and uploading files to the server. Remote debugging isn't covered in this book; for more details, see *Essential ActionScript* by Colin Moock (O'Reilly).

Window

This menu is command central for opening and closing the many windows you use when working in Flash. Checkmarks appear next to the names of currently open windows. Clicking next to the name opens or closes the window.

Duplicate Window

Windows: Ctrl+Alt+K

Mac: Option-⌘-K

Creates a second program window. Use this command when you want more than one view of your animation or timeline. It's useful for side-by-side comparisons of two separate frames or other aspects of your Flash animation.

Toolbars

Leads to a submenu with the following commands:

Controller

Opens the Controller toolbar, which you use to play, pause, and navigate through the frames of your animation.

Edit Bar

Opens the Edit Bar, which appears between the timeline and the stage in your program window.

Timeline

Windows: Ctrl+Alt+T

Mac: Option-⌘-T

Displays the timeline in your program window, which you use to work with frames and layers in your animation.

Motion Editor

Opens the Motion Editor panel, which you use to fine-tune motion tweens. The Motion Editor uses graphs to show how properties change over time. In particular, the Motion Editor gives you greater control over the easing applied to property changes.

Tools

Windows: Ctrl+F2

Mac: ⌘-F2

Shows and hides the Tools palette, which holds tools for: selection, drawing, shape creation, text, color application, and color picking.

Properties

Windows: Ctrl+F3

Mac: ⌘-F3

Opens the Properties window, where you view—and edit—various aspects of objects in your animation.

Library

Windows: Ctrl+L

Mac: ⌘-L

Opens the Library window, which stores objects used in your animation like graphics, movie clips, buttons, and sound clips.

Common Libraries

Opens the Common Library windows, which hold buttons, classes, and sounds.

Motion Presets

Opens a panel with predesigned motion tweens like Fly-in, Fly-out and Bounce. You can use Adobe-designed presets or store your own custom designed presets using this panel.

Actions

Windows: F9

Mac: Option-F9

Opens the Actions panel, from which you define and edit actions used in your animation.

Behaviors

Windows: Shift+F3

Mac: Shift-F3

Opens the Behaviors panel, which automates the process of applying actions to objects in your animation. (Behaviors aren't available with ActionScript 3.0.)

Compiler Errors

Windows: Alt+F2

Mac: Option-F2

Opens the Compiler Errors window, where Flash displays the problems that may happen during the compilation of your animation.

Debug Panels

Opens the Debug panels, which you use to find errors in your ActionScript programs. The Debug panel displays the lines of your code, variables, values, and properties while giving you the opportunity to execute code a line at a time. The Debug subpanels are: Debug Console, Variables, and ActionScript 2.0 Debugger.

Movie Explorer

Windows: Alt+F3

Mac: Option-F3

Displays the Movie Explorer window, where you see a hierarchical representation of your Flash animation, breaking it down into scenes and objects.

Windows: F2

Mac: F2

Opens the Output window, which is used in combination with *trace( )* statements to debug ActionScript code.

Align

Windows: Ctrl+K

Mac: ⌘-K

Displays the Align window, which you use to align, distribute and position objects on the stage. The Align commands are identical to those in the Modify → Align submenu, except the window displays icons that visually indicate the alignment command.

Color

Windows: Shift+F9

Mac: Shift-F9

Opens the Color window, from which you pick stroke, fill, and gradient colors. The Color window provides several tools to identify colors including color pickers, swatches, and RBG color tools.

Info

Windows: Ctrl+I

Mac: ⌘-I

Opens the Info panel, which continually provides details on the position of the mouse cursor and the colors at that location. The info panel also provides height, width, and location information for selected objects on the stage.

Swatches

Windows: Ctrl+F9

Mac: ⌘-F9

Opens the Swatch window, from which you can pick colors to apply them to objects in your animation. You use the Swatch panel to create and save custom colors for your animation.

Transform

Windows: Ctrl+T

Mac: ⌘-T

Opens the Transform window, which you use to resize, rotate, and skew objects in your animation.

Components

Windows: Ctrl+F7

Mac: ⌘-F7

Opens the Components window, from which you choose components to add to your animation. Components are grouped in four categories: data, media, user interface, and video.

Component Inspector

Windows: Shift+F7

Mac: Shift-F7

Displays the Component Inspector window, which you use to set parameters, bindings, and XML schema for components you add to your animation.

Other Panels

Leads to a submenu with additional panels, including the following:

Accessibility

Windows: Shift+F11

Mac: Shift-F11

Opens the Accessibility window, which you use to provide accessibility information to screen readers and set accessibility options for individual Flash objects.

History

Windows: Ctrl+F10

Mac: ⌘-F10

Displays the History panel, where you see a record of actions performed during the current Flash authoring session. Use the slider to the left of the list to backtrack and undo these actions. By selecting and saving multiple actions in the History panel, you can create *commands* (reusable actions, similar to macros) that you run from the Commands menu.

Scene

Windows: Shift+F2

Mac: Shift-F2

Opens the Scene window, which lists all the scenes in your animation. Reorganize the list of scenes to change the order in which scenes play in your animation.

Screens

Opens and closes the Screens panel, used to create PowerPoint-type slideshows with Flash. Use the Screens panel to arrange and organize the slides in your presentation.

Strings

Windows: Ctrl+F11

Mac: ⌘-F11

Opens the Strings panel, where you can create and update multilingual content for your animation. Using Strings, you specify content for text fields that accommodate multiple languages. Flash can automatically determine which language to use based on the language used by the computer running Flash Player.

Web Services

Windows: Ctrl+F10

Mac: Shift-⌘-F10

This panel helps to connect your Flash application to Web-based services, like those provided by the SOAP protocol or RESTful design architecture.

Extensions

Leads to a submenu with additional Adobe services and community-based tools.

Kuler

A community-based tool that lets Flash fans share, rate, and reuse color palettes. You can use this resource when you're looking for inspiration.

Connections

Used to log into Adobe's Web-based resources. To make a connection, you provide your email address and a password. (These are the same details you use to purchase Adobe products online.)

Workspace

Leads to a submenu of commands that let you customize the Flash workspace and save your favorite workspace layouts for use with later projects.

Hide Panels

Windows: F4

Mac: F4

Hides all panels and toolbars, leaving only the main program window visible.

Help

The Help menu provides access to Flash help files included with the product and links to the Adobe Web site. (Many of the Help and Support resources were still in the works at the time this book went to press.)

Search Field (Mac Only)

The first Help option on the Mac is a search field. Type words to find help on that subject.

Flash Help

Windows: F1

Mac: F1

Opens the Help window in Flash, where you can find and view the help information that's included with the Flash program. Use the panels on the left to select books and type in search words and phrases. Help articles appear on the right side of the Help window.

Adobe Product Improvement Program

Opens a dialog box where, if you wish, you can give Adobe permission to anonymously collect information about how you use their products. The company then uses this information to develop future products. If you choose to participate, you can later turn this feature off through the same menu command.

Flash Exchange

Opens Adobe's Extension manager and provides access to Flash Exchange, where you can download components and other extensions that add to Flash's features.

Manage Extensions

Opens Adobe's Extension Manager, where you can add components and features to Flash.

Flash Support Center

Opens your browser to the Flash Support pages, where you can find tech support.

Flash Developer Center

Opens your browser to the Flash Developer Center, which contains articles, tutorials, and other resources for developing Flash programs.

Adobe Training

Takes you to a Web page listing resources for getting Adobe-certified training or becoming an Adobe-certified professional.

Register/Activate/Deactivate

Registration

Opens a form you can use to register Flash CS4 Professional.

Activate

Opens a window where you can activate Flash. Activation is part of Adobe's copy and piracy protection system. Products that aren't activated won't run.

Deactivate

Opens a window where you can deactivate Flash. After deactivation, you can install Flash on another computer.

Updates

Runs Adobe's product update tool. You have to have an activated product and Internet access to download updates from Adobe's Web site.

About Adobe Flash CS4 Professional (Mac: Flash → About Flash)

Opens the About Adobe Flash CS4 Professional window, where you see the product name and version as well as copyright information.

Index

Window menu commands *(continued)*
Behaviors, 700
Color, 209, 701
Common Libraries, 700
Compiler Errors, 700
Component Inspector, 371, 504, 702
Components, 501, 513–529, 702
Debug Panels, 700
Duplicate Window, 698
Extensions, 703
Hide Panels, 704
Info, 701
Library, 699
Motion Editor, 286, 699
Motion Presets, 271, 700
Movie Explorer, 700
Other Panels, 489, 702–703
Output, 701
Properties, 206, 699
Swatches, 221, 701
Timeline, 90, 699
Toolbars, 239, 596, 698–699
Tools, 699
Transform, 702
Workspace, 704

WMF format, 322, 353
words, replacing in strings, 553
work area, 22
workflow for tweens, 288
Workspace command (Window menu), 704
Workspace Switcher, 39–40

X

XE "animations"
See also drawings; frame-by-frame animations; tweens

Z

Zoom In command (View menu - Flash Player), 607
Zoom In command (View menu), 679
Zoom Out command (View menu - Flash Player), 607
Zoom Out command (View menu), 679
zooming in/out
selecting, 28
tutorial, 42–43